Long-Term Debt-Paying Ability

$$\text{Times Interest Earned} = \frac{\text{Recurring Earnings, Excluding Interest Expense, Tax Expense,}}{\text{Interest Expense, Including Capitalized Interest}}$$
$$\text{Equity Earnings, and Minority Earnings}$$

$$\text{Fixed Charge Coverage} = \frac{\text{Recurring Earnings, Excluding Interest Expense, Tax Expense,}}{\text{Interest Expense, Including Capitalized}}$$
$$\text{Equity Earnings, and Minority Income} + \text{Interest Portion of Rentals}$$
$$\text{Interest} + \text{Interest Portion of Rentals}$$

$$\text{Debt Ratio} = \frac{\text{Total Liabilities}}{\text{Total Assets}}$$

$$\text{Debt/Equity} = \frac{\text{Total Liabilities}}{\text{Shareholders' Equity}}$$

$$\text{Debt to Tangible Net Worth} = \frac{\text{Total Liabilities}}{\text{Shareholders' Equity} - \text{Intangible Assets}}$$

$$\text{Operating Cash Flow/Total Debt} = \frac{\text{Operating Cash Flow}}{\text{Total Debt}}$$

Profitability

$$\text{Net Profit Margin} = \frac{\text{Net Income Before Minority Share of Earnings and Nonrecurring Items}}{\text{Net Sales}}$$

$$\text{Total Asset Turnover} = \frac{\text{Net Sales}}{\text{Average Total Assets}}$$

$$\text{Return on Assets} = \frac{\text{Net Income Before Minority Share of Earnings and Nonrecurring Items}}{\text{Average Total Assets}}$$

$$\text{DuPont Return on Assets} = \text{Net Profit Margin} \times \text{Total Asset Turnover}$$

$$\text{Operating Income Margin} = \frac{\text{Operating Income}}{\text{Net Sales}}$$

$$\text{Operating Asset Turnover} = \frac{\text{Net Sales}}{\text{Average Operating Assets}}$$

$$\text{Return on Operating Assets} = \frac{\text{Operating Income}}{\text{Average Operating Assets}}$$

$$\text{DuPont Return on Operating Assets} = \frac{\text{Operating Income}}{\text{Margin}} \times \frac{\text{Operating Asset}}{\text{Turnover}}$$

$$\text{Sales to Fixed Assets} = \frac{\text{Net Sales}}{\text{Average Net Fixed Assets}}$$

(Ratios continue at back of book.)

FINANCIAL STATEMENT ANALYSIS

Using Financial Accounting Information

Fifth Edition

Charles H. Gibson
The University of Toledo

COLLEGE DIVISION South-Western Publishing Co.

Cincinnati Ohio

This book is dedicated to my wife Patricia
and daughters Anne Elizabeth and Laura.

AM63EA

Copyright © 1992 by South-Western Publishing Company

This text was originally developed and produced by PWS-KENT Publishing Company. South-Western will market and sell this and future editions.

Sponsoring Editor: Mark Hubble
Production Coordinator: Patricia Adams
Marketing Manager: Randy Haubner
Production: David Hoyt, Hoyt Publishing Services
Interior Design: Patricia Adams
Cover Designer: Lindgren Design Associates
Manufacturing Coordinator: Lisa M. Flanagan

ISBN: 0-538-82160-4

1 2 3 4 5 6 7 8 AB 7 6 5 4 3 2 1 0

Printed in the United States of America

Library of Congress Cataloging-in-Publication Data

Gibson, Charles H.
   Financial statement analysis : using financial accounting information / Charles H. Gibson.—5th ed.
     p. cm.
   Includes bibliographical references and index.
   ISBN 0-538-82160-4
   1. Financial statements. I. Title.
HF5681.B2G49 1991
657′.3—dc20
                                  91-27904
                                      CIP

PREFACE

The objective of this book is to present a realistic and organized approach to financial reporting, with particular emphasis on the analysis of the end result of financial reporting—financial statements. Students and professionals often become too involved in statement preparation, without ever really reading the statements to interpret results. Typical financial accounting textbooks take a procedural rather than an analytical approach. This book emphasizes the interpretation of the end result. Typical textbook presentations oversimplify financial statements, so readers are not prepared to understand or analyze actual financial reports. This book utilizes actual statements extensively in illustrations, problems, cases, and complete analyses.

The Financial Accounting Standards Board has specified understandability as a desirable quality of financial reporting. It is my goal to enhance the user's understanding and to make the analysis of financial reporting meaningful, interesting, and exciting.

My major objective in writing this book has been to make a clear and balanced presentation of the material. Manufacturing, retailing, and service firms, including regulated and nonregulated industries, are presented. All discussion is based on accounting principles, in an effort to have students understand the methods used as well as their implications for analysis. Consideration has been given to current financial reporting problems, including lease presentation, pension presentation, options, social reporting, postretirement benefits, financial instruments disclosures, and deferred taxes.

ORGANIZATION

The first chapter develops the basic principles of accounting on which financial statements are based. Chapter 1 also introduces the basic financial statements and a number of topics related to them.

Chapter 2 is an in-depth review of the balance sheet, and Chapter 3 covers the income statement and statement of retained earnings in detail. Chapter 4 is an introduction to analysis and comparative statistics.

An important feature of this book is that one firm, Cooper Tire & Rubber Company, is used extensively as an illustration, so readers can become familiar with a particular firm and industry and view the analysis as a whole. This firm and its industry are introduced in Chapter 5, which contains most of the 1989 Cooper Tire & Rubber Company statements. Chapter 6 covers short-term liquidity; Chapter 7, long-term debt-paying ability; Chapter 8, profitability; Chapter 9, analysis for the investor; and Chapter 10, the statement of cash flows. The Cooper Tire & Rubber Company illustration is synthesized in Chapter 11 with a ratio summary comparing the company with industry statistics. Summary comments guide readers through the methodology of comprehensive analysis.

Chapter 12 analyzes the impact of inflation on financial statements; Chapter 13 introduces the expanded utility of financial ratios. Some topics covered there are financial ratios as perceived by commercial loan departments and financial executives, financial ratios used in annual reports, and forecasting financial failure.

Regulated industries present analytical problems different from those of other firms and require special analysis. Therefore, banks, utilities, and transportation, insurance, and oil and gas companies are discussed in Chapter 14, which offers suggestions for reviewing these industries.

Chapter 15 introduces personal financial statements and accounting for governments and other nonprofit-oriented businesses. A comprehensive case concludes the book.

USING THE BOOK AS A TEXT

The book provides the flexibility necessary to meet the needs of accounting and finance courses varying in content and length. Sufficient text and problem materials are presented to allow the instructor latitude in the depth of coverage during a course. The materials have been tested in the classroom and by faculty. I hope that professors and students enjoy using this text as much as I have enjoyed preparing it.

SUPPLEMENTARY MATERIALS

For the student:

1. A Study Guide, prepared by the author, includes objective problems that will aid in reviewing chapter material. The following types of problems are provided: (1) fill-ins, (2) multiple choice, (3) true/false, (4) matching, (5) classification, and (6) effect of selected transactions.

2. A Computer-Assisted Financial Statement Analysis Package has been prepared by the author and Professor Don Saftner of the University of Toledo. This software package can result in substantial time savings when working applicable problems and class projects. Students will find this software to be a valuable aid in other courses involving ratio or common size analysis. It can also be of substantial value at work. The software can be used with Lotus 1-2-3.

For the instructor:

1. A Solutions Manual for all homework materials has been prepared by the author. It includes a suggested solution for each question, problem, and case.
2. A Test Bank, also prepared by the author, contains examination materials for each chapter. The Test Bank includes problems, multiple-choice and true/false questions, and other objective material.

ACKNOWLEDGMENTS

I am grateful to many people for help and encouragement during the writing of this book. Many changes were made as a result of helpful comments received from colleagues and students who used the first four editions. I want to extend my appreciation to Cooper Tire & Rubber Company for permission to use its statements as illustrations. I am also grateful to the numerous other firms and organizations that granted permission to reproduce their materials. Special thanks go to the American Institute of Certified Public Accountants, the Institute of Chartered Financial Analysts, and the Institute of Certified Management Accountants for permission to use material from their respective professional examinations.

I sincerely appreciate the helpful comments made by the reviewers of this edition: Kung Chen, University of Nebraska-Lincoln; Grace M. Conway, Adelphi University; J. Larry Hagler, East Carolina University; Joanna L. Ho, University of California at Irvine; Wesley Sampson, University of Toledo; and Waymond Rogers, University of California at Irvine.

Permission to reprint material has been granted by the following companies and organizations:

American Institute of Certified Public Accountants, Inc.	Cooper Tire & Rubber Company
Georgia-Pacific Corp.	Ford Motor Company
Johnson & Johnson	Dresser Industries, Inc.
J.C. Penney Company Inc.	Lands' End Inc.
Merck & Co., Inc.	Fluor Corp.
National Association of Accountants	Kinder Care Learning Centers Inc.
American Accounting Association	W.W. Grainger, Inc.
VR Corporation	Hillenbrand Industries Inc.
Time Inc.	Tempo Enterprises Inc.
CBS, Inc.	NCR Corporation
GTE Corporation	Goodyear Tire & Rubber Company
Barnes Group Inc.	Panhandle Eastern Corporation
Dana Corporation	The Procter & Gamble Company
Delta Air Lines, Inc.	Ameritech
Warner Lambert Company	Echlin Inc.
International Business Machines Corporation	Caterpillar Inc.
	Commercial Intertech Corp
	Occidental Petroleum Corporation

Knape & Vogt Manufacturing Co.
United Technologies Corp.
United Industrial Inc.
Standard & Poor's Corporation
Hartford Courant
Wisconsin Electric Utilities
Prentice-Hall Corp.
Kroger Co.
McDonnell Douglas Corporation
American Software, Inc.
Snap-On Tools Corporation
Georgia Power Co.
F. W. Woolworth Co.
General Host Corporation
Halliburton Company
Phelps Dodge Corporation
Lukens Inc.
Englehard Corporation
Chrysler Corp.
May Department Stores Co.
The Hannaford Bros. Co.
Trinova Corporation
Dun and Bradstreet Corp.
Arbor Drugs, Inc.
Kelly Services, Inc.
Union Carbide Corporation
The Institute of Chartered Financial
    Analysts

PepsiCo, Inc.
The Lubrizol Corporation
Utilicorp United
Chevron Corporation
Mosinee Paper Corporation
Wausau Paper Mills Co.
ConAgra Inc.
The Coca-Cola Company
Collins Indus. Inc.
U S T Corp.
Huntington Bancshares Incorporated
Public Service Company of Colorado
Aetna Life & Casualty Co.
Mid Am, Inc.
Lucas County Government,
    Department of Finance
The Institute of Internal Auditors
National Association of Accountants
The Robert Morris Associates
The Institute of Chartered Financial
    Analysts
Institute of Certified Management
    Accountants
City of Toledo
Worthington Industries

THE AUTHOR

Charles Gibson, Professor of Accounting at The University of Toledo, is a certified public accountant who practiced with a Big Six accounting firm for four years and has had more than twenty-five years of teaching experience. His teaching experience encompasses a variety of accounting courses, including financial, managerial, tax, cost, and financial statement analysis.

Professor Gibson teaches seminars on financial statement analysis to company presidents, financial executives, bank commercial loan officers, and lawyers. He has also taught financial reporting seminars for CPAs and review courses for both CPAs and certified management accountants. He has authored several problems used on the certified management accountants exam.

Charles Gibson has written more than fifty articles in such journals as the *Journal of Accountancy, Accounting Horizons, Journal of Commercial Bank Lending, CPA Journal, Ohio CPA, Management Accounting, Risk Management, Taxation for Accountants, Advanced Management Journal, Taxation for Lawyers, California Management Review,* and *Journal of Small Business Management.* He is a co-author of a Financial Executives Research Foundation study, "Discounting in Financial Accounting and Reporting."

Dr. Gibson has co-authored *Cases in Financial Reporting,* published by PWS-KENT Publishing Company. He has also co-authored two continuing education courses consisting of books and cassette tapes, published by the American Institute of Certified Public Accountants. These courses are entitled "Funds Flow Evaluation" and "Profitability and the Quality of Earnings."

The author is a member of the American Accounting Association, American Institute of Certified Public Accountants, National Association of Accountants, Ohio Society of Certified Public Accountants, Institute of Internal Auditors, and Financial Executives Institute. He has been particularly active in the American Accounting Association and the Ohio Society of Certified Public Accountants.

Dr. Gibson received the 1989 Outstanding Ohio Accounting Educator Award, jointly presented by the Ohio Society of Certified Public Accountants and the Ohio Regional American Accounting Association.

CONTENTS

FUNDAMENTAL CONCEPTS AND INTRODUCTION TO FINANCIAL STATEMENTS

CHAPTER TOPICS

Development of Generally Accepted Accounting Principles

American Institute of Certified Public Accountants (AICPA)

Financial Accounting Standards Board (FASB)

Operating Procedure for Statements of Financial Accounting Standards (SFAS)

FASB Conceptual Framework

Additional Input—American Institute of Certified Public Accountants

Emerging Issues Task Force (EITF)

Traditional Assumptions of the Accounting Model

Business Entity

Going Concern or Continuity

Time Period

Monetary Unit

Historical Cost

Conservatism

Realization

Matching

Consistency

Full Disclosure

Materiality

Industry Practices

Transaction Approach

Present Value Considerations

Accrual Basis

The Financial Statements

Balance Sheet

Income Statement

Statement of Retained Earnings

Statement of Cash Flows

Footnotes

Subsequent Events

Human Resource and Social Accounting

Auditor's Report

Management's Responsibility for Financial Statements

The SEC's Integrated Disclosure System

Summary Annual Report

Ethics

There are many users of financial statements. These include the firm's managers, stockholders, bondholders, security analysts, suppliers, lending institutions, employees, labor unions, regulatory authorities, and the general public.

These users of the financial statements use them to make decisions. For example, a potential investor interested in the company's stock could use the financial statements as input in deciding whether to buy the stock. A supplier might use the financial statements as input in deciding whether to sell the company merchandise. A labor union could use them in determining what demands to negotiate for employees. Management could use the statements to determine the company's profitability.

There is a demand for financial statements because these users perceive an improvement in decision making by using them. In addition to the financial statements, users often consult competing information sources, such as new wage contracts and economy-oriented releases.

This textbook concentrates on using financial accounting information properly. Users must have a basic understanding of generally accepted accounting principles and traditional assumptions of the accounting model. Without such an understanding, users will not recognize the limits of financial statements.

The ideas that underlie financial statements have developed over several hundred years. This development continues today, to meet the needs of a changing society. A review of the evolution of generally accepted accounting principles and the traditional assumptions of the accounting model should help the reader understand the statements and thus analyze them better. This chapter reviews the ideas that underlie the financial statements.

The form of business entity is usually a sole proprietorship, a partnership, or a corporation. The corporation is the dominant form of business entity.

A sole proprietorship is a business entity owned by one person. A sole proprietorship is not a legal entity separate from its owner; the owner is responsible for the debts of the proprietorship. However, the accountant treats the sole owner and the business as separate accounting entities.

A partnership is a business owned by two or more individuals. Each owner is called a *partner,* and each partner is personally responsible for the debts of the partnership. The accountant treats the partners and the business as separate accounting entities.

In the United States, a business corporation is a legal entity incorporated in a particular state. Ownership is evidenced by shares of stock. A corporation is considered to be a legal entity separate and distinct from the stockholders. The stockholders risk only their investment; they are not responsible for the debt of the corporation.

In this book, the corporate form of business is assumed unless specifically stated otherwise. The accounting for corporations, sole proprietorships, and partnerships is practically the same, except for the owners' equity.

The major published financial statements of a corporation are the balance sheet, income statement, and statement of cash flows. These financial statements are accompanied by footnotes. A statement of retained earnings is also included with the published financial statements of a corporation, but it explains only the change in the retained earnings account on the balance sheet. In order to evaluate an entity, it is necessary to understand these statements and to be aware of their problems and limitations. This chapter includes an introduction to financial statements. A detailed review of individual statements is included in subsequent chapters: Chapter 2, balance sheet; Chapter 3, income statement and statement of retained earnings; and Chapter 10, statement of cash flows.

An accountant's report is the formal presentation of all the effort that goes into an audit. The types of accountant's reports are reviewed in this chapter. Although the auditor is responsible for conducting an independent examination of the statements, the responsibility for the preparation and integrity of financial statements rests with management.

The Securities and Exchange Commission has a goal of integrating the reporting requirements regarding the annual report to stockholders and the annual report to the Securities and Exchange Commission. A reporting option available to public companies is to issue a summary report. Both this reporting option and the SEC's integrated disclosure system are reviewed in this chapter.

DEVELOPMENT OF GENERALLY ACCEPTED ACCOUNTING PRINCIPLES

Generally accepted accounting principles (GAAP) are accounting principles that have substantial authoritative support. The accountant must be familiar with acceptable reference sources in order to decide whether any particular accounting principle has substantial authoritative support.

Although accounting principles have developed over hundreds of years, the formal process that exists today started with the Securities Act of 1933. This act was designed to protect investors from abuses in financial reporting that developed during the 1920s. The Securities Act of 1933 was intended to regulate the initial offering and sale of securities in interstate commerce.

The Securities Act of 1933 was followed by the Securities Exchange Act of 1934. In general, the Securities Act of 1934 was intended to regulate securities trading on the national exchanges, and it was under this authority that the Securities and Exchange Commission (SEC) was created. In effect, the SEC was given the authority to determine generally accepted accounting principles and to regulate the accounting profession. The SEC has elected to leave much of the determination of generally accepted accounting principles and the regulation of the accounting profession to the private sector. At times, the SEC issues its own standards. Thus, the formal process that exists today is a blend of the private and public sectors.

A number of parties in the private sector have played a role in the development of GAAP. We will address the roles of the two that have had the most influence: the American Institute of Certified Public Accountants (AICPA) and the Financial Accounting Standards Board (FASB).

American Institute of Certified Public Accountants (AICPA)

The AICPA has played a vital role in the development of GAAP. During the 1930s, the AICPA had a special committee working with the New York Stock Exchange on matters of common interest. An outgrowth of this special committee was the establishment in 1939 of two standing committees of the AICPA, the Committee on Accounting Procedures and the Committee on Accounting Terminology. These committees were active from 1939 to 1959 and issued fifty-one Accounting Research Bulletins. These committees took a problem-by-problem approach; because they tended to review an area only when there was a problem, this method became known as the *brushfire* approach. They were only partially successful in developing a well-structured body of accounting.

In 1959, the AICPA terminated the two committees and in their place created the Accounting Principles Board (APB) and the Accounting Research Division. The Accounting Research Division was to provide research to aid the APB in making decisions regarding accounting principles. It was thought that this approach would be sounder than the previous one. Basic postulates would be developed to aid in the development of accounting principles, and the entire process would be based on research prior to an APB decision. However, the approach of the Accounting Principles Board and the Accounting Research Division turned out to be much like that of the earlier committees, because the Accounting Research Division was not successful in establishing basic postulates or in formulating broad principles.

Pressure was generated from various sources, including the public, to find another way of developing generally accepted accounting principles. The combination of the Accounting Principles Board and the Accounting Research Division lasted from 1959 to 1973. During this time, the Accounting Research Division issued fourteen Accounting Research Studies. The Accounting Principles Board issued thirty-one Opinions and four Statements. The Opinions represented official positions of the Board, whereas the Statements represented the views of the Board but not the official positions.

Still another approach was recommended by a special study group of the AICPA in the spring of 1972—the establishment of a new board called the Financial Accounting Standards Board (FASB). This recommendation was adopted by the AICPA and implemented in 1973.

Financial Accounting Standards Board (FASB)

The Financial Accounting Standards Board is an independent organization. The FASB is governed by the Financial Accounting Foundation (FAF), which consists of a representative from each of nine organizations (AICPA, Financial Executives Institute, National Association of Accountants, Financial Analysts Federation, American Accounting Association, Security Industry Association, and three not-for-profit organizations). The FAF appoints the seven members of the FASB and the Financial Accounting Standards Advisory Council (FASAC). The FASAC is responsible for advising the FASB.

The FASB issues four types of pronouncements:

1. *Statements of Financial Accounting Standards (SFAS)*. These Statements establish GAAP for specific accounting issues.

2. *Interpretations.* These pronouncements provide clarifications of previously issued standards, including FASB Statements of Standards, APB Opinions, and Accounting Research Bulletins. The interpretations have the same authority and require the same majority votes for passage as standards (a supermajority of five or more of the seven members).

3. *Technical bulletins.* Technical bulletins provide timely guidance on financial accounting and reporting problems. They may be used when they will not cause a major change in accounting practice for a number of companies and when they do not conflict with any fundamental accounting principle.

4. *Statements of Financial Accounting Concepts (SFACs).* These Statements provide a theoretical foundation upon which to base GAAP. They are the output of the FASB's Conceptual Framework project, but they are not part of GAAP.

Operating Procedure for Statements of Financial Accounting Standards (SFAS)

The process of considering an SFAS begins when the Board elects to add a topic to its technical agenda. The Board receives suggestions and advice on topics from many sources, including the Financial Accounting Standards Advisory Council, the SEC, the AICPA, and industry organizations.

For its technical agenda, the Board considers only items that are "broke." In other words, the Board must be convinced that there is a major issue to be addressed in a new area or that an old issue needs to be reexamined.

The Board must rely on staff members for the day-to-day work on projects. A project is assigned a staff project manager, and informal discussions frequently take place between Board members, the staff project manager, and staff. In this way, Board members gain an understanding of the accounting issues and the economic relationships that underlie those issues.

On projects with a broad impact, a Discussion Memorandum or an Invitation to Comment is issued. A Discussion Memorandum is a presentation of all known facts and points of view on a topic. An Invitation to Comment sets forth the Board's tentative conclusions on issues related to the topic or represents the views of others.

The Discussion Memorandum or Invitation to Comment is distributed as a basis for public comment. There is usually a sixty-day period for written comments, followed by a public hearing. A transcript of the public hearing and the written comments become part of the public record. Then the Board begins deliberations on an Exposure Draft of a proposed Statement of Financial Accounting Standards. When completed, the Exposure Draft is issued for public comment. The Board may call for written comments only, or it may announce another public hearing. After considering the written comments and the public hearing comments, the Board resumes deliberations in one or more public Board meetings. The final Statement must receive affirmative votes from five of the seven members of the Board. The Rules of Procedure require dissenting Board members to set forth their reasons in the Statement. Developing a Statement on a major project generally takes at least two years and sometimes much longer. Some people believe that the time should be shortened to permit faster decision making.

The FASB standard-setting process includes aspects of accounting theory and political aspects. Many organizations, companies, and individuals have input into the process. Some of this input is directed toward achieving a standard that is less than desirable in terms of a strict accounting perspective. Often, the end result is a standard that is not the best representation of economic reality.

FASB Conceptual Framework

The Conceptual Framework for Accounting and Reporting was on the agenda of the FASB from its inception in 1973. The Framework is intended to set forth a system of interrelated objectives and underlying concepts to serve as the basis for evaluating existing standards of financial accounting and reporting.

Under this project, the FASB has established a series of pronouncements known as Statements of Financial Accounting Concepts (SFACs). These are intended to provide the Board with a common foundation and basic reasons for considering the merits of various alternative accounting principles. SFACs do not establish GAAP; rather, the FASB intends eventually to evaluate current principles in terms of the concepts established.

To date, the Framework project has six Concept Statements. There may be additional Concept Statements in the future, and Concept Statements are expected to undergo periodic review with a view toward improvement. The six Concept Statements issued to date are the following:

1. Statement of Financial Accounting Concepts No. 1, "Objectives of Financial Reporting by Business Enterprises"
2. Statement of Financial Accounting Concepts No. 2, "Qualitative Characteristics of Accounting Information"
3. Statement of Financial Accounting Concepts No. 3, "Elements of Financial Statements of Business Enterprises"
4. Statement of Financial Accounting Concepts No. 4, "Objectives of Financial Reporting by Nonbusiness Organizations"
5. Statement of Financial Accounting Concepts No. 5, "Recognition and Measurement in Financial Statements of Business Enterprises"
6. Statement of Financial Accounting Concepts No. 6, "Elements of Financial Statements" (a replacement of No. 3)

The Concept Statements will be reviewed briefly.

Concept Statement No. 1 deals with identifying the objectives of financial reporting for business entities and establishes the focus for subsequent projects for business entities. Concept Statement No. 1 pertains to general-purpose external financial reporting and is not restricted to financial statements. The highlights of Concept Statement No. 1 are as follows:[1]

1. Financial reporting is not an end in itself but is intended to provide information that is useful in making business and economic decisions.

2. The objectives of financial reporting are not immutable—they are affected by the economic, legal, political, and social environment in which financial reporting takes place.

3. The objectives are also affected by the characteristics and limitations of the kind of information that financial reporting can provide.
    a. The information pertains to business enterprises rather than to industries or the economy as a whole.
    b. The information often results from approximate, rather than exact, measures.
    c. The information largely reflects the financial effects of transactions and events that have already happened.
    d. The information is but one source of information needed by those who make decisions about business enterprises.
    e. The information is provided and used at a cost.

4. The objectives in this Statement are those of general-purpose external financial reporting by business enterprises.
    a. The objectives stem primarily from the needs of external users who lack the authority to prescribe the information they want and must rely on information management communicates to them.
    b. The objectives are directed toward the common interests of many users in the ability of an enterprise to generate favorable cash flows but are phrased using investments and credit decisions as a reference to give them a focus. The objectives are intended to be broad rather than narrow.
    c. The objectives pertain to financial reporting and are not restricted to financial statements.

5. The objectives state that
    a. Financial reporting should provide information that is useful to present and potential investors and creditors and other users in making rational investment, credit, and similar decisions. The information should be comprehensible to those who have a reasonable understanding of business and economic activities and are willing to study the information with reasonable diligence.

---

[1]"Objectives of Financial Reporting by Business Enterprises," FASB Statement of Financial Accounting Concepts No. 1 (Stamford, Conn.: Financial Accounting Standards Board, 1978). This reprint does not include the appendices to FASB Concept No. 1. These appendices are an integral part of the document.

    b. Financial reporting should provide information to help present and potential investors and creditors and other users in assessing the amounts, timing, and uncertainty of prospective cash receipts from dividends or interest and the proceeds for the sale, redemption, or maturity of securities or loans. Since investors' and creditors' cash flows are related to enterprise cash flows, financial reporting should provide information to help investors, creditors, and others assess the amounts, timing, and uncertainty of prospective net cash inflows to the related enterprise.

    c. Financial reporting should provide information about the economic resources of an enterprise, the claims against those resources (obligations of the enterprise to transfer resources to other entities and owners' equity), and the effects of transactions, events, and circumstances that change its resources and claims to those resources.

6. "Investors" and "creditors" are used broadly and include not only those who have or contemplate having a claim to enterprise resources but also those who advise or represent them.

7. Although investment and credit decisions reflect investors' and creditors' expectations about future enterprise performance, those expectations are commonly based at least partly on evaluations of past enterprise performance.

8. The primary focus of financial reporting is information about earnings and its components.

9. Information about enterprise earnings based on accrual accounting (described later in this chapter) generally provides a better indication of an enterprise's present and continuing ability to generate favorable cash flows than information limited to the financial effects of cash receipts and payments.

10. Financial reporting is expected to provide information about an enterprise's financial performance during a period and about how management of an enterprise has discharged its stewardship responsibility to owners.

11. Financial accounting is not designed to measure directly the value of a business enterprise, but the information it provides may be helpful to those who wish to estimate its value.

12. Investors, creditors, and others may use reported earnings and information about the elements of financial statements in various ways to assess the prospects for cash flows. They may wish, for example, to evaluate management's performance, estimate "earning power," predict future earnings, assess risk, confirm change, or reject earlier predictions or assessments. Although financial reporting should provide basic information to aid them, they do their own evaluating, estimating, predicting, assessing, confirming, changing, or rejecting.

13. Management knows more about the enterprise and its affairs than investors, creditors, or other "outsiders" and accordingly can often increase the usefulness of financial information by identifying certain events and circumstances and explaining their financial effects on the enterprise.

The second SFAC, issued in May 1980, is entitled "Qualitative Characteristics of Accounting Information" (SFAC No. 2). This SFAC examines the characteristics that make accounting information useful for investment, credit, and similar decisions. Those characteristics of information that make it a desirable commodity can be viewed as a hierarchy of qualities, with *understandability* and *usefulness for decision making* of most importance. The hierarchy of qualities is shown in Exhibit 1-1.

Relevance and reliability are the two primary qualities that make accounting information useful for decision making. SFAC No. 2 indicates that, to be relevant, the information must have predictive and feedback value and must be timely. The SFAC also indicates that, to be reliable, the information must be verifiable, subject to representational faithfulness, and neutral. Comparability, which includes consistency, interacts with relevance and reliability to contribute to the usefulness of information.

Two constraints are included in the hierarchy. To be useful and worth providing, the information should have benefits that exceed its cost. In addition, all of the qualities of information shown are subject to a materiality threshold.

In December 1980, the third SFAC was issued, entitled "Elements of Financial Statements of Business Enterprises" (SFAC No. 3). The elements of financial statements are the building blocks from which financial statements are constructed. SFAC No. 3 was replaced in 1985 by SFAC No. 6, "Elements of Financial Statements." This statement defines ten interrelated elements that are directly related to measuring performance and status of an enterprise. The ten elements are defined as follows:[2]

1. *Assets.* Assets are probable future economic benefits obtained or controlled by a particular entity, as a result of past transactions or events.

2. *Liabilities.* Liabilities are probable future sacrifices of economic benefits arising from present obligations of a particular entity to transfer assets or provide services to other entities in the future, as a result of past transactions or events.

3. *Equity.* Equity is the residual interest in the assets of an entity that remains after deducting its liabilities—that is, Equity = Assets − Liabilities.

4. *Investments by owners.* Investments by owners are increases in equity of a particular business enterprise, resulting from transfers to the enterprise from other entities of something of value to obtain or increase ownership interests (or equity) in it. Assets are most commonly received as investments by owners, but that which is received may also include services or satisfaction or conversion of liabilities of the enterprise.

5. *Distribution to owners.* Distribution to owners is a decrease in equity of a particular business enterprise, resulting from transferring assets, rendering ser-

---

[2]"Elements of Financial Statements," FASB Statement of Financial Accounting Concepts No. 6 (Stamford, Conn.: Financial Accounting Standards Board, 1985). This reprint does not include the appendices to FASB Concept No. 6. These appendices are an integral part of the document.

EXHIBIT 1-1

A Hierarchy of Accounting Qualities

Users of accounting information	**Decision makers and their characteristics** (for example, understanding or prior knowledge)
Pervasive constraint	Benefits > Costs
	Understandability
User specific qualities	Decision usefulness
Primary decision specific qualities	Relevance ⟷ Reliability
Ingredients of primary qualities	Predictive value / Feedback value / Timeliness — Verifiability / Representational faithfulness
Secondary and interactive qualities	Comparability (including consistency) — Neutrality
Threshold for recognition	Materiality

Source: "Qualitative Characteristics of Accounting Information." Adapted from Figure 1 in FASB Statement of Financial Accounting Concepts No. 2 (Stamford, Conn.: Financial Accounting Standards Board, 1980). This reprint does not include the appendices of FASB Concept No. 2. These appendices are an integral part of the document.

vices, or incurring liabilities by the enterprise to owners. Distributions to owners decrease ownership interest (or equity) in an enterprise.

6. *Comprehensive income.* Comprehensive income is the change in equity (net assets) of a business enterprise during a period, resulting from transactions and other events and circumstances from nonowner sources. It includes all changes in equity during a period except those resulting from investments by owners and distributions to owners.

7. *Revenues.* Revenues are inflows or other enhancements of assets of an entity or settlements of its liabilities (or a combination of both), resulting from de-

livering or producing goods, rendering services, or other activities that constitute the entity's ongoing major or central operations.

8. *Expenses.* Expenses are outflows or other consumption or using up of assets or incurrence of liabilities (or a combination of both), resulting from delivering or producing goods, rendering services, or carrying out other activities that constitute the entity's ongoing major or central operations.

9. *Gains.* Gains are increases in equity (net assets) resulting from peripheral or incidental transactions of an entity and from all other transactions and other events and circumstances from revenues or investments by owners.

10. *Losses.* Losses are decreases in equity (net assets) resulting from peripheral or incidental transactions of an entity and from all other transactions and other events and circumstances affecting the entity during a period, except those that result from expenses or distributions to owners.

The project establishing objectives of general-purpose external financial reporting by nonbusiness organizations was completed in December 1980. This is Concept Statement No. 4, entitled "Objectives of Financial Reporting by Nonbusiness Organizations" (SFAC No. 4). Examples of organizations that fall within the focus of this concept statement are churches, foundations, and human service organizations. Performance indicators for nonbusiness organizations usually include such items as formal budgets and donor restrictions. These types of indicators are not ordinarily related to competition in markets.

The fifth SFAC was issued in December 1984 and is entitled "Recognition and Measurement in Financial Statements of Business Enterprises" (SFAC No. 5). Statement No. 5 sets forth recognition criteria and discusses certain measurement issues that are related to recognition. SFAC No. 5 indicates that an item, to be recognized, should meet four criteria, subject to the cost-benefit constraint and the materiality threshold. These criteria are:[3]

1. *Definition.* The item fits one of the definitions of the elements.
2. *Measurability.* The item has a relevant attribute measurable with sufficient reliability.
3. *Relevance.* The information is relevant.
4. *Reliability.* The information is reliable.

SFAC No. 5 identifies five different measurement attributes currently used in practice.[4] These measurement attributes are the following:

1. *Historical cost* (historical proceeds). Property, plant, and equipment and most inventories are reported at their historical cost, which is the amount of cash, or

---

[3]"Recognition and Measurement of Financial Statements of Business Enterprises," FASB Statement of Financial Accounting Concepts No. 5 (Stamford, Conn.: Financial Accounting Standards Board, 1984), paragraph 63. This reprint does not include the appendices to FASB Concept No. 5. These appendices are an integral part of the document.

[4]Ibid., paragraph 67.

its equivalent, paid to acquire an asset, commonly adjusted after acquisition for amortization or other allocations. Liabilities that involve obligations to provide goods or services to customers are generally reported at historical proceeds, which is the amount of cash, or its equivalent, received when the obligation was incurred and may be adjusted after acquisition for amortization or other allocations.

2. *Current cost.* Some inventories are reported at their current (replacement) cost, which is the amount of cash, or its equivalent, that would have to be paid if the same or an equivalent asset were acquired currently.

3. *Current market value.* Some investments in marketable securities are reported at their current market value, which is the amount of cash, or its equivalent, that could be obtained by selling an asset in orderly liquidation. Current market value is also generally used for assets expected to be sold at prices lower than previous carrying amounts. Some liabilities that involve marketable commodities and securities—for example, the obligations of writers of options or sellers of common shares who do not own the underlying commodities or securities—are reported at current market value.

4. *Net realizable (settlement) value.* Short-term receivables and some inventories are reported at their net realizable value, which is the nondiscounted amount of cash, or its equivalent, into which an asset is expected to be converted in due course of business less direct costs, if any, necessary to make that conversion. Liabilities that involve known or estimated amounts of money payable at unknown future dates, for example, trade payables or warranty obligations, generally reported at their net settlement value, which is the nondiscounted amounts of cash, or its equivalent, expected to be paid to liquidate an obligation in the due course of business, including direct costs, if any, necessary to make that payment.

5. *Present (or discounted) value of future cash flows.* Long-term receivables are reported at their present value (discounted at the implicit or historical rate), which is the present or discounted value of future cash inflows into which an asset is expected to be converted in due course of business, less present values of cash outflows necessary to obtain those inflows. Long-term payables are similarly reported at their present value (discounted at the implicit or historical rate), which is the present or discounted value of future cash outflows expected to be required to satisfy the liability in due course of business.

A great deal was expected from SFAC No. 5, but it probably accomplished little, because a firm, consistent position on recognition and measurement could not be agreed upon. SFAC No. 5 states: "Rather than attempt to select a single attribute and force changes in practice so that all classes of assets and liabilities use that attribute, this concept statement suggests that use of different attributes will continue."[5]

The FASB Conceptual Framework for Accounting and Reporting project rep-

---

[5]Ibid., pp. 24–25.

resents the most extensive effort that has ever been undertaken to provide a conceptual framework for financial accounting. Potentially, the project can have a significant influence on financial accounting.

Additional Input—American Institute of Certified Public Accountants

As indicated earlier in this chapter, the AICPA played the primary role in the private sector in establishing GAAP until 1973. In that year, the FASB assumed that role. However, the AICPA continues to play a substantial part, primarily through its Accounting Standards Division. The Accounting Standards Division Executive Committee (ACSEC) serves as the official voice of the AICPA in matters relating to financial accounting and reporting standards.

The Accounting Standards Division publishes numerous documents that may be considered as sources of generally accepted accounting principles. These include Industry Audit Guides, Industry Accounting Guides, and Statements of Position (SOP).

Industry Audit Guides and Industry Accounting Guides are designed to assist auditors in examining and reporting on financial statements of companies in specialized industries, such as insurance. SOPs are issued to influence the development of accounting standards. Some SOPs are revisions or clarifications to recommendations on accounting standards contained in Industry Audit Guides and Industry Accounting Guides.

Industry Audit Guides, Industry Accounting Guides, and SOPs are considered a lower level of authority than FASB Statements of Financial Accounting Standards (SFASs), FASB Interpretations, Accounting Principles Board Opinions, and Accounting Research Bulletins. However, since the Industry Audit Guides, Industry Accounting Guides, and SOPs deal with material not covered in the primary sources, in effect they become the guide to standards for the areas they cover.

Emerging Issues Task Force (EITF)

The FASB established the Emerging Issues Task Force in July 1984, to help identify emerging issues affecting reporting and problems in implementing authoritative pronouncements. The Task Force has 15 members—senior technical partners of major national CPA firms and representatives of major associations of preparers of financial statements. The FASB's Director of Research and Technical Activities serves as Task Force chairman. The SEC's Chief Accountant and the chairman of the AICPA's Accounting Standards Executive Committee participate in Task Force meetings as observers.

The SEC's Chief Accountant has stated that any accounting that conflicts with the position of a consensus of the Task Force would be challenged by the SEC. Agreement of the Task Force is recognized as a consensus if no more than two members disagree with a position.

Task Force meetings are held about once every six weeks. Issues come to the

Task Force from a variety of sources, including the EITF members, the SEC, and other federal agencies. The FASB also brings issues to the EITF in response to issues submitted by auditors and preparers of financial statements.

The EITF has become a very important source of GAAP. The Task Force has the capability of reviewing a number of issues within a relatively short period of time, in contrast to the lengthy deliberations that go into an SFAS.

EITF statements are considered to be less authoritative than the sources previously discussed in this chapter. However, since the EITF addresses issues not covered by the other sources, its statements become important guidelines to standards for the areas they cover.

TRADITIONAL ASSUMPTIONS OF THE ACCOUNTING MODEL

The FASB's Conceptual Framework was influenced by several underlying assumptions. Some of these assumptions were addressed in the Conceptual Framework, and others are implicit in the Framework. These assumptions, along with the Conceptual Framework, are considered when a GAAP is established. Accountants are often confronted with a situation in which there is no explicit standard. Such situations should be resolved by considering the Conceptual Framework and the traditional assumptions of the accounting model.

In all cases, accountants are required to make a "fair representation." Even when there is an explicit GAAP, following the GAAP is not appropriate unless the end result is a fair representation.

Business Entity

The concept of separate entity means that the business or entity for which the financial statements are prepared is separate and distinct from the owners of the entity. In other words, the entity is viewed as an economic unit that stands on its own.

For example, a sole proprietor may own a grocery store, a farm, and numerous personal assets. In order to determine the economic success of the grocery store, we would view it as separate from the other resources that are owned by the individual. The grocery store would be treated as a separate entity.

A corporation such as the Ford Motor Company has many owners (stockholders). The entity concept enables us to account for the Ford Motor Company entity separately from the transactions of the owners of the Ford Motor Company.

Going Concern or Continuity

The assumption is made that the entity in question will remain in business for an indefinite period of time. This assumption provides perspective on the future of the entity.

By making the going-concern assumption, we deliberately disregard the possibility that the entity will go bankrupt or be liquidated. If a particular entity is in fact threatened with bankruptcy or liquidation, then the going-concern assumption should be dropped. In such a case, the reader of the financial statements is interested in the liquidation values, not the values that can be used when making the assumption that the business will continue indefinitely. If the going-concern assumption has not been used for a particular set of financial statements, because of the threat of liquidation or bankruptcy, the financial statement must clearly disclose that the statements were prepared with the view that the entity would be liquidated or that it is a failing concern. In this case, conventional financial statement analysis would not apply.

Many of our present financial statement figures would be misleading if it were not for the going-concern assumption. For instance, prepaid insurance is computed by spreading the cost of the insurance over the period of time of the policy. If the entity is liquidated, then only the cancellation value of the policy will be meaningful. Inventories are basically carried at their accumulated cost. If the entity were liquidated, the amount realized from the sale of the inventory, in a manner other than through the usual channels, would usually be substantially less than the cost. Therefore, to carry the inventory at cost would fail to recognize the loss that is represented by the difference between the liquidation value and the cost.

Intangible assets would often have no liquidation value, but the conventional balance sheet may have substantial amounts for intangible assets. This is because the conventional balance sheet assumes a going concern, so that the entity is expected to receive benefits from these intangibles in the future.

The going-concern assumption influences liabilities as well as assets. If the entity were liquidating, some long-term liabilities would have to be stated at amounts in excess of those stated on the conventional statement. Also, the amounts provided for warranties and guarantees would not be realistic if the entity were liquidating.

The classification of assets and liabilities is also influenced by the going-concern assumption. Without the going-concern assumption, all assets and liabilities would be current, with the expectation that the assets would be liquidated and the liabilities paid in the near future.

The audit opinion for a particular firm may indicate that the auditors have reservations as to the going-concern status of the firm. This puts the reader on guard that the statements are misleading if the firm does not continue as a going concern. For example, the 1989 annual report of Calumet Industries indicated a concern over the company's ability to continue as a going concern.

Time Period

The only accurate way to account for the success or failure of an entity is to accumulate all transactions from the opening of business until the business eventually liquidates. Many years ago, this time period for reporting was acceptable, because a business might have been the venture type; it would be feasible to account for and divide up what remained at the completion of the venture. Today, the typical business has a relatively long duration, so it is not feasible to wait until the business liquidates before accounting for its success or failure.

This presents a problem: Accounting for the success or failure of the business in midstream involves inaccuracies. Many transactions and commitments are incomplete at any particular time between the opening and the closing of business. An attempt is made to eliminate the inaccuracies when statements are prepared for a particular period of time short of an entity's life span, but the inaccuracies cannot be eliminated completely. For example, the entity typically carries accounts receivable on the balance sheet. Only when the receivables are eventually collected can the entity account for them accurately. Until the receivable is collected, there is always the possibility that collection cannot be made. The entity will have outstanding obligations at any particular time, and these cannot be accurately accounted for until they are met. An example would be a warranty on products sold. An entity may also have a considerable investment in the production of inventories. Usually, until the inventory is sold in the normal course of business, the entity cannot accurately account for the investment in inventory.

With the time period assumption, we accept some inaccuracies of accounting for the entity short of its complete life span. The assumption is made that the entity can be accounted for reasonably accurately for a particular period of time. In other words, the decision is made to accept some inaccuracy, because of incomplete information about the future, in exchange for more timely reporting.

Some businesses select an accounting period that ends when operations are at a low ebb, in order to facilitate a better measurement of income and financial position. This type of period is known as a *natural business year*. Other businesses use the calendar year and end their accounting time period on December 31, whereas others select a twelve-month accounting period closing at the end of a month other than December; this is known as a *fiscal year*. The accounting period may be shorter than a year—for example, a month. The shorter the period of time, the more inaccuracies we typically expect in the reporting.

Monetary Unit

Accountants need some standard of measure to bring financial transactions together in a meaningful way. Without some standard of measure, accountants would be forced to report in such terms as five cars, one factory, and one hundred acres. This type of reporting would not be very meaningful.

There are a number of standards of measure, such as a yard, a gallon, and money. Of the possible standards of measure, accountants have concluded that money is the best for the purpose of measuring financial transactions.

Different countries call their monetary units by different names: Germany calls its money the *mark*, France calls its money the *franc*, and Japan calls its money the *yen*. Different countries also have different values to their money; one mark is not equal to one yen. Thus, financial transactions may be measured in terms of money in each country, but the statements from various countries cannot be compared directly or added together until they are converted to a common measure of money, such as the U.S. dollar.

In various countries, stability of value of the monetary unit has been a problem. The loss in value of money is called *inflation*. In some countries, inflation has been more than 300% per year. In countries where inflation has been significant, financial statements are adjusted by an inflation factor, restoring the significance of money as a measuring unit to a material extent. However, a completely acceptable restoration of money as a measuring unit cannot be made in such cases, because of the problems involved in determining an accurate index. To indicate one such problem, consider the price of a Ford in 1982 and in 1992. The price of the car in 1992 would be higher, but the explanation would not be simply that prices increased. Part of the reason for the price increase would be that the equipment and the quality of the equipment have changed between 1982 and 1992. Thus, when an index is arrived at relating the 1992 price to the 1982 price, the resulting index is a mixture of inflation, technological advancement, and quality changes.

The rate of inflation in the United States prior to the 1970s was relatively low. Therefore, it was thought that an adjustment of money as a measuring unit was not appropriate, because the added expense and inaccuracy of adjusting for inflation were greater than the benefits. During the 1970s, however, the United States experienced double-digit inflation in some years, and inflation that approached double digits in other years. This made it increasingly desirable that some formal recognition of inflation be implemented.

In September 1979, the FASB issued Statement of Financial Accounting Standards No. 33, "Financial Reporting and Changing Prices." This Statement required that certain large, publicly held companies disclose specified supplementary information, concerning the impact of changing prices, in their annual reports for fiscal years ending on or after December 25, 1979. This disclosure was later made optional in 1986, when SFAS No. 89 was issued. (Inflation accounting is discussed in Chapter 12.)

Historical Cost

SFAC No. 5 identified five different measurement attributes currently used in practice. These measurement attributes are historical cost, current cost, current market value, net realizable value, and present value. Usually, historical cost is used in practice, because it is objective and determinable. A deviation from historical cost is accepted when it becomes apparent that the historical cost cannot be recovered. This deviation is justified by the conservatism concept.

Conservatism

The accountant is often faced with a choice of different measurements of a situation, with each measurement having reasonable support. According to the concept of conservatism, the accountant must select the measurement with the least favorable effect on net income and financial position in the current period.

In order to apply the concept of conservatism to any given situation, there must be alternative measurements, each of which must have reasonable support. This means that the conservatism concept cannot be used to justify arbitrarily low figures. For example, to write the inventory down to an arbitrarily low figure in order to recognize any possible loss from selling the inventory could not be justified under the concept of conservatism. To do so would constitute inaccurate accounting, and the concept of conservatism cannot be used to justify inaccurate accounting.

It would be conservative to value inventory at the lower of historical cost or market value. By doing so, any anticipated loss from selling the inventory will be recognized in the current period. The conservatism concept is used in many other situations. For instance, obsolete inventory is written down or off prior to the point of sale; a loss is recognized for long-term construction contracts when the loss can be reasonably anticipated; and a conservative approach is taken in determining the overhead application to inventory. In determining the lives of fixed assets, a conservative view is taken. In estimating warranty expense, the conservative approach requires that the estimate be a larger figure, in order to reflect the least favorable effect on net income and the financial position of the current period.

Realization

Accountants face the problem of when to recognize revenue. All parts of the entity have contributed to the revenue earned by the entity, including the janitor, the receiving department, and the production employees. The problem is how to determine objectively the contribution of each of the segments toward revenue. Since such separate determinations are not practical, we are left with the question of *when* it is practical to recognize revenue. The general conclusion is to determine the point at which the revenue can be reasonably objectively determined, and then to recognize all of the revenue at that point in time—the point of recognition. The realization principle is that revenue should be recognized when:

1. The earning process is virtually complete, and
2. The exchange value can be objectively determined.

Point of Sale

In practice, revenue is usually recognized at the point of sale. At this time, the earning process is virtually complete, and the exchange value can be determined. It is essential that there be some uniformity between firms regarding when revenue is recognized, so as to make financial statements meaningful.

There are times when the use of the point-of-sale approach does not give a fair result. An example is the selling of land on credit to a buyer who does not have a reasonable ability to pay. If revenue were recognized at the point of sale, there would be a reasonable chance that sales had been overstated, because of the material risk of default. In such cases, there are other acceptable methods of recognizing revenue, such as the following:

1. End of production
2. Receipt of cash

3. Revenue recognized during production
4. Cost of recovery

End of Production

The recognition of revenue at the completion of the production process is acceptable when the price of the item is known and there is a ready market. The mining of gold or silver is an example, and the harvesting of some farm products would also fit these criteria. If corn is harvested in the fall and held over the winter in order to obtain a higher price in the spring, the realization of revenue from the growing of the corn should be recognized in the fall, at the point of harvest. The gain or loss from the holding of the corn represents a separate consideration from the growing of the corn.

Receipt of Cash

The receipt of cash is another basis for revenue recognition. This method should be used only when the prospects of collection are especially doubtful at the time of sale. The land sales business, where the purchaser makes only a nominal down payment, is one type of business in which the collection of the full amount is especially doubtful; experience has shown that many purchasers default on the contract.

During Production

In some long-term construction projects, revenue is recognized as the construction progresses. This exception is allowed because it tends to give a fairer picture of the results for a given period of time. The building of a utility plant, which may take several years, is an example; recognizing revenue as work progresses gives a fairer picture of the results for a given time period than does having the entire revenue recognized in the period when the plant is completed.

Cost Recovery

The cost recovery approach is acceptable for highly speculative transactions. For example, the entity may invest in a venture search for gold, the outcome of which is completely unpredictable. In this case, the first return can be handled as a return of the investment. When and if more is returned than has been invested, this amount is considered revenue.

Matching

The revenue realization concept involves when to recognize revenue. Accountants need a related concept that addresses when to recognize the costs that are associated with the recognized revenue: the *matching concept*. The basic intent is to determine the revenue first and then match the appropriate costs against this revenue.

Some costs, such as the cost of inventory, fit in well with this concept; when we sell the inventory and recognize the revenue, the related cost of the inventory should be matched against the revenue. Other costs have no direct connection with revenue, so some systematic policy must be adopted in order to allocate these costs reasonably against revenues. Examples are research and development costs and public relations costs. Both research and development costs and public relations costs are charged off in the period incurred. This is inconsistent with the matching concept, but it is in accordance with the concept of conservatism.

Consistency

The consistency concept requires that the entity give the same treatment to comparable transactions from period to period. This adds to the usefulness of the reports when they are compared from period to period, and it also facilitates the detection of trends.

There are many accounting methods that could be used for any single item, such as inventory. If inventory were determined in one period on the FIFO basis (first-in, first-out) and in the next period on the LIFO basis (last-in, first-out), the resulting inventory, profits, and working capital would not be comparable from period to period.

Entities sometimes have a need to change particular accounting methods in order to adapt to changing environments. If the entity can justify the use of an alternative accounting method, the change can be made. The entity must be prepared to defend the justification for the change—a responsibility that should not be taken lightly, in view of the liability for misleading financial statements. Sometimes the justification will be based on a new accounting pronouncement. When a change in accounting methods is made, the justification for the change must be disclosed, along with an explanation of the effect on the statements, such as the effect on income.

Full Disclosure

The accounting reports must disclose all facts that might influence the judgment of an informed reader. Usually, this is a judgment decision for the accountant to make. Significant accounting policies must be disclosed either in the first footnote or just prior to it.

Several methods of disclosure are available, such as parenthetical explanations, supporting schedules, cross-reference, and footnotes. Often, the additional disclosures must be made by a footnote in order to explain the situation properly. Examples are details of a pension plan, long-term leases, and provisions of a bond issue.

If the entity uses an accounting method that represents a departure from the official position of the FASB, disclosure of the departure must be made, along with the justification for it.

The financial statements are expected to summarize significant financial information. If all the financial information were presented in detail, it could be misleading; excessive disclosure could violate the concept of full disclosure. Therefore, a reasonable summarization of financial information is required.

Because of the complexity of many businesses and the increased expectations of the public, full disclosure has become one of the most difficult concepts for the accountant to apply. Lawsuits frequently charge accountants with failure to make proper disclosure. Since disclosure is often a judgment decision, it is not surprising that others (especially those who have suffered losses) would disagree with the adequacy of the disclosure.

Materiality

The accountant must consider many concepts and principles when determining how to handle a particular item. The proper use of the various concepts and principles may be costly and time-consuming. The materiality concept involves the relative size and importance of an item to a firm. An item that is material to one entity may not be material to another. For example, an asset that costs $100 might be expensed by General Motors, but the same asset might be capitalized and depreciated by a small entity.

It is essential that material items be properly handled on the financial statements. Immaterial items are not subject to the concepts and principles that bind the accountant; they may be handled in the most economical and expedient manner possible. However, the accountant is faced with a judgment situation when determining materiality. It is better to err in favor of an item being material than the other way around.

A basic question when determining whether an item is material is: "Would this item influence an informed reader of the financial statements?" In answering this question, the statements as a whole should generally be considered, rather than isolated parts of the statements.

Industry Practices

Some industry practices lead to accounting reports that do not conform to the general theory that underlies accounting. These practices are few in number, and the accounting profession is making an effort to eliminate them.

Some industry practices that differ from the customary accounting for a particular type of transaction result from government regulation. For example, some differences can be found in the insurance, railroad, and utility industries, which are highly regulated.

In the utility industry, the practice is to reflect an allowance for funds used during the construction period of a new plant as part of the cost of the plant. The offsetting amount is reflected on the income statement as other income. This amount is computed based on the utility's hypothetical cost of funds, including funds from debt, preferred stock, and common stock. This type of accounting is found only in the utility industry.

In some industries, it is very difficult to determine the cost of inventory. Examples are the meat-packing industry, the flower industry, and farming. In these areas, it may be necessary to determine the inventory value by working backward from the anticipated selling price and subtracting the estimated cost to complete and dispose of the item. The inventory would thus be valued at net realizable value, which would depart from the cost concept and the usual interpretation of the revenue realization concept. If inventory is valued at net realizable value, the profit has already been recognized and is part of the inventory amount.

Industry practices that depart from typical accounting procedures will probably never be eliminated completely. Some industries have legitimate peculiarities that call for accounting procedures other than the customary ones.

Transaction Approach

The accountant records only events that affect the financial position of the entity and, at the same time, can be reasonably determined in monetary terms. For example, if the entity purchases merchandise on account, the financial position of the entity changes. This change can be determined in monetary terms as the inventory asset is obtained and the liability, accounts payable, is incurred.

Many important events that influence the prospects for the entity are not recorded and therefore are not reflected in the financial statements, because they fall outside the transaction approach. If a top executive of the entity dies, this could have a material influence on the future prospects of the entity, especially if it is a small company. One of the company's major suppliers could go bankrupt at a time when the entity does not have an alternative source. The entity may experience a long strike by its employees or have a history of labor problems. A major competitor may go out of business. All these events may be significant to the entity, but they are not recorded, because they do not come under the transaction approach that is applied by accountants. When projecting the future prospects of an entity, it is necessary to go beyond financial statement analysis.

Present Value Considerations

Some assets and most liabilities represent current purchasing power or legal obligations to pay out a fixed number of dollars. These assets and liabilities are known as *monetary items*. Examples of monetary assets are cash, investments in marketable debt securities, and accounts receivable. The timing of when the cash is received for a monetary asset and paid out to extinguish a liability is important to the worth of the asset and the value of the liability. The characteristic that money received or paid out in the future is not worth as much as money available today is referred to as the *time value of money* or the *present value*.

Accountants must reflect the time value of money on monetary assets and liabilities when there is a material difference between the monetary amount that is involved in the transaction and the present value of the item. For example, if a sale is made for $1,000, receiving a three-year, non-interest-bearing note, the note and the sales price would need to be adjusted downward to reflect the present value of the money. For this purpose, the entity would use the interest rate that reflected the going rate of interest to the entity. If the entity had accepted a one-year, non-interest-bearing note, no adjustment to the $1,000 amount would be made. The difference between the stated monetary amount and the projected present value would be considered immaterial, since the note would be classified as a current asset. This illustrates that the time value of money consideration is not applied to current assets or current liabilities (described in Chapter 2).

Accountants take into consideration the time value of money when preparing the financial statements for such areas as long-term leases, pensions, and other long-term situations in which the future payments or receipts are not indicative of the present value of the asset or obligation. However, the way accountants consider the time value of money is not always consistent. For example, an interest rate at the time of the original transaction is used for leases, whereas an annual consideration of the interest rate is used for pensions.

Accrual Basis

The accrual basis of accounting dictates that revenue is recognized when it is realized (realization concept) and expenses are recognized when incurred (matching concept). The point of cash receipt for revenue and cash disbursement for expenses is not important under the accrual basis for income determination. If the difference between the accrual basis and the cash basis is not material, the entity may use the cash basis as an alternative to the accrual basis for income determination. Usually, the difference between the accrual basis and the cash basis is material.

The cash basis is simpler to apply than the accrual basis, because under the cash basis, revenue is recognized when cash is received, and expenses are recognized when payment is made. Because the accrual basis is used, there is a need for numerous adjustments at the end of the accounting period. For instance, if insurance has been paid, the accountant must determine the amount that belongs to prepaid insurance and the amount that belongs to insurance expense. If employees have not been paid all of their wages, it is necessary to determine the unpaid wages and record the amount as an expense and as an accrued liability. If revenue has been collected in advance (for example, rent received in advance), it is necessary to defer to future periods the recognition of the revenue that is for future periods. At the end of the accounting period, the unearned rent would be considered to be a liability.

The use of the accrual basis complicates the accounting process, but the end result is considered more representative than the cash basis. Without the accrual basis, accountants would not be able to make the time period assumption—that the entity can be accounted for reasonably accurately for a particular period of time.

The following illustration indicates why the accrual basis is generally regarded as a better measure of a firm's performance than the cash basis.

Assumptions:

1. Sold inventory for $25,000 on credit this year
2. The inventory sold cost $12,500 when purchased in the prior year

3. Purchased inventory this year in the amount of $30,000, on credit
4. Paid suppliers $18,000 this year
5. Collected $15,000 from sales

Accrual Basis		Cash Basis	
Sales	$25,000	Receipts	$15,000
Cost of sales (expenses)	(12,500)	Expenditures	(18,000)
Income	$12,500	Loss	$ (3,000)

For this example, the accrual basis indicates a profitable business, whereas the cash basis indicates a loss. The cash basis does not reasonably indicate when the revenue was earned or when to recognize the cost that relates to the earned revenue. The cash basis does indicate when the receipts were received and when payment was made. The points in time when cash is received and payment made do not usually constitute a good gauge of profitability. However, knowing the points in time is important; the flow of cash will be presented in the cash flow statement.

THE FINANCIAL STATEMENTS

The major financial statements of a corporation are the balance sheet, the income statement, and the statement of cash flows. A statement of retained earnings is usually included with the financial statements, but it explains only the change in the retained earnings account on the balance sheet. These financial statements are accompanied by footnotes. In order to evaluate the financial condition of an entity, it is necessary to understand these statements and footnotes and to be aware of their problems and limitations. An introduction to these statements is included in this chapter. A detailed explanation of the balance sheet is in Chapter 2; Chapter 3 covers the income statement and statement of retained earnings; and the statement of cash flows is covered in Chapter 10.

Balance Sheet

The purpose of a balance sheet is to show the financial condition of an accounting entity as of a particular date. The balance sheet consists of assets, which are the resources of the firm; liabilities, which are the debts of the firm; and stockholders' equity, which is the owners' interest in the firm.

At any point in time, the assets must equal the contributions of the creditors and owners. This is expressed in the accounting equation:

$$\text{Assets} = \text{Liabilities} + \text{Equity}$$

In simplistic form, the stockholders' equity is as follows:

Stockholders' equity	
Common stock	$200,000
Retained earnings	50,000
	$250,000

This indicates that stockholders contributed (invested) $200,000, and prior earnings less dividends have been reinvested in the entity in the net amount of $50,000.

Income Statement

An income statement is a summary of revenues and expenses and gains and losses, ending with net income for a particular period of time. It summarizes the results of operations for an accounting period. Net income is closed to the retained earnings account in the stockholders' equity section of the balance sheet. (This is necessary for the balance sheet to balance.)

Statement of Retained Earnings

Since net income is closed to the retained earnings account, this account is the link between the balance sheet and the income statement. Retained earnings is reduced by declared dividends to stockholders. There are some other possible increases or decreases to retained earnings besides income (losses) and dividends. For the purposes of this chapter, it is adequate to describe retained earnings as prior earnings less prior dividends.

The retained earnings statement is not a required financial statement, but it is usually presented whenever the income statement, balance sheet, and statement of cash flows are presented. The statement of retained earnings is a reconciliation of beginning retained earnings (retained earnings at the end of the prior period) to the retained earnings balance at the end of the current period.

Statement of Cash Flows

The statement of cash flows details the sources and uses of cash during a specified period of time—the same period that is used for the income statement. The period of time represented in annual reports would be one year.

The statement of cash flows is presented with three major sections: cash flows from operating activities, cash flows from investing activities, and cash flows from financing activities.

Exhibit 1-2 illustrates the interrelationship of the balance sheet, income statement, statement of retained earnings, and statement of cash flows. The most basic statement is the balance sheet. The other three statements explain the changes between two balance sheet dates in some way. Each of the statements in Exhibit 1-2 is highly simplified. As previously indicated, detailed explanations of these statements are included in subsequent chapters.

ABC COMPANY
The Interrelationship of Financial Statements

Balance Sheet December 31, 1991		Statement of Cash Flows For the Year Ended December 31, 1992		Balance Sheet December 31, 1992	
Assets		Cash flows from operating activities		Assets	
Cash	$25,000	Net income	$20,000	Cash	$40,000
Receivables	20,000	+ Decrease in		Receivables	20,000
Inventory	30,000	inventory	10,000	Inventory	20,000
Land	10,000	− Decrease in		Land	20,000
Other assets	10,000	accounts payable	(5,000)	Other assets	10,000
Total assets	$95,000	Net cash flow from operating activities	25,000	Total assets	$110,000
Liabilities		Cash flow from investing activities		Liabilities	
Accounts payable	$25,000	− Increase in land	(10,000)	Accounts payable	$20,000
Wages payable	5,000	Net cash flow from investing activities	(10,000)	Wages payable	5,000
Total liabilities	$30,000	Cash flow from financing activities		Total liabilities	$25,000
Stockholders' equity		+ Capital stock	10,000	Stockholders' equity	
Capital stock	$40,000	− Dividends	(10,000)	Capital stock	$50,000
Retained earnings	25,000	Net cash flow from financing activities	—0—	Retained earnings	35,000
Total stockholders' equity	$65,000	Net increase in cash	$15,000	Total stockholders' equity	$85,000
Total liabilities and stockholders' equity	$95,000	Cash at beginning of year	25,000	Total liabilities and stockholders' equity	$110,000
		Cash at end of year	$40,000		

**Income Statement
For the Year Ended
December 31, 1992**

Revenues	$120,000
− Expenses	(100,000)
Net income	$20,000

**Statement of
Retained Earnings
For the Year Ended
December 31, 1992**

Beginning balance	$25,000
+ Net income	20,000
− Dividends	(10,000)
Ending balance	$35,000

Footnotes

The footnotes to the financial statements are useful for presenting additional information on items included in the financial statements or other financial information. Footnotes are an integral part of financial statements; a detailed review of footnotes is absolutely essential in order to understand the financial statements.

Certain information must be presented in footnotes, according to generally accepted accounting principles. Specifically, APB Opinion No. 22 requires disclosure of accounting policies as the first footnote to financial statements. Accounting policies include such items as the method of inventory valuation and depreciation policies. Other information specifically required to be disclosed in the footnotes is the existence of contingent liabilities and some subsequent events.

Contingent liabilities are those that may result in payment, depending on a particular occurrence such as the settlement of litigation or the ruling of a tax court. Signing as guarantor on a loan creates another type of contingent liability. SFAS No. 5 recommends that an estimated loss from a contingent liability be charged to income, and that it be established as a liability only if the loss is considered probable and the amount is reasonably determinable. Otherwise, the contingent liability is footnoted. Exhibit 1-3 illustrates a contingent liability footnote.

Subsequent Events

Subsequent events are those that occur after the balance sheet date but before the statements are issued. There are two varieties of subsequent events. The first type consists of events that existed at the balance sheet date, affect the estimates in the statements, and require adjustment of the statements before issuance. The second type consists of events that provide evidence about conditions that did not exist at the balance sheet date, and do not require adjustment of the statements. If failure to disclose these events would be misleading, disclosure should take the form of footnotes or supplementary schedules. Examples of such events include the sale of securities, the settlement of litigation, a casualty loss, or the purchase of a subsidiary. Other categories of subsequent events might be debt—incurred, reduced, or refinanced; business combinations pending or effected; discontinued operations; employee benefit plans; and capital stock issued or purchased.[6] Exhibit 1-4 describes subsequent events for Johnson Controls, Inc., which has a September 30 year end.

Human Resource and Social Accounting

American business has become acutely aware of the influence of social pressures and of the value of its employees. This has been reflected by two developments in the accounting area—human resource accounting and social accounting. Human

---

[6]*Accounting Trends and Techniques* (New York: AICPA, 1989), p. 65.

EXHIBIT 1 - 3

GEORGIA-PACIFIC
Commitments and Contingencies
1989 Annual Report

Note 11. Commitments and Contingencies

The Corporation is a party to various legal proceedings generally incidental to its business. Although the ultimate disposition of these proceedings is not presently determinable, management does not believe that adverse determinations in any or all of such proceedings would have a material adverse effect upon the financial condition of the Corporation.

The Corporation is self-insured for general liability claims up to $25 million per claim.

The Corporation is a 50% partner in a joint venture (GA-MET) with Metropolitan Life Insurance Company (Metropolitan). GA-MET owns and operates the Corporation's office headquarters complex in Atlanta, Georgia. The Corporation accounts for its investment in GA-MET under the equity method.

During 1986, GA-MET borrowed $170 million from Metropolitan for the primary purpose of retiring debt incurred from the acquisition and construction of the Atlanta headquarters complex. The note bears interest at $9\frac{1}{2}$% and requires monthly payments of principal and interest with a final installment due in 2011. The note is secured by the land and building of the Atlanta headquarters complex. In the event of foreclosure, each partner has severally guaranteed payment of one-half of any shortfall of collateral value to the outstanding secured indebtedness. Based on the present market conditions and building occupancy, the likelihood of any obligation to the Corporation with respect to this guarantee is considered remote.

EXHIBIT 1 - 4

JOHNSON & JOHNSON
Subsequent Events

In January 1990, the Johnson & Johnson-Merck Consumer Pharmaceuticals Co. joint venture completed the acquisition of the U.S. over-the-counter (OTC) business of ICI Americas, Inc. The OTC business includes the MYLANTA line of antacid products and the MYLICON line of anti-gas products. The consideration involved $395 million in cash and the transfer of the U.S. rights to the Merck prescription anti-depressant drug ELAVIL to ICI Americas, Inc.

Additionally in January 1990, the Company announced that it had agreed in principle to sell the Devro edible sausage casing business. Devro is an industrial business which does not complement the Company's strategic objective of expanding its position as the world's leading health care products company. The terms of the agreement have not been finalized. The disposition of Devro will not have a material effect on the Company's financial position or operating results.

Reprinted with permission of Johnson & Johnson.

resource accounting attempts to account for the services of employees, and social accounting attempts to account for benefits to the social environment within which the firm operates. Although reporting of these areas is still in the development stage, many firms have begun to include such information on their annual reports. Such information may enhance the analyst's subjective opinion regarding the company. Exhibit 1-5 is an example of one firm's attempt to show its human and social concern.

Auditor's Report

The auditor who signs the audit report is a certified public accountant or an accounting firm that conducts an independent examination of the accounting information presented by the business and issues a report thereon. An auditor's report is the formal presentation of all the effort that goes into an audit. Audit opinions are classified as shown on the next page.

E X H I B I T   1 - 5

J.C. PENNEY
Social Concern
1989 Annual Report

The Company continued to reinforce its commitment to the health and vitality of the communities in which it does business through charitable contributions, community service programs, and minority supplier development.

In 1989, charitable contributions were $17.8 million Company-wide. Approximately 65 per cent of the contributions were made by JCPenney stores and facilities to local community programs. The remainder was granted to national organizations with programs that impact communities across the country. JCPenney employees pledged an additional $6.5 million to local United Ways through payroll deduction and one-time gifts.

Community service programs were augmented by the second production of the Golden Rule Network. The Network utilizes the Company's business television network to provide information and materials on social issues to the communities where we do business. The initial broadcast in 1988 dealt with teenage substance abuse. The 1989 program focused on the issue of stress among teenagers.

The Company continues to promote volunteerism through the James Cash Penney Awards, which recognize JCPenney employees for outstanding volunteer activities in their communities. The Golden Rule Awards program provides similar recognition to volunteers outside the Company. This program was expanded to 110 markets in 1989 and contributed $432 thousand to local organizations.

The Company is committed to expanding the purchase of merchandise and services from minority-owned companies. During 1989, purchases from minority-owned businesses were $335 million, representing relationships with 1,830 suppliers.

1. *Unqualified opinion.* This opinion states that the financial statements present fairly, in all material respects, the financial position, results of operations, and cash flows of the entity, in conformity with generally accepted accounting principles.

In certain circumstances, an unqualified opinion on the financial statements may require that the auditor add an explanatory paragraph or explanatory language to the report. This paragraph or explanatory language is added when the auditor's opinion is based in part on the report of another auditor. The auditor may agree with a departure from a designated principle, an expression of material uncertainty or doubt as to the going-concern assumption, or a change in accounting principle. Explanatory language may also be added to emphasize a matter.

2. *Qualified opinion.* A qualified opinion states that, except for the effects of the matters to which the qualification relates, the financial statements present fairly, in all material respects, the financial position, results of operations, and cash flows of the entity, in conformity with generally accepted accounting principles.

3. *Adverse opinion.* This opinion states that the financial statements do not present fairly the financial position, results of operations, or cash flows of the entity, in conformity with generally accepted accounting principles.

4. *Disclaimer of opinion.* A disclaimer of opinion states that the auditor does not express an opinion on the financial statements. This type of opinion is rendered when the auditor has not performed an audit sufficient in scope to form an opinion.

The typical unqualified (or *clean*) opinion has three paragraphs. The first paragraph indicates the financial statements that have been audited and states that these statements are the responsibility of the company's management. This paragraph indicates that the auditors have the responsibility to express an opinion on these statements based on the audit or to disclaim an opinion.

The second paragraph indicates that the audit has been conducted in accordance with generally accepted auditing standards. It indicates that these standards require the auditor to plan and perform the audit to obtain reasonable assurance that the financial statements are free of material misstatement. The second paragraph also includes a brief description of what is included in an audit.

The third paragraph gives an opinion on the statements—that they are in conformity with generally accepted accounting principles. A typical unqualified report is illustrated in Exhibit 1-6.

When examining financial statements, review the independent auditor's report; it can be important to your analysis. From the point of view of analysis, the unqualified opinion without an explanatory paragraph or explanatory language carries the highest degree of reliability. It indicates that the financial statements do not contain limitation on scope or a material departure from generally accepted accounting principles. When an unqualified opinion contains an explanatory paragraph or explanatory language, try to decide how seriously to regard the departure from a straight unqualified opinion. For example, an explanatory paragraph because of a change in accounting principle would not usually be regarded as serious, although it would be important to your analysis. An explanatory paragraph because of a material uncertainty would often be regarded as a serious qualification.

You are likely to regard a qualified opinion or an adverse opinion as casting

EXHIBIT 1-6

MERCK & CO., INC.
Accountant's Report—Unqualified Report

Report of Independent Public Accountants

To the Stockholders and Board of Directors of Merck & Co., Inc.:

We have audited the accompanying consolidated balance sheets of Merck & Co., Inc. (a New Jersey Corporation) and Subsidiaries as of December 31, 1989 and 1988, and the related statements of income, retained earnings, and cash flows for each of the three years in the period ended December 31, 1989. These financial statements are the responsibility of the Company's management. Our responsibility is to express an opinion on these financial statements based on our audits.

We conducted our audits in accordance with generally accepted auditing standards. Those standards require that we plan and perform the audit to obtain reasonable assurance about whether the financial statements are free of material misstatement. An audit includes examining, on a test basis, evidence supporting the amounts and disclosures in the financial statements. An audit also includes assessing the accounting principles used and significant estimates made by management, as well as evaluating the overall financial statement presentation. We believe that our audits provide a reasonable basis for our opinion.

In our opinion, the financial statements referred to above present fairly, in all material respects, the financial position of Merck & Co., Inc. and Subsidiaries as of December 31, 1989 and 1988, and the results of its operations and its cash flows for each of the three years in the period ended December 31, 1989, in conformity with generally accepted accounting principles.

New York, New York   ARTHUR ANDERSEN & CO.
January 23, 1990

serious doubt on the reliability of the financial statements. In each case, you must read the auditor's report carefully to form your opinion.

A disclaimer of opinion indicates that you should not look to the auditor's report as an indication of the reliability of the statements. When this type of report is rendered, the auditor has not performed an audit sufficient in scope to form an opinion, or the auditor is not independent.

In some cases, outside accountants are associated with financial statements when they have performed less than an audit. The accountant's report then indicates that they have either reviewed or compiled the financial statements.

A review consists principally of inquiries made to company personnel and analytical procedures applied to financial data. It has substantially less scope than an examination in accordance with generally accepted auditing standards, the objective of which is the expression of an opinion regarding the financial statements taken as a whole. Accordingly, the accountant does not express an opinion. The accountant's report indicates that the accountant is not aware of any material modifications that should be made to the financial statements in order for them to be in conformity with generally accepted accounting principles, or the report indicates departures from GAAP. A departure from GAAP is described as using one or more accounting principles without reasonable justification, or the omission of the statement of cash flows.

In general, the reliance that can be placed on the accountant's report for financial statements that have been reviewed is substantially less than for those that have been audited. Remember that the accountant's report does not express an opinion on reviewed financial statements.

When the outside accountant presents only financial information as represented by management, the accountant's report is described as a *compilation*. Such a report states that the accountant has not audited or reviewed the financial statements. Therefore, the accountant does not express an opinion or any other form of assurance about them. If an accountant performs a compilation and becomes aware of deficiencies in the statements, the accountant's report characterizes the deficiencies, as follows:

- Omission of substantially all disclosures
- Omission of statement of cash flows
- Accounting principles not generally accepted

Do not place reliance on the accountant's report for financial statements that have been compiled. Such statements have not been audited or reviewed. Accordingly, the accountant does not express an opinion or any other form of assurance about them.

Sometimes financial statements are presented without an accompanying accountant's report. This means that the statements have not been audited, reviewed, or compiled. Such statements are solely the representation of management.

Management's Responsibility for Financial Statements

The responsibility for the preparation and integrity of financial statements rests with management. The auditor is responsible for conducting an independent examination of the accounting statements. In an attempt to make this responsibility of management known to the users of financial statements, companies have acknowledged this responsibility through management statements to shareholders. An example is shown in Exhibit 1-7.

The SEC's Integrated Disclosure System

In general, the SEC has the authority to prescribe external financial reporting requirements for companies with securities sold to the general public. Under this jurisdiction, the SEC requires that certain financial statement information be in-

EXHIBIT 1-7

MERCK & CO., INC.
Management's Report

Primary responsibility for the integrity and objectivity of the Company's financial statements rests with management. The financial statements report on management's stewardship of Company assets. They are prepared in conformity with generally accepted accounting principles and accordingly include amounts that are based on management's best estimates and judgments. Nonfinancial information included in the annual report has also been prepared by management and is consistent with the financial statements.

To assure that financial information is reliable and assets are safeguarded, management maintains an effective system of internal controls and procedures, important elements of which include: careful selection, training, and development of operating and financial managers; an organization that provides appropriate division of responsibility; and communications aimed at assuring that Company policies and procedures are understood throughout the organization. In establishing internal controls, management weighs the costs of such systems against the benefits it believes such systems will provide. A staff of internal auditors regularly monitors the adequacy and application of internal controls on a worldwide basis.

To insure that personnel continue to understand the system of internal controls and procedures and policies concerning good and prudent business practices, the Company periodically conducts the Management's Stewardship Program for key management and financial personnel. This program reinforces the importance and understanding of internal controls by reviewing key corporate policies, procedures, and systems. Included is a review of corporate policies on ethical business practices and management controls which stress the Company's high standards in the conduct of its business.

The independent public accountants have audited the Company's consolidated financial statements as described in their report. Their audits included a review of the Company's accounting systems, procedures and internal controls, and tests and other auditing procedures sufficient to enable them to render their opinion on the Company's financial statements.

P. Roy Vagelos, M.D.   Francis H. Spiegel, Jr.
Chairman and   Senior Vice President
Chief Executive Officer

cluded in the annual report to shareholders. This annual report, along with certain supplementary information, must then be included in an annual filing to the SEC known as the 10-K report. The 10-K report is available to the public, usually on request only. The SEC has adopted major changes in its disclosure system, intended to promote an integrated disclosure system. The changes significantly affect the information content of annual reports to shareholders and the annual form 10-K filed with the SEC. The goals of the plan are to improve the quality of disclosure, lighten the disclosure load, standardize information requirements, and achieve uniformity of annual reports and 10-K filings.

In addition to the company's primary financial statements, the form 10-K and shareholder annual reports must include the following:

1. Information on the market for holders of common stock and related securities, including high and low sales price, frequency and amount of dividends, and number of shares.

2. Five-year summary of selected financial data, including net sales or operating revenues, income from continuing operations, total assets, long-term obligations, redeemable preferred stock, and cash dividends per share. (Some companies elect to present data for more than five years and/or expand the disclosure.) Trend analysis is emphasized.

3. Management's discussion and analysis of financial condition and results of operations. Specifically required is discussion of liquidity, capital resources, and results of operations.

4. Two years of audited balance sheets and three years of audited statements of income and changes in financial position.

5. Disclosure of the domestic and foreign components of pretax income.

The changes in the SEC requirements force management to focus on the financial statements as a whole, rather than just looking at the income statement and operations. Where trend information is relevant, discussion should center on the new five-year summary. Emphasis should be on favorable or unfavorable trends and on identification of significant events or uncertainties. This discussion should provide the analyst with a reasonable summary of the position of the firm. The specific management discussion for Cooper Tire & Rubber Company is presented and discussed in Chapter 11.

Summary Annual Report

A reporting option available to public companies is to issue a summary annual report. The concept of a summary annual report was approved by the Securities and Exchange Commission in January 1987.

A summary annual report is a condensed report that omits much of the financial information otherwise included in an annual report. When a company issues a summary annual report, the proxy materials it sends to shareholders must include a set of fully audited statements and other required financial disclosures. The proxy is the solicitation sent to stockholders for the election of directors and for the approval of other corporation actions. The 10-K report submitted to the SEC is also available to the public.

A summary annual report is substantially shorter than a full annual report. The greatest reduction in pages is usually in the financial pages: A typical annual report has more financial pages than nonfinancial pages, but a summary annual report generally has more nonfinancial pages than financial pages.[7] For example, the 1987 summary annual report of the Kroger Company had 17 nonfinancial pages and a single financial page, which included only data on sales, earnings, return on average equity from continuing operations, dividends per common share, and capital expenditures.

A summary annual report is not adequate for reasonable analysis. For companies that issue a summary annual report, request a copy of the proxy materials and the 10-K. This will provide more comprehensive material for analysis than is provided in a normal annual report.

Ethics

"Ethics and morals are synonymous. While ethics is derived from Greek, morals is derived from Latin. They are interchangeable terms referring to ideals of character and conduct. These ideals, in the form of codes of conduct, furnish criteria for distinguishing between right and wrong."[8] Ethics has been a subject of investigation for hundreds of years. It is important that individuals in financial positions be able to recognize ethical issues and resolve them in an appropriate manner.

Ethics is an everyday issue that affects all individuals, from the financial clerk to the high-level financial executive. Daily decisions are made by individuals based on the individuals' values. Ten essential values can be considered central to relations between people:[9]

1. Caring
2. Honesty
3. Accountability
4. Promise keeping
5. Pursuit of excellence
6. Loyalty
7. Fairness
8. Integrity
9. Respect for others
10. Responsible citizenship

Some companies and professional organizations have formulated a code of ethics for their employees—a statement of aspirations and a standard of integrity beyond that required by law (which can be viewed as the minimum standard of ethics).

Ethics can be a particular problem with financial reports. Accepted accounting principles leave ample room for arriving at different results in the short run. Highly

[7]Charles H. Gibson and Nicholas Schroeder, "How 21 Companies Handled Their Summary Annual Reports," *Financial Executive* (November/December 1989), Financial Executive's Institute, New York, pp. 45–46.
[8]Mary E. Guy, *Ethical Decision Making in Everyday Work Situations* (New York: Quarum Books, 1990), p. 5.
[9]Ibid., p. 14.

subjective estimates can substantially influence earnings. What provision should be made for warranty costs? What should be the loan loss reserve? What should be the allowance for doubtful accounts?

Example 1: Questionable Ethics in Savings and Loans

In connection with the savings and loan scandal, it has been revealed that several auditors of thrift institutions borrowed substantial amounts from the S & L that their firm was auditing. It is charged that some of the loans involved special consideration.[10] In one case, dozens of partners of a major accounting firm borrowed money for commercial real estate loans, and some of the partners defaulted on their loans when the real estate market collapsed.[11] It is not clear whether these particular loans violated professional ethics standards, but the AICPA has proposed a rule banning all such loans.

An accounting firm paid $1.5 million to settle charges by the California State Board of Accountancy that the accounting firm was grossly negligent in its 1987 audit of Lincoln Savings & Loan. The accounting board charged that the firm had agreed to the improper recognition of approximately $62 million in profits.[12]

Example 2: Questionable Ethics in the Motion Picture Industry

Hollywood's accounting practices have often been labeled "mysterious."[13] A case in point is Art Buchwald's lawsuit against Paramount Pictures for breach of contract regarding the film *Coming to America*. When Paramount took an option on Buchwald's story "King for a Day" in 1983, Buchwald was promised 1.5% of the net profits. Buchwald's attorney, Pierce O'Donnell accused Paramount Studios of "fatal subtraction" in determining the amount of profit. Although the film grossed $350 million worldwide, Paramount claimed an $18 million net loss. As a result of the studio's accounting practices, Buchwald was to get 1.5% of nothing.[14] The outcome of the case was uncertain as this book went to press.

The American Accounting Association initiated a project in 1988 on professionalism and ethics. One of the goals of the project was to provide students with a framework for evaluating their courses of action when such dilemmas are encountered. The American Accounting Association developed a decision model for focusing on ethical issues:[15]

1. Determine the facts—what, who, where, when, how
2. Define the ethical issues (includes identifying the identifiable parties affected by the decision made or action taken)

[10]"Regulators Investigate Peat on Its Auditing of S & L," *New York Times*, May 23, 1991, p. D-1.
[11]"S.E.C. Inquiry Is Reported on Loans to Accountants," *New York Times*, February 7, 1991, p. D-1.
[12]"Ernst & Young Settles Negligence Charge," *Business Insurance*, May 6, 1991, p. 2.
[13]Ronald Grover, "Curtains for Tinseltown Accounting?" *Business Week*, January 14, 1991, p. 35.
[14]Shahram Victory, "Pierce O'Donnell Pans 'Fatal Subtraction,' " *American Lawyer* (March 1991), p. 43.
[15]William W. May, Ed., *Ethics in the Accounting Curriculum: Cases & Readings* (Sarasota, Fla.: American Accounting Association, 1990), pp. 1–2.

3. Identify major principles, rules, and values
4. Specify the alternatives
5. Compare norms, principles, and values with the alternatives to see if a clear decision can be reached
6. Assess the consequences
7. Make your decision

SUMMARY

This chapter has reviewed the development of generally accepted accounting principles and the traditional assumptions of the accounting model. A broad understanding of generally accepted accounting principles and the traditional assumptions is needed to understand financial statements. The financial statements can be no better than the accounting principles and the assumptions of the accounting model that are the basis for their preparation.

An introduction to the basic financial statements has been included in this chapter. Subsequent chapters will cover these statements in detail.

Although management is responsible for financial statements, the auditor's report also covers the financial statements. The auditor's report often points out key factors that can affect financial statement analysis.

The SEC has begun a program to integrate the form 10-K requirements with those of the annual report. These requirements are incorporated in the numerous reporting examples in the chapters that follow, especially in Chapters 5 and 12.

A reporting option available to public companies is to issue a summary annual report. A summary annual report is a condensed annual report that omits much of the financial information included in a typical annual report.

It is important that individuals in financial positions be able to recognize ethical issues and resolve them appropriately.

QUESTIONS

Q 1-1   Discuss the role of each of the following in the formulation of accounting principles:
a. American Institute of Certified Public Accountants
b. Financial Accounting Standards Board
c. Securities and Exchange Commission

Q 1-2   A typical accrual adjusting entry for salaries is as follows:

Salary expense	$1,000 (increase)
Salaries payable	1,000 (increase)

Explain how the matching concept applies in this situation.

Q 1-3   According to Financial Accounting Standards Board Statement No. 12, the lower of cost or market must be applied to marketable equity securities on a portfolio basis. Why is this statement considered an application of the concept of conservatism?

Q 1-4   How does the concept of consistency aid in the analysis of financial statements? What type of accounting disclosure is required if this concept is not applied?

Q 1-5   The president of your firm, Lesky and Lesky, has little background in accounting. Today he walked into your office and said, "A year ago we bought a piece of land for $100,000. This year inflation has driven prices up by 6%, and an appraiser just told us we could easily resell the land for $115,000. Yet our balance sheet still shows it at $100,000. It should be valued at $115,000. That's what it's worth. Or, at a minimum, at $106,000." Respond to this statement with specific reference to accounting principles applicable in this situation.

Q 1-6   Identify the accounting principle(s) applicable to each of the following situations:
   a. Tim Roberts owns a bar and a rental apartment and operates a consulting service. He has separate financial statements for each.
   b. Adjustments are made to the allowance for doubtful accounts at the end of the year at 1¼% of credit sales for the period.
   c. An advance collection for magazine subscriptions is reported as a liability titled unearned subscriptions.
   d. Purchases of office or store equipment for less than $25 are entered in miscellaneous expense.
   e. Patent costs are recorded as intangible assets and written off against future income.
   f. A company uses the lower of cost or market for valuation of its inventory.
   g. Although inflation of 6% occurred during the year, no adjustment for this was made on the books.
   h. Partially completed television sets are carried at the sum of direct materials, direct labor, and factory overhead incurred to date.
   i. Land purchased fifteen years ago for $40,500 is now worth $346,000. It is still carried on the books at $40,500.
   j. The manager insists that the petty cash fund be replenished at year end before statements are prepared.
   k. Zero Corporation is being sued for $1,000,000 for breach of contract. Its lawyers believe that the damages will be minimal. Zero reports the possible loss in a footnote.
   l. Although Kaufman's Restaurant maintains three bank accounts, it reports a single cash balance on its balance sheet.

Q 1-7   A corporation such as General Motors has many owners (stockholders). Which concept enables the accountant to account for transactions of General Motors, separate and distinct from the personal transactions of the owners of General Motors?

Q 1-8   The Zebra Company has incurred substantial financial losses in recent years. Because of its financial condition, the ability of the company to keep operating is in question. Management prepares a set of financial statements that conform to generally accepted accounting principles. Comment on the use of GAAP under these conditions.

Q 1-9   Discuss why the following accounts would be overstated using historical cost if the firm is not a going concern.
   a. intangible assets
   b. inventories
   c. prepaid insurance

Q 1-10   Because of assumptions and estimates that go into the preparation of financial statements, the statements turn out to be inaccurate and are therefore not a very meaningful tool to determine the profits or losses of an entity or the financial position of an entity. Comment.

Q 1-11   The only accurate way to account for the success or failure of an entity is to accumulate all transactions from the opening of business until the business eventually liquidates. Comment on whether this is true. Discuss the necessity of having completely accurate statements.

Q 1-12   Define the following terms, which indicate the period of time included in financial statements:
    a. natural business year
    b. calendar year
    c. fiscal year

Q 1-13   When a warranty liability is found on the balance sheet, you can be sure that the amount stated is an accurate amount. Comment.

Q 1-14   Which standard of measure is the best for measuring financial transactions?

Q 1-15   Various countries have had problems with the stability of their money. Briefly describe the problem caused for financial statements when money does not hold a stable value.

Q 1-16   In some countries where inflation has been material, an effort has been made to retain the significance of money as a measuring unit by adjusting the financial statements by an inflation factor. Can an accurate adjustment for inflation be made to the statements? Can a reasonable adjustment to the statements be made? Discuss.

Q 1-17   An arbitrary write-off of inventory can be justified under the conservatism concept. True or false? Discuss.

Q 1-18   Inventory that has a market value below the historical cost should be written down in order to recognize a loss. Comment.

Q 1-19   There are other acceptable methods of recognizing revenue when the point of sale is not acceptable. List and discuss the other methods, and indicate when they can be used.

Q 1-20   The matching concept involves the determination of when to recognize the costs associated with the revenue that is being recognized. For some costs, such as administrative costs, the matching concept is difficult to apply. Comment on when it is difficult to apply the matching concept. What do accountants often do under these circumstances?

Q 1-21   The consistency concept requires the entity to give the same treatment to comparable transactions from period to period. Under what circumstances can an entity change its accounting methods, provided it makes full disclosure?

Q 1-22   Discuss why the concept of full disclosure is difficult to apply.

Q 1-23   No estimates or subjectivity are allowed in the preparation of financial statements. Discuss.

Q 1-24   It is proper to handle immaterial items in the most economical, expedient manner possible. In other words, generally accepted accounting principles do not apply. Comment, including a concept to support your answer.

Q 1-25   The same generally accepted accounting principles apply to all companies. Comment.

Q 1-26 Many important events that influence the prospects for the entity are not recorded in the financial records. Comment and give an example.

Q 1-27 If a company has a long-term lease and the lease payments are $20,000 a year for the next ten years, then the amount of the liability that appears on the financial statement would be $200,000. Comment.

Q 1-28 An entity may choose between the use of the accrual basis of accounting and the cash basis. Comment.

Q 1-29 Generally accepted accounting principles are accounting principles that have substantial authoritative support. Indicate the problem in determining substantial authoritative support.

Q 1-30 Would an accountant record the personal assets and liabilities of the owners on the accounts of the business? Explain.

Q 1-31 Fixed assets are reported on the balance sheet of the Jason Company at a cost of $300,000 less accumulated depreciation of $100,000. Why aren't fixed assets reported on the balance sheet at market value?

Q 1-32 At which point is revenue from sales on account commonly recognized?

Q 1-33 The Elliott Company constructed a building at a cost of $50,000. A local contractor had submitted a bid to construct it for $60,000.
   a. At what amount should the building be recorded?
   b. Should revenue be recorded for the savings between the cost of $50,000 and the bid of $60,000?

Q 1-34 The Dexter Company charges to expense all fixed assets that cost $25 or less. What concept supports this policy?

Q 1-35 The cost of inventory at the close of the calendar year of the first year of operation is $40,000, using LIFO inventory, resulting in a profit of $100,000. If the FIFO inventory would have been $50,000, what would the reported profit have been? If the average cost method would have resulted in an inventory of $45,000, what would the reported profit have been? Should the inventory costing method be disclosed? Why?

Q 1-36 What is the basic problem with the monetary assumption when there has been significant inflation?

Q 1-37 Explain the matching principle. How is the matching principle related to the realization concept?

Q 1-38 Briefly explain the term *generally accepted accounting principles.*

Q 1-39 Briefly describe the operating procedure for Statements of Financial Accounting Standards.

Q 1-40 What is the FASB Conceptual Framework for Accounting and Reporting intended to provide?

Q 1-41 Briefly describe the following:
   a. Committee on Accounting Procedures
   b. Committee on Accounting Terminology
   c. Accounting Principles Board
   d. Financial Accounting Standards Board

Q 1-42   Describe the role of Statements of Financial Accounting Concepts (SFACs) in the development of generally accepted accounting principles.

Q 1-43   The objectives of general-purpose external financial reporting are primarily to serve the needs of management. Comment.

Q 1-44   Financial accounting is designed to measure directly the value of a business enterprise. Comment.

Q 1-45   According to Concept Statement No. 2, relevance and reliability are the two primary qualities that make accounting information useful for decision making. Comment on what is meant by *relevance* and *reliability*.

Q 1-46   SFAC No. 5 indicates that, to be recognized, an item should meet four criteria, subject to the cost-benefit constraint and materiality threshold. List these criteria.

Q 1-47   SFAC No. 5 identifies five different measurement attributes currently used in practice. List these measurement attributes.

Q 1-48   Briefly explain the difference between an accrual basis income statement and a cash basis income statement.

Q 1-49   The cash basis does not reasonably indicate when the revenue was earned and when the cost should be recognized. Comment.

Q 1-50   It is not important to know when cash is received and when payment is made. Comment.

Q 1-51   Name the type of opinion indicated by each of the following situations.
   a. There is a material uncertainty.
   b. There was a change in accounting principle.
   c. There is no material scope limitation or material departure from GAAP.
   d. The financial statements do not present fairly the financial position, results of operations, or cash flows of the entity in conformity with GAAP.
   e. Except for the effects of the matter(s) to which the qualification relates, the financial statements present fairly, in all material respects, the financial position, results of operations, and cash flows of the entity, in conformity with GAAP.

Q 1-52   What are the roles of management and the auditor in the preparation and integrity of the financial statements?

Q 1-53   What is the purpose of the SEC's integrated disclosure system for financial reporting?

Q 1-54   Why do some unqualified opinions have explanatory paragraphs?

Q 1-55   Describe an auditor's review of financial statements.

Q 1-56   Does the accountant express an opinion on reviewed financial statements? Describe the accountant's report for reviewed financial statements.

Q 1-57   What type of opinion is expressed on a compilation?

Q 1-58   Are all financial statements presented with some kind of an accountant's report?

Q 1-59   What are the major financial statements of a corporation? Briefly describe the purpose of each statement.

Q 1-60 Why are footnotes to statements necessary?

Q 1-61 What are contingent liabilities? Are lawsuits contingent liabilities?

Q 1-62 Which of the following events, occurring subsequent to the balance sheet date, would require a footnote?
   a. major fire in one of the firm's plants
   b. increase in competitor's advertising
   c. purchase of a subsidiary
   d. introduction of new management techniques
   e. death of the corporate treasurer

Q 1-63 Why are the firm's employees not valued as assets on the balance sheet?

Q 1-64 Briefly describe a summary annual report.

Q 1-65 If a company issues a summary annual report, where can the more extensive financial information be found?

Q 1-66 Comment on the typical number of financial pages in a summary annual report, as compared to a full annual report.

Q 1-67 Indicate the major sections of a statement of cash flows.

Q 1-68 Which major financial statements explain the differences between two balance sheet dates?

Q 1-69 What are the three major categories on a balance sheet?

Q 1-70 Can cash dividends be paid from retained earnings? Comment.

Q 1-71 Why review footnotes to financial statements?

Q 1-72 Where do we find a description of a firm's accounting policies?

Q 1-73 Describe the relationship between the terms *ethics* and *morals*.

Q 1-74 What is the relationship between ethics and law?

| PROBLEMS

P 1-1 FASB Statement of Concepts No. 2 indicates several qualitative characteristics of useful accounting information. Below is a list of some of these qualities, as well as a list of statements and phrases describing the qualities.
   a. benefits > costs
   b. decision usefulness
   c. relevance
   d. reliability
   e. predictive value, feedback value, timeliness
   f. verifiability, neutrality, representational faithfulness
   g. comparability
   h. materiality

     i. relevance, reliability

    ____ 1. Without usefulness, there would be no benefits from information to set against its cost.

    ____ 2. Pervasive constraint imposed upon financial accounting information.

    ____ 3. Constraint that guides the threshold for recognition.

    ____ 4. A quality requiring that the information be timely and that it also have predictive value or feedback value, or both.

    ____ 5. A quality requiring that the information have representational faithfulness and that it be verifiable and neutral.

    ____ 6. These are the two primary qualities that make accounting information useful for decision making.

    ____ 7. These are the ingredients needed to ensure that the information is relevant.

    ____ 8. These are the ingredients needed to ensure that the information is reliable.

    ____ 9. Includes consistency and interacts with relevance and reliability to contribute to the usefulness of information.

Required   Place the appropriate letter identifying each quality on the line in front of the statement or phrase describing the quality.

P 1-2   Certain underlying considerations have had an important impact on the development of generally accepted accounting principles. Below is a list of these underlying considerations, as well as a list of statements describing them.

    a. going concern or continuity
    b. monetary unit
    c. conservatism
    d. matching
    e. full disclosure
    f. materiality
    g. transaction approach
    h. accrual basis
    i. industry practices
    j. verifiability
    k. consistency
    l. realization
    m. historical cost
    n. time period
    o. business entity

    ____ 1. The business for which the financial statements are prepared is separate and distinct from the owners of the entity.

    ____ 2. The assumption is made that the entity in question will remain in business for an indefinite period of time.

    ____ 3. Accountants need some standard of measure to bring financial transactions together in a meaningful way.

    ____ 4. Revenue should be recognized when the earning process is virtually complete and the exchange value can be objectively determined.

    ____ 5. This concept deals with when to recognize the costs that are associated with the recognized revenue.

    ____ 6. Accounting reports must disclose all facts that may influence the judgment of an informed reader.

____ 7. This concept involves the relative size and importance of an item to a firm.

____ 8. The accountant is required to adhere as closely as possible to verifiable data.

____ 9. Leads to accounting reports that do not conform to the general theory that underlies accounting.

____ 10. The accountant records only events that affect the financial position of the entity and, at the same time, can be reasonably determined in monetary terms.

____ 11. Revenue must be recognized when it is realized (realization concept) and expenses are recognized when incurred (matching concept).

____ 12. The entity must give the same treatment to comparable transactions from period to period.

____ 13. The measurement with the least favorable effect on net income and financial position in the current period must be selected.

____ 14. Of the various values that could be used, this value has been selected because it is objective and determinable.

____ 15. With this assumption, inaccuracies of accounting for the entity short of its complete life span are accepted.

Required   Place the appropriate letter identifying each quality on the line in front of the statement describing that quality.

P 1-3

Required   Answer the following multiple-choice questions.

a. Which of the following is a characteristic of information provided by external financial reports?
  1. The information is exact and not subject to change.
  2. The information is frequently the result of reasonable estimates.
  3. The information pertains to the economy as a whole.
  4. The information is provided at the least possible cost.
  5. None of the above.

b. Which of the following is not an objective of financial reporting?
  1. Financial reporting should provide information that is useful to present and potential investors and creditors and other users in making rational investment, credit, and similar decisions.
  2. Financial reporting should provide information to help present and potential investors and creditors and other users in assessing the amounts, timing, and uncertainty of prospective cash receipts from dividends or interest and the proceeds from the sale, redemption, or maturity of securities or loans.
  3. Financial reporting should provide information about the economic resources of an enterprise, the claims against those resources, and the effects of transactions, events, and circumstances that change the resources and claims against those resources.
  4. Financial accounting is designed to measure directly the value of a business enterprise.
  5. None of the above.

c. According to FASB Statement of Concepts No. 2, which of the following is an ingredient of the quality of relevance?

1. verifiability
2. representational faithfulness
3. neutrality
4. timeliness
5. none of the above

d. The primary current source of generally accepted accounting principles for nongovernment operations is the
1. New York Stock Exchange
2. Financial Accounting Standards Board
3. Securities and Exchange Commission
4. American Institute of Certified Public Accountants
5. none of the above

e. What is the underlying concept that supports the immediate recognition of a loss?
1. matching
2. consistency
3. judgment
4. conservatism
5. going concern

f. The balance sheet equation can be defined as
1. assets + stockholders' equity = liabilities
2. assets + liabilities = stockholders' equity
3. assets = liabilities − stockholders' equity
4. assets = liabilities + stockholders' equity
5. assets − liabilities = stockholders' equity

g. If assets are $40,000 and stockholders' equity is $10,000, then liabilities are
1. $30,000
2. $50,000
3. $20,000
4. $60,000
5. $10,000

P 1-4   Each of the following statements represents a decision made by the accountant of Growth Industries.

a. A tornado destroyed $200,000 in uninsured inventory. This loss is included in cost of goods sold.

b. Land was purchased ten years ago for $50,000. The accountant adjusts the land account to $100,000, which is the estimated current value.

c. The cost of machinery and equipment is charged to a fixed asset account. The machinery and equipment will be expensed over the period of use.

d. The value of equipment increased this year, so no depreciation of equipment was recorded this year.

e. During the year, inventory that cost $5,000 was stolen by employees. This loss has been included in cost of goods sold for the financial statements. The total amount of cost of goods sold was $1,000,000.

f. The president of the company, who owns the business, used company funds to buy a car for his use. The car was recorded on the company's books.

Required   a. State whether you agree or disagree with the decision.
              b. Indicate why you agree or disagree with the decision.

P 1-5   These data relate to the Jones Company for the year ended December 31, 1992:

Sales on credit	$80,000
Cost of inventory sold on credit	$65,000
Collections from customers	$60,000
Purchase of inventory on credit	$50,000
Payment for purchases	$55,000
Cash collections for common stock	$30,000
Dividends paid	$10,000
Payment to sales clerk	$10,000

Required   a. Determine income on an accrual basis.
b. Determine income on a cash basis.

CASES

Case 1-1   URANIUM MINING COMPANY

The Uranium Mining Company was founded in 1960 to mine and market uranium, and it purchased a mine in 1961 for $900 million. It was estimated that the uranium had a market value of $150 per ounce. By 1992, the market value had increased to $300 per ounce. Records for 1992 indicate the following:

Production	200,000 ounces
Sales	230,000 ounces
Deliveries	190,000 ounces
Cash collection	210,000 ounces
Costs of production including depletion*	$50,000,000
Selling expenses	2,000,000
Administrative expenses	1,250,000
Tax rate	50%

*Production cost per ounce has remained constant over the last few years, and the company has maintained the same production level.

Required   a. Compute the income for 1992, using each of the following bases:
1. receipt of cash
2. point of sale
3. end of production
4. based on delivery
b. Comment on when each of the above methods should be used. Which method should be used by the Uranium Mining Company?

Case 1-2   BIG GAAP—LITTLE GAAP

Even though accounting records go back hundreds of years, there was little effort to develop accounting standards until the 1900s. The first major effort to develop accounting standards in the United States came in 1938, when the American Institute of Certified Public Accountants formed the Committee on Accounting Procedure (CAP). This committee issued pronouncements that were published as Accounting Research Bulletins. Fifty-one Accounting Research Bulletins were issued.

The Committee on Accounting Procedure was replaced by the Accounting Principles Board (APB) in 1959. The workings of the Accounting Principles Board were to be more formal than the workings of the Committee on Accounting Procedure. The pronouncements of the APB were termed Opinions of the Accounting Principles Board. Thirty-one Opinions were issued by the Accounting Principles Board. The Accounting Principles Board was replaced in 1973 by the Financial Accounting Standards Board (FASB). By the end of 1989 the FASB had issued 103 statements.

As the number of Statements issued by the FASB increased, "standards overload" emerged—a charge that there are too many accounting standards and that the standards are too complicated. The individuals who charge standards overload maintain that more professional judgment should be allowed in financial accounting. Some claim that certain standards should not apply to nonpublic companies. Others feel that "little" companies should be exempt from certain standards.

Required
a. Financial statements should aid the user of the statement in making decisions. Do you think the user of the statement would be aided or hindered if there were a distinction between the financial reporting standards for little and big companies?
b. Would small business owner-managers favor a distinction between financial reporting standards for small and large companies? Discuss.
c. Would accountants in small CPA firms view standards overload as a bigger problem than accountants in large CPA firms? Discuss.

Case 1-3   THE WATCHMAN*

UNITED STATES OF AMERICA
Before the
SECURITIES AND EXCHANGE COMMISSION

SECURITIES EXCHANGE ACT OF 1934
Release No. 20364/November 14, 1983

ACCOUNTING AND AUDITING ENFORCEMENT
Release No. 16/November 14, 1983

Administrative Proceedings File No. 3-6303

In the Matter of TOUCHE ROSS & CO. 1633 Broadway New York, New York	ORDER INSTITUTING PROCEEDINGS PURSUANT TO RULE 2(e) OF THE COMMISSION'S RULES OF PRACTICE AND OPINION AND ORDER OF THE COMMISSION

*NOTE: This case includes the first three and one-fourth pages of the Securities & Exchange Commission Release No. 16, November 14, 1983. The total release includes more detail and background information.

Case adapted from "Cases in Financial Reporting," 2nd Edition, Gibson and Frishkoff, Kent Publishing, Inc., 1985.

The Commission deems it appropriate and in the public interest that administrative proceedings be, and they hereby are, instituted against Touche Ross & Co. ("Touche") pursuant to Rule 2(e) of the Commission's Rules of Practice.[A] These proceedings arise out of Touche's examination of financial statements issued by Litton Industries, Inc. ("Litton") and Gelco Corporation ("Gelco").

Simultaneous with the institution of these proceedings, and without any evidentiary hearing, trial or arguments or adjudication of any issue of law or fact, Touche, without admitting or denying any statements or conclusions herein, submitted a letter to the Commission in which it discussed various matters and consented to the issuance of this Opinion and Order. Based on the foregoing, the Commission has determined to conclude and terminate these proceedings by the issuance of this Opinion and Order.

LITTON INDUSTRIES, INC.

Introduction and Summary

On March 12, 1981, the Securities and Exchange Commission announced the filing and settlement of a civil action against Litton Industries, Inc., a Delaware corporation with its principal offices located in Beverly Hills, California.[B] The Commission's complaint filed in that action concerned Litton's accounting for costs in excess of contract values on commercial and military shipbuilding contracts between 1971 and 1978, and the Company's disclosures relating thereto.[C]

With respect to a major shipbuilding contract with the U.S. Navy (the "LHA contract")

[A]Rule 2(e). 17 CFR 201.2(e), provides in part:

The Commission may deny, temporarily or permanently, the privilege of appearing or practicing before it in any way to any person who is found by the Commission after notice of an opportunity for hearing in the matter (i) not to possess the requisite qualifications to represent others, or (ii) to be lacking in character and integrity or to have engaged in unethical or improper professional conduct, or (iii) to have willfully violated, or willfully aided and abetted the violation of any provision of the federal securities laws [15 U.S.C. 77a to 80b-20], or the rules and regulations thereunder.

[B]*SEC* v. *Litton Industries, Inc.,* (DDC, Civil Action No. 81-0589), Litigation Release No. 9322. The Commission's Complaint alleged that Litton failed to comply with Section 13(a) of the Exchange Act and Rules 12b-20, 13a-1 and 13a-13 promulgated thereunder. Litton, without admitting or denying any of the Commission's allegations, consented to the entry of a Final Order directing Litton to comply with Section 13(a) of the Exchange Act.

[C]Litton reported the following revenues and net earnings (loss) during the 1971–1978 period:

Year	Reported Revenues ($000 omitted)	Reported After-Tax Net Earnings Loss ($000 omitted)
1971	$2,466,120	$50,003
1972	2,202,327	1,118
1973	2,392,261	43,030
1974	3,002,781	(47,783)
1975	3,002,781	19,338
1976	3,354,552	28,297
1977	3,442,924	55,906
1978	3,653,204	(90,843)

awarded in 1969, Litton incurred costs in excess of the contract value which grew from approximately $75 million in fiscal 1973 to approximately $500 million by fiscal 1978. Litton contended that such excess costs were caused by Navy delay and disruption in the construction process, and the financial statements contained in the annual and periodic reports which Litton filed with the Commission between 1973 and 1978 were presented on the assumption that the company would recover all of its costs under the LHA contract. The Commission's Complaint alleged that the costs in excess of the LHA contract value were largely caused by factors for which the Navy was not responsible under the express terms of the contract, and that the uncertainties relating to Litton's recovery of its excess costs were such that the company did not have adequate grounds for not providing for a loss on that contract prior to 1978, at which time it provided for a pre-tax loss of $200 million as a result of a settlement with the Navy.

With respect to two commercial shipbuilding contracts awarded in 1968, Litton incurred costs in excess of the contract values amounting to $128 million by the end of its fiscal year 1972. Between 1972 and 1978, at which time the entire amount was written off, Litton deferred recognition of such costs on the basis that they would benefit later military contracts to be performed on its new shipbuilding facility. The Commission's Complaint alleged that Litton did not have adequate grounds for deferring the $128 million of excess costs for financial reporting purposes in light of the nature of the excess costs, the lack of assured revenues against which to absorb the costs.

Touche examined and rendered opinions with respect to the annual financial statements of Litton throughout the period in question. The firm's report on Litton's financial statements for each of the years 1972 through 1977 was qualified with respect to the uncertainties to Litton's contract disputes with the Navy. The evidence developed in the Commission's investigation establishes that Touche failed to examine Litton's financial statements in accordance with generally accepted auditing standards.[D] Touche accepted, without adequate basis, Litton's judgment that the entire cost overrun which incurred on the Navy contracts would be recovered pursuant to a claim. Touche further accepted, without adequate basis, Litton's judgment to defer $128 million in costs with the expectation that they would be recovered through future new shipyard revenues without appropriately verifying that such amounts represented specific costs which would benefit Litton in future periods.

Required

a. Were the cost overruns in question material in relation to the after-tax net earnings (loss) for the period 1971–1978?

b. Comment on generally accepted accounting principles regarding a situation in which estimated costs on long-term construction contacts exceed projected revenues.

c. 1. Where does the Securities and Exchange Commission get its authority to deny, temporarily or permanently, the privilege of appearing or practicing before it?

2. How important is this authority?

3. The administrative proceeding that this case was based on (File No. 3-6303) was concluded by the issuance of an opinion and order. The order was to censure the accounting firm with respect to the audits. Do you think that the issuance of an opinion and order of censure is effective in controlling those who appear or practice before the Commission? Why or why not?

[D]As used in this document, "Touche" refers to the firm as a whole, including the engagement partner, other partners in the practice office, and partners from Touche's national staff, all of whom were involved in many of the matters described herein.

Case 1-4   WHICH RESPONSIBILITIES TAKE PRECEDENCE?*

A large accounting firm has granted permission for the partner in charge of financial reporting, Raymond Manley, to serve on the accounting policy committee of the national organization representing professional accountants. At the next meeting of the policy committee, a vote is to be taken to determine what stance the committee should take regarding the valuation of certain assets held by banks and other financial institutions. The existing policy allows these financial institutions to value long-term debt securities held as long-term investments at their cost on year-end balance sheets. The policy committee has discussed the issue at length and in depth and appears to be favoring the position that these debt securities should be valued at the lower of cost or market in order to provide investors and depositors better information to assess the financial strength of institutions holding such debt securities. The policy committee has determined that banks and other financial institutions which have significant investments in such securities were valuing these securities at cost even though their market value was considerably less due to various economic factors. By not taking a writedown for the depressed market for these securities, the financial institutions were showing higher profits than would be the case if these investments were written down to market.

The day before going to the policy committee meeting, Manley expressed his concern about how he should vote on the debt security valuation issue since his firm has a number of banks and other financial institutions as audit clients and realizes that valuing these debt securities at the lower of cost or market will cause a significant decline in the earnings of some of the financial institutions which are his firm's clients. In fact, he had a call a few days ago from the audit engagement partner for one of the banks that would be adversely affected by a change in valuation policy. The audit partner indicated that this particular client would surely change auditors if it learned that Manley voted in favor of changing the valuation policy. The audit partner did not believe that the bank officers would distinguish between Manley's position on the policy committee and what the auditing firm's internal policies are.

After talking with the audit partner, Manley feels very depressed. After studying the valuation issue very carefully, he feels strongly that the accounting profession should raise its standards regarding the valuation of investments in debt securities and should value such investments the same way that investments in long-term equity securities are valued, namely at the lower of cost or market. Yet his loyalty to his firm suggests that he should not push this position in tomorrow's policy committee discussion that will take place just prior to this vote.

What are the ethical issues in the case? What should Manley do?

Required
a. Determine the facts.
b. Define the ethical issues.
c. Identify major principles, rules, and values.
d. Specify the alternatives.
e. Compare norms, principles, and values with the alternatives to see if a clear decision can be reached.
f. Assess the consequences.
g. Make your decision.

*From *Ethics in the Accounting Curriculum: Cases & Readings,* edited by William W. May. American Accounting Association, 1990. Included with permission.

Case 1-5   THE DANGEROUS MORALITY OF MANAGING EARNINGS*

The Majority of Managers Surveyed Say It's Not Wrong to Manage Earnings

Occasionally, the morals and ethics executives use to manage their businesses are examined and discussed. Unfortunately, the morals that guide the timing of nonoperating events and choices of accounting policies largely have been ignored.

The ethical framework used by managers in reporting short-term earnings probably has received less attention than its operating counterpart because accountants prepare financial disclosures consistent with laws and generally accepted accounting principles (GAAP). Those disclosures are reviewed by objective auditors.

Managers determine the short-term reported earnings of their companies by:

- Managing, providing leadership, and directing the use of resources in operations.
- Selecting the timing of some nonoperating events, such as the sale of excess assets or the placement of gains or losses into a particular reporting period.
- Choosing the accounting methods that are used to measure short-term earnings.

Casual observers of the financial reporting process may assume that time, laws, regulation, and professional standards have restricted accounting practices to those which are moral, ethical, fair, and precise. But most managers and their accountants know otherwise—that managing short-term earnings can be part of a manager's job.

To understand the morals of short-term earnings management, we surveyed general managers and finance, control, and audit managers. The results are frightening.

We found striking disagreements among managers in all groups. Furthermore, the liberal definitions revealed in many responses of what is moral or ethical should raise profound questions about the quality of financial information that is used for decision-making purposes by parties both inside and outside a company. It seems many managers are convinced that if a practice is not explicitly prohibited or is only a slight deviation from rules, it is an ethical practice regardless of who might be affected either by the practice or the information that flows from it. This means that anyone who uses information on short-term earnings is vulnerable to misinterpretation, manipulation, or deliberate deception.

The Morals of Managing Earnings

To find a "revealed" consensus concerning the morality of engaging in earnings management activities, we prepared a questionnaire describing 13 earnings-management situations we had observed either directly or indirectly. The actions described in the incidents were all legal (although some were in violation of GAAP), but each could be construed as involving short-term earnings management.

A total of 649 managers completed our questionnaire. Table 1 shows a rough classification of respondents by job function. A summary of the views on the acceptability of various earnings management practices is shown in Table 2.

A major finding of the survey was a striking lack of agreement. None of the respondent groups viewed any of the 13 practices unanimously as an ethical or unethical practice. The

*By William J. Bruns, Jr., Professor of Business Administration, Harvard University Graduate School of Business Administration, and Kenneth A. Merchant, Professor of Accounting, University of Southern California. Reprinted by permission from *Management Accounting* (August 1990), pp. 22–25. Copyright by National Association of Accountants, Montvale, N.J.

TABLE   1

Survey Respondents

	Total Sample
General managers	119
Finance, control, & audit managers	262
Others or position not known	268
	649

TABLE   2

Managing Short-Term Earnings

		Proportion of Managers Who Judge the Practice	
	Ethical	Questionable, or a Minor Infraction	Unethical, or a Serious Infraction
1. Managing short-term earnings by changing or manipulating operating decisions or procedures:			
When the result is to reduce earnings	79%	19%	2%
When the result is to increase earnings	57%	31%	12%
2. Managing short-term earnings by changing or manipulating accounting methods:			
When the change to earnings is small	5%	45%	50%
When the change to earnings is large	3%	21%	76%
3. Managing short-term earnings by deferring discretionary expenditures into the next accounting period:			
To meet an interim quarterly budget target	47%	41%	12%
To meet an annual budget target at year-end	41%	35%	24%
4. Increasing short-term earnings to meet a budget target:			
By selling excess assets and realizing a profit	80%	16%	4%
By ordering overtime work at year-end to ship as much as possible	74%	21%	5%
By offering customers special credit terms to accept delivery without obligation to pay until the following year	43%	44%	15%

Percentages are calculated from *Harvard Business Review* reader sample.

dispersion of judgments about many of the incidents was great. For example, here is one hypothetical earnings-management practice described in the questionnaire:

In September, a general manager realized that his division would need a strong performance in the last quarter of the year in order to reach its budget targets. He decided to implement a sales program offering liberal payment terms to pull some sales that would normally occur next year into the current year. Customers accepting delivery in the fourth quarter would not have to pay the invoice for 120 days.

The survey respondents' judgments of the acceptability of this practice were distributed as follows:

Ethical	279
Questionable	288
Unethical	82
Total	649

Perhaps you are not surprised by these data. The ethical basis of an early shipment/ liberal payment program may not be something you have considered, but, with the prevalence of such diverse views, how can any user of a short-term earnings report know the quality of the information?

Although the judgments about all earnings management practices varied considerably, there are some other generalizations that can be made from the findings summarized in Table 2.

- On average, the respondents viewed management of short-term earnings by *accounting* methods as significantly less acceptable than accomplishing the same ends by changing or manipulating *operating decisions or procedures.*
- The direction of the effect on earnings matters. *Increasing* earnings is judged less acceptable than *reducing* earnings.
- Materiality matters. Short-term earnings management is judged less acceptable if the earnings effect is *large* rather than *small.*
- The time period of the effect may affect ethical judgments. Managing short-term earnings at the end of an interim *quarterly* reporting period is viewed as somewhat more acceptable than engaging in the same activity at the end of an *annual* reporting period.
- The method of managing earnings has an effect. Increasing profits by offering *extended credit terms* is seen as less acceptable than accomplishing the same end by *selling excess assets or using overtime* to increase shipments.

Managers Interviewed

Were the survey results simply hypothetical, or did managers recognize they can manage earnings and choose to do so? To find the answers, we talked to a large number of the respondents. What they told us was rarely reassuring.

On accounting manipulations, a profit center controller reported: "Accounting is grey. Very little is absolute. . . . You can save your company by doing things with sales and expenses, and, if it's legal, then you are justified in doing it."

A divisional general manager spoke to us about squeezing reserves to generate additional reported profit: "If we get a call asking for additional profit, and that's not inconceivable, I would look at our reserves. Our reserves tend to be realistic, but we may have a product claim that could range from $50,000 to $500,000. Who knows what the right amount for something like that is? We would review our reserves, and if we felt some were on the high side, we would not be uncomfortable reducing them."

We also heard about operating manipulations. One corporate group controller noted: "[To boost sales] we have paid overtime and shipped on Saturday, the last day of the fiscal quarter. If we totally left responsibility for the shipping function to the divisions, it could even slip over to 12:30 A.M. Sunday. There are people who would do that and not know it's wrong."

Managers often recognize that such actions "move" earnings from one period to another. For example, a division controller told us: "Last year we called our customers and asked if they would take early delivery. We generated an extra $300,000 in sales at the last minute. We were scratching for everything. We made our plans, but we cleaned out our backlog and started in the hole this year. We missed our first quarter sales plan. We will catch up by the end of the second quarter."

And a group vice president said: "I recently was involved in a situation where the manager wanted to delay the production costs for the advertising that would appear in the fall [so that he could meet his quarterly budget]."

Thus, in practice, it appears that a large majority of managers use at least some methods to manage short-term earnings. Although these methods are legal, they do not seem to be consistent with a strict ethical framework. While the managers' actions have the desired effect on reported earnings, the managers know there are no real positive economic benefits and the actions might actually be quite costly in the long run. These actions are at best questionable because they involve deceptions that are not disclosed. Most managers who manage earnings, however, do not believe they are doing anything wrong.

We see two major problems. The most important is the generally high tolerance for operating manipulations. The other is the dispersion in managers' views about which practices are moral and ethical.

The Dangerous Allure

The essence of a moral or ethical approach to management is achieving a balance between individual interests and obligations to those who have a stake in what happens in the corporation (or what happens to a division or group within the corporation). These stakeholders include not only people who work in the firm, but customers, suppliers, creditors, shareholders, and investors as well.

Managers who take unproductive actions to boost short-term earnings may be acting totally within the laws and rules. Also they may be acting in the best interest of the corporation. But, if they fail to consider the adverse effects of their actions on other stakeholders, we may conclude that they are acting unethically.

The managers we interviewed explained that they rated accounting manipulations harshly because in such cases the "truth" has somehow been denied or misstated. The recipients of the earnings reports do not know what earnings would have been if no manipulation had taken place. Even if the accounting methods used are consistent with GAAP, they reason, the actions are not ethical because the interests of major stakeholder groups—including the recipients of the earnings reports—have been ignored.

The managers judge the operating manipulations more favorably because the earnings numbers are indicative of what actually took place. The operating manipulations have changed reality, and "truth" is fairly reported.

We see flaws in that reasoning. One is that the truth has not necessarily been disclosed completely. When sales and profits are borrowed from the future, for example, it is a rare company that discloses the borrowed nature of some of the profits reported.

A second flaw in the reasoning about the acceptability of operating manipulations is that it ignores a few or all of the effects of some types of operating manipulations on the full range of stakeholders. Many managers consider operating manipulations as a kind of "victimless crime."

But victims do exist. Consider, for example, the relatively common operating manipulation of early shipments. As one manager told us: "Would I ship extra product if I was faced with a sales shortfall? You have to be careful there; you're playing with fire. I would let whatever happened fall to the bottom line. I've been in companies that did whatever they could to make the sales number, such as shipping lower quality product. That's way too short-term. You have to draw the line there. You must maintain the level of quality and customer service. You'll end up paying for bad shipments eventually. You'll have returns, repairs, adjustments, ill will that will cause you to lose the account. . . . [In addition] it's tough to go to your employees one day and say ship everything you can and then turn around the next day and say that the quality standards must be maintained."

Another reported: "We've had to go to [one of our biggest customers] and say we need an order. That kills us in the negotiations. Our last sale was at a price just over our cost of materials."

These comments point out that customers—and sometimes even the corporation—may be victims.

Without a full analysis of the costs of operating manipulations, the dangers of such manipulations to the corporation are easily underestimated. Mistakes will be made because the quality of information is misjudged. The short term will be emphasized at the expense of the long term. If managers consistently manage short-term earnings, the messages sent to other employees create a corporate culture that lacks mutual trust, integrity, and loyalty.

A Lack of Moral Agreement

We also are troubled by the managers' inability to agree on the types of earnings-management activities that are acceptable. This lack of agreement exists even within corporations.

What this suggests is that many managers are doing their analyses in different ways. The danger is obfuscation of the reality behind the financial reports. Because managers are using different standards, individuals who try to use the information reported may be unable to assess accurately the quality of that information.

If differences in opinions exist, it is likely that financial reporting practices will sink to their lowest and most manipulative level. As a result, managers with strict definitions of what is moral and ethical will find it difficult to compete with managers who are not playing by the same rules. Ethical managers either will loosen their moral standards or fail to be promoted into positions of greater power.

Actions for Concerned Managers

We believe most corporations would benefit if they established clearer accounting and operating standards for all employees to follow. The standard-setting process should involve managers in discussions of the practices related to short-term earnings measurements.

Until these standards are in place, different managers will use widely varying criteria in assessing the acceptability of various earnings-management practices. These variations will have an adverse affect on the quality of the firm's financial information. Companies can use a questionnaire similar to the one in our study to encourage discussion and to communicate corporate standards and the reason for them. (See Short-Term Earnings Practices.)

Standards also enable internal and external auditors and management to judge whether or not the desired quality of earnings is being maintained. In most companies, auditors can depend on good standards to identify and judge the acceptability of the operating manipulations.

Ultimately, the line management chain-of-command, not auditors or financial staff, bears the primary responsibility for controlling operating manipulations. Often managers must rely on their prior experience and good judgment to distinguish between a decision that will have positive long-term benefits and one that has a positive short-term effect but a deleterious long-term effect.

Finally, it is important to manage the corporate culture. A culture that promotes openness and cooperative problem solving among managers is likely to result in less short-term earnings management than one that is more competitive and where annual, and even quarterly, performance shortfalls are punished. A corporate culture that is more concerned with managing for excellence rather than for reporting short-term profits will be less likely to support the widespread use of immoral earnings-management practices.

Required

a. Time, laws, regulation, and professional standards have restricted accounting practices to those which are moral, ethical, fair, and precise. Comment.

b. Most managers surveyed had a conservative, strict interpretation of what is moral or ethical in financial reporting. Comment.

c. The managers surveyed exhibited a surprising agreement as to what constitutes an ethical or unethical practice. Comment.

d. List the five generalizations from the findings in this study relating to managing earnings.

e. Comment on management's ability to manage earnings in the long run by influencing financial accounting.

CHAPTER 2

BALANCE SHEET

CHAPTER TOPICS

Consolidated Statements	Owners' Equity
Balance Sheet	Problems in Balance Sheet
Assets	Presentation
Liabilities	

As previously indicated, the major financial statements are the balance sheet, income statement, and statement of cash flows. The focus of this chapter is to review the balance sheet in detail.

CONSOLIDATED STATEMENTS

Financial statements of legally separate entities may be issued to show financial position, income, and cash flow as they would appear if the companies were one entity. Such statements reflect an economic, rather than a legal, concept of the entity.

When one corporation holds substantial voting rights in another, the corporation that owns the stock is described as the *parent corporation,* and the corporation that is invested in is described as the *subsidiary.* When a parent corporation has control of voting rights, the financial statements of the parent and the subsidiary are combined into what are termed *consolidated financial statements.* If control of voting rights is not evident, as might be the case with less than 50% ownership (or even with more than 50% ownership when there are restrictions imposed on the stock), the subsidiaries are not consolidated. When a subsidiary is not consolidated, it is accounted for as an investment on the parent's balance sheet. Such subsidiaries are termed *unconsolidated.*

When a subsidiary is less than 100% owned, and the subsidiary is consolidated, minority shareholders must be recognized in the consolidated financial statements. This is done by showing the minority interest in net assets on the balance sheet and the minority share of earnings on the income statement. These minority-related accounts are discussed in detail later in this and the next chapter.

BALANCE SHEET

As indicated in Chapter 1, the purpose of a balance sheet is to show the financial condition of an accounting entity as of a particular date. The balance sheet consists of assets, which are the resources of the firm; liabilities, which are the debts of the firm; and stockholders' equity, which is the owners' interest in the firm.

The assets are derived from two sources—creditors and owners. At any point in time, the assets must equal the contribution of the creditors and owners. This is expressed in the accounting equation (shown on the next page):

E X H I B I T   2 - 1

GTE CORPORATION AND SUBSIDIARIES
Consolidated Balance Sheets (Statement of Financial Position)
Account Form

(thousands of dollars)	December 31	
	1989	1988
Assets		
Current assets:		
Cash and temporary cash investments	$ 395,802	$ 306,979
Receivables, less allowances of $99,496 and $98,297	3,191,091	2,893,661
Inventories	1,416,118	1,263,934
Deferred income tax benefits	307,884	266,232
Other	286,402	881,101
Total current assets	5,597,297	5,611,907
Property, plant and equipment, at cost:		
Telephone subsidiaries	33,381,095	31,739,842
Accumulated depreciation	(11,504,742)	(10,400,217)
	21,876,353	21,339,625
Other subsidiaries	3,280,560	2,941,798
Accumulated depreciation	(1,456,694)	(1,294,537)
	1,823,866	1,647,261
Total property, plant and equipment, net	23,700,219	22,986,886
Investments and other assets:		
Investments in unconsolidated companies	858,344	811,613
Deferred charges	831,231	774,462
Bonds, at amortized cost	369,690	388,094
Noncurrent receivables	280,334	245,069
Intangibles and other	349,381	285,895
Total investments and other assets	2,688,980	2,505,133
Total assets	$31,986,496	$31,103,926

Assets = Liabilities + Equity

The balance sheet is presented with the assets equal to liabilities plus equity. This presentation is usually side by side (called the *account form*) or top and bottom (called the *report form*). A typical account form format is presented in Exhibit 2-1, and a typical report form format is presented in Exhibit 2-2.

E X H I B I T   2 - 1   (continued)

(thousands of dollars)	December 31	
	1989	1988
Liabilities and shareholders' equity		
Current liabilities:		
Short-term obligations, including current maturities	$ 1,049,857	$ 1,757,738
Accounts and payrolls payable	1,918,604	1,514,144
Accrued taxes	708,325	622,751
Dividends payable	271,787	244,084
Advance billings	239,531	227,546
Accrued interest	233,397	237,373
Other	1,281,675	1,266,439
Total current liabilities	5,703,176	5,870,075
Long-term debt	10,909,397	9,704,710
Reserves and deferred credits:		
Deferred income taxes	3,742,593	3,668,964
Deferred investment tax credits	585,500	735,058
Other	1,296,883	1,329,993
Total reserves and deferred credits	5,624,976	5,734,015
Minority interests in equity of subsidiaries	1,070,302	861,821
Preferred stock, subject to mandatory redemption	275,958	301,958
Shareholders' equity:		
Preferred stock	468,043	504,833
Common stock—shares issued 351,971,990 and 349,289,499	35,197	34,929
Amounts paid in, in excess of par value	5,348,840	5,067,310
Reinvested earnings	4,428,072	3,978,219
Foreign currency translation adjustment	(11,036)	(16,665)
Guaranteed ESOP obligation	(700,000)	—
Common stock held in treasury—21,670,255 and 23,000,000, at cost	(1,166,429)	(937,279)
Total shareholders' equity	8,402,687	8,631,347
Total liabilities and shareholders' equity	$31,986,496	$31,103,926

EXHIBIT   2 - 2

BARNES GROUP INC.
Consolidated Balance Sheet (Statement of Financial Position)
Report Form

	December 31	
(dollars in thousands)	1989	1988
Assets		
Current assets		
Cash and cash equivalents	$ 18,017	$ 18,133
Accounts receivable, less allowances (1989—		
$1,953; 1988—$2,296)	79,315	73,312
Inventories		
Finished goods	36,794	37,329
Work-in-process	26,131	25,358
Raw materials and supplies	11,126	11,960
	74,051	74,647
Deferred income taxes	11,772	9,321
Prepaid expenses	5,636	6,634
Total current assets	188,791	182,047
Property, plant and equipment		
Land	4,575	4,312
Buildings	55,002	50,063
Machinery and equipment	164,094	148,926
	223,671	203,301
Less accumulated depreciation	116,180	102,898
	107,491	100,403
Investments in excess of net assets of businesses		
acquired	24,663	24,956
Other assets	7,171	4,470
	$328,116	$311,876
Liabilities and shareholders' equity		
Current liabilities		
Notes and overdrafts payable	$ 25,896	$ 12,928
Accounts payable	26,588	27,736
Accrued income taxes	2,376	3,232
Accrued liabilities	43,051	35,729
Guaranteed ESOP obligation—current	1,469	—
Long-term debt—current	217	296
Total current liabilities	99,597	79,921
Long-term debt	79,088	79,287
Guaranteed ESOP obligation	19,181	—
Deferred income taxes	8,408	6,920
Other liabilities	9,274	11,938

EXHIBIT 2-2 (continued)

(dollars in thousands)	December 31	
	1989	1988
Redeemable preferred stock at stated and redemption value	—	21,000
Common shareholders' equity		
Common stock—par value $1.00 per share		
Authorized: 30,000,000 shares		
Issued: 7,345,923 shares stated at	15,737	15,737
Additional paid-in capital	29,166	26,468
Retained earnings	139,531	136,503
Foreign currency translation adjustments	(3,643)	(3,629)
	180,791	175,079
Treasury stock at cost (1989—1,278,911; 1988—1,802,949 shares)	(47,573)	(62,269)
Guaranteed ESOP obligation	(20,650)	—
	112,568	112,810
	$328,116	$311,876

Assets

Assets are probable future economic benefits obtained or controlled by a particular entity as a result of past transactions or events.[1] Assets may be of a physical nature, such as land, buildings, inventory of supplies, material, or finished products. Assets may also be intangible, such as patents and trademarks.

Assets are divided into two major categories: current and noncurrent (long term). Current assets are assets (1) in the form of cash, (2) that will normally be realized in cash, or (3) that conserve the use of cash during the operating cycle of a firm or for one year, whichever is longer. The operating cycle is the time between the acquisition of inventory and the realization of cash from selling the inventory. Noncurrent or long-term assets are those assets that do not qualify as current. Noncurrent assets are usually divided into the categories of tangible assets, investments, intangibles, and other.

Current Assets

Current assets are listed on the balance sheet in order of liquidity (the ability to be converted to cash). Current assets typically include cash, marketable securities, short-

[1]Financial Accounting Standards Board, Statement of Financial Accounting Concepts No. 6, "Elements of Financial Statements of Business Enterprises," December 1980, par. 25.

term receivables, inventories, and prepaids. In some cases, assets other than these may be classified as current; if so, management is indicating that it expects the asset to be converted into cash during the operating cycle or within a year, whichever is longer. An example is land held for immediate disposal. The definition of current assets implies the exclusion of restricted cash, investments for purposes of control, long-term receivables, the cash surrender value of life insurance, land and other natural resources, depreciable assets, and long-term prepayments.

Cash.   Cash, the most liquid of the assets, includes negotiable checks and unrestricted balances in checking accounts, as well as any cash on hand. Savings accounts are also usually classified as cash, even though the bank may not release the money for a specified period of time. Exhibit 2-3 illustrates the presentation of cash.

Marketable Securities.   Marketable securities are ownership and debt instruments of the government and other companies that can be readily converted into cash. They might also be labeled short-term investments. They are held by a firm to earn a return on near-cash resources and are characterized by their marketability at a readily determinable market price. It must be the intent of management to convert these assets to cash during the current period in order for them to be classified as marketable securities. Marketable debt securities are carried at cost (or the lower of cost or market), with market price shown parenthetically or in footnotes. Marketable equity securities (stocks or the right to purchase stocks) must be carried at the lower of aggregate cost or market, according to FASB Statement No.

EXHIBIT 2-3

DANA CORPORATION AND CONSOLIDATED SUBSIDIARIES
Illustration of Cash, Marketable Securities, and Accounts Receivable

	December 31	
(dollars in thousands)	1989	1988
Assets		
Current assets		
Cash	$ 35,623	$ 28,484
Marketable securities, at cost plus accrued		
interest which approximates market	45,569	35,922
Accounts receivable, less allowance for doubtful		
accounts of $17,583 (1988—$17,610)	681,968	736,911
Inventories		
Raw materials	155,372	138,104
Work in process and finished goods	556,149	589,820
Total inventories	711,521	727,924
Other current assets	23,482	40,436
Total current assets	$1,498,163	$1,569,677

12. The other valuation, cost or market, must be shown parenthetically or in footnotes. Refer to Exhibit 2-3 for a presentation for marketable securities. Note that the securities are carried at cost, but that cost approximates market price.

Accounts Receivable.   Monies due on accounts from customers arise from sales or services rendered. Accounts receivable are shown net of allowances to reflect their realizable value. This is the amount that is expected to be collected. The most typical allowances are for bad debts or uncollectible accounts. Other allowances may account for expected sales discounts, which are given for prompt payment, or for sales returns. Expenses of these types are recognized in the period of sale, at which time the allowance is established. In future periods when the losses occur, they are charged to the allowance. The accounts receivable of Dana Corporation is presented in Exhibit 2-3. The receivables are shown less allowances. At year end 1989, $681,968,000 is what the firm expects to realize. The gross receivables can be reconciled as follows:

Receivables, net	$681,968,000
Plus allowances	17,583,000
Receivables, gross	$699,551,000

Other types of receivables may exist besides trade receivables: tax refund claims, contracts, investees, finance installment notes or accounts, employees, and sale of assets.[2]

Inventories.   Inventories are the balance of goods on hand. In a manufacturing firm, they include the items described in the paragraphs that follow.

Raw Materials.   These are goods purchased for direct use in manufacturing a product, and they become part of the product. For example, in the manufacture of shirts, the fabrics and buttons are raw materials.

Work in Process.   Goods started, but not ready for sale, are in process. Work in process includes the cost of materials, labor costs for workers directly involved in the manufacture, and a portion of costs (termed *overhead*) that include rent, depreciation, indirect wages, maintenance, and the like.

Finished Goods.   These are items ready for sale. These inventory costs also include the cost of materials, labor costs for workers directly involved in the manufacture, and a portion of overhead costs including rent, depreciation, indirect wages, maintenance, and so on. Raw materials, work in process, and finished goods are carried at cost or the lower of cost or market.

Supplies.   These are items used indirectly in the production of goods or services. They could include register tapes, pencils, or sewing machine needles for the shirt factory.

[2]American Institute of Certified Public Accountants, *Accounting Trends and Techniques*, 1989, p. 111. Copyright 1989 by the American Institute of Certified Public Accountants, Inc. Material is reprinted with permission.

Since retailing or wholesaling firms are not engaged in the manufacture of a product but only in the sale, finished goods and supplies are their only inventory items. There are no raw materials or work in process inventory in these firms.

The valuation of inventory is a particularly difficult problem. Consider a firm that buys two units of raw materials, initially costing $5 and then $7. If, at the end of the year, the firm has used only one of them, what is the cost (expense) of the unit used? What is the cost assigned to the unit in inventory? Various valuation methods exist; four of them are explained briefly in the paragraphs that follow.

FIFO. The flow pattern assumed here is that the first unit purchased is the first sold—first-in, first-out. By necessity, this would be the flow pattern for a product such as bananas. In the above example, the cost of sales would be $5 and inventory $7. FIFO can be selected as the cost flow assumption even if this assumption does not agree with the actual physical flow.

LIFO. "Last-in, first-out" assumes that those units purchased last are sold first. This would apply to the sale of bulk nails, where new shipments are poured on top of old ones and subsequently sold first. In our example, cost of goods sold would be $7 and inventory $5. Again, this method can be selected as the cost flow assumption even if this assumption does not agree with the actual physical flow.

Average. Averaging methods lump the costs to determine a midpoint. In the example, the average is $6. Cost of goods sold would be $6; inventory would also be $6.

Specific Identification. With the specific identification method, the items in inventory are identified as coming from specific purchases. Assume that the item in inventory was the second item, costing $7. Therefore, the inventory cost would be $7, and cost of sales would be $5.

In a period of rising prices, LIFO results in the most realistic figure for cost of goods sold, in terms of current cost. LIFO also has the advantage of providing the largest tax break during such periods. FIFO results in the most realistic current value for inventory, but it also results in higher taxes. An average method, obviously, falls in between LIFO and FIFO.

The inventory costing method can have a material effect not only on the inventory account on the balance sheet, but also on cost of goods sold and therefore on reported income. The inventory costing method can be particularly important during times of significant inflation. During times of inflation, LIFO can result in materially lower income and lower inventory balance than would FIFO.

When using LIFO, a reduction in inventory can have a substantial influence on the current year's reported income. This is because the reduction in inventory brings out old costs that are matched against the current year's revenue. The old costs are often substantially less than the current costs to replace the inventory. Thus, income is increased as revenue is matched with old cost. The effect of matching old cost, when LIFO inventory is reduced, against the current revenue is referred to as the *LIFO layers effect*.

Footnote 2 of the 1989 annual report of Ingersoll Rand Company described a reduction in LIFO inventory. This footnote reads in part as follows:

> During the periods presented, inventory quantities were reduced, resulting in partial liquidations of LIFO layers. This decreased cost of goods sold by $2,229,000 in 1989, $7,678,000 in 1988 and $17,681,000 in 1987. These liquidations increased net earnings in 1989, 1988, and 1987 by approximately $1,383,000 ($.03 per share), $4,763,000 ($.09 per share) and $10,078,000 ($.20 per share), respectively.

The inventory presentation of Dana Corporation is shown in Exhibit 2-4. This includes the footnote description of valuation (costing), which is required. Notice that more than one costing method is used by Dana. Also note the disclosure that if all inventories were valued at replacement cost, inventories would be increased by $95,335,000 at December 31, 1989.

Prepaids. A prepaid is an expenditure made in advance of the use of the service or goods. For example, if insurance is paid in advance for three years, at

EXHIBIT 2-4

DANA CORPORATION AND CONSOLIDATED SUBSIDIARIES
Inventory

	December 31	
(dollars in thousands)	1989	1988
Assets		
Current assets		
Cash	$ 35,623	$ 28,484
Marketable securities, at cost plus accrued		
interest which approximates market	45,569	35,922
Accounts receivable, less allowance for doubtful		
accounts of $17,583 (1988—$17,610)	681,968	736,911
Inventories		
Raw materials	155,372	138,104
Work in process and finished goods	556,149	589,820
Total inventories	711,521	727,924
Other current assets	23,482	40,436
Total current assets	$1,498,163	$1,569,677

Inventories

Inventories are valued at the lower of cost or market. Cost is determined generally on the last-in, first-out basis for domestic inventories and on the first-in, first-out or average cost basis for international inventories. If all inventories were valued at replacement cost, inventories would be increased by $95,335,000 and $79,855,000 at December 31, 1989 and 1988, respectively.

the end of the first year, two years' worth of the outlay will be prepaid. The entity retains the right to be covered by insurance for two more years.

Typical prepaids include advertising, taxes, insurance, promotion costs, and early payments on long-term contracts. Prepaids are often not disclosed separately but are part of "other." In Exhibit 2-2, the prepaid account is disclosed separately. In Exhibit 2-1, prepaids are part of "other."

Other Current Assets.   As previously indicated, current assets typically include cash, marketable securities, short-term accounts and notes receivable, and prepaids. Management can classify as current only an asset it expects to convert into cash during the operating cycle or within one year, whichever is longer. This leads to many other items occasionally being classified as current. Exhibit 2-5 includes the items that *Accounting Trends and Techniques* reported as being disclosed as other current assets in the 1989 edition.

Long-Term Assets

Long-term or noncurrent assets take longer than a year to be converted to cash or to conserve cash in the long run. They are divided into four categories: tangible assets, investments, intangibles, and other.

Tangible Assets.   These are the physical facilities used in the operations of the business.

Land.   Land is shown at acquisition cost and is not depreciated, because in theory land does not get used up. Lands containing resources that will be used up, however, such as mineral deposits and timberlands, are subject to depletion. Depletion expense attempts to measure the wearing away of these resources. It is similar to depreciation, except that depreciation deals with a tangible fixed asset, whereas depletion deals with a natural resource.

Buildings.   Structures are valued at cost plus the cost of permanent improvements. Buildings are depreciated over their estimated useful life.

EXHIBIT   2 - 5

Other Current Asset Captions

	Number of Companies			
Nature of Asset	1988	1987	1986	1985
Deferred income taxes	143	140	147	129
Property held for sale	49	53	52	42
Unbilled costs	28	34	31	34
Advances or deposits	7	8	11	8
Other—identified	35	25	29	36

Source: American Institute of Certified Public Accountants, *Accounting Trends and Techniques*, 1989, p. 129.

Machinery. Equipment is listed at historical cost, including delivery and installation, plus any material improvements that extend its life or increase the quantity or quality of service. Machinery is also depreciated over its estimated useful life.

Accumulated Depreciation. Depreciation is the process of allocating the cost of buildings and machinery over the periods of benefit, the depreciable life. The depreciation expense taken each period is accumulated in this account. Accumulated depreciation is a contra asset that is subtracted from plant and equipment. The net value shown simply gives the cost minus the apportioned cost that has been taken as a reduction in income. It does not purport to represent current market value of the asset.

There are a number of depreciation methods that a firm can use. Often a firm depreciates an asset under one method for financial statements and another for income tax returns. A firm often wants to depreciate slowly for the financial statements, because this results in the highest immediate income and highest asset balance. The same firm would want to depreciate at a fast pace for income tax returns, because this results in the lowest immediate income and thus lower income taxes. Over the life of an asset, the total depreciation will be the same regardless of the depreciation method selected.

Three factors are usually considered when computing depreciation: the asset cost, length of the life of the asset, and the salvage value when it is retired from service. The length of the asset's life and the salvage value must be estimated at the time that the asset is placed in service.

Exhibit 2-6 indicates the depreciation methods used for financial reporting purposes by the firms surveyed for the 1989 edition of *Accounting Trends and Techniques.* The most popular methods used by these firms were straight-line, declining balance, sum of the years' digits, and unit of production. Many firms use more than one depreciation method.

E X H I B I T   2 - 6

Depreciation Methods, 1985–1988

	Number of Companies			
	1988	**1987**	**1986**	**1985**
Straight-line	563	559	561	563
Declining-balance	44	44	49	53
Sum-of-the-years'-digits	11	12	14	16
Accelerated method—not specified	70	76	77	73
Unit-of-production	53	51	48	54
Other	9	12	12	12

Source: American Institute of Certified Public Accountants, *Accounting Trends and Techniques,* 1989, p. 279.

The following assumptions will be made to illustrate these four depreciation methods:

1. Cost of asset—$10,000
2. Estimated life of asset—five years
3. Estimated salvage value—$2,000
4. Estimated total hours of use—16,000

Straight-Line Method. With the straight-line method, depreciation is recognized in equal amounts over the estimated life of the asset. The following formula can be used to compute the straight-line method:

$$\frac{\text{Cost} - \text{Salvage value}}{\text{Estimated life}} = \text{Annual depreciation}$$

For the asset used for illustration, the annual depreciation would be computed as follows:

$$\frac{\$10,000 - \$2,000}{\text{Five years}} = \$1,600$$

The $1,600 depreciation amount would be recognized each year of the five-year life of the asset.

Declining-Balance Method. The declining-balance method applies double the straight-line depreciation rate times the declining book value (cost minus accumulated depreciation) to achieve a declining depreciation charge over the estimated life of the asset. The following formula can be used to compute the declining-balance method:

$$\frac{1}{\text{Estimated life of asset}} \times 2 \times \begin{pmatrix} \text{Book value at beginning} \\ \text{of the year} \end{pmatrix} = \frac{\text{Annual}}{\text{depreciation}}$$

For the asset used for illustration, the first year's depreciation would be computed as follows:

$$\frac{1}{5} \times 2 \times (\$10,000 - 0) = \$4,000$$

The declining-balance method results in the following depreciation amounts for each of the five years of the asset's life.

Year	Cost	Accumulated Depreciation at Beginning of Year	Book Value at Beginning of Year	Depreciation for Year	Book Value at End of Year
One	$10,000	—	$10,000	$4,000	$6,000
Two	10,000	$4,000	6,000	2,400	3,600
Three	10,000	6,400	3,600	1,440	2,160
Four	10,000	7,840	2,160	160	2,000
Five	10,000	8,000	2,000	—	2,000

Estimated salvage value is not considered in the formula, but the asset should not be depreciated below the estimated salvage value. For the sample asset, the formula produced a depreciation amount of $864 in the fourth year. Only $160 depreciation can be used in the fourth year, because the $160 amount brings the book value of the asset down to the salvage value. Once the book value is equal to the salvage value, no additional depreciation may be taken.

Sum-of-the-Years'-Digits Method. The sum-of-the-years'-digits method is an accelerated depreciation method, as is the declining-balance method. Thus, the depreciation expense declines steadily over the estimated life of the asset. For this method, a fraction is taken each year times the cost less salvage value. The numerator of the fraction changes each year. It is the remaining number of years of the asset's life. The denominator of the fraction remains constant; it is the sum of the digits representing the years of the asset's life. The following formula can be used to compute depreciation by the sum-of-the-years'-digits method:

$$\frac{\text{Remaining number of years of life}}{\text{Sum of the digits representing the years of life}} \times (\text{Cost} - \text{Salvage}) = \text{Annual depreciation}$$

For the asset used for illustration, the first year's depreciation would be computed as follows:

$$\frac{5}{15 = (5 + 4 + 3 + 2 + 1)} \times (\$10,000 - \$2,000) = \$2,666.67$$

The sum-of-the-years'-digits method results in the following depreciation amounts for each of the five years of the asset's life.

Year	Cost Less Salvage Value	Fraction	Depreciation for Year	Accumulated Depreciation at End of Year	Book Value at End of Year
One	$8,000	5/15	$2,666.67	$2,666.67	$7,333.33
Two	8,000	4/15	2,133.33	4,800.00	5,200.00
Three	8,000	3/15	1,600.00	6,400.00	3,600.00
Four	8,000	2/15	1,066.67	7,466.67	2,533.33
Five	8,000	1/15	533.33	8,000.00	2,000.00

Unit-of-Production Method. The unit-of-production method relates depreciation to the output capacity of the asset, estimated for the life of the asset. The capacity should be in terms that are most appropriate for the particular asset, such as units of production, hours of use, or miles. Hours of use will be used for the asset in our example. For the life of the asset, it is estimated that there will be 16,000 hours of use. The output capacity estimated is divided into the cost of the asset less the salvage value to determine the depreciation per unit of output capacity. For the example, the depreciation per hour of use would be $.50 [(cost of asset $10,000 — salvage $2,000) divided by 16,000 hours].

The depreciation for each year is then determined by multiplication of the depreciation per output capacity by the output for that year. For the asset in our example, assuming that the output was 2,000 hours during the first year, the depreciation for that year would be $1,000 ($.50 × 2,000). Further depreciation cannot be taken when the accumulated depreciation equals the cost of the asset less the salvage value. For the example, this will be when accumulated depreciation equals $8,000.

In Exhibit 2-7, Dana Corporation lists three categories of tangible property—land and improvements to land, building and building fixtures, and machinery and equipment. Dana uses primarily the straight-line method of depreciation for financial reporting purposes and accelerated depreciation methods for federal income tax purposes.

Leases.   From the standpoint of the lessee, leases are classified as operating or capital leases. If the lease is in substance an ownership arrangement, it is a capital lease; otherwise it is an operating lease. Leased equipment under capital leases, according to the provisions of FASB Statement No. 13, are classified as long-term assets. They are shown net of the related amortization. They are usually grouped with plant, property, and equipment. The discounted value of the obligation, a liability, will be part current and part long term. The topic of leases is discussed at more length in Chapter 7 on long-term debt.

Investments.   Long-term investments are usually stocks and bonds of other companies, held for the purpose of maintaining a business relationship or exercising control. For an investment to be classified as long term, management must intend

EXHIBIT   2 - 7

DANA CORPORATION AND CONSOLIDATED SUBSIDIARIES
Properties and Depreciation

Depreciation is computed over the estimated useful lives of property, plant and equipment using primarily the straight-line method for financial reporting purposes and accelerated depreciation methods for federal income tax purposes.
     Property, plant and equipment consisted of the following:

	December 31	
(dollars in thousands)	1989	1988
Land and improvements to land	$ 48,322	$ 46,412
Buildings and building fixtures	417,566	384,289
Machinery and equipment	1,708,053	1,534,105
	2,173,941	1,964,806
Less—accumulated depreciation	1,055,802	928,055
	$1,118,139	$1,036,751

to hold the assets for a long time. Long-term assets are differentiated from marketable securities, where the intent is to hold the assets for short-term profits and to achieve liquidity.

Investments in bonds are carried at cost, with the premium or discount being amortized over the life of the bond. Equity investments are carried at the lower of cost or market if there is no substantial control. Equity investments are carried at equity if control is evident. Under the equity method, the cost is adjusted for the proportionate share of the rise in retained profits. For example, a parent company owns 40% of a subsidiary company, purchased at a cost of $400,000. When the subsidiary company earns $100,000, the parent company increases the investment account by 40% of $100,000, or $40,000. When the subsidiary company declares dividends of $20,000, the parent company decreases the investment account by 40% of $20,000, or $8,000. This decrease occurs because the investment account changes in direct proportion and in the same direction as the retained earnings of the subsidiary.

If the investment is carried at cost or equity, then the book amount may be more than the market value of the investment. In this case, management must judge whether the market value of the investment will improve sufficiently in the future to cover the book amount. If it is management's opinion that the market value will recover sufficiently, no write-down is taken. If it is management's opinion that the market value will not recover sufficiently, a write-down is taken. This write-down could be to the book amount or only partway to the book amount, depending on management's opinion as to subsequent recovery in market value.

When an investment is carried at more than the market value, the market value should be disclosed. In analyzing a company, it is important to consider whether investments are carried substantially above market value.

Investments can also include tangible assets not currently used in operations, such as an idle plant, as well as monies set aside in special funds, such as sinking funds or pensions.

The investments of Delta Air Lines, Inc. are illustrated in Exhibit 2-8.

Intangibles. Intangibles are nonphysical assets, such as legal rights. Intangibles are recorded at historical cost, which is then reduced by systematic amortization. Intangibles are generally amortized over their useful lives or their legal lives, whichever is shorter. Current generally accepted accounting principles require amortization for intangibles over a period of time that cannot exceed forty years (APB Opinion No. 17). Intangibles purchased before 1970 (the year of passage of APB Opinion No. 17) do not have to be amortized. Also, research and development must be expensed immediately as incurred (FASB Statement No. 2). The following paragraphs give examples of intangibles.

Goodwill. Goodwill arises from the acquisition of a business for a sum greater than the physical asset value, usually because the business has unusual earning power. It may result from good customer relations, a well-respected owner, or similar intangible factors.

E X H I B I T   2 - 8

DELTA AIR LINES, INC.
Consolidated Balance Sheets June 30, 1989, and 1988 (partial)
Investments

(dollars in thousands)	1989	1988
Assets		
Investments in associated companies (Note 10)	$66,651	$63,017

Note 10. Investments in Associated Companies

In prior fiscal years, the Company purchased approximately 20% of the stock of Atlantic Southeast Airlines, Inc. (ASA); Comair, Inc.; and Sky West, Inc., the parent company of Sky West Airlines. Included in the carrying amount of the investments in these three Delta Connection Commuter carriers is $28 million, which represents the amounts by which the costs of the investments exceeded the values of the underlying net assets when the investments were made. This amount is being amortized over 30 years. The investments in ASA, Comair and Sky West are being accounted for under the equity method.

Patents.   These are exclusive legal rights granted to an inventor for a period of seventeen years. Patents are valued at their cost to acquire, not their future benefits.

Trademarks.   Distinctive names or symbols are termed *trademarks.* Rights are granted to the holder for twenty-eight years, with an option for renewal.

Organizational Costs.   The legal costs incurred when a business is organized are carried as an asset and are usually written off over a period of five years or longer.

Franchises.   These are the legal rights to operate under a particular corporate name, providing trade-name products or services.

The Warner Lambert intangibles are displayed in Exhibit 2-9. They consist of intangibles resulting from purchased patents, trademarks, and other intangibles, plus goodwill.

Other Assets.   Firms occasionally have assets that do not fit into one of the classifications previously discussed. These assets, termed "other," might include noncurrent receivables and noncurrent prepaids. Exhibit 2-10 summarizes types of other assets from a financial statement compilation in *Accounting Trends and Techniques.*

Liabilities

Liabilities are probable future sacrifices of economic benefits arising from present obligations of a particular entity to transfer assets or provide services to other

EXHIBIT 2-9

WARNER LAMBERT
Consolidated Balance Sheet (Partial)
Intangibles

(millions of dollars)	December 31	
	1989	1988
Intangible assets	$140.1	$148.7

Note 1. Significant Accounting Policies (Partial)

Intangible assets—Intangible assets are recorded at cost and are amortized over appropriate periods not exceeding 40 years.

(in millions)	December 31	
	1989	1988
Purchased patents, trademarks and other intangibles	$116.5	$118.2
Goodwill	61.1	66.3
	177.6	184.5
Less accumulated amortization	(37.5)	(35.8)
	$140.1	$148.7

Amortization expense for the years 1989, 1988, and 1987 totaled $63 million, $5.8 million, and $2.4 million, respectively. The decrease in goodwill reflects the sale of the hair care products business in the United Kingdom and exchange rate changes, partially offset by the acquisition of Pagna in Italy as discussed in Note 2.

entities in the future, as a result of past transactions or events.[3] Liabilities are classified as either current or long term.

Current Liabilities

Current liabilities are obligations whose liquidation is reasonably expected to require the use of existing current assets or the creation of other current liabilities within a year or an operating cycle, whichever is longer. They include the items discussed in the paragraphs that follow.

Payables. These include short-term obligations created by the acquisition of goods and services, such as accounts payable (for materials or goods bought for use or resale), wages payable, taxes payable, and the like. Payables may also be in the form of a written promissory note—notes payable.

[3]FASB, Concept Statement No. 6, par. 35.

EXHIBIT 2-10

Other Noncurrent Assets

	Number of Companies			
	1988	1987	1986	1985
Property held for sale	49	56	58	64
Prepaid pension costs	49	51	23	—
Segregated cash or securities	36	52	46	62
Assets leased to others	34	18	21	23
Debt issue costs	26	22	20	15
Deferred income taxes	12	16	16	13
Assets of nonhomogeneous operations	11	—	—	—
Cash surrender value of life insurance	10	11	10	10
Prepaid expenses	9	2	6	6
Start-up costs	7	4	7	4
Other identified noncurrent assets	56	44	62	71

Source: American Institute of Certified Public Accountants, *Accounting Trends and Techniques*, 1989, p. 157.

Unearned Income.   Collections in advance of the performance of service are termed *unearned;* they include rent income and subscription income. Rather than owing cash, a future service or good is due the customer. The current liabilities of Warner Lambert, which are very typical, are shown in Exhibit 2-11.

Other Current Liabilities.   There are many other current obligations requiring payment during the year. Other current liabilities reported by *Accounting Trends and Techniques* in 1989 are displayed in Exhibit 2-12.

EXHIBIT 2-11

**WARNER LAMBERT
Consolidated Balance Sheets (Partial)
Current Liabilities**

	December 31	
(millions of dollars)	1989	1988
Notes payable—banks and other	$ 190.9	$ 187.1
Current portion of long-term debt	11.6	7.1
Accounts payable, trade	292.4	298.0
Other current liabilities	416.9	397.0
Federal, state and foreign income taxes	119.5	136.0
Total current liabilities	$1,031.3	$1,025.2

EXHIBIT 2-12

Other Current Liabilities

	Number of Companies			
	1988	1987	1986	1985
Taxes other than federal income taxes	148	168	186	186
Interest	125	125	128	122
Dividends payable	94	89	86	87
Estimated costs related to discontinued operations	80	84	85	78
Customer advances, deposits	53	59	60	61
Insurance	50	50	49	47
Deferred taxes	48	49	50	57
Warranties	47	46	40	40
Deferred revenue	33	24	37	32
Billings on uncompleted contracts	30	28	31	27
Advertising	26	32	28	24
Due to affiliated companies	15	15	15	26
Other—described	99	98	84	85

Source: American Institute of Certified Public Accountants, *Accounting Trends and Techniques*, 1989, p. 169.

Long-Term Liabilities

Long-term liabilities are those due in a period exceeding one year or one operating cycle, whichever is longer. Long-term liabilities are generally of two types: financing arrangements of assets and operations obligations.

Liabilities Relating to Financing Agreements. The long-term liabilities that are financing arrangements of assets usually require systematic payment of principal and interest. They include notes payable, bonds payable, and credit agreements.

Notes Payable. Promissory notes due in periods greater than one year or one operating cycle, whichever is longer, are classified as long term. If secured by a claim against real property, they are called *mortgage notes*.

Bonds Payable. A bond is a debt security normally issued with $1,000 par and requiring semiannual interest payments based on the coupon rate.

Bonds are not necessarily sold at par. They are sold at a premium if the stated rate exceeds market rate, and at a discount if the stated rate is less than the market rate. If they are sold for more than par, an account, premium on bonds payable, is created. This account is added to bonds payable to obtain the current carrying value. Similarly, if bonds are sold at less than par, there arises a discount on bonds payable that is subtracted from bonds payable on the balance sheet. Each of these accounts, discount or premium, will be gradually written off (amortized) to interest expense over the life of the maturity of the bond. Amortization of bond discount increases interest expense; amortization of premium reduces it. APB Opinion No.

21 establishes the accounting and reporting requirements for discount and premium.

Some bonds are convertible into common stock. At the option of the bondholder (creditor), the bond is exchanged for a specified number of common shares (and the bondholder becomes a common stockholder). Often, convertible bonds are issued when the common stock price is low, in management's opinion, and the firm eventually wants to increase its common equity. By issuing a convertible bond, the firm may get more for the specified number of common shares than could be obtained by issuing the specified number of common shares. The conversion feature allows the firm to issue the bond at a more favorable interest rate than would be the case with a bond lacking the conversion feature. Also, the interest paid on the convertible bond is tax deductible, thus reducing the cost to the firm for these funds. If common stock had been issued instead of the convertible bond, the dividend on the common stock would not be tax deductible. Thus, a firm may find that issuing a convertible bond can be an attractive means of raising common equity funds in the long run. However, if the firm's stock price stays depressed after issuing a convertible bond, the firm will be left with the convertible bond liability until the bond comes due. Convertible bonds of IBM are displayed in Exhibit 2-13.

Credit Agreements. Many firms arrange loan commitments from banks or insurance companies for future loans. Often, the firm does not intend to obtain these loans but has arranged the credit agreement just in case there is a need for additional funds. Such credit agreements do not represent a liability unless the firm actually requests the funds. From the point of view of analysis, the existence of a substantial

EXHIBIT 2-13

IBM
Convertible Bonds

	(dollars in millions)	
Long-Term Debt	**December 31, 1989**	**December 31, 1988**
U.S. dollars:		
7⅞% convertible subordinated debentures due 2004*	$ 1,254	$1,254
8⅜% debentures due 2019	750	—
6¾% notes due 1990	500	500
10¼% notes due 1995	500	500
9% notes due 1998	500	500
8⅝% notes due 1992	450	450
7¾% notes due 1992	400	—
8⅝% notes due 1992	400	—
9⅜% debentures due 2004 (with sinking fund payments to 2003)	300	363
7⅛% notes due 1989	—	300

EXHIBIT 2-13 (continued)

Long-Term Debt	(dollars in millions)	
	December 31, 1989	December 31, 1988
8⅜% notes due 1990	300	300
7¾% notes due 1991	250	250
9½% notes due 1992	250	—
9⅝% notes due 1992	250	—
8⅝% notes due 1991	250	250
8⅞% notes due 1991	250	250
9% notes due 1992	250	—
9.32% notes due 2000	203	205
6⅝% notes due 1989	—	200
10% notes due 1992	200	—
8% notes due 1990	200	200
12¼% notes due 1992	—	200
Medium-term note program, payable 1990–2008 (7.5%–15.0%)	1,057	667
Other U.S. dollars, due 1990–2012 (7.3%)	948	954
	9,462	7,343
Other (average interest rate at December 31, 1989, in parentheses), payable in:		
European currency units, due 1990–1994 (8.6%)	599	176
Australian dollars, due 1990–1993 (14.4%)	539	509
Japanese yen, due 1990–2019 (5.3%)	489	355
French francs, due 1990–2002 (10.2%)	486	513
Canadian dollars, due 1991–1994 (10.1%)	443	261
Swiss francs, due 1992–1996 (5.0%)	317	232
Other currencies, due 1990–2010 (9.8%)	379	261
	12,714	9,650
Less: net unamortized discount	6	13
	12,708	9,637
Less: current maturities	1,883	1,119
Total	$10,825	$8,518

Annual maturity and sinking fund requirements in millions of dollars on long-term debt outstanding at December 31, 1989, are as follows:
1990, $1,883; 1991, $1,598; 1992, $3,261; 1993, $1,203; 1994, $578; 1995 and beyond, $4,191.

*The 7⅞% convertible subordinated debentures are unsecured subordinated obligations of IBM, which are convertible into IBM capital stock at a conversion price of $153.6563 per share. They are redeemable, at the option of the company, as of November 1989 at a price of 103.938% of the principal amount, and at decreasing prices thereafter. Sinking fund payments starting in 1994 are intended to retire 75% of the debentures prior to maturity. During 1989, conversions of debentures resulted in the issuance of 106 shares of IBM capital stock.

credit agreement is a positive condition, in that it could relieve pressure on the firm if there is a problem in meeting existing liabilities.

In return for giving a credit agreement, the bank or insurance company obtains a fee, called a *commitment fee*. This fee is usually a percentage of the unused portion of the commitment. Also, banks often require the firm to keep a specified sum in its bank account. These bank balances are referred to as *compensating balances*. An example of a credit agreement is shown in Exhibit 2-14.

Liabilities Relating to Operational Obligations.   Long-term liabilities include obligations arising from the operation of a business, mostly of a service nature, such as pension obligations, deferred taxes, and service warranties.

Pensions are discussed at length in Chapter 7, "Long-Term Debt-Paying Ability."

Deferred taxes are caused by using different accounting methods for tax and reporting purposes. For example, a firm may use accelerated depreciation for tax purposes and straight-line depreciation for reporting purposes. This causes tax expense for reporting purposes to be higher than taxes payable according to the tax return. The difference is deferred tax. Any situation in which revenue or expense is recognized in the financial statements in a different time period than for the tax return creates a deferred tax situation. If only one timing difference exists, the deferred tax becomes payable as the situation reverses. In the later years of the life of a fixed asset, for example, straight-line depreciation will give higher depreciation and therefore lower net income than an accelerated method. Then tax expense for reporting purposes will be lower than taxes payable, and the deferred tax will be reduced. Since firms often buy more and higher-priced assets, however, the increase in deferred taxes may exceed the decrease. In this case, a partial or a total reversal

---

E X H I B I T   2 - 1 4

COOPER TIRE & RUBBER COMPANY
Credit Agreements
1989 Annual Report
Long-Term Debt (Financial Review—Partial)

The Company has a revolving credit agreement with four banks authorizing borrowings up to $85,000,000 with interest rates at prime or lower under optional rate provisions. The agreement, which permits the issuance of commercial paper, provides that on July 31, 1992 the Company may convert any outstanding borrowings under the agreement into a four-year term loan. A commitment fee ranging from 1/4 percent to 3/8 percent per year on the daily unused portion of the $85,000,000 is payable quarterly. There were no borrowings under the revolving credit agreement during the years ended December 31, 1989 and 1988.

will not occur. The taxes may be deferred for a very long time, perhaps permanently. The possibility of permanent or very long deferral raises a question concerning classification. Because the deferred tax may require future payment, it is recommended that deferred taxes be classified as a liability for purposes of financial statement analysis. Deferred taxes are discussed in more detail in Chapter 7.

Warranty obligations are estimated obligations arising out of product warranties. Product warranties require the seller to correct over a specified period of time after the sale any deficiency in quantity, quality, or performance of the product or service. Warranty obligations need to be estimated in order to recognize the obligation at the balance sheet date and to charge the expense to the period of the sale.

Warranty obligations of the Ford Motor Company are shown in Exhibit 2-15. Notice that these obligations are disclosed in both current liabilities and noncurrent liabilities as "dealer and customer allowances and claims."

Minority Interest. Minority interest reflects the ownership of minority shareholders in the equity of consolidated subsidiaries that are less than wholly owned. Minority interest does not represent a liability or stockholders' equity in the firm being analyzed. Consider the following simple example. Parent P owns 90% of the common stock of Subsidiary S, as shown on the next page.

EXHIBIT 2-15

FORD MOTOR COMPANY
Warranty Obligations

Note 9. Liabilities—Automotive

Current Liabilities. Included in accrued liabilities at December 31 were the following:

(in millions)	1989	1988
Dealer and customer allowances and claims	$3,621.8	$3,478.2
Employee benefit plans	1,735.8	1,778.7
Social Security, state, and local taxes	344.7	368.2
Salaries and wages	196.1	206.7
Other	896.3	1,024.4
Total accrued liabilities	$6,794.7	$6,856.2

Noncurrent Liabilities. Automotive noncurrent liabilities at December 31, 1989 and 1988 included $2,432 million and $2,187 million, respectively, of employee benefit plan liabilities and $2,098 million and $1,705 million, respectively, of dealer and customer allowances and claims. Automotive noncurrent liabilities at December 31, 1989 also include $832 million to reflect the unfunded pension obligation for plans whose benefits exceeded assets. A corresponding intangible asset is included in noncurrent assets in the Automotive section of the balance sheet.

	Parent P Balance Sheet December 31, 1991	Subsidiary S Balance Sheet December 31, 1991
	(in millions)	
Current assets	$100	$10
Investment in Subsidiary S	18	—
Other long-term assets	382	40
	$500	$50
Current liabilities	$100	$10
Long-term liabilities	200	20
Stockholders' equity	200	20
	$500	$50

In consolidation, the assets and liabilities of the subsidiary are added to those of the parent, with the elimination of the investment in Subsidiary S. The net assets ($50–$30) of the subsidiary do not all belong to Parent P, however; the minority owners hold 10%. This is shown on the consolidated balance sheet as follows:

PARENT P AND SUBSIDIARY
Consolidated Balance Sheet
December 31, 1991 (in millions)

Current assets	$110
Long-term assets	422
	$532
Current liabilities	$110
Long-term liabilities	220
Minority interest	2
Stockholders' equity	200
	$532

Because of the nature of minority interest, it is usually presented after liabilities and before stockholders' equity. Some firms include minority interest in liabilities; others present minority interest in stockholders' equity. Since minority interest is seldom material, it is recommended that it be considered a liability, to simplify the analysis. In a firm where the minority interest is material, the analysis can be performed twice—once with minority interest as a liability, and then with minority interest as a stockholders' equity item.

Including minority interest as a long-term liability is also conservative when analyzing a firm. For primary analysis, it is recommended that the analysis be conservative. Refer to Exhibit 2-16 for an illustration of minority interest.

DRESSER INDUSTRIES
Liabilities and Shareholders' Investment
Minority Interest

	October 31		
(In millions of dollars)	1989	1988	1987
Current liabilities			
[Detail of current liabilities omitted by author]			
Total current liabilities	971.5	926.0	896.3
Long-term debt—Note H	238.2	255.2	283.4
Pension plans—Note L	56.1	65.3	70.2
Property and casualty insurance reserves	47.6	46.2	55.3
Deferred compensation and other liabilities—Note I	53.7	69.0	72.5
Minority interest—Note C	80.8	77.7	71.1
Shareholders' investment—Notes H, I, J and M			
[Detail of shareholders' investment omitted by author]			

Note C—Business Combinations

On January 11, 1988, the Company acquired substantially all of the business of
The M. W. Kellogg Company, a process engineering and construction firm, from
The Henley Group, Inc. for a cash outlay of $114.1 million and the assumption of
non-interest bearing liabilities of $345.5 million. The acquisition has been accounted
for as a purchase and, accordingly, the consolidated statement of earnings includes
the results of operations since the date of acquisition. The acquisition cost exceeded
the fair value of the net assets acquired by approximately $256.0 million. The excess
was recorded as goodwill and is being amortized on a straight-line basis over forty
years.

    As of September 1, 1987, the Company and Geolograph-Pioneer, Inc. combined
the Company's Swaco operations and Geolograph-Pioneer, Inc.'s fluids processing,
pressure control and rig instrumentation businesses into a new partnership named
Swaco Geolograph Company. The partnership was owned 65 percent by the
Company and 35 percent by Geolograph-Pioneer, Inc. and is included as a
consolidated subsidiary from formation through October 31, 1989. Geolograph-
Pioneer's equity is included in the Minority Interest accounts on the balance sheets
and statements of earnings. On November 1, 1989, the Company purchased
Geolograph-Pioneer's 35% interest in Swaco Geolograph Company and certain re-
lated inventories and fixed assets owned by Geolograph-Pioneer.

    As of December 1, 1986, the Company and the Halliburton Company combined
their drilling fluid operations and formed M-I Drilling Fluids Company, which is a
partnership owned 60 percent by the Company and 40 percent by Halliburton. M-I
Drilling Fluids is included as a consolidated subsidiary. Halliburton's equity is
included in the Minority Interest accounts on the balance sheets and statements of
earnings. Halliburton contributed approximately $75 million of net assets, including
approximately $45 million of working capital, for its investment.

Other Noncurrent Liabilities.   Many other noncurrent liabilities may be disclosed. It would not be practical to discuss all of the possibilities, but some examples are deferred compensation, estimated warranties, and deferred profit on sales.

Redeemable Preferred Stock.   Redeemable preferred stock is subject to mandatory redemption requirements or has a redemption feature that is outside the control of the issuer. If this feature is coupled with such characteristics as no vote or fixed return (often characteristics of preferred stock and bonds), this type of preferred stock is more like debt than equity. For this reason, in 1979 the SEC issued Accounting Series Release No. 268, which requires that the three categories of stock—redeemable preferred stock, nonredeemable preferred stock, and common stock—not be totaled in the balance sheet. Further, the stockholders' equity section is not to include redeemable preferred stock. This is illustrated in the partial balance sheet of GTE Corporation, shown in Exhibit 2-17. Because redeemable preferred stock is more like debt than equity, consider it as part of total liabilities for purposes of financial statement analysis.

Owners' Equity

Ownership equity is the residual ownership interest in the assets of an entity that remains after deducting its liabilities.[4] It is usually divided into two basic categories: paid-in capital and retained earnings. In addition to these two basic categories, owners' equity may contain other accounts that are usually presented separately from paid-in capital and retained earnings. These accounts are foreign currency translation adjustments, unrealized decline in market value of noncurrent equity investments, equity-oriented deferred compensation, and employee stock ownership plans (ESOPs).

Corporations do not use a standard title for owners' equity. Exhibit 2-18 indicates the titles for owners' equity that were used by the companies surveyed by *Accounting Trends and Techniques.*

Paid-In Capital

The first type of paid-in capital account is capital stock. There are two basic types of capital stock: preferred and common.

Both preferred stock and common stock may be issued as par-value stock. (Some states call this *stated value stock.*) The par value of stock is a designated dollar amount per share, established in the articles of incorporation. Most states stipulate that the par value of issued stock times the number of shares outstanding constitutes the legal capital. Also in most states, if original-issue stock is sold below par value, the buyer is contingently liable for the difference between the par value and the lower amount paid. This does not usually pose a problem, because the par value has no direct relationship to market value, the price at which the stock is sold. To

---

[4]FASB, Concept Statement No. 6, par. 212.

EXHIBIT 2-17

GTE CORPORATION
Redeemable Preferred Stock

(thousands of dollars)	December 31	
	1989	1988
Preferred stock, subject to mandatory redemption	$ 275,958	$ 301,958
Shareholders' equity:		
Preferred stock	468,043	504,833
Common stock—shares issued 351,971,990 and 349,289,499	35,197	34,929
Amounts paid in, in excess of par value	5,348,840	5,067,310
Reinvested earnings	4,428,072	3,978,219
Foreign currency translation adjustment	(11,036)	(16,665)
Guaranteed ESOP obligation	(700,000)	—
Common stock held in treasury—21,670,255 and 23,000,000, at cost	(1,166,429)	(937,279)
Total shareholders' equity	8,402,687	8,631,347
Total liabilities and shareholders' equity	$31,986,496	$31,103,926

avoid the problem of selling a stock below par, the par value is usually set very low in relation to the intended selling price. For example, the intended selling price may be $25.00, and the par value may be $1.00.

Some states allow the issuance of no-par stock (either common or preferred).

EXHIBIT 2-18

Title of Stockholders' Equity Section

	1988	1987	1986	1985
Shareholders' Equity	239	249	247	235
Stockholders' Equity	237	228	217	223
Shareowners' Equity	18	22	20	22
Common Shareholders' Equity	16	18	20	24
Common Stockholders' Equity	17	20	18	21
Shareholders' Investment	11	14	19	18
Stockholders' Investment	15	14	13	12
Other or not titled	47	35	46	45
Total companies	600	600	600	600

Source: American Institute of Certified Public Accountants, *Accounting Trends and Techniques*, 1989, p. 204.

Some of these states require that the entire proceeds received from the sale of the no-par stock be designated as legal capital.

Additional paid-in capital arises from the excess of amounts paid for stock over the par or stated value of the common and preferred stock. Also included here are amounts over cost from the sale of treasury stock (discussed later in this chapter), capital arising from the donation of assets to the firm, and transfer from retained earnings through stock dividends when the market price of the stock exceeds par.

Common Stock.   Common stock is capital stock that shares in all the stockholders' rights. It is a representation of ownership which has voting and liquidation rights.

Common stockholders elect the board of directors and vote on major corporate decisions. In the event of liquidation, the liquidation rights of common stockholders give them claims to company assets after all creditors' and preferred stockholders' rights have been fulfilled.

Preferred Stock.   Preferred stock seldom has voting rights. When preferred stock has voting rights, it is usually because of missed dividends. For example, the preferred stockholders may receive voting rights if their dividend has been missed two consecutive times. Some other preferred stock characteristics are the following:

- Preference as to dividends
- Accumulation of dividends
- Participation in excess of stated dividend rate
- Convertibility into common stock
- Callability by the corporation
- Redemption at future maturity date (see the previous discussion of redeemable preferred stock)
- Preference in liquidation

Preference as to Dividends.   When preferred stock has a preference as to dividends, the current year's preferred dividend must be paid before a dividend can be paid to common stockholders. For par-value (or stated value) stock, the dividend rate is usually stated as a percentage of par. For example, if the dividend rate were 9% and the par $100, then the dividend per share would be $9.00. For no-par stock, the dividend rate is stated as $7.00, so each share should receive $7.00 if a dividend is paid. A preference as to dividends does not guarantee that a preferred dividend will be paid in a given year; the board of directors must first declare a dividend. The lack of a fixed commitment to pay dividends and the lack of a due date on the principal are the primary reasons that many firms elect to issue preferred stock instead of bonds. Preferred stock usually represents an expensive source of funds, compared to bonds. This is because preferred stock dividends are not tax deductible, whereas interest on bonds is tax deductible.

Accumulation of Dividends.   If dividends are not declared by the board of directors in a particular year, a holder of noncumulative preferred stock will never be paid that dividend. To make the preferred stock more attractive to investors, the preferred stock is typically issued as cumulative. If a corporation fails to declare the usual dividend on the cumulative preferred stock, the amount of passed dividends becomes dividends in arrears. Common stockholders cannot be paid any dividends until the preferred dividends in arrears and the current preferred dividends are paid.

To illustrate dividends in arrears, assume that a corporation has outstanding 10,000 shares of 8%, $100 par, cumulative preferred stock. Should dividends not be declared in 1991 and 1992, but be declared in 1993, then the preferred stockholders would be entitled to dividends in arrears of $160,000 and current dividends in 1993 of $80,000 before any dividends could be paid to common shareholders.

Participation in Excess of Stated Dividend Rate. When preferred stock is participating, preferred stockholders may receive an extra dividend beyond the stated dividend rate. The terms of the participation depend on the terms included with the stock certificate. For example, the terms may be that any dividend to common stockholders over $10 per share will also be given to preferred stockholders.

To illustrate participating preferred stock, assume that a corporation has 8%, $100 par, preferred stock. The terms of the participation are that any dividend paid on common shares over $10 per share will also be given to preferred stockholders. For the current year, a dividend of $12 per share is declared on the common stock. Therefore, a dividend of $10 must be paid per share of preferred stock for the current year: 8% × 100 = $8.00 + $2.00 = $10.00.

Convertibility into Common Stock. Convertible preferred stock contains a provision that allows the preferred stockholders, at their option, to convert the share of preferred stock at a specific exchange ratio into another security of the corporation. The other security is almost always common stock. The conversion feature is very attractive to investors. For example, the terms may be that each share of preferred stock can be converted to four shares of common stock.

Convertible preferred stock is similar to a convertible bond, except that fixed payout commitments are not present with the convertible preferred stock. The preferred dividend need not be declared, and the preferred stock does not have a due date. The major reason for issuing convertible preferred stock is similar to that for issuing convertible bonds: If the current common stock price is low, in the opinion of management, and the firm eventually wants to increase its common equity, then the firm can raise more money for a given number of common shares by first issuing convertible preferred stock.

A firm usually prefers to issue convertible bonds rather than convertible preferred stock if its capital structure can carry more debt without taking on too much risk. The reason for this is that the interest on the convertible bond is tax deductible, whereas the dividend on the preferred stock is not.

Callability by the Corporation. Callable preferred stock may be retired (recalled) by the corporation at its option. The call price is part of the original stock contract. When the preferred stock is also cumulative, the call terms normally require payment of dividends in arrears before the call is executed.

The call provision favors the company, because the company makes the election to call. Investors do not like call provisions. Therefore, to make a security that has a call provision marketable, the call provision can usually not be exercised for a given number of years. For example, callable preferred stock issued in 1990 may have a provision that the call option cannot be exercised prior to 1995.

Preference in Liquidation. Should the corporation liquidate, the preferred stockholders normally have priority over common stockholders for settlement of claims. However, the claims of preferred stockholders are secondary to the claims of creditors, including bondholders.

Preference in liquidation for preferred stock over common stock is not usually considered to be an important provision. This is because in liquidation there are often insufficient funds to pay claims of preferred stock. Even creditors may receive only a few cents on the dollar in satisfaction of their claims.

Disclosures. It is possible for preferred stock to carry various combinations of provisions. The provisions of each preferred stock issue should be disclosed either parenthetically in the stockholders' equity section of the balance sheet or in a footnote. A company may have various preferred stock issues, each with different provisions.

Donated Capital. Donated capital may be present within the paid-in capital. Donated capital results from donations to the company by stockholders, creditors, or other parties (such as a city). For example, a city may offer land to a company as an inducement to locate a factory in the city, to increase the level of employment.

The firm would record the donated land at the appraised amount and would record an equal amount as donated capital in stockholders' equity.

Another example would be a company that needs to increase its available cash. A plan is devised, calling for existing common stockholders to donate a percentage of their stock to the company, to be sold to raise needed funds. When the stock is sold, the proceeds are added to the cash account, and the donated capital in stockholders' equity is increased. Exhibit 2-19 illustrates the presentation of donated capital by Lands' End, Inc.

Retained Earnings

Retained earnings are the undistributed earnings of the corporation—that is, the net income for all past periods minus the dividends (both cash and stock) that have been declared. Retained earnings are legally available as a basis for dividends unless they have been restricted. A firm may elect, or be required by law or contract, to restrict dividends. For example, bond indenture agreements frequently contain dividend restrictions to require the firm to conserve cash for debt coverage. A restriction of retained earnings is accomplished through an appropriation of retained earnings, making the amount unavailable for dividends. Appropriated retained earnings are shown separately. Caution should be exercised not to confuse retained earnings or appropriated retained earnings with cash or any other asset.

EXHIBIT   2 - 1 9

LANDS' END
Donated Capital

(dollars in thousands)	January 31 1989	1988
Shareholders' investment		
Common stock, 20,040,294 shares issued	$ 200	$ 200
Donated capital	7,000	—
Paid-in capital	22,308	22,308
Retained earnings	62,440	34,166
Total shareholders' investment	$91,948	$56,674

Exhibit 2-19: Lands' End, Inc. Shareholders' Investment, January 31, 1989 annual report. © Copyright 1989, Lands' End, Inc.

Quasi-Reorganization

A quasi-reorganization is an accounting procedure equivalent to an accounting fresh start. A company with a deficit balance in retained earnings "starts over" with a zero balance rather than a deficit. A quasi-reorganization involves the reclassification of a deficit in retained earnings. The deficit is removed, and an equal amount is removed from paid-in capital. A quasi-reorganization may also include a restatement of the carrying values of assets and liabilities to reflect current values.

When a quasi-reorganization is performed, the retained earnings should be dated as of the readjustment date. This dating should be disclosed in the financial statements for a period of 5 to 10 years.

A quasi-reorganization of the Fluor Company is illustrated in Exhibit 2-20.

Foreign Currency Translation

The expansion of international business and extensive currency realignments have created special accounting problems. The biggest difficulty has involved the translation of foreign currency financial statements that are incorporated into the financial statements of an enterprise by consolidation, combination, or the equity method of accounting. Through 1981, following SFAS No. 8, financial statements were translated, and the resulting unrealized exchange gains or losses were included in determining net income. This mandate caused income statement amounts that fluctuated widely. These fluctuations and public sentiment about the impact of changes on earnings caused the FASB to rethink this matter.

After considerable deliberation and research effort, the FASB passed SFAS No. 52 in late 1981. It calls for postponing the recognition of unrealized exchange gains and losses until the foreign operation is substantially liquidated. This postponement is accomplished by creating a stockholders' equity account to carry

EXHIBIT 2-20

FLUOR
Quasi-Reorganization

	October 31	
(dollars in thousands)	1989	1988
Shareholders' equity		
Capital stock		
Preferred—authorized 20,000,000 shares without par value, none issued		
Common—authorized 150,000,000 shares of $.625 par value; issued and outstanding in 1989—79,792,996 shares and in 1988—79,051,744 shares	$ 49,871	$ 49,407
Additional capital	522,615	497,907
Retained earnings (since October 31, 1987)	152,172	54,814
Unamortized executive stock plan expense	(4,439)	(3,117)
Cumulative translation adjustments	144	2,736
Total shareholders' equity	$720,363	$601,747

Restructuring

Quasi-Reorganization   At October 31, 1987, the company adjusted its balance sheet to fair value and transferred the accumulated deficit of $141 million to Additional capital in accordance with quasi-reorganization accounting principles. The fair value adjustments to the October 31, 1987 balance sheet resulted in a net charge to Additional capital of $438 million.

unrealized exchange gains and losses. This method eliminates the wide fluctuations in earnings from translation adjustments for most firms. For subsidiaries operating in highly inflationary economies, translation adjustments are charged to net earnings. Also, actual foreign currency exchange gains or losses are included in net income. Exhibit 2-21 illustrates the presentation of translation adjustments in stockholders' equity.

Unrealized Decline in Market Value of Noncurrent Equity Investments

The use of the lower of cost or market value is appropriate for long-term equity investments (common or preferred stock) when the investment is not consolidated. According to SFAS No. 12, the adjustment to bring the equity securities to the lower of cost or market value is offset with an unrealized loss account that is charged to stockholders' equity. The exception would be when, in the opinion of management, the decline in value is permanent; then the write-down of the investment is considered to be permanent, and the resulting loss is charged to net income.

EXHIBIT   2-21

WARNER LAMBERT COMPANY
Foreign Currency Translation

(millions of dollars)	1989	1988
Stockholders' equity:		
Preferred stock—none issued	—	—
Common stock—80,165,134 shares issued	$ 80.2	$ 80.2
Capital in excess of par value	142.6	143.0
Retained earnings	1,816.8	1,577.1
Cumulative translation adjustments	(120.6)	(75.5)
	1,919.0	1,725.1
Treasury stock, at cost: 1989—12,743,744 and		
1988—2,369,006 shares	(789.2)	(726.5)
Total stockholders' equity	$1,129.8	$ 998.6

Exhibit 2-22 shows a lower of cost or market value adjustment for long-term equity investments for the Kinder Care Learning Centers.

Equity-Oriented Deferred Compensation

Equity-oriented deferred compensation arrangements encompass a wide variety of plans. The deferred compensation element of an equity-based deferred compensa-

EXHIBIT   2-22

KINDER CARE LEARNING CENTERS
Unrealized Loss

	December 29, 1989	December 30, 1988
Stockholders' equity:		
Common stock, par value $.01; authorized 100,000,000 shares; issued and outstanding 51,740,400, shares at December 29, 1989 and December 30, 1988	$ 517,000	$ 517,000
Additional paid-in capital	117,769,000	123,203,000
Unrealized loss on non-current marketable equity securities	—	(6,941,000)
Retained earnings (deficit)	(14,490,000)	8,794,000
	$103,796,000	$125,573,000

tion arrangement is the amount of compensation cost deferred and amortized (expensed) to future periods as the services are provided. APB Opinion No. 25 directs that if stock is issued in a plan before some or all of the services are performed, the unearned compensation should be shown as a separate contra (reduction) item to stockholders' equity.

This unearned compensation amount should be accounted for as an expense of the future period(s) as services are performed. Thus, the unearned compensation amount is removed out of stockholders' equity (amortized) and is recognized as an expense in future periods.

When a plan involves the potential issuance of only stock, the unearned compensation is shown as a reduction in stockholders' equity, and the offsetting amount is also in the stockholders' equity section. If the plan involves cash or a subsequent election of either cash or stock, the unearned compensation is presented as a reduction in stockholders' equity, and the offsetting amount is presented as a liability.

Exhibit 2-23 illustrates an equity-oriented deferred compensation plan for Georgia-Pacific. It is a stock plan only.

Employee Stock Ownership Plans (ESOPs)

An ESOP is a qualified stock-bonus, or combination stock-bonus and money-purchase, pension plan designed to invest primarily in the employer's securities. A qualified plan must satisfy certain qualification requirements of the Internal Revenue Code. An ESOP must be a permanent trusteed plan for the exclusive benefit of the employees.

The trust that is part of the plan is exempt from tax on its income, and the employer/sponsor gets a current deduction for contributions to the plan. The plan participants become eligible for favorable taxation of distributions from the plan.

An ESOP may borrow the funds necessary to purchase the employer stock, borrowing from the company, its shareholders, or a third party such as a bank. The company can guarantee the loan to the ESOP. Financial leverage—the ability of the ESOP to borrow to buy employer securities—is an important aspect.

The Internal Revenue Code is favorable to borrowing for an ESOP. Commercial lending institutions, insurance companies, and mutual funds are permitted an exclusion from income for 50% of the interest received on loans used to finance an ESOP's acquisition of company stock. Thus, these institutions are willing to charge a reduced rate of interest for the loan.

From a company's perspective, there are advantages and disadvantages to an ESOP. One advantage is that it is a source of funds for expansion at a reasonable rate; other possible advantages are the following:

1. A means to buy the stock from a major shareholder or possibly an unwanted shareholder
2. Help financing a leveraged buyout
3. Reduction of potential of an unfriendly takeover
4. Help in creating a market for the company's stock

EXHIBIT 2-23

GEORGIA-PACIFIC
Equity-Oriented Deferred Compensation

(millions, except shares and per share amounts)	December 31 1989	December 31 1988
Shareholders' equity		
Common stock, par value $.80; authorized 150,000,000 shares; 86,664,000 and 94,967,000 shares issued	$ 69	$ 76
Additional paid-in capital	1,009	1,046
Retained earnings	1,713	1,533
Less—Common stock held in treasury, at cost; 139,000 shares in 1988	—	(4)
Long-term incentive plan deferred compensation	(56)	(11)
Accumulated translation adjustments	(18)	(5)
Total shareholders' equity	2,717	2,635
Total liabilities and shareholders' equity	$7,056	$7,115

Long-Term Incentive Plan

The 1988 Long-Term Incentive Plan (Incentive Plan) initially reserved 3,000,000 shares for issue with 1,835,000 shares allocated to the plan participants. Specified portions of the shares allocated under this plan are issued as restricted stock, at no cost to the employee, based on increases in the average market value of the Corporation's common stock. At the time restricted shares are issued, the market value of the stock is added to common stock and additional paid-in capital and an equal amount is deducted from shareholders' equity (long-term incentive plan deferred compensation). Long-term incentive plan deferred compensation is amortized over the vesting (restriction) period, generally five years, with adjustments made quarterly for market price fluctuations. The Corporation recognized long-term incentive plan compensation expense of $14 million in 1989 and $3 million in 1988. Additional information relating to the Incentive Plan is as follows:

	Year ended December 31 1989	Year ended December 31 1988
Shares allocated and unissued at January 1	1,401,000	—
Shares allocated	290,000	1,835,000
Shares cancelled	(110,000)	(90,000)
Restricted shares issued, net of cancellations	(1,045,000)	(344,000)
Shares allocated and unissued at December 31	536,000	1,401,000
Shares available for allocation at December 31	1,075,000	1,255,000
Total shares reserved	1,611,000	2,656,000

Some firms do not find an ESOP attractive, because it can result in a significant amount of voting stock in the hands of their employees. Existing stockholders may not find an ESOP desirable, because it will probably dilute their proportional ownership.

The employer contribution to an ESOP is charged to expense on the income statement. When an ESOP borrows funds and the firm (in either an informal or a formal guarantee) commits to future contributions to the ESOP to meet the debt-service requirements, the firm records this commitment as a liability and as a deferred compensation deduction within stockholders' equity. As the debt is liquidated, the liability and deferred compensation are reduced.

Exhibit 2-24 shows the reporting of the ESOP of W.W. Grainger, Inc.

Treasury Stock

When a firm repurchases its own stock and does not retire it, the stock is called *treasury stock*. Since treasury stock lowers the stock outstanding, it is subtracted from stockholders' equity, usually as the last item in the section. Treasury stock is, in essence, a reduction in paid-in capital.

There are two basic ways that a firm may record treasury stock. One is to record the treasury stock at par or stated value. When this method is used, the

EXHIBIT 2-24

W.W. GRAINGER, INC.
Employee Stock Ownership Plan

(thousands of dollars)	December 31		
	1989	1988	1987
Shareholders' equity			
Cumulative Preferred Stock—1989, 1988, and 1987, $10 par value— authorized, 3,000,000 shares, issued and outstanding, none	—	—	—
Common stock—$1 par value— authorized, 75,000,000 shares, 1989, 1988 and 1987; issued and outstanding, 27,248,869 shares in 1989, 27,172,185 shares in 1988, and 27,712,084 shares in 1987	$ 27,249	$ 27,172	$ 27,712
Additional contributed capital	47,378	40,163	34,467
Guarantee of ESOP debt	(659)	—	—
Retained earnings	657,696	568,147	519,034
Total shareholders' equity	731,664	635,482	581,213
Total liabilities and shareholders' equity	$1,065,245	$936,213	$832,067

EXHIBIT 2-24 (continued)

Note 8—Long-Term Debt

Long-term debt consisted of the following at December 31:

(thousands of dollars)	1989	1988	1987
Industrial development revenue bonds	$26,825	$27,107	$38,675
ESOP debt	659	—	—
Other	1,941	4,969	4,037
	29,425	32,076	42,712
Less current maturities	26,649	15,544	35,700
	$ 2,776	$16,532	$ 7,012

The industrial development revenue bonds include various issues that bear interest at either a fixed rate of 6.125% or variable rates up to 80% of the prime rate. Eight of the bonds bear interest at a variable rate up to 15%. One of the bonds matures at the rate of $75,000 each year through 1994, with the remaining bonds due in various amounts from 2001 through 2011. Interest rates on some of the issues are subject to change at certain dates in the future. Also, at such dates, the bond-holders may require the Company to redeem these bonds. The Company classified $26,450,000, $14,650,000, and $34,570,000 of bonds currently subject to redemption options in current maturities of long-term debt at December 31, 1989, 1988, and 1987, respectively.

In 1989, as part of an acquisition, the Company assumed the liability for a combined Section 401(k) and Employee Stock Ownership Plan (ESOP). The shares held by the ESOP Trust were exchanged for shares of the Company's Common Stock. The ESOP loans are guaranteed by the Company and are included in long-term debt, offset by a like amount included in Shareholders' Equity as Guarantee of ESOP debt. As principal payments are made on the loans by the ESOP Trust, long-term debt and the offset in Shareholders' Equity, Guarantee of ESOP debt, are both reduced.

The aggregate amounts of long-term debt maturing in each of the five years subsequent to December 31, 1989 are as follows:

(In thousands of dollars)	Amounts Payable Under Terms of Agreements	Amounts Subject to Redemption Options
1990	$ 199	$26,450
1991	195	—
1992	1,499	—
1993	173	—
1994	457	—

paid-in capital in excess of par from the original issue is removed. The treasury stock is presented as a reduction of stockholders' equity. This method is referred to as the *par value method* of recording treasury stock.

The other method of presenting treasury stock is to record it at the cost of the stock (presented as a reduction of stockholders' equity). This is referred to as the *cost method*. Most firms record treasury stock at cost.

Exhibit 2-25 illustrates the presentation of treasury stock for Hillenbrand Industries. Note that a firm cannot record gains or losses from dealing in its own stock.

Owners' Equity in Unincorporated Firms

Owners' equity in an unincorporated firm is termed *capital*. The amount invested by the owner plus the retained earnings may be shown as one sum, since there is no restriction on the removal (drawing or withdrawal) of profits.

Problems in Balance Sheet Presentation

The problems inherent in balance sheet presentation are numerous and may cause difficulty in analysis. First, most assets are valued at cost, so one cannot determine the market value or replacement cost of many assets and should not assume that their balance sheet value approximates this current valuation.

Second, varying methods are used for asset valuation. For example, inventories may be valued differently from firm to firm and, within a firm, from product to

---

EXHIBIT 2-25

HILLENBRAND INDUSTRIES
Treasury Stock

(dollars in thousands)	December 2, 1989	December 3, 1988
Shareholders' equity		
Common stock—without par value		
Authorized—45,000,000 shares		
Issued—40,161,956 shares in 1989 and 1988	$ 4,442	$ 4,442
Additional paid-in capital	1,752	1,470
Retained earnings	460,117	403,757
Unearned restricted stock compensation	(1,333)	(2,237)
Foreign currency translation adjustment	2,284	2,013
Treasury stock, at cost: 1989—3,048,714 shares;		
1988—2,866,834 shares	(62,188)	(56,137)
Total shareholders' equity	$405,074	$353,308

product. A simple illustration may help. In a period, a firm buys two units of goods for resale, the first at $10 and the second at $12. The goods are placed on the shelf and are indistinguishable. After sales for the period, there is one unit left. Different methods of inventory valuation allow a cost of $10, $12, or the average of $11 to be used. This lack of uniformity causes problems in comparison. Similar problems exist with long-term asset valuation and the related depreciation alternatives. Methods of alleviating these problems will be discussed in connection with the ratios where these asset valuations are used.

A third and different type of problem arises because not all items of value to the firm are included as assets. For example, such characteristics as good employees, outstanding management, and a well-chosen location do not appear on the balance sheet. In the same vein, liabilities related to contingencies also may not appear on the balance sheet. Many of the problems of the balance sheet are discussed in Chapters 6 and 7.

These problems do not make statement analysis impossible. They merely require that qualitative judgment be applied to quantitative ratio and trend analyses, in order to assess the impact of these problem areas.

SUMMARY

The balance sheet shows the financial condition of an accounting entity as of a particular date. It is the most basic financial statement, which is read by various users as part of their decision-making process.

QUESTIONS

Q 2-1   Name and describe the three major categories of balance sheet accounts.

Q 2-2   Are the following balance sheet items (A) assets, (L) liabilities, or (E) stockholders' equity?

a. dividends payable
b. mortgage notes payable
c. investments in stock
d. cash
e. land
f. inventory
g. unearned rent
h. marketable securities
i. patents
j. capital stock
k. retained earnings

l. lease obligations that are recorded
m. accounts receivable
n. taxes payable
o. accounts payable
p. organizational costs
q. prepaid expenses
r. goodwill
s. tools
t. buildings
u. donated capital

Q 2-3   Classify the following as (a) current asset, (b) investment, (c) intangible asset, or (d) tangible asset.

a. land
b. cash
c. copyrights
d. marketable securities
e. goodwill
f. inventories

g. tools
h. prepaids
i. buildings
j. accounts receivable
k. long-term investment in stock
l. machinery

Q 2-4   Current assets are listed in a specific order, starting with cash. What is the objective of this order of listing?

Q 2-5   Differentiate between marketable securities and long-term investments. What is the purpose of owning each?

Q 2-6   Differentiate between accounts receivable and accounts payable.

Q 2-7   What types of inventory will a retailing firm have? A manufacturing firm?

Q 2-8   Why does LIFO result in a very unrealistic ending inventory figure in a period of rising prices?

Q 2-9   What is depreciation? Which tangible assets are depreciated and which are not? Why?

Q 2-10   For reporting purposes, management prefers higher profits; for tax purposes, lower taxable income is desired. To meet these goals, firms often use different methods of depreciation for tax and reporting purposes. Which depreciation method is best for reporting and which for tax purposes? Why?

Q 2-11   A rental agency collects rent in advance. Why is the rent collected treated as a liability?

Q 2-12   A bond carries a stated rate of interest of 6% and par of $1,000. It matures in twenty years. It is sold at 83 (83% of $1,000, or $830).
a. Under normal conditions, why would the bond sell at less than par?
b. How would the discount be disclosed on the statements?

Q 2-13   To be conservative, how should minority interest on the balance sheet be handled for primary analysis?

Q 2-14   Firms value many assets at historical cost. Why does this accounting principle cause difficulties in financial statement analysis?

Q 2-15   Explain how the issuance of a convertible bond can be a very attractive means of raising common equity funds.

Q 2-16   Classify each of the following as a current asset, noncurrent asset, current liability, noncurrent liability, or equity account. Choose the best or most frequently used classification.

a. supplies
b. notes receivable
c. unearned subscription revenue
d. accounts payable
e. retained earnings

f. accounts receivable
g. preferred stock
h. plant
i. prepaid rent
j. capital

k. wages payable
l. mortgage bonds payable
m. unearned interest
n. marketable securities
o. paid-in capital from sale of treasury
   stock

p. land
q. inventories
r. taxes accrued
s. cash

Q 2-17   Explain these preferred stock characteristics:
   a. accumulation of dividends
   b. participation in excess of stated dividend rate
   c. convertibility into common stock
   d. callability by the corporation
   e. preference in liquidation

Q 2-18   Describe the account "unrealized exchange gains or losses."

Q 2-19   What is treasury stock? Why is it deducted from stockholders' equity?

Q 2-20   A firm, with no opening inventory, buys ten units at $6 each during the period. In which
         accounts might the $60 appear on the financial statements?

Q 2-21   Consolidated statements may be issued to show financial position as it would appear if the
         companies were one entity. What is the objective of such a statement?

Q 2-22   How is a subsidiary that is not consolidated presented on a balance sheet?

Q 2-23   Why would minority interest be presented on a balance sheet?

Q 2-24   What is the basic guideline for consolidation?

Q 2-25   DeLand Company owns 100% of Little Florida, Inc. Will DeLand Company show a mi-
         nority interest on its balance sheet? Would the answer change if it owned only 60%? Will
         there ever be a case in which the subsidiary, Little Florida, is not consolidated?

Q 2-26   Describe the account "unrealized decline in market value of noncurrent equity investments."

Q 2-27   What is redeemable preferred stock? Why should it be included with debt for purposes of
         financial statement analysis?

Q 2-28   Describe donated capital.

Q 2-29   Assume that land was donated to a company by a city. What accounts would be affected by
         this donation, and what would be the measurement amount?

Q 2-30   In general, describe quasi-reorganization.

Q 2-31   Assume that an equity-oriented deferred compensation plan involves cash or a subsequent
         election of either cash or stock. Describe the presentation of this plan on the balance sheet.

Q 2-32   Describe employee stock ownership plans (ESOPs).

Q 2-33   Why are commercial lending institutions, insurance companies, and mutual funds willing to
         grant loans to an employee stock ownership plan at favorable rates?

Q 2-34   Indicate possible disadvantages of an employee stock ownership plan.

Q 2-35   How does a company recognize, either in an informal or a formal way, that it has guaranteed commitments to future contributions to an ESOP to meet debt-service requirements?

Q 2-36   Describe the difference between depreciation, amortization, and depletion.

Q 2-37   Indicate the three factors usually considered when computing depreciation.

Q 2-38   An accelerated system of depreciation is often used for income tax purposes but is usually not used for financial reporting. Why?

Q 2-39   Which depreciation method will result in the most depreciation over the life of an asset?

Q 2-40   Should depreciation be recognized on a building in a year in which the cost of replacing the building rises? Explain.

| PROBLEMS

P 2-1   The following are the inventory records of Herrick House.

	Units	Cost	Total
January 1	10	8	$ 80
Purchases			
April 18	32	9	288
November 3	41	10	410
December 10	4	11	44

Ending inventory is 6 units. These units are from the November purchase.

Required   Calculate ending inventory and cost of sales using: (a) FIFO, (b) LIFO, (c) average, and (d) specific identification.

P 2-2   The following information was obtained from the accounts of Airlines International as of December 31, 1992. It is presented in scrambled order.

Accounts payable	$ 77,916
Accounts receivable	67,551
Accrued expenses	23,952
Accumulated depreciation	220,541
Allowance for doubtful accounts	248
Capital in excess of par	72,913
Cash	28,837
Common stock (par $.50, authorized 20,000 shares, issued 14,304 shares)	7,152
Current installments of long-term debt	36,875
Deferred income tax liability (long term)	42,070
Inventory	16,643
Investments and special funds	11,901
Long-term debt, less current portion	393,808
Marketable securities	10,042

Other assets	727
Prepaid expenses	3,963
Property, plant, and equipment at cost	809,980
Retained earnings	67,361
Unearned transportation revenue (airline tickets expiring within one year)	6,808

Required Prepare a classified balance sheet.

P 2-3 The following information was obtained from the accounts of Lukes as of December 31, 1992. It is presented in scrambled order.

Common stock, no par value, 10,000 shares authorized, 5,724 shares issued	$ 3,180
Retained earnings	129,950
Deferred income tax liability (long-term)	24,000
Long-term debt	99,870
Accounts payable	35,000
Buildings	75,000
Machinery and equipment	300,000
Land	11,000
Accumulated depreciation	200,000
Cash	3,000
Receivables, less allowance of $3,000	58,000
Accrued income taxes	3,000
Inventories	54,000
Other accrued expenses	8,000
Current portion of long-term debt	7,000
Prepaid expenses	2,000
Other assets (long term)	7,000

Required Prepare a classified balance sheet. For assets, use the classifications of current assets, plant and equipment, and other assets. For liabilities, use the classifications of current liabilities and long-term liabilities.

P 2-4 The following information was obtained from the accounts of Alleg as of December 31, 1992. It is presented in scrambled order.

Common stock, authorized 21,000 shares at $1 par value, issued 10,000 shares	$ 10,000
Additional paid-in capital	38,000
Cash	13,000
Marketable securities	17,000
Accounts receivable	26,000
Accounts payable	15,000
Current maturities of long-term debt	11,000
Mortgages payable	80,000
Bonds payable	70,000
Inventories	30,000
Land and buildings	57,000
Machinery and equipment	125,000

Goodwill	8,000
Patents	10,000
Other assets	50,000
Deferred income taxes (long-term liability)	18,000
Retained earnings	33,000
Accumulated depreciation	61,000

Required   Prepare a classified balance sheet. For assets, use the classifications of current assets, plant and equipment, intangibles, and other assets. For liabilities, use the classifications of current liabilities and long-term liabilities.

P 2-5   The following is the balance sheet of Ingram Industries.

INGRAM INDUSTRIES
Balance Sheet
June 30, 1992

Assets			
Current assets:			
Cash (including $13,000 in sinking fund)		$ 70,000	
Marketable securities (cost $20 000) at market		23,400	
Investment in subsidiary company		23,000	
Accounts receivable		21,000	
Inventories (lower of cost or market)		117,000	$254,400
Plant assets:			
Land and buildings		$160,000	
Less: accumulated depreciation		100,000	60,000
Investments:			
Treasury stock			4,000
Deferred charges:			
Discount on bonds payable		$ 6,000	
Prepaid expenses		2,000	8,000
Total assets			$326,400
Liabilities and equity			
Liabilities:			
Notes payable to bank		$ 60,000	
Accounts payable		18,000	
Bonds payable		61,000	
Total liabilities			$139,000
Stockholders' equity:			
Preferred and common (each $10 par, 5,000			
shares preferred and 6,000 shares common)		$110,000	
Capital in excess of par		61,000	
Retained earnings, beginning of year	$11,400		
Net income	15,000		
Less: dividends	10,000	16,400	187,400
Total liabilities and stockholders' equity			$326,400

Required   Indicate your criticisms of the balance sheet and briefly explain the proper treatment of any item criticized.

P 2-6   The following is the balance sheet of Rubber Industries.

RUBBER INDUSTRIES
Balance Sheet
For the Year Ended December 31, 1992

Assets	
Current assets:	
Cash	$ 50,000
Marketable securities (market $25,000) at lower of cost or market	19,000
Accounts receivable, net	60,000
Inventories (lower of cost or market)	30,000
Treasury stock	20,000
Total current assets	$179,000
Plant assets:	
Land and buildings, net	160,000
Investments:	
Short-term U.S. notes	20,000
Other assets:	
Supplies	4,000
Total assets	$363,000
Liabilities and stockholders' equity	
Liabilities:	
Bonds payable	$120,000
Accounts payable	40,000
Wages payable	10,000
Premium on bonds payable	3,000
Total liabilities	173,000
Stockholders' equity:	
Common stock ($20 par, 20,000 shares authorized, 6,000 shares outstanding)	120,000
Retained earnings	30,000
Minority interest	20,000
Redeemable preferred stock	20,000
Total liabilities and stockholders' equity	$363,000

Required   Indicate your criticisms of the balance sheet and briefly explain the proper treatment of any item criticized.

P 2-7   The balance sheet of McDonald Company is shown on the next page.

MCDONALD COMPANY
December 31, 1992

Assets:
  Current assets:
    Cash (including $10,000 restricted for

payment of note)		$ 40,000	
Marketable securities (market of $18,000)			
at lower of cost or market		20,000	
Accounts receivable, less allowance for			
doubtful accounts of $12,000		70,000	
Inventory (lower of cost or market)		60,000	
Total current assets			$190,000
Plant assets:			
Land		$ 40,000	
Buildings, net		100,000	
Equipment	$80,000		
Less: accumulated depreciation	20,000	60,000	
Patents		20,000	
Organizational costs		15,000	
			235,000
Other assets			
Prepaid insurance			5,000
Total assets			$430,000
Liabilities and stockholders' equity			
Current liabilities:			
Accounts payable		$ 60,000	
Wages payable		10,000	
Notes payable, due July 1, 1993		20,000	
Bonds payable, due December 1993		100,000	
Total current liabilities			$190,000
Dividends payable			4,000
Deferred tax liability, long term			30,000
Stockholders' equity:			
Common stock ($10 par, 10,000 shares			
authorized, 5,000 shares outstanding)		$ 50,000	
Retained earnings		156,000	
Total stockholders' equity			206,000
Total liabilities and stockholders' equity			$430,000

Required   Indicate your criticisms of the balance sheet and briefly explain the proper treatment of any item criticized.

P 2-8   You have just started as a staff auditor for a small CPA firm. During the course of the audit, you discover the following items related to a single client firm.

a. During the year, the firm declared and paid $10,000 in dividends.
b. Your client has been named defendant in a legal suit involving a material account; you have received from the client's counsel a statement indicating little likelihood of loss.
c. Because of cost control actions and general employee dissatisfaction, it is likely that the client will suffer a costly strike in the near future.
d. During the year, the firm changed its inventory method from average to LIFO.
e. Twenty days after closing, the client suffered a major fire in one of its plants.
f. The cash account includes a substantial amount set aside for payment of pension obligations.
g. Marketable securities include a large quantity of shares of stock purchased for control purposes.
h. Land is listed on the balance sheet at market of $1,000,000. It cost $670,000 to purchase twelve years ago.
i. During the year, the government of Uganda expropriated a plant located in that country. There was substantial loss.

Required   How would each of these items be reflected in the year-end balance sheet, including footnotes?

P 2-9   Corvallis Corporation owns 80% of the stock of Little Harrisburg, Inc. At December 31, 1992, Little Harrisburg had the following summarized balance sheet:

LITTLE HARRISBURG, INC.
Balance Sheet
December 31, 1992

Current assets	$100,000	Current liabilities	$ 50,000
Property, plant, and equipment (net)	400,000	Long-term debt	150,000
	$500,000	Capital stock	50,000
		Retained earnings	250,000
			$500,000

The earnings of Little Harrisburg, Inc., for 1992 were $50,000 after tax.

Required   a. What would be the amount of minority interest on the balance sheet of Corvallis Corporation? How should minority interest be classified for financial statement analysis purposes?
b. What would be the minority share of earnings on the income statement of Corvallis Corporation?

P 2-10   The Aggarwal Company has had 10,000 shares of 10%, $100 par-value preferred stock and 80,000 shares of $5 stated-value common stock outstanding for the last three years. During that period, dividends paid totaled $0, $200,000, and $220,000 for each year, respectively.

Required   Compute the amount of dividends that must have been paid to preferred stockholders and common stockholders in each of the three years, given the following four independent assumptions:

a. Preferred stock is nonparticipating and cumulative.
b. Preferred stock participates up to 12% of its par value and is cumulative.
c. Preferred stock is fully participating and cumulative.
d. Preferred stock is nonparticipating and noncumulative.

P 2-11   The Rosewell Company has had 5,000 shares of 9%, $100 par-value preferred stock and 10,000 shares of $10 par-value common stock outstanding for the last two years. During the most recent year, dividends paid totaled $65,000; in the prior year, dividends paid totaled $40,000.

Required   Compute the amount of dividends that must have been paid to preferred stockholders and common stockholders in each of the years, given the following independent assumptions:
a. Preferred stock is fully participating and cumulative.
b. Preferred stock is nonparticipating and noncumulative.
c. Preferred stock participates up to 10% of its par value and is cumulative.
d. Preferred stock is nonparticipating and cumulative.

P 2-12   An item of equipment acquired on January 1 at a cost of $100,000 has an estimated life of ten years.

Required   Assuming that the equipment will have a salvage value of $10,000, determine the depreciation for each of the first three years by the:
a. straight-line method
b. declining-balance method
c. sum-of-the-years'-digits method

P 2-13   An item of equipment acquired on January 1 at a cost of $60,000 has an estimated use of 25,000 hours. During the first three years, the equipment was used 5,000, 6,000, and 4,000 hours, respectively. The estimated salvage value of the equipment is $10,000.

Required   Determine the depreciation for each of the three years, using the straight-line method, the declining-balance method, and the sum-of-the-years'-digits method.

P 2-14   An item of equipment acquired on January 1 at a cost of $50,000 has an estimated life of five years and an estimated salvage of $10,000.

Required   a. From a management perspective, from among the straight-line method, declining-balance method, and the sum-of-the-years'-digits method of depreciation, which method should be chosen for the financial statements if income is to be at a maximum the first year? Which method should be chosen for the income tax returns, assuming that the tax rate stays the same each year? Explain and show computations.
b. Is it permissible to use different depreciation methods in financial statements than in tax returns?

CASES

Case 2-1   COMPREHENSIVE BALANCE SHEET

The January 3, 1987, and January 4, 1986, consolidated balance sheets of VR Corporation follow.

(dollars in thousands)	January 3 1987	January 4 1986
Assets		
Current assets		
Cash and short-term investments	$ 126,097	$ 68,483
Accounts receivable, less allowances of $7,705 in 1986 and $6,785 in 1985	261,559	148,423
Inventories	476,175	208,745
Other current assets	20,518	11,153
Total current assets	884,349	436,804
Property, plant and equipment		
Land	33,402	14,340
Buildings	211,210	133,687
Machinery and equipment	413,747	324,242
	658,359	472,269
Less accumulated depreciation	198,095	156,731
	460,264	315,538
Intangible assets	448,414	100,297
Other assets	40,734	7,554
	$1,833,761	$860,193
Liabilities and shareholders' equity		
Current liabilities		
Short-term borrowings	$ 169,840	$ 3,948
Accounts payable	109,121	48,124
Employee compensation	23,151	19,903
Federal and state income taxes	10,124	19,440
Other current liabilities	35,430	15,161
Current portion of long-term debt	82,427	38,476
Total current liabilities	430,093	145,052
Long-term debt	436,468	124,280
Other liabilities	143,059	36,638
Shareholders' equity		
Common stock	67,556	31,097
Additional paid-in capital	207,421	36,073
Foreign currency translation	(6,282)	(12,354)
Retained earnings	555,446	499,407
	824,141	554,223
	$1,833,761	$860,193

See notes to consolidated financial statements.

Required

a. The statement is entitled Consolidated Balance Sheets. What does it mean to have consolidated balance sheets?

b. Does it appear that the subsidiaries are wholly owned by VF Corporation? Explain.

c. What are the gross receivables at January 3, 1987?

d. What is the estimated amount that will be collected on receivables outstanding at January 3, 1987?
e. What is the gross cost of property, plant, and equipment at January 3, 1987?
f. What is the net property, plant, and equipment at January 3, 1987?
g. How much expense has been recognized on the cost of property, plant, and equipment as of January 3, 1987?
h. Speculate on the reason for the significant increase in total assets and intangible assets.
i. Why is a portion of long-term debt included in current liabilities?
j. What does the balance in the foreign currency translation account represent?

Case 2-2   INSIGHT ON LIABILITIES AND SHAREHOLDERS' EQUITY

The December 31, 1985, and 1984 consolidated balance sheets of Time Inc. included the following liabilities and shareholders' equity.

(dollars in thousands)	1985	1984
Liabilities and shareholders' equity		
Current liabilities:		
Accounts payable and accrued expenses	$ 577,282	$ 564,987
Employee compensation and benefits	121,224	99,516
Loans and current portion of long-term debt	70,364	26,710
Total current liabilities	768,870	691,213
Unearned portion of paid subscriptions	333,673	258,764
Long-term debt	464,530	383,195
Deferred federal income taxes	248,132	150,695
Other liabilities	45,899	69,022
Redeemable preferred stock—series B; authorized 4,000,000 shares; issued and outstanding 990,700 shares in 1984		29,460
Shareholders' equity:		
Common stock—$1 par value; authorized 200,000,000 shares; issued 62,797,400 shares in 1985 and 62,142,300 shares in 1984; outstanding 62,772,600 in 1985 and 60,786,900 shares in 1984	62,797	62,142
Additional paid-in capital	235,114	221,133
Foreign currency translation	(7,133)	(9,696)
Deferred compensation—restricted stock	(5,767)	(7,329)
Retained income	926,026	814,183
Treasury stock—at cost; common shares—24,800 in 1985 and 1,373,400 in 1984	(526)	(47,970)
Total shareholders' equity	1,210,511	1,032,463
Total liabilities and shareholders' equity	$3,071,615	$2,614,812

© 1986 Time Inc. Reproduced with permission.

Required   a. The statement is entitled Consolidated Balance Sheets. What does it mean to have consolidated balance sheets?
b. Does it appear that the subsidiaries are wholly owned by Time Inc.? Explain.

c. Why is a portion of long-term debt included in current liabilities?
d. Speculate on the nature of the unearned portion of the paid subscription account.
e. Describe the deferred federal income taxes account.
f. Describe the redeemable preferred stock—series B account. Why is redeemable preferred stock not classified with shareholders' equity?
g. What is the dollar amount of shareholders' equity at December 31, 1985, that relates to the common stockholders? Would this amount be the market value of the total common stock at December 31, 1985?
h. Describe the retained income account. Is there cash in this account?
i. Describe the treasury stock account. Why did it significantly decrease between December 31, 1984, and December 31, 1985?

Case 2-3   INSIGHT ON ASSETS

The December 31, 1985 and 1984 consolidated balance sheets of CBS, Inc., included the following assets.

(dollars in millions)	December 31	
	1985	1984
Assets		
Current assets:		
Cash and cash equivalents:		
Cash and cash items	$ 75.8	$ 14.0
Short-term marketable securities, at cost plus accrued interest (approximates market)	44.3	265.6
	120.1	279.6
Notes and accounts receivable, less allowances for doubtful accounts, returns, and discounts: 1985, $155.9; 1984, $153.3; 1983, $146.9	785.0	849.8
Inventories (Note 11)	173.3	290.5
Program rights and feature film productions	483.9	462.0
Recoverable income taxes	130.9	
Prepaid expenses	142.9	144.0
Total current assets	1,836.1	2,025.9
Property, plant, and equipment:		
Land	27.6	31.4
Buildings	304.0	333.6
Machinery and equipment	620.4	596.9
Leasehold improvements	53.0	51.8
	1,005.0	1,013.7
Less accumulated depreciation	445.7	414.4
Net property, plant, and equipment	559.3	599.3
Investments and other assets:		
Investments (Notes 3, 4, and 12)	252.9	200.7
Excess of the cost over the fair value of net assets of businesses acquired, less amortization (Note 3)	420.8	67.0
Other intangible assets (Note 3)	70.9	25.7

Other program rights and feature film productions	169.6	170.3
Other assets	199.1	172.9
Total investments and other assets	1,113.3	636.6
Total assets	$3,508.7	$3,261.8

Reproduced with the permission of CBS, Inc.

Required

a. The statement is entitled Consolidated Balance Sheets. What does it mean to have consolidated balance sheets?

b. What is the gross amount of notes and accounts receivable at December 31, 1985?

c. What is the estimated amount that will be collected from notes and accounts receivable at December 31, 1985?

d. Describe the program rights and feature film productions account that is included in current assets. Why is the other program rights and feature film productions account included in long-term assets?

e. Speculate on the nature of the accounts receivable income taxes.

f. What is the gross amount of property, plant, and equipment at December 31, 1985?

g. What is the net amount of property, plant, and equipment at December 31, 1985?

h. What is the total depreciation expense that has been recognized as of December 31, 1985?

i. What is the unamortized balance for goodwill at December 31, 1985?

Case 2-4   SELECTIVE REVIEW OF BALANCE SHEET

The consolidated balance sheet and selected footnotes from the 1989 annual report of Johnson & Johnson follow.

At December 31, 1989 and January 1, 1989 (dollars in millions) (Note 1)	1989	1988
Assets		
Current assets		
Cash and cash equivalents (Note 1)	$ 452	$ 529
Marketable securities, at cost, which approximates market value	131	131
Accounts receivable, trade, less allowances $88 (1988, $71)	1,320	1,135
Inventories (Notes 1 and 3)	1,353	1,273
Deferred taxes on income	196	183
Prepaid expenses and other receivables	324	252
Total current assets	3,776	3,503
Marketable securities, non-current, at cost, which approximates market value	254	188
Property, plant and equipment, net (Notes 1 and 4)	2,846	2,493
Intangible assets, net (Notes 1 and 5)	704	609
Deferred taxes on income	26	46
Other assets	313	280
Total assets	$7,919	$7,119

Liabilities and stockholders' equity

Current liabilities

Loans and notes payable (Note 6)	$ 570	$ 522
Accounts payable	622	651
Accrued liabilities	624	615
Taxes on income	111	80
Total current liabilities	1,927	1,868
Long-term debt (Note 6)	1,170	1,166
Certificates of extra compensation (Note 13)	85	77
Other liabilities	589	505

Stockholders' equity (Note 12)

Preferred stock—without par value (authorized and unissued 2,000,000 shares)	—	—
Common stock—par value $1.00 per share (authorized 540,000,000 shares; issued 383,670,000 shares)	384	384
Cumulative currency translation adjustments (Note 8)	(9)	(22)
Retained earnings	5,260	4,625
	5,635	4,987
Less common stock held in treasury, at cost (50,616,000 and 50,601,000 shares)	1,487	1,484
Total stockholders' equity	4,148	3,503
Total liabilities and stockholders' equity	$7,919	$7,119

Selected Notes to Consolidated Financial Statements

Note 1. Summary of Significant Accounting Policies

Principles of Consolidation   The consolidated financial statements include the accounts of Johnson & Johnson and subsidiaries. Intercompany accounts and transactions are eliminated.

Cash Equivalents   The Company considers securities with maturities of three months or less, when purchased, to be cash equivalents.

Inventories   While cost is determined principally by the first-in, first-out (FIFO) method, the majority of domestic inventories are valued using the last-in, first-out (LIFO) method. Inventories are valued at the lower of cost or market.

Depreciation of Property   In the second quarter of 1989, the Company adopted the straight-line method of depreciation for financial statement purposes for all additions to property, plant and equipment after January 1, 1989. Depreciation of property, plant and equipment for assets placed in service prior to January 1, 1989 is generally determined using an accelerated method. The Company believes that the new method of depreciation is preferable and more consistent with the method prevalent in the Company's lines of business. The effect of the change on 1989 net earnings and earnings per share is not material.

Intangible Assets   The excess of the cost over the fair value of net assets of purchased businesses is recorded as goodwill and is amortized on a straight-line basis over periods of 40 years or less.

The cost of other acquired intangibles is amortized on a straight-line basis over their estimated useful lives.

Income Taxes   Domestic investment tax credits and certain international tax incentives are deferred and amortized over the estimated useful lives of the related assets.

The Company intends to continue to reinvest its undistributed international earnings to expand its international operations; therefore, no tax has been provided to cover the repatriation of such undistributed earnings. At December 31, 1989, the cumulative amount of undistributed international earnings for which the Company has not provided United States income taxes was approximately $1.4 billion.

Net Earnings Per Share   Net earnings per share are calculated using the average number of shares outstanding during each year. Shares issuable under stock option and compensation plans would not materially reduce net earnings per share.

Annual Closing Date   The Company follows the concept of a fiscal year which ends on the Sunday nearest to the end of the month of December. Normally each fiscal year consists of 52 weeks, but every five or six years, as was the case in 1987, the fiscal year consists of 53 weeks.

Note 3.   Inventories

At the end of 1989 and 1988, inventories comprised:

(dollars in millions)	1989	1988
Raw materials and supplies	$ 435	$ 388
Goods in process	259	238
Finished goods	659	647
	$1,353	$1,273

Inventories valued on the LIFO basis were approximately 19% and 22% of total inventories at the end of 1989 and 1988, respectively. If all inventories were valued on the FIFO basis, total inventories would have been $1,482 million and $1,385 million at December 31, 1989 and January 1, 1989, respectively.

Note 4. Property, Plant and Equipment

At the end of 1989 and 1988, net property, plant and equipment comprised:

(dollars in millions)	1989	1988
Land and land improvements	$ 226	$ 191
Buildings and building equipment	1,737	1,576
Machinery and equipment	2,231	1,853
Construction in progress	323	349

	4,517	3,969
Less accumulated depreciation	1,671	1,476
	$2,846	$2,493

The Company capitalizes interest expense as part of the cost of construction of facilities and equipment. Interest expense capitalized in 1989, 1988 and 1987 was $41, $31 and $24 million, respectively.

Note 5. Intangible Assets

At the end of 1989 and 1988, intangible assets, consisting primarily of patents and goodwill, comprised:

(dollars in millions)	1989	1988
Intangible assets	$880	$729
Less accumulated amortization	176	120
	$704	$609

Required

a. The statement is entitled Consolidated Balance Sheet. What does it mean to have a consolidated balance sheet?
b. Does it appear that the subsidiaries are wholly owned? Explain.
c. What is the dollar amount of stockholders' equity at December 31, 1989? How much of this amount relates to common stock?
d. Would the dollar amount of stockholders' equity at December 31, 1989 equal the market value of the common stock at December 31, 1989? Explain.
e. Describe the retained earnings account. Is there cash in this account?
f. Describe the treasury stock account.
g. What was the approximate market value of marketable securities at December 31, 1989?
h. What are the gross receivables at December 31, 1989?
i. What would have been the total inventories at December 31, 1989 if all inventories had been valued on the FIFO basis?
j. What is the gross amount of property, plant, and equipment at December 31, 1989?
k. For property, plant, and equipment on hand at December 31, 1989, what has been the depreciation recognized?
l. Will the adoption of straight-line depreciation result in a faster or slower recognition of depreciation expense? Comment.
m. Intangible assets
   1. What is the amortization period for goodwill?
   2. What is the gross amount for intangible assets at December 31, 1989?
   3. What is the net amount for intangible assets at December 31, 1989?

CHAPTER 3

INCOME STATEMENT AND STATEMENT OF RETAINED EARNINGS

CHAPTER TOPICS

Income Statement	Income Taxes
Sales or Revenues	Special Income Statement Items
Cost of Goods Sold or Cost of Sales	Earnings Per Share
Operating Expense	*Statement of Retained Earnings*
Other Income and Expense	*Dividends and Stock Splits*

In practice, the income statement is frequently considered to be the most important financial statement. This statement and the statement of retained earnings are covered in this chapter.

INCOME STATEMENT

As previously indicated, an income statement is a summary of revenues and expenses and gains and losses, ending with net income for a particular period of time.

A simplified multiple-step income statement might look as follows:

	Sales or revenue	$XXX
−	*Cost of goods sold (cost of sales)*	XXX
	Gross profit	(XXX)
−	*Operating expenses (selling and administration)*	XXX
	Income from operations	XXX
+(−)	*Other income or expense*	XXX
	Net income before income taxes	XXX
−	*Income taxes*	XXX
	Net income	$XXX
	Earnings per share	$XXX

With a multiple-step income statement, gross profit, income from operations, net income before income taxes, and net income are usually presented separately.

Many firms use a single-step income statement, in which all revenues and gains (sales, other income) are first totaled, and then total expenses and losses (cost of goods sold, operating expenses, other expenses) are deducted. A simplified single-step income statement might look as follows:

Sales or revenue	$XXX
Other income	XXX
Total revenue	XXX
Cost of goods sold (cost of sales)	XXX
Operating expense (selling and	
administrative)	XXX
Other expense	XXX
Income tax expense	XXX
Total expenses	XXX
Net income	$XXX
Earnings per share	$XXX

The basic approach to a single-step income statement is to list all revenues and gains (usually in order of amount), then list all expenses and losses (usually in order of amount). With total expense and loss items deducted from total revenue and gain items, the net income is determined. Most firms that present a single-step income statement modify it in some way, such as by presenting federal income tax expense as a separate item.

Exhibits 3-1 and 3-2 illustrate the different types of income statements. In Exhibit 3-1, Ameritech uses a single-step income statement; in Exhibit 3-2, Echlin uses a multiple-step format.

To permit comparison, the formats of income statements must be similar. The multiple-step format is recommended, because it provides intermediate profit figures useful in financial statement analysis. It is necessary to become familiar with the types of income statement accounts in order to construct the restatement from single-step to multiple-step format. This is especially important because 240 of 600 firms surveyed in *Accounting Trends and Techniques* in 1988 used some type of single-step format.[1]

Sales or Revenues

Sales represent revenue from goods or services sold to a customer. They may also include lease revenue or royalties, depending on the product of the business. Revenues included here are for the principal products of the firm. Sales are usually shown net of any discounts, returns, or allowances.

[1]American Institute of Certified Public Accountants, *Accounting Trends and Techniques,* 1989, p. 231.

EXHIBIT 3-1

AMERITECH
Consolidated Statements of Income
Single-Step Income Statement

(dollars in millions, except per share amounts)	1989	1988	1987
Revenues	$10,211.3	$9,903.3	$9,547.5
Costs and expenses			
Depreciation	1,796.6	1,757.4	1,840.8
Network operations	2,539.8	2,516.0	2,365.0
Selling, general and administrative	3,132.1	2,873.0	2,523.5
Taxes other than income taxes	588.1	624.7	553.2
Interest expense	401.4	384.0	379.7
Other income, net	(31.6)	(70.4)	(20.5)
	8,426.4	8,084.7	7,641.7
Income before income taxes	1,784.9	1,818.6	1,905.8
Income taxes	546.7	581.2	717.7
Net income	$ 1,238.2	$1,237.4	$1,188.1
Earnings per share	$ 4.59	$ 4.55	$ 4.24
Dividends declared per share	$ 2.98	$ 2.76	$ 2.55

EXHIBIT 3-2

ECHLIN INC.
Consolidated Statements of Income
Multiple-Step Income Statement

(dollars in thousands, except per share data)	Year Ended August 31,		
	1989	1988	1987
Net sales	$1,454,492	$1,294,297	$1,099,703
Cost of goods sold	1,054,650	935,531	790,152
Gross profit on sales	399,842	358,766	309,551
Selling and administrative expenses	326,221	263,605	234,255
Income from operations	73,621	95,161	75,296
Interest expense	24,594	13,229	11,676
Interest income	13,677	11,368	9,395
Interest expense, net	10,917	1,861	2,281
Income before taxes	62,704	93,300	73,015
Provision for taxes	18,285	31,228	27,381
Net income	$ 44,419	$ 62,072	$ 45,634
Earnings per share of common stock	$0.80	$1.12	$0.88

Cost of Goods Sold or Cost of Sales

This shows the cost of goods that were sold to produce the sales. For a retailing firm, this is equal to beginning inventory, plus purchases, minus ending inventory. In a manufacturing firm, purchases are replaced by the cost of goods manufactured, since the goods are produced rather than purchased.

Operating Expense

Operating expenses consist of two types: selling and administrative. These are expenses not specifically identifiable with or assigned to production. Selling expenses, resulting from the company's effort to create sales, include advertising, sales commissions, depreciation on sales equipment, sales supplies used, and so on.

Administrative expenses relate to the general administration of the company's operations. They include office salaries, insurance, depreciation on office equipment, telephone, and the like. Also included are bad debt expense and other costs that are difficult to allocate.

Other Income and Expense

These categories are nonoperating in nature; they are secondary activities of the firm, not directly related to the operations. For example, if a manufacturing firm has a warehouse rented, this lease income would be other income. Dividend and interest income is also included here. Interest expense is categorized as other expense. Amortization of bond premium and bond discount decrease and increase, respectively, the amount of interest expense in the "other expense" category. Many types of gains and losses, such as those from the sale of assets or write-downs of inventory, are also included here.

Income Taxes

Federal, state, and local income taxes, based on reported accounting profit, are shown here. Income tax expense includes both tax paid and tax deferred.

Special Income Statement Items

In order to comprehend and analyze profits, it is necessary to understand income statement items that require disclosure. Exhibit 3-3 contains an example, with all of the income statement items that require special disclosure. These items are lettered to identify them for discussion.

(A) Unusual or Infrequent Item Disclosed Separately

Certain income statement items are unusual or occur infrequently, but not both. The financial disclosure for these items is covered in APB Opinion No. 30. They might include such items as a gain on the sale of securities or write-downs of

EXHIBIT 3-3

Illustration of Special Items

G and F COMPANY
Income Statement (Multiple-Step Format)
For the Year Ended December 31, 1992

Revenue from sales		$XXX
Cost of products sold		(XXX)
Gross margin		$XXX
Operating expenses:		
Selling expenses	$XXX	
General expenses	XXX	(XXX)
Operating Income		$XXX
Other income (includes interest income)		XXX
Other expenses (includes interest expense)		(XXX)
[A] Unusual or infrequent item disclosed separately [loss]		(XXX)
[B] Equity in earnings of nonconsolidated subsidiaries [loss]		XXX
Operating income before taxes		$XXX
Taxes related to operations		(XXX)
Net income from operations		$XXX
[C] Discontinued operations:		
Income [loss] from operations of discontinued segment (less applicable income taxes of $XXX)	($XXX)	
Income [loss] on disposal of division X (less applicable income taxes of $XXX)	(XXX)	(XXX)
Income before extraordinary items		$XXX
[D] Extraordinary gain [loss] (less applicable income taxes of $XXX)		(XXX)
Income before change in accounting principle		$XXX
[E] Cumulative effect of change in accounting principle [loss] (less applicable income taxes of $XXX)		XXX
Net income before minority interest		$XXX
[F] Minority share of earnings		(XXX)
Net income		$XXX
Earnings per share		$XXX

inventory. These items are shown with normal, recurring revenues and expenses, and gains and losses. If they are material, they are disclosed separately, before tax. Presenting an item after tax, with the related tax deducted, is called *net-of-tax presentation*; this is not acceptable for these unusual or infrequent items. It is recommended that these items be removed from the income statement for primary analysis, because they are nonrecurring. The analysis may indicate that the item has had a substantial influence on the profitability analysis.

In supplementary analysis, unusual or infrequent items should be considered, as this approach avoids completely disregarding these items.

Remove these items net of tax. The tax effect of these items may be disclosed in a footnote. Usually, an estimate of the tax effect is necessary. A reasonable estimate of the tax effect can typically be accomplished by using the effective income tax rate, which is usually disclosed in a footnote, or by comparing income taxes to income before income taxes.

Refer to Exhibit 3-4, which illustrates an unusual or infrequent item disclosed

EXHIBIT 3-4

THE PROCTER & GAMBLE COMPANY
Consolidated Statement of Earnings
Unusual or Infrequent Item (Provision for Restructuring)

(millions of dollars except per share amounts)	Years Ended June 30		
	1989	1988	1987
Income:			
Net sales	$21,398	$19,336	$17,000
Interest and other income	291	155	163
	21,689	19,491	17,163
Costs and expenses:			
Cost of products sold	13,371	11,880	10,411
Marketing, administrative, and other			
expenses	5,988	5,660	4,977
Interest expense	391	321	353
Provision for restructuring	—	—	805
	19,750	17,861	16,546
Earnings before income taxes	1,939	1,630	617
Income taxes	733	610	290
Net earnings	$ 1,206	$ 1,020	$ 327
Per common share			
Net earnings	$7.12	$5.96	$1.87
Dividends	$3.00	$2.75	$2.70

Courtesy of the Procter & Gamble Company.

separately for 1987. Comparing 1987 income taxes to income before income taxes results in a tax estimate of 47% ($290/$617 = 47%).

The Procter & Gamble Company item for 1987 would be removed as follows:

Unusual item	$805.00
Estimated tax effect (47% × $805.00)	378.35
Provision for restructuring, net of tax	$426.65

Income from continuing operations would be increased by $426.65 million, resulting in an adjusted income from continuing operations of $753.65 ($327.00 + $426.65).

(B) Equity in Earnings of Nonconsolidated Subsidiaries

When a firm has investments in stocks, where the equity method of accounting is utilized and the investment is not consolidated, the investor reports equity earnings. Equity earnings are the proportionate share of the earnings of the investee. If the investor owns 20% of the stock of the investee, for example, and the investee reports income of $100,000, then the investor reports $20,000 on its income statement.

To the extent that equity earnings are not accompanied by cash dividends, the investor is reporting earnings that are greater than the cash flow from the investment. If an investor company reports material equity earnings, its net income could be much greater than its ability to pay dividends or cover maturing liabilities.

For purposes of ratio analysis, the equity in net income of nonconsolidated subsidiaries raises practical problems. For one thing, the equity earnings represent earnings of other companies, not earnings that come directly from the operations of the business in question. Thus, equity earnings can distort the success of a business in its own operations, apart from investing in other companies. For each ratio that is influenced by equity earnings, a recommended approach is suggested in this book.

Refer to Exhibit 3-5, which illustrates equity in earnings of nonconsolidated subsidiaries. Leaving these accounts in the statements presents a problem for the profitability analysis, because most of the profitability measures relate income figures to other figures (usually, balance sheet figures). Because these earnings are from nonconsolidated subsidiaries, an inconsistency can result between the numerator and the denominator when computing a ratio.

Some ratios will be distorted more than others by equity earnings. One ratio frequently computed relates income to sales; this ratio can be particularly distorted because of equity earnings. If earnings are related to sales, for example, there will be an inconsistency between the numerator, which includes the earnings of the operating company and equity earnings of nonconsolidated subsidiaries, and the denominator (sales), which includes only the sales of the operating company. The sales of the unconsolidated subsidiaries do not appear on the statement, because the subsidiary is not consolidated.

EXHIBIT 3-5

CATERPILLAR
Consolidated Results of Operations
Equity in Earnings of Nonconsolidated Subsidiaries

	Years Ended December 31	
(millions of dollars except per share data)	1989	1988
Sales	$10,882	$10,255
Revenues of financial subsidiaries	244	180
Sales and revenues	11,126	10,435
Operating costs:		
Cost of goods sold	8,727	8,011
Selling, general, and administrative expenses:		
Excluding financial subsidiaries	1,242	1,153
Financial subsidiaries	96	89
Research and development expenses (note 2)	235	182
Interest expense of financial subsidiaries	121	76
	10,421	9,511
Operating profit	705	924
Interest expense—excluding financial subsidiaries	251	264
	454	660
Other income (note 4)	167	182
	621	842
Provision for income taxes (note 5)	162	262
Profit of consolidated companies	459	580
Equity in profit of affiliated companies		
(notes 1A and 6)	38	36
Profit	$ 497	$ 616
Profit per share of common stock	$ 4.90	$ 6.07
Dividends paid per share of common stock	$ 1.20	$ .75

© 1990 Caterpillar Inc. Used with permission.

(C) Discontinued Operations

A common type of unusual item is the disposal of a business or product line. APB Opinion No. 30 established disclosure requirements to provide the information necessary to assess the impact of discontinued operations on the business enterprise. If the disposal meets the criteria of APB Opinion No. 30, a separate income statement category for the gain or loss from disposal of a segment of the business must be provided. In addition, the results of operations of the segment that has been or will be disposed of are reported in conjunction with the gain or loss on disposal. These effects are shown as a separate category—after continuing operations, but before extraordinary items.

Discontinued operations pose a problem when performing profitability analysis. Ideally, income from continuing operations would be the better income figure to use to project the future from the analysis of historical statements. There are several practical problems associated with the removal of a gain or loss from the discontinued operations in the primary profitability analysis. These problems revolve around two points: (1) frequently, an inadequate disclosure of data related to the discontinued operations, in order to remove the balance sheet amounts associated with the discontinued operations; and (2) the lack of past profit and loss data associated with the discontinued operations. The exceptions are for the year that the discontinued operations are first disclosed and for the prior years when a three-year comparison of income statements is presented.

The presentation of discontinued operations in net income is illustrated in Exhibit 3-6. The best analysis would remove the income statement item that relates to the discontinued operations.

EXHIBIT 3-6

COMMERCIAL INTERTECH CORP.
Statements of Consolidated Income
Discontinued Operations

	Year Ended October 31,		
(in thousands, except per-share data)	1989	1988	1987
Net sales	$434,775	$398,666	$321,348
Less costs and expenses:			
Cost of products sold	291,464	274,313	218,316
Selling, administrative and general expenses	92,756	84,007	74,459
	384,220	358,320	292,775
Operating income	50,555	40,346	28,573
Non-operating income (expense):			
Interest income	2,713	2,123	1,476
Interest expense	(6,595)	(7,309)	(7,905)
Other	(2,240)	(4,574)	(2,879)
	(6,122)	(9,760)	(9,308)
Income from continuing operations before income taxes	44,433	30,586	19,265
Provision for income taxes—Note F			
Current	19,717	13,017	3,230
Deferred	597	805	4,811
	20,314	13,822	8,041

E X H I B I T   3 - 6   (continued)

(in thousands, except per-share data)	Year Ended October 31,		
	1989	1988	1987
Income from continuing operations	24,119	16,764	11,224
Loss on discontinued operation—Note K	(17,389)	(200)	0
Net income	$ 6,730	$ 16,564	$ 11,224
Per share of common stock:			
Primary:			
Income from continuing operations	$2.03	$1.51	$1.02
Net income	0.57	1.49	1.02
Fully diluted:			
Income from continuing operations	1.95	1.45	1.00
Net income	0.57	1.43	1.00

Note K—Discontinued Operations

During 1988 the Company acquired a minority interest in the business of Watermark Corporation, a California development company engaged in the retailing of bottled water products. Subsequent to the initial investment the Company purchased interest bearing subordinated notes which were convertible to shares of Watermark common stock and further agreed to advance funds or arrange outside financing for the purpose of expanding the business. Pursuant to this agreement, additional financing of up to $15,000,000 was arranged for and guaranteed by Commercial Intertech Corp. during fiscal 1989. The equity method was used to account for the Company's proportionate share of Watermark's losses in the 1988 and interim 1989 financial statements.

Startup costs, cash requirements and ongoing operating losses for the retailing venture ultimately proved to be in excess of expectations. Consequently, the Company elected during the fourth fiscal quarter not to extend financial assistance beyond the previously agreed amount and concurrently decided to write off its total investment in the Watermark Corporation in fiscal 1989. The write-off is being accounted for as a discontinued operation in the accompanying financial statements and includes charges over and above equity losses for loan guarantee exposure, interest receivable on the convertible notes and accounts receivable owed to Company subsidiaries as suppliers of water filtration products. Write-off of the outstanding exposure occurred in the fourth quarter and amounted to $14,903,000 while equity losses for the year totaled $2,486,000. The combined effect on consolidated earnings amounted to a $1.38 per-share loss in 1989 and a $.02 per-share loss in 1988. Additional long-term debt has been arranged through existing credit lines to satisfy the Company's loan guarantee obligation (see Note B).

This action will eliminate from future financial results any ongoing equity losses from the Company's remaining minority interest in Watermark. Future involvement with Watermark will be limited to attempts to recover investment losses through whatever means available.

The income statement items that relate to a discontinued operation are always presented net of applicable income taxes. Therefore, the items as presented on the income statement are removed without a further adjustment for income taxes. In supplementary analysis, discontinued operations should be considered, as this approach avoids completely disregarding these items.

Ideally, the balance sheet accounts that relate to the discontinued operations should be removed for primary analysis. These items should ideally be considered on a supplemental basis, because they will not contribute to future operating revenue. However, it is often impossible to remove these items from your analysis, because of inadequate disclosure.

The balance sheet items related to discontinued operations are frequently disposed of prior to the year-end balance sheet date; when the business or product line has been disposed of. In this case, the balance sheet accounts related to a disposal (discontinued operations) do not present a problem for the current year.

(D) Extraordinary Items

APB Opinion No. 30 established criteria for extraordinary items—that is, material events and transactions distinguished by their unusual nature and by the infrequency of their occurrence. Examples include a major casualty, such as a fire, prohibition under a newly enacted law, or an expropriation. These items, net of their tax effects, must be shown separately. Other pronouncements have specified items that must be considered extraordinary, including material tax loss carryovers and gains and losses from extinguishment of debt. The effect on earnings per share must also be shown separately. Refer to Exhibit 3-7, where an extraordinary gain from the tax benefit of loss carryovers is presented.

In analysis of income for purposes of determining a trend, extraordinary items should be eliminated, since the extraordinary item is not expected to recur. In supplementary analysis, these extraordinary items should be considered, as this approach avoids completely disregarding such items.

Extraordinary items are always presented net of applicable income taxes. Therefore, the items as presented on the income statement are removed without a further adjustment for income taxes.

(E) Cumulative Effect of Change in Accounting Principle

Some changes in accounting principles do not require retroactive adjustments to reflect the new accounting principle. For these changes, the new principle is used for the current year, and the prior years continue to be presented based on the prior accounting principle. This practice presents a problem of comparability. Also, for these changes, the comparability problem is compounded by the additional reporting guideline that directs that the income effect on prior years be reported as a cumulative effect of change in accounting principle on the income statement in the year of change. The cumulative effect is shown separately on the income statement in the year of change, usually just prior to net income.

When there is a cumulative effect of change in accounting principle, the re-

EXHIBIT 3-7

OCCIDENTAL PETROLEUM CORPORATION AND CONSOLIDATED SUBSIDIARIES
Consolidated Statements of Operations
Extraordinary Gain (Loss)

	For the Years Ended December 31,		
(In millions, except per-share amounts)	1989	1988	1987
Revenues:			
Net sales and operating revenues—			
Oil and gas operations	$ 2,804	$ 2,798	$ 3,386
Natural gas transmission operations	2,489	2,456	2,794
Chemical operations	5,163	4,617	2,798
Agribusiness operations	9,131	9,068	7,681
Coal operations	656	658	590
Interdivisional sales elimination	(175)	(180)	(153)
	20,068	19,417	17,096
Interest, dividends and other income	186	276	149
Gains on dispositions of assets, net (Note 2)	81	14	234
Gain on issuance of common stock of			
subsidiaries (Note 2)	—	176	200
Equity in net income of affiliates	29	50	67
	20,364	19,933	17,746
Costs and other deductions:			
Cost of sales	16,364	15,782	13,792
Selling, general and administrative and other			
operating expenses	1,358	1,456	1,136
Depreciation, depletion and amortization of			
assets	1,031	990	995
Exploration expense	144	148	144
Interest and debt expense, net	966	940	922
Minority interests in net income of subsidiaries			
and partnerships	26	43	10
	19,889	19,359	16,999
Income before taxes and extraordinary gain (loss)	475	574	747
Provision for domestic and foreign income and			
other taxes (Notes 1 and 10)	219	261	563
Income before extraordinary gain (loss)	256	313	184
Extraordinary gain (loss) (Note 3)	29	(11)	56
Net income	$ 285	$ 302	$ 240
Earnings applicable to common stock	$ 278	$ 295	$ 213
Earnings per common share:			
Income before extraordinary gain (loss)	$ .92	$ 1.26	$ .78
Extraordinary gain (loss)	.11	(.05)	.28
Earnings per common share (Note 1)	$ 1.03	$ 1.21	$ 1.06

The accompanying notes are an integral part of these statements.

porting standards require that income before extraordinary items and net income, computed on a pro forma basis (that is, as if the new principle had been in effect), should be shown on the face of the income statements for all periods, presented as if the newly adopted accounting principle had been applied during all periods affected. In practice, this pro forma material is often not presented or is only partially presented.

The accounting principle of not changing the statements retroactively when there has been a change in accounting principle was intended to be the general case when an accounting principle is changed. APB Opinion No. 20 is the basis of this reporting standard, and it provides for only a few exceptions. For most exceptions, the prior statements are retroactively changed using the new accounting principle. An exception to this is when the cumulative effect cannot be determined; in that case, the firm is to include a footnote explaining the change in accounting principle and the fact that the cumulative effect is not determinable.

The most common situation in which the cumulative effect is not determinable has been a switch to LIFO inventory. The base-year inventory is the opening inventory in the year that LIFO is adopted; there is no restatement of prior years or cumulative effect treatment. Thus, when a firm switches to LIFO inventory, a major problem develops in profitability analysis, because the year of change and subsequent years are in LIFO, whereas years prior to the change are reported using the previous inventory principle. Be aware that these years are not comparable with the years that are using LIFO.

In practice, the accounting principle of not changing the statements retroactively when there has been a change in accounting principle has not always been used. This is because APBs subsequent to No. 20 and later SFASs frequently directed that the new principles included in the respective pronouncement be handled retroactively, with a change in prior statements.

The accounting principle of not changing the statements retroactively when there has been a change in accounting principle is unfortunate: It is not good theory, and it presents major problems for analysis. It is not good theory because it places on the income statement, in the year of change, a potentially material income or loss amount that has nothing to do with the operations of that year. It is also not good theory because of the comparability problem with prior years (consistency).

Statement of Financial Accounting Concepts No. 5 (December 1985) recommends that the cumulative effects of changes in accounting principles not be included in earnings in the year of change in principle. To date, this recommendation has not been acted on with a FASB statement.

There is no ideal way to handle the analysis problem when a change in accounting principle is not handled retroactively. The recommendation is to remove the cumulative effect of change in accounting principle from the income statement for primary analysis. This still leaves the comparability problem that the income in the year of change and subsequent years is based on the new principle, whereas the years prior to the change are based on the prior principle. When it is your opinion that the income effect is so extreme that comparability is materially distorted, do not use years prior to the change for comparability analysis. Also note the pro forma presentation at the bottom of the income statement when it is presented; the pro forma numbers will be comparable, but limited. Refer to Exhibit 3-8, in which a cumulative effect of change is illustrated.

EXHIBIT 3-8

KNAPE & VOGT MANUFACTURING COMPANY
Consolidated Statements of Income
Cumulative Effect of Change in Accounting Principle

	Year Ended June 30,		
	1989	1988	1987
Net sales	$114,887,069	$101,351,530	$84,732,724
Cost of sales	84,504,222	75,115,963	60,984,400
Gross profit	30,382,847	26,235,567	23,748,324
Expenses:			
Selling and shipping	14,779,271	13,229,126	10,997,462
Administrative and general	5,993,560	5,016,692	4,248,902
Total expenses	20,772,831	18,245,818	15,246,364
Operating income	9,610,016	7,989,749	8,501,960
Other income (expense)—net (primary interest)	(1,267,857)	(708,090)	(230,992)
Income before income taxes and cumulative effect of change in accounting principle	8,342,159	7,281,659	8,270,968
Income taxes (Note 6)	3,018,000	2,689,000	3,925,000
Income before cumulative effect of change in accounting principle	5,324,159	4,592,659	4,345,968
Cumulative effect of change in accounting principle (Note 1)	—	708,000	—
Net income	$ 5,324,159	$ 5,300,659	$ 4,345,968
Income per share before cumulative effect of change in accounting principle	$ 1.31	$ 1.13	$ 1.10
Cumulative effect of change in accounting principle	—	.18	—
Net income per share	$ 1.31	$ 1.31	$ 1.10
Weighted average shares outstanding	4,079,373	4,051,500	3,964,155
Dividends per share:			
Common stock	$ .66	$ .66	$ .52
Class B common stock	$ .59	$ .59	$ .49

Note 1—Summary of Significant Accounting Policies [Partial]

Income Taxes   The 1988 and 1989 financial statements reflect adoption of the liability method of accounting for income taxes pursuant to Statement of Financial Accounting Standards No. 96. "Accounting for Income Taxes," issued in December 1987. Financial statements presented for 1987 reflect income taxes under the deferred method previously required. In conformity with SFAS No. 96 transition rules, the Company elected to adopt the liability method for income tax accounting in 1988. The cumulative effect to July 1987 of $708,000 is shown separately in the 1988 consolidated statement of income. Also, as required, quarterly earnings reported for 1988 have been restated for the effect of this change on interim quarters in 1988 as if the change had occurred at July 1, 1987. The effect of this change was not material to net income for 1988.

   Deferred taxes are recorded for temporary differences in the recognition of revenues and expenses for tax and financial reporting purposes.

   Tax credits and recapture of tax credits are reflected in income currently as reductions or additions of the income tax provision.

(F) Minority Share of Earnings

If a firm consolidates subsidiaries that are not wholly owned, the total revenues and expenses of the subsidiaries are included with those of the parent. However, to determine the income that would accrue to the parent, it is necessary to deduct the portion of income that belongs to the minority owners. This is labeled minority share of earnings or minority interest in net income. It should be noted that this item sometimes appears before and sometimes after the tax provision on the income statement. Refer to Exhibit 3-9, in which minority share of earnings is illustrated.

   Some ratios can be distorted because of minority share of earnings. For each ratio that is influenced by minority share of earnings, a recommended approach is suggested in this book.

Earnings Per Share

Earnings per share is the earnings per share of outstanding common stock. The capital structure of a firm may be termed simple or complex; this structure determines whether a firm presents a single earnings per share figure or a dual earnings per share figure. Companies with a complex capital structure must report primary and fully diluted earnings per share (which are discussed in Chapter 9).

   Earnings per share must also be shown before and after discontinued operations, before and after extraordinary items, and before and after the cumulative effect of a change in accounting principle.

   These comments are intended as an introduction to earnings per share. Earnings per share will be discussed in depth in Chapter 9 (Analysis for the Investor), which gives a detailed explanation of how to compute earnings per share. Mean-

EXHIBIT 3-9

UNITED TECHNOLOGIES
Consolidated Statement of Income
Minority Share of Earnings

	Years Ended December 31,		
(In millions of dollars except per share amounts)	1989	1988	1987
Revenues:			
Sales	$19,532.1	$18,000.1	$17,170.2
Financing revenues and other income, less other deductions	224.4	517.8	266.0
	$19,756.5	$18,517.9	$17,436.2
Costs and expenses:			
Cost of goods and services sold	$14,382.2	$13,486.0	$12,665.5
Research and development	956.6	932.4	878.8
Selling, service and administrative	2,810.8	2,622.5	2,468.3
Interest	346.5	312.1	331.7
	$18,496.1	$17,353.0	$16,344.3
Income before income taxes and minority interests	$ 1,260.4	$ 1,164.9	$ 1,091.9
Income taxes	497.8	460.1	458.0
Income before minority interests	$ 762.6	$ 704.8	$ 633.9
Less—minority interests in subsidiaries' earnings	60.5	45.7	42.2
Net income	$ 702.1	$ 659.1	$ 591.7
Preferred stock dividend requirement	$ 14.8	$ —	$ —
Earnings applicable to common stock	$ 687.3	$ 659.1	$ 591.7
Per share of common stock:			
Primary	$5.34	$5.05	$4.52
Fully diluted	$5.20	$5.05	$4.52

while, use the formula of net income divided by outstanding shares of common stock.

STATEMENT OF RETAINED EARNINGS

Retained earnings are all the undistributed earnings of the corporation. The statement of retained earnings summarizes the changes to retained earnings. It shows the retained earnings at the beginning of the year, the net income for the year as an addition, and the dividends as a subtraction and concludes with end-of-year retained earnings. Also included, if appropriate, are adjustments of prior periods and some adjustments for changes in accounting principles. These restate beginning retained earnings.

Sometimes a portion of retained earnings is unavailable for dividends because this portion has been appropriated (restricted). Retained earnings that have been appropriated remain part of retained earnings. The appropriation of retained earnings may or may not have significance.

Appropriations that are the result of legal requirements (usually state law) and appropriations that are the result of contractual agreements are potentially significant. This is because they may leave an inadequate amount of unappropriated retained earnings from which to pay dividends. (Note: A corporation will not be able to pay a cash dividend, even with an adequate unrestricted balance in retained earnings, unless it has adequate cash.)

Most appropriations are the result of management discretion. These are usually not significant, because management can change its mind and remove the appropriation.

The reason for an appropriation is disclosed either in the statement of retained earnings or in a footnote. From this disclosure, try to arrive at an opinion as to the significance, if any. For example, the Cooper Tire & Rubber Company had retained earnings of $263,894,759 at December 31, 1989. A footnote indicates that part of the retained earnings is restricted because of loan agreements. The amount of retained earnings not restricted was $123,415,000 at December 31, 1989. This is probably not significant, because the dividends paid were only $7,080,479 in 1989.

The statement of retained earnings is sometimes combined with the income statement. Exhibit 3-10 gives an example of a statement of retained earnings, and Exhibit 3-11 illustrates a combined income statement and statement of retained earnings. This clearly shows the connection between the income statement and the retained earnings account on the balance sheet.

EXHIBIT 3-10

MERCK & CO., INC.
Consolidated Statement of Retained Earnings

($ in millions)	Years Ended December 31		
	1989	1988	1987
Balance, January 1	$4,580.3	$3,919.8	$3,378.6
Net income	1,495.4	1,206.8	906.4
Common stock dividends declared	(681.5)	(546.3)	(365.2)
Balance, December 31	$5,394.2	$4,580.3	$3,919.8

EXHIBIT 3-11

UNITED INDUSTRIAL
Statement of Income and Retained Earnings

(dollars in thousands, except per share data)	Year Ended December 31		
	1989	1988	1987
Net sales	$280,783	$314,986	$297,501
Operating costs and expenses:			
Cost of sales	207,837	236,541	230,264
Write-off of claim receivable	9,992	—	—
Selling and administrative	51,781	54,668	47,952
Other income—net	(747)	(266)	(975)
Interest expense (income)—net	14	(1,128)	(2,895)
Total operating costs and expenses	268,877	289,815	274,346
Income before federal income taxes	11,906	25,171	23,155
Provision (credit) for federal income taxes:			
Current	8,183	9,946	6,899
Deferred	(4,281)	(1,644)	1,954
Federal income taxes	3,902	8,302	8,853
Net income	8,004	16,869	14,302
Retained earnings (deficit) at beginning of year	598	(7,892)	(13,687)
Dividends: 64¢ per share	8,362	8,379	8,507
Retained earnings (deficit) at end of year	$ 240	$ 598	$ (7,892)
Earnings per share	$ .61	$ 1.29	$ 1.07

DIVIDENDS AND STOCK SPLITS

Dividends return profits to the owners of a corporation. When a cash dividend is declared by the board of directors, the retained earnings account is reduced by the amount of the dividends declared, and the current liability account (dividends payable) is increased. The date of payment occurs after the date of declaration. On the date of dividend payment, the liability account (dividends payable) is paid off, and cash is reduced. Note that it is the date of the declaration of dividends that affects retained earnings and creates the liability, not the date of dividend payment.

The board of directors may elect to declare and issue another type of dividend, termed a *stock dividend*. In this situation, the firm issues a percentage of outstanding stock as new shares to existing shareholders. In a 10% stock dividend, for example, an owner holding 1,000 shares would receive an additional 100 shares of new stock. The accounting for a stock dividend, assuming that the distribution is relatively small (such as below 25% of the existing stock), requires that the fair market value of the stock at the date of declaration be removed from retained earnings and transferred to paid-in capital. (With a material stock dividend, the amount removed from retained earnings and transferred to paid-in capital is determined by multiplying the par value of the stock times the additional shares.) Note that the overall effect of a stock dividend is to leave total stockholders' equity and each owner's share of stockholders' equity unchanged, although the total number of shares increases.

A stock dividend should reduce the market value of individual shares by the percentage of the stock dividend. (Total market value, considering all outstanding shares, should not change.) A more drastic device to change the market value of individual shares is to declare a stock split. (A 2-for-1 split should reduce the market value per share to one-half the amount prior to the split.)

Lowering the market value is sometimes desirable for stocks selling at high prices (as perceived by management). This is because stocks with high prices are less readily traded.

A stock split merely increases the number of shares of stock; it does not usually change retained earnings or paid-in capital. For example, if a firm had 1,000 shares of common stock, a 2-for-1 stock split would result in 2,000 shares.

The firm effecting a stock split capitalizes retained earnings (transfer from retained earnings to the additional paid-in capital or capital stock) only to the extent required by law. Thus, the par or stated value is usually changed in proportion to the stock split, and no change is made to retained earnings, additional paid-in capital, or capital stock. For example, if a firm with $10 par common stock declared a 2-for-1 stock split, it would normally reduce the par value to $5.

Since the number of shares changes under both a stock dividend and a stock split, any ratio based on the number of shares must be restated. For example, if a firm had earnings per share of $4.00 in 1991, a 2-for-1 stock split in 1992 would require restatement of the earnings per share to $2.00 because of the increase in the number of shares. Restatement is made for all prior financial statements presented, including a five- or ten-year summary. This restatement has been done for published financial statements.

SUMMARY

The income statement is a required, published financial statement used by the public. The income statement summarizes the profit for a particular period of time. In order to understand and analyze profitability, the reader must be familiar with the components of income, as well as income statement items that require special disclosure. This chapter has discussed special income statement items, such as unusual or infrequent items disclosed separately, equity in earnings of nonconsolidated subsidiaries, discontinued operations, extraordinary items, changes in accounting principle, and minority share of earnings. This chapter also introduces the statement of retained earnings, dividends, and stock splits. Analysis of profitability will be discussed extensively in Chapter 8.

| QUESTIONS

Q 3-1   What are extraordinary items? How are they shown on the income statement and why?

Q 3-2   Which of the following would be classified as extraordinary?
   a. selling expense
   b. interest expense
   c. gain on the sale of marketable securities
   d. loss from flood
   e. income tax expense
   f. loss from prohibition of red dye
   g. loss from the write-down of inventory

Q 3-3   Give three examples of unusual or infrequent items that are disclosed separately. Why are they shown separately? Are they presented before or after tax? Why, or why not?

Q 3-4   Why is the equity in earnings of nonconsolidated subsidiaries sometimes a problem in profitability analysis? Discuss with respect to income versus cash flow.

Q 3-5   A health food distributor selling wholesale dairy products and vitamins decides to discontinue in July the division that sells vitamins. How should this discontinuance be classified on the income statement?

Q 3-6   Jones Company presents both primary and fully diluted earnings per share. What does this indicate about its capital structure?

Q 3-7   In 1989, Jensen Company decided to change its depreciation method from units of production to sum of the years' digits. The cumulative effect of the change to the new method, prior to 1989, was to increase depreciation by $30,000 before tax. How would the change be presented in the financial statements?

Q 3-8   How does the declaration of a cash dividend affect the financial statements? How does the payment of a cash dividend affect the financial statements?

Q 3-9   What is the difference in the impact on financial statements of a stock dividend versus a stock split?

Q 3-10   Why is minority share of earnings deducted before arriving at net income?

Q 3-11   Explain the relationship between the income statement and the statement of retained earnings.

Q 3-12   List the three types of appropriated retained earnings accounts. Which of these types is most likely not a detriment to the payment of a dividend? Explain.

Q 3-13   The date on a balance sheet is as of a specific date, such as December 31, while the date on an income statement is for a period of time, such as For the Year Ended December 31, 1989. Why does this difference exist?

Q 3-14   Describe the following items:
  a. minority interest
  b. equity in earnings of nonconsolidated subsidiaries
  c. minority share of earnings

Q 3-15   An income statement is a summary of revenues and expenses and gains and losses, ending with net income for a particular period of time. Indicate the two traditional formats for presenting the income statement. Which of these formats is preferable for analysis? Why?

Q 3-16   The Melcher Company reported earnings per share in 1990 and 1989 of $2.00 and $1.60, respectively. In 1991, there was a 2-for-1 stock split, and the earnings per share for 1991 were reported to be $1.40. Present a three-year presentation of earnings per share (1989–1991).

| PROBLEMS

P 3-1   The following information for Decher Automotive is for the year ended 1992.

Administrative expenses	$ 62,000
Dividend income	10,000
Income taxes	100,000
Interest expense	20,000
Merchandise inventory, 1/1	650,000
Merchandise inventory, 12/31	440,000
Flood loss (net of tax)	30,000
Purchases	460,000
Sales	1,000,000
Selling expenses	43,000

Required   a. Prepare a multiple-step income statement.
  b. Assuming that 100,000 shares of common stock are outstanding, calculate the earnings per share before extraordinary items and the net earnings per share (simple capital structure).
  c. Prepare a single-step income statement.

P 3-2

LESKY CORPORATION
Income Statement
For the Year Ended December 31, 1992

Revenue:	
Revenues from sales	$362,000
Rental income	1,000
Interest	2,400
Total revenue	$365,400

Expenses:		
Cost of products sold	$242,000	
Selling expenses	47,000	
Administrative and general expenses	11,400	
Interest expense	2,200	
Federal and state income taxes	$ 20,300	
Total expenses		322,900
Net income		$ 42,500

Required Recategorize this statement to multiple-step format, as illustrated in this chapter.

P 3-3 The accounts of Consolidated Can contain the following amounts at December 31, 1992.

Cost of products sold	$410,000
Dividends	3,000
Extraordinary gain (net of tax)	1,000
Income taxes	9,300
Interest expense	8,700
Other income	1,600
Retained earnings 1/1	270,000
Sales	480,000
Selling and administrative expense	42,000

Required Prepare a multiple-step income statement combined with a statement of retained earnings for the year ended December 31, 1992.

P 3-4 The following items are from an adjusted trial balance of Taperline Corporation on December 31, 1992. Assume a flat 40% corporate tax rate on all items, including the casualty loss.

Sales	$670,000
Rental income	3,600
Gain on the sale of fixed assets	3,000
General and administrative expenses	110,000
Selling expenses	97,000
Interest expense	1,900
Depreciation for the period	10,000
Extraordinary item (casualty loss—pretax)	30,000
Cost of sales	300,000
Common stock (30,000 shares outstanding)	150,000

Required
a. Prepare a single-step income statement for the year ended December 31, 1992. Include earnings per share for earnings before extraordinary items and net income (simple capital structure).
b. Prepare a multiple-step income statement. Include earnings per share for earnings before extraordinary items and net income (simple capital structure).

P 3-5 The income statement of Rawl Company for the year ended December 31, 1992, is as follows:

Net sales	$360,000
Cost of sales	190,000
Gross profit	170,000
Selling, general, and administrative expense	80,000
Income before unusual write-offs	90,000
Provision for unusual write-offs	50,000
Earnings from operations before income taxes	40,000
Income taxes	20,000
Net earnings from operations before extraordinary charge	20,000
Extraordinary charge, net of tax of $10,000	50,000
Net earnings (loss)	($30,000)

Required   Compute the net earnings remaining after removing the nonrecurring items. Remove unusual items net of tax. Estimate the tax rate based on the taxes on operating income.

P 3-6   At year end 1992, your financial records were destroyed by vandals who set fire to the file cabinet. Fortunately, the controller had kept certain statistical data related to the income statement, as follows:

a. Cost of goods sold was $2,000,000.
b. Administrative expenses were 20% of cost of sales, but only 10% of sales.
c. Selling expenses were 150% of administrative expenses.
d. Bonds payable were $1,000,000, with an average interest rate of 11%.
e. The tax rate was 48%.
f. 50,000 shares of common stock were outstanding for the entire year.

Required   From the information given, reconstruct a multiple-step income statement for the year. Include earnings per share (simple capital structure).

P 3-7   The following information is known about the Bowling Green Metals Corporation for the year ended December 31, 1992:

Total revenues from regular operations	$832,000
Total expenses from regular operations	776,000
Extraordinary gain, net	30,000
Dividends paid	20,000
Number of shares of common stock outstanding during the year	10,000

Required   Compute earnings per share before extraordinary items and net earnings. Show how this might be presented in the financial statements (simple capital structure).

P 3-8   You were recently hired as the assistant treasurer for Victor, Inc. Yesterday the treasurer was injured in a bicycle accident and is now hospitalized, unconscious. Your boss, Mr. Fernandes, just informed you that the financial statements are due today. Searching through the treasurer's desk, you find the following notes:

a. Income from continuing operations, based on computations done so far, is $400,000. No taxes are accounted for yet; tax rate is 30%.

b. Dividends declared and paid were $20,000, based on 100,000 shares of stock outstanding all year.

c. The corporation experienced an uninsured loss from a freak hail storm for $20,000 pretax. Such a storm is considered to be unusual and infrequent.

d. The company decided to change its inventory pricing method from average cost to the FIFO method. The effect of this change is to increase prior years' income by $30,000 pretax. The FIFO method has been used for 1992. (*Hint:* This adjustment should be placed just prior to net income.)

e. In 1992, the company settled a lawsuit against it for $10,000 pretax. The settlement was not previously accrued and is due for payment in February 1993.

f. In 1992, the firm sold a portion of its long-term securities at a gain of $30,000 pretax.

g. The corporation disposed of its consumer products division in August 1992, at a loss of $90,000 pretax. The loss from operations through August was $60,000 pretax.

Required   Prepare an income statement for 1992, in good form, starting with income from continuing operations. Compute earnings per share for income from continuing operations, discontinued operations, extraordinary loss, cumulative change in accounting principle, and net income (simple capital structure).

P 3-9   List the statement on which each of these may appear. Choose from (a) income statement, (b) balance sheet, or (c) neither.

a. net income	l. interest payable
b. cost of goods sold	m. loss from flood
c. gross profit	n. land
d. retained earnings	o. taxes payable
e. paid-in capital in excess of par	p. interest income
f. sales	q. gain on sale of property
g. supplies expense	r. dividend income
h. investment in G. Company	s. depreciation expense
i. dividends	t. accounts receivable
j. inventory	u. accumulated depreciation
k. common stock	v. sales commissions

P 3-10   List the statement on which each of these may appear. Choose from (a) income statement, (b) balance sheet, or (c) statement of retained earnings.

a. dividends paid	k. unrealized exchange gains and losses
b. notes payable	l. equity in net income of affiliates
c. minority share of earnings	m. goodwill
d. accrued payroll	n. unrealized decline in market value of noncurrent equity investment
e. loss on disposal of discontinued operations	o. cumulative effect of change in accounting principle
f. minority interest in consolidated subsidiary	p. common stock
g. adjustments of prior periods	q. cost of goods sold
h. redeemable preferred stock	r. supplies
i. treasury stock	s. land
j. extraordinary loss	

P 3-11   The income statement of Tawls Company for the year ended December 31, 1992, is as follows:

Revenue from sales		$980,000
Cost of products sold		510,000
Gross profit		$470,000
Operating expenses		
Selling expenses	$110,000	
General expenses	140,000	250,000
Operating income		220,000
Equity on earnings of nonconsolidated		
subsidiary		60,000
Operating income before income taxes		280,000
Taxes related to operations		100,000
Net income from operations		180,000
Extraordinary loss from flood (less		
applicable taxes of $50,000)		(120,000)
Minority share of earnings		(40,000)
Net income		$ 20,000

Required   a. Compute the net earnings remaining after removing nonrecurring items.
      b. Determine the earnings from the nonconsolidated subsidiary.
      c. For the subsidiary that was not consolidated, what amount of income would have been included if this subsidiary had been consolidated?
      d. What earnings relate to minority shareholders of a subsidiary that was consolidated?
      e. Determine the total tax amount.

P 3-12   The income statement of Jones Company for the year ended December 31, 1992, is as follows:

Revenue from sales		$790,000
Cost of products sold		410,000
Gross profit		380,000
Operating expenses		
Selling expenses	$40,000	
General expenses	80,000	120,000
Operating income		260,000
Equity in earnings of nonconsolidated		
subsidiaries (loss)		(20,000)
Operating income before income taxes		240,000
Taxes related to operations		(94,000)
Net income from operations		146,000
Discontinued operations		
Loss from operations discontinued		
segment (less applicable income tax		
credit of $30,000)	($70,000)	

Loss on disposal of segment (less
applicable income tax credit of
$50,000) | ($100,000) | (170,000)

Loss on disposal of segment (less applicable income tax credit of $50,000)	($100,000)	(170,000)
Income before cumulative effect of change in accounting principle		(24,000)
Cumulative effect of change in accounting principle (less applicable income taxes of $25,000)		50,000
Net income		$ 26,000

Required
a. Compute the net earnings remaining after removing nonrecurring items.
b. Determine the earnings (loss) from the nonconsolidated subsidiary.
c. Determine the total tax amount.

P 3-13   The Uranium Mining Company was founded in 1970 to mine and market uranium, and it purchased a mine in 1971 for $900 million. It was estimated that the uranium had a market value of $150 per ounce. By 1992, the market value had increased to $300 per ounce. Records for 1992 indicate the following:

Production	200,000 ounces
Sales	230,000 ounces
Deliveries	190,000 ounces
Cash collection	210,000 ounces
Costs of production, including depletion*	$50,000,000
Selling expense	$ 2,000,000
Administrative expenses	$ 1,250,000
Tax rate	50%

*Production cost per ounce has remained constant over the last few years, and the company has maintained the same production level.

Required
a. Compute the income for 1992, using each of the following bases:
   1. receipt of cash
   2. point of sale
   3. end of production
   4. based on delivery
b. Comment on when each of the methods should be used. Which method should be used by the Uranium Mining Company?

| CASES

Case 3-1   REVIEW OF INCOME

The Procter & Gamble Company presented this consolidated statement of earnings for 1989.

(millions of dollars except per share amounts)	Years Ended June 30		
	1989	**1988**	**1987**
Income:			
Net sales	$21,398	$19,336	$17,000
Interest and other income	291	155	163
	21,689	19,491	17,163
Costs and expenses:			
Cost of products sold	13,371	11,880	10,411
Marketing, administrative, and other expenses	5,988	5,660	4,977
Interest expense	391	321	353
Provision for restructuring	—	—	805
	19,750	17,861	16,546
Earnings before income taxes	1,939	1,630	617
Income taxes	733	610	290
Net earnings	$ 1,206	$ 1,020	$ 327
Per common share			
Net earnings	$7.12	$5.96	$1.87
Dividends	$3.00	$2.75	$2.70

Average shares outstanding (in millions): 1989—167.2; 1988—169.3; 1987—168.6.

Courtesy of the Proctor & Gamble Company.

Required   a. Does it appear that there is 100% ownership in all consolidated subsidiaries? Discuss.
b. Present a multiple-step income statement.
c. Estimate net earnings on a recurring basis for 1987–1989.

Case 3-2   COMPLEX INCOME STATEMENT

Tempo Enterprises, Inc., presented this consolidated statement of income on its 1986 annual report.

	Year Ended December 31		
	1986	**1985**	**1984**
Income:			(Note 1a)
Subscriptions and fees	$27,286,000	$29,678,000	$24,389,000
Interest and dividends	372,000	493,000	1,270,000
Other—net	556,000	233,000	412,000
Total income	28,214,000	30,404,000	26,071,000
Costs and expenses:			
Selling, general and administrative	11,957,000	10,802,000	10,302,000
Cable television operating	1,843,000	2,126,000	342,000
Pay television operating	—	569,000	2,948,000
Satellite rental	4,164,000	4,516,000	2,656,000
Provision for doubtful accounts	1,967,000	2,001,000	1,016,000
Depreciation and amortization	2,451,000	2,342,000	1,585,000
Interest	1,450,000	1,239,000	145,000

	Year Ended December 31		
	1986	**1985**	**1984**
Share of loss of unconsolidated affiliates	—	277,000	226,000
Total costs and expenses	23,832,000	23,872,000	19,220,000
Income before unusual charge, taxes on income, and extraordinary item	4,382,000	6,532,000	6,851,000
Unusual charge (Note 10)	64,000	2,422,000	—
Income before taxes on income and extraordinary item	4,318,000	4,110,000	6,851,000
Taxes on income (Note 11)	2,009,000	2,034,000	2,776,000
Extraordinary item			
Income before extraordinary item	2,309,000	2,076,000	4,075,000
Reduction in income taxes resulting from net operating loss carryforward	—	—	38,000
Net income	$ 2,309,000	$ 2,076,000	$ 4,113,000
Income per common share:			
Income before extraordinary item	$ .40	$ .36	$ .71
Extraordinary item	—	—	—
Net income	$ .40	$ .36	$ .71
Weighted average number of shares outstanding	5,750,000	5,749,204	5,719,430

Required

a. Describe the share of loss of unconsolidated affiliates account.
b. Identify the nonrecurrent items in 1986, 1985, and 1984.
c. Compute net income for 1986, 1985, and 1984 with the nonrecurring items removed.

Case 3-3   GROSS PROFIT TRENDS

The 1984 consolidated statement of income for the NCR Corporation is as follows.

	Year Ended December 31		
(in thousands, except per share figures)	**1984**	**1983**	**1982**
Revenue			
Net sales	$2,527,538	$2,245,867	$2,112,099
Rentals	286,941	313,721	326,292
Services	1,259,848	1,171,363	1,087,826
	4,074,327	3,730,951	3,526,217
Costs and expenses			
Cost of products sold	1,147,508	1,019,849	997,804
Cost of rentals	92,203	97,367	104,583
Cost of services	789,272	738,953	680,076
Selling, general, and administrative	1,233,325	1,140,023	1,100,651
Research and development	288,948	257,522	248,647

(in thousands, except per share figures)	Year Ended December 31		
	1984	**1983**	**1982**
Interest expense	42,707	45,889	51,616
Other (income) expenses, net	(81,076)	(91,717)	(86,971)
	3,512,887	3,207,886	3,096,406
Income before income taxes	561,440	523,065	429,811
Income taxes	218,800	235,400	195,400
Net income	$ 342,640	$ 287,665	$ 234,411

Required

a. Is this a single-step or a multiple-step income statement?

b. Calculate the 1984 gross profit and gross profit percentage for each of sales, rentals, and services, and then for the three combined. (Determine the gross profit percentage by dividing the gross profit by the respective revenue.)

c. Which of the three lines of business provides the largest gross profit in 1984?

d. Which of the three lines of business has the largest gross profit percentage in 1984?

e. For each of the three lines of business, what is the trend of gross profit and the gross profit percentage?

f. What is the trend of total gross profit and the total gross profit percentage?

Case 3-4   EXAMINATION OF INCOME STATEMENT

Panhandle Eastern Corporation presented this consolidated statement of income (loss) with its 1989 annual report.

(millions, except per share amounts)	Years Ended December 31		
	1989	**1988**	**1987**
Operating revenues:			
Sales of natural gas (Note 4)	$1,830.1	$ 835.2	$1,249.1
Transportation of natural gas (Note 4)	399.8	240.4	165.1
Petroleum products (Note 3)	109.6	—	—
Natural gas liquids	67.8	59.7	25.7
Other	373.7	126.3	123.2
Total	2,781.0	1,261.6	1,563.1
Cost and expenses:			
Gas purchased	1,196.8	537.9	659.7
Operating	693.1	353.8	365.7
Maintenance	71.5	38.9	43.5
General and administrative	177.3	99.6	92.6
Depreciation and amortization (Note 11)	203.3	114.2	114.7
Miscellaneous taxes	54.9	31.4	29.6
	2,396.9	1,175.8	1,305.8
Take-or-pay settlement/contract reformation charges (Note 10)	—	369.6	—
Total	2,396.9	1,545.4	1,305.8

(millions, except per share amounts)	Years Ended December 31		
	1989	**1988**	**1987**
Operating income (loss)	384.1	(283.8)	257.3
Other income			
Equity in earnings of unconsolidated affiliates (Note 12)	26.1	39.3	41.6
Interest and miscellaneous, net (Note 14)	80.9	114.7	13.6
Total	107.0	154.0	55.2
Gross income (loss)	491.1	(129.8)	312.5
Interest expense (Note 14)	362.9	144.5	132.7
Income (loss) from continuing operations before income taxes	128.2	(274.3)	179.8
Taxes on income (loss) (Note 6)	58.7	(102.4)	70.1
Continuing operations, before extraordinary items, income (loss)	69.5	(171.9)	109.7
Discontinued operations (Note 7)	(11.1)	—	(1.5)
Income (loss) before extraordinary items	58.4	(171.9)	108.2
Extraordinary items (Note 8)	(29.2)	14.8	—
Net income (loss)	$ 29.2	$ (157.1)	$ 108.2
Average shares outstanding (thousands)	71,894	54,968	53,088
Earnings (loss) per common share:			
Continuing operations, before extraordinary items	$ 0.97	$ (3.13)	$ 2.07
Discontinued operations	(0.15)	—	(0.03)
Extraordinary items	(0.41)	0.27	—
Total	$ 0.41	$ (2.86)	$ 2.04

Required

a. Identify nonrecurring items to be excluded from primary analysis.
b. Describe equity in earnings of unconsolidated affiliates.
c. Describe how unconsolidated affiliates would influence net income (loss) if they were consolidated.
d. Estimate the net income (loss) for each year from 1987 to 1989 if the nonrecurring items were excluded.
e. Comment on the net income (loss) and the trend in net income (loss) as reported and the income (loss) without nonrecurring items.

Case 3-5   TREND IN INCOME

The Goodyear Tire & Rubber Company presented the following consolidated statement of income with its 1989 annual report.

(dollars in millions, except per share)	Year Ended December 31		
	1989	1988	1987
Net sales	$10,869.3	$10,810.4	$ 9,905.2
Other income	175.4	184.5	179.9
	11,044.7	10,994.9	10,085.1
Cost and expenses:			
Cost of goods sold	8,234.7	8,291.0	7,374.6
Selling, administrative and general expense	1,863.7	1,745.1	1,634.9
Interest expense	271.4	238.0	282.5
Unusual items	109.7	78.8	(135.0)
Foreign currency exchange	75.7	85.3	38.9
Minority interest in net income of subsidiaries	18.6	19.2	16.8
	10,573.8	10,457.4	9,212.7
Income from continuing operations before income taxes and extraordinary item	470.9	537.5	872.4
United States and foreign taxes on income	281.5	187.4	358.5
Income from continuing operations before extraordinary item	189.4	350.1	513.9
Discontinued operations	—	—	257.0
Income before extraordinary item	189.4	350.1	770.9
Extraordinary item—tax benefit of loss carryovers	17.4	—	—
Net income	$ 206.8	$ 350.1	$ 770.9
Per share of common stock:			
Income from continuing operations before extraordinary item	$3.28	$6.11	$8.49
Discontinued operations	—	—	4.24
Income before extraordinary item	3.28	6.11	12.73
Extraordinary item—tax benefit of loss carryovers	.30	—	—
Net income	$3.58	$6.11	$12.73
Average shares outstanding	57,727,577	57,322,165	60,564,981

Source: The Goodyear Tire & Rubber Company, 1989 Annual Report. Reprinted with permission.

Required

a. Determine income from continuing operations before extraordinary item, with the unusual items removed.

b. Identify the nonrecurrent items in 1989, 1988, and 1987.

c. Have subsidiaries been consolidated in which the Goodyear Tire & Rubber Company did not own 100%? What account indicates the answer to this question? Explain.

d. If subsidiaries were not consolidated but rather accounted for using the equity method, would this change net income? Explain.

CHAPTER 4

BASICS OF ANALYSIS

CHAPTER TOPICS

Ratio Analysis

*Common Size Analysis
(Vertical and Horizontal)*

Comparisons

Trend Analysis
Industry Averages and
   Comparison with
   Competitors
Caution in Using Industry
   Averages

Library Sources

Standard Industrial
   Classification Manual (SIC)
Standard & Poor's Report
Standard & Poor's Register
   of Corporations, Directors,
   and Executives
Standard & Poor's Analyst's
   Handbook
Standard & Poor's Corporation
   Records

America's Corporate Families:™
   The Billion Dollar Directory®
Million Dollar Directory®
Directory of Corporate
   Affiliations
Thomas Register of American
   Manufacturers and Thomas
   Register
Moody's Investors Services
Securities Owner's Stock Guide
Wall Street Transcript
Predicasts F & S Index
Reference Book of Corporate
   Managements
Compact Disclosure

Relative Size of Firm

*Financial Statement Variations
by Type of Industry*

Descriptive Information

*The Users of Financial
Statements*

Various techniques are used in the analysis of financial data to emphasize the comparative and relative importance of the data presented and to evaluate the position of the firm. These techniques include ratio analysis, common size analysis, examination of relative size among firms, comparison of results with other types of data, the study of differences of components of financial statements among industries, and review of descriptive material. The information derived from these types of analyses should be blended to determine the overall financial position. No one type of analysis is best or sufficient to support overall findings or to serve all types of users. This chapter provides an introduction to different analyses and uses of financial information.

Financial statement analysis is a judgmental process. One of the primary objectives is identification of major changes (turning points) in trends, amounts, and relationships and of the reasons underlying those changes. Often a turning point may be an early warning signal of a significant shift in the success or failure of the business. The judgment process can be improved by experience and the use of analytical tools.

RATIO ANALYSIS

Financial ratios are usually expressed in percentages or "times." Several of the following types will be discussed fully in future chapters.

1. Liquidity ratios are measures of a firm's ability to meet its current obligations. They may include ratios that measure the efficiency of the use of current assets. These ratios are discussed in Chapter 6.
2. Borrowing capacity (leverage) ratios measure the degree of protection of suppliers of long-term funds. They will be discussed in Chapter 7.
3. Profitability ratios measure the earning ability of a firm, including the use of assets in general. These will be discussed in Chapter 8.
4. Investors are interested in a special group of profitability ratios. Special types of analyses for the investor will be discussed in Chapter 9.
5. Cash flow ratios can indicate liquidity, borrowing capacity, or profitability. These will be discussed in Chapter 10.

A ratio can be computed from any pair of numbers. Given the large quantity of variables included in financial statements, a very long list of meaningful ratios can be derived. There is no standard list of ratios or standard computation of them; each author and source on financial statement analysis uses a different list. The ratios discussed in this text are among the most frequently utilized and discussed.

Comparison of income statement and balance sheet numbers, in the form of ratios, can create difficulties due to the timing of the financial statements. Specifically, the income statement covers the entire fiscal period, whereas the balance sheet is for a single point in time, the end of the period. Ideally, then, to compare an income statement figure such as sales to a balance sheet figure such as receivables, we usually need a reasonable measure of average receivables for the year that the sales figure covers. However, these data are not available to the external analyst. In some cases, the analyst should take the next best approach, by using an average of beginning and ending balance sheet figures. This approach smooths out changes from beginning to end, but it does not eliminate problems due to seasonal and cyclical changes. It also does not reflect changes that occur unevenly throughout the year.

COMMON SIZE ANALYSIS
(VERTICAL AND HORIZONTAL)

Common size analysis involves expressing comparisons in percentages. For example, if cash is $40,000 and total assets is $1,000,000, then cash is 4% of total assets. The use of percentages is usually preferable to the use of absolute figures. An illustration will make this clear. If Firm A earns $10,000 and Firm B earns $1,000, which is more profitable? Firm A is probably your response. However, the total owners' equity of A is $1,000,000, and B's is $10,000, the return on owners' equity is as follows:

$$\text{Firm A} \qquad\qquad\qquad \text{Firm B}$$

$$\frac{\text{Earnings}}{\text{Owners' Equity}} \quad \frac{\$10,000}{\$1,000,000} = 1\% \qquad \frac{\$1,000}{\$10,000} = 10\%$$

The use of common size analysis can make comparisons of firms of different sizes much more meaningful, since the numbers are brought to a common base: percent.

Care must be exercised in the use of common size analysis when the absolute figures are small, because a small absolute change can result in a very substantial percentage change. For instance, if profits last year amounted to $100 and increased this year to $500, this would be an increase of only $400 in profits, but it would represent a substantial increase in percentage terms.

In vertical analysis, a figure from a year is compared with a base selected from the same year. For example, if advertising expenses were $1,000 in 1992 and sales were $100,000, the advertising would be 1% of sales.

In horizontal analysis, a dollar figure for an account is expressed in terms of that same account figure for a selected base year. For example, if sales were $400,000 in 1991 and $600,000 in 1992, then sales increased to 150% of the 1991 level in 1992, an increase of 50%.

Exhibit 4-1 illustrates common size analysis (vertical and horizontal).

COMPARISONS

Absolute figures or ratios are nearly meaningless unless compared to another figure. If you were asked if ten dollars is a lot of money, the frame of reference would determine the answer. To a small child, still in awe of a quarter, ten dollars is a lot; to a millionaire, a ten-dollar bill is nothing. Similarly, having 60% of total assets composed of buildings and equipment would be normal for some firms but disastrous for others. One must have a guide to determine the meaning of the ratios and other measures that are computed. Several types of comparisons offer insight into the financial position.

E X H I B I T   4 - 1

MELCHER COMPANY
Income Statement
Illustration of Common Size Analysis (Vertical and Horizontal)

(absolute dollars)	For the Years Ended December 31		
	1991	1990	1989
Revenue from sales	$100,000	$95,000	$91,000
Cost of products sold	65,000	60,800	56,420
Gross profit	35,000	34,200	34,580
Operating expenses			
Selling expenses	14,000	11,400	10,000
General expenses	16,000	15,200	13,650
Total operating expenses	30,000	26,600	23,650
Operating income before income taxes	5,000	7,600	10,930
Taxes related to operations	1,500	2,280	3,279
Net income	$ 3,500	$ 5,320	$ 7,651
Vertical Common Size			
Revenue from sales	100.0%	100.0%	100.0%
Cost of goods sold	65.0	64.0	62.0
Gross profit	35.0	36.0	38.0
Operating expenses			
Selling expenses	14.0	12.0	11.0
General expenses	16.0	16.0	15.0
Total operating expenses	30.0	28.0	26.0
Operating income before income taxes	5.0	8.0	12.0
Taxes related to operations	1.5	2.4	3.6
Net income	3.5	5.6	8.4
Horizontal Common Size			
Revenue from sales	109.9%	107.7%	100.0%
Cost of goods sold	115.2	107.8	100.0
Gross profit	101.2	98.9	100.0
Operating expenses			
Selling expenses	139.9	113.9	100.0
General expenses	117.2	111.4	100.0
Total operating expenses	126.8	112.3	100.0
Operating income before income taxes	45.7	69.5	100.0
Taxes related to operations	45.7	69.5	100.0
Net income	45.7	69.5	100.0

Trend Analysis

Using the past history of a firm for comparison is called *trend analysis*. By looking at a trend in a particular ratio, one sees whether that ratio is falling, rising, or remaining relatively constant. From this, a problem is detected, or good management is observed.

Industry Averages and Comparison with Competitors

The analysis of an entity's financial statements can be more meaningful if the results are compared with industry averages and with the results of competitors. Several financial services provide composite data on various industries.

A problem the analyst sometimes faces is that the industries reported do not clearly include the company being examined, because the company is diversified into many industrial areas. It is often necessary to choose the industry that the firm best fits. The financial services have a similar problem in selecting an industry in which to place a company. Many companies do not clearly fit into any one industry. The financial service uses its best judgment as to which industry the firm best fits.

This section includes a brief description of some financial services. For a more extensive explanation, consult the service's literature. Each service explains in some detail how it computes its ratios and the data provided.

The Department of Commerce Financial Report (Exhibit 4-2) is a publication of the federal government for manufacturing, mining, and trade corporations. It includes income statement data and balance sheet data in total industry dollars. It also includes an industry-wide common size vertical income statement (called an *income state*) in ratio format and an industry-wide common size vertical balance sheet ("selected balance sheet ratios"). This source also includes selected operating and balance sheet ratios and common size vertical balance sheet data.

This report is updated quarterly and probably offers the most current source. It is a unique source of industry data in total dollars and would enable a company to compare its dollars (such as sales) with the industry dollars (sales).

Robert Morris Associates Annual Statement Studies (Exhibit 4-3) is another source for comparison. A particular advantage is that this source provides simple, common size income statements and balance sheets as well as sixteen selected ratios.

Industries in manufacturing, wholesaling, retailing, and construction are presented, with the data divided into different categories by size of firm, including an all-sizes category. This is particularly useful, as the financial position of small firms is often quite different from that of larger firms. Comparative historical data are also provided for use in trend analysis.

In each size category, the ratios are computed for the median and the upper and lower quartiles. For example:

- Number of firms: 9
- Ratio: Return on total assets

(continues on p. 156)

E X H I B I T   4 - 2

DEPARTMENT OF COMMERCE QUARTERLY FINANCIAL REPORT
(Presented in Part Only)

Table 14.0—Income Statement
For Corporations Included in Manufacturing, by Asset Size

Item	All Manufacturing[1]				
	4Q 1988[2]	1Q 1989[2]	2Q 1989[2]	3Q 1989[2]	4Q 1989
	(million dollars)				
Net sales, receipts, and operating revenues	680,244	662,741	703,864	677,519	687,701
Less: Depreciation, depletion and amortization of property, plant, and equipment	26,136	25,595	26,044	25,942	26,680
Less: All other operating costs and expenses, including cost of goods sold and selling, general, and administrative expenses	607,401	589,294	625,293	605,466	626,403
Income (or loss) from operations	46,707	47,852	52,527	46,111	34,618
Net nonoperating income (expense)	5,542	6,075	604	677	1,267
Income (or loss) before income taxes	52,249	53,927	53,131	46,788	35,885
Less: Provision for current and deferred domestic income taxes	14,839	15,439	16,669	13,297	6,955
Income (or loss) after income taxes	37,410	38,488	36,463	33,491	28,930
Cash dividends charged to retained earnings in current quarter	16,509	16,517	17,437	15,786	15,703
Net income retained in business	20,901	21,971	19,025	17,705	13,227
Retained earnings at beginning of quarter	708,964	713,914	715,690	717,097	720,585
Other direct credits (or charges) to retained earnings (net), including stock and other noncash dividends, etc.	(12,180)	(17,069)	(11,705)	(6,479)	(5,955)
Retained earnings at end of quarter	717,685	718,815	723,010	728,323	727,857
Income Statement in Ratio Format	(percent of net sales)				
Net sales, receipts, and operating revenues	100.0	100.0	100.0	100.0	100.0

Less: Depreciation, depletion, and amortization of property, plant, and equipment	3.8	3.9	3.7	3.8	3.9
Less: All other operating costs and expenses	89.3	88.9	88.8	89.4	91.1
Income (or loss) from operations	6.9	7.2	7.5	6.8	5.0
Net nonoperating income (expense)	0.8	0.9	0.1	0.1	0.2
Income (or loss) before income taxes	7.7	8.1	7.5	6.9	5.2
Less: Provision for current and deferred domestic income taxes	2.2	2.3	2.4	2.0	1.0
Income (or loss) after income taxes	5.5	5.8	5.2	4.9	4.2
Operating Ratios (see explanatory notes)			(percent)		
Annual rate of profit on stockholders' equity at end of period:					
Before income taxes	21.33	21.93	21.55	18.80	14.26
After income taxes	15.27	15.65	14.79	13.46	11.50
Annual rate of profit on total assets:					
Before income taxes	8.93	9.00	8.78	7.64	5.78
After income taxes	6.40	6.42	6.02	5.47	4.66
Balance Sheet Ratios (based on succeeding table)					
Total current assets to total current liabilities	1.52	1.47	1.50	1.48	1.47
Total cash, U.S. Government and other securities to total current liabilities	0.21	0.19	0.19	0.18	0.19
Total stockholders' equity to total debt	1.48	1.40	1.37	1.36	1.36
Assets			(million dollars)		
Cash and demand deposits in the United States	37,406	34,462	34,686	36,123	39,410
Time deposits in the United States, including negotiable certificates of deposit	24,295	25,370	24,283	20,654	22,887
Total cash on hand and in U.S. banks	61,700	59,832	58,969	56,777	62,297
Other short-term financial investments, including marketable and government securities, commercial paper, etc.	64,720	60,997	61,912	56,053	59,501
Total cash, U.S. Government and other securities	126,421	120,829	120,881	112,830	121,798

E X H I B I T　4 - 2　(continued)

Item	All Manufacturing[1]				
	4Q 1988[2]	1Q 1989[2]	2Q 1989[2]	3Q 1989[2]	4Q 1989
	(million dollars)				
Trade accounts and trade notes receivable (less allowances for doubtful receivables)	350,048	355,862	365,171	368,259	363,195
Inventories	358,012	369,351	372,415	372,046	366,868
All other current assets	79,524	72,572	76,518	79,345	83,134
Total current assets	914,005	918,613	934,986	932,481	934,995
Depreciable and amortizable fixed assets, including construction in progress	1,331,973	1,345,819	1,366,264	1,387,731	1,407,911
Land and mineral rights	103,371	104,492	105,251	104,662	105,572
Less: Accumulated depreciation, depletion, and amortization	648,743	657,756	669,491	682,547	688,731
Net property, plant, and equipment	786,601	792,556	802,024	809,846	824,752
All other noncurrent assets, including investment in nonconsolidated entities, long-term investments, intangibles, etc.	639,085	685,174	684,290	707,898	723,189
Total assets	2,339,690	2,396,343	2,421,300	2,450,225	2,482,936
Liabilities and Stockholders' Equity					
Short-term debt, original maturity of 1 year or less:					
a. Loans from banks	45,561	46,830	49,493	50,475	50,253
b. Other short-term debt, including commercial paper	43,274	59,856	52,421	54,713	52,140
Trade accounts and trade notes payable	189,305	187,321	188,955	187,529	193,669
Income taxes accrued, prior and current years, net of payments	31,203	34,640	30,581	29,696	27,029
Installments, due in 1 year or less, on long-term debt:					
a. Loans from banks	15,457	15,154	17,575	17,736	19,973
b. Other long-term debt	22,589	26,295	25,676	27,827	24,787
All other current liabilities, including excise and sales taxes, and accrued expenses	255,247	253,454	258,292	261,045	266,998
Total current liabilities	602,636	623,551	622,993	629,020	634,848

Long-term debt (due in more than 1 year):				
a. Loans from banks	163,657	166,960	175,047	178,023	180,948
b. Other long-term debt	371,700	385,374	397,459	405,400	413,913
All other noncurrent liabilities, including deferred income taxes, capitalized leases, and minority stockholders' interest in consolidated domestic corporations	221,765	236,685	239,486	242,392	246,961
Total liabilities	1,359,759	1,412,569	1,434,984	1,454,836	1,476,671
Capital stock and other capital (less treasury stock)	262,247	264,958	263,306	267,067	278,408
Retained earnings	717,685	718,815	723,010	728,323	727,857
Stockholders' equity	979,932	983,773	986,316	995,389	1,006,266
Total liabilities and stockholders' equity	2,339,690	2,396,343	2,421,300	2,450,225	2,482,936
Net Working Capital					
Excess of total current assets over total current liabilities	311,368	295,063	311,993	303,461	300,147
Selected Balance Sheet Ratios					
(percent of total assets)					
Total cash, U.S. Government and other securities	5.4	5.0	5.0	4.6	4.9
Trade accounts and trade notes receivable	15.0	14.9	15.1	15.0	14.6
Inventories	15.3	15.4	15.4	15.2	14.8
Total current assets	39.1	38.3	38.6	38.1	37.7
Net property, plant, and equipment	33.6	33.1	33.1	33.1	33.2
Short-term debt including installments on long-term debt	5.4	6.2	6.0	6.1	5.9
Total current liabilities	25.8	26.0	25.7	25.7	25.6
Long-term debt	22.9	23.1	23.6	23.8	24.0
Total liabilities	58.1	58.9	59.3	59.4	59.5
Stockholders' equity	41.9	41.1	40.7	40.6	40.5

[1] In the first quarter 1989, a number of corporations were reclassified by industry. To provide comparability, data for quarters in 1988 were restated to reflect these reclassifications.
[2] Revised principally to reflect respondents corrections of submitted data subsequent to original publication.
[3] Revised.

EXHIBIT 4-3
ROBERT MORRIS ASSOCIATES ANNUAL STATEMENT STUDIES

MANUFACTURERS—RUBBER & PLASTIC FOOTWEAR & FABRICATED RUBBER PRODUCTS   SIC# 3021 (63)

	Current Data					Comparative Historical Data				
	66(6/30-9/30/88)			80(10/1/88-3/31/89)		6/30/84-3/31/85	6/30/85-3/31/86	6/30/86-3/31/87	6/30/87-3/31/88	6/30/88-3/31/89
Type of Statement	0-1MM	1-10MM	10-50MM	50-100MM	ALL	ALL	ALL	ALL	ALL	ALL
Unqualified		29	17	2	48	62	60	52	64	48
Qualified	1	1	2		4	1	2	3	6	4
Reviewed	6	26	3		35	23	36	33	37	35
Compiled	13	15	1		29	32	25	24	35	29
Other	7	12	11		30	14	11	15	27	30
Asset Size	0-1MM	1-10MM	10-50MM	50-100MM	ALL	ALL	ALL	ALL	ALL	ALL
Number of Statements	27	83	34	2	146	132	134	127	169	146
	%	%	%	%	%	%	%	%	%	%
Assets										
Cash & Equivalents	9.3	5.6	4.7		6.1	8.7	7.2	7.8	7.2	6.1
Trade Receivables - (net)	34.4	29.5	23.0		28.7	27.9	29.5	28.5	28.9	28.7
Inventory	20.6	25.1	23.6		23.8	25.1	25.0	24.9	24.0	23.8
All Other Current	1.4	2.4	4.2		2.6	1.6	1.9	1.7	2.4	2.6
Total Current	65.7	62.5	55.4		61.3	63.3	63.5	62.9	62.4	61.3
Fixed Assets (net)	25.9	31.3	35.9		31.5	28.6	28.3	28.4	30.5	31.5
Intangibles (net)	.2	1.5	2.4		1.4	.5	.8	.6	.7	1.4
All Other Non-Current	8.2	4.7	6.3		5.8	7.6	7.4	8.1	6.4	5.8
Total	100.0	100.0	100.0		100.0	100.0	100.0	100.0	100.0	100.0
Liabilities										
Notes Payable-Short Term	10.6	10.9	10.2		10.7	9.0	9.9	10.1	10.5	10.7
Cur. Mat.-L/T/D	3.1	4.2	3.3		3.8	3.3	3.6	3.4	3.8	3.8
Trade Payables	21.3	15.9	11.2		15.7	15.2	15.0	15.5	16.8	15.7
Income Taxes Payable	.4	1.5	1.5		1.3	1.2	1.2	1.6	1.1	1.3
All Other Current	9.3	8.2	9.9		8.8	8.8	9.3	8.0	8.0	8.8
Total Current	44.6	40.7	36.1		40.2	37.6	39.0	38.6	40.3	40.2
Long Term Debt	18.4	15.2	19.2		16.8	15.3	15.8	13.3	16.5	16.8
Deferred Taxes	.1	.5	2.1		.8	1.0	1.1	1.2	1.1	.8
All Other Non-Current	2.3	2.9	3.7		3.0	1.0	1.6	2.1	1.9	3.0
Net Worth	34.6	40.6	39.0		39.1	45.1	42.4	44.7	40.2	39.1
Total Liabilities & Net Worth	100.0	100.0	100.0		100.0	100.0	100.0	100.0	100.0	100.0
Income Data										
Net Sales	100.0	100.0	100.0		100.0	100.0	100.0	100.0	100.0	100.0
Gross Profit	34.1	29.0	23.1		28.6	27.3	29.7	28.6	29.2	28.6
Operating Expenses	29.3	22.9	16.2		22.5	20.7	23.6	22.3	23.7	22.5
Operating Profit	4.8	6.0	6.9		6.1	6.6	6.1	6.3	5.5	6.1
All Other Expenses (net)	.6	1.6	1.7		1.5	1.4	1.3	1.1	1.2	1.5
Profit Before Taxes	4.2	4.4	5.2		4.6	5.2	4.8	5.2	4.3	4.6

Ratios (comparison) — values shown as upper quartile / median / lower quartile; figures in parentheses are number of statements.

Upper section

Ratio	Col 1	Col 2	Col 3	Col 4	Col 5
Current	2.6 / 1.7 / 1.2	2.3 / 1.7 / 1.2	2.5 / 1.7 / 1.3	2.3 / 1.5 / 1.2	2.2 / 1.6 / 1.2
Quick	1.6 / 1.0 / .7	1.5 / 1.0 / .7	1.5 / 1.0 / .7	1.4 / .8 / .6	1.2 / .9 / .6
Sales/Receivables	(37/46/59) 9.9 / 8.0 / 6.2	(36/45/54) 10.2 / 8.2 / 6.7	(35/44/55) 10.4 / 8.3 / 6.6	(35/47/57) 10.4 / 7.7 / 6.4	(39/49/59) 9.4 / 7.5 / 6.2
Cost of Sales/Inventory	(28/53/87) 13.0 / 6.9 / 4.2	(30/53/76) 12.2 / 6.9 / 4.8	(33/54/81) 11.1 / 6.8 / 4.5	(31/54/81) 11.7 / 6.8 / 4.5	(32/51/85) 11.3 / 7.2 / 4.3
Cost of Sales/Payables	(19/30/43) 19.1 / 12.3 / 8.5	(18/29/48) 20.0 / 12.6 / 7.6	(18/28/43) 19.8 / 13.1 / 8.4	(22/33/53) 16.6 / 11.1 / 6.9	(21/33/47) 17.0 / 11.2 / 7.8
Sales/Working Capital	5.2 / 9.7 / 21.9	6.1 / 9.8 / 21.0	5.9 / 8.4 / 21.3	5.9 / 11.4 / 29.4	6.2 / 10.1 / 32.0
EBIT/Interest	(113) 9.1 / 3.8 / 1.7	(122) 10.7 / 3.7 / 1.5	(118) 10.4 / 4.0 / 1.9	(146) 7.2 / 4.2 / 1.6	(129) 8.6 / 4.0 / 1.9
Net Profit + Depr., Dep., Amort./Cur. Mat. L/T/D	(83) 5.8 / 3.2 / 1.7	(90) 5.9 / 3.0 / 1.4	(81) 8.1 / 3.3 / 1.8	(101) 7.7 / 3.6 / 1.6	(86) 9.3 / 3.2 / 1.6
Fixed/Worth	.3 / .6 / 1.3	.3 / .7 / 1.2	.3 / .6 / 1.2	.4 / .8 / 1.4	.3 / .9 / 1.7
Debt/Worth	.6 / 1.3 / 2.8	.7 / 1.5 / 2.7	.6 / 1.3 / 2.6	.8 / 1.5 / 3.6	.8 / 1.6 / 3.3
% Profit Before Taxes/Tangible Net Worth	(129) 37.5 / 20.8 / 8.0	(130) 43.3 / 21.5 / 9.7	(123) 37.2 / 22.0 / 9.9	(162) 42.0 / 23.5 / 9.6	(136) 40.3 / 22.0 / 9.9
% Profit Before Taxes/Total Assets	16.1 / 8.5 / 2.8	17.8 / 9.3 / 3.1	18.4 / 9.4 / 2.9	15.9 / 8.6 / 2.5	14.7 / 7.9 / 3.2
Sales/Net Fixed Assets	15.6 / 8.1 / 5.1	15.8 / 10.3 / 5.0	16.4 / 8.3 / 4.6	14.9 / 7.0 / 4.5	15.0 / 7.3 / 4.5

(A further column at far side repeats Col 5: 2.2 / 1.6 / 1.2 ... 15.0 / 7.3 / 4.5)

Lower section

Ratio	Col 1	Col 2	Col 3
Current	2.2 / 1.6 / 1.3	2.1 / 1.6 / 1.1	2.2 / 1.5 / 1.2
Quick	1.1 / .9 / .6	1.1 / .8 / .5	1.4 / 1.1 / .8
Sales/Receivables	(38/46/60) 9.6 / 8.0 / 6.1	(40/49/58) 9.2 / 7.5 / 8.3	(36/51/61) 10.2 / 7.1 / 6.0
Cost of Sales/Inventory	(31/56/99) 11.7 / 6.5 / 3.7	(33/51/96) 11.2 / 7.2 / 3.8	(26/42/64) 14.0 / 8.7 / 5.7
Cost of Sales/Payables	(19/29/38) 18.9 / 12.5 / 9.6	(22/32/48) 16.6 / 11.3 / 7.6	(23/35/56) 10.2 / 10.3 / 6.5
Sales/Working Capital	5.3 / 9.9 / 18.8	6.2 / 10.2 / 42.7	6.7 / 14.4 / 29.6
EBIT/Interest	(33) 8.8 / 4.1 / 2.4	(71) 9.6 / 4.2 / 1.8	(23) 6.5 / 3.2 / 1.1
Net Profit + Depr., Dep., Amort./Cur. Mat. L/T/D	(24) 12.9 / 3.1 / 1.9	(50) 9.0 / 2.7 / 1.4	(10) 9.0 / 7.9 / 2.9
Fixed/Worth	.6 / 1.0 / 1.9	.3 / .8 / 1.7	.3 / .9 / 1.7
Debt/Worth	1.0 / 1.6 / 3.0	.8 / 1.6 / 3.4	.9 / 1.5 / 4.0
% Profit Before Taxes/Tangible Net Worth	(31) 40.6 / 22.2 / 9.1	(80) 39.4 / 22.4 / 11.6	(23) 49.4 / 18.9 / 5.5
% Profit Before Taxes/Total Assets	16.4 / 7.4 / 3.5	13.6 / 8.6 / 3.4	15.8 / 8.1 / 1.5
Sales/Net Fixed Assets	7.4 / 5.6 / 4.1	17.8 / 7.8 / 4.5	22.5 / 13.8 / 6.2

EXHIBIT 4 - 3 (continued)

Current Data					Type of Statement	Comparative Historical Data				
3.5	2.8	2.2		2.8	Sales/Total Assets	2.9	2.9	2.9	2.9	2.8
2.8	2.3	1.8		2.1		2.1	2.4	2.1	2.2	2.1
2.0	1.6	1.4		1.6		1.7	1.8	1.7	1.7	1.6
1.0	1.3	1.8		1.4	% Depr., Dep., Amort./Sales	1.5	1.6	1.4	1.7	1.4
(23) 2.5	(73) 2.4	(27) 2.6		(125) 2.4		(120) 2.4	(122) 2.4	(117) 2.4	(147) 2.5	(125) 2.4
3.8	3.8	3.6		3.7		3.6	3.5	3.0	3.7	3.7
3.5	2.1			2.2	% Officers' Comp/Sales	2.5	3.0	2.9	2.1	2.2
(12) 6.6	(27) 4.4			(42) 5.1		(30) 4.4	(38) 5.2	(39) 4.4	(51) 3.3	(42) 5.1
11.1	7.5			9.7		7.6	8.8	7.3	5.6	9.7
36435M	597707M	2409865M	229985M	3273992M	Net Sales ($)	2405169M	2559305M	2539671M	3031928M	3273992M
14175M	285835M	860707M	159878M	1320595M	Total Assets ($)	1234425M	1332048M	1344170M	1551854M	1320595M

M = $ thousand; MM = $ million.

E X H I B I T   4 - 3   (continued)

Interpretation of Statement Studies Figures

RMA recommends that Statement Studies data be regarded only as general guidelines and not as absolute industry norms. There are several reasons why the data may not be fully representative of a given industry:

(1) The financial statements used in the *Statement Studies* are not selected by any random or statistically reliable method. RMA member banks voluntarily submit the raw data they have available each year, with these being the only constraints: (a) The fiscal year-ends of the companies reported may not be from April 1 through June 29, and (b) their total assets must be less than $100 million.

(2) Many companies have varied product lines; however, the *Statement Studies* categorize them by their primary product Standard Industrial Classification (SIC) number only.

(3) Some of our industry samples are rather small in relation to the total number of firms in a given industry. A relatively small sample can increase the chances that some of our composites do not fully represent an industry.

(4) There is the chance that an extreme statement can be present in a sample, causing a disproportionate influence on the industry composite. This is particularly true in a relatively small sample.

(5) Companies within the same industry may differ in their method of operations which in turn can directly influence their financial statements. Since they are included in our sample, too, these statements can significantly affect our composite calculations.

(6) Other considerations that can result in variations among different companies engaged in the same general line of business are different labor markets; geographical location; different accounting methods; quality of products handled; sources and methods of financing; and terms of sale.

For these reasons, RMA does not recommend the Statement Studies figures be considered as absolute norms for a given industry. Rather the figures should be used only as general guidelines and in addition to the other methods of financial analysis. RMA makes no claim as to the representativeness of the figures printed in this book.

- Results for the nine firms (in order, from highest to lowest): 12%, 11%, 10.5%, 10%, 9.8%, 9.7%, 9.6%, 7.0%, 6.5%
- The middle result is the median: 9.8%
- The result halfway between the top result and the median is the upper quartile: 10.5%
- The result halfway between the bottom result and the median is the lower quartile: 9.6%

For ratios in which a low ratio is desirable, the results are presented from low values to high: for example, 2% (upper quartile), 5% (median), and 8% (lower quartile).

Because of the combination of common size statements, selected ratios, and comparative historical data, *Robert Morris Associates Annual Statement Studies* is one of the most extensively used sources of industry data. Commercial loan officers in banks frequently use this source.

Notice the section called "Interpretation of Statement Studies Figures," which indicates that statement studies should be "regarded only as general guidelines and not as absolute industry norms." It then proceeds to list reasons why the data may not be fully representative of a given industry. This word of caution is useful in keeping the user from concluding that the data represent an absolute norm for a given industry.

Standard and Poor's Industry Surveys contains a five-year summary on several firms within an industry group. Exhibit 4-4 illustrates the type of data provided. *Standard and Poor's Industry Surveys* are of particular interest to investors. Some of the data included are the following:

1. Operating revenues
2. Net income
3. Return on revenues (%)
4. Return on assets (%)
5. Return on equity (%)
6. Current ratio
7. Debt/capital ratio (%)
8. Debt as percent of net working capital
9. Price-earnings ratio (high-low)
10. Dividend payout ratio (%)
11. Yield (high %-low %)
12. Earnings per share
13. Book value per share
14. Share price (high-low)

The Almanac of Business and Industrial Financial Ratios (Exhibit 4-5), by Leo Troy, presents twenty-four statistics for eleven size categories of firms. These statistics include twelve common size operating factors. There are also ten ratios and

E X H I B I T 4 - 4

STANDARD AND POOR'S INDUSTRY SURVEY
Aerospace and Air Transport

Company	Yr. End	Price-Earnings Ratio (High-Low)					Dividend Payout Ratio (%)				
		1984	1985	1986	1987	1988	1984	1985	1986	1987	1988
Diversified Aerospace											
*Allied Signal Inc	Dec	8– 6	NM–NM	17–11	16– 8	12– 9	35	NM	55	59	58
*EG&G Inc	Dec	19–14	21–15	26–17	23–14	17–12	21	23	32	28	26
General Motors-Class H	Dec	NA–NA	21–16	17–11	15–12	NA–NA	NA	0	20	22	NA
*Martin Marietta Corp	Dec	10– 6	10– 6	13– 9	13– 8	8– 6	28	22	27	25	18
*Raytheon Co	Dec	12– 9	12– 9	14–10	14– 9	10– 8	26	35	33	29	34
*Rockwell Intl Corp	Sep	10– 7	10– 7	12– 8	14– 6	8– 5	29	27	28	28	23
*TRW Inc	Dec	11– 8	26–18	15–11	17– 9	13– 9	40	79	42	40	39
*Teledyne Inc	Dec	8– 4	7– 5	18–14	12– 8	10– 9	0	0	0	12	12
Components & Systems											
AAR Corp	†May	16–11	14– 8	18–11	19–10	NA–NA	32	32	31	26	NA
Fairchild Industries Inc	Dec	NM–NM	NM–NM	NM–NM	NM–NM	29–14	NM	NM	NM	667	35
Hexcel Corp	Dec	18–10	18–13	20–12	21–11	18–10	36	32	26	21	18
Hi-Shear Industries	†May	15–10	10– 7	28–20	29–15	NA–NA	43	22	54	52	NA
Rohr Industries	Jul	9– 6	12– 7	13– 9	26– 8	18– 9	0	0	0	0	0
Sequa Corp -CL A	Dec	10– 7	75–55	26–11	21–10	11– 8	14	92	15	14	10
Sierracin Corp	Dec	13– 8	NM–NM	20–12	19– 8	NA–NA	32	NM	0	0	NA
Sundstrand Corp	Dec	14– 9	14–10	27–20	35–19	NM–NM	50	45	74	97	NM
UNC Inc	Dec	NM–NM	38–29	25–15	25– 8	25–13	NM	0	0	0	0
Wyman-Gordon Co	Dec	18–13	66–44	NM–NM	26–14	52–39	44	174	NM	98	242
Airframe											
*Boeing Co	Dec	7– 4	14–10	15–11	18–11	17– 9	17	28	28	45	39
*General Dynamics Corp	Dec	9– 5	10– 7	NM–NM	8– 4	7– 5	12	11	NM	10	11
*Grumman Corp	Dec	8– 6	14– 9	14–10	49–26	10– 7	26	38	43	149	40
*Lockheed Corp	Dec	9– 6	10– 7	10– 7	9– 4	7– 5	9	12	15	20	21
*McDonnell Douglas Corp	Dec	9– 6	10– 7	13–10	11– 7	9– 6	20	21	30	30	28
*Northrop Corp	Dec	11– 7	12– 7	58–41	26–12	NM–NM	25	26	135	60	NM
Propulsion, Engines											
*United Technologies Corp	Dec	9– 6	10– 7	NM–NM	13– 7	8– 7	28	29	NM	31	31

E X H I B I T 4 - 4 (continued)

Company	Yr. End	Price-Earnings Ratio (High-Low)					Dividend Payout Ratio (%)				
		1984	1985	1986	1987	1988	1984	1985	1986	1987	1988
Shipbuilding											
American Ship Building Co	Sep	36–22	12–9	23–16	NM–NM	NM–NM	178	63	145	NM	NM
*Litton Industries Inc	Jul	12–9	13–9	37–28	21–12	14–11	28	28	0	0	0
Todd Shipyards Corp	†Mar	8–7	NM–NM	NM–NM	NM–NM	NA–NA	30	NM	NM	NM	NA
Major Carriers											
*AMR Corp-Del	Dec	9–6	9–6	13–8	20–8	NA–NA	0	0	0	0	NA
Continental Airlines Inc	Dec	9–4	15–8	NA–NA	NA–NA	NA–NA	0	0	NA	NA	NA
*Delta Air Lines Inc	Jun	10–6	8–6	44–32	11–5	9–6	14	11	85	17	19
Eastern Air Lines	Dec	NM–NM	NM–NM	NA–NA	NA–NA	NA–NA	NM	NM	NA	NA	NA
*NWA Inc	Dec	13–9	19–12	19–13	21–9	12–8	22	28	28	25	19
*Pan Am Corp	Dec	NM–NM	21–10	NM–NM	NM–NM	NM–NM	NM	0	NM	NM	NM
Texas Air Corp	Dec	8–5	8–4	63–22	NM–NM	NA–NA	0	0	0	NM	NA
Trans World Airlines	Dec	82–45	NM–NM	NM–NM	NM–NM	NA–NA	0	NM	NM	NM	NA
*UAL Corp	Dec	7–4	NM–NM	NM–NM	NM–NM	5–3	7	NM	400	NM	0
*USAir Group	Dec	7–4	10–7	12–9	10–5	11–7	2	3	4	2	3
National Carriers											
Alaska Airgroup Inc	Dec	8–4	13–7	16–10	33–14	10–6	6	7	11	19	7
America West Airlines Inc	Dec	NM–NM	30–16	NM–NM	NM–NM	NM–NM	NM	0	NM	NM	NM
HAL Inc	Dec	3–1	NM–NM	12–4	NM–NM	NM–NM	0	NM	0	NM	NM
Midway Airlines Inc	Dec	NM–NM	NM–NM	44–18	18–9	NA–NA	NM	NM	0	0	NA
Southwest Airlines	Dec	17–9	20–14	18–12	40–19	11–7	8	8	8	21	7
Worldcorp Inc	Dec	NM–NM	NM–NM	2–1	5–2	10–7	NM	NM	0	0	0
Air Cargo											
Airborne Freight Corp	Dec	16–7	18–13	14–7	40–12	22–13	32	43	27	67	59
*Consolidated Freightways Inc	Dec	11–7	13–9	16–10	21–12	12–8	35	35	35	46	32
*Federal Express Corp	†May	29–17	23–12	23–16	21–10	NA–NA	0	0	0	0	NA

Note: Data as originally reported.
*Company included in the Standard & Poor's 500.
†Of the following calendar year.

Company	Yr. End	Current Ratio					Debt/Capital Ratio (%)				
		1984	1985	1986	1987	1988	1984	1985	1986	1987	1988
Diversified Aerospace											
*Allied Signal Inc	Dec	1.2	1.6	1.3	1.2	1.3	30.2	23.4	33.1	34.5	33.9
*EG&G Inc	Dec	1.2	1.5	1.6	1.6	2.1	8.6	6.6	7.4	6.9	4.2
General Motors-Class H	Dec	NA	1.0	1.1	1.2	NA	NA	4.4	5.4	2.3	NA
*Martin Marietta Corp	Dec	1.1	1.3	1.2	1.4	1.4	25.9	15.8	14.9	16.3	22.4
*Raytheon Co	Dec	1.5	1.3	1.3	1.1	1.1	4.1	3.7	2.4	2.4	1.9
*Rockwell Intl Corp	Sep	1.3	1.1	1.1	1.2	1.3	8.0	18.0	16.6	18.7	16.8
*TRW Inc	Dec	1.6	1.2	1.3	1.3	1.5	10.7	31.3	32.3	31.5	30.0
*Teledyne Inc	Dec	2.1	1.7	1.8	2.1	NA	44.9	28.8	25.0	21.0	20.2
Components & Systems											
AAR Corp	†May	2.3	2.0	2.1	2.0	NA	14.9	19.5	8.1	13.0	NA
Fairchild Industries Inc	Dec	1.9	1.6	2.0	2.5	2.1	30.3	45.6	41.4	40.2	34.9
Hexcel Corp	Dec	3.1	2.4	2.7	2.3	2.5	39.9	36.6	41.2	36.2	42.0
Hi-Shear Industries	†May	3.9	5.5	4.9	4.4	NA	0.0	0.0	0.0	0.0	NA
Rohr Industries	Jul	1.8	2.3	2.3	3.0	3.5	20.7	8.1	6.3	30.6	43.9
Sequa Corp -CL A	Dec	2.0	1.4	2.1	2.0	1.9	41.2	48.0	29.7	41.7	45.6
Sierracin Corp	Dec	2.0	1.2	1.6	1.9	NA	38.1	26.3	26.6	26.7	NA
Sundstrand Corp	Dec	2.1	1.9	2.6	2.1	1.7	19.4	23.0	27.4	26.0	24.6
UNC Inc	Dec	2.7	2.0	1.6	2.0	2.6	21.5	33.0	56.8	60.4	53.7
Wyman-Gordon Co	Dec	4.8	4.5	3.9	4.0	2.9	6.4	5.8	6.4	5.6	5.8
Airframe											
*Boeing Co	Dec	1.5	1.5	1.5	1.3	1.3	6.4	0.3	4.9	4.7	4.3
*General Dynamics Corp	Dec	1.6	1.2	1.2	1.4	1.8	0.9	1.2	22.6	17.9	29.0
*Grumman Corp	Dec	2.2	1.9	2.1	2.3	2.5	24.1	25.9	32.1	42.1	46.3
*Lockheed Corp	Dec	1.1	1.0	1.0	0.9	0.9	17.2	2.3	40.0	29.8	18.5
*McDonnell Douglas Corp	Dec	0.9	1.1	1.1	1.1	NA	1.7	18.6	21.1	20.6	42.8
*Northrop Corp	Dec	0.6	0.7	0.7	0.8	1.1	1.0	0.6	0.5	0.3	34.1
Propulsion, Engines											
*United Technologies Corp	Dec	1.6	1.7	1.5	1.6	1.6	20.4	21.4	29.2	27.8	23.2
Shipbuilding											
American Ship Building Co	Sep	1.7	1.5	1.9	2.4	1.1	26.6	22.8	22.1	25.0	28.6
*Litton Industries Inc	Jul	1.5	1.6	1.6	1.5	1.7	9.3	61.3	59.1	54.4	51.9
Todd Shipyards Corp	†Mar	1.6	1.8	0.7	3.9	NA	20.3	42.3	5.0	0.0	NA

EXHIBIT 4 - 4 (continued)

Company	Yr. End	Current Ratio					Debt/Capital Ratio (%)				
		1984	1985	1986	1987	1988	1984	1985	1986	1987	1988
Major Carriers											
*AMR Corp-Del	Dec	1.4	1.3	1.1	1.0	NA	43.4	41.6	44.6	45.0	NA
Continental Airlines Inc	Dec	1.9	1.6	1.0	0.8	NA	126.9	95.5	97.2	85.1	NA
*Delta Air Lines Inc	Jun	0.6	0.7	0.8	1.0	1.2	30.4	22.0	31.6	27.9	20.5
Eastern Air Lines	Dec	0.9	0.9	1.0	0.9	NA	87.6	85.0	78.1	83.5	NA
*NWA Inc	Dec	0.8	0.6	0.5	0.6	0.6	7.9	29.3	50.8	34.4	32.1
*Pan Am Corp	Dec	0.8	1.1	0.7	0.7	0.7	82.2	60.5	99.0	132.8	153.0
Texas Air Corp	Dec	1.9	2.4	1.0	0.9	NA	93.3	81.8	79.1	83.9	NA
Trans World Airlines	Dec	1.1	0.8	1.1	1.5	1.0	62.0	70.0	82.1	82.1	101.3
*UAL Corp	Dec	0.7	1.0	0.8	1.0	0.8	31.0	56.7	45.7	32.7	62.6
*USAir Group	Dec	1.4	1.7	1.5	0.9	0.7	31.7	27.7	24.0	44.5	35.6
National Carriers											
Alaska Airgroup Inc	Dec	1.3	2.1	0.9	1.2	0.8	41.5	54.1	56.6	39.5	32.7
America West Airlines Inc	Dec	0.6	1.7	1.8	1.0	1.0	75.7	66.1	81.5	89.0	86.9
HAL Inc	Dec	1.4	1.0	1.0	0.7	0.8	82.7	74.5	66.7	80.5	67.5
Midway Airlines Inc	Dec	1.3	1.3	1.3	0.9	NA	62.3	44.1	34.9	50.8	NA
Southwest Airlines	Dec	1.3	1.6	1.5	1.8	1.7	25.7	40.3	35.3	29.5	35.6
Worldcorp Inc	Dec	0.5	0.4	0.5	1.7	1.5	90.4	96.0	123.6	309.2	220.4
Air Cargo											
Airborne Freight Corp	Dec	1.3	1.3	1.2	1.5	1.4	23.2	35.1	43.6	47.1	57.2
*Consolidated Freightways Inc	Dec	1.5	1.6	1.5	1.4	1.3	8.7	7.8	6.8	5.8	5.0
*Federal Express Corp	†May	1.3	1.4	1.0	1.1	NA	38.4	33.9	40.8	38.7	NA

Note: Data as originally reported.
*Company included in the Standard & Poor's 500.
†Of the following calendar year.

E X H I B I T   4 - 5

THE ALMANAC OF BUSINESS AND INDUSTRIAL FINANCIAL RATIOS
by Leo Troy

Table I: Corporations with and without Net Income, 1989 Edition
1150 Mining:
Coal mining

Item Description For Accounting Period 7/85 Through 6/86	A Total	B Zero Assets	C Under 100	D 100 to 250	E 250 to 500	F 500 to 1,000	G 1,000 to 5,000	H 5,000 to 10,000	I 10,000 to 25,000	J 25,000 to 50,000	K 50,000 to 100,000	L 100,000 to 250,000	M 250,000 and over
1. Number of Enterprises	3575	323	1478	477	407	314	313	132	48	38	20	11	15
2. Total receipts	18764.7	507.8	325.1	82.2	316.8	390.7	1130.9	1279.4	1298.4	1532.8	978.9	1223.3	9698.5
(in millions of dollars)													
						Selected Operating Factors in Percent of Net Sales							
3. Cost of operations	73.2	77.2	68.1	—	36.9	39.2	67.1	74.5	83.1	76.5	76.8	80.3	73.1
4. Compensation of officers	0.8	0.2	—	—	2.1	6.6	1.8	1.3	0.9	0.8	0.8	0.4	0.4
5. Repairs	1.1	0.2	1.7	—	5.2	9.5	0.9	0.8	0.3	1.3	0.5	0.5	0.9
6. Bad debts	0.4	7.8	—	—	2.7	—	—	—	0.2	0.1	0.3	0.2	0.2
7. Rent on business property	1.4	0.1	0.4	—	0.8	2.8	0.4	0.1	1.1	0.5	1.7	0.2	2.1
8. Taxes (excl Federal tax)	5.0	2.8	4.1	—	5.1	6.0	6.0	5.7	2.6	3.8	4.9	3.9	5.5
9. Interest	3.6	2.0	3.0	—	3.2	2.1	1.8	1.9	1.4	3.9	3.7	4.3	4.4
10. Deprec/Deplet/Amortiz†	8.6	9.2	1.6	—	8.2	10.4	5.5	8.4	4.4	9.5	8.2	8.9	9.6
11. Advertising	0.1	—	0.1	—	—	—	—	—	—	0.1	0.1	—	0.1
12. Pensions & other benef plans	2.0	8.9	—	—	—	1.4	0.6	1.1	0.8	1.3	1.1	0.8	2.6
13. Other expenses	11.9	3.2	24.5	—	51.3	39.2	19.1	9.1	9.9	8.9	10.0	7.6	10.1
14. Net profit before tax	*	*	*	*	*	*	*	*	*	*	*	*	*
						Selected Financial Ratios (number of times ratio is to one)							
15. Current ratio	1.3	—	—	—	—	0.8	1.3	1.1	1.5	1.1	1.5	1.3	1.4
16. Quick ratio	1.0	—	—	—	—	0.7	1.1	0.9	1.2	0.7	0.9	0.7	1.1
17. Net sls to net wkg capital	9.9	—	—	—	—	—	21.7	32.1	9.8	26.2	8.1	15.7	5.6
18. Coverage ratio	0.5	—	—	—	—	—	2.0	1.7	—	1.5	0.3	0.2	0.5
19. Asset turnover	0.7	—	—	—	—	1.6	1.9	1.3	1.8	1.1	0.7	0.7	0.5

EXHIBIT 4 - 5 (continued)

Table I: Corporations with and without Net Income, 1989 Edition
1150 Mining:
Coal mining

Item Description For Accounting Period 7/85 Through 6/86	A Total	B Zero Assets	C Under 100	D 100 to 250	E 250 to 500	F 500 to 1,000	G 1,000 to 5,000	H 5,000 to 10,000	I 10,000 to 25,000	J 25,000 to 50,000	K 50,000 to 100,000	L 100,000 to 250,000	M 250,000 and over
							Size of Assets in Thousands of Dollars (000 Omitted)						
20. Total liab to net worth	1.3		—	—	—	2.7	2.3	1.4	1.7	2.3	1.2	2.1	1.1
							Selected Financial Factors in Percentages						
21. Debt ratio	56.9		—	—	—	73.3	70.0	58.1	62.2	70.1	54.9	67.7	51.1
22. Return on assets	1.2		—	—	—	—	6.7	4.2	—	6.5	0.7	0.5	1.2
23. Return on equity	—		—	—	—	—	4.1	0.4	—	5.7	—	—	—
24. Return on net worth	2.8		—	—	—	—	22.2	10.1	—	21.6	1.5	1.5	2.4

From *Almanac of Business and Industrial Financial Ratios*, 1989 Edition, by Leo Troy, Ph.D. © 1989. Used by permission of the publisher, Prentice Hall/A division of Simon & Schuster, Englewood Cliffs, New Jersey 07632.

†Depreciation largest factor

Each industry is subdivided by assets size, as follows:

	headlined in the charts as	Size of Assets in Thousands of Dollars (000 Omitted)
Total		A. Total
Zero	"	B. Zero
Under $100,000	"	C. Under 100
$100,000 to $249,999	"	D. 100 to 250
$250,000 to $499,999	"	E. 250 to 500
$500,000 to $999,999	"	F. 500 to 1,000
$1,000,000 to $4,999,999	"	G. 1,000 to 5,000
$5,000,000 to $9,999,999	"	H. 5,000 to 10,000
$10,000,000 to $24,999,999	"	I. 10,000 to 25,000
$25,000,000 to $49,999,999	"	J. 25,000 to 50,000
$50,000,000 to $99,999,999	"	K. 50,000 to 100,000
$100,000,000 to $249,999,999	"	L. 100,000 to 250,000
$250,000,000 and over	"	M. 250,000 and over

For each industry, both for the total and only those operating at a profit, the *Almanac* first provides the total number of returns (designated as "enterprises" in the text) in each subdivision, and total receipts in millions of dollars. The 22 ratios and percentages relate to all returns, and are given in three groups. All Operating Factors (numbers 3 to 14) are expressed as percentages of *net sales.* The percentages covered under Operating Factors are:

3. Cost of operations
4. Compensation of officers
5. Repairs
6. Bad debts
7. Rent on business property
8. Taxes (excluding Federal tax)
9. Interest
10. Depreciation/Depletion/Amortization (The most significant of these for each industry is indicated in a footnote to each table.)
11. Advertising
12. Pensions and other benefit plans
13. Other expenses
14. Net profit before Federal income tax.

E X H I B I T   4 - 5   (continued)

Note:: For industries in Finance, Insurance and Real Estate, the Operating Factors are expressed as a percent of total receipts. This was necessary because companies in these industries receive their income from a number of sources rather than a predominantly single source such as Sales.

Items 15 through 20 are Financial Ratios, expressed as the number of times the first factor in computation is to the second. The method of computation of each ratio is explained in the following pages. The ratios given are:

15. Current ratio
16. Quick ratio
17. Net sales to net working capital
18. Coverage ratio (times interest earned)
19. Asset turnover
20. Total liabilities to net worth.

Note: For industries in Finance, Insurance and Real Estate, Financial Ratios 15 through 17 and 19 are not calculated because these were not applicable.

Selected Financial Factors are given in items 21 through 24. These percentage relations are as follows:

21. Debt ratio
22. Return on assets
23. Return on equity
24. Return on net worth.

statistics on numbers of firms and total receipts to indicate market size. A broader range of industries is covered by this source than by other surveys, including manufacturing, wholesaling, construction, mining, utilities, financial institutions, insurance, and real estate.

Dun & Bradstreet publishes *Industry Norms and Key Business Ratios*. This source includes over 800 different lines of business as defined by the U.S. Standard Industrial Classification (SIC) code numbers. The Industry Norms books are published separately in the following five major industry segments:

1. Agriculture/Mining/Construction/Transportation/Communication/Utilities
2. Manufacturing
3. Wholesaling
4. Retailing
5. Finance/Real Estate/Services

All five segments are available in three different formats, for a total of fifteen books. The three formats are as follows:

1. Industry Norms for last three years
2. Industry Norms for the most recent year
3. Key Business Ratios (only) for the most recent year

Exhibit 4-6 contains a sample page from *Industry Norms and Key Business Ratios*. Notice that this includes a vertical common size balance sheet and a limited vertical common size income statement. It also includes fourteen ratios that are presented for the upper quartile, median, and lower quartile.

Value Line Investment Service contains profitability and investment data for 1,700 individual firms and for industries in general. Companies are placed in one of ninety-one industries. This service rates each stock's timeliness and safety. It is very popular with investors.

The data included in *Value Line* for a company are largely for a relatively long period of time (five to ten years). Some of the data provided for each company are as follows:

1. Sales per share
2. Cash flow per share
3. Earnings per share
4. Dividends declared per share
5. Capital spending per share
6. Book value per share
7. Common shares outstanding
8. Average annual P/E ratio
9. Relative P/E ratio
10. Average annual dividend yield
11. Sales

(continues on p. 168)

EXHIBIT 4-6

INDUSTRY NORMS AND KEY BUSINESS RATIOS

	SIC 2951 Aspt Pving Mix & Blok (No Breakdown) 1989 (217 Estab)		SIC 2952 Aspt Felts & Coatings (No Breakdown) 1989 (83 Estab)		SIC 2992 Lubrcting Oils & Greas (No Breakdown) 1989 (178 Estab)		SIC 3052 Rubr & Plstc Hs & Blt (No Breakdown) 1989 (97 Estab)	
	$	%	$	%	$	%	$	%
Cash	260,528	15.5	91,858	9.5	106,324	12.3	184,673	10.1
Accounts receivable	418,526	24.9	294,912	30.5	257,597	29.8	466,253	25.5
Notes receivable	15,127	0.9	967	0.1	2,593	0.3	3,657	0.2
Inventory	151,274	9.0	219,492	22.7	184,986	21.4	462,596	25.3
Other current	89,084	5.3	41,578	4.3	40,628	4.7	54,853	3.0
Total current	934,540	55.6	648,807	67.1	592,127	68.5	1,172,032	64.1
Fixed assets	413,483	24.6	174,047	18.0	141,765	16.4	402,257	22.0
Other non-current	332,804	19.8	144,072	14.9	130,527	15.1	254,154	13.9
Total assets	1,680,827	100.0	966,925	100.0	864,419	100.0	1,828,443	100.0
Accounts payable	226,912	13.5	150,840	15.6	153,002	17.7	274,266	15.0
Bank loans	—		8,702	0.9	11,237	1.3	12,799	0.7
Notes payable	75,637	4.5	31,909	3.3	36,306	4.2	74,966	4.1
Other current	210,103	12.5	132,469	13.7	95,951	11.1	235,869	12.9
Total current	512,652	30.5	323,920	33.5	296,496	34.3	597,901	32.7
Other long term	315,995	18.8	152,774	15.8	114,968	13.3	334,605	18.3
Deferred credits	5,042	0.3	7,735	0.8	864	0.1	7,314	0.4
Net worth	847,137	50.4	482,496	49.9	452,091	52.3	888,623	48.6
Total liab & net worth	1,680,827	100.0	966,925	100.0	864,419	100.0	1,828,443	100.0
Net sales	3,402,377	100.0	2,981,524	100.0	2,747,665	100.0	3,000,000	100.0
Gross profit	905,032	26.6	879,550	29.5	983,664	35.8	1,056,000	35.2
Net profit after tax	197,338	5.8	86,464	2.9	104,411	3.8	156,000	5.2
Working capital	421,888	—	324,887	—	295,631	—	574,131	—

Ratios	UQ	MED	LQ	UQ	MED	LQ	UQ	MED	LQ	UQ	MED	LQ
Solvency												
Quick ratio (times)	2.6	1.2	0.8	2.0	1.2	0.8	2.0	1.3	0.8	1.8	1.1	0.7
Current ratio (times)	3.8	1.9	1.2	3.5	2.4	1.3	3.4	2.2	1.4	3.0	2.1	1.4
Curr liab to NW (%)	20.1	49.0	129.9	27.8	61.2	136.1	28.1	48.9	101.1	29.8	59.0	140.7
Curr liab to inv (%)	116.0	235.5	411.8	84.9	144.7	232.7	70.3	136.8	205.8	81.5	115.2	167.8
Total liab to NW (%)	30.7	96.1	217.9	39.4	85.7	190.2	34.7	66.9	152.6	40.8	97.1	219.3
Fixed assets to NW (%)	32.4	73.3	137.5	17.0	34.9	87.6	13.2	32.5	55.7	24.1	52.7	85.4
Efficiency												
Coll period (days)	18.9	41.5	59.4	22.7	51.8	78.2	27.4	40.5	55.9	32.3	48.2	62.4
Sales to inv (times)	74.4	31.5	13.9	14.8	9.1	6.6	20.5	12.4	7.4	11.2	7.0	5.1
Assets to sales (%)	34.0	47.3	69.3	35.4	47.9	66.7	28.9	38.2	54.1	35.5	49.9	90.5
Sales to NWC (times)	15.6	7.6	3.9	16.5	6.7	4.4	15.9	6.7	4.3	11.0	5.5	4.1
Acct pay to sales (%)	2.8	5.3	9.1	3.0	6.0	11.8	3.7	5.5	8.3	3.8	6.1	9.4
Profitability												
Return on sales (%)	8.5	4.7	1.8	7.1	2.5	0.2	5.6	2.8	0.6	10.9	4.6	2.0
Return on assets (%)	18.5	8.3	3.5	10.1	4.2	0.1	11.0	6.7	1.5	8.4	5.4	3.4
Return on NW (%)	42.7	19.0	7.6	20.3	10.9	(0.1)	20.9	13.3	3.0	22.0	12.4	6.7

Final Note

The SIC categories in this directory reflect those appearing in the 1987 edition of the *Standard Industrial Classification Manual.*

The Dun & Bradstreet Financial Data Base includes over one million U.S. companies and is the most extensive and complete source of financial information of its kind. This compilation of data should be regarded only as a source of financial information, to be used in conjunction with other sources of data, when performing financial analysis. When utilizing these figures, remember:

■ Because of the size of this data base, and in order to facilitate the many calculations and rankings, many of the very large group samples have been randomly reduced.

■ On the other hand, some of the samples from our file are very small, and, therefore, may not present a true picture of an entire line of business. In these small groups there is a chance that a few extreme variations might have an undue influence on the overall figures in a particular category.

■ The companies composing our data base are organized by principal line of business without consideration for multiple-operation functions.

■ Within the primary SIC numbers, no allowance has been made for differing accounting methods, terms of sale, or fiscal-year closing date, all of which might have had an effect on the composite data.

Therefore, Dun & Bradstreet advises users that the Industry Norms and Key Business Ratios be used as yardsticks and not as absolutes.

12. Operating margin
13. Depreciation
14. Net profit
15. Income tax rate
16. Net profit margin
17. Working capital
18. Long-term debt
19. Net worth
20. Percent earned total capital
21. Percent earned net worth
22. Percent retained to common equity
23. Percent all dividends to net profit

As indicated previously, comparison has become more difficult in recent years, as more firms have become conglomerates and branched into many lines. To counteract this problem, the Securities and Exchange Commission has implemented line-of-business reporting requirements for companies that must submit their reports to the SEC. These reports are made available to the public. SFAS No. 14 has also approved line-of-business reporting requirements that will include all firms that obtain certified audits. Such reporting requirements ease the analysis problem created by conglomerates but cannot eliminate it, because the entity must use judgment in the allocation of administrative and joint costs. If line-of-business reporting is not available, one must try to select that industry most similar to the firm in question.

If industry figures are unavailable, or if comparison with a competitor is desired, another firm's statements may be analyzed for comparative purposes. Remember, however, that the other firm is not necessarily good or bad, nor does it represent a norm or standard.

As mentioned previously, alternative accounting methods are acceptable in many situations. Since identical companies may use different valuation or expense methods, one must read statements and footnotes carefully to determine the comparability of statements.

Ideally, the use of all types of comparison would be best. Using trend analysis, industry averages, and comparisons with a major competitor gives support to findings and provides a concrete basis for problem solving.

In analyzing ratios, negative profit figures will sometimes be encountered. *Analysis of ratios that have negative numerators or denominators is meaningless, and the negative sign of the ratio should simply be noted.*

Caution in Using Industry Averages

Financial statement analysis is an art; it requires judgment decisions on the part of the analyst. Caution must be taken so as not to place complete confidence in ratios computed or comparisons made. A number of situations require the analyst to use care.

Remember that ratios are simply fractions with a numerator (top) and a denominator (bottom). There are as many for financial analysis as there are pairs of figures. There is no set group, nor is a particular analysis always computed using the same figures. Even the industry ratio formulas vary from source to source. Adequate detailed disclosure of how the industry ratios are computed is often lacking. Major comparability problems can result from analyzing a firm according to the recommendations of a book and then making comparisons to industry ratios that may have been computed differently.

One problem is the use of different accounting methods. Since identical firms may use different valuation or revenue recognition methods, one must read statements and footnotes carefully to determine the degree of comparability between statements. For example, if one firm uses FIFO and another uses LIFO inventory, their inventory and cost of sales figures will be so different that comparisons of ratios that utilize these figures will be useless in an absolute sense. Trend analysis for each firm, however, will be meaningful. In preparation of industry averages, these firms are all grouped together.

Dissimilar year ends can also produce diverse results. Consider the difference in the inventory of two toy stores if one year end is November 30 and the other is December 31. The ratios of firms with differing year ends are all grouped together in industry averages.

Firms with differing financial policies might be included in the same industry average. Capital-intensive firms are grouped with labor-intensive companies. Firms utilizing large amounts of debt may be included in the same average as firms that prefer to avoid the risk of debt.

Some industry averages come from small samples that may not be representative of the industry. An extreme statement, such as one containing a large loss, can also distort industry data.

Ratios may have alternative forms of computation. In comparing from one year to the next, one firm to another, or a company to its industry, it is vital to meaningful analysis that the ratios be computed using the same formula. For example, Robert Morris computes income ratios before tax; Dun and Bradstreet profit figures are after tax. Ideally, the analyst should compute the enterprise ratios on the same basis as is used for industry comparisons, but this is often not possible.

Finally, ratios are not absolute norms. They are general guidelines, to be combined with other methods in formulating an evaluation of the financial condition of a firm.

LIBRARY SOURCES

The typical business library has many sources of information relating to a particular company, industry, and product. Some of these sources are described here to aid you in your search for information about a company, its industry, and its products.

Standard Industrial Classification Manual (SIC)

The standard industrial classification was developed for use in the classification of establishments by type of activity in which they are engaged. Determining a company's SIC is a good starting point in your research about a company, industry, or product. Many library sources use the SIC number as a method of classification; so knowing a company's SIC will be necessary in order to use these sources.

Standard & Poor's Report

The Standard & Poor's Reports cover companies on the New York Stock Exchange, American Stock Exchange, over-the-counter companies, and regional exchanges. They are arranged alphabetically by stock exchange and contain a brief narrative analysis of companies regularly traded, with key financial data provided. Company information is updated four times per year, on a rotating basis.

Standard & Poor's Register of Corporations, Directors, and Executives

This annual source is arranged in three volumes. Volume 1 contains corporate listings. This is an alphabetical list of approximately 55,000 corporations, including such data as zip codes, telephone numbers, and functions of officers, directors, and other principals.

Volume 2 contains an alphabetical list of individuals serving as officers, directors, trustees, partners, and so on. Such data as principal business affiliations, business addresses, and residence addresses are provided.

Volume 3 contains seven sections, as follows:

- *Section 1* explains the constructions and use of the SIC code numbers and lists these numbers by major groups and by alphabetical and numerical divisions of major groups.
- *Section 2* lists corporations under the four-digit standard industrial classification codes, which are arranged in numerical order.
- *Section 3* lists companies geographically, by states and by major cities.
- *Section 4* lists and cross-references subsidiaries, divisions, and affiliates in alphabetical sequence and links them to their ultimate parent company, listed in Volume 1.
- *Section 5* lists deaths of which the publishers have been notified in the past year.
- *Section 6* lists individuals whose names appear in the register for the first time.
- *Section 7* lists the companies appearing in the register for the first time.

Standard & Poor's Analyst's Handbook

This source contains selected income account and balance sheet items and related ratios as applied to the Standard & Poor's industry group stock price indexes. It is possible to compare the progress of a given company with a composite of its industry groups. Brief monthly updates for selected industries supplement the annual editions of the handbook.

Standard & Poor's Corporation Records

This source provides background information and detailed financial statistics on U.S. corporations. For some corporations, the coverage is extensive. Historical information is arranged in a multi-value section, separate from the "Daily News" section. The contents and the index are dynamic, with updates throughout the year.

America's Corporate Families:™
The Billion Dollar Directory®

The directory listings include 9,000 parent companies that have $500,000 or more of net worth, at least one subsidiary, and at least two principal business locations. Corporate family listings are alphabetical, geographical, and by product (SIC) classification. A cross-reference index of divisions, subsidiaries, and ultimate parent companies is also provided. This annual directory provides such data as lines of business for parent and subsidiary companies and telephone numbers of parent and subsidiary companies.

Million Dollar Directory®

This directory provides information on more than 160,000 U.S. companies that have a net worth of over $500,000. Company listings are shown alphabetically, geographically, and by SIC classification. Data include lines of business, accounting firm, legal counsel, stock ticker symbol, and names of officers.

Directory of Corporate Affiliations

This directory gives an in-depth view of companies and their divisions, subsidiaries, and affiliates. It contains an alphabetical index, a geographical index, and SIC classifications. The parent company listing consists of address, telephone number, ticker symbol, stock exchange(s), approximate sales, number of employees, type of business, and top corporate officers.

Thomas Register of American Manufacturers
and Thomas Register

This is a comprehensive "yellow pages" of products and services, as follows:

- *Red section*—Products and services listed alphabetically.
- *Yellow section*—Company profiles with addresses, zip codes, telephone numbers, branch officials, asset ratings, and company officials.
- *Blue section*—Catalogs of companies, cross-referenced to the red volumes.

Moody's Investors Services

Moody's manuals examine 22,000 corporations, with detailed summary coverage of the history, principal products and services, and detailed financial tables. They are color-coded and arranged in major industry/service groups: Bank and finance, Industrial, OTC industrial, OTC unlisted, International, Municipal government, Public utility, and Transportation.

Also available from Moody's are the following:

- *Moody's Bond Record*
- *Moody's Bond Survey*
- *Moody's Dividend Record*
- *Moody's Handbook of Common Stock*

Securities Owner's Stock Guide

This is a monthly guide, published by Standard & Poor's, to over 5,300 common and preferred stocks. It contains trading activity, price range, dividends, and so on for companies traded on the New York Stock Exchange (NYSE), American Stock Exchange (AMEX), over the counter (OTC), and regional exchanges. The information is displayed with numerous abbreviations and footnotes, in order to fit concisely into a single line, for each publicly traded security.

Wall Street Transcript

The *Wall Street Transcript* is a newspaper providing access to corporate management presentations to financial analysts and brokerage house assessment reports of corporations and industries. Each issue contains a cumulative index for the current quarter. Each issue also has a reference to the cumulative index for a relatively long period of time, such as for the prior year.

Predicasts F & S Index

This family of indexes was previously known as the "Funk & Scott Index of Corporations and Industries." It includes:

- Predicasts F & S Index—United States
- Predicasts F & S Index—Europe
- Predicasts F & S Index—International

This is a comprehensive family of index to articles on corporations and industries from 1965 to the present. The listing includes business periodicals, newspapers, government documents, and investment services reports. The material is arranged by company and industry by SIC code. It is issued monthly.

Reference Book of Corporate Managements

The four volumes contain profile information on over 200,000 principal corporate officers in over 12,000 companies. The information includes the year of birth, education, military service, present business position, and previous positions. Names and titles of other officers, as well as names of directors who are not officers, are also provided.

Compact Disclosure

This is a database of textual and financial information on over 13,000 public companies. It is accessed by a menu-driven screen. The information is taken from annual and periodic reports filed by each company with the Securities and Exchange Commission. A company can be accessed by typing the company name. A full printout for a company is approximately fourteen pages. It includes many items, including the major financial statements (annual and quarterly), twenty-nine financial ratios for the prior three years, institutional holdings, ownership by insiders, president's letter, and financial footnotes.

In addition to company name or ticker symbol, the system can be searched by type of business (S.I.C.), by geographic area (state, city, zip code or telephone area code), by stock price, by financial ratios, and much more.

RELATIVE SIZE OF FIRM

Comparisons of firms of different sizes may be more difficult than comparison of firms of equal size. For example, larger firms often have access to wider and more sophisticated capital markets, can buy in large quantities, and service wider markets. Ratios and common size analysis help to eliminate some of the problems related to the use of absolute numbers, thus alleviating certain size difficulties.

It is nonetheless important to be aware of the different sizes of firms under comparison. These differences can be seen by looking at relative sales, assets, or profit sizes. Another meaningful figure is percent of market. This is often available in investment services such as Value Line, a securities analysis and rating service.

FINANCIAL STATEMENT VARIATIONS BY TYPE OF INDUSTRY

The components of financial statements vary by type of industry. Exhibits 4-7, 4-8, and 4-9 illustrate, respectively, a merchandising firm (Arbor Drugs, Inc.), a service firm (Kelly Services, Inc.), and a manufacturing firm (Union Carbide Corporation).

EXHIBIT   4 - 7

ARBOR DRUGS, INC. AND SUBSIDIARIES
Financial Statements—Merchandising Firm
Consolidated Balance Sheets and Statements of Income

CONSOLIDATED BALANCE SHEETS

ARBOR DRUGS, INC.
AND SUBSIDIARIES

July 31,	1989	1988
(Dollars in thousands)		
ASSETS		
Current assets:		
Cash and cash equivalents	$ 9,977	$ 9,630
Short-term investments	13,000	—
Accounts receivable	7,011	6,336
Inventory	39,845	36,214
Prepaid expenses	1,641	1,173
Total current assets	71,474	53,353
Property and equipment:		
Land and land improvements	1,995	1,979
Building	5,307	5,358
Furniture, fixtures and equipment	22,755	19,139
Leasehold improvements	16,077	14,341
Less accumulated depreciation	(12,613)	(9,384)
	33,521	31,433
Other assets:		
Intangible assets	13,039	13,041
Land held for future development	855	211
Other	24	565
	13,918	13,817
	$118,913	$98,603
LIABILITIES		
Current liabilities:		
Notes payable, current portion	$ 853	$ 144
Accounts payable	26,562	17,507
Accrued expenses	2,441	1,384
Accrued compensation and benefits	2,465	1,609
Income tax payable	483	259
Total current liabilities	32,804	20,903
Notes payable, net of current portion	29,966	30,619
Deferred income tax	3,079	2,229
Minority interest in subsidiary	590	575
	33,635	33,423
SHAREHOLDERS' EQUITY		
Preferred stock: $.01 par value; 2,000,000 shares authorized; none issued	—	—
Common stock: $.01 par value; 20,000,000 shares authorized; 9,520,937 and 6,342,353 issued and outstanding, respectively	95	63
Additional paid-in capital	17,585	17,573
Retained earnings	34,794	26,641
	52,474	44,277
	$118,913	$98,603

ARBOR DRUGS, INC.
AND SUBSIDIARIES

CONSOLIDATED STATEMENTS OF INCOME

Fiscal Years Ended July 31,	1989	1988	1987
(Dollars in thousands, except per share data)			
Net sales	$300,198	$246,514	$215,291
Costs and expenses:			
Cost of sales	214,365	175,829	153,352
Selling, general and administrative	69,936	58,593	51,479
Income from operations	15,897	12,092	10,460
Interest expense	(3,119)	(2,639)	(1,121)
Interest and dividend income	1,411	661	22
Other income (expense)	(193)	42	77
Income before income tax	13,996	10,156	9,438
Provision for income tax	4,828	3,498	4,288
Net income	$ 9,168	$ 6,658	$ 5,150
Weighted average number of common shares outstanding (in thousands)	9,515	9,514	9,514
Net income per common share	$.96	$.70	$.54

KELLY SERVICES, INC. AND SUBSIDIARIES
Financial Statements—Service Firm
Consolidated Balance Sheets and Consolidated Statements of Earnings

Consolidated Balance Sheets

(in thousands)	1989	1988
Assets		
Current assets:		
Cash and cash equivalents	$ 67,420	$ 56,053
Short-term investments	121,867	91,193
Accounts receivable, less allowances of $2,780 and $2,375, respectively	154,403	135,526
Prepaid expenses and other current assets	10,248	9,397
Total current assets	353,938	292,169
Property and Equipment:		
Land and buildings	12,996	11,802
Equipment, furniture and leasehold improvements	42,502	40,951
Less—accumulated depreciation	(24,010)	(24,509)
	31,488	28,244
Land for future expansion	2,512	2,512
	34,000	30,756
Other assets	6,345	3,476
	$394,283	$326,401

E X H I B I T   4 - 8   (continued)

Consolidated Balance Sheets

(in thousands)	1989	1988
Liabilities and Stockholders' Equity		
Current liabilities:		
Accounts payable	$ 17,369	$ 15,193
Payroll and related taxes	41,725	37,827
Insurance	39,805	33,146
Income and other taxes	11,673	10,320
Total current liabilities	110,572	96,486
Stockholders' equity:		
Capital stock, $1 par value—		
Class A common stock, issued 29,174 shares in		
1989 and 22,729 in 1988	29,174	22,729
Class B common stock, issued 2,919 shares in 1989		
and 3,602 in 1988	2,919	3,602
Paid-in capital	575	690
Earnings invested in the business	257,054	226,381
	289,722	253,402
Less—Treasury stock, at cost—		
Class A common stock, 2,037 shares in 1989 and		
1,663 in 1988	(6,011)	(5,425)
Class B common stock, 655 shares in 1988		(18,062)
	(6,011)	(23,487)
Total stockholders' equity	283,711	229,915
	$394,283	$326,401

Consolidated Statements of Earnings

(in thousands, except per share items)	Fiscal Years		
	1989	1988	1987
Sale of services	$1,377,453	$1,269,427	$1,161,438
Cost of services	1,017,268	944,313	861,913
Gross profit	360,185	325,114	299,525
Selling, general and administrative expenses	247,264	225,761	207,589
Earnings before income taxes	112,921	99,353	91,936
Income taxes:			
Federal	33,700	31,100	33,490
State and other	8,420	7,945	7,985
	42,120	39,045	41,475
Net earnings	70,801	60,308	50,461
Earnings per share	2.36	2.01	1.68

EXHIBIT 4-9

UNION CARBIDE CORPORATION AND SUBSIDIARIES
Financial Statements—Manufacturing Firm
Consolidated Balance Sheet and Statement of Income

Consolidated Balance Sheet

Millions of dollars at December 31,	1989	1988
Assets		
Cash and cash equivalents	$ 142	$ 146
Notes and accounts receivable	1,474	1,413
Inventories		
Raw materials and supplies	262	275
Work in process	207	191
Finished goods	463	566
	932	1,032
Prepaid expenses	239	292
Total current assets	2,787	2,883
Property, plant and equipment	9,530	9,009
Less: Accumulated depreciation	4,946	4,593
Net fixed assets	4,584	4,416
Companies carried at equity	727	680
Other investments and advances	135	139
Total investments and advances	862	819
Other assets	313	323
Total assets	$8,546	$8,441
Liabilities and stockholders' equity		
Accounts payable	$ 689	$ 756
Short-term debt	445	270
Payments due within one year on long-term debt	210	192
Accrued income and other taxes	146	193
Other accrued liabilities	838	1,044
Total current liabilities	2,328	2,455
Long-term debt	2,080	2,295
Other long-term obligations	342	355
Deferred credits	807	915
Minority stockholders' equity in consolidated subsidiaries	606	585
UCC stockholders' equity		
Common stock		
Authorized—500,000,000, shares		
Issued—141,577,588 shares (214,409,782 shares in 1988)	142	214

E X H I B I T 4 - 9 (continued)

Consolidated Balance Sheet

Millions of dollars at December 31,	1989	1988
Additional paid-in capital	$ 38	$1,322
Equity adjustment from foreign currency translation	(90)	(106)
Retained earnings	2,293	2,605
	2,383	4,035
Less: Treasury stock, at cost—none in 1989 (76,808,221 shares in 1988)	—	2,199
Total UCC stockholders' equity	2,383	1,836
Total liabilities and stockholders' equity	$8,546	$8,441

Consolidated Statement of Income

Millions of dollars (except per share figures), year ended December 31,	1989	1988*	1987*
Net sales	$8,744	$8,324	$6,914
Cost of sales, exclusive of depreciation shown separately below	5,875	5,480	4,788
Research and development	181	159	159
Selling, administrative and other expenses	924	807	764
Depreciation	498	473	463
Interest on long-term and short-term debt	304	300	311
Other expenses—net	84	1	50
Income before provision for income taxes	878	1,104	379
Provision for income taxes	284	415	121
Income of consolidated companies	594	689	258
Less: Minority stockholders' share of income	59	64	40
Plus: UCC share of income of corporate ventures carried at equity	38	37	14
Net income	$ 573	$ 662	$ 232
Earnings per share			
Primary	$ 4.07	$ 4.88	$ 1.76
Fully diluted	$ 3.92	$ 4.66	$ 1.75
Dividends declared per share	$ 1.00	$ 1.15	$ 1.50

*Certain amounts have been reclassified to conform to the 1989 presentation.

Merchandising (retail-wholesale) firms sell a product purchased from another firm. Therefore, a principal asset is inventory, which consists basically of finished goods. For some merchandising firms, a large amount of sales may be for cash; in this case, the receivable balance will be relatively low. Other merchandising firms may have a large amount of sales charged but also accept credit cards such as Visa, so they also have a relatively low balance in receivables. Some other merchandising firms accept credit sales and carry the account receivable and thus have a relatively large amount in receivables. Because of the competitive nature of the industry, profit ratios on the income statement are often quite low, with cost of sales and operating expenses constituting a large portion of expenses. Refer to the balance sheet and income statement of Arbor Drugs in Exhibit 4-7.

A service firm generates its revenue from the service provided. Because service cannot usually be stored, inventory is low or nonexistent. In people-intensive services, such as consulting, investment in property and equipment may also be relatively low compared with that of manufacturing firms. Refer to the balance sheet and income statement of Kelly Services, Inc. in Exhibit 4-8.

A manufacturing firm usually has large inventories composed of raw materials, work in process, and finished goods, as well as a material investment in property, plant, and equipment. Cost of goods sold often represents the major expense. Refer to the Union Carbide Corporation statements in Exhibit 4-9.

DESCRIPTIVE INFORMATION

The descriptive information found in an annual report, in trade periodicals, and in industry reviews is helpful in understanding the financial position of a firm. Descriptive material might discuss the role of research and development in producing future sales, present data on capital expansion and the goals related thereto, discuss aspects of employee relations such as minority hiring or union negotiations, or help explain the dividend policy of the firm.

THE USERS OF FINANCIAL STATEMENTS

The financial statements just discussed are prepared for a group of diversified users. Each user of financial data has his or her own objectives in statement analysis.

Management, among the obvious users of financial data, must analyze the data from the point of view of both investors and creditors. Management must be concerned about the current position of the entity and its ability to meet its obligations, as well as the future earning prospects of the firm.

Management is interested in the financial structure of the entity in order to determine a proper mix of short-term debt, long-term debt, and equity from owners. Also of interest is the asset structure of the entity—that is, the combination of cash, inventory, receivables, investments, and fixed assets.

Management must guide the entity toward sound short-term and long-term financial policies and also earn a profit. These competing objectives must be satisfied at the same time. For example, liquidity and profitability are competitive, since the assets that are most highly liquid (cash and marketable securities) are usually the least profitable. It does the entity little good to be guided toward a maximum profitability goal if resources are not made available to meet current obligations. The entity would soon find itself in bankruptcy as creditors cut off lines of credit and demand payment. Similarly, management must utilize resources properly to obtain a reasonable return.

The investing public is another category of users of financial statements interested in specific types of analysis. Investors are concerned with the financial position of the entity and its ability to earn future profits. An analysis of past trends and the current position of the entity helps the investor project the future prospects of the entity.

Credit grantors have an interest in the financial statements of the entity. Pure credit grantors obtain a limited return from extending credit to the entity: a fixed rate of interest (as in the case of banks) or the profit on the merchandise or services provided (as in the case of suppliers). Since these rewards are limited and there is the possibility that the principal will not be repaid, credit grantors tend to be conservative in extending credit.

The same principle is true for suppliers that extend credit. If merchandise with a 20% markup is sold on credit, it takes five successful sales of the same amount to make up for one sale not collected. In addition, the creditor has the cost of the funds to consider when extending credit. Extending credit really amounts to financing the entity.

There is a difference between the objectives of short-term grantors of credit and those of long-term grantors. The short-term grantor of credit can look primarily to current resources that appear on the financial statements in order to determine if credit should be extended. Long-term grantors of credit must usually look to the future prospects of earnings in order to be repaid. For example, if bonds are issued that are to be repaid in thirty years, the current resources of the entity will not be an indication of the entity's ability to meet this obligation successfully. The repayment for this obligation will need to come from future earnings. Thus, the objectives of financial statement analysis by credit grantors vary based on such factors as the term of the credit and the purpose. Profitability of the entity may not be a major consideration, as long as the resources for repayment can be projected.

The financial structure of the entity is of interest to creditors, because the amount of equity capital in relation to debt is an indication of the risk that the owners bear in relation to the creditors. The equity capital provides creditors with a cushion against loss. When this equity cushion is small, creditors are bearing the risk of the entity.

There are many other parties that have an interest in analyzing financial statements. One of these is the unions that represent employees. Unions are interested in the ability of the entity to grant wage increases and fringe benefits, such as pension plans. The government also has an interest in analyzing financial statements for tax and antitrust purposes.

SUMMARY

Financial statement analysis consists of the quantitative and qualitative aspects of measuring the relative financial position among firms and among industries. Analysis can be done in different ways, depending on the type of firm or industry and the specific needs of the user.

The chapter introduced ratio and common size analyses; these techniques will be utilized throughout the book. The need to make comparisons in financial statement analysis was stressed. Various types of comparisons were discussed, and industry average sources were illustrated.

Financial statements vary by size of firm and among industries. These differences were presented through explanation and illustration.

These basics of analysis will be extensively illustrated. Chapter 5 presents an actual set of financial statements for Cooper Tire & Rubber Company. Financial statement analysis is applied to the firm in Chapters 6 through 11.

QUESTIONS

Q 4-1 What is a ratio? How do ratios help to alleviate the problems of size differences among firms?

Q 4-2 State what each of the following categories of ratios attempts to measure: (a) liquidity; (b) long-term borrowing capacity; (c) profitability. Name a group of users who might be interested in each category.

Q 4-3 Brown Company earned 5.5% on sales in 1992. What further information would be needed to evaluate this result?

Q 4-4 Differentiate between absolute and percentage changes. Which is generally a better measure of change, and why?

Q 4-5 Differentiate between horizontal and vertical analyses. Using sales as a component for each type, give an example that explains the difference.

Q 4-6 What is trend analysis? Can it be used for ratios? For absolute figures?

Q 4-7 Suppose you are comparing two firms within an industry. One is large; the other is small. Will relative or absolute numbers be of more value in each case? What kinds of statistics can help evaluate relative size?

Q 4-8 Are managers the only users of financial statements? Discuss.

Q 4-9   Briefly describe how each of these groups might use financial statements: managers, investors, and creditors.

Q 4-10   Refer to Exhibits 4-7, 4-8, and 4-9 to answer the following questions.
   a. For each of the firms illustrated, what is the single largest asset category? Does this seem typical of this type of firm?
   b. Which of the three firms has the largest amount in current assets in relation to the amount in current liabilities? Does this seem logical? Explain.

Q 4-11   Differentiate between the types of inventory typically held by a retailing and a manufacturing firm.

Q 4-12   Sometimes manufacturing firms have only raw materials and finished goods listed on their balance sheets. This is true of Avon Products, a manufacturer of cosmetics, and it might be true of food canners also. Explain the absence of work in process.

Q 4-13   Using the sample industry ratios from *Robert Morris Associates Annual Statement Studies* (Exhibit 4-3), answer the following:
   a. Describe the common size statements included in Exhibit 4-3.
   b. Describe some possible uses of these common size statements by a firm in the same industry.
   c. Speculate on why the current data are broken down by size of firm.
   d. The sales/total assets ratio for all firms for the current year has three numbers (2.8, 2.1, 1.6). Explain these three numbers.
   e. For the following ratios in Exhibit 4-3, indicate if the ratio is expressed in percent, times, or days:
      1. current
      2. fixed/worth
      3. sales/receivables
      4. sales/total assets

Q 4-14   Using Standard and Poor's Industry Survey for Aerospace and Air Transport (Exhibit 4-4) and the text discussion of Standard and Poor's Industry Surveys, answer the following:
   a. For Airborne Freight Corp. in the period 1984–1988, comment on the trend in the following:
      1. dividend payout ratio (%)
      2. current ratio (%)
      3. debt/capital(%)
   b. Which firm had the highest current ratio in 1988?
   c. Which firm had the highest dividend payout ratio in 1988?
   d. Which firm had the highest debt/capital ratio in 1988?

Q 4-15   Answer the following concerning *The Almanac of Business and Industrial Financial Ratios:*
   a. This service presents twenty-four statistics for how many size categories of firms?
   b. Indicate the industries covered by this service.

Q 4-16   Using the *Department of Commerce Quarterly Financial Report* (Exhibit 4-2) and the discussion of it in the text, answer the following:
   a. Could we determine the percentage of total income after income taxes that a particular firm had in relation to the total industry? Explain.

b. Could we determine the percentage of total assets that a particular firm had in relation to the total industry? Explain.

c. What statements are presented in common size format? Are they in vertical or horizontal format?

d. For the first quarter of 1989, a firm in the same industry as illustrated in Exhibit 4-2 has a 5.0% annual rate of profit on total assets after taxes. How does this compare with the industry?

Q 4-17 What is the SIC? How can it aid in the search of a company, industry, or product?

Q 4-18 You want to know if there have been any reported deaths of officers of a company you are researching. What library source will aid you in your search?

Q 4-19 You want to compare the progress of a given company with a composite of that company's industry group for selected income statement and balance sheet items. Which library source will aid you?

Q 4-20 You are considering buying the stock of a large publicly traded company. You need an opinion of the timeliness of the industry and the company. Which publication could you use?

Q 4-21 You want to know the trading activity (volume of stock sold) for a company. Which service provides this information?

Q 4-22 You need to research articles on a company that you are analyzing. Which source will aid you?

Q 4-23 You read in your local newspaper that an executive of a company that you are interested in is giving a presentation to financial analysts in New York. How could you learn the content of the presentation without getting in touch with the company?

Q 4-24 You would like to determine the principal business affiliations of the president of a company you are analyzing. Which reference service may have this information?

Q 4-25 Indicate some sources that contain an appraisal of the outlook for particular industries.

Q 4-26 You want to determine if there is a fairly recent brokerage house assessment report on a company that you are analyzing. Which reference may aid you?

Q 4-27 You want profile information on the president of a company. Which reference book should be consulted?

| *PROBLEMS*

P 4-1 The Arbor Drugs balance sheet from its 1989 annual report is presented in Exhibit 4-7.

Required
a. Using the balance sheet, prepare a vertical common size analysis for 1989 and 1988. Use total assets as a base.
b. Using the balance sheet, prepare a horizontal common size analysis for 1989 and 1988. Use 1988 as the base.
c. Comment on significant trends that appear in (a) and (b).

P 4-2   The Arbor Drugs income statement from its 1989 annual report is presented in Exhibit 4-7.

Required   a. Using the income statement, prepare a vertical common size analysis for 1989, 1988, and 1987. Use net sales as a base.
                 b. Using the income statement, prepare a horizontal common size analysis for 1989, 1988, and 1987. Use 1984 as the base.
                 c. Comment on significant trends that appear in (a) and (b).

P 4-3   The Kelly Services balance sheet from its 1989 annual report is presented in Exhibit 4-8.

Required   a. Using the balance sheet, prepare a vertical common size analysis for 1989 and 1988. Use total assets as a base.
                 b. Using the balance sheet, prepare a horizontal common size analysis for 1989 and 1988. Use 1988 as the base.
                 c. Comment on significant trends that appear in (a) and (b).

P 4-4   The Kelly Services income statement from its 1989 annual report is presented in Exhibit 4-8.

Required   a. Using the income statement, prepare a vertical common size analysis for 1989, 1988, and 1987. Use net sales as a base.
                 b. Using the income statement, prepare a horizontal common size analysis for 1989, 1988, and 1987. Use 1987 as the base.
                 c. Comment on significant trends that appear in (a) and (b).

CHAPTER 5

AN ILLUSTRATION OF STATEMENT ANALYSIS: PART I—COOPER TIRE & RUBBER COMPANY

CHAPTER TOPICS

Cooper Tire & Rubber Company

Introduction

Industry

Operations

1989 Financial Statements

Financial statement analysis is an applied tool; one must be able to apply as well as understand it. Ratio and trend analysis must be studied for meaning. This analysis is the difficult aspect of interpreting financial statements.

In order to aid in the technique of calculations and interpretation, Cooper Tire & Rubber Company (Cooper) will be used as an example firm in Chapters 5 through 11. The statements of Cooper are presented in this chapter.[1]

An actual firm was selected to provide a real-world situation. Illustrative financial statements are often oversimplified and therefore of limited value in learning to analyze actual statements received by users. Thus, although the statements of Cooper may seem difficult because of their comprehensiveness, they provide a typical and meaningful example for financial statement analysis.

The objectives of this chapter are to present information pertaining to Cooper and the tire industry and to indicate some sources of extensive data relating to the tire industry.

COOPER TIRE & RUBBER COMPANY

Introduction

The original company from which Cooper evolved was started in 1914. On March 26, 1930, the company was incorporated as Master Tire & Rubber Company. Master Tire & Rubber Company changed its name to Cooper Tire & Rubber Company on July 20, 1946.

---

[1]All the financial statements, and parts thereof, that appear in this chapter are reproduced with permission of Cooper Tire & Rubber Company.

Fortune magazine's list of America's 500 largest industrial companies ranked Cooper 367 in sales for 1989. Cooper is ranked fifth in terms of U.S. tire manufacturing capacity.

Industry

Radial tires are the fastest-growing product segment in the industry. The trend toward radial tires has been substantial, and it is expected to continue.

Within the market for radial tires for passenger cars, all-season tread designs are filling a growing consumer demand. This applies to the light truck tire market as well. The trend toward radial tires has slowed the total demand for replacement tires, because radial tires provide up to twice the mileage as bias-belted tires.

For each industry, there are usually just a few sources of data that provide particularly extensive information. For the tire industry, sources of extensive industry data are the following:

1. *Modern Tire Dealer.* Published fourteen times a year by Bill Communications, Rubber/Automotive Division, 633 Third Ave., New York, NY 10017.
2. *Tire Industry Quarterly.* Published by Merrill Lynch, Pierce, Fenner & Smith, Inc., One Liberty Plaza, 165 Broadway, New York, NY 10080.
3. *Standard & Poor's Industry Surveys, Autos—Auto Parts;* includes *Rubber Fabricating.* Published by Standard & Poor's, Equity Research Department, 25 Broadway, New York, NY 10004.
4. *Rubber & Plastics News.* Published by Crain Communications, Inc., Executive Offices, 1725 Merriman Road, Suite 300, Akron, OH 44313.

Operations

Products and Sales

The primary business of Cooper Tire & Rubber Company is the conversion of natural and synthetic rubbers into a variety of carbon black reinforced rubber products. The Company manufactures and markets automobile and truck tires, inner tubes, vibration control products, hoses and tubing, automotive body sealing products, and specialty seating components. Its nontransportation products accounted for less than 1% of sales in 1989, 1988, and 1987.

The company's tires are sold internationally in the replacement tire market, primarily through independent dealers and distributors. This channel of marketing accounted for 67% of all replacement passenger tires sold in the United States during 1989.

Cooper also supplies original equipment manufacturers with a wide range of rubber products. Rubber parts are manufactured for automobile companies, and tires are produced for mobile home and travel trailer manufacturers.

Market research conducted by the company indicates an increasing demand for tires and industrial rubber products. Essentially, there are no economical or practical substitutes for tires or certain rubber automotive parts.

During recent years, Cooper has exported to approximately sixty countries. These include Canada and countries in Latin America, Western Europe, the Middle East, Asia, Africa, and Oceania. Net sales from international operations accounted for approximately 4% of Cooper's sales in 1989, 1988, and 1987.

During 1989, Cooper's ten largest customers accounted for approximately 52% of total sales. There were no sales of 10% or more to an individual customer in 1989, 1988, or 1987.

The company operates successfully in a competitive industry. A number of its competitors are larger than Cooper. The four largest domestic tire products are believed to account for approximately 60% of all original equipment and replacement tires in the United States. The company's shipments of automobile and truck tires in 1989 represented approximately 7.7% of all such industry shipments.

Raw Materials

The primary raw materials used by the company include synthetic and natural rubbers, polyester and nylon fabrics, steel tire cord, and carbon black, which the company acquires from multiple sources. The company's contractual relationships with its raw material suppliers are generally based on purchase order arrangements.

Research, Development, and Product Improvement

Cooper generally directs its research activities toward product development, improvements in quality, and better operating efficiency. A significant portion of basic research for the rubber industry is performed by raw material suppliers.

The company continues active development of new passenger and truck tires. Cooper conducts extensive testing of current tire lines, as well as new concepts in tire design and construction. The company continues to design and develop specialized equipment to fit its precise manufacturing and quality control requirements.

Properties

Cooper owns and leases properties in various sections of the United States for use in the ordinary course of business, including three tire manufacturing facilities, three industrial rubber products manufacturing facilities, and one inner tube manufacturing facility. Six of these facilities are owned, and one is leased by the company under long-term agreements with purchase options. Cooper leases five of its eleven regional distribution centers under long-term leases and owns its headquarters facility, which is adjacent to its Findlay, Ohio, tire manufacturing plant. Cooper also owns an inner tube manufacturing facility in Mexico.

1989 Financial Statements

The 1989 annual report of Cooper included the following sections:

1. *Financial Highlights.* A summary of selected items that would be used in analysis, especially if you are not doing your own analysis. (Not included in this chapter.)

2. *To the Stockholders.* Management comments to stockholders. (Not included in this chapter.)

3. *Operations Review.* (Some of this information has been included in this chapter under Operations.)

4. *Financial Review.* (Included in this chapter.) This review includes Management's Analysis (financial condition and results of operations). The SEC requires firms to prepare a management discussion and analysis (MD&A) as part of the annual report. The MD&A discusses issues and trends relating to the firm's liquidity, capital resources, and operating results.

5. *Eleven-Year Summary of Operations and Financial Data.* (Included in this chapter.)

6. *Directory.* (Not included in this chapter.)

The 1989 annual report of Cooper Tire & Rubber Company is partially reproduced in the pages that follow.

FINANCIAL REVIEW
INCLUDING MANAGEMENT'S ANALYSIS
AND NOTES TO FINANCIAL STATEMENTS

MANAGEMENT'S RESPONSIBILITY FOR FINANCIAL REPORTING

The management of Cooper Tire & Rubber Company is responsible for the integrity, objectivity and accuracy of the financial statements of the Company. The statements have been prepared by the Company in accordance with generally accepted accounting principles and, where appropriate, are based on management's best estimates and judgment. The financial information presented in this report is consistent with the statements.

The accounting systems established and maintained by the Company are supported by adequate internal controls augmented by written policies, internal audits and the training of qualified personnel.

The accompanying financial statements have been audited by Ernst & Young, independent auditors, whose report appears below.

The Audit Committee of the Board of Directors is composed solely of directors who are not officers or employees of the Company. The committee meets regularly with management, the Company's internal auditors and its independent auditors to discuss their evaluations of internal accounting controls and the quality of financial reporting. The independent auditors and the internal auditors have free access to the committee, without management's presence, to discuss the results of their respective audits.

REPORT OF INDEPENDENT AUDITORS

Board of Directors
Cooper Tire & Rubber Company

We have audited the accompanying consolidated balance sheets of Cooper Tire & Rubber Company at December 31, 1989 and 1988, and the related consolidated statements of income, stockholders' equity and cash flows for each of the three years in the period ended December 31, 1989. These financial statements are the responsibility of the Company's management. Our responsibility is to express an opinion on these financial statements based on our audits.

We conducted our audits in accordance with generally accepted auditing standards. Those standards require that we plan and perform the audit to obtain reasonable assurance about whether the financial statements are free of material misstatement. An audit includes examining, on a test basis, evidence supporting the amounts and disclosures in the financial statements. An audit also includes assessing the accounting princi-

ples used and significant estimates made by management, as well as evaluating the overall financial statement presentation. We believe that our audits provide a reasonable basis for our opinion.

In our opinion, the financial statements referred to above present fairly, in all material respects, the consolidated financial position of Cooper Tire & Rubber Company at December 31, 1989 and 1988, and the consolidated results of operations and cash flows for each of the three years in the period ended December 31, 1989 in conformity with generally accepted accounting principles.

Ernst & Young

Toledo, Ohio
February 12, 1990

Financial Condition

The year-end financial position of the Company reflects continued excellent operating results in 1989. Funds provided by operating activities (net income plus depreciation) were $81.6 million for the year, a $20.7 million increase over the $60.9 million in the prior year. These strong operating flows provided funds for modernization and expansion, and contributed significantly to the strong financial position at December 31, 1989.

Working capital amounted to $150.3 million at year-end 1989 compared to $143.1 million one year earlier. A current ratio of 2.5 and a quick asset ratio (total cash and receivables divided by current liabilities) of 1.8 reflect the excellent financial liquidity position of the Company. These ratios compare favorably to the 2.7 current ratio and 1.8 quick asset ratio in 1988.

Accounts receivable reached $126.4 million, up from $120.4 million at year-end 1988, reflecting higher fourth quarter sales in 1989. Generally, collection experience has been excellent and payment terms are comparable to the prior year. Customer balances are collectible and adequate provisions have been made for possible collection losses.

Total inventories at $70.7 million were up $2.8 million from $67.9 million at year-end 1988. Finished goods inventories were $2.3 million higher than one year ago while work in process inventories were down slightly. Raw material and supplies inventories increased moderately at year-end 1989.

In 1989 additions to property, plant and equipment were a record $73.2 million, a slight increase of $2.6 million from the previous record of $70.6 million in 1988. These expenditures included amounts for expansion and modernization projects begun in 1989 as well as carry over amounts from 1988 projects. Depreciation and amortization was $23.4 million in 1989, an 18 percent increase from $19.9 million in 1988, reflecting the significant capital expenditures in recent years.

Current liabilities of $98.9 million were $12.8 million higher than the $86.1 million at year-end 1988. This increase was primarily due to increases in trade payables and accrued liabilities. Long-term debt decreased $2.1 million from year-end 1988 to $65.7 million reflecting scheduled payments of debt maturities.

Common stockholders' equity increased $52.3 million during the year reaching $310.1 million at year end. Earnings retentions for 1989 (net income less dividends paid) added $51.2 million to common equity while stock issued for the exercise of employee stock options added $1.1 million. Common equity per share was $15.08 at year-end 1989, an increase of 20 percent over $12.60 per share at year-end 1988.

Long-term debt, as a percent of total capitalization, decreased to 17.5 percent at December 31, 1989 from 20.8 percent one year earlier. Total capitalization, comprised of long-term debt and common stockholders' equity, was $375.8 million at year-end 1989. This total compares favorably to $325.5 million at December 31, 1988.

Results of Operations

Sales increased 15.9 percent in 1989 to a record $866.8 million, following an increase of 12.4 percent in 1988, due to escalating customer demand for the Company's tire products.

Sales margins were slightly higher for 1989 as compared to 1988 which was slightly higher than 1987. The effects of changes in product mix, price increases and production efficiencies in 1989 and 1988 exceeded increased raw material costs. In 1987 significant increases in raw material costs were offset by production efficiencies and some modest increases in product prices.

Increases in 1989 and 1988 selling, general and administrative expenses reflected increased sales activity levels, increased advertising and general inflation.

Other income was lower in 1989 compared with 1988, and lower in 1988 than in 1987. These changes reflect differences related to the investments of cash reserves.

Effective income tax rates differed in 1989, 1988 and 1987 due to differences in the statutory Federal tax rates and tax credits. The Financial Accounting Standards Board has issued Statement of Financial Accounting Standards No. 96, ''Accounting for Income Taxes,'' which significantly modifies certain aspects of accounting for income taxes. The Company has not elected to comply with this statement in 1989 and is not required to do so until 1992. It is expected, if financial statements for prior years are not restated, that the cumulative effect of the change in accounting will increase net income.

Increases in net income during 1989 and 1988 resulted from record high sales levels, efficient production schedules and ongoing cost containment programs. Net income during 1988 also benefited from reduced Federal income taxes.

Significant Accounting Policies

Accounting policies employed by the Company are based on generally accepted accounting principles. The following summary of significant accounting policies is presented for assistance in the evaluation and interpretation of the financial statements and supplementary data. Certain amounts for prior years have been reclassified to conform to 1989 presentations.

Consolidation—The consolidated financial statements include the accounts of the Company and its subsidiaries all of which are wholly-owned. All material intercompany accounts and transactions have been eliminated.

Inventories—Substantially all inventories are valued at cost, using the last-in, first-out (LIFO) cost method, which is not in excess of market.

Property, plant and equipment—Assets are recorded at cost and depreciated or amortized using the straight-line method over their expected useful lives. For income tax purposes accelerated depreciation methods and shorter lives are used.

Warranties—Estimated costs for product warranties are charged to income at the time of sale.

Research and development—These costs are charged to expense as incurred and amounted to approximately $10,300,000, $11,200,000 and $10,300,000 in 1989, 1988 and 1987, respectively.

Statement of Cash Flows—For purposes of the Statement of Cash Flows, the Company considers all highly liquid investments with a maturity of three months or less at date of purchase to be short-term investments. The effect of changes in foreign exchange rates on cash balances was not significant.

Business

The Company is a specialist in the rubber industry manufacturing and marketing automobile and truck tires, inner tubes, vibration control products, hose and tubing, automotive body sealing products and specialty seating components.

The Company manufactures products primarily for the transportation industry. Its non-transportation products accounted for less than one percent of sales in 1989, 1988 and 1987. There were no sales of 10 percent or more to an individual customer in 1989, 1988 or 1987.

Inventories

Under the LIFO method, inventories have been reduced by approximately $52,204,000 and $49,001,000 at December 31, 1989 and 1988, respectively, from current cost which would be reported under the first-in, first-out method.

Long-term Debt

The 9% Senior Notes, due October 1, 2001, provide for semiannual interest payments on April 1 and October 1 and annual principal prepayments of $4,545,000 commencing on October 1, 1991.

The 9% Senior Notes, due February 1, 1992, provide for semiannual interest payments on February 1 and August 1 and annual principal prepayments of $700,000 on February 1 through 1991.

Other long-term debt at December 31 was as follows:

	1989	1988
Industrial Development Revenue Bonds maturing to 2014 with interest at variable rates - 6.75% at December 31, 1989	$ 4,000,000	$ 4,000,000
8⅞% mortgage note, payable $47,083 monthly including interest	3,098,801	3,386,792
Other	535,324	717,058
	$ 7,634,125	$ 8,103,850

Mortgages and bonds are secured by real and personal property with a carrying value of $12,550,000 at December 31, 1989.

The Company has a revolving credit agreement with four banks authorizing borrowings up to $85,000,000 with interest rates at prime or lower under optional rate provisions. The agreement, which permits the issuance of commercial paper, provides that on July 31, 1992 the Company may convert any outstanding borrowings under the agreement into a four-year term loan. A commitment fee ranging from $1/4$ percent to $3/8$ percent per year on the daily unused portion of the $85,000,000 is payable quarterly. There were no borrowings under the revolving credit agreement during the years ended December 31, 1989 and 1988.

The most restrictive covenants under the loan agreements require the maintenance of $65,000,000 in working capital and restrict the payment of dividends; the amount of retained earnings not restricted was $123,415,000 at December 31, 1989.

Interest paid on debt during 1989, 1988 and 1987 was $6,335,000, $5,497,000 and $8,218,000, respectively. The amount of interest capitalized was $1,902,000, $1,923,000 and $480,000 during 1989, 1988 and 1987, respectively.

The required principal payments for long-term debt, including capitalized lease obligations, during the next five years are as follows: 1990-$2,060,000; 1991-$6,702,000; 1992-$6,800,000; 1993-$6,130,000; 1994-$6,080,000. See the note on lease commitments for information on capitalized lease obligations.

Accrued Liabilities

Accrued liabilities at December 31, were as follows:

	1989	1988
Payroll	$ 19,372,055	$ 13,848,745
Other	14,899,740	14,152,956
	$ 34,271,795	$ 28,001,701

Preferred Stock

At December 31, 1989, 5,000,000 shares of preferred stock were authorized but unissued. The rights of the preferred stock will be determined upon issuance by the board of directors.

Preferred Stock Purchase Right

Each stockholder is entitled to the right to purchase 1/100th of a newly-issued share of Series A preferred stock of the Company at an exercise price of $67.50. The rights will be exercisable only if a person or group acquires beneficial ownership of 20 percent or more of the Company's outstanding common stock, or commences a tender or exchange offer which upon consummation would result in such person or group beneficially owning 30 percent or more of the Company's outstanding common stock.

If any person becomes the beneficial owner of 25 percent or more of the Company's outstanding common stock, or if a holder of 20 percent or more of the Company's common stock engages in certain self-dealing transactions or a merger transaction in which

the Company is the surviving corporation and its common stock remains outstanding, then each right not owned by such person or certain related parties will entitle its holder to purchase a number of shares of the Company's Series A preferred stock having a market value equal to twice the then current exercise price of the right. In addition, if the Company is involved in a merger or other business combination transaction with another person after which its common stock does not remain outstanding, or sells 50 percent or more of its assets or earning power to another person, each right will entitle its holder to purchase a number of shares of common stock of such other person having a market value equal to twice the then current exercise price of the right.

The Company will generally be entitled to redeem the rights at one cent per right at any time until the tenth day following public announcement that a person or group has acquired 20 percent or more of the Company's common stock.

Common Stock

There were 2,216,179 common shares reserved for the exercise of stock options and contributions to the Company's Thrift and Profit Sharing Plan at December 31, 1989.

Stock Options

The Company's 1981 and 1986 incentive stock option plans provide for granting options to key employees to purchase common shares at prices not less than market at the date of grant. The plans were amended in 1988 to allow the granting of nonqualified stock options. Nonqualified stock options are not intended to qualify for the tax treatment applicable to incentive stock options under Section 422 A(b) of the Internal Revenue Code.

The options may have terms of up to ten years becoming exercisable in whole or in consecutive installments, cumulative or otherwise. The plans also permit the granting of stock appreciation rights with the options. Stock appreciation rights enable an optionee to surrender exercisable options and receive common stock and/or cash measured by the difference between the option price and the market value of the common stock on the date of surrender.

All options issued prior to 1988, which have been granted under the plans, have a term of five years and become exercisable 25 percent annually on a cumulative basis starting one year from the date of grant. Options granted in 1988 and 1989 have a term of 10 years and become exercisable 50 percent in the second year from the date of grant and 100 percent in the third year and thereafter.

Options granted prior to 1987 include stock appreciation rights. The appreciation on each right is limited to 25 percent of the option exercise price, during each year of the option period, on a cumulative basis.

Summarized information for the plans follows:

	Number of Shares	Price Range Per Share
Outstanding at December 31, 1987	538,060	$ 6.44 - $ 17.75
Granted under 1986 plan	41,920	20.38
Exercised	(109,479)	6.44 - 17.75
Cancelled	(24,450)	6.44 - 20.38
Outstanding at December 31, 1988	446,051	$ 6.44 - $ 20.38
Granted under 1986 plan	17,500	32.25
Exercised	(109,544)	6.44 - 20.38
Cancelled	(10,250)	13.81 - 17.75
Outstanding at December 31, 1989	343,757	$ 9.13 - $ 32.25

At December 31, 1989, under the 1981 plan, options were exercisable on 3,000 shares and 22,400 shares were available for future grants. At December 31, 1988, options were exercisable on 70,000 shares and 22,400 shares were available for future grants.

Under the 1986 plan, at December 31, 1989, options were exercisable on 146,266 shares and 409,580 shares were available for future grants. At December 31, 1988, options were exercisable on 84,600 shares and 416,830 shares were available for future grants.

Earnings Per Share

Net income per share is based upon the weighted average number of shares outstanding which were 20,519,236 in 1989, 20,395,635 in 1988 and 20,314,392 in 1987. The effect of common stock equivalents is not significant for any period presented.

Federal Income Taxes

The effective income tax rate differs from the statutory Federal tax rate as follows:

	1989	1988	1987
Statutory Federal tax rate	34.0%	34.0%	40.0%
State and local income taxes, net of Federal income tax benefit	2.9	3.0	2.7
Other	0.2	(0.3)	(0.5)
Effective income tax rate	37.1%	36.7%	42.2%

Statement of Financial Accounting Standards No. 96, "Accounting for Income Taxes," significantly modified certain aspects of accounting for income taxes. The new standard requires, among other things, that deferred income taxes be provided under the liability method, whereas the current standard follows the deferred method. The new standard is effective for fiscal years beginning after December 15, 1991. The Company has not elected to comply with this statement in 1989 and is not required to do so until 1992. Restatement of financial statements for years prior to adoption is permitted, but is not required. Based on current income tax rates, and assuming financial statements for prior years are not restated, it is expected that the cumulative effect of the change in accounting would increase net income.

Payments for income taxes in 1989, 1988 and 1987 were $29,497,000, $20,918,000 and $20,531,000, respectively.

Items giving rise to deferred Federal income taxes were as follows:

	1989	1988	1987
Excess of tax over book depreciation .	$ 4,625,000	$ 4,065,000	$ 3,644,000
Installment sales	(882,000)	(1,510,000)	(81,000)
Other	(946,000)	(1,081,000)	(1,543,000)
	$ 2,797,000	$ 1,474,000	$ 2,020,000

Pensions

The Company has defined benefit plans covering substantially all employees. The salary plan provides pension benefits based on an employee's years of service and average earnings for the five highest calendar years during the ten years immediately preceding retirement. The hourly plans provide benefits of stated amounts for each year of service. The Company's general funding policy is to contribute amounts deductible for Federal income tax purposes.

In 1989 the Company adopted the minimum liability provisions of Statement of Financial Accounting Standards No. 87, ''Employers' Accounting for Pensions.'' The minimum liability and a corresponding intangible asset of $7,850,000 have been recorded for those pension plans for which accumulated benefits exceed the related plan assets. Pension expense increased in 1989 due to increased benefits. Pension expense for 1989, 1988 and 1987 included the following components:

	1989	1988	1987
Service cost — benefits earned during period . . .	$ 4,534,000	$ 3,919,000	$3,838,000
Interest cost on projected benefit obligation	10,086,000	8,829,000	7,931,000
Actual return on assets	(20,023,000)	(13,505,000)	674,000
Net amortization and deferral	13,025,000	7,469,000	(5,950,000)
Net periodic pension cost	$ 7,622,000	$ 6,712,000	$6,493,000

The plans' assets consist of cash, cash equivalents and marketable securities. The funded status of the Company's plans at December 31, 1989 and 1988 was as follows:

	December 31, 1989		December 31, 1988	
	Plans for Which		Plans for Which	
	Assets Exceed Accumulated Benefits	Accumulated Benefits Exceed Assets	Assets Exceed Accumulated Benefits	Accumulated Benefits Exceed Assets
Actuarial present value of benefit obligations:				
Vested benefit obligation	$ (70,866,000)	$ (35,394,000)	$ (53,115,000)	$ (41,277,000)
Accumulated benefit obligation	$ (72,332,000)	$ (35,776,000)	$ (54,153,000)	$ (41,793,000)
Projected benefit obligation	$ (100,968,000)	$ (37,142,000)	$ (80,400,000)	$ (42,638,000)
Plan assets at fair value	98,489,000	24,788,000	68,763,000	29,370,000
Projected benefit obligation in excess of plan assets	$ (2,479,000)	$ (12,354,000)	$ (11,637,000)	$ (13,268,000)
Unrecognized transition amount . . .	8,404,000	6,020,000	9,665,000	5,847,000
Unrecognized prior service cost . . .	1,130,000	3,369,000	129,000	3,989,000
Unrecognized net (gain) loss	(5,871,000)	(698,000)	(303,000)	413,000
Adjustment for minimum liability .	—	(7,850,000)	—	—
Pension liability recognized in the Balance Sheet	$ 1,184,000	$ (11,513,000)	$ (2,146,000)	$ (3,019,000)

The assumed rate of increase in future compensation levels and the assumed discount rate used in determining the actuarial present value of the projected benefit obligation at December 31, 1989 and 1988 were 6 percent and 8 percent, respectively; the assumed rate of return on plan assets was 10 percent.

The information presented above includes an unfunded nonqualified supplemental executive retirement plan covering certain employees whose participation in the qualified plan is limited by Section 415 of the Internal Revenue Code.

Lease Commitments

The Company leases certain manufacturing facilities, equipment and warehouse facilities under long-term leases expiring at various dates to 1997. The leases generally contain renewal or purchase options and provide that the Company shall pay for insurance, property taxes and maintenance.

Included in property, plant and equipment are the following capitalized lease amounts at December 31, 1989 and 1988:

	1989	1988
Land and land improvements	$ 1,023,933	$ 1,023,933
Buildings	14,849,359	14,849,359
Machinery and equipment	20,338,483	25,196,158
	36,211,775	41,069,450
Less accumulated amortization	29,999,711	34,344,319
	$ 6,212,064	$ 6,725,131

Rental expense for all operating leases was $6,010,000 for 1989, $5,634,000 for 1988 and $5,361,000 for 1987.

Future minimum payments for all noncancelable leases at December 31, 1989 are summarized below:

	Capital Leases	Operating Leases
1990	$ 1,359,000	$ 2,869,000
1991	1,348,000	2,100,000
1992	1,347,000	1,176,000
1993	1,338,000	736,000
1994	1,355,000	482,000
1995 and later	2,760,000	268,000
	9,507,000	$7,631,000
Less amount representing interest	1,925,000	
Present value of minimum lease payments	$7,582,000	

SELECTED QUARTERLY DATA [Unaudited]

Quarterly data on financial performance, dividends and stock prices (in thousands of dollars except per share amounts) for 1989 and 1988 is as follows:

	Net Sales	Gross Margin	Net Income	Net Income Per Share	Dividend Per Share	Stock Price High	Low
1989							
Fourth	$ 208,288	$ 39,177	$ 17,968	$ .88	$ .090	$ 39	$ 32¼
Third	233,554	36,019	14,891	.72	.090	39	28¾
Second	229,446	36,296	15,059	.74	.090	31⅜	25
First	195,517	27,990	10,326	.50	.075	27⅝	22½
1988							
Fourth	$ 195,157	$ 31,820	$ 13,898	$ .68	$ .075	$ 27¼	$ 20½
Third	208,072	27,570	10,520	.51	.075	25¾	18⅝
Second	183,822	26,098	9,820	.48	.065	19⅜	16¾
First	160,981	20,931	6,824	.34	.065	19⅜	14⅛

The common stock of the Company (CTB) is traded on the New York Stock Exchange.

STATEMENT OF INCOME
Years ended December 31

	1989	1988	1987
Revenues:			
Net sales	$ 866,805,462	$ 748,032,206	$ 665,774,644
Other income	2,809,069	2,832,616	3,536,185
	869,614,531	750,864,822	669,310,829
Costs and expenses:			
Cost of products sold	727,323,386	641,613,558	571,897,675
Selling, general and administrative	45,293,867	39,843,514	37,846,130
Interest and debt expense	4,373,398	4,495,464	6,477,277
	776,990,651	685,952,536	616,221,082
Income before income taxes	92,623,880	64,912,286	53,089,747
Provision for income taxes:			
Current:			
Federal	27,503,000	19,386,000	18,040,000
State and local	4,080,000	2,990,000	2,350,000
Deferred—Federal	2,797,000	1,474,000	2,020,000
	34,380,000	23,850,000	22,410,000
Net income	$ 58,243,880	$ 41,062,286	$ 30,679,747
Net income per share	$ 2.84	$ 2.01	$ 1.51

BALANCE SHEET
December 31

Assets	1989	1988
Current assets:		
Cash, including short-term investments of $39,500,000 in 1989 and $30,500,000 in 1988	$ 49,586,311	$ 38,690,586
Accounts receivable, less allowance for doubtful accounts of $2,100,000 in 1989 and $1,350,000 in 1988	126,431,368	120,407,633
Inventories:		
Finished goods	43,133,543	40,790,473
Work in process	5,791,595	6,355,139
Raw materials and supplies	21,765,727	20,763,883
	70,690,865	67,909,495
Prepaid expenses	2,506,518	2,218,956
Total current assets	249,215,062	229,226,670
Investments and other assets	8,232,809	432,883
Property, plant and equipment:		
Land and land improvements	12,103,807	10,269,635
Buildings	97,809,403	88,941,688
Machinery and equipment	304,453,628	246,701,282
Molds, cores and rings	11,897,000	10,442,660
	426,263,838	356,355,265
Less accumulated depreciation and amortization	163,819,099	143,432,356
Net property, plant and equipment	262,444,739	212,922,909
	$519,892,610	$442,582,462

Liabilities and Stockholders' Equity	1989	1988
Current liabilities:		
Accounts payable	$ 58,855,787	$ 51,882,143
Income taxes	3,742,010	3,709,599
Accrued liabilities	34,271,795	28,001,701
Current portion of long-term debt	2,060,000	2,532,000
Total current liabilities	98,929,592	86,125,443
Long-term debt:		
9% senior notes payable, due 2001	50,000,000	50,000,000
9% senior notes payable, due 1992	1,400,000	2,100,000
Capitalized lease obligations	6,692,725	7,586,000
Other	7,634,125	8,103,850
Total long-term debt	65,726,850	67,789,850
Other long-term liabilities	16,204,000	6,793,000
Deferred Federal income taxes	28,968,508	24,118,000
Commitments	—	—
Stockholders' equity:		
Preferred stock, $1 par value; 5,000,000 shares authorized; none issued	—	—
Common stock, $1 par value; 70,000,000 shares authorized (30,000,000 in 1988); 20,564,837 shares outstanding (20,455,293 in 1988)	20,564,837	20,455,293
Capital in excess of par value	25,604,064	24,569,518
Retained earnings	263,894,759	212,731,358
Total stockholders' equity	310,063,660	257,756,169
	$ 519,892,610	$ 442,582,462

STATEMENT OF STOCKHOLDERS' EQUITY
Years ended December 31

	Common Stock $1 Par Value	Capital In Excess of Par Value	Retained Earnings
Balance at December 31, 1986	$ 10,143,962	$ 33,632,283	$ 151,374,510
Net income			30,679,747
Exercise of stock options	28,945	380,153	
Cash dividends—$ .23 per share			(4,673,146)
Balance at December 31, 1987	10,172,907	34,012,436	177,381,111
Net income			41,062,286
Exercise of stock options	81,335	758,133	
Two-for-one stock split	10,201,051	(10,201,051)	
Cash dividends—$ .28 per share			(5,712,039)
Balance at December 31, 1988	20,455,293	24,569,518	212,731,358
Net income			58,243,880
Exercise of stock options	109,544	1,034,546	
Cash dividends—$ .345 per share			(7,080,479)
Balance at December 31, 1989	$ 20,564,837	$ 25,604,064	$ 263,894,759

STATEMENT OF CASH FLOWS
Years ended December 31

	1989	1988	1987
Operating activities:			
Net income	$ 58,243,880	$ 41,062,286	$ 30,679,747
Adjustments to reconcile net income to net cash provided by operating activities:			
Depreciation and amortization	23,393,307	19,872,614	18,436,182
Deferred taxes	2,797,000	1,474,000	2,020,000
Increase in accounts receivable	(6,023,735)	(5,779,124)	(15,607,028)
Decrease (increase) in inventories and prepaid expenses	(3,068,932)	(6,843,493)	962,701
Increase (decrease) in accounts payable and accrued liabilities	13,243,738	(4,106,154)	22,602,888
Increase in other long-term liabilities and other	3,904,508	2,253,798	513,644
Net cash provided by operating activities	92,489,766	47,933,927	59,608,134
Investing activities:			
Additions to property, plant and equipment	(73,181,647)	(70,620,543)	(41,507,210)
Other	58,995	105,792	142,420
Net cash used in investing activities	(73,122,652)	(70,514,751)	(41,364,790)
Financing activities:			
Payments on long-term debt	(2,535,000)	(6,460,836)	(5,720,244)
Issuance of common stock	1,144,090	839,468	409,098
Dividends paid	(7,080,479)	(5,712,039)	(4,673,146)
Net cash used in financing activities	(8,471,389)	(11,333,407)	(9,984,292)
Increase (decrease) in cash and short-term investments	10,895,725	(33,914,231)	8,259,052
Cash and short-term investments at beginning of year	38,690,586	72,604,817	64,345,765
Cash and short-term investments at end of year	$ 49,586,311	$ 38,690,586	$ 72,604,817

ELEVEN-YEAR SUMMARY OF OPERATIONS AND FINANCIAL DATA

(All dollar amounts in thousands except per share figures)

	Net Sales	Gross Margin	Operating Margin	Pretax Income	Income Taxes	Net Income	Common Dividends
1989	$ 866,805	$ 139,482	$ 94,188	$ 92,624	$ 34,380	$ 58,244	$ 7,080
1988	748,032	106,419	66,575	64,912	23,850	41,062	5,712
1987	665,775	93,877	56,031	53,090	22,410	30,680	4,673
1986	577,517	81,515	46,432	43,138	20,120	23,018	4,146
1985	522,639	64,862	34,492	31,151	12,680	18,471	4,013
1984	555,388	73,030	43,447	41,978	17,400	24,578	3,799
1983	457,780	67,666	41,009	39,796	18,390	21,406	3,392
1982	430,354	63,727	38,716	34,898	15,890	19,008	2,521
1981	393,945	56,193	33,828	31,196	13,930	17,266	2,071
1980	323,953	47,714	28,014	24,545	11,720	12,825	1,543
1979	283,236	28,301	11,447	7,812	2,650	5,162	1,493

	Stockholders' Equity	Total Assets	Working Capital	Net Property, Plant & Equipment	Capital Expenditures	Depreciation & Amortization	Long-term Debt
1989	$ 310,064	$ 519,893	$ 150,285	$ 262,445	$ 73,182	$ 23,393	$ 65,727
1988	257,756	442,582	143,101	212,923	70,621	19,873	67,790
1987	221,566	413,306	154,283	162,447	41,507	18,436	70,059
1986	195,151	367,715	153,538	139,721	26,548	16,666	76,795
1985	175,711	295,161	110,300	123,380	23,660	14,955	41,910
1984	160,526	279,857	92,920	115,329	57,239	11,605	36,501
1983	139,601	243,665	111,586	69,839	18,502	9,527	33,414
1982	121,451	220,901	105,058	60,917	11,978	8,370	38,480
1981	81,806	185,523	71,787	57,475	15,166	7,067	43,461
1980	60,438	181,784	70,638	49,386	7,122	5,870	51,649
1979	48,705	149,855	59,912	48,339	5,183	5,382	51,708

	Return On Beginning Equity	Return On Beginning Assets	Current Ratio	Pretax Margin	Effective Tax Rate	Return On Sales	Long-term Debt To Capitalization
1989	22.6%	13.2%	2.5	10.7%	37.1%	6.7%	17.5%
1988	18.5	9.9	2.7	8.7	36.7	5.5	20.8
1987	15.7	8.3	2.6	8.0	42.2	4.6	24.0
1986	13.1	7.8	3.1	7.5	46.6	4.0	28.2
1985	11.5	6.6	2.8	6.0	40.7	3.5	19.3
1984	17.6	10.1	2.3	7.6	41.4	4.4	18.5
1983	17.6	9.7	2.8	8.7	46.2	4.7	19.3
1982	23.2	10.2	2.9	8.1	45.5	4.4	24.1
1981	28.5	9.5	2.3	7.9	44.7	4.4	34.7
1980	25.8	8.6	2.2	7.6	47.7	4.0	44.1
1979	10.8	3.3	2.6	2.8	33.9	1.8	48.7

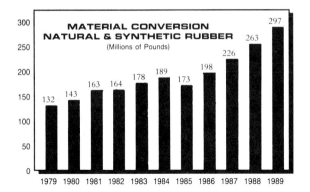

	Stock Price*		Price/Earnings
	High	Low	Average Ratio
1989	$ 39.00	$ 22.50	10.8
1988	27.25	14.13	10.3
1987	19.88	11.13	10.3
1986	14.38	8.63	10.1
1985	10.19	7.31	9.5
1984	9.50	6.31	6.4
1983	11.38	6.19	8.2
1982	9.44	3.47	5.9
1981	5.22	3.06	4.0
1980	3.47	1.20	2.8
1979	2.13	1.27	5.2

	Net Income Per Share*	Equity Per Share*	Assets Per Share*	Dividends Per Share*	Common Shares Average [OOO]*	Common Shares Year End [OOO]*	Number of Stockholders
1989	$ 2.84	$ 15.08	$ 25.28	$ .35	20,519	20,565	3,871
1988	2.01	12.60	21.64	.28	20,396	20,455	3,627
1987	1.51	10.89	20.31	.23	20,314	20,346	3,516
1986	1.14	9.62	18.12	.21	20,216	20,288	3,138
1985	.92	8.72	14.64	.20	20,064	20,156	3,526
1984	1.23	8.02	13.98	.19	19,995	20,017	3,872
1983	1.07	6.99	12.20	.17	19,952	19,976	4,028
1982	1.10	6.09	11.08	.15	17,212	19,939	3,500
1981	1.03	4.79	10.87	.13	16,697	17,072	3,845
1980	.84	4.01	12.05	.11	14,942	15,081	3,721
1979	.33	3.26	10.04	.10	14,930	14,930	4,478

	Number of Employees	Wages & Benefits	Total Taxes†	Research & Development
1989	6,041	$ 233,257	$ 53,907	$ 10,300
1988	6,031	217,062	41,743	11,200
1987	5,720	189,045	39,056	10,300
1986	5,398	165,458	34,801	8,900
1985	4,876	153,825	26,275	7,300
1984	4,805	148,139	30,845	6,700
1983	4,455	128,844	29,660	6,400
1982	4,169	118,019	25,644	5,900
1981	3,869	103,901	22,802	5,300
1980	3,885	83,030	18,285	3,900
1979	3,687	77,564	8,830	3,100

FORM 10-K

A copy of the Company's annual report to the Securities and Exchange Commission on Form 10-K, including the financial statements and schedules thereto, will be furnished after March 31, 1990, upon written request to: Secretary, Cooper Tire & Rubber Company, Findlay, Ohio 45839.

Share data reflects stock splits in 1988, 1983 and 1981.   † *Excluding Federal Excise Taxes.*

| *QUESTIONS*

Q 5-1 Cooper—Significant Accounting Policies—Research and Development.
"These costs are charged to expense as incurred and amounted to approximately $10,300,000, $11,200,000 and $10,300,000 in 1989, 1988 and 1987, respectively."
  a. Would this policy be considered conservative? Comment.
  b. Is the policy of expensing research and development a policy chosen by management?
  c. Rationalize how research and development expenditures could be viewed as a hidden asset.

Q 5-2 Cooper—Significant Accounting Policies—Inventory Valuation.
"Substantially all inventories are valued at cost, using the last-in, first-out (LIFO) cost method, which is not in excess of market."
  a. Would this policy usually be considered conservative? Comment.
  b. Would the use of LIFO usually result in a reasonable matching of current cost against revenue?
  c. What would the balance of inventory be at December 31, 1989, if Cooper had costed its 1989 inventory using FIFO?

Q 5-3 Cooper—Significant Accounting Policies—Property, Plant, and Equipment.
"Assets are recorded at cost and depreciated or amortized using the straight-line method over their expected useful lives. For income tax purposes accelerated depreciation methods and shorter lives are used."
  a. Would this policy usually be considered conservative? Comment.
  b. Would this policy result in depreciation being recognized on a slower basis for the financial statements or for the tax return? Comment.
  c. Speculate on why management might want to select a different policy for the financial statements than for the tax return.
  d. How much did tax depreciation exceed book (financial) depreciation in 1989, 1988, and 1987?

Q 5-4 Cooper—Significant Accounting Policies—Warranties.
"Estimated costs for product warranties are charged to income at the time of sale."
  a. Does this result in warranty expense being recognized in the same period that warranty costs are incurred? Explain.
  b. Explain this policy in terms of the matching concept.

Q 5-5 Comment on the materiality of Cooper's sales of nontransportation products.

Q 5-6 Comment on the concentration of sales by Cooper to an individual customer.

Q 5-7 Does Cooper have any retained earnings restricted at December 31, 1989? If so, indicate the amount and the purpose of the restriction.

Q 5-8 Comment on the materiality of export sales in 1989, 1988, and 1987.

Q 5-9 Using the statement of stockholders' equity for Cooper, comment on the significance of cash dividends in relation to net income for the three-year period ended December 31, 1989.

| *PROBLEMS*

P 5-1 The Cooper Tire & Rubber Company income statement from the 1989 annual report is included in this chapter.

Required
a. Using the income statement, prepare a vertical common size analysis for 1989, 1988, and 1987. Use net sales as the base.
b. Using the income statement, prepare a horizontal common size analysis for 1989, 1988, and 1987. Use 1987 as the base year.
c. Comment on significant trends that appear in the common size statements prepared in (a) and (b).

P 5-2 The Cooper Tire & Rubber Company balance sheet from the 1989 annual report is included in this chapter.

Required
a. Using the balance sheet, prepare a vertical common size analysis for 1989 and 1988. Use total assets as the base.
b. Using the balance sheet, prepare a horizontal common size analysis for 1989 and 1988. Use 1988 as the base year.
c. Comment on significant trends that appear in the common size statements prepared in (a) and (b).

P 5-3 An eleven-year summary of operations and financial data for Cooper Tire & Rubber Company is included in this chapter.

Required
a. Prepare a vertical common size analysis, using 1979 as the base for the following items:
   1. net sales
   2. net income
   3. common dividends
   4. stockholders' equity
b. Comment on significant trends in (a).

P 5-4 An eleven-year summary of operations and financial data for Cooper Tire & Rubber Company is included in this chapter.

Required
a. Prepare a vertical common size analysis, using 1979 as the base for the following items:
   1. number of employees
   2. wages and benefits
   3. research and development
b. Comment on significant trends in (a).

CHAPTER **6**

LIQUIDITY OF SHORT-TERM ASSETS AND THE RELATED SHORT-TERM DEBT-PAYING ABILITY

CHAPTER TOPICS

Current Assets, Current Liabilities, and the Operating Cycle
Cash
Marketable Securities
Receivables
Days' Sales in Receivables
Accounts Receivable Turnover
Accounts Receivable Turnover in Days
Credit Sales versus Cash Sales
Inventories
Inventory Cost
Days' Sales in Inventory
Merchandise Inventory Turnover
Inventory Turnover in Days

Operating Cycle Computed
Prepayments
Other Current Assets
Current Liabilities

Current Assets Compared with Current Liabilities
Working Capital
Current Ratio
Acid Test Ratio (Quick Ratio)
Cash Ratio

Other Liquidity Considerations
Sales to Working Capital (Working Capital Turnover)
Liquidity Considerations Not on the Face of the Statements

The ability of an entity to maintain its short-term debt-paying ability is important to all users of financial statements. If the entity cannot maintain a short-term debt-paying ability, naturally it will not be able to maintain a long-term debt-paying ability, nor will it be able to satisfy its stockholders. Even an entity on a very profitable course will find itself bankrupt if it fails to meet its obligations to short-term creditors.

In this chapter, procedures are suggested for analyzing short-term assets and the short-term debt-paying ability of an entity. The procedures require an understanding of current assets, current liabilities, and notes to financial statements.

This chapter also includes a detailed discussion of four very important assets: cash, marketable securities, accounts receivable, and inventory. Accounts receivable and inventory are two critical assets that often substantially influence the liquidity and profitability of a firm.

CURRENT ASSETS, CURRENT LIABILITIES, AND THE OPERATING CYCLE

Current assets are assets that (1) are in the form of cash, (2) will be realized in cash, or (3) conserve the use of cash *within the operating cycle of a business or for one year, whichever is longer*.

There are five categories of assets that are usually found in current assets: cash, marketable securities, receivables, inventories, and prepayments. The order of listing represents their order of liquidity. Other assets may also be classified in current assets, such as assets held for sale. Each of the types of assets that are classified as current assets will be examined in detail in this chapter.

The operating cycle is the time between the acquisition of inventory and the realization of cash from selling the inventory. For example, a food store purchases inventory and then sells the inventory for cash. The average length of time that the inventory remains an asset of the food store is relatively short and represents a very short operating cycle. In another example, a car manufacturer purchases materials and then uses labor and overhead to convert these materials into a finished car. The car is sold to a dealer on credit, and then the dealer pays the manufacturer. The operating cycle of the car manufacturer is much longer than that of the food store, but it is still less than a year. Only in a few businesses is the operating cycle longer than a year. For instance, if a business is involved in selling resort property, the average time period that the property is held before sale, plus the average collection period, is typically longer than a year.

Cash

Cash is a medium of exchange that a bank will accept for deposit and a creditor will accept for payment. In order to classify cash as a current asset, it must be free from any restrictions that would prevent its deposit or use to pay creditors classified as current. If restrictions on cash are for specific short-term creditors, many firms still classify this cash under current assets, but the restrictions are disclosed. Cash restricted for short-term creditors should be eliminated along with the related amount of short-term debt when determining the short-term debt-paying ability of the entity. Cash should be available to pay general short-term creditors if it is to be considered part of the firm's short-term debt-paying ability.

It has become common for banks to require a portion of any loan to remain on deposit in the bank for the duration of the loan period. These deposits are termed *compensating balances*. Compensating balances reduce the amount of cash available to the borrower to meet obligations, and they increase the effective interest rate for the borrower.

Compensating balances against short-term borrowings are separately stated in the current asset section or footnoted, whereas compensating balances for long-term borrowings are separately stated as noncurrent assets under either investments or other assets.

The cash account on the balance sheet is usually entitled *cash, cash and equivalents, cash and certificates of deposit*, or *time deposits*. The cash classification typically includes currency and unrestricted funds on deposit with a bank.

Two major problems encountered when analyzing a current asset are determining a fair valuation for the asset and determining the liquidity of the asset. Neither of these problems applies to the asset cash unless it is restricted. Thus it is usually a simple matter to decide on the amount of cash to use when determining the short-term debt-paying ability of the entity.

Marketable Securities

The entity has varying cash needs throughout the year. Because there is an inferred cost from keeping money available, management does not want to keep all of the entity's cash needs in the form of cash throughout the year. The available alternative is to put some of the cash to productive use through short-term investments, which can be converted into cash as the need arises.

To qualify as a marketable security, the investment must be readily marketable, and it must be the intent of management to convert the investment to cash within the current operating cycle or one year, whichever is longer. The key element of this test is managerial intent. At times, the analyst may detect that the same securities have been classified as marketable securities year after year. It is highly likely that these securities should be classified as long-term investments rather than marketable securities under current assets.

In terms of liquidity, it is to management's advantage to show investments under marketable securities instead of long-term investments, because this classification improves the appearance of liquidity of the firm. When it is detected that the same securities are carried as marketable securities year after year, to be conservative, it is better to reclassify these securities as investments for analysis purposes. It is likely that these securities are held for a business purpose—for example, the other company may be a major supplier or customer of the firm being analyzed. Thus, the firm being analyzed would not want to sell these securities in order to pay short-term creditors.

Investments classified as marketable securities should be temporary. Examples of investments that are found in marketable securities are treasury bills, short-term notes of corporations, government bonds, corporate bonds, preferred stock, and common stock. Preferred stock and common stock investments are referred to as *marketable equity securities*.

Determining a fair valuation and the liquidity of the asset is more of a problem with marketable securities than with cash, but these determinations are not normally major problems. The valuation of marketable securities will usually be at cost or the lower of cost or market.[1] According to SFAS No. 12, marketable equity

---

[1] The market value method is used by a few industries: mutual funds, insurance companies, and securities brokers.

securities should be carried at the lower of the aggregate cost or aggregate market value. If the marketable equity securities are material, a footnote usually discloses the cost and market value of each security. Since marketable securities are an extension of cash, the market value figure is the more realistic amount to use when determining the amount of resources that are available.

Equity securities are the ownership shares in a corporation. Examples of equity securities are common stock and preferred stock that is not redeemable by the corporation. (The phrase "not redeemable" refers to the fact that the holders of these securities are not entitled to a repayment of the securities' purchase price from the issuing corporation.)

As previously indicated, SFAS No. 12 directs that marketable equity securities should be carried at the lower of the aggregate cost or aggregate market value. This means that the total cost and the total market value of the securities are compared. The lower of these two total figures is used for statement presentation. If the aggregate market value is lower than the aggregate cost, a valuation allowance account is offset against the original cost account to achieve a lower of cost or market presentation.

The result of the lower of cost or market presentation (required by SFAS No. 12 for marketable equity securities) is that the securities are presented on the balance sheet at lower of cost or market, and the resulting unrealized loss and possibly later an unrealized loss recovery (gain) are recognized on the income statement. Management finds this to be a disadvantage, because market forces determine when these gains and losses are reported. *Generally accepted accounting principles do not usually require unrealized losses to be reported on the income statement for long-term investments; such unrealized losses are reported in the stockholders' equity section of the balance sheet.*

Thus, management may gain a liquidity appearance advantage by classifying marketable securities under current assets, but there is an income statement disadvantage because of the lack of control over reporting unrealized losses and possibly later unrealized loss recoveries (gains).

SFAS No. 12 did not address itself to marketable securities other than marketable equity securities. The other marketable securities are carried by some companies at cost; other companies carry them at the lower of cost or market. The market value is often disclosed; as previously indicated, the market value figure is the more realistic amount to use when determining the amount of resources that are available. Marketable securities, other than marketable equity securities, may actually be carried at a cost figure that is substantially above market. When these securities are carried at cost, it is up to management to write them down to market when they think that there has been a permanent impairment. Conservative analysis uses the lower of cost or market figure even if management has decided not to recognize the lower market figure. Unfortunately, for external analysis, this valuation is not always possible, because the cost and market figures may not be disclosed.

For a security to be classified as a marketable security, its liquidity must be determined. When analyzing financial statements, it must generally be assumed that securities classified as marketable securities are readily marketable. When the detail of the marketable securities account is available for review, it is important to determine whether each of the securities is readily marketable.

The presentation of marketable securities on the 1988 annual report of American Software, Inc. is presented in Exhibit 6-1. It is a thorough disclosure of the detail of the marketable securities account. Many companies do not disclose the detail of the marketable securities accounts.

Receivables

An entity usually has a number of claims to future inflows of cash. These claims are usually classified as accounts receivable and notes receivable on the financial statements. The primary claim that most entities have comes from the selling of merchandise or services on account to customers, with the customer promising to pay within a limited period of time, such as thirty days. These claims are referred to as *trade receivables*. Other claims may be from sources such as loans to employees or a federal tax refund.

Claims from customers are usually in the form of accounts receivable. These accounts are non-interest-bearing and do not have any particular claims against specific resources of the customer. In some cases, however, the customer is requested to sign a note instead of being granted the privilege of having an open account. Usually, the note is for a longer period of time than an account receivable and is interest-bearing. In some cases, a customer who does not pay the account receivable when due is asked to sign a note receivable in place of the account receivable.

The common characteristic of receivables is that the cash is expected to be received at some time in the future. This increases the valuation problem of a receivable. Two problems exist in the valuation of a receivable. One is that a period of time must pass before the receivable can be collected, so the entity incurs costs for the use of the funds. The other problem is that collection may not be made.

The valuation problem from waiting to collect is ignored in the valuation of receivables and of notes that are classified in current assets, because the waiting period is short and the difference in value is therefore immaterial. The waiting period problem is not ignored if the receivable or note is long term and thus classified as an investment. These situations are covered by APB Opinion No. 21, which states that the stipulated rate of interest is presumed to be fair.

Under the following conditions, this presumption can be overcome:

1. No interest is stated, or
2. The stated rate of interest is clearly unreasonable, or
3. The face value of the note is materially different from the cash sales price of the property, goods, or services, or the market value of the note at the date of the transaction.[2]

---

[2]American Institute of Certified Public Accountants, Accounting Principles Board Opinion No. 21, "Interest on Receivables and Payables," 1971, par. 11.

EXHIBIT 6-1

AMERICAN SOFTWARE, INC.
Marketable Securities (Short-Term Investments)

	1988	1987
Current assets:		
Cash	$ 193,353	$ 586,620
Investments (note 2)	43,582,848	36,822,019
Trade accounts receivable, less allowance for doubtful accounts of $800,000 in 1988 and $600,000 in 1987	14,363,557	12,083,836
Unbilled accounts receivable	1,648,601	3,562,956
Prepaid expenses and other current assets	1,052,018	750,978
Total current assets	$60,840,377	$53,806,409

Notes to Consolidated Financial Statements

1 (In Part): Summary of Significant Accounting Policies

(d) Investments   Investments are recorded at the lower of aggregate cost or market. The cost of the investments sold is based on the earliest acquisition cost of each security held at the time of sale.

2 Investments

Investments consist of the following:

	April 30,	
	1988	1987
Commercial paper and money market funds	$19,406,986	$12,049,015
Obligations of the U.S. Government	12,324,674	1,196,750
State and municipal bonds	10,353,188	15,183,254
Common and preferred stocks	1,498,000	8,393,000
	$43,582,848	$36,822,019

Marketable equity securities are carried at market for both years presented, which is lower than cost. These investments had an aggregate cost of approximately $1,770,000 and $9,309,000 at April 30, 1988 and 1987, respectively. To reduce the carrying amount of the portfolio to market a valuation allowance in the amount of approximately $916,000 was established in 1987 with a corresponding charge to net earnings. At April 30, 1988, the necessary valuation allowance was approximately $272,000 and the decrease in the valuation allowance between the periods of approximately $644,000 has been included in the determination of net earnings in 1988. At April 30, 1988, the gross unrealized gains and losses pertaining to marketable equity securities were approximately $8,000 and $280,000, respectively.

Net realized losses of $694,441 and net realized gains of $909,967 and $405,002 from the sale of marketable equity securities are included in the determination of net earnings in 1988, 1987, and 1986, respectively.

Source: American Institute of Certified Public Accountants, *Accounting Trends and Techniques*, 1989, pp. 107–108.

Under the condition that the face amount of the note does not represent the fair value of the consideration exchanged, the note is recorded as a present value amount on the date of the original transaction. This means that the note is recorded at less than (or more than) the face amount, taking into consideration the time value of money. The difference between the recorded amount and the face amount is subsequently amortized to interest income (note receivable) or to interest expense (note payable). APB Opinion No. 21 applies to both notes receivable and notes payable.

The second problem on the valuation of receivables or notes is that collection may not be made; this situation must be considered. Usually an allowance is provided for the estimated uncollectible accounts. SFAS No. 5 requires that estimated losses be accrued against income and that the impairment of the asset be recognized (or liability recorded) under the following conditions:

1. Information available prior to the issuance of the financial statements indicates that it is probable that an asset has been impaired, or a liability has been incurred at the date of the financial statements.
2. The amount of the loss can be reasonably estimated.[3]

Both of these conditions are normally met with respect to the uncollectibility of receivables, and the amount subject to being uncollectible is usually material. Thus, in most cases, the company must estimate bad debt expense and indicate the impairment of the receivable. The expense is placed on the income statement, and the impairment of the receivable is disclosed by the use of an account called *allowance for doubtful accounts*, which is subtracted from the gross receivable account. Later, when a specific customer's account is identified as being uncollectible, the account is charged against the allowance for doubtful accounts account, and the receivable account is removed from the balance sheet. (This does *not* mean that the firm will stop efforts to collect.)

Estimating the collectibility of any individual receivable is difficult, but when all of the receivables are considered in setting up the allowance, the total estimate should be reasonably accurate. The problem of collection applies to each of the types of receivables accounts, including the notes receivable. The company normally provides for only one allowance account as a matter of convenience, but possible collection problems with all types of receivables and notes must be considered when determining the allowance account.

The impairment of the receivable asset may arise from causes other than uncollectibility. Examples of other causes would be cash discounts allowed, sales returns, and allowances given. Frequently, all of the causes that impair the asset account receivable are considered in the allowance for doubtful accounts account, rather than setting up a separate allowance account for each cause.

Cooper presented its receivable account as follows for December 31, 1989 and 1988:

[3]Financial Accounting Standards Board, Statement of Financial Accounting Standards No. 5, "Accounting for Contingencies," 1975, par. 8.

	1989	1988
Accounts receivable, less allowance for doubtful accounts of $2,100,000 in 1989 and $1,350,000 in 1988	$126,431,368	$120,407,633

This indicates that net receivables were $126,431,368 at December 31, 1989, and $120,407,633 at December 31, 1988, after subtracting allowances for doubtful accounts of $2,100,000 in 1989 and $1,350,000 in 1988.

The use of the allowance for doubtful accounts approach results in the bad debt expense being charged to the period of sale, thus matching this expense in the period of sale. It also results in the recognition of the impairment of the asset. The later charge-off of a specified account receivable does not influence the income statement or the net receivable on the balance sheet. (The charge-off reduces the accounts receivable account and the allowance for doubtful accounts.)

According to the Federal Tax Return Act of 1986, deductions for bad debt expense are allowed only for bad debt write-offs. Since the bad debt expense on the income statement results from an estimate of bad debts, the result is a deferred income tax relating to bad debt expense.

When both conditions specified in SFAS No. 5 are not met, or the receivables are immaterial, the entity uses a method of recognizing bad debt expense by the direct write-off method. Under this method, the bad debt expense is recorded as a specific customer's account is determined to be noncollectible. At this time, the bad debt expense is recognized on the income statement, and the account receivable is removed from the balance sheet. (This method recognizes the bad debt expense in the same period for both the income statement and the tax return.)

The direct write-off method frequently results in the bad debt expense being recognized in the year subsequent to the sale and thus does not result in a proper matching of expense with revenue. Under this method, the receivable account is also carried gross, which means that the impairment of the asset from noncollectibility has not been recognized.

When a company has receivables that are due beyond one year (or accounting cycle) from the balance sheet date, and when it is the industry practice to include these receivables in current assets, they are included in current assets even though they do not technically meet the guidelines to qualify as a current asset. The company should disclose these receivables that do not meet the technical guidelines to be current. Exhibit 6-2 indicates the disclosure made by Snap-On Tools Corporation in its 1988 annual report.

When a company has receivables classified as current, based on industry practice, special note should be made of this when comparing with competitors. Competitors may not have the same type of receivables, so the receivables may not be comparable. For example, if a retail company has substantial installment receivables, with many of them over a year from their due date, the company is not comparable to a retail company that does not have installment receivables. The receivables of the company with the installment receivables are normally considered to be of lower quality than the receivables of the company that does not have the installment

EXHIBIT 6 - 2

SNAP-ON TOOLS CORPORATION
Accounts Receivable Due beyond One Year

(in thousands)	1988	1987
Current assets		
Cash and cash equivalents	$ 16,895	$ 64,575
Accounts receivable, less allowance for doubtful accounts of $2.4 million in 1988 and $2.2 million in 1987 (Note 1e)	336,588	277,357
Inventories	139,460	120,083
Prepaid expenses	12,037	8,501
Total current assets	$504,980	$470,516

Notes to Consolidated Financial Statements

1 (In Part): Summary of Accounting Policies

e. Installment receivables: Installment receivables include amounts which are due subsequent to one year from balance sheet dates. These amounts were approximately $28 million and $24 million at the end of 1988 and 1987. A portion of unearned finance charges is recognized as income in the month of sale to offset initial direct costs incurred in processing the installment contract. The remaining finance charges are recognized as income over the life of the installment contract on the "liquidation method." Under this method, finance charges are recognized as income in the ratio of monthly collections to installment receivables.

Gross installment receivables amounted to $360.2 million and $290.1 million at the end of 1988 and 1987. Of this amount, $71.8 million and $55.9 million represented unearned finance charges at the end of 1988 and 1987.

Source: American Institute of Certified Public Accountants, *Accounting Trends and Techniques*, 1989, p. 115.

receivables. This is because of the length of time of the installment receivables. It is important that the company with installment receivables have high standards as to what customers are given credit, and it is also important that this company closely monitor its receivables.

Customer concentration can be an important consideration in the quality of receivables. When a large proportion of receivables is from a few customers, the firm can be highly dependent on those customers. This information is usually not available when doing external analysis, but it is readily available when doing internal analysis.

The liquidity of the trade receivables for a company can be examined by making two computations. One computation determines the number of days' sales in receivables at the end of the accounting period, and the other computation determines the accounts receivable turnover. The turnover figure can be computed in relation to times per year or in terms of how many days on the average it takes to turn over the receivables.

Days' Sales in Receivables

The number of days' sales in receivables relates the amount of the accounts receivable to the average daily sales on account. Trade notes receivable should be included with the accounts receivable for this computation, since the two are very much related. Other receivables should not be included in this computation, because they are not related to sales on account.

The formula for determining the days' sales in receivables is as follows:

$$\text{Days' Sales in Receivables} = \frac{\text{Gross Receivables}}{\text{Net Sales}/365}$$

This formula indicates that the number of days in a year should be divided into net sales on account, and the resulting figure divided into gross receivables. The ratio is computed in Exhibit 6-3 for Cooper at the end of 1989 and 1988. The decrease in days' sales in receivables from 59.41 days at the end of 1988 to 54.12 days at the end of 1989 appears to indicate an improvement in the control of receivables. It could also indicate a decrease in sales late in 1989.

For internal analysis, days' sales in receivables should be compared with the company's credit terms to obtain an indication of how efficiently the company is managing its receivables. For example, if the credit term is thirty days, days' sales in receivables should not be materially over thirty days. If days' sales in receivables are materially longer than the credit terms, this indicates a collection problem. An effort should be made to keep the days' sales in receivables from extending materially beyond the credit terms.

Consider the influence on the quality of receivables from any change in the credit terms. A shortening of the credit terms is an indication that there will be less

EXHIBIT 6-3

COOPER TIRE & RUBBER COMPANY
Days' Sales in Receivables
December 31, 1989 and 1988

	1989	1988
Receivables, less: allowance for doubtful accounts of $2,100,000 in 1989 and $1,350,000 in 1988	$126,431,368	$120,407,633
Gross receivables (net plus allowance) [A]	128,531,368	121,757,633
Net sales	866,805,462	748,032,206
Average daily sales on account (net sales on account divided by 365) [B]	2,374,809	2,049,403
Days' sales in receivables [A ÷ B]	54.12 days	59.41 days

risk in the collection of future receivables, and a lengthening of the credit terms indicates that there will be a greater risk in the collection of future receivables. Credit term information is readily available when doing internal analysis and may be available in footnotes.

Right of return privileges can also be important to the quality of receivables. Liberal right of return privileges can be a negative factor in the quality of receivables and on sales that have already been booked. Pay particular attention to any change in the right of return privileges. Right of return privileges can readily be determined for internal analysis, and this information should be available in a footnote if it is considered to be material.

The net sales figure includes collectible and uncollectible accounts. The uncollectible accounts would not exist if there were an accurate way of determining, prior to sale, accounts that would not pay. An effort is made to determine credit standing when the customer is approved for credit. Since the net sales figure includes both collectible and uncollectible accounts (gross sales), the comparable receivables figure should include gross receivables, rather than the net receivables figure that remains after allowance for doubtful accounts.

The days' sales in receivables ratio gives an indication of the length of time that the receivables have been outstanding at the end of the year. *The indication can be misleading if sales are seasonal and/or the company uses a natural business year.* If the company uses a natural business year for its accounting period, the days' sales in receivables tends to be understated, based on the formula computation, because the actual sales per day at the end of the year are at a low point when compared to the average sales per day for the year from the formula. The understatement of days' sales in receivables can also be explained by the fact that gross receivables tend to be below average at that time of year.

The following is an example of how days' sales in receivables tend to be understated when a company uses a natural business year:

Average sales per day considering the entire year	$ 2,000
Sales per day at the end of the natural business year	1,000
Gross receivables at the end of the year	100,000
Days' sales in receivables based on the formula:	

$$\frac{\$100,000}{\$2,000} = 50 \text{ Days}$$

Days' sales in receivables based on sales per day at the end of the natural business year:

$$\frac{\$100,000}{\$1,000} = 100 \text{ Days}$$

The liquidity of a company that uses a natural business year tends to be overstated in comparison with a company that uses a calendar year; such companies should not be compared for liquidity of receivables. However, the only positive way to know if a company is on a natural business year is through familiarity. When doing internal analysis, the information is readily determinable.

It is unlikely that a company that has a seasonal business will close the accounting year when activity is at a peak, for good reasons. At the peak of the business cycle, company personnel are busy, and receivables are likely to be at their highest levels. If a company closed when activities are at a peak, the days' sales in receivables would tend to be overstated—in short, the liquidity would be understated.

The length of time that the receivables have been outstanding gives an indication of the collectibility of the receivables. The days' sales should be compared for several years. A comparison should also be made between the days' sales in receivables for a particular company and comparable figures for other firms in the industry and industry averages. This type of comparison can be made when doing either internal or external analysis.

Assuming that the days' sales in receivables computation is not distorted because of a seasonal business and/or the company's use of a natural business year, the following should be considered as possible reasons why the receivables appear to be abnormally high:

1. Sales volume expanded materially late in the year.
2. Receivables have collectibility problems, and possibly some should have been written off.
3. The company seasonally dates invoices. (An example would be a toy manufacturer that ships in August, with the receivable due at the end of December.)
4. Material amount of receivables are on the installment basis.

Assuming that the distortion is not from a seasonal situation or the company's use of a natural business year, the following should be considered as possible reasons why the receivables appear to be abnormally low:

1. Sales volume decreases materially late in the year.
2. Material amount of sales are on a cash basis.
3. The company has a factoring arrangement in which a material amount of the receivables are sold. (With a factoring arrangement, the receivables are sold to an outside party.)

When doing external analysis, many of the reasons why the days' sales in receivables are abnormally high or low cannot be determined without access to internal information.

Accounts Receivable Turnover

The second computation that indicates the liquidity of the receivables is the accounts receivable turnover. The formula for determining the accounts receivable turnover in times per year is as follows:

$$\text{Accounts Receivable Turnover} = \frac{\text{Net Sales}}{\text{Average Gross Receivables}}$$

The ratio is computed in Exhibit 6-4 for Cooper at the end of 1989 and 1988. There was an increase in the turnover of receivables between 1988 and 1989, from 6.29 times to 6.93 times.

Computing the average gross receivables based on beginning-of-year and end-of-year receivables can be misleading if the business has seasonal fluctuations or if the company uses a natural business year. To avoid problems of seasonal fluctuations, or of comparing a company that uses a natural business year with one that uses a calendar year, the monthly balances of accounts receivable should be used in the computation. This is feasible when performing internal analysis, but not when performing external analysis. In the latter case, quarterly figures are often available, and these can be used to help eliminate these problems. If these problems cannot be eliminated, companies that are not on the same basis should not be compared. The company with the natural business year tends to overstate its accounts receivable turnover, thus overstating its liquidity.

Accounts Receivable Turnover in Days

The accounts receivable turnover can be expressed in terms of days instead of times per year. Some individuals find it easier to relate to number of days; turnover in number of days also gives a comparison with the number of days' sales in the ending receivables. The accounts receivable turnover in days also results in an answer that can be directly related to the firm's credit terms.

EXHIBIT 6-4

COOPER TIRE & RUBBER COMPANY
Accounts Receivable Turnover
For the Years Ended December 31, 1989 and 1988

	1989	1988
Net sales [A]	$866,805,462	$748,032,206
End-of-year receivables, less allowance for doubtful accounts	126,431,368	120,407,633
Beginning-of-year receivables, less allowance for doubtful accounts	120,407,633	114,628,509
Allowance for doubtful accounts		
End of 1989 $2,100,000		
End of 1988 $1,350,000		
End of 1987 $1,300,000		
Ending gross receivables (net plus allowance)	128,531,368	121,757,633
Beginning gross receivables (net plus allowance)	121,757,633	115,928,509
Average gross receivables [B]	125,144,501	118,843,071
Accounts receivable turnover [A ÷ B]	6.93 times	6.29 times

This formula for determining the accounts receivable turnover in days is as follows:

$$\text{Accounts Receivable Turnover in Days} = \frac{\text{Average Gross Receivables}}{\text{Net Sales/365}}$$

Notice that this formula is the same as that for determining number of days' sales in receivables, except that the accounts receivable turnover in days is computed using the average gross receivables. The ratio is computed in Exhibit 6-5 for Cooper at the end of 1989 and 1988. Accounts receivable turnover in days decreased from 57.99 in 1988 to 52.70 days in 1989.

The accounts receivable turnover in times per year and days can both be computed by alternative formulas, as follows:

1. Accounts Receivable Turnover (Times)

(1989 Cooper)

$$\frac{365}{\text{Accounts Receivable Turnover in Days}} \qquad \frac{365}{52.70 \text{ Days}} = 6.93 \text{ Times}$$

2. Accounts Receivable Turnover in Days

(1989 Cooper)

$$\frac{365}{\text{Accounts Receivable Turnover in Times}} \qquad \frac{365}{6.93 \text{ Times}} = 52.67 \text{ Days}$$

The answer in both accounts receivable turnover in times and accounts receivable turnover in days, using the alternative formulas, differ slightly from the respective answers obtained with the previous formulas. The difference comes from additional rounding with the alternative formulas, which sometimes makes them slightly less accurate than the previous formulas.

EXHIBIT 6-5

COOPER TIRE & RUBBER COMPANY
Accounts Receivable Turnover in Days
For the Years Ended December 31, 1989 and 1988

	1989	1988
Net sales	$866,805,462	$748,032,206
Average gross receivables [A]	125,144,501	118,843,071
Sales per day (net sales divided by 365) [B]	2,374,809	2,049,403
Accounts receivable turnover in days [A ÷ B]	52.70 days	57.99 days

Credit Sales versus Cash Sales

A difficulty in computing receivables' liquidity is the problem of credit sales versus cash sales. Both credit sales and cash sales are included in net sales. In order to have a realistic indication of the liquidity of receivables, only the credit sales should be included in the computations. If cash sales are included, the liquidity will be overstated.

When performing internal analysis, the credit sales figure can be determined, thus eliminating the problem of credit sales versus cash sales. When performing external analysis, the analyst should be aware of this problem, so as not to be misled by the liquidity figures. The distinction between cash sales and credit sales is not usually a major problem when performing external analysis, because certain types of businesses tend to sell only on cash terms, and others sell only on credit terms. For instance, a retail food store usually sells only on cash terms, while a manufacturer usually sells only on credit terms. Some businesses have a mixture of credit sales and cash sales—for instance, a retail department store.

In cases of mixed sales, the problem is usually reduced because the proportion of credit and cash sales tends to stay rather constant. Therefore, the liquidity figures are comparable (but overstated), enabling the analyst to compare figures from period to period as well as figures of similar companies.

Inventories

Inventory is usually the most significant asset in determining the short-term debt-paying ability of an entity. Often the inventory account is more than half of the total current assets. Because of the significance of inventories, a special effort should be made to analyze this important area properly.

To be classified as inventory, the asset should be for sale in the ordinary course of business or used or consumed in the production of goods. A firm that purchases merchandise in a form to sell to customers is called a *trading concern*. Inventories of a trading concern, whether it is wholesale or retail, are usually classified in one inventory account called *merchandise inventory*. A firm that produces goods to be sold is called a *manufacturing concern*. Inventories of a manufacturing concern are normally classified in three inventory accounts. These inventory accounts distinguish between inventory available to use in production (raw material inventory), inventory in production (work in process inventory), and inventory completed (finished goods inventory). Usually, the determination of the inventory figures is much more difficult in a manufacturing concern than in a trading concern. The manufacturing concern is dealing with materials, labor, and overhead when determining the inventory figures, whereas the trading concern is dealing only with purchased merchandise. The overhead portion of the work in process inventory and the finished goods inventory is often a particular problem when determining a manufacturer's inventory. The overhead consists of all the costs of the factory other than direct materials and direct labor. From an analysis viewpoint, however, many of the problems of determining the proper inventory have already been handled by the time the entity publishes financial statements.

Inventory is particularly sensitive to changes in business activity, so management must keep inventory in balance with business activity. Failure to do so leads to excessive costs (such as storage cost), production disruptions, and the related layoff of employees. An example of how inventories get out of hand when business activities decrease is the situation that occasionally exists for the automobile manufacturers. When sales decline rapidly, the industry has difficulty adjusting production and resulting inventory in accordance with the decline in sales. The result is a large buildup of inventory that leads to price rebates in order to get the inventory back to a manageable level. Inventory problems also arise when business activity increases; inventory shortages can soon occur, leading to overtime costs. The increase in activity can also lead to cash shortages because of the delay between the acquiring of inventory, the receivable from the sale, and the collection from the sale.

Valuation and liquidity are the two problems that have been emphasized in examining current assets in the determination of the short-term debt-paying ability of an entity. Both of these problems are fairly complicated when dealing with inventories.

The basic approach to the valuation of inventory is to use cost. The cost figure is often difficult to determine, especially when dealing with manufacturing inventory. Because of the concept of conservatism, the cost figure may not be acceptable if it cannot be recovered. Therefore, if the market figure is below cost, the inventory has been reduced to market. This means that the inventory is being stated at the lower of cost or market on the financial statements.

Inventory Cost

The most critical problem that most entities face is determining which cost to use, since the cost prices have usually varied over time. If it were practical to determine the specific cost of any particular item, this would be the cost figure to use, and our valuation problems with inventory would be substantially reduced. In practice, because of the different types of inventory items and the constant flow of these items, it is not practical to determine the specific costs. Exceptions to this are large and/or expensive items. For example, it would be practical to determine the specific cost of a new car in the dealer's showroom or the specific cost of an expensive diamond in a jewelry store.

Because the cost of specific items is not usually practical to determine, it is necessary to use a cost flow assumption. The most common cost flow assumptions are first-in, first-out (FIFO); last-in, first-out (LIFO); or some average computation. These assumptions can produce substantially different results, especially over the years, primarily because of changing prices in an upward direction (inflation). If it were not for the inflation problem, the cost determined would be approximately the same regardless of the cost flow assumption.

As indicated, the FIFO method assumes that the first inventory acquired is the first to be sold. This means that the costs of the first items are taken to the cost of goods sold account as sales are made, and the latest items remain in inventory. These latest costs are usually fairly representative of the current costs to replace the inventory. If the inventory revolves slowly, or if there has been substantial inflation, even FIFO may not produce an inventory figure for the balance sheet that is representative of the replacement cost. If the entity is a manufacturing concern, part of the inventory cost consists of overhead, some of which may represent costs from several years prior, such as depreciation on the plant and equipment. Often the costs taken to cost of goods sold under FIFO are too low in relation to current costs, so there has not been an ideal matching of current costs against current revenue. To the extent that such an ideal matching has not been achieved during a time of inflation, the resulting profit has been overstated. To the extent that the resulting inventory is not representative of the replacement cost, there is also an understatement of the inventory cost in relation to the short-term debt-paying ability.

The LIFO method assumes that the costs of the latest item bought or produced are matched against current sales. This assumption materially improves the matching of current costs against current revenue, so the resulting profit figure is usually fairly realistic. Because the first items (and oldest costs) remain in inventory, there can be a material distortion of the reported inventory figure in comparison with the cost to replace the inventory. A firm that has been on LIFO for many years may have some inventory costs that go back ten years or more. Considering the inflation that the firm has experienced, it is obvious that the resulting inventory figure is not realistic in relation to the current replacement costs.

An average cost computation for inventories results in an inventory amount and a cost of goods sold amount somewhere between the figures for FIFO and LIFO. The resulting inventory amount is more than the LIFO inventory and less than the FIFO inventory. The resulting costs of goods sold amount is less than the LIFO amount and more than the FIFO amount.

Exhibit 6-6 summarizes the inventory methods used by the 600 companies that are surveyed by *Accounting Trends and Techniques*. The table covers the years 1988, 1987, 1986, and 1985. (Notice that the number of companies in the table do not add up to 600. This is because many companies use more than one method.) Exhibit 6-6 indicates that the most popular inventory methods are FIFO and LIFO. There was a slight trend toward the use of FIFO during the period from 1985 to 1988. This would be expected, because these were years of relatively low inflation. It is perceived that LIFO requires more cost to administer than FIFO. Therefore, it is not as popular during times of relatively low inflation as during times of relatively high inflation. During times of relatively high inflation, LIFO becomes more popular, because it matches the latest costs against revenue, resulting in a better earnings recognition. LIFO also results in tax benefits because of the lower taxes during a period of inflation. The tax benefits result from the matching of recent higher costs against the revenue. LIFO represents a unique tax situation. In order to use LIFO for federal taxes, the company must get the permission of the Internal Revenue Service. When the company gets permission to use LIFO, it must

EXHIBIT 6-6

Inventory Cost Determination
Number of Companies, 1988, 1987, 1986, and 1985

	1988	1987	1986	1985
Methods				
First-in, first-out (FIFO)	396	392	383	381
Last-in, first-out (LIFO)	379	393	393	402
Average cost	213	216	223	223
Other	50	49	53	48
Use of LIFO				
All inventories	20	18	23	26
50% or more of inventories	207	221	229	231
Less than 50% of inventories	90	86	74	83
Not determinable	62	68	67	62
Companies using LIFO	379	393	393	402

Source: American Institute of Certified Public Accountants, *Accounting Trends and Techniques*, 1989, p. 119.

also use LIFO for this same inventory for financial reporting purposes. Thus, the election to use LIFO for taxes governs the firm's financial reporting. To change from LIFO, the company also must get permission from the Internal Revenue Service. To receive this permission, the company will be required to pay back the past tax benefits that were achieved from the use of LIFO, plus interest on the funds. The payback period is negotiated with the Internal Revenue Service—typically, ten years or longer.

Exhibit 6-6 includes a summary of companies that use LIFO for all inventories, 50% or more of inventories, less than 50% of inventories, and not determinable. This summary indicates that only a small percentage of companies that use LIFO use it for all of their inventory.

To illustrate the major costing methods for determining which costs apply to the units remaining in inventory at the end of the year and which costs are allocated to cost of goods sold, consider the following data:

Date	Description	Number of Units	Cost per Unit	Total Cost
January 1	Beginning inventory	200	$ 6	$ 1,200
March 1	Purchase	1,200	7	8,400
July 1	Purchase	300	9	2,700
October 1	Purchase	400	11	4,400
		2,100		$16,700

A physical inventory on December 31 indicates that 800 units are on hand. There were 2,100 units available during the year, and 800 remained at the end of the year; therefore, 1,300 units were sold.

Four cost assumptions will be used to illustrate the determination of the ending inventory costs and the related cost of goods sold. These cost assumptions are first-in, first-out (FIFO), last-in, first-out (LIFO), average cost, and specific identification.

First-in, First-Out (FIFO)

		Inventory	Cost of Goods Sold
October 1	Purchase 400 @ $11	$4,400	
July 1	Purchase 300 @ 9	2,700	
March 1	Purchase 100 @ 7	700	
		$7,800	
Remaining cost in cost of goods sold ($16,700 − $7,800) =			$8,900

Last-In, First-out (LIFO)

There are several ways to compute LIFO inventory cost. The method illustrated here is called the *periodic system*. Physical counts are taken periodically—at least once a year. The cost of the ending inventory is found by attaching costs to the physical quantities on hand, based on the LIFO cost flow assumption used. The cost of goods sold is calculated by subtracting the ending inventory cost from the cost of goods available for sale.

		Inventory	Cost of Goods Sold
October 1	Purchase 200 @ $ 6	$1,200	
March 1	Purchase 600 @ 7	4,200	
		$5,400	
Remaining cost in cost of goods sold ($16,700 − $5,400) =			$11,300

Average Cost

There are several ways to compute the average cost. The method illustrated here is called the *weighted average*. With the weighted average, the total units are divided into the total cost to get the average cost per unit.

		Inventory	Cost of Goods Sold
Total cost	$\frac{\$16,700}{2,100} = \$7.95$		
Total units			
Inventory	(800 × $7.95)	$6,360	
Remaining cost in cost of goods sold ($16,700 − $6,360) =			$10,340

Specific Identification

With the specific identification method, the items in inventory are identified as coming from specific purchases. In the example, it is assumed that the 800 items in inventory can be identified with the March 1 purchase.

	Inventory	Cost of Goods Sold
Inventory (800 × $7.00)	$5,600	
Remaining cost in cost of goods sold ($16,700 − $5,600) =		$11,100

The difference in results on the inventory and cost of goods sold may be material or immaterial. The major impact on the results usually comes from the rate of inflation. In general, the more material the inflation, the greater the differences between the inventory methods.

Because the inventory amounts can be substantially different under the various inventory flow assumptions, the analyst should be cautious when comparing the liquidity of firms that have different inventory flow assumptions. Caution is particularly necessary when one of the firms is using the LIFO inventory method, because LIFO may prove meaningless with regard to the firm's short-term debt-paying ability. If it is necessary to compare two firms that have different inventory flow assumptions, this problem should be kept in mind to avoid being misled by the indicated short-term debt-paying ability.

Since the resulting inventory amount is not equal to the cost of replacing the inventory, regardless of the cost method, there is another problem to consider when determining the short-term debt-paying ability of the firm: The inventory must be sold for more than cost in order to realize a profit. To the extent that the inventory is sold for more than cost, the point could be made that the short-term debt-paying ability has been understated. This is partially true, but the extent of the understatement is materially reduced by several factors. One factor is that the firm will incur substantial selling and administrative costs in addition to the inventory cost, thereby reducing the understatement of liquidity to the resulting net profit. The other factor is that the replacement cost of the inventory is usually more than the reported inventory cost, even if FIFO is used; therefore, funds will be required to replace the inventory that is in excess of the cost of the inventory sold. This will reduce the future short-term debt-paying ability of the firm. Also, it must be considered that accountants support the conservatism concept, so they would rather have a slight understatement of the short-term debt-paying ability of the firm than an overstatement.

It is very important that the impact on the entity of the different inventory methods be understood. Since the extremes in inventory costing are LIFO and FIFO, these methods have been summarized as to their influence on the entity. This summary assumes that the entity faces an inflationary condition. The conclusions arrived at in this summary would be reversed if the entity faced a deflationary condition.

A summary of a LIFO-FIFO comparison follows:

1. LIFO generally results in a lower profit than does FIFO, and this difference can be substantial.

2. Generally, reported profit under LIFO is closer to reality than the profit reported under FIFO, because the cost of goods sold is closer to replacement under LIFO than FIFO. This is the case under both inflationary and deflationary conditions.

3. FIFO reports a higher inventory ending balance, which makes it closer to replacement cost, but this figure falls short of a true replacement cost.

4. LIFO results in a lower profit figure than does FIFO. This is the result of a higher cost of goods sold.

5. The cash flow under LIFO is greater than the cash flow under FIFO by the difference in the resulting tax between the two methods. This is one of the important reasons why a company might select LIFO.

6. Some companies use a periodic inventory system, in which the inventory is updated in the general ledger once a year. When the periodic inventory system is used, purchases late in the year can have a substantial influence on profits. The effect is to reduce profits, as the most recent purchases end up in the cost of goods sold on the income statement. It is important that accountants keep management informed of the depression in profits that results from substantial year-end purchases of inventory when this is the case.

7. A company using LIFO could be faced with a severe tax problem and a severe cash problem if sales reduce or eliminate the amount of inventory that is normally carried. This is because the reduction in inventory would result in older cost being matched against current sales, resulting in a high reported profit. This is a distortion of profits on the high side. Because of the high reported profit, income taxes would be increased. When the firm has to replenish the inventory, it has an additional, unexpected cash need. These problems can be reduced by planning and close supervision of production and purchases.[4]

8. LIFO would probably not be used for inventory that has a high turnover rate, because there would be an immaterial difference in the results between LIFO and FIFO.

A firm using LIFO must disclose a LIFO reserve account (usually in a footnote). Usually, the amount disclosed must be added to inventory to approximate the inventory at FIFO. An inventory at FIFO is usually a reasonable approximation of the current replacement cost of the inventory.

The footnote must be examined closely to determine specifically what the result approximates when the amount disclosed is adjusted to the inventory amount on the balance sheet. The Cooper footnote reads, "Under the LIFO method inven-

---

[4]A method called *dollar value LIFO* is now frequently applied by companies that use LIFO. This method can essentially eliminate the problem addressed in item 7. The dollar value LIFO method uses price indexes related to the inventory instead of units and unit costs. With dollar value LIFO, inventory during each period is determined for pools of inventory dollars.

tories have been reduced by approximately $52,204,000 and $49,001,000 at December 31, 1989 and 1988, respectively, from amounts which would have been reported under the first-in, first-out method." The Cooper footnote indicates that the approximate current costs can be determined by adding the disclosed amounts to the inventory amount included on the balance sheet.

The approximate current costs of the Cooper inventory for December 31, 1989 and 1988 are determined as follows:

	1989	1988
Balance sheet inventories	$ 70,690,865	$ 67,909,495
Additional amount in footnote (LIFO reserve)	52,204,000	49,001,000
Approximate current costs	$122,894,865	$116,910,495

Later in the book, we will examine the possibility of using the adjusted inventory amount in analysis to improve the analysis of inventory and the analysis of the liquidity of the firm in general.

The liquidity of the inventories can be approached in a manner similar to that taken to analyze the liquidity of accounts receivable. One computation determines the number of days' sales in inventory at the end of the accounting period; another computation determines the inventory turnover in times per year; and a third determines the inventory turnover in days.

Days' Sales in Inventory

The number of days' sales in inventory ratio relates the amount of the ending inventory to the average daily cost of goods sold. All of the inventory accounts should be included in the computation. The computation gives an indication of the length of time that it will take to use up the inventory through sales. This indication can be misleading; sales may be seasonal, or the company may be using a natural business year.

If the company uses a natural business year for its accounting period, the number of days' sales in inventory tends to be understated, because the average daily cost of goods sold is at a low point at this time of year. If the days' sales in inventory is understated, the liquidity of the inventory is overstated. The same caution should be observed here as was suggested for determining the liquidity of receivables; companies should not be compared for liquidity of inventory when one is on a natural business year and the other is on a calendar year.

If the company closes the year when the activities are at a peak, the number of days' sales in inventory tends to be overstated and the liquidity understated. As indicated with receivables, there is no good business reason for closing the year when activities are at a peak, so this situation should rarely occur.

A formula for determining the number of days' sales in inventory is as follows:

$$\text{Days' Sales in Inventory} = \frac{\text{Ending Inventory}}{\text{Cost of Goods Sold}/365}$$

The formula indicates that the number of days in a year should be divided into cost of goods sold and that the resulting figure should be divided into ending inventory. Using the 1989 and 1988 figures from the Cooper data, the number of days' sales in inventory is computed in Exhibit 6-7.

The days' sales in inventory is an estimate of the number of days that it will take to sell the current inventory. This estimate may not be very accurate, for several reasons. One is that the cost of goods sold figure is based on last year's sales, divided by the number of days in a year. Sales next year may not be at the same pace as last year. Also, the ending inventory figure may not be representative of the quantity of inventory actually on hand, especially if LIFO is used. This is possibly the case with Cooper, because of the large LIFO reserve in relation to the reported inventory.

A seasonal situation, in which the inventory is unusually low or high at the end of the year, would also result in an unrealistic figure for days' sales in inventory. A natural business year in which the inventory is low at the end of the year would also result in an unrealistic figure for days' sales in inventory. Therefore, the resulting answer should be taken as a rough estimate, but it is usually very helpful when comparing periods or similar companies.

The number of days' sales in inventory is computed in Exhibit 6-7 for Cooper for December 31, 1989, and December 31, 1988. This comparison indicates that the number of days' sales in inventory decreased from 38.63 days at the end of 1988 to 35.48 days at the end of 1989. If sales are approximately constant, then the lower the number of days' sales in inventory, the better the inventory is under control. An inventory buildup can be burdensome if business volume is decreasing. However, it can be good if business volume is expanding, since the increased inventory would be needed to give acceptable service to customers. Because Cooper's sales are expanding, an inventory buildup may be in order.

The number of days' sales in inventory could become too low, resulting in lost sales caused by unavailable inventory. A good knowledge of the industry and the company is required to determine if the number of days' sales in inventory is too low.

E X H I B I T   6 - 7

COOPER TIRE & RUBBER COMPANY
Days' Sales in Inventory
December 31, 1989 and 1988

	1989	1988
Inventories, end of year [A]	$ 70,690,865	$ 67,909,495
Cost of goods sold	727,323,386	641,613,558
Average daily cost of goods sold (cost of goods sold divided by 365) [B]	1,992,667	1,757,845
Number of days' sales in inventory [A ÷ B]	35.48 days	38.63 days

In some cases, not only will the cost of goods sold not be reported separately, but the figure reported will not be a close approximation of cost of goods sold. This, of course, presents a problem when doing external analysis. If the published financial statements present this problem, use net sales in place of cost of goods sold. The result is not a realistic number of days' sales in inventory, but it can be useful in comparing periods within one firm and in comparing one firm with another. Using net sales produces a much lower number of days' sales in inventory, which materially overstates the liquidity of the ending inventory. Therefore, it is important that only the trend determined from comparing one period with another, and one firm with other firms, be taken seriously, not the actual figures.

When you suspect that the days' sales in inventory computation does not result in a reasonable answer because of one of the distortions, consider using this ratio only to indicate a trend. The ratio is almost always reasonable to use in determining a trend.

When doing internal analysis, distortions may be caused if the dollar figures for inventory and/or cost of goods sold are not reasonable. These distortions can be eliminated to some extent by using quantities rather than dollars in the computation. The use of quantities in the computation may work very well for single products or groups of similar products; it does not work very well for a large diversified inventory, because of the change in the mix of the inventory.

An example of the use of quantities, instead of dollars, follows:

$$\begin{array}{ll} \text{Ending Inventory} & \text{50 units} \\ \text{Cost of Goods Sold} & \text{500 units} \end{array}$$

$$\text{Days' Sales in Inventory} = \frac{50}{500/365} = 36.50 \text{ Days}$$

Merchandise Inventory Turnover

Another computation that indicates the liquidity of the inventory is that of inventory turnover. This computation is similar to the receivable turnover computation that was used to indicate the liquidity of receivables.

The merchandise inventory turnover formula is as follows:

$$\text{Merchandise Inventory Turnover} = \frac{\text{Cost of Goods Sold}}{\text{Average Inventory}}$$

Using the 1989 and 1988 figures for Cooper, the merchandise inventory turnover is computed in Exhibit 6-8.

Computing the average inventory based on beginning-of-year and end-of-year inventories can be misleading if the company has seasonal fluctuations or if the company uses a natural business year. The solution to the problem is similar to that used when computing the receivable turnover—that is, to use the monthly balances of inventory. Monthly estimates of inventory are typically available when

EXHIBIT 6-8

COOPER TIRE & RUBBER COMPANY
Merchandise Inventory Turnover
December 31, 1989 and 1988

	1989	1988
Cost of goods sold [A]	$727,323,386	$641,613,558
Inventory:		
Beginning of year	67,909,495	60,977,373
End of year	70,690,865	67,909,495
Total	138,600,360	128,886,868
Average inventory [B]	69,300,180	64,443,434
Merchandise inventory turnover [A ÷ B]	10.50 times	9.96 times

performing internal analysis, but not when performing external analysis. Quarterly figures may be available for external analysis and should be used. If adequate information is not available, avoid comparing a company on a natural business year with a company on a calendar year. The company with the natural business year tends to overstate inventory turnover and therefore liquidity of inventory.

Over time, the difference between the merchandise inventory turnover ratio for a firm that uses LIFO can become very material in comparison with a firm that uses a method that results in a higher inventory figure. The LIFO firm will have a much lower inventory. Therefore, it is not logical to compare the merchandise inventory turnover of a firm that uses LIFO with a firm that does not. Nor is it logical to compare a firm in one industry with a firm in another industry.

When you suspect that the merchandise inventory turnover computation is not resulting in a reasonable answer because inventory and/or cost of goods sold dollar figures are not reasonable, the computation may be performed using quantities rather than dollars. As with the days' sales in inventory, this alternative is feasible only when performing internal analysis. (It may not be feasible even for internal analysis because of product line changes.)

Inventory Turnover in Days

The inventory turnover figure can be expressed in number of days instead of times per year. This is comparable to the computation that expressed accounts receivable turnover in days.

The formula for determining the inventory turnover in days is as follows:

$$\text{Inventory Turnover in Days} = \frac{\text{Average Inventory}}{\text{Cost of Goods Sold}/365}$$

Notice that this is the same formula for determining the days' sales in inventory, except that the average inventory is used. The 1989 and 1988 Cooper data are used in Exhibit 6-9 to compute the inventory turnover in days. Considering that Cooper is a manufacturing concern, the turnover figures appear to be relatively good.

The inventory turnover in terms of times per year can be computed using the following formula, which is directly related to the turnover in days:

$$\frac{365}{\text{Inventory Turnover in Days}} = \text{Inventory Turnover per Year}$$

Using the 1989 Cooper data, the inventory turnover is determined as follows:

$$\frac{365}{\text{Inventory Turnover in Days}} = \frac{365}{34.78} = 10.49 \text{ Times}$$

Operating Cycle Computed

As indicated earlier, the operating cycle is considered to be the time between the acquisition of inventory and the realization of cash from the selling of the inventory. An approximation of the operating cycle can be determined from the receivable liquidity figures and the inventory liquidity figures. The formula for computing the operating cycle is as follows:

$$\text{Operating Cycle} = \frac{\text{Accounts Receivable}}{\text{Turnover in Days}} + \frac{\text{Inventory Turnover}}{\text{in Days}}$$

The 1989 and 1988 Cooper data are used in Exhibit 6-10 to compute the operating cycle.

The accounts receivable turnover in days, plus the inventory turnover in days, gives an approximation of the operating cycle. Using Cooper figures for 1989 produced an accounts receivable turnover of 52.70 days and an inventory turnover of 34.78 days. From this, the operating cycle can be estimated at 87.48 days. This is not a realistic estimate of the operating cycle, of course, if the accounts receivable turnover in days and the inventory turnover in days are not realistic. It should be

E X H I B I T 6 - 9

COOPER TIRE & RUBBER COMPANY
Inventory Turnover in Days
December 31, 1989 and 1988

	1989	1988
Cost of goods sold	$727,323,386	$641,613,558
Average inventory [A]	69,300,180	64,443,434
Sales of inventory per day (cost of goods sold divided by 365) [B]	1,992,667	1,757,845
Inventory turnover in days [A ÷ B]	34.78 days	36.66 days

EXHIBIT   6 - 1 0

COOPER TIRE & RUBBER COMPANY
Operating Cycle
For the Years Ended December 31, 1989 and 1988

	1989	1988
Accounts receivable turnover in days [A]	52.70	57.99
Inventory turnover in days [B]	34.78	36.66
Operating cycle [A + B]	87.48	94.65

remembered that the accounts receivable turnover in days and the inventory turnover in days are understated, and thus the liquidity overstated, if the company uses a natural business year and the averages were computed based on start-of-year and end-of-year data. It should also be remembered that the inventory turnover in days is understated, and the liquidity of the inventory overstated, if the company uses LIFO inventory. Also note that accounts receivable turnover in days is understated, and liquidity of receivables overstated, if the sales figures used included cash and credit sales.

The indicated operating cycle should be helpful when comparing a firm from period to period and when comparing a firm with similar companies. This would be the case, even if it is understated or overstated, as long as the figures in the computation are comparable.

Related to the operating cycle figure, which was computed from a combination of accounts receivable turnover in days and inventory turnover in days, is a computation that indicates how long it will take to realize cash from the ending inventory. This computation consists of combining the number of days' sales in ending receivables and the number of days' sales in ending inventory. The 1989 Cooper data produced a days' sales in ending receivables of 54.12 days and a days' sales in ending inventory of 35.48 days, for a total of 89.60 days. In this case, there is no material difference between this figure and the operating cycle figure. It is therefore likely that the receivables and inventory at the end of the year are representative of the receivables and inventory carried during the year.

Prepayments

Prepayments consist of unexpired costs, for which payment has been made, which are expected to be consumed within the period that has been used to determine current assets—namely, the operating cycle or one year, whichever is longer. Prepayments normally represent an immaterial portion of the current assets; they therefore have an immaterial influence on the short-term debt-paying ability of the firm.

Since prepayments have been paid and will not generate cash in the future, they are quite different from other assets classified as current assets. Prepayments are related to the short-term debt-paying ability of the entity, because they conserve the use of cash.

Because of the nature of prepayments, the problems of valuation and liquidity are handled in a simple manner. Valuation is taken as the cost that has been paid. Since prepayments are a current asset that has been paid for in a relatively short period prior to the balance sheet date, the cost paid is fairly representative of the cash that will be saved because of the prepayment. Except in rare circumstances, a prepayment will not result in cash coming in; therefore, no liquidity computation is called for. An example of a circumstance where cash comes in would be an insurance policy that is going to be canceled in advance. No liquidity computation is possible, even in this exceptional case.

Other Current Assets

Current assets other than the normal current assets of cash, marketable securities, receivables, inventories, and prepayments may be found. These other current assets may be very material in any one year and therefore, unless they are recurring, may distort the firm's liquidity in terms of liquidity from normal sources.

These other current assets will, in management's opinion, be realized in cash or conserve the use of cash within the operating cycle of the business or for one year, whichever is longer. Examples of assets sometimes found listed as current assets, other than the normal ones previously discussed, are property held for sale and advances or deposits. Often these other current assets are explained in a footnote.

Current Liabilities

Current liabilities are those obligations whose liquidation is reasonably expected to require the use of existing resources properly classified as current assets, or the creation of other current liabilities, within the normal operating cycle or one year, whichever is longer.[5] Thus, the definition of current liabilities is correlated with the definition of current assets. Typical items found in current liabilities are accounts payable, notes payable, accrued wages, accrued taxes, collections received in advance, and current portions of long-term liabilities.

The 1989 Cooper report listed current liabilities as follows:

Current liabilities:	
Accounts payable	$58,855,787
Income taxes	3,742,010
Accrued liabilities	34,271,795
Current portion of long-term debt	2,060,000
Total current liabilities	$98,929,592

[5]"Restatement and Revision of Accounting Research Bulletins," *Accounting Research and Terminology Bulletins, Final Edition*, No. 43 (New York: AICPA, 1961), Chap. 3, Sec. A, par. 7.

Two major problems are encountered when analyzing a current asset: determining a fair valuation and determining the liquidity of the asset. Only the valuation problem applies when analyzing a current liability, but even the valuation problem turns out to be immaterial and is therefore disregarded.

Theoretically, the valuation of a current liability should be the present value of the required future outlay of money. Since the difference between the present value and the amount that will be paid in the future is immaterial, the current liability is carried at its face value.

CURRENT ASSETS COMPARED WITH CURRENT LIABILITIES

A comparison of current assets with current liabilities gives an indication of the short-term debt-paying ability of the entity. Several comparisons can be made to determine this ability:

1. Working capital
2. Current ratio
3. Acid test ratio
4. Cash ratio

Working Capital

The working capital of a business is the excess of current assets over current liabilities; this is computed by subtracting the current liabilities from the current assets. The resulting working capital figure is taken as one of the primary indications of the short-run solvency of the business. The working capital formula is as follows:

$$\text{Working Capital} = \text{Current Assets} - \text{Current Liabilities}$$

The working capital for Cooper at the end of 1989 and 1988 is computed in Exhibit 6-11. The exhibit indicates that Cooper had $150,285,470 in working

EXHIBIT 6-11

COOPER TIRE & RUBBER COMPANY
Working Capital
December 31, 1989 and 1988

	1989	1988
Current assets [A]	$249,215,062	$229,226,670
Current liabilities [B]	98,929,592	86,125,443
Working capital [A − B]	$150,285,470	$143,101,227

capital in 1989 and $143,101,227 in working capital in 1988. These figures tend to be understated, because some of the current assets are understated based on the book figures. The current assets that may be understated are marketable securities and inventory.

Some of the marketable securities may be carried at cost, and others may be carried at the lower of cost or market. If the market value of those securities is not used, and if it is above the cost figure, then it must be disclosed. This market value figure should be used, if it is materially above the book figure, in order to determine the value of the resources that are available to pay the current liabilities.

Another figure that may be understated is the inventory figure, which, as reported, may be much less than the cost of replacing the inventory. The difference between the reported inventory amount and the replacement amount is normally material when the firm is using LIFO inventory. The difference may also be material when one of the other cost methods is used.

The current working capital amount should be compared with past amounts to determine if working capital is reasonable. Caution must be exercised, because the relative size of the firm may be expanding or contracting. Comparing working capital of one firm with that of another firm is usually meaningless because of size differences. If the working capital appears to be out of line, the reasons can be found by analyzing the individual current asset and current liability accounts.

Current Ratio

Another indicator of the short-term debt-paying ability of the firm is the current ratio. The current ratio is determined by dividing the current assets by the current liabilities. The current ratio formula is as follows:

$$\text{Current Ratio} = \frac{\text{Current Assets}}{\text{Current Liabilities}}$$

The current ratio computation for Cooper at the end of the 1989 and 1988 years is shown in Exhibit 6-12. Cooper's current ratio was 2.52 times at the end of 1989 and 2.66 times at the end of 1988.

For many years, the guideline for the minimum current ratio has been 2.00. The typical firm successfully maintained a current ratio of 2.00 or better until approximately the mid-1960s. Since that time, the current ratio of many firms has declined to a point below the 2.00 guideline. Currently, many firms are not successful in staying above a current ratio of 2.00. This indicates that there has been a decline in the liquidity of many firms.

A comparison with industry averages should be made to determine the typical current ratio for similar firms. In some industries, a current ratio substantially below 2.00 is adequate, while other industries require a ratio much larger than 2.00. In general, the shorter the operating cycle, the lower the normal current ratio. The longer the operating cycle, the higher the normal current ratio.

A comparison of the firm's current ratio with prior current ratios, and a comparison with industry averages, can help determine if the current ratio is high or low at this period in time. These comparisons do not indicate why the current ratio

EXHIBIT 6-12

COOPER TIRE & RUBBER COMPANY
Current Ratio
December 31, 1989 and 1988

	1989	1988
Current assets [A]	$249,215,062	$229,226,670
Current liabilities [B]	98,929,592	86,125,443
Current ratio [A ÷ B]	2.52 times	2.66 times

is high or low. Possible reasons for the current ratio being out of line can be found from an analysis of the individual accounts that are used when computing the current ratio—namely, the current asset and the current liability accounts. Often, the major reasons for the current ratio being out of line are found in the detailed analysis that has been performed for accounts receivables and inventory.

The current ratio is considered to be more indicative of short-term debt-paying ability than is the working capital. Working capital determines only the absolute difference between the current assets and liabilities. The current ratio takes into consideration the relative relation between the size of the current assets and the size of the current liabilities, making it feasible to compare the current ratio, for instance, between General Motors and Chrysler. A comparison of the working capital of these two firms would be meaningless, because of the material differences in company size.

When marketable securities appear in the current assets, the current assets should be adjusted to reflect the market value of these securities (when this information is available). This is the same adjustment that was suggested in the determination of working capital.

LIFO inventory can cause major problems with the current ratio, because of the understatement of inventory. The result would be a current ratio that is understated. Extreme caution should be exercised when comparing a firm that uses LIFO and a firm that uses some other inventory costing method.

Before computing the current ratio, the accounts receivable turnover and the merchandise inventory turnover should be computed. These computations enable the analyst to formulate an opinion as to whether there are liquidity problems with receivables and/or inventory. An opinion as to the quality of receivables and inventory should then have an influence on the analyst's opinion of an adequate current ratio. Liquidity problems with receivables and/or inventory indicate that the current ratio needs to be much higher than when there are no such liquidity problems.

Acid Test Ratio (Quick Ratio)

The current ratio is generally used to evaluate an enterprise's overall liquidity position. At times, it is desirable to access a more immediate position than that indicated by the current ratio. This is done by relating the most liquid assets to current liabilities. The resulting ratio is called the acid test (or quick) ratio.

Inventory should be removed from current assets when computing the acid test. Some of the reasons for this are that inventory may be slow moving or possibly obsolete, and parts of the inventory may have been pledged to specific creditors. For example, a winery has inventory that requires considerable time for aging and therefore a considerable time before sale. To include the wine inventory in the acid test computation would overstate the liquidity.

There is also a valuation problem with inventory, because it is stated at a cost figure that is likely to be materially different from a fair current valuation. In summary, inventory should be left out of the computation because of possible misleading liquidity indications.

The acid test ratio is as follows:

$$\text{Acid Test} = \frac{\text{Current Assets} - \text{Inventory}}{\text{Current Liabilities}}$$

The acid test ratio is computed in Exhibit 6-13 for Cooper at the end of 1989 and 1988. For Cooper, the acid test was 1.80 times at the end of 1989 and 1.87 times at the end of 1988.

It may also be desirable to achieve a view of liquidity that excludes some other items in current assets that may not represent relatively current cash flow. Examples of items to eliminate are prepaids and miscellaneous items such as assets held for sale.

The more conservative manner of computing the acid test is to combine cash equivalents, marketable securities, and net receivables and then relate the total of these items to current liabilities. Usually there is a very immaterial difference between the acid test computed under the first method and this second method. This is because frequently the only difference in the computation is the inclusion of prepaids in the first computation. Sometimes there is a very material difference in the computation. The more conservative acid test ratio is computed as follows:

$$\text{Acid Test} = \frac{\text{Cash Equivalents} + \text{Marketable Securities} + \text{Net Receivables}}{\text{Current Liabilities}}$$

EXHIBIT 6-13

COOPER TIRE & RUBBER COMPANY
Acid Test
December 31, 1989 and 1988

	1989	1988
Current assets	$249,215,062	$229,226,670
Less: ending inventory	70,690,865	67,909,495
Remaining current assets [A]	178,524,197	161,317,175
Current liabilities [B]	98,929,592	86,125,443
Acid test [A ÷ B]	1.80 times	1.87 times

The conservative acid test ratio is computed in Exhibit 6-14 for Cooper at the end of 1989 and 1988. This approach to determining the acid test resulted in 1.78 times at the end of 1989 and 1.85 times at the end of 1988.

For Cooper, the difference in the results between the two alternative computations is immaterial. From this point on in this text, the more conservative computations will be used for computing the acid test. When a company needs to view liquidity with only inventory removed, the alternative computation should be used.

The usual guideline for the acid test ratio is 1.00, and the conservative approach to computing the acid test ratio is usually used. Here again a comparison should be made with the past acid test of the firm. A comparison should also be made with major competitors and the industry averages. Some industries find that a ratio less than 1.00 is adequate, while others need a ratio greater than 1.00. For example, the typical grocery store sells only for cash and therefore does not have receivables. This type of business can have an acid test substantially below the 1.00 guideline and still have adequate liquidity.

Before computing the acid test, the accounts receivable turnover should be computed. This is to get an idea of whether there are liquidity problems with receivables. An opinion as to the quality of receivables should then help the analyst form an opinion of an adequate acid test.

There has been a major decline in the liquidity of companies in the United States, as measured by the current ratio and the acid test ratio. This is illustrated in Exhibit 6-15, which shows the dramatically reduced liquidity of U.S. companies. A reduced liquidity position leads to more bankruptcies; in general, it means more risk for creditors and investors.

Cash Ratio

Sometimes there is a need to view the liquidity of a firm from an extremely conservative point of view. This may be the case when the company has pledged its receivables and its inventory, or severe liquidity problems with inventory and re-

EXHIBIT 6 - 1 4

COOPER TIRE & RUBBER COMPANY
Acid Test (Conservative Approach)
December 31, 1989 and 1988

	1989	1988
Cash, including short-term investments	$ 49,586,311	$ 38,690,586
Net receivables	126,431,368	120,407,633
Total quick assets [A]	$176,017,679	$159,098,219
Current liabilities [B]	98,929,592	86,125,443
Acid test ratio [A ÷ B]	1.78 times	1.85 times

EXHIBIT 6-15

**Trends in Current Ratio and Acid Test
All U.S. Manufacturing Companies, 1947–1989**

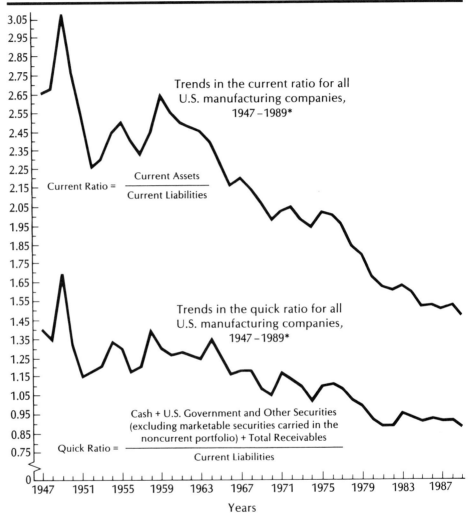

Years

*1980–1989 extended by author.
Source: Financial Accounting Standards Board, "FASB Discussion Memorandum—Reporting Funds Flows, Liquidity, and Financial Flexibility," 1980, p. 7.

ceivables may be suspected. In this case, the best indicator of the company's short-run liquidity may possibly be a ratio called the *cash ratio*.

The cash ratio relates cash equivalents and marketable securities to current liabilities. This ratio is seldom given much weight when evaluating the liquidity of a firm. This is because it is not realistic to expect a firm to have enough cash equivalents and marketable securities to cover current liabilities. This ratio indicates the "last resort" liquidity of the firm if it must depend on cash equivalents and marketable securities.

Significant weight is seldom given to the cash ratio unless the firm is in financial trouble. Exceptions to this are companies that have naturally slow-moving inventories and receivables and highly speculative companies. For instance, a land development company in Florida may sell lots that are paid for over a number of years on an installment basis; or the success of a new company may be in doubt, such as the Bricklin car company that was started in Canada during the early 1970s.

The cash ratio indicates the immediate liquidity of the firm. A high cash ratio indicates that the firm is not using its resource cash to best advantage; that cash should be put to work in the operations of the company. Detailed knowledge of the firm is required, however, before drawing a definite conclusion. Management may possibly have plans for the cash—for example, a building expansion program. A cash ratio that is too low could indicate an immediate problem with paying bills.

The cash ratio is computed as follows:

$$\text{Cash Ratio} = \frac{\text{Cash Equivalents} + \text{Marketable Securities}}{\text{Current Liabilities}}$$

This ratio is computed in Exhibit 6-16 for Cooper at the end of 1989 and 1988. For Cooper, the cash ratio was .50 times at the end of 1989 and .45 times at the end of 1988. Cooper's cash ratio increased at the end of 1989 in relation to the end of 1988. The increase in the very liquid assets between 1989 and 1988 approximately equals the increase in the acid test ratio between these two years for Cooper. Thus, the increase in liquidity for Cooper was in its most liquid assets. The cash ratio was very strong at the end of 1989.

EXHIBIT 6-16

COOPER TIRE & RUBBER COMPANY
Cash Ratio
December 31, 1989 and 1988

	1989	1988
Cash, including short-term investments [A]	$49,586,311	$38,690,586
Current liabilities [B]	98,929,592	86,125,443
Cash ratio [A ÷ B]	0.50 times	0.45 times

Management would usually not want the cash ratio to be abnormally high, because it would want to use the cash actively in operations. A very high cash ratio could indicate plans for a capacity increase or an acquisition.

OTHER LIQUIDITY CONSIDERATIONS

Another liquidity ratio is cash flow/current maturities of long-term debt and notes payable. This ratio is discussed in connection with the statement of cash flows in Chapter 10.

Sales to Working Capital (Working Capital Turnover)

Relating sales to working capital gives an indication of the turnover in working capital per year. This ratio needs to be compared with the past, competitors, and industry averages in order to form an opinion as to the adequacy of the working capital turnover. Like many ratios, there are no rules of thumb as to what this ratio should be. Since this ratio relates a balance sheet number (working capital) to an income statement number (sales), there is a problem if the balance sheet number is not representative of the year. To avoid this type of distortion, use the average monthly working capital figure when it is available.

A low working capital turnover ratio tentatively indicates an unprofitable use of working capital. In other words, sales are not adequate in relation to the available working capital. A high ratio is a tentative indication that the firm is undercapitalized (overtrading). An undercapitalized firm is particularly susceptible to liquidity problems when there is a major adverse change in business conditions.

The formula for determining the working capital turnover is as follows:

$$\text{Sales to Working Capital} = \frac{\text{Sales}}{\text{Average Working Capital}}$$

This ratio is computed in Exhibit 6-17 for Cooper at the end of 1989 and 1988. The sales to working capital ratio increased for Cooper between 1988 and 1989. (Working capital was lower in relation to sales.) This tentatively indicates a more profitable use of working capital in 1989 than in 1988.

Liquidity Considerations Not on the Face of the Statements

A firm may have a better liquidity position than is indicated by the face of the financial statements. Several examples are discussed in the paragraphs that follow.

1. Unused bank credit lines would be a positive addition to liquidity. Unused bank credit lines are frequently disclosed in footnotes.

EXHIBIT   6 - 1 7

COOPER TIRE & RUBBER COMPANY
Sales to Working Capital
For the Years Ended December 31, 1989 and 1988

	1989	1988
Net sales [A]	$866,805,462	$748,032,206
Working capital at beginning of year	143,101,227	154,283,213
Working capital at end of year	150,285,470	143,101,227
Average working capital [B]	146,693,348	148,692,220
Sales to working capital [A ÷ B]	5.91 times	5.03 times

2. Cooper includes the following statement in the long-term debt footnote: "The Company has a revolving credit agreement with four banks authorizing borrowings up to $85,000,000 with interest rates at prime or lower under optional rate provisions. The agreement, which permits the issuance of commercial paper, provides that on July 31, 1992 the Company may convert any outstanding borrowings under the agreement into a four-year term loan. . . . There were no borrowings under the revolving credit agreement during the years ended December 31, 1989 and 1988."

3. A firm may have some long-term assets that could be converted to cash quickly. This would add to the firm's liquidity. Extreme caution is advised if there is any reliance on long-term assets for liquidity. For one thing, the long-term assets are usually needed in operations. Second, even excess long-term assets may not be easily converted into cash in a short period of time. An exception might be investments, depending on the nature of the investments.

4. A firm may be in a very good long-term debt position and therefore have the capability to issue debt or stock. Thus, the firm could relieve a severe liquidity problem in a reasonable amount of time.

A firm may not be in as good a position of liquidity as is indicated by the ratios, as the following examples show.

1. A firm may have notes discounted on which the other party has full recourse against the firm. Discounted notes should be disclosed in a footnote.

2. A firm may have major contingent liabilities that have not been booked. An example would be a disputed tax claim. Unbooked contingencies that are material are disclosed in a footnote.

3. A firm may have guaranteed a bank note for another company. This would be disclosed in a footnote.

An example of additional potential liabilities that are not disclosed on the face of the statements is the following footnote of Federal-Mogul Corporation in its 1988 annual report.

Note L: Litigation

In June 1988, a trial court in Boston, Massachusetts issued a decision against the Company in the amount of $28.5 million in compensatory damages and interest. The Company intends to pursue all available remedies to set aside or reverse this decision that the Company had breached a letter of intent and committed unfair practices in selling a small division in 1981. In the opinion of the Company's counsel, the decision awarding the judgment is erroneous and should be reversed or substantially reduced upon appeal. In management's opinion, this judgment, when finally concluded, will not have a material adverse effect on the consolidated financial position of the Company.

The ability to pay current obligations when due is related to the cash-generating ability of the firm. This will be discussed in Chapter 10.

SUMMARY

The ratios related to liquidity of short-term assets and the related short-term debt-paying ability are as follows:

$$\text{Days' Sales in Receivables} = \frac{\text{Gross Receivables}}{\text{Net Sales}/365}$$

$$\text{Accounts Receivable Turnover} = \frac{\text{Net Sales}}{\text{Average Gross Receivables}}$$

$$\text{Accounts Receivable Turnover in Days} = \frac{\text{Average Gross Receivables}}{\text{Net Sales}/365}$$

$$\text{Days' Sales in Inventory} = \frac{\text{Ending Inventory}}{\text{Cost of Goods Sold}/365}$$

$$\text{Merchandise Inventory Turnover} = \frac{\text{Cost of Goods Sold}}{\text{Average Inventory}}$$

$$\text{Inventory Turnover in Days} = \frac{\text{Average Inventory}}{\text{Cost of Goods Sold}/365}$$

$$\text{Operating Cycle} = \frac{\text{Accounts Receivable}}{\text{Turnover in Days}} + \frac{\text{Inventory Turnover}}{\text{in Days}}$$

$$\text{Working Capital} = \text{Current Assets} - \text{Current Liabilities}$$

$$\text{Current Ratio} = \frac{\text{Current Assets}}{\text{Current Liabilities}}$$

$$\text{Acid Test} = \frac{\text{Cash Equivalents} + \text{Marketable Securities} + \text{Net Receivables}}{\text{Current Liabilities}}$$

$$\text{Cash Ratio} = \frac{\text{Cash Equivalents} + \text{Marketable Securities}}{\text{Current Liabilities}}$$

$$\text{Sales to Working Capital} = \frac{\text{Sales}}{\text{Average Working Capital}}$$

| QUESTIONS

Q 6-1   It is proposed at a stockholders' meeting that the firm slow its rate of payments on accounts payable in order to make more funds available for operations. It is contended that this procedure will enable the firm to expand inventory, which will in turn enable the firm to generate more sales. Comment on this proposal.

Q 6-2   The Jones Wholesale Company has been one of the fastest-growing wholesale firms in the United States for the last five years in terms of sales and profits. The firm has maintained a current ratio above the average for the wholesale industry. Mr. Jones has asked you to explain possible reasons why the firm is having difficulty meeting its payroll and its accounts payable.

Q 6-3   What is the reason for separating current assets from the rest of the assets found on the balance sheet?

Q 6-4   Define operating cycle.

Q 6-5   Define current assets.

Q 6-6   List the major categories of items usually found in current assets.

Q 6-7   The Rachit Company has cash that has been frozen in a bank in Cuba. Should this cash be classified as a current asset? Discuss.

Q 6-8   The A. B. Smith Company has marketable securities that cost $80,000 and now have a market value of $85,000. The company carries the marketable securities on its balance sheet at $80,000 and discloses the market value in parentheses. For statement analysis, which figure should be used when determining the company's short-term debt-paying ability? Why?

Q 6-9   The Arrow Company has invested funds in a supplier to help ensure a steady supply of needed materials. Would this investment be classified as a marketable security?

Q 6-10   List the two computations that are used to determine the liquidity of the receivables.

Q 6-11   List the two computations that are used to determine the liquidity of the inventory.

Q 6-12   Would a company that uses a natural business year tend to overstate or understate the liquidity of its receivables? Explain.

Q 6-13   The T. Melcher Company uses the calendar year. Sales are at a peak during the Christmas holiday season, and T. Melcher Company extends thirty-day credit terms to customers. Comment on the expected liquidity of its receivables, based on the days' sales in receivables and the accounts receivable turnover.

Q 6-14   A company that uses a natural business year, or ends its year when business is at a peak, will tend to distort the liquidity of its receivables when end-of-year and beginning-of-year receivables are used in the computation. Explain how a company that uses a natural business year or ends its year when business is at a peak can eliminate the distortion in its liquidity computations.

Q 6-15   If a company has substantial cash sales and credit sales, is there any meaning to the receivable liquidity computations that are based on gross sales?

Q 6-16   Describe the difference in inventories between a firm that is a trading concern and a firm that is a manufacturing concern.

Q 6-17   During times of inflation, which of the inventory costing methods listed below would give the most realistic valuation of inventory? Which method would give the least realistic valuation of inventory? Explain.
a. LIFO
b. average
c. FIFO

Q 6-18   The number of days' sales in inventory relates the amount of the ending inventory to the average daily cost of goods sold. Explain why this computation may be misleading under the following conditions:
a. The company uses a natural business year for its accounting period.
b. The company closes the year when the activities are at a peak.
c. The company uses LIFO inventory, and inflation has been a problem for a number of years.

Q 6-19   The days' sales in inventory is an estimate of the number of days that it will take to sell the current inventory.
a. What is the ideal number of days' sales in inventory?
b. In general, does a company want many days' sales in inventory?
c. Can days' sales in inventory be too low?

Q 6-20   Some firms do not report cost of goods sold separately on their income statements. In such a case, how should you proceed to compute days' sales in inventory? Will this procedure produce a realistic figure for days' sales in inventory?

Q 6-21   One of the computations to determine the liquidity of inventory determines the merchandise inventory turnover. This computation is done by dividing the average inventory into the cost of goods sold. Usually, the average inventory is determined by using the beginning-of-the-year and the end-of-the-year inventory figures, but this computation can be misleading if the company has seasonal fluctuations or uses a natural business year. Suggest how to eliminate these distortions.

Q 6-22   Explain the influence of the use of LIFO inventory on the merchandise inventory turnover.

Q 6-23   Define working capital.

Q 6-24   Define current liabilities.

Q 6-25   Several comparisons can be made to determine the short-term debt-paying ability of an entity. Some of these comparisons are:
a. working capital
b. current ratio
c. acid test ratio

       d. cash ratio
          1. Define each of these terms.
          2. If the book figures are based on cost, will the results of the preceding computations tend to be understated or overstated? Explain.
          3. What figures should be used in order to avoid the problem referred to in (2)?

Q 6-26   Discuss how to use working capital in analysis.

Q 6-27   Both current assets and current liabilities are used in the computation of working capital and the current ratio, yet the current ratio is considered to be more indicative of the short-term debt-paying ability. Explain.

Q 6-28   In determining the short-term liquidity of a firm, the current ratio is usually considered to be a better guide than the acid test ratio, and the acid test ratio is considered to be a better guide than the cash ratio. Discuss when the acid test ratio would be preferred over the current ratio and when the cash ratio would be preferred over the acid test ratio.

Q 6-29   Discuss some benefits that may accrue to a firm from reducing its operating cycle. Suggest some ways that may be used to reduce a company's operating cycle.

Q 6-30   Discuss why some firms have longer natural operating cycles than other firms.

Q 6-31   Would a firm with a relatively long operating cycle tend to charge a higher markup in its inventory cost than a firm with a short operating cycle? Discuss.

Q 6-32   Is the profitability of the entity considered to be of major importance in determining the short-term debt-paying ability? Discuss.

Q 6-33   Does the allowance method for bad debts or the direct write-off method result in the fairest presentation of receivables on the balance sheet and the fairest matching of expenses against revenue?

Q 6-34   When a firm faces an inflationary condition and the LIFO inventory method is based on a periodic basis, purchases late in the year can have a substantial influence on profits. Comment.

Q 6-35   Why could a current asset such as "net assets of required business held for sale" distort a firm's liquidity, in terms of working capital or the current ratio?

Q 6-36   Before computing the current ratio, the accounts receivable turnover and the merchandise inventory turnover should be computed. Why?

Q 6-37   Before computing the acid test ratio, the accounts receivable turnover should be computed. Comment.

Q 6-38   Which inventory costing method results in the highest balance sheet amount for inventory? (Assume inflationary conditions.)

Q 6-39   Indicate the single most important factor that motivates a company to select LIFO.

Q 6-40   A relatively low sales to working capital ratio is a tentative indication of an efficient use of working capital. Comment. A relatively high sales to working capital ratio is a tentative indication that the firm is undercapitalized. Comment.

Q 6-41   List three situations in which the liquidity position of the firm may be better than that indicated by the liquidity ratios.

Q 6-42   List three situations in which the liquidity position of the firm may not be as good as that indicated by the liquidity ratios.

Q 6-43   Indicate the objective of the ratio of sales to working capital.

| PROBLEMS

P 6-1   In this problem, the acid test ratio is computed as follows:

$$\frac{\text{Current Assets} - \text{Inventory}}{\text{Current Liabilities}}$$

Required   Determine the cost of sales of a firm with the financial data given below:

Current ratio	2.5
Quick ratio or acid test	2.0
Current liabilities	$400,000
Inventory turnover	3 times

P 6-2   The Hawk Company is interested in determining the liquidity of its receivables. It has supplied you with the following data regarding selected accounts for December 31, 1989 and 1988.

Net sales	$1,180,178	$2,200,000
Receivables, less allowance for losses and discounts		
Beginning of year (allowance for losses and discounts, 1989—$12,300; 1988—$7,180)	240,360	230,180
End of year (allowance for losses and discounts 1989—$11,180; 1988—$12,300)	220,385	240,360

Required   a. Compute the number of days' sales in receivables at December 31, 1989 and 1988.
b. Compute the accounts receivable turnover for 1989 and 1988.
c. Comment on the liquidity of the Hawk Company receivables.

P 6-3   Mr. Williams, the owner of Williams Produce, is interested in keeping control over accounts receivable. He understands that days' sales in receivables and accounts receivable turnover will give a good indication of how well receivables are being managed. Williams Produce does 60% of its business during June, July, and August.

Required   a. Compute the days' sales in receivables for July 31, 1989 and December 31, 1989, based on the accompanying data.
b. Compute the accounts receivable turnover for the periods ended July 31, 1989, and December 31, 1989.
c. Comment on the results from (a) and (b).

	For Year Ended December 31, 1989	For Year Ended July 31, 1989
Net sales	$800,000	$790,000
Receivables, less allowance for doubtful accounts		
Beginning of period (allowance January 1, 3,000; August 1, 4,000)	50,000	89,000
End of period (allowance December 31, 3,500; July 31, 4,100)	55,400	90,150

P 6-4 The L. Solomon Company would like to compare its days' sales in receivables with that of a competitor, L. Konrath Company. Both companies have had similar sales results in the past, but the L. Konrath Company has had better profit results. The L. Solomon Company suspects that one reason for this is that the L. Konrath Company did a better job of managing receivables. The L. Solomon Company uses a calendar year that ends on December 31, and L. Konrath Company uses a fiscal year that ends on July 31.

	For Year Ended December 31, 19XX
L. Solomon Company	
Net sales	$1,800,000
Receivables, less allowance for doubtful accounts of $8,000	110,000

	For Year Ended July 31, 19XX
L. Konrath Company	
Net sales	$1,850,000
Receivables, less allowance for doubtful accounts of $4,000	60,000

Required a. Compute the days' sales in receivables for both companies.
b. Comment on the results.

P 6-5a The P. Gibson Company has computed its accounts receivable turnover in days to be 36.

Required Compute the accounts receivable turnover per year.

P 6-5b The P. Gibson Company has computed its accounts receivable turnover per year to be 12.

Required Compute the accounts receivable turnover in days.

P 6-5c The P. Gibson Company has gross receivables at the end of the year of $280,000 and net sales for the year of $2,158,000.

Required Compute the days' sales in receivables at the end of the year.

P 6-5d The P. Gibson Company has net sales of $3,500,000 and average gross receivables of $324,000.

Required Compute the accounts receivable turnover.

P 6-6 The J. Shaffer Company has an ending inventory of $360,500 and a cost of goods sold for the year of $2,100,000. It has used LIFO inventory for a number of years because of persistent inflation.

Required   a. Compute the days' sales in inventory.
                 b. Is the J. Shaffer Company days' sales in inventory as computed realistic in comparison
                    with the actual days' sales in inventory?
                 c. Would the days' sales in inventory computed for the J. Shaffer Company be a helpful
                    guide?

P 6-7   The J. Szabo Company had an average inventory of $280,000 and a cost of goods sold of
                 $1,250,000.

Required   Compute the following:
                 a. inventory turnover in days
                 b. inventory turnover

P 6-8   The following are inventory and sales data for this year for G. Rabbit Company.

	End of Year	Beginning of Year
Net sales	$3,150,000	
Gross receivables	180,000	$160,000
Inventory	480,000	390,000
Cost of goods sold	2,250,000	

Required   Using the above data from the G. Rabbit Company, compute:
                 a. the accounts receivable turnover in days
                 b. the inventory turnover in days
                 c. the operating cycle

P 6-9   The Anna Banana Company would like to estimate how long it will take to realize cash
                 from its ending inventory. For this purpose, the following data are submitted:

Accounts receivable, less allowance for	
doubtful accounts of $30,000	$ 560,000
Ending inventory	680,000
Net sales	4,350,000
Cost of goods sold	3,600,000

Required   Estimate how long it will take to realize cash from the ending inventory.

P 6-10   The Laura Badora Company has been using LIFO inventory. The company is required to
                 disclose the replacement cost of its inventory and the replacement cost of its cost of goods
                 sold on its annual statements. Selected data for the year ended 1989 are as follows:

Accounts receivable, less allowance for	
doubtful accounts of $25,000	$ 480,000
Ending inventory, LIFO (estimated	
replacement cost $900,000)	570,000
Net sales	3,650,000
Cost of goods sold (estimated replacement	
cost $3,150,000)	2,850,000

Required   a. Compute the days' sales in receivables.
                 b. Compute the days' sales in inventory, using the cost figure.
                 c. Compute the days' sales in inventory, using the replacement cost for the inventory and
                    the cost of goods sold.

d. Should replacement cost of inventory and cost of goods sold be used, when possible, when computing days' sales in inventory? Discuss.

P 6-11   A partial balance sheet and income statement for the King Corporation are as follows:

KING CORPORATION
Partial Balance Sheet
December 31, 1989

Assets	
Current assets:	
Cash	$ 33,493
Marketable securities—at lower of cost or market (estimated	
market value $265,000)	215,147
Trade receivables, less allowance of $6,000	255,000
Inventories, LIFO	523,000
Prepaid expenses	26,180
Total current assets	$1,052,820
Liabilities	
Current liabilities	
Trade accounts payable	$ 103,689
Notes payable (primarily to banks) and commercial paper	210,381
Accrued expenses and other liabilities	120,602
Income taxes payable	3,120
Current maturities of long-term debt	22,050
Total current liabilities	$ 459,842

KING CORPORATION
Partial Income Statement
For Year Ended December 31, 1989

Net sales	$3,050,600
Miscellaneous income	45,060
	$3,095,660
Cost and expenses:	
Cost of sales	$2,185,100
Selling, general, and administrative expenses	350,265
Interest expense	45,600
Income taxes	300,000
	2,880,965
Net income	$ 214,695

Note: The trade receivables at December 31, 1988 were $280,000, less an allowance of $8,000, for a gross receivable figure of $288,000. The inventory at December 31, 1988 was $565,000.

Required   Compute the following:

a. working capital
b. current ratio
c. acid test ratio
d. cash ratio
e. days' sales in receivables

f. accounts receivable turnover in days
g. days' sales in inventory
h. inventory turnover in days
i. operating cycle

P 6-12   Individual transactions often have a significant impact on ratios. This problem will consider the direction of such an impact.

	Total Current Assets	Total Current Liabilities	Net Working Capital	Current Ratio
a. Cash is acquired through issuance of additional common stock.	_____	_____	_____	_____
b. Merchandise is sold for cash. (Assume a profit.)	_____	_____	_____	_____
c. A fixed asset is sold for more than book value.	_____	_____	_____	_____
d. Payment is made to trade creditors for previous purchases.	_____	_____	_____	_____
e. A cash dividend is declared and paid.	_____	_____	_____	_____
f. A stock dividend is declared and paid.	_____	_____	_____	_____
g. Cash is obtained through long-term bank loans.	_____	_____	_____	_____
h. A profitable firm increases its fixed assets depreciation allowance account.	_____	_____	_____	_____
i. Current operating expenses are paid.	_____	_____	_____	_____
j. Ten-year notes are issued to pay off accounts payable.	_____	_____	_____	_____
k. Accounts receivable are collected.	_____	_____	_____	_____
l. Equipment is purchased with short-term notes.	_____	_____	_____	_____
m. Merchandise is purchased on credit.	_____	_____	_____	_____
n. The estimated taxes payable are increased.	_____	_____	_____	_____
o. Marketable securities are sold below cost.	_____	_____	_____	_____

Required   Indicate the effects of the transactions listed above on each of the following: total current assets, total current liabilities, net working capital, and current ratio. Use + to indicate an increase, − to indicate a decrease, and 0 to indicate no effect. Assume an initial current ratio of more than 1 to 1.

P 6-13   Current assets and current liabilities for companies D and E are summarized as follows:

	Company D	Company E
Current assets	$400,000	$900,000
Current liabilities	200,000	700,000
Working capital	$200,000	$200,000

Required   Evaluate the relative solvency of companies D and E.

P 6-14   Current assets and current liabilities for companies R and T are summarized as follows:

	Company R	Company T
Current assets	$400,000	$800,000
Current liabilities	200,000	400,000
Working capital	$200,000	$400,000

Required   Evaluate the relative solvency of companies R and T.

P 6-15   The accompanying financial data were taken from the annual financial statements of Smith Corporation.

	1987	1988	1989
Current assets	$ 450,000	$ 400,000	$ 500,000
Current liabilities	390,000	300,000	340,000
Sales	1,450,000	1,500,000	1,400,000
Cost of goods sold	1,180,000	1,020,000	1,120,000
Inventory	280,000	200,000	250,000
Accounts receivable	120,000	110,000	105,000

Required   a. Based on these data, calculate the following for 1988 and 1989:
  1. working capital
  2. current ratio
  3. acid test ratio
  4. accounts receivable turnover
  5. merchandise inventory turnover
  6. inventory turnover in days
 b. Evaluate the results of your computations in regard to the short-term liquidity of the firm.

P 6-16   The Anne Elizabeth Corporation is engaged in the business of making toys. A high percentage of its products are sold to consumers during November and December. Therefore, retailers need to have the toys in stock prior to November. The corporation produces on a relatively stable basis during the year in order to retain skilled employees and to minimize the investment in plant and equipment. The seasonal nature of the business requires a substantial capacity to store inventory.

   The Anne Elizabeth Corporation uses a natural business year that ends on April 30. Inventory and accounts receivable data are given in the following table for the year ended April 30, 1990.

   The gross receivables balance at April 30, 1989, was $75,000, and the inventory balance was $350,000 on this date. Sales for the year ended April 30, 1990, totaled $4,000,000 and cost of goods sold totaled $1,800,000.

| | Month-End Balance | |
Month End	Gross Receivables	Inventory
May, 1989	$ 60,000	$525,000
June, 1989	40,000	650,000
July, 1989	50,000	775,000
August, 1989	60,000	900,000
September, 1989	200,000	975,000
October, 1989	800,000	700,000
November, 1989	1,500,000	400,000
December, 1989	1,800,000	25,000
January, 1990	1,000,000	100,000
February, 1990	600,000	150,000
March, 1990	200,000	275,000
April, 1990	50,000	400,000

Required

a. Computing averages based on the year-end figures, compute the following:
  1. accounts receivable turnover in days
  2. accounts receivable turnover per year
  3. inventory turnover in days
  4. inventory turnover per year
b. Computing averages based on monthly figures, compute the following:
  1. accounts receivable turnover in days
  2. accounts receivable turnover per year
  3. inventory turnover in days
  4. inventory turnover per year
c. Comment on the difference between the ratios computed in (a) and (b).
d. Compute the days' sales in receivables.
e. Compute the days' sales in inventory.
f. How realistic are the days' sales in receivables and the days' sales in inventory that were computed in (d) and (e)?

P 6-17   The following data relate to inventory for the year ended December 31, 1989.

Date	Description	Number of Units	Cost Per Unit	Total Cost
January 1	Beginning inventory	400	$5.00	$ 2,000
March 1	Purchase	1,000	6.00	6,000
August 1	Purchase	200	7.00	1,400
November 1	Purchase	200	7.50	1,500
		1,800		$10,900

A physical inventory on December 31, 1989 indicates that 400 units are on hand and that they came from the March 1 purchase.

Required   Compute the cost of goods sold for the year ended December 31, 1989 and the ending inventory under the following cost assumptions.

a. first-in, first-out (FIFO)
b. last-in, first-out (LIFO)
c. average cost (weighted average)
d. specific identification

P 6-18   The following data relate to inventory for the year ended December 31, 1989.

Date	Description	Number of Units	Cost Per Unit	Total Cost
January 1	Beginning inventory	1,000	$4.00	$ 4,000
February 20	Purchase	800	4.50	3,600
April 1	Purchase	900	4.75	4,275
July 1	Purchase	700	5.00	3,500
October 22	Purchase	500	4.90	2,450
December 10	Purchase	500	5.00	2,500
		4,400		$20,325

A physical inventory on December 31, 1989 indicates that 600 units are on hand and that they came from the July 1 purchase.

Required   Compute the cost of goods sold for the year ended December 31, 1989 and the ending inventory under the following cost assumptions:
a. first-in, first-out (FIFO)
b. last-in, first-out (LIFO)
c. average cost (weighted average)
d. specific identification

P 6-19   The J. A. Appliance Company has supplied you with the following data regarding working capital and sales for the years 1989, 1988, and 1987.

	1989	1988	1987
Working capital	$270,000	$260,000	$240,000
Sales	650,000	600,000	500,000
Industry average for the ratio sales to working capital	4.10 times	4.05 times	4.00 times

Required   a. Compute the sales to working capital ratio for each year.
b. Comment on the sales to working capital ratio for J. A. Appliance in relation to the industry average and what this may indicate.

P 6-20   The following data apply to items (a) through (e). Depoole Company is a manufacturer of industrial products and employs a calendar year for financial reporting purposes. Items (a) through (e) present several of Depoole's transactions during 1989. Total quick assets exceeded total current liabilities both before and after each transaction described. Depoole had positive profits in 1989 and a credit balance throughout 1989 in its retained earnings account.

Required   Answer the following multiple-choice questions.
a. Payment of a trade account payable of $64,500 would:
1. increase the current ratio, but the quick ratio would not be affected.

  2. increase the quick ratio, but the current ratio would not be affected.
  3. increase both the current and quick ratios.
  4. decrease both the current and quick ratios.
  5. have no effect on the current and quick ratios.
  b. The purchase of raw materials for $85,000 on open account would:
  1. increase the current ratio.
  2. decrease the current ratio.
  3. increase net working capital.
  4. decrease net working capital.
  5. increase both the current ratio and net working capital.
  c. The collection of a current account receivable of $29,000 would:
  1. increase the current ratio.
  2. decrease the current ratio.
  3. increase the quick ratio.
  4. decrease the quick ratio.
  5. not affect the current or quick ratios.
  d. Obsolete inventory of $125,000 was written off during 1989. This would:
  1. decrease the quick ratio.
  2. increase the quick ratio.
  3. increase net working capital.
  4. decrease the current ratio.
  5. decrease both the current and quick ratios.
  e. The early liquidation of a long-term note with cash would:
  1. affect the current ratio to a greater degree than the quick ratio.
  2. affect the quick ratio to a greater degree than the current ratio.
  3. affect the current and quick ratio to the same degree.
  4. affect the current ratio but not the quick ratio.
  5. affect the quick ratio but not the current ratio.

CMA Adapted

P 6-21   The following data apply to items (a) and (b). Mr. Sparks, the owner of School Supplies, Inc., is interested in keeping control over accounts receivable. He understands that accounts receivable turnover will give a good indication of how well receivables are being managed. School Supplies, Inc., does 70% of its business during June, July, and August. The terms of sale are 2/10, net/60.

Net sales for the year ended December 31, 1989, and receivables balances are given below.

Net Sales	$1,500,000
Receivables, less allowance for doubtful accounts of $8,000 at January 1, 1989	72,000
Receivables, less allowance for doubtful accounts of $10,000 at December 31, 1989	60,000

Required   Answer the following multiple-choice questions.
  a. The average accounts receivable turnover calculated from the data above is:
  1. 20.0 times

       2. 25.0 times

       3. 22.7 times

       4. 18.75 times

       5. 20.8 times

b. The average accounts receivable turnover computed for School Supplies, Inc., in item (a) is:

    1. representative for the entire year

    2. overstated

    3. understated

c. If a firm has a high current ratio but a low quick ratio, one can conclude that:

    1. the firm has a large outstanding accounts receivable balance.

    2. the firm has a large investment in inventory.

    3. the firm has a large amount of current liabilities.

    4. the cash ratio is extremely high.

    5. the two ratios must be recalculated, because both conditions cannot occur simultaneously.

d. Investment instruments used to invest temporarily idle cash balances should have the following characteristics:

    1. high expected return, low marketability, and a short term to maturity.

    2. high expected return, ready marketability, and no maturity date.

    3. low default risk, low marketability, and a short term to maturity.

    4. low default risk, ready marketability, and a long term to maturity.

    5. low default risk, ready marketability, and a short term to maturity.

e. The primary objective in the management of accounts receivable is:

    1. to achieve the combination of sales volume, bad debt experience, and receivables turnover that maximizes the profits of the corporation.

    2. to realize no bad debts, because of the opportunity cost involved.

    3. to provide the treasurer of the corporation with sufficient cash to pay the company's bills on time.

    4. to coordinate the activities of manufacturing, marketing, and financing so that the corporation can maximize its profits.

    5. to allow the most liberal credit acceptance policy, because increased sales mean increased profits.

f. A firm requires short-term funds to cover payroll expenses. These funds can come from:

    1. trade credit

    2. collections of receivables

    3. bank loans

    4. delayed payments of accounts payable

    5. all of the above

g. If, just prior to a period of rising prices, a company changed its inventory measurement method from FIFO to LIFO, the effect in the next period would be to:

    1. increase both the current ratio and inventory turnover.

    2. decrease both the current ratio and inventory turnover

    3. increase the current ratio and decrease inventory turnover

    4. decrease the current ratio and increase inventory turnover.

    5. leave the current ratio and inventory turnover unchanged.

CMA Adapted

P 6-22   Information from Greg Company's balance sheet is as follows:

Current assets:	
Cash	$ 2,400,000
Marketable securities	7,500,000
Accounts receivable	57,600,000
Inventories	66,300,000
Prepaid expenses	1,200,000
Total current assets	$135,000,000

Current liabilities:	
Notes payable	$ 1,500,000
Accounts payable	19,500,000
Accrued expenses	12,500,000
Income taxes payable	500,000
Payments due within one year on long-term debt	3,500,000
Total current liabilities	$ 37,500,000

Required   Answer the following multiple-choice questions.

a. What is the quick (acid test) ratio for Greg Company?
1. 1.60 to 1
2. 1.80 to 1
3. 1.99 to 1
4. 3.60 to 1

b. What is the effect of the collection of accounts receivable on the current ratio and net working capital, respectively?

	Current Ratio	Net Working Capital
1.	No effect	No effect
2.	Increase	Increase
3.	Increase	No effect
4.	No effect	Increase

c. Delta Corporation wrote off a $100 uncollectible account receivable against the $1,200 balance in the allowance account. Compare the current ratio before the write-off (x) with the current ratio after the write-off (y).
1. x greater than y
2. x equals y
3. x less than y
4. cannot be determined

d. Epsilon Company has a current ratio of 2 to 1. A transaction reduces the current ratio. Compare the working capital before this transaction (x) and the working capital after this transaction (y).
1. x greater than y
2. x equals y
3. x less than y
4. cannot be determined

e. Information from Guard Company's financial statements is as follows:

	1988	1989
Current assets at December 31	$2,000,000	$2,100,000
Current liabilities at December 31	1,000,000	900,000
Stockholders' equity at December 31	2,500,000	2,700,000
Net sales for year	8,300,000	8,800,000
Cost of goods sold for year	6,200,000	6,400,000
Operating income for year	500,000	550,000

What is the current ratio at December 31, 1989?

1. 1.20 to 1
2. 2.25 to 1
3. 2.33 to 1
4. 7.33 to 1

f. Which of the following accounts would be included in the calculation of the acid test (quick) ratio?

	Accounts Receivable	Inventories
1.	No	No
2.	No	Yes
3.	Yes	No
4.	Yes	Yes

AICPA Adapted

P 6-23   Items (a) through (d) are based on the following information:

ALPHA CORPORATION
Selected Financial Data

	As of December 31	
	1989	1988
Cash	$ 10,000	$ 80,000
Accounts receivable (net)	50,000	150,000
Merchandise inventory	90,000	150,000
Short-term marketable securities	30,000	10,000
Land and buildings (net)	340,000	360,000
Mortgage payable (no current portion)	270,000	280,000
Accounts payable (trade)	70,000	110,000
Short-term notes payable	20,000	40,000
Cash sales	1,800,000	1,600,000
Credit sales	500,000	800,000
Cost of goods sold	1,000,000	1,400,000

Required   Answer the following multiple-choice questions.

a. Alpha's quick (acid test) ratio as of December 31, 1989 is:
1. 0.5 to 1
2. 0.7 to 1
3. 1.0 to 1
4. 2.0 to 1

b. Alpha's receivable turnover for 1989 is:
   1. 5 times
   2. 10 times
   3. 23 times
   4. 46 times
c. Alpha's merchandise inventory turnover for 1989 is:
   1. 8.3 times
   2. 10.0 times
   3. 11.1 times
   4. 13.3 times
d. Alpha's current ratio at December 31, 1989 is:
   1. 0.5 to 1
   2. 0.7 to 1
   3. 1.0 to 1
   4. 2.0 to 1
e. Selected information for 1989 for the Prince Company is as follows:

Cost of goods sold	$5,400,000
Average inventory	1,800,000
Net sales	7,200,000
Average receivables	960,000
net income	720,000

Assuming a business year consisting of 360 days, what was the average number of days in the operating cycle for 1989?
   1. 72
   2. 84
   3. 144
   4. 168
f. If current assets exceed current liabilities, payments to creditors made on the last day of the month will:
   1. decrease current ratio.
   2. increase current ratio.
   3. decrease net working capital.
   4. increase net working capital.
g. Selected information from the accounting records of the Code Company is as follows:

Cost of goods sold for 1989	$1,200,000
Inventories at December 31, 1988	350,000
Inventories at December 31, 1989	310,000

Assuming a business year consisting of 300 days, what was the number of days' sales in average inventories for 1989?
   1. 36.5
   2. 77.5
   3. 82.5
   4. 87.5

AICPA Adapted

P 6-24

Required   Answer the following multiple-choice questions.
   a. A company's current ratio is 2.2 to 1 and quick (acid test) ratio is 1.0 to 1 at the

beginning of the year. At the end of the year, the company has a current ratio of 2.5 to 1 and a quick ratio of .8 to 1. Which of the following could help explain the divergence in the ratios from the beginning to the end of the year?
1. an increase in inventory levels during the current year
2. an increase in credit sales in relation to cash sales
3. an increase in the use of trade payables during the current year
4. an increase in the collection rate of accounts receivable
5. the sale of marketable securities at a price below cost

b. If, just prior to a period of rising prices, a company changed its inventory measurement method from FIFO to LIFO, the effect in the next period would be to:
1. increase both the current ratio and inventory turnover.
2. decrease both the current ratio and inventory turnover.
3. increase the current ratio and decrease inventory turnover.
4. decrease the current ratio and increase inventory turnover.
5. leave the current ratio and inventory turnover unchanged.

c. Selected year-end data for the Bayer Company are as follows:

Current liabilities	$600,000
Acid test ratio	2.5
Current ratio	3.0
Cost of sales	$500,000

Bayer Company's inventory turnover ratio based on this year-end data is:
1. 1.20
2. 2.40
3. 1.67
4. some amount other than those given above
5. not determinable from the data given

CMA Adapted

P 6-25* Text-of-the-Quarter, Inc. (TQI) is a new retailer of accounting texts. Sales are made via contracts that provide for TQI to send the customer an accounting text each quarter for twelve quarters. The selling price of each text is $15, with payment due within thirty days of delivery. Sales can be accurately estimated because of the contracts.

The number of contracts TQI sold in its first four quarters of existence, along with the number of texts purchased by TQI, were as follows:

	Contracts Sold	Texts Purchased	Texts Remaining from Each Quarter's Purchases at End of First Year
First Qtr	10,000	50,000	0
Second Qtr	20,000	40,000	0
Third Qtr	30,000	50,000	10,000
Fourth Qtr	40,000	120,000	50,000

*Material from CFA Examination I, June 6, 1987, is adapted here with permission from the Association for Investment Management and Research and the Institute of Chartered Financial Analysts.

All deliveries start in the quarter of contract sale, and all deliveries are up-to-date. Texts were purchased from the publisher at an average cost of $9 for the first quarter, $10 for the second and third quarters, and $11 for the fourth quarter. Selling and administrative costs for the year were $270,000. TQI's tax rate is 40%.

Required   Using generally accepted accounting principles for revenue and expense recognition and inventory accounting, prepare an income statement in such a way as to minimize the company's taxes.

CFA Adapted
June 1987

CASES

Case 6-1   LIFO-FIFO

The current assets and current liabilities section of the Kroger Co.'s balance sheet is presented below for 1984, along with the inventory footnote.

(in thousands of dollars)	December 29, 1984	December 31, 1983
Assets		
Current assets		
Cash and temporary cash investments	$ 163,209	$ 142,106
Receivables	204,062	156,359
Inventories:		
FIFO cost	1,463,626	1,338,939
Less LIFO reserve	(217,641)	(187,808)
	1,245,985	1,151,131
Property held for resale	10,724	105,075
Prepaid and other current assets	116,049	110,188
Total current assets	$1,740,029	$1,664,859

	December 29, 1984	December 31, 1983
Liabilities		
Current liabilities		
Current portion of long-term debt	$ 57,233	$ 6,084
Current portion of obligations under capital leases	5,601	6,057
Accounts payable	906,758	842,155
Other current liabilities	424,132	418,600
Accrued income taxes	69,783	52,262
Total current liabilities	$1,463,507	$1,325,158

Inventories

Inventories are stated at the lower of cost (principally LIFO) or market. Approximately 87% of inventories for 1984 and 75% of inventories for 1983 were valued using the LIFO method. The application of the LIFO method to the Company's Drug Store inventories, beginning in 1984, had no material effect on the financial statement. Cost for the balance of the inventories is determined by the FIFO method of inventory valuation.

Required

a. What is the working capital at the end of 1984?
b. What is the LIFO reserve account?
c. If the LIFO reserve account were added to the inventory at LIFO, what would be the resulting working capital at the end of 1984? Which working capital answer do you consider to be more realistic?
d. Does the use of LIFO or FIFO produce higher, lower, or the same income during (1) price increases, (2) price decreases, and (3) constant prices? (Assume no decrease or increase in inventory quantity.)
e. Does the use of LIFO or FIFO produce higher, lower, or the same amount of cash flow during (1) price increases, (2) price decreases, and (3) constant prices? Answer the question for both pretax cash flows and after-tax cash flows. (Assume no decrease or increase in inventory quantity.)
f. Assume that the company purchased inventory on the last day of the year, beginning inventory equaled ending inventory, and inventory records for the item purchased were maintained periodically on the LIFO basis. Would that purchase be included on the income statement or the balance sheet at year end?

Case 6-2 RISING PRICES, A TIME TO SWITCH OFF LIFO?

The following information was taken directly from an annual report of a firm that wishes to remain anonymous.

Financial Summary

Effects of LIFO Accounting

For a number of years, the corporation has used the Last-In, First-Out (LIFO) method of accounting for its steel inventories. In periods of extended inflation, coupled with uncertain supplies of raw materials from foreign sources, and rapid increases and fluctuations in prices of raw materials such as nickel and chrome nickel scrap, earnings can be affected unrealistically for any given year.

Because of these factors, the corporation will apply to the Internal Revenue Service for permission to discontinue using the LIFO method of accounting for valuing those inventories for which this method has been used. If such application is granted, the LIFO reserve at December 31, 1989, of $12,300,000 would be eliminated, which would require a provision for income taxes of approximately $6,150,000. The corporation will also seek permission to pay the increased taxes over a ten-year period. If the corporation had not used the LIFO method of accounting during 1989, net earnings for the year would have been increased by approximately $1,500,000.

The 1989 annual report also disclosed the following:

	1989	1988
1. Sales and revenues	$536,467,782	$487,886,449
2. Earnings per common share		
Primary	$3.44	$3.58
Fully diluted	$3.27 .	$3.35

Required

a. The corporation indicates that earnings can be affected unrealistically by rapid increases and fluctuations in prices when using LIFO. Comment.

b. How much taxes will need to be paid on past earnings because of the switch from LIFO? How will the switch from LIFO influence taxes in the future?

c. How will a switch from LIFO affect 1989 profits?

d. How will a switch from LIFO affect future profits?

e. How will a switch from LIFO affect 1989 cash flow?

f. How will a switch from LIFO affect future cash flow?

g. Speculate on the real reason that the corporation wishes to switch from LIFO.

Case 6-3   THE OTHER SIDE OF LIFO

What happens when a company using LIFO sells a greater quantity of goods than it purchases? In the following article,* Allen I. Schiff, Ph.D., Associate Professor of Accounting at Fordham University, New York City, discusses the implications of this phenomenon, which is known as LIFO liquidation.

Discussion of the LIFO cost basis for inventory valuation usually focuses on the superiority of this method and its widespread adoption. The conventional rationale for LIFO is its consistency with the matching principle during a period of rising prices. Historically, the most significant adoption of LIFO by U.S. corporations occurred during the period from 1973 to 1974, which was characterized by rapidly rising prices and sharp increases in interest rates. However, the motivation for the widespread use of LIFO didn't derive from the desire to achieve better matching of cost and revenue but, rather, from the reduced reported income that led to tax savings and increased cash flow.

Recently, another facet of LIFO has appeared in the annual reports of some companies. Known as LIFO liquidation, this process occurs during a reporting period when a company sells (withdraws) goods in a greater quantity than the quantity purchased (entered). As a result, inventories are reduced to a point at which cost layers of prior years are related to current inflated sales prices.

Relatively little attention has been given to the implications of LIFO inventory liquidations. Accounting texts discuss LIFO liquidations in a superficial fashion—and for good reason; it wasn't a phenomenon frequently encountered in the past. Indeed, until recently the only significant attempted LIFO liquidation related to the steel industry during the Korean War period. During this period, the demand for steel was strong, prices were high and a steelworkers' strike contributed to decreasing inventory levels. Congress was petitioned to modify the tax result from a matching of "old" costs against their then-current high selling prices. Congress refused and steel inventories weren't liquidated despite market demand.

The Incentives for LIFO Liquidation

The economic environment at this writing is quite different. Possible factors causing LIFO liquidations at present are:

- Decreased expected demand associated with a recessionary economy.
- High interest rates resulting in high inventory carrying costs. These high rates also present alternative economic opportunities for funds invested in inventories if there is a belief that the inflation rate will decrease in relation to interest rates.
- A sluggish economy that could lead management to minimize losses or improve reported profit.

To get a notion about the extent, if any, to which companies that recorded a LIFO liquidation increased net income, the financial reports of seventeen LIFO companies for the years 1980 and 1981 were randomly selected. Nine of these companies reported an increase in pretax income (or a reduction of loss) of at least 10 percent for either 1980, 1981 or both as a direct result of LIFO liquidation. What these preliminary results suggest is that there are other aspects of LIFO which require more extensive study. The original justification for LIFO was its superiority in reflecting results consistent with the matching principle. The liquidation of LIFO layers in recent years has had the opposite effect; it mismatches current revenues and historical costs, which results in the inclusion of inventory holding gains in reported income.

Conclusion

Thus, we have come full circle. FIFO valuation methods, originally criticized for poor matching when compared to LIFO, may actually be superior in the sense that, compared to companies experiencing LIFO liquidations, FIFO companies match costs and revenues relatively well. Furthermore, it may be argued that the sole motivation attributed to companies for switching to LIFO—to improve cash flows—may need broadening. Since the timing of the decision to liquidate LIFO inventories is entirely up to management, it would appear that such liquidations may give rise to income smoothing; it must be stressed that the smoothing may enhance the image conveyed by financial statements, but it has a negative impact on cash flow to the extent that taxes are paid (or loss carry-forwards reduced) on the incremental profit associated with the sale of the liquidated inventories.

More extensive research is, of course, needed to fully document the incidence of LIFO inventory liquidation during the last two years. Even my limited examination of reports suggests the need to emphasize the "other side of LIFO."

Required

a. Briefly describe why an inventory method that uses historical costs (such as LIFO) can distort profits.

b. Indicate probable reasons why the steel industry did not sell its available inventory during the steel strike.

c. For the firms that were using LIFO, explain the anticipated effect on the following variables because of reducing inventories during 1980 and 1981:
   1. profits
   2. taxes paid
   3. cash flow

d. In your opinion, what effect did the LIFO firms' reduction in inventories during 1980 and 1981 have on the quality of earnings?

e. Explain why many firms voluntarily reduced their inventories during 1980 and 1981.

Case 6-4   **THE FLYING MACHINE**

The Consolidated Balance Sheet and Selected Notes to the December 31, 1977 and 1976 financial statements of McDonnell Douglas Corporation follow:

Partial Consolidated Balance Sheet

Assets	December 31 1977	December 31 1976
Current assets		
Cash including time deposits	$ 161,424,208	$ 8,022,433
Short-term investments	238,413,136	50,986,910
Receivables:		
Accounts receivable—U.S. Government	113,661,224	88,024,299
Accounts and notes receivable—		
commercial	78,838,264	65,905,704
	192,499,488	153,930,003
Contracts in process and inventories		
(Note C)		
Commercial products in process	1,200,708,836	1,052,105,630
Government contracts in process	837,416,243	992,160,570
Materials and spare parts	346,933,715	353,480,025
Progress payments to subcontractors	250,465,590	231,195,245
	2,635,524,384	2,628,941,470
Less applicable progress payments	1,223,576,912	1,134,844,075
	1,411,947,472	1,494,097,395
Prepaid expenses	14,061,685	14,746,411
Total current assets	$2,018,345,989	$1,721,783,152

Current Liabilities	December 31 1977	December 31 1976
Current liabilities		
Accounts and drafts payable	$ 285,803,100	$ 234,269,395
Accrued expenses	76,914,276	68,026,387
Employee compensation	111,629,717	95,770,597
Income taxes, principally deferred	409,837,488	387,795,647
Progress payments received	174,034,771	56,324,243
Estimated modification, completion, and		
other contract adjustments	266,329,785	198,293,499
Current maturities of long-term debt	7,678,988	5,811,871
Total current liabilities	$1,332,228,125	$1,046,291,639

Selected Notes to Consolidated Financial Statements
31 December 1977 and 1976

[Partial] Note A: Summary
of Accounting Policies

Long-Term Contracts. In accordance with industry practice, substantial amounts applicable to long-term Government contracts and commercial aircraft programs are classified as current assets or liabilities in the balance sheet, even though some portion is not expected to be realized within one year.

Adjustments of costs and earnings may be made during and after completion of such long-term contracts; therefore, earnings recorded in the current year may include adjustments applicable to sales recorded in prior years.

Government Contracts. Government contracts are primarily accounted for on a percentage-of-completion method wherein sales are recorded at their estimated contract price as the work is performed. Under this method, all costs (including general and administrative expenses) are charged to Costs and Expenses as incurred, and the recorded sales values (equal to incurred costs plus estimated earnings) are carried in the account, Government contracts in process. At the time the item is completed and accepted by the customer, the sales value of the item is transferred to accounts receivable—U.S. Government.

Certain contracts contain incentive provisions which provide increased or decreased earnings based upon performance in relation to established targets. Incentives based upon cost performance are recorded currently and other incentives are recorded when the amounts can reasonably be determined.

Title to certain items, included in the captions of materials and progress payments to subcontractors, is vested in the U.S. Government by reason of progress payment provisions of related contracts.

Commercial Programs. Commercial products in process (including military versions of commercial aircraft) are stated on the basis of production and tooling costs incurred less cost allocation to delivered items, reduced (where applicable) to realizable market after giving effect to the estimated costs of completion.

Cost of sales for the DC-9 commercial aircraft program is determined on a specific-unit cost method, while the cost of sales of the DC-10 commercial aircraft program is determined on a program-average cost method. Inasmuch as the DC-10 program involves several models with differing sales prices and costs and the contracts contain escalation clauses based upon the future cost of materials and labor, the cost of sales for a particular DC-10 aircraft is computed at the percentage of the sales price that the total of the estimated tooling and production costs for the entire program bears to the total estimated sales price for all aircraft in the program.

Materials and spare parts are stated at the lower of cost (priced generally on a moving average method) or market.

Note C. Commercial Products in Process

A summary of commercial products in process at the end of 1977 is presented below, with comparable amounts at the end of 1976.

31 December	1977	1976
Commercial aircraft programs:		
Aircraft in process	$ 498,140,996	$ 343,326,903
Deferred production costs applicable		
to delivered DC-10 aircraft	458,908,000	474,985,000
Unamortized tooling, principally		
DC-10	169,983,112	176,879,729
	1,172,032,108	995,191,632
Other commercial programs	73,676,728	56,913,998
	$1,200,708,836	$1,052,105,630

DC-10 tooling and production costs were charged to cost of sales based upon the estimated average unit cost for the program. The costs incurred to produce DC-10 aircraft delivered prior to the end of 1973 were higher than average, which is normal in a new aircraft program. The costs incurred in excess of the estimated average unit cost were deferred to be recovered by production and sale of lower-than-average cost units. DC-10 aircraft delivered from 1 January 1974 through 30 June 1976 were produced at less than program average in the aggregate and, consequently, absorbed a portion of the deferred costs of the program.

From 30 June 1976 through the end of 1977, the DC-10 aircraft delivered were produced at such a low production rate that production costs exceeded program-average on most of the aircraft. The costs of $21,295,000 in excess of program-average in 1977 and the $16,100,000 in 1976 were charged direct to cost of sales upon delivery of these aircraft in order to prevent deferred production costs from increasing during this 18-month period. The thirty DC-10 aircraft under firm order at 31 December 1977, in the aggregate, are expected to be produced at less than program-average and to absorb approximately $120,400,000 of the $629,000,000 deferred tooling and early production units of new models.

The 400 aircraft accounting pool is in excess of the 275 DC-10 aircraft ordered (of which 245 had been delivered) plus the 31 DC-10 conditional orders and options at 31 December 1977. Comparable quantities at 31 December 1976 were 246 orders (of which 231 had been delivered) plus 12 conditional orders and options.

Estimated sales proceeds from undelivered aircraft of a 400 aircraft program exceed the production and tooling costs in inventory at 31 December 1977 plus the estimated additional production and tooling costs to be incurred. However, if less than 400 DC-10 aircraft are sold, or if the sales proceeds are overestimated, or if the costs to complete the program are underestimated, substantial amounts of unrecoverable costs may be charged to expense in subsequent fiscal periods. MDC continues to believe that the sale of 400 DC-10 aircraft is realistic and achievable in the early 1980s.

Required   a. The note on long-term contracts indicates that "In accordance with industry practice, substantial amounts applicable to long-term contracts and commercial aircraft programs are classified as current assets or liabilities in the balance sheet, even though some portion is not expected to be realized within one year."

1. Give a reasonable definition of current assets and current liabilities.
2. Indicate specific references in accounting standards that allow for the indicated interpretation of current assets and current liabilities as quoted.
3. Discuss the implications to traditional liquidity measures when current assets and current liabilities include items that are normally classified as long-term. Support your discussion with specific examples from this case.

b. Indicate specific references to parts of the summary of accounting policies that indicate subjectivity in the determination of income.

c. Footnote C, "Commercial Products in Process," states, "From 30 June 1976 through the end of 1977, the DC-10 aircraft delivered were produced at such a low production rate that production costs exceeded program-average on most of the aircraft. The costs of $21,295,000 in excess of program-average in 1977 and the $16,100,000 in 1976 were charged direct to cost of sales upon delivery of these aircraft in order to prevent deferred production costs from increasing during this 18-month period."

1. Prior to 1976, where had substantial production costs that exceeded program-average been charged?
2. Discuss the method for determining where to charge production costs that exceed program-average.

d. 1. Why is unamortized tooling an asset?
   2. Why is unamortized tooling classified by McDonnell Douglas as a current asset?

e. "Deferred production costs applicable to delivered DC-10 aircraft" and "Unamortized tooling, principally DC-10" are part of the current asset "Commercial Products in Process." When will these costs be recognized as expenses on the income statement?

Case 6-5   BOOMING RETAIL

The Grand retail firm reported the following financial data for the past several years (amounts are in thousands):

	Year				
	5	4	3	2	1
Sales	$1,254,131	$1,210,918	$1,096,152	$979,458	$920,797
Net accounts receivable	419,731	368,267	312,776	272,450	230,427

The Grand firm had a decentralized credit operation, allowing each store to administer its own credit. Many stores provided installment plans allowing the customer up to 36 months to pay. Gross profits on installment sales were reflected in the financial statements in the period when the sales were made.

Required   a. Using year 1 as the base, prepare a horizontal common size analysis for sales and net accounts receivable.

b. Compute the accounts receivable turnover for years 2–5. (Use net accounts receivable.)

c. Would financial control of accounts receivable be more important with installment sales than with sales on 30-day credit? Comment.

d. Comment on what is apparently happening at the Grand retail firm.

CHAPTER 7

LONG-TERM DEBT-PAYING ABILITY

CHAPTER TOPICS

Income Statement Consideration When Determining Long-Term Debt-Paying Ability

Times Interest Earned
Fixed Charge Coverage
Variations of Fixed Charge Coverage

Balance Sheet Consideration When Determining Long-Term Debt-Paying Ability

Debt Ratio
Debt/Equity
Debt to Tangible Net Worth

Other Long-Term Debt-Paying Ability Ratios

Special Items That Influence a Firm's Long-Term Debt-Paying Ability

Long-Term Assets versus Long-Term Debt
Long-Term Leasing
Pension Plans
Joint Ventures
Contingencies
Financial Instruments Disclosures and Credit Risk Concentrations

This chapter covers two approaches to viewing a firm's long-term debt-paying ability. One approach views the firm's ability to carry debt as indicated by the income statement, and the other considers the firm's ability to carry debt as indicated by the balance sheet.

In the long run, there is usually a relationship between the reported income that is the result of accrual accounting and the ability of the firm to meet its long-term obligations. Although the reported income does not agree with the cash available in the short run, the revenue and expense items eventually do result in cash movements. Because of the close relationship between the reported income and the ability of the firm to meet its long-run obligations, the entity's profitability is an important factor when determining long-term debt-paying ability.

In addition to the profitability of the firm, the amount of debt in relation to the size of the firm should be analyzed. This analysis indicates the amount of funds provided by outsiders in relation to those provided by owners of the firm. If a high proportion of the resources has been provided by outsiders, this indicates that the risks of the business have been shifted to the outsiders. If a large proportion of debt is in the capital structure, the risk of not meeting the principal or interest obligation is increased, because the company may not generate adequate funds to meet these obligations.

When analyzing the short-term debt-paying ability of the firm, a close relationship is found between the current assets and the current liabilities. It is generally expected that the current liabilities will be paid with cash generated from the current assets. The profitability of the firm is not considered important in determining the short-term debt-paying ability, since profitability is the end result of accrual accounting. In other words, using accrual accounting, the entity may report very high profits but may not have the ability to pay its current bills, because of a lack of available funds. It also may be the case that the entity has a reported loss but still has the ability to pay short-term obligations.

INCOME STATEMENT CONSIDERATION WHEN DETERMINING LONG-TERM DEBT-PAYING ABILITY

Times Interest Earned

A ratio that indicates a firm's long-term debt-paying ability from the income statement view is the times interest earned. If the times interest earned is adequate, there is little danger that the firm will not be able to meet its interest obligation. If the firm has good coverage of the interest obligation, it should also be able to refinance the principal when it comes due. In effect, the funds will probably never be required to pay off the principal if the company can show a good record of covering the interest expense. A good record is indicated by a relatively high, stable coverage of interest over the years. A poor record is indicated by a low, fluctuating coverage from year to year. Companies that maintain a good record can finance a relatively high proportion of debt in relation to stockholders' equity and, at the same time, obtain funds at favorable rates. Utility companies have traditionally been examples of companies that have financed a relatively high debt structure, in relation to stockholders' equity, at reasonable interest rates. They accomplished this because of their relatively high, stable coverage of interest over the years. This stable coverage evolved from a regulated profit situation in an industry with relatively stable demand. During the 1970s and 1980s, utilities experienced a severe strain on their profits, as rate increases did not keep pace with inflation. In addition, the demand was not as predictable as in prior years, because of soaring energy costs. The strain on profits and the uncertainty of demand influenced investors to require higher interest rates from utilities than had been previously required, in relation to other firms.

Basically, a company issues debt obligations to obtain funds at an interest rate that is less than the earnings from these funds. This is called *trading on the equity* or *leverage*. When the interest rate is high, there is the added risk that the company will not be able to earn more on the funds than the interest cost on them.

The primary formula for determining times interest earned is the following:

$$\text{Times Interest Earned} = \frac{\begin{array}{c}\text{Recurring Earnings, Excluding Interest Expense,}\\\text{Tax Expense, Equity Earnings, and Minority Earnings}\end{array}}{\begin{array}{c}\text{Interest Expense,}\\\text{Including Capitalized Interest}\end{array}}$$

The income statement contains several figures that might be used in analysis. In general, the primary analysis of the firm's ability to carry the debt as indicated by the income statement should include only income that is expected to occur in subsequent periods. Thus, the following nonrecurring items should be excluded:

1. Unusual or infrequent items
2. Discontinued operations
3. Extraordinary items
4. Cumulative effect of change in accounting principle

In addition to these nonrecurring items, additional items that should be excluded for the times interest earned computation are the following:

1. *Interest expense.* This is excluded from the income statement because the interest coverage would be distorted by a coverage of one if interest expense were deducted before computing times interest earned.
2. *Income tax expense.* Income taxes are computed after deducting interest expense, so they do not affect the safety of the interest payments.
3. *Equity earnings (losses) of nonconsolidated subsidiaries.* These are excluded because they are not available to cover interest payments, except to the extent that the equity earnings are accompanied by cash dividends.
4. *Minority income (loss).* This adjustment at the bottom of the income statement should be excluded; use income before minority interest. Minority income (loss) results from consolidating a firm in which a company has control but less than 100% ownership. All of the interest expense of the firm consolidated is included in the consolidated income statement. Therefore, all of the income of the firm consolidated should be considered in the coverage.

In 1979, the Financial Accounting Standards Board issued SFAS No. 34, which requires the capitalization of interest in certain circumstances. Capitalization of interest results in interest being added to a fixed asset instead of being expensed. The interest capitalized should be included with the total interest in the denominator of the times interest earned ratio, because it is part of the interest payment. In order to do this, the capitalized interest must be added to the interest expense that is disclosed on the income statement or in footnotes.

An example of capitalized interest would be interest during the current year on a bond issued to build a factory. Following the guidelines of SFAS No. 34, as long as the factory is under construction, this interest would be added to the asset account construction in process on the balance sheet. This interest does not appear on the income statement, but it is as much of a commitment as the interest expense that is deducted on the income statement.

When the factory is completed, the annual interest on the bond that was issued to build it will be expensed. When interest is expensed, it appears on the income statement.

If a company has capitalized interest, this fact is usually disclosed in a footnote. Some firms describe the capitalized interest on the face of the income statement. Cooper disclosed in footnotes that the amount of interest capitalized was $1,902,000, $1,923,000, and $480,000 during 1989, 1988, and 1987, respectively.

Times interest earned is computed in Exhibit 7-1 for Cooper for the years 1989 and 1988. Note that the ratio has substantially improved from an already high coverage. To evaluate the adequacy of coverage, times interest earned should be computed for a relatively long period of time (three to five years) and then compared to competitors and the industry average.

Times interest earned should be computed for approximately a five-year period in order to gain insight into the stability of the interest coverage. Usually, the lowest times interest coverage in the period is used as the primary indication of the interest coverage. This is because the firm needs to cover interest in the bad years as well as the good years. A firm that is cyclical may have a very high times interest in highly profitable years, but this does not help in low-profit years.

Interest coverage on long-term debt is sometimes computed separately from the normal times interest earned. This is done by dividing the recurring earnings before interest and tax by the interest on long-term debt, thus focusing on the long-term interest coverage. Since times interest earned is an indicator of long-term debt-paying ability, this revised computation helps focus on the long-term position. For external analysis, times interest coverage on long-term debt is usually not a

EXHIBIT 7-1

COOPER TIRE & RUBBER COMPANY
Times Interest Earned
For the Years Ended December 31, 1989 and 1988

	1989	1988
Income before income tax	$92,623,880	$64,912,286
Plus: Interest expense	4,373,398	4,495,464
Earnings before interest and tax [A]	$96,997,278	$69,407,750
Interest expense	$ 4,373,398	$ 4,495,464
Capitalized interest	1,902,000	1,923,000
Total interest paid [B]	$ 6,275,398	$ 6,418,464
Times interest earned [A ÷ B]	15.46 times	10.81 times

practical computation, because of a lack of data. However, this computation can be made for internal analysis.

In the long run, a firm must have the funds to meet all of its expenses. In the short run, a firm can often meet its interest obligations even when the times interest earned is less than 1.00, because some of the expenses do not require funds in the short run: depreciation expense, amortization expense, and depletion expense. The airline industry has had several bad periods when the times interest earned was less than 1.00, but the interest payments were maintained.

To get a better indication of a firm's ability to cover interest payments in the short run, the noncash charges for depreciation, depletion, and amortization can be added back to the numerator of the times interest earned ratio. The resulting ratio, which is less conservative, gives a type of cash basis times interest earned that is useful for evaluating the firm in the short run.

The short-run times interest earned is computed for Cooper in Exhibit 7-2. Cooper's short-run times interest earned is substantially higher than its long-run times interest earned. When performing analysis, the short-run times interest earned is normally computed only when the analyst is concerned about the long-run times interest earned coverage.

Fixed Charge Coverage

Another ratio that indicates a firm's long-term debt-paying ability from the income statement view is the fixed charge coverage, which is an extension of the times

EXHIBIT 7 - 2

COOPER TIRE & RUBBER COMPANY
Times Interest Earned (Short-Run Perspective)
For the Years Ended December 31, 1989 and 1988

	1989	1988
Income before income tax	$ 92,623,880	$64,912,286
Plus: Interest expense	4,373,398	4,495,464
Depreciation and amortization	23,393,307	19,872,614
Earnings adjusted [A]	$120,390,585	$89,280,364
Interest expense	$ 4,373,398	$ 4,495,464
Capital interest	1,902,000	1,923,000
Total interest paid [B]	$ 6,275,398	$ 6,418,464
Times interest earned (short-run perspective) [A ÷ B]	19.18 times	13.91 times

interest earned ratio. The fixed charge coverage is an indication of a firm's ability to cover fixed charges, including interest expense and similar fixed charges.

There is a difference of opinion in practice as to what should be included in the fixed charges. A portion of operating lease payments is an item frequently included in the fixed charge coverage, in addition to interest expense.

Leases are handled by the lessee by capitalizing the lease or by reporting as an operating lease. A capitalized lease is handled as if the lessee bought the asset. The leased asset is included in the fixed assets, and the related obligation is included in liabilities. When lease payments are made, part of the payment is considered to be for interest expense. Therefore, the interest expense reflected on the income statement includes interest related to capitalized leases. Operating leases are not reflected on the balance sheet, but they are reflected on the income statement in the rent expense. Usually, many operating leases are for a relatively long term.

An operating lease for a relatively long term is a type of long-term financing, so a part of the lease payment is really a financing charge called interest. When a portion of operating lease payments is included in fixed charges, it is an effort to recognize the true total interest that the firm is paying.

SEC reporting may require a more conservative computation than the times interest earned in order to determine the firm's long-term debt-paying ability. The SEC refers to its ratio as the *ratio of earnings to fixed charges*. The major difference between the times interest earned computation and the ratio of earnings to fixed charges is that the latter computation includes a portion of the operating leases rental charges.

Usually, one-third of the operating leases rental charges is included in the fixed charges because this is an approximation of the proportion of lease payments that is interest. The SEC does not accept the one-third approximation automatically but requires a more specific estimate of the interest portion, based on the terms of the lease. Individuals interested in a company's ratio of earnings to fixed charges can find this ratio on the face of the income statement that is included with the SEC registration statement (Form S-7) when debt securities are registered.

The fixed charge coverage with this added interest included would be computed as follows:

$$\text{Fixed Charge Coverage} = \frac{\begin{array}{c}\text{Recurring Earnings, Excluding}\\ \text{Interest Expense, Tax Expense,}\\ \text{Equity Earnings, and Minority Income}\\ \text{+ Interest Portion of Rentals}\end{array}}{\begin{array}{c}\text{Interest Expense,}\\ \text{Including Capitalized Interest}\\ \text{+ Interest Portion of Rentals}\end{array}}$$

The adjusted earnings figure in the fixed charge coverage is the same as used in the times interest earned, except that interest portion of rentals is added to adjusted earnings, because this amount had previously been deducted on the income statement as rental charges.

Cooper's 1989 annual report disclosed its rent expense attributable to all operating leases as $6,010,000 and $5,634,000, respectively, for 1989 and 1988. Using one-third as the approximation of the rent expense, which would be interest expense if financed, the interest expense would be increased by $2,003,333 in 1989 and by $1,878,000 in 1988.

The fixed charge coverage for Cooper for 1989 and 1988, with the interest portion of rentals considered, is computed in Exhibit 7-3. This figure is more conservative than the times interest earned, but it shows the same improving trend.

Variations of Fixed Charge Coverage

The methods of computing fixed charge coverage vary widely. Among the items sometimes considered as fixed charges in this ratio are interest expense, a portion of lease payments, all lease payments, depreciation, depletion and amortization, debt principal payments, and pension payments. If preferred dividends are substantial, they may also be included, or a separate ratio may be computed to consider their coverage. The more items that are considered as fixed charges, the more conservative the ratio. The trend is usually similar to that found for the times interest earned ratio. Caution should be taken to compute the ratio the same way as the financial service does when comparing to any industry average. If trend analysis is done, the ratio must also be computed the same way each year to produce meaningful results.

EXHIBIT 7-3

COOPER TIRE & RUBBER COMPANY
Fixed Charge Coverage
For the Years Ended December 31, 1989 and 1988

	1989	1988
Income before income tax	$92,623,880	$64,912,286
Plus: Interest expense	4,373,398	4,495,464
Interest portion of rentals	2,003,333	1,878,000
Earnings adjusted [A]	$99,000,611	$71,285,750
Interest expense	$ 4,373,398	$ 4,495,464
Capitalized interest	1,902,000	1,923,000
Interest portion of rental	2,003,333	1,878,000
Adjusted interest [B]	$ 8,278,731	$ 8,296,464
Fixed coverage [A ÷ B]	11.96 times	8.59 times

> ## BALANCE SHEET CONSIDERATION
> ## WHEN DETERMINING LONG-TERM
> ## DEBT-PAYING ABILITY

Debt Ratio

One computation to determine the firm's long-term debt-paying ability is called the *debt ratio*. It is a comparison of a company's total liabilities with its total assets. The debt ratio indicates the percentage of assets that were financed by creditors, and it helps determine how well creditors are protected in case of insolvency of the company. If creditors are not well protected, the company is not in a position to issue additional long-term debt. From the perspective of long-term debt-paying ability, the lower this ratio is, the better the company's position.

In practice, there is substantial disagreement on the details of the formula to compute the debt ratio. Some of the disagreement revolves around whether short-term liabilities should be included in the formula. Some firms take the position that short-term liabilities should be excluded because they are not long-term sources of funds and are therefore not a valid indication of the firm's debt position in a long-term sense. Other firms take the position that short-term funds in total become part of the total sources of outside funds in the long run. For example, individual accounts payable are relatively short term, but accounts payable in total becomes a rather permanent part of the entire sources of funds. This book takes a conservative position that includes the short-term liabilities in the debt ratio.

Another issue involves whether certain other items should be included in liabilities. The problem is that liabilities are not equal in their commitment to pay out funds in the future. Under current generally accepted accounting principles, some liabilities clearly represent a commitment to pay out funds in the future, whereas other liabilities may never result in a future payment. Items that present particular problems as to a future payment of funds are reserves, deferred taxes, minority shareholders' interests, and redeemable preferred stock. Each of these items will be reviewed in the subsections that follow.

Reserves

The reserve accounts classified under liabilities result from an expense charge to the income statement and an equal increase in the reserve account on the balance sheet. These reserve accounts do not represent definite commitments to pay out funds in the future, but they do represent an estimate of funds that will be paid out in the future.

An example of a reserve account is the long-term liability account entitled general aviation product liability in the 1989 annual report of General Dynamics. The balance in this account at the end of 1989 was $258,200,000. This represents an estimate of the general aviation product liability as of December 31, 1989. Thus, this account is not a definite future commitment; it represents an estimate of the future general aviation product liability.

This book takes a conservative position that includes the reserves in liabilities in the debt ratio.

Deferred Taxes (Interperiod Tax Allocation)

Many items are expensed by a firm (or recognized as income) for the financial statements in a different period than they are expensed (or recognized as income) for the federal income tax return. This can result in financial statement income in any one period that is substantially different from the tax return income. Therefore, taxes payable based on the tax return can be substantially different from taxes payable based on the financial statement income. Current generally accepted accounting principles direct that the tax expense for the financial statements be based on the tax-related items on the financial statements. Taxes payable are based on the actual current taxes payable, which are determined by the tax return. (The Internal Revenue Code specifies the procedures for determining taxable income.)

The tax expense for the financial statements often does not agree with the taxes payable. The difference between tax expense and taxes payable is booked as deferred income taxes. The concept that results in deferred income taxes is called *interperiod tax allocation*.

As an illustration of deferred taxes, consider the following facts:

Machinery purchased for $100,000
Three-year write-off for tax purposes

1st year	$ 25,000
2nd year	38,000
3rd year	37,000
	$100,000

Five-year write-off for financial
  statements

1st year	$ 20,000
2nd year	20,000
3rd year	20,000
4th year	20,000
5th year	20,000
	$100,000

Over the five-year period, both the tax return and the financial statements deducted $100,000 for the equipment, but the write-off on the tax return was much faster than the write-off on the financial statements. The faster write-off on the tax return resulted during the first three years in lower taxable income than income for the income statement. During the last two years, the income statement income is lower than the tax return income.

In addition to temporary differences, the tax liability can be influenced by an operating loss carryback and/or operating loss carryforward. The tax code allows a corporation reporting an operating loss for income tax purposes in the current year to carry this loss back and forward to offset other reported taxable income. The company may first carry an operating loss back three years (in sequential order, starting with the earliest of the three years). If the taxable income for the past three years is not enough to offset the amount of the operating loss, the remaining loss is sequentially carried forward fifteen years and offset against future taxable income.

When an operating loss is carried back to prior years, it is called an *operating loss carryback*. When carried forward, it is called an *operating loss carryforward*. A company can elect to forgo a carryback and, instead, only carry forward an operating loss.

A company would not normally forgo a carryback, because an operating loss carryback results in a definite and immediate income tax refund. A carryforward will reduce income taxes payable in future years to the extent that taxable income is earned. A company could possibly benefit from forgoing a carryback if prospects in future years are good and there is an anticipated increase in the tax rate.

The specific guidelines for accounting for deferred taxes are provided by SFAS No. 96, "Accounting for Income Taxes." This SFAS directs that interperiod tax allocation should be used for all temporary differences. A temporary difference is the difference between the tax basis of an asset or liability and its reported amount in the financial statements that will result in taxable or deductible amounts in future years when the reported amount of the asset or liability is recovered or settled, respectively.

Deferred taxes are classified on the balance sheet as current or noncurrent, depending on when the underlying temporary differences reverse. Usually, a firm has both a short-term and a long-term deferred account. Generally, the current amount of deferred taxes is the deferred tax attributable to temporary differences reversing in the next year. The long-term amount of deferred taxes is the deferred tax attributable to temporary differences reversing after the next year.

The short-term deferred tax account is classified as a current asset or a current liability, depending on the nature of the temporary differences reversing in the next year. The long-term deferred tax account is classified as a long-term asset or liability, depending on the nature of the temporary differences reversing after the next year. Most firms will have two deferred tax accounts, one classified as a short-term liability and one as a long-term liability.

General Dynamics Corporation disclosed deferred taxes in current liabilities and noncurrent liabilities in its 1989 annual report, as follows:

Current liabilities:	(dollars in millions)
Commercial paper	$ 194.0
Current maturities of debt-finance operations	84.0
Accounts payable	1,012.5
Accrued salaries and wages	245.2
Other accrued liabilities	385.3
Deferred income taxes	156.7
Total current liabilities	$2,077.7

Noncurrent liabilities:	
Long-term debt	$ 623.8
Long-term debt-finance operations	281.7
General aviation product liability	258.2
Deferred income taxes	639.9
Other	541.7
Total noncurrent liabilities	$2,345.3

Notice on the Cooper balance sheet (see Chapter 5) that Cooper discloses deferred taxes in long-term liabilities in the amounts of $28,968,508 in 1989 and $24,118,000 in 1988. For many firms, the long-term liability deferred taxes has grown to a substantial amount, which often increases each year. This is because of the growth in the temporary differences that cause the timing difference.

In accordance with Statement No. 96, deferred taxes are accounted for using the liability method, which focuses on the balance sheet. Deferred taxes are recorded at the amounts at which they will be settled when the underlying temporary differences reverse. One important aspect of Statement No. 96 is that deferred taxes are adjusted for tax rate changes, whereas they were not under the prior deferred method. A change in tax rates can result in a material adjustment to the deferred account and can substantially influence income in the year of the tax rate change.

Some individuals disagree with the concept of deferred taxes (interperiod tax allocation). Some of their objections are that it is uncertain that the deferred tax will ever be paid—and, if it will in fact be paid, it is uncertain *when* this will take place. The deferred tax accounts are therefore often referred to as *soft accounts*.

Because of the uncertainty over whether (and when) a deferred tax liability will be paid, some individuals elect to exclude deferred tax liabilities from liabilities when performing analysis. This book takes a conservative position that includes deferred tax liabilities in the debt ratios. This conservative position is consistent with generally accepted accounting principles that do recognize deferred taxes.

There are some revenue and expense items that never go on the tax return, but do go on the income statement. Examples would be premiums on life insurance and life insurance proceeds. Federal tax law does not allow these items to be included in expense and revenue, respectively. Revenue and expense items that never go on the tax return are referred to as *permanent differences*. These items never influence either the tax expense or the tax liability, so they never influence the deferred tax accounts.

Minority Shareholders' Interest

The account minority shareholders' interest results when the firm has consolidated another company of which it owns less than 100%. The proportion of the company consolidated that is not owned is usually shown on the balance sheet just prior to stockholders' equity.

Some firms exclude the minority shareholders' interest when computing debt ratios; the reasoning followed is that this amount does not represent a commitment to pay funds to outsiders. Other firms include the minority shareholders' interest when computing debt ratios, reasoning that these funds came from outsiders and are part of the total funds that the firm is using. This book takes the conservative position of including minority shareholders' interest in the primary computation of debt ratios. (To review minority shareholders' interest, refer to the section of Chapter 2 on minority interest.)

Redeemable Preferred Stock

Redeemable preferred stock is subject to mandatory redemption requirements or has a redemption feature that is outside the control of the issuer. Some redeemable preferred stock agreements require the firm to purchase certain amounts of the preferred stock on the open market.

Securities and Exchange Commission Accounting Series Release No. 268 dictates that redeemable preferred stock not be disclosed under shareholders' equity.

The nature of redeemable preferred stock leaves open to judgment how it should be handled when computing debt ratios. One view is to exclude it from debt and include it in stockholders' equity, on the grounds that it does not represent a normal debt relationship. A conservative position is to include it as debt when computing the debt ratios. This book uses the conservative approach and includes redeemable preferred stock in debt for the primary computation of debt ratios. (For a more detailed review, refer to the section of Chapter 3 that describes redeemable preferred stock.)

In this book, the debt ratio is computed as follows:

$$\text{Debt Ratio} = \frac{\text{Total Liabilities}^1}{\text{Total Assets}}$$

The debt ratio for Cooper for December 31, 1989, and December 31, 1988, is computed in Exhibit 7-4. The exhibit indicates that less than one-half of the Cooper assets were financed by outsiders in both 1989 and 1988, and the proportion financed by outsiders was approximately the same in the two years. This debt ratio is a conservative computation, because all of the liabilities and near liabilities have been included. At the same time, the assets are understated, because no adjustments have been made for assets that have a value greater than book value.

The debt ratio should be compared with industry averages. Industries that have stable earnings can handle more debt than industries that have cyclical earnings. This comparison can be misleading if one firm has substantial hidden assets that other firms do not (such as substantial land that is carried at historical cost).

---

[1]Total liabilities includes short-term liabilities, reserves, deferred tax liabilities, minority shareholders' interests and redeemable preferred stock, and any other noncurrent liability. It does not include shareholders' equity (convertible preferred stock, preferred stock, common stock, capital in excess of stated value, foreign currency equity accounts, long-term investment equity accounts, retained earnings, or treasury stock).

EXHIBIT 7-4

COOPER TIRE & RUBBER COMPANY
Debt Ratio
December 31, 1989 and 1988

	1989	1988
Total liabilities compiled:		
Current liabilities	$ 98,929,592	$ 86,125,443
Long-term debt	65,726,850	67,789,850
Other long-term liabilities	16,204,000	6,793,000
Deferred federal income taxes	28,968,508	24,118,000
Total liabilities [A]	$209,828,950	$184,826,293
Total assets [B]	$519,892,610	$442,582,462
Debt ratio [A ÷ B]	40.36%	41.76%

Debt/Equity

Another computation that is used to determine the entity's long-term debt-paying ability is called the *debt/equity ratio*. In this computation, the total debt is compared with the total shareholders' equity. The debt/equity ratio also helps determine how well creditors are protected in case of insolvency of the company. From the perspective of long-term debt-paying ability, the lower this ratio is, the better the company's position.

In this book, the computation of the debt/equity ratio is conservative, as was the debt ratio, because all of the liabilities and near liabilities that have been booked are included, and the shareholders' equity is understated to the extent that assets have a value greater than book value. This ratio should also be compared with industry averages and competitors. The debt/equity ratio is computed as follows:

$$\text{Debt/Equity} = \frac{\text{Total Liabilities}^2}{\text{Shareholders' Equity}}$$

The debt/equity ratio for Cooper for December 31, 1989, and December 31, 1988, is computed in Exhibit 7-5. Using a conservative approach to computing debt/equity, Exhibit 7-5 indicates that a smaller amount of funds came from outsiders than was provided by shareholders' equity. Also, the proportion of funds provided by outsiders was slightly reduced in 1989. The debt/equity ratio was 67.67% at the end of 1989, down from 71.71% at the end of 1988.

The debt ratio and the debt/equity ratio have the same objectives and use the

[2]This is the same liability figure as is used in the debt ratio.

EXHIBIT 7-5

COOPER TIRE & RUBBER COMPANY
Debt/Equity Ratio
December 31, 1989 and 1988

	1989	1988
Total liabilities (Exhibit 7-4) [A]	$209,828,950	$184,826,293
Shareholders' equity [B]	310,063,660	257,756,169
Debt/equity [A ÷ B]	67.67%	71.71%

same figures, except in a different form. Therefore, these ratios are alternatives to each other if computed in the manner recommended here. Because some financial services may be reporting the debt ratio, and others may be reporting the debt/equity ratio, the reader should be familiar with both.

It was indicated previously that there is a problem with a lack of uniformity in the way some ratios are computed. This is especially true with the debt ratio and the debt/equity ratio. When comparing the debt ratio and the debt/equity ratio with industry ratios, try to determine how the industry ratios were computed. A reasonable comparison may not be possible, because the financial sources do not indicate what elements of debt are included in the computations.

Debt to Tangible Net Worth

The debt to tangible net worth ratio is also used to determine the entity's long-term debt-paying ability. This ratio also indicates how well creditors are protected in case of insolvency of the firm. As with the debt ratio and the debt/equity ratio, from the perspective of long-term debt-paying ability, the lower this ratio is, the better.

The debt to tangible net worth ratio is a more conservative ratio than either the debt ratio or the debt/equity ratio, because it eliminates intangible assets such as goodwill, trademarks, patents, and copyrights. These assets are left out on the assumption that they provide no resources to pay creditors—a very conservative position. The debt to tangible net worth ratio is computed as follows:

$$\text{Debt to Tangible Net Worth} = \frac{\text{Total Liabilities}}{\text{Shareholders' Equity} - \text{Intangible Assets}}$$

In this book, the computation of the debt to tangible net worth ratio is conservative, as in the case of the debt ratio and the debt/equity ratio. All of the liabilities and near liabilities are included, and the shareholders' equity is understated to the extent that assets have a value greater than book value.

The debt to tangible net worth ratio for Cooper for December 31, 1989 and December 31, 1988 is computed in Exhibit 7-6. Because Cooper does not list any

EXHIBIT 7-6

COOPER TIRE & RUBBER COMPANY
Debt to Tangible Net Worth
December 31, 1989 and 1988

	1989	1988
Total liabilities (Exhibit 7-4) [A]	$209,828,950	$184,826,293
Shareholders' equity	$310,063,660	$257,756,169
Less: intangibles	—	—
Adjusted shareholders' equity [B]	$310,063,660	$257,756,169
Debt to tangible net worth [A ÷ B]	67.67%	71.71%

intangible assets, there is no difference between its debt/equity ratio and its debt to tangible net worth ratio.

Other Long-Term Debt-Paying Ability Ratios

There are a number of additional ratios that give perspective on the long-term debt-paying ability of a firm. In this section, some of these ratios are described.

One of these ratios is the current debt/net worth ratio, which indicates a relationship between current liabilities and funds contributed by shareholders. The higher the proportion of funds provided by current liabilities, the greater the risk.

Another ratio is the total capitalization ratio. Total capitalization is usually considered to be long-term debt, preferred stock, and common shareholders' equity. Long-term debt is compared to total capitalization in this ratio. The lower the ratio, the lower the risk. Cooper reported that long-term debt, as a percent of total capitalization, decreased to 17.5% at December 31, 1989 from 20.8% one year earlier.

Another of these ratios is the fixed asset/equity ratio, which indicates the extent to which shareholders have provided funds in relation to fixed assets. Some firms subtract intangibles from shareholders' equity to obtain tangible net worth. This results in a more conservative view of this ratio. The higher the fixed assets in relation to equity, the greater the risk.

Another long-term debt ratio is cash flow/total debt, which will be described in Chapter 10.

Exhibit 7-7 indicates the trend in current liabilities, total liabilities, and stockholders' equity of firms in the United States between 1964 and 1989. It shows that there has been a major shift in the capital structure of firms, toward a higher proportion of debt in relation to total assets. It also shows a higher proportion of current liabilities in relation to total assets. This indicates a substantial increase in risk, as management is more frequently faced with debt coming due. It also indi-

E X H I B I T   7 - 7

Trends in Current Liabilities, Total Liabilities, and Stockholders' Equity, 1964–1989

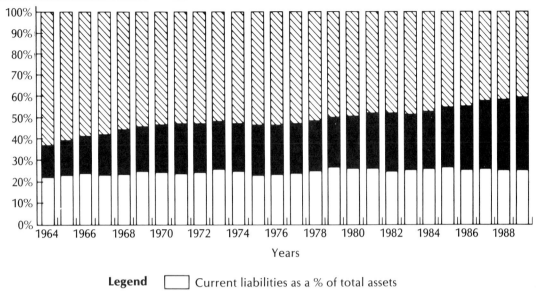

Source: *Quarterly Financial Reports of Manufacturing, Mining, & Trading,* Department of Commerce. Washington, D.C.: Government Printing Office.

cates that short-term debt is a permanent part of the financial structure of firms. This supports the decision to include short-term liabilities in the long-term debt ratios of debt ratio, debt/equity, and debt to tangible net worth.

SPECIAL ITEMS THAT INFLUENCE A FIRM'S LONG-TERM DEBT-PAYING ABILITY

Long-Term Assets versus Long-Term Debt

The specific assets of the firm are important if the firm turns unprofitable and the assets are sold. Therefore, consider the assets of the firm when determining the long-term debt-paying ability. The assets are insurance should the firm turn unprofitable. The ability to analyze the assets, in relation to the long-term debt-paying ability, is limited, based on the information reported in the published financial statements. The statements do not extensively disclose market or liquidation values;

they disclose only unrecovered cost for many items. Over the years, the market value figure reported for some investments has been an exception.

Because of a lack of information on the market value of assets, it is not feasible to compute a ratio that relates market value of assets to debt for external analysis; indeed, it is often not even feasible for internal analysis.

A review of the financial statements is often of value if the firm liquidates or decides to reduce the scope of its operations. Examples of assets that may have substantial value would be land, timberlands, and investments.

When the Penn Central Company went bankrupt, it had substantial debt and operating losses. Yet because of assets that had substantial market values, creditors were repaid in the bankruptcy. In other cases, creditors receive nothing or only nominal amounts when a firm goes bankrupt.

Substantial assets that have a potential value higher than the book figures may also indicate an earnings potential that will be realized later. For example, knowing that a railroad owns land that contains millions or billions of tons of coal could indicate substantial profit potential, even if the coal is not economical to mine at the present time. In future years, as the prices of competitive products such as oil and gas increase, the coal may become economical to mine. This is what happened in the United States in the late 1970s. Several railroads that owned millions or billions of tons of unmined coal found that the coal became very valuable as the price of oil and gas increased.

Long-Term Leasing

The influence of long-term leasing was explained in relation to the income statement earlier in this chapter. Now we will consider the influence of long-term leasing from the balance sheet perspective.

First, review some points made previously. Leases are handled by the lessee by capitalizing the lease or by reporting it as an operating lease. A capitalized lease is handled as if the lessee bought the asset. The leased asset is in the fixed assets, and the related obligation is included in liabilities. Operating leases are not reflected on the balance sheet, but they are reflected in a footnote and on the income statement in the rent expense.

An operating lease for a relatively long term is a type of long-term financing. Therefore, operating leases should be considered in a supplemental manner, as to their influence on the debt structure of the firms. The capital leases have already been considered in the debt ratios computed, because the capitalized leases were part of the total assets and also part of the total liabilities on the balance sheet.

Cooper disclosed capitalized leases included in property, plant, and equipment of $6,212,064 at December 31, 1989.

Notice that the capitalized asset amount does not agree with the capitalized liability amount. This is because the liability is reduced, based on payments, and the asset is reduced, based on depreciation taken. Usually, a company depreciates capitalized leases faster than payments are made. This would result in the capitalized asset amount being lower than the capitalized liability amount. On the original date of the capitalized lease, the capitalized asset amount and the capitalized liability amount are the same.

The Cooper footnote relating to long-term leases indicates that the minimum future rentals under operating leases for years subsequent to December 31, 1989, were as follows:

	Operating Leases
1990	$2,869,000
1991	2,100,000
1992	1,176,000
1993	736,000
1994	482,000
1995 and later	268,000
	$7,631,000

This does not include an amount for any possible contingent rentals, because they are not practical to estimate.

If these leases had been capitalized, the amount added to fixed assets and the amount added to liabilities would be the same at the time of the initial entry. As indicated previously, the amounts would not be the same subsequently, because the asset is depreciated at some selected rate, while the liability is reduced as payments are made. As we observed for capitalized leases for Cooper at the end of 1989, $6,212,064 was under property, plant, and equipment, and $7,582,000 was under long-term liabilities. When incorporating the operating leases into the debt ratios, it is necessary to assume that the asset and the liability amount would be the same, since there is no realistic way to compute the difference. Use the liability amount.

It would not be realistic to include the total future rentals that relate to operating leases on the face of the balance sheet, because part of the commitment would be an interest consideration. Earlier in this chapter, it was indicated that some firms estimate that one-third of the operating lease commitment is for interest. With a one-third estimate for interest, approximately two-thirds could be estimated for principal. For Cooper, this would amount to approximately $5,082,246 ($7,631,000 × 2/3). This amount can be added to fixed assets and long-term liabilities in order to obtain a supplemental view of the debt ratios that relate to the balance sheet. In Exhibit 7-8, the adjusted debt ratio and debt/equity ratio are computed for Cooper at the end of 1989; this increases the debt position by a modest amount. For some firms, the adjusted debt position would be materially higher than the unadjusted position.

Pension Plans

The Employee Retirement Income Security Act (ERISA) became law in 1974 and substantially influenced the administration of pension plans, while elevating their liability status for the firm.

EXHIBIT 7-8

COOPER TIRE & RUBBER COMPANY
Adjusted Debt Ratio and Debt/Equity Considering Operating Leases
December 31, 1989

	1989
Debt ratio:	
Unadjusted total liabilities (Exhibit 7-4)	$209,828,950
Plus: Estimated for operating leases	5,082,246
Adjusted liabilities [A]	$214,911,196
Unadjusted total assets	$519,892,610
Plus: Estimated for operating leases	5,082,246
Adjusted assets [B]	$524,974,856
Adjusted debt ratio [A ÷ B]	40.94%
Unadjusted debt ratio (Exhibit 7-4)	40.36%
Debt/equity	
Adjusted liabilities (above) [A]	$214,911,196
Shareholders' equity [B]	310,063,660
Adjusted debt/equity [A ÷ B]	69.31%
Unadjusted debt/equity (Exhibit 7-5)	67.67%

Included in the act are provisions requiring minimum funding of plans, minimum rights of employees upon termination of their employment, and the creation of a special federal agency, the Pension Benefit Guaranty Corporation (PBGC), to help fund employee benefits when pension plans are terminated. The PBGC receives a fee for every employee covered by a pension plan that is subject to the PBGC. The PBGC has the right to impose a lien against a covered firm of 30% of the firm's assets. This lien has the status of a tax lien and therefore ranks high among creditor claims. In practice, the PBGC has been reluctant to impose this lien except when a firm is in bankruptcy proceedings. This has resulted in the PBGC receiving a relatively small amount of assets when it has imposed the lien.

An important provision in a pension plan is the vesting provision. When an employee is vested in the pension plan, he or she is eligible to receive some pension benefits at retirement, regardless of whether the employee continues working for the employer. ERISA has had a major impact on reducing the vesting time. The original ERISA has been amended several times to increase the responsibility of firms regarding their pension plans.

In 1980, Congress passed the Multiemployer Pension Plan Amendment Act. Multiemployer pension plans are plans maintained jointly by two or more unrelated employers. This act provided for significantly increased employer obligations for multiemployer pension plans and made PBGC coverage mandatory for multiemployer plans.

When a firm has a multiemployer pension plan, it normally covers union employees. Such a firm usually has other pension plans that cover nonunion employees. When disclosing a multiemployer pension plan, the firm normally includes the cost of the plan with the cost of the other pension plans. It is usually not practical to isolate the cost of these plans based on the footnote disclosure because of commingling. The plans are usually on a pay-as-you-go basis, so there is no liability booked unless a payment has not been made. A potential significant liability is possible if the company withdraws from the multiemployer plan. Unfortunately, the amount of this liability cannot be ascertained from the pension footnote.

Maury Federal Savings Bank included the following comment in a footnote with its 1989 annual report.

> All contributions to the fund are commingled with other employers' contributions and all assets of the fund are invested on a pooled basis, without allocation to individual employers or employees. The bank's relative position with respect to this multiemployer plan is not determinable, and therefore, certain actuarially-determined information is not disclosed.

The financial influence of pension plans is one of the most difficult areas to consider in financial reporting, especially as related to long-term borrowing ability. A reasonable understanding of pension accounting is required in order to interpret pension plan disclosure. Therefore, a brief description is included at this point.

In 1966, the Accounting Principles Board passed APB Opinion No. 8. This standard improved pension accounting, as it provided for recognition of pension expense in all periods, while still providing management with much flexibility in determining the pension expense. APB Opinion No. 8 did not provide for the recognition of a pension liability except when a firm provided funding (payments to trustee or similar) at a rate less than the current expense and also when there was a legal liability.

Under APB Opinion No. 8, there were only limited disclosure requirements. FASB Statements No. 35 and No. 36 were passed in 1980 and provided for significant disclosure improvements.

In 1985, FASB Statement No. 87 was passed. It further improved the financial reporting of pensions, including the determination of the expense for the income statement, limited balance sheet recognition of pension liabilities, and disclosure. Despite these improvements, significant additional improvements in financial reporting could be achieved in the area of pensions.

Firms were allowed a three-year period to conform with the financial reporting requirements of FASB No. 87. They could elect to implement immediately the financial reporting requirements under FASB No. 87. Some firms used FASB No. 87 for their 1985 financial statements, other firms did not fully implement FASB No. 87 requirements until their fiscal year beginning after December 15, 1988.

Defined Contribution Plan versus Defined Benefit Plan

A company-sponsored pension plan is either a defined contribution plan or a defined benefit plan.

A defined contribution plan defines the contributions of the company to the pension plan. Once this defined contribution is made, the company has no further obligation to the pension plan. This type of plan shifts the risk to the employee as to whether the pension funds will grow to provide for a reasonable pension payment upon retirement. With this type of plan, which gained popularity during the 1980s, there is no problem of estimating the company's pension liability or pension expense. Thus, defined contribution plans do not present major financial reporting problems.

Firms should disclose the following for any defined contribution plan:

1. Description of the plan
2. The amount of cost recognized during the period

For firms with defined contribution plans, try to grasp the significance by doing the following:

1. For approximately a three-year period, compare pension expense with net sales (operating revenue). This will indicate the part of each sales dollar that is needed to cover pension expense.
2. Note any balance sheet items.

The Procter & Gamble Company disclosed the following in a footnote to its 1989 annual report.

> Most employees are covered by Company-funded defined contribution profit sharing plans which provide retirement benefits. Company contributions are based on a percentage of earnings, not to exceed 15% of the salaries and wages of participants and, in millions, amounted to $204 in 1989, $203 in 1988 and $190 in 1987. In 1990, the Company will begin contributions to the newly formed employee stock ownership plan which is part of the U.S. profit sharing plan. Other employees, primarily outside the U.S., are covered by local pension or retirement plans.

Procter & Gamble had net sales for 1989 and 1988 of $21,398,000,000 and $19,336,000,000, respectively. Thus, pension cost from defined contribution plans was .95% and 1.05% in 1989 and 1988, respectively. These costs do not appear to be material in relation to sales, and the trend is positive.

A defined benefit plan defines the benefits to be received by the participants in the plan. For example, the plan may call for the participant to receive 40% of his or her average pay for the three years before retirement. This type of plan leaves the company with the risk of having sufficient funds in the pension fund to meet the defined benefit. This type of plan was the predominant type of plan prior to the 1980s. Most companies still have a defined benefit plan, partly because of the difficulties involved in switching to a defined contribution plan. Some companies have terminated their defined benefit plan by funding the obligations of the plan and starting a defined contribution plan. In some cases, this has resulted in millions of dollars being transferred to the company from the pension plan after the defined benefit plan obligations have been met.

A number of assumptions about future events must be made regarding a defined benefit plan. Some of these assumptions that relate to the future are interest rates, employee turnover, mortality rates, compensation, and pension benefits set by law. Assumptions about future events contribute materially to the financial reporting problems in the pension area. Two firms with the same plan may make significantly different assumptions, resulting in major differences in pension expense and liability.

Several terms that should be understood in order to have a reasonable understanding of the financial reporting of defined benefit plans are explained in the paragraphs that follow.

1. Vested Benefits and Unvested Benefits. A vested pension benefit is one that the employee is entitled to even if he or she leaves the firm prior to retirement. This benefit is usually due either at normal retirement age or after a minimum number of years of work. The typical pension plan requires several years of work with the firm before the employee receives a vested benefit, although an unvested benefit is accruing. This means that the employee is in the pension plan, but rights under the plan will be lost if the employee leaves the firm prior to receiving a vested interest.

2. Prior Service Cost. When a defined benefit plan is adopted or amended, credit is often given to employees for years of service provided before the date of adoption or amendment. The cost of taking on this added commitment is called the *prior service cost.*

3. Accumulated Benefit Obligation. This is the actuarial present value of benefits attributed by the pension benefit formula to employee service rendered before a specified date and based on employee service and compensation (if applicable) prior to that date. The interest rate used for the present value computation is very important. A high interest rate results in a low present value for the accumulated benefit obligation. This could give the appearance that the pension plan is overfunded when it is not. Too low an interest rate could give the appearance that the pension plan is underfunded.

4. Projected Benefit Obligation. This is the actuarial present value as of a date of all benefits attributed by the pension benefit formula to employee service rendered prior to that date. The projected benefit obligation is measured using assumptions as to future compensation levels if the pension benefit formula is based on those future compensation levels. For plans with flat-benefit or non-pay-related pension benefit formulas, the accumulated benefit obligation and the projected benefit obligation are the same. The interest rate used for the present value computation is very important, as it is for the accumulated benefit obligation.

5. Net Periodic Pension Cost (Expense). The amount of net periodic pension cost for a period is the sum of the following six components:

a. Service cost (increases pension expense): the actuarial present value of benefits attributed by the pension benefit formula to services rendered by the employees during that period. (Future compensation levels must be considered if the plan benefit formula incorporates them.)

b. Interest cost (increases pension expense): the increase in the projected benefit obligation due to the passage of time. The assumed discount rate should reflect the rates at which pension benefits could be effectively settled.

c. Actual return on plan assets (decreases pension expense): the difference between the fair value of plan assets at the end of the period and the fair value at the beginning of the period, adjusted for contributions and payments of benefits during the period.

d. Amortization of unrecognized prior service cost (increases pension expense): Prior service cost is the cost of retroactive benefits granted in a plan amendment or at the initial adoption of the plan.

e. Amortization of net gains or losses (could increase or decrease pension expense): Gains and losses result from changes in the amount of either the projected benefit obligation or plan assets that are caused by differences between what was assumed would occur and what actually occurred or from changes in assumptions about the future of the plan.

f. Amortization of the unrecognized net obligation (and loss or cost) or unrecognized net asset (and gain) existing at the date of initial application of the statement: This is the loss or gain associated with the unrecognized net obligation or unrecognized net asset at the beginning of the fiscal year in which Statement No. 87 is first applied.

6. Balance Sheet Liabilities/Assets.

a. If the pension expense for the period exceeds the funding for the period, the difference is recognized as a liability.

b. If the pension expense for the period is less than the funding for the period, the difference is recognized as an asset.

c. An additional balance sheet liability is recognized if the accumulated benefit obligation exceeds the fair market value of plan assets less the balance in the accrued pension liability account or plus the balance in the deferred pension asset account (a or b above).

If an additional liability is recognized, an equal amount is recognized as an intangible asset if the amount recognized does not exceed the amount of unrecognized prior service cost. If it does, the excess would be reported separately as a reduction of stockholders' equity.

Note that the additional balance sheet liability considers the accumulated benefit obligation, not the projected benefit obligation. Thus, any additional balance sheet liability is a very conservative estimate of the liability if the projected benefit obligation is greater than the accumulated benefit obligation.

7. Footnote Disclosure.   Included in the required disclosures are the following:

a. Description of the plan.
b. The amount of the net periodic pension cost, including the components. (The detail of all six components of pension cost will usually be disclosed only when they are material.)
c. A schedule reconciling the funded status of the plan with amounts reported in the statement of financial position.

For purposes of the disclosure regarding the reconciliation of the funded status of the plan with amounts reported in the firm's balance sheet, the disclosures are required to be presented in two groups:

1. Aggregate amounts for plans with assets in excess of the accumulated benefit obligation.
2. Aggregate amounts for plans that have an accumulated benefit obligation that exceeds plan assets.

For firms with defined benefit plans, try to grasp the significance by doing the following:

1. For approximately a three-year period, compare the pension cost with net sales (operating revenue). This will indicate the significance of pension expense in relation to sales.
2. Compare the accumulated benefit obligations in relation to the plan assets at year end. Observe the part of the accumulated benefit obligations that is vested.
3. Note the projected benefit obligations in relation to the plan assets. Observe the part of the projected benefit obligations that is vested.
4. Note the interest rate used to compute the actuarial present value of the accumulated benefit obligation and the projected benefit obligation. The higher the interest rate used, the lower the present value of the liability and the lower the immediate pension cost. Changes in this interest rate could significantly increase or decrease the present value of the liability and increase or decrease the pension cost. *The Wall Street Journal* included these comments in an article entitled "Pension Funds Boost Projected Returns Even Though Experts Take a Dim View."[3]

   General Motors Corp., for example, was able to add $75 million to its first-quarter earnings largely by raising its annual pension earnings estimate to 11%

---

[3]"Pension Funds Boost Projected Return Even Though Experts Take a Dim View," *The Wall Street Journal*, October 23, 1990, pp. C1, C12.

from 10%. . . . International Business Machines Corp., for example, thinks it will earn 9% a year on its $26 billion pension fund. But if the computer maker made a more conservative long-term return forecast of, say 8%, its pension costs would soar $228 million this year.

5. Note the rate of compensation increase used in computing the projected benefit obligation. If the rate is too low, the projected benefit obligation is too low. If the rate is too high, the projected benefit obligation is too high.
6. Note the assumed rate of return on plan assets.
7. Note the unrecognized gains or losses. Unrecognized gains will reduce future pension cost, and unrecognized losses will increase future pension cost.
8. Note whether the unrecognized transition amount is an asset or a liability. Amortization of an asset will reduce future pension cost. Amortization of a liability will increase future pension cost.
9. Note the unrecognized prior service cost. This amount will be amortized to pension expense in subsequent years.
10. Note the prepaid (accrued) pension cost. Keep in mind that the balance sheet account has been computed using the accumulated benefit obligation, which has not considered assumptions as to the future compensation levels. Consider the impact on the balance sheet account if the projected benefit obligation were considered instead of the accumulated benefit obligation.

The Cooper pension footnote is shown in Exhibit 7-9. We note that Cooper's pension plans are defined benefit plans. Cooper implemented the reporting requirements of SFAS No. 87 with its 1989 report.

EXHIBIT 7 - 9

COOPER TIRE & RUBBER COMPANY
Pension Footnote
1989 Annual Report

Pensions

The Company has defined benefit plans covering substantially all employees. The salary plan provides pension benefits based on an employee's years of service and average earnings for the five highest calendar years during the ten years immediately preceding retirement. The hourly plans provide benefits of stated amounts for each year of service. The Company's general funding policy is to contribute amounts deductible for Federal income tax purposes.

In 1989 the Company adopted the minimum liability provisions of Statement of Financial Accounting Standards No. 87, "Employers' Accounting for Pensions." The minimum liability and a corresponding intangible asset of $7,850,000 have been recorded for those pension plans for which accumulated benefits exceed the related plan assets. Pension expense increased in 1989 due to increased benefits. Pension expense for 1989, 1988 and 1987 included the following components:

EXHIBIT 7-9 (continued)

	1989	1988	1987
Service cost—benefits earned during period	$ 4,534,000	$ 3,919,000	$3,838,000
Interest cost on projected benefit obligation	10,086,000	8,829,000	7,931,000
Actual return on assets	(20,023,000)	(13,505,000)	674,000
Net amortization and deferral	13,025,000	7,469,000	(5,950,000)
Net periodic pension cost	$ 7,622,000	$ 6,712,000	$6,493,000

The plans' assets consist of cash, cash equivalents and marketable securities. The funded status of the Company's plans at December 31, 1989 and 1988 was as follows:

	December 31, 1989		December 31, 1988	
	Plans for Which		Plans for Which	
	Assets Exceed Accumulated Benefits	Accumulated Benefits Exceed Assets	Assets Exceed Accumulated Benefits	Accumulated Benefits Exceed Assets
Actuarial present value of benefit obligations:				
Vested benefit obligation	$ (70,866,000)	$(35,394,000)	$(53,115,000)	$(41,277,000)
Accumulated benefit obligation	$ (72,332,000)	$(35,776,000)	$(54,153,000)	$(41,793,000)
Projected benefit obligation	$(100,968,000)	$(37,142,000)	$(80,400,000)	$(42,638,000)
Plan assets at fair value	98,489,000	24,788,000	68,763,000	29,370,000
Projected benefit obligation in excess of plan assets	$ (2,479,000)	$(12,354,000)	$(11,637,000)	$(13,268,000)
Unrecognized transition amount	8,404,000	6,020,000	9,665,000	5,847,000
Unrecognized prior service cost	1,130,000	3,369,000	129,000	3,989,000
Unrecognized net (gain) loss	(5,871,000)	(698,000)	(303,000)	413,000
Adjustment for minimum liability	—	(7,850,000)	—	—
Pension liability recognized in the balance sheet	$ 1,184,000	$(11,513,000)	$ (2,146,000)	$ (3,019,000)

The assumed rate of increase in future compensation levels and the assumed discount rate used in determining the actuarial present value of the projected benefit obligation at December 31, 1989 and 1988 were 6 percent and 8 percent, respectively; the assumed rate of return on plan assets was 10 percent.

The information presented above includes an unfunded nonqualified supplemental executive retirement plan covering certain employees whose participation in the qualified plan is limited by Section 415 of the Internal Revenue Code.

The following is observed relating to the pension plans of Cooper:

1. Pension cost in relation to sales:

	1989	1988	1987
Pension cost	$ 7,622,000	$ 6,712,000	$ 6,493,000
Net sales	$866,805,462	$748,032,206	$665,774,644
Pension cost/net sales	.88%	.90%	.98%

Cooper's pension expense does not appear to be significant in relation to sales. In relation to net sales, pension cost actually decreased in 1989.

2. Comparison of accumulated benefit obligations in relation to the plan assets at December 31, 1989:

	Assets Exceed Accumulated Benefits	Accumulated Benefits Exceed Assets
Accumulated benefit obligation	$72,332,000	$35,776,000
Plan assets at fair value	98,489,000	24,788,000
Plan assets in excess (less) than accumulated benefit obligation	$26,157,000	($10,988,000)

In total, Cooper's plan assets are in excess of accumulated benefit obligations. Cooper does have some plans for which the accumulated benefits obligation is in excess of plan assets, the the excess for these plans does not appear to be material. Approximately 98% of the accumulated benefit obligation is vested.

3. Comparison of projected benefit obligation in relation to the plan assets at December 31, 1989:

	Plans for Which Projected Benefit Obligation Exceeds Assets
Projected benefit obligations	$138,110,000
Plan assets at fair value	123,277,000
Projected benefit obligations exceed plan assets at fair value	($ 14,833,000)

Projected benefit obligations exceed plan assets at fair value by approximately $15 million. This would probably not be considered material. Approximately 77% of projected benefit obligations are vested.

4. The interest rate used to compute the actuarial present value of the accumulated benefit obligation and the projected benefit obligation was 8% in 1989 and 1988. This rate did not change between 1988 and 1989, and it appears to be reasonable. According to the 1989 *Accounting Trends and Techniques*, most firms were using a rate of 8% to 9% in 1988.[4]

---

[4]American Institute of Certified Public Accountants, *Accounting Trends and Techniques*, 1989, p. 255.

5. The compensation rate of increase in computing the projected benefit obligation was 6%. This rate appears reasonable; it was the rate most commonly used by the 600 companies included by *Accounting Trends and Techniques*.[5]

6. The assumed rate of return on plan assets was 10%. This rate appears to be reasonable, but it is slightly higher than the 9% most firms used.[6]

7. Unrecognized net gains totaled $6,569,000 at December 31, 1989. These unrecognized net gains will reduce pension expense in subsequent years when amortized to the income statement.

8. Unrecognized transition amount totaled $14,424,000 at December 31, 1989. This amount will be amortized to pension expense in subsequent years.

9. Unrecognized prior service cost totaled $4,499,000 at December 31, 1989. This amount will be amortized to pension expense in subsequent years.

10. Balance sheet booking of pension assets and pension liability has been $7,850,000 and $11,513,000, respectively. The asset appears to have been booked under investments and other assets, and the liability appears to have been booked under other long-term liabilities.

A review of the significance of a firm's pension expense and pension obligations can yield only a subjective insight into the significance of the firm's pensions. An attempt should be made to obtain this insight, since it can be material to a firm's profitability and debt position. For Cooper, a subjective conclusion is that the pension plans do not currently have a significant influence on profitability and debt position. Material pension cost could serve as a drag on future earnings. This could be a problem during a recession period if earnings are down but pension costs continue.

Employer's Accounting for Settlements and Curtailments

SFAS No. 88 was passed in December 1985, at the same time that SFAS No. 87 was passed. SFAS No. 88 covers how to account for settlements and curtailments and for termination benefits of a defined benefit plan.

Hundreds of companies have terminated their defined benefit plans because the plan assets were in excess of accumulated plan benefits. Companies are allowed to keep the difference between the amount necessary to settle the accumulated plan benefits and the assets in the plan. They must meet requirements that are intended to protect the employee before they can obtain funds by curtailing a plan. Some companies have benefited by hundreds of millions of dollars from a termination.

Prior to SFAS No. 88, companies spread these gains over subsequent years. Under SFAS No. 88, they can report the gains immediately as profit. These gains should be considered nonrecurring.

Panhandle Eastern Corporation disclosed the following in a footnote to its 1989 annual report:

[5]Ibid., p. 255.
[6]Ibid., p. 255.

During 1988, the Company received $15.5 million for the final settlement of pension plans of discontinued operations and paid $0.2 million related to such plans. The net result of the final pension settlements for these operations, after income tax and 10-percent excise tax on asset reversions of $8.5 million, has been credited to the previously established reserve for discontinued operations.

Postretirement Benefits Other Than Pensions

Some benefits other than pensions accrue to employees upon retirement, such as medical insurance and life insurance contracts. These benefits can be substantial; many firms have obligations in the millions of dollars. Most firms do not have these obligations funded; therefore, for these firms, there is a potential for a significant liability.

Historically, most firms followed a pay-as-you-go basis for postretirement benefits other than pensions. One of the reasons for this practice was that, unlike pension benefits, such costs are not tax deductible until paid. Usually, no recognition was given to the potential liability for these postretirement benefits. Thus, the accounting for the obligations related to postretirement benefits was one of the major weaknesses in financial reporting.

For most firms, the substantial postretirement benefit other than pensions is medical insurance. In December 1990, the FASB passed SFAS No. 106, which substantially improved the financial reporting of medical insurance for retirees. Beginning in 1993, most firms must accrue, or set up a reserve for, future medical benefits of retirees rather than deduct these costs when paid.

Under SFAS No. 106, firms can usually spread the catch-up accrual costs over twenty years or take the charge in one lump sum. The amount involved is frequently material, so this choice can represent a major problem when comparing financial results of two or more firms.

For some firms, the catch-up charge for medical insurance is so material that it can result in a deficit in retained earnings, or even a deficit to the entire stockholders' equity section.

Many firms are reducing costs by changing their plans to limit health care benefits to retirees to a maximum fixed amount. This type of plan, in contrast to open-ended medical benefits, could materially reduce the firm's health care costs for retirees.

Review the footnotes closely to determine how the firm is recording health care costs for retirees. The health care benefits to retirees are usually disclosed in a footnote. Compare this cost to net sales to grasp its significance in relation to sales.

Cooper did not disclose postretirement benefits other than pensions in its 1989 annual report. This indicates either that it did not have such obligations or that the obligations were insignificant.

In a footnote to its 1989 annual report, the Procter & Gamble Company disclosed the following in relation to postretirement benefits other than pensions:

Certain health care and life insurance benefits are provided for many retired employees. The cost of these benefits is charged against earnings in the year the claims and premiums are paid. This cost, in millions, amounted to $21 in 1989, $16 in 1988 and $10 in 1987.

For Procter & Gamble, the cost of these postretirement benefits other than pensions is insignificant as of 1989 (net sales $21,398,000,000 and $19,336,000,000 in 1989 and 1988, respectively). Procter & Gamble probably had an unbooked liability for postretirement benefits other than pensions at the end of 1989.

Joint Ventures

A joint venture is an association of two or more businesses, established for a special purpose. Some joint ventures are in the form of partnerships and unincorporated joint ventures; others are in the form of corporations that are jointly owned by two or more other firms. Usually, the joint venture is jointly owned by only two firms.

The accounting principles for accounting for a joint venture are flexible. This is necessary because of the many forms of joint ventures. The typical problem is whether a joint venture should be carried as an investment or consolidated. Some joint ventures are very significant in relation to the parent firm, but there is usually a question as to whether the parent firm has control or only significant influence. Joint ventures in which the parent firm feels that it has control are usually consolidated, but sometimes by using a pro rata share. Other joint ventures are usually carried in an investment account by using the equity method. In either case, there is often disclosure of significant information in a footnote.

When a firm enters into a joint venture, it frequently makes commitments, such as guaranteeing a bank loan for the joint venture or a long-term contract to purchase materials with the joint venture. This type of action can give the parent company significant potential liabilities or commitments that are not on the face of the balance sheet. This is a potential problem with all joint ventures, including those that have been consolidated. In order to be aware of these significant potential liabilities or commitments, read the footnote that relates to the joint venture. Then try to consider this information subjectively in relation to the additional liabilities or commitments that the joint venture may commit the firm to.

The Fluor Corporation disclosed in footnotes the following in its 1986 annual report:

> The company consolidates its 50 percent proportionate share of the accounts of Massey Coal Company. . . . At October 31, 1986, $480,000,000 of net assets of subsidiaries, including $72,000,000 of working capital, have restrictions which affect the ability to transfer them to the parent company in the form of loans, advances, or dividends. A substantial portion of these restricted net assets relate to the requirement of the Massey Coal Company joint venture agreement to obtain approval of all parties prior to the transfer of joint venture assets.

Contingencies

"Accounting for Contingencies," SFAS No. 5, defines a contingency as an existing condition, situation, or set of circumstances involving uncertainty as to possible gain or loss to an enterprise that will ultimately be resolved when one or more future events occur or fail to occur.[7]

A contingency is characterized by an existing condition, uncertainty as to the ultimate effect, and its resolution depending on one or more future events. SFAS No. 5 directs that a loss contingency be accrued if two conditions are met:[8]

1. Information prior to issuance of the financial statements indicates that it is probable that an asset has been impaired or a liability has been incurred at the date of the financial statements.
2. The amount of the loss can be reasonably estimated.

If a contingency loss meets one, but not both, of the criteria for recording and is therefore not accrued, disclosure by footnote is made when it is at least reasonably possible that there has been an impairment of assets or that a liability has been incurred. Examples of contingencies that are usually recorded are warranty obligations and collectibility of receivables. Guarantees of indebtedness of others is a case for which the contingency is usually recorded in a footnote.

When examining financial statements, a footnote that describes contingencies should be closely reviewed for possible significant liabilities that are not disclosed on the face of the balance sheet.

There is no contingency footnote for Cooper at the end of 1989. This indicates that the company did not have significant contingency problems that it considered necessary to disclose in a footnote. Practically all firms have addressed the contingency problem. Even the account, allowance for doubtful accounts, has been recorded under the contingency standard.

Westinghouse described contingencies in a footnote to its 1989 annual report. This footnote, entitled "Commitments and Contingent Liabilities," reads in part:

> During the course of its normal business activities, WFSI [Westinghouse Financial Services, Inc. and its subsidiaries] issues various guarantees, standby letters of credit and standby commitments. At December 31, 1989, WFSI was contingently liable under guarantees of $838 million associated primarily with real estate projects. In addition, WFSI was contingently liable for $323 million under standby agreements issued on behalf of various customers. Funding under the above guarantees and standby agreements generally would result in a secured receivable or a right to proceed against an outside party.

Gain contingencies are covered in ARB No. 50, and the position taken there was reaffirmed in SFAS No. 5. Paragraphs 3 and 5 of ARB No. 50 indicate the following:

---

[7]Financial Accounting Standards Board, Statement of Financial Accounting Standards No. 5, "Accounting for Contingencies," 1975, par. 1.
[8]Ibid., par. 8.

1. Contingencies that might result in gains usually are not reflected in the accounts, since to do so might be to recognize revenue prior to its realization.
2. Adequate disclosure shall be made of contingencies that might result in gains, but care shall be exercised to avoid misleading implications as to the likelihood of realization.

The footnotes of the firm being examined should be reviewed for gain contingencies. Parkway Company disclosed the following in the notes to its 1989 annual report:

> The Company has available net operating loss carryforwards of approximately $27,365,000 for financial reporting purposes. For federal income tax reporting purposes, the Company has net operating loss carryforwards of approximately $12,771,000.

Financial Instruments Disclosures and Credit Risk Concentrations

SFAS No. 105 requires disclosure of matters relating to off-balance-sheet financial instruments and credit risk concentrations, which can result in disclosure of significant financial risk. This SFAS addresses credit and market risk for all financial instruments with off-balance-sheet risk. For these financial instruments, the following disclosure is required:

1. The face, contract or national amount
2. The nature and terms including, at a minimum, a discussion of credit and market risk, cash requirements, and accounting policies

SFAS No. 105 also requires disclosure of the following regarding financial instruments with off-balance-sheet credit risk:

1. The amount of accounting loss the entity would incur if any party failed completely to perform according to the terms of the contract and the collateral or other security, if any, proved worthless
2. The entity's policy of requiring collateral and a brief description of the collateral it currently holds

Accounting loss is a new term used in this SFAS. It represents the worst-case loss, if everything related to a contract went wrong. This includes the possibility that a loss may occur from the failure of another party to perform according to the terms of a contract, as well as the possibility that changes in market prices may make a financial instrument less valuable or more troublesome.

In addition to requiring disclosure of matters relating to off-balance-sheet financial instruments, SFAS No. 105 requires disclosure of credit risk concentration. This disclosure includes information on the extent of risk from exposures to individuals or groups of counter parties in the same industry or region. A narrative description of the activity, region, or economic characteristic that identifies a concentration is required. The provision of requiring disclosure of credit risk concentration can be particularly significant to small companies. Examples are a retail store whose receivables are substantially with local residents and a local bank with a loan portfolio that is concentrated with debtors that are dependent on the local tourist business.

SUMMARY

This chapter covered two approaches to a firm's long-term debt-paying ability. One approach considers the firm's ability to carry debt as indicated by the income statement, and the other approach views it as indicated by the balance sheet. The ratios related to debt that were covered in this chapter are the following:

$$\text{Times Interest Earned} = \frac{\text{Recurring Earnings, Excluding Interest Expense, Tax Expense, Equity Earnings, and Minority Income}}{\text{Interest Expense, Including Capitalized Interest}}$$

$$\text{Fixed Charge Coverage} = \frac{\text{Recurring Earnings, Excluding Interest Expense, Tax Expense, Equity Earnings, and Minority Income} + \text{Interest Portion of Rentals}}{\text{Interest Expense, Including Capitalized Interest} + \text{Interest Portion of Rentals}}$$

$$\text{Debt Ratio} = \frac{\text{Total Liabilities}}{\text{Total Assets}}$$

$$\text{Debt/Equity} = \frac{\text{Total Liabilities}}{\text{Shareholders' Equity}}$$

$$\text{Debt to Tangible Net Worth} = \frac{\text{Total Liabilities}}{\text{Shareholders' Equity} - \text{Intangible Assets}}$$

QUESTIONS

Q 7-1   Is profitability important to a firm's long-term debt-paying ability? Discuss.

Q 7-2   List the two approaches to examining a firm's long-term debt-paying ability. Discuss why each of these approaches gives an important view of a firm's ability to carry debt.

Q 7-3   What type of times interest earned ratio would be desirable? What type would not be desirable?

Q 7-4   Would you expect an auto manufacturer to finance a relatively high proportion of its long-term funds from debt? Discuss.

Q 7-5   Would you expect a telephone company to have a high debt ratio? Discuss.

Q 7-6   Why should capitalized interest be added to interest expense when computing times interest earned?

Q 7-7   Discuss how noncash charges for depreciation, depletion, and amortization can be used to obtain a short-run view of times interest earned.

Q 7-8   Why is it difficult to determine the value of assets?

Q 7-9   Is it feasible to get a precise measurement of the funds that could be available from long-term assets to pay long-term debts? Discuss.

Q 7-10   One of the ratios used to indicate long-term debt-paying ability is total liabilities to total assets. What is the intent of this ratio? How precise is this ratio in achieving its intent?

Q 7-11   For a given firm, would you expect the debt ratio to be as high as the debt/equity ratio? Explain.

Q 7-12   Explain how the debt/equity ratio indicates the same relative long-term debt-paying ability as does the debt ratio, only in a different form.

Q 7-13   Why is it important to compare long-term debt ratios of a given firm with industry averages?

Q 7-14   Under SFAS No. 13, how should operating leases be accounted for by lessees? Capital leases? Include both income statement and balance sheet accounts.

Q 7-15   A firm that has substantial leased assets that have not been capitalized may be overstating its long-term debt-paying ability. Explain.

Q 7-16   Capital leases that have not been capitalized will decrease the times interest earned ratio. Comment.

Q 7-17   Indicate the status of pension liabilities under the Employee Retirement Income Security Act.

Q 7-18   Why is the vesting provision an important provision of a pension plan? How has the Employee Retirement Income Security Act influenced vesting periods?

Q 7-19   Indicate the risk to a company if it withdraws from a multiemployer pension plan or if the multiemployer pension plan is terminated.

Q 7-20   Operating leases are not reflected on the balance sheet, but they are reflected on the income statement in the rent expense. Comment on why an interest expense figure that relates to long-term operating leases should be considered when determining a fixed charge coverage.

Q 7-21   What portion of net worth can the federal government require a company to use to pay for pension obligations?

Q 7-22   Consider the debt ratio. Explain a position for including short-term liabilities in the debt ratio. Explain a position for excluding short-term liabilities from the debt ratio. Which of these approaches would be more conservative?

Q 7-23   Consider the accounts of bonds payable and reserve for rebuilding furnaces. Explain how one of these accounts could be considered a firm liability and the other could be considered a soft liability.

Q 7-24   Explain why deferred taxes that are disclosed as long-term liabilities may not result in actual cash outlays in the future.

Q 7-25   A firm has a high current debt/net worth ratio in relation to prior years, competitors, and the industry. Comment on what this tentatively indicates.

Q 7-26   Comment on the implications of relying on a greater proportion of short-term debt in relation to long-term debt.

Q 7-27   When a firm guarantees a bank loan for a joint venture that it participates in, and the joint venture is handled as an investment, then the overall potential debt position will not be obvious from the face of the balance sheet. Comment.

Q 7-28   When examining financial statements, a footnote that describes contingencies should be reviewed closely for possible significant liabilities that are not disclosed on the face of the balance sheet. Comment.

Q 7-29   There is a chance that a company may be in a position to have large sums transferred from the pension fund to the company. Comment.

| PROBLEMS

P 7-1   Consider the following operating figures:

Net sales	$1,079,143
Cost and deductions:	
Cost of sales	792,755
Selling and administration	264,566
Interest expense, net	4,311
Income taxes	5,059
	1,066,691
	$ 12,452

Note: Depreciation expense totals $40,000.

Required   Compute the times interest earned and the cash basis times interest earned.

P 7-2   The Jones Petro Company reports the following consolidated statement of income:

Operating revenues	$2,989
Costs and expenses:	
Cost of rentals and royalties	543
Cost of sales	314
Selling, service, administrative, and general expense	1,424
Total costs and expenses	2,281
Operating income	708
Other income	27
Other deductions (interest)	60
Income before income taxes	675
Income taxes	309

Income before outside shareholders' interests	366
Outside shareholders' interests	66
Net income	$ 300

Note: Depreciation expense totals $200; operating lease payments total $150; and preferred dividends total $50. Assume that 1/3 of operating lease payments is for interest.

Required
a. Compute the times interest earned.
b. Compute the fixed charge coverage.

P 7-3   The Sherwill statement of consolidated income is as follows:

Net sales		$658
Other income		8
		666
Costs and expenses:		
Cost of products sold		418
Selling, general, and administrative expenses		196
Interest		16
		630
Income before income taxes and extraordinary charges		36
Income taxes		18
Income before extraordinary charge		18
Extraordinary charge-losses on tornado damage (net)		4
Net income		$ 14

Required
a. Compute the times interest earned.
b. Compute the fixed charge coverage.

P 7-4   The Kaufman Company balance sheet is as follows:

Assets		
Current assets		
Cash		$ 13,445
Short-term investments—at cost (approximate market)		5,239
Trade accounts receivable, less allowance of $1,590		88,337
Inventories—at lower of cost (average method) or market:		
Finished merchandise	$113,879	
Work in process, raw materials and supplies	47,147	
		160,915
Prepaid expenses		8,221
Total current assets		276,157
Other assets:		
Receivables, advances, and other assets		4,473
Intangibles		2,324
Total other assets		6,797

Property, plant, and equipment:	
Land	$ 5,981
Buildings	78,908
Machinery and equipment	162,425
	247,314
Less allowances for depreciation	106,067
Net property, plant, and equipment	141,247
Total assets	$424,201

Liabilities and shareholders' equity	
Current liabilities:	
Notes payable	$ 2,817
Trade accounts payable	23,720
Pension, interest, and other accruals	33,219
Taxes, other than income taxes	4,736
Income taxes	3,409
Total current liabilities	67,901
Long-term debt, 12% debentures	86,235
Deferred income taxes	8,768
Minority interest in subsidiaries	12,075
Shareholders' equity:	
Capital stock	
Serial preferred	9,154
Common, $5.25 par value	33,540
Additional paid-in capital	3,506
Retained earnings	203,712
Total shareholders' equity	249,912
Less cost of common shares in treasury	690
	249,222
Total liabilities and shareholders' equity	$424,201

Required

a. Compute the debt ratio.
b. Compute the debt/equity ratio.
c. Compute the ratio of total debt to tangible net worth.
d. Comment on the amount of debt that the Kaufman Company has.

P 7-5 Individual transactions often have a significant impact on ratios. This problem will consider the direction of such an impact.

Ratio Transaction	Times Interest Earned	Debt Ratio	Debt/ Equity	Total Debt Tangible Net Worth
a. Purchase of buildings financed by mortgage	___	___	___	___
b. Purchase of inventory on short-term loan at 1% over the prime rate	___	___	___	___
c. Declaration and payment of cash dividend	___	___	___	___
d. Declaration and payment of stock dividend	___	___	___	___

Ratio Transaction	Times Interest Earned	Debt Ratio	Debt/ Equity	Total Debt Tangible Net Worth
e. Firm increases profits by cutting cost of sales	_____	___	___	_____
f. Appropriation of retained earnings	_____	___	___	_____
g. Sale of common stock	_____	___	___	_____
h. Repayment of long-term bank loan	_____	___	___	_____
i. Conversion of bonds to common stock outstanding	_____	___	___	_____
j. Sale of inventory at greater than cost	_____	___	___	_____

Required   Indicate the effect of each of the transactions on the ratios listed. Use + to indicate an increase, − to indicate a decrease, and 0 to indicate no effect. Assume an initial times interest earned of more than 1 to 1, and a debt ratio, a debt/equity ratio, and a total debt to tangible net worth of less than 1 to 1.

P 7-6   For the year ended June 30, 1989, A.E.G. Enterprises presented the following financial statements:

A.E.G. ENTERPRISES
Balance Sheet for June 30, 1989 (in thousands)

Assets		
Current assets:		
Cash	$ 50,000	
Accounts receivable	60,000	
Inventory	106,000	
Total current assets		$216,000
Property, plant, and equipment	$504,000	
Less: accumulated depreciation	140,000	364,000
Patents and other intangible assets		20,000
Total assets		$600,000
Liabilities and stockholders' equity		
Current liabilities:		
Accounts payable	$ 46,000	
Taxes payable	15,000	
Other current liabilities	32,000	
Total current liabilities		$ 93,000
Long-term debt		100,000
Stockholders' equity: Preferred stock ($100 par, 10% cumulative, 500,000 shares authorized and issued)		50,000
Common stock ($1 par, 200,000,000 shares authorized, 100,000,000 issued)		100,000
Premium on common stock		120,000
Retained earnings		137,000
Total liabilities and stockholders' equity		$600,000

A.E.G. ENTERPRISES
Income Statement for the Year Ended June 30, 1989
(in thousands except earnings per share)

Sales		$936,000
Cost of sales		671,000
Gross profit		$265,000
Operating expenses		
Selling	$62,000	
General	41,000	103,000
Operating income		$162,000
Other items:		
Interest expense		20,000
Earnings before provision for income tax		$142,000
Provision for income tax		56,800
Net income		$ 85,200
Earnings per share		$.83

Early in the new fiscal year, the officers of the firm formalized a substantial expansion plan. The plan will increase fixed assets by $190,000,000. In addition, extra inventory will be needed to support expanded production. The increase in inventory is purported to be $10,000,000.

The firm's investment bankers have suggested three alternative financing plans:

Plan A: Sell preferred stock at par.
Plan B: Sell common stock at $10 per share.
Plan C: Sell long-term bonds, due in 20 years, at par ($1,000), with a stated interest rate of 16%.

Required

a. For the year ended June 30, 1989, compute:
   1. times interest earned
   2. debt ratio
   3. debt/equity ratio
   4. debt to tangible net worth ratio
b. Assuming the same financial results and statement balances, except for the increased assets and financing, compute the same ratios as in (a) under each financing alternative. Do not attempt to adjust retained earnings for the next year's profits.
c. Changes in earnings and number of shares will give the following earnings per share: Plan A—.73; Plan B—.69; Plan C—.73. Based on the information given, discuss the advantages and disadvantages of each alternative.
d. Why does the 10% preferred stock cost the company more than the 16% bonds?

P 7-7   A Mr. Parks has asked you to advise him on the long-term debt-paying ability of the Arodex Company. He provides you with the following ratios:

	1989	1988	1987
Times interest earned	8.2	6.0	5.5
Debt ratio	40%	39%	40%
Debt to tangible net worth	80%	81%	81%

Required a. Give the implications and the limitations of each item separately and then the collective inference one may draw from them about the Arodex Company's long-term debt position.

b. What warnings should you offer Mr. Parks about the limitations of ratio analysis for the purpose stated here?

P 7-8 The Allen Company and the Barker Company are competitors in the same industry. Selected financial data from their 1989 statements are as follows:

Balance Sheet
December 31, 1989

	Allen Company	Barker Company
Cash	$ 10,000	$ 35,000
Accounts receivable	45,000	120,000
Inventory	70,000	190,000
Investments	40,000	100,000
Intangibles	11,000	20,000
Property, plant, and equipment, net	180,000	520,000
Total assets	$356,000	$985,000
Accounts payable	$ 60,000	$165,000
Bonds payable	100,000	410,000
Preferred stock, $1 par	50,000	30,000
Common stock, $10 par	100,000	280,000
Retained earnings	46,000	100,000
Total liabilities and capital	$356,000	$985,000

Income Statement
For the Year Ended December 31, 1989

	Allen Company	Barker Company
Sales	$1,050,000	$2,800,000
Cost of goods sold	725,000	2,050,000
Selling and administrative expenses	230,000	580,000
Interest expense	10,000	32,000
Income taxes	42,000	65,000
Net income	$ 43,000	$ 43,000

Income Statement   (continued)

Industry averages:	
Times interest earned	7.2 times
Debt ratio	40.3%
Debt/equity	66.6%
Debt to tangible net worth	72.7%

Required   a. Compute the following ratios for each company:
 1. times interest earned
 2. debt ratio
 3. debt/equity
 4. debt to tangible net worth
 b. Is Barker Company in a position to take on additional long-term debt? Explain.
 c. Which company has the better long-term debt position? Explain.

P 7-9   The consolidated statement of earnings of Anonymous Corporation for the year ended December 31, 1989 is as follows:

Net sales	$1,550,010,000
Other income, net	10,898,000
	1,560,908,000
Cost of expenses:	
Cost of goods sold	1,237,403,000
Depreciation and amortization	32,229,000
Selling, general, and administrative	178,850,000
Interest	37,646,000
	1,486,128,000
Earnings from continuing operations before income taxes and equity earnings	74,780,000
Income taxes	37,394,000
Earnings from continuing operations before equity earnings	37,386,000
Equity in net earnings of unconsolidated subsidiaries and affiliated companies	27,749,000
Earnings from continuing operations	65,135,000
Earnings (losses) from discontinued operations, net of applicable income taxes	6,392,000
Net earnings	$ 71,527,000

Required   a. Compute the times interest earned for 1989.
 b. Compute the times interest earned for 1989, including the equity income in the coverage.
 c. What is the impact of excluding equity earnings from the coverage? Why should equity income be excluded from the times interest earned coverage?

P 7-10   The following are a number of terms that relate to pensions and a definition of the term. Match the appropriate definition with each term.

Term

_____ 1. Employee Retirement Income Security Act (ERISA)

_____ 2. Multiemployer pension plan

_____ 3. Defined contribution plan

_____ 4. Defined benefit plan

_____ 5. Vested pension plan

_____ 6. Prior service cost

_____ 7. Projected benefit obligation

_____ 8. Amortization of the unrecognized net obligation (and loss or cost) or unrecognized net asset (and gain) existing at the date of initial application of SFAS No. 87

Definition

a. Defines the benefits to be received by the participants in the plan

b. A pension benefit that the employee is entitled to even if the employee leaves the firm prior to retirement

c. The loss or gain associated with the unrecognized net obligation or unrecognized net asset at the beginning of the fiscal year in which SFAS No. 87 is first applied

d. Federal pension law passed in 1974

e. Credit given to employees for years of service provided before the date of adoption or amendment of the defined benefit plan

f. Pension plan maintained jointly by two or more unrelated employers

g. Defines the contributions of the company to the pension plan

h. The actuarial present value, as of a date, of all benefits attributed by pension benefit formula to employee service rendered prior to that date; computed using assumptions as to future compensation levels if the pension benefit formula is based on those future compensation levels

CASES

Case 7-1   DEFERRED TAXES? THE ANSWER IS YES*

GEORGIA POWER COMPANY
Position Paper on Accounting for Income Taxes

Comprehensive Allocation

Comprehensive interperiod tax allocation is necessary to properly recognize the economic substance of a taxable transaction or event. Income taxes are an expense of doing business. It would be inconsistent with accrual accounting to not recognize the appropriate income tax expense at the time of a transaction, when the revenues and other expenses are recognized. The fact that the taxes are not

---

*Note: Georgia Power Company Position Paper on Accounting for Income Taxes, submitted to the Financial Accounting Standards Board.

currently payable does not eliminate the expense. If an asset is being depreciated at an accelerated rate for tax purposes, there is a clear economic event that must be recognized. In addition to a reduction in current taxes payable, part of the value of that asset has been consumed, and that fact must be recognized under accrual accounting. The current reduction in taxes payable is not income, it is simply the proceeds from the disposal of a portion of the asset. To recognize only the amount of taxes paid in a particular year would ignore the economic fact that income taxes are based on the separate revenue and expense transactions as measured by the tax laws.

Criticisms and concerns expressed in current articles and accounting literature have focused both on the complexities of current accounting requirements and the meaningfulness of the results of applying the requirements. Accrual accounting is obviously more complex than a listing of cash receipts and payments. However, Concepts Statement No. 1, Objectives of Financial Reporting, states that "Information about enterprises' earnings based on accrual accounting generally provides a better indication of an enterprise's present and continuing ability to generate favorable cash flows than information limited to the financial effects of cash receipts and payments." Flow-through accounting or any method of partial allocation is inconsistent with accrual accounting.

Conceptual Definition

The Accounting Principles Board (APB) recognized that income taxes were an expense of doing business, and that comprehensive tax allocation or accrual accounting was the most meaningful way to recognize this expense. However, the Board members had differing opinions on the conceptual definition of the balance sheet effect of tax allocations and selected the deferred method as a compromise. The deferred method properly dealt with the effect of income taxes on the income statement, but it gave only secondary consideration to the balance sheet effect. However, at the time of APB 11 the accounting profession was more concerned with the income statement.

Current accounting concepts place much more emphasis on the balance sheet. Concepts Statement No. 3 states that deferred taxes, as defined under APB 11, do not meet the definition for proper elements of financial reporting. Deferred taxes must be defined as either liabilities or valuation accounts to be properly recorded on the balance sheet. This does not necessarily mean that the deferred "method" must be abandoned. It simply means that the balance sheet results must be defined under a different concept. For example, Concepts Statement No. 3 states that "Some proponents of the deferred method hold that it is actually a variation of the net-of-tax method despite rejection of that method in Opinion 11. They view the deferred tax charges and credits as the separate display of the effects of interperiod tax allocation instead of as reductions of the related assets, liabilities, revenues, expenses, gains, and losses. They argue that separate display is necessary or desirable, but it is a matter of geography in financial statements rather than a matter of the nature of deferred income tax credits."

The APB could not agree on whether the tax effects of timing differences were liabilities or valuation accounts, and the reasons for this disagreement seem obvious. Not all timing differences are the same; some are liabilities (or assets) and some are valuations of other balance sheet accounts. The conceptual definition of a timing difference should be based on the economic substance of the particular timing difference.

Generally speaking, if an existing asset or liability is directly impacted by the timing difference, the tax effect of the timing difference should be considered a valuation of the asset or liability (but not necessarily netted against the asset or liability). If the timing difference is not related to an existing asset or liability, the tax effect of the timing difference would have to be evaluated based on the characteristics of an asset or a liability.

The valuation concept is based on the fact that taxability and tax deductibility are factors in the determination of the carrying amounts of individual assets and liabilities. Concepts Statement No. 3 defines assets as "probable future economic benefits obtained or controlled by a particular entity as a result of past transactions or events." The Statement goes on to explain, "The common characteristics possessed by all assets and economic resources is service potential or future economic benefit, the capacity to provide services or benefits to the entities that use them. In a business enterprise, that service potential or future economic benefit eventually results in net cash inflows to the enterprise. That characteristic is the primary basis of the definition of assets in this Statement." Part of the value (future cash flow) of an asset is its tax deductibility. Any businessman understands that an asset with a tax basis has more value than an asset with no tax basis. This fact was made explicitly clear with the provision of the Economic Recovery Tax Act of 1981, which allowed an enterprise to sell the tax benefits of an asset. When a portion of an asset's value has been consumed or sold, the future cash flow from that asset has been reduced. Under accrual accounting, financial statements should reflect this fact.

Concepts Statement No. 3 defines liabilities as "probable future sacrifices of economic benefits arising from present obligations . . . as a result of past transactions or events." Since income taxes are based on separate revenue and expense transactions, the tax effects of timing differences do meet the definitions of assets and liabilities. A good example is an installment sale that is recognized for financial accounting in the period of the sale but included in taxable income of a later period, when cash is collected. The "past transaction" is the sale which makes future tax payment "probable" (but not certain). Certainly future taxes are dependent on future taxable income; however, for this one item there will be taxes payable and the elimination of future taxable income will require future tax deductions or changes in the laws. This timing difference also could be viewed as a valuation of the receivable, and as explained above this would be the preferable treatment.

Presentation

The conceptual nature of the timing difference does not necessarily dictate the method of recording the timing difference. The tax effects of timing differences, which are in fact valuations of fixed assets, should be reported as a component of, or offset to, the fixed asset. The presentation would more properly reflect the future cash flows expected from the fixed asset. However, timing differences which are valuations of other assets or liabilities may be better recorded in a separate account similar to current deferred taxes, separated between current and noncurrent (see example of balance sheet presentation). This approach would avoid the problems of netting payables with future tax benefits or having other potentially misleading combinations. Furthermore, the adoption of the valuation concept would not necessarily change the current treatment of income taxes in the income statement. All income taxes (current and deferred) could still be recorded as tax expense.

Tax Rate

Under either concept of interperiod tax allocation, an important issue is the tax rate to be used in calculating the tax timing difference. However, the conceptual nature of the timing difference should not dictate how the tax rate is determined. The tax impact of a transaction is determined at the time the transaction affects the tax return. Once an item has been reflected in the tax return, its economic impact is fixed and this will not change regardless of changes in the income tax laws. Therefore, timing differences arising from transactions recognized first for tax purposes would be measured using the tax rate at that time. Timing differences arising from transactions recognized first for financial reporting purposes would be measured based on the tax rate expected to be in effect when the revenue or expense is to be reflected in the tax return. The economic impact of these timing differences would change if the tax rate changes. The tax rate change would be handled as would any other change in accounting estimate.

Discounting

In addition to the tax rate, another measurement question is whether the tax allocation balance should be discounted. The question normally arises when tax allocations are viewed as liabilities, however, the question is also relevant when using the valuation method. In APB Opinion No. 10, Omnibus Opinion-1966 (Tax Allocation Accounts—Discounting), the Board concluded that pending further consideration of the broader aspects of discounting as it related to financial accounting in general, deferred taxes should not be discounted. The accounting profession (APB or FASB) has not yet reviewed the broad issue of discounting. Tax timing differences should not be considered independent of the broader issue. The FASB should defer this question until the completion of the Concept Statement on accounting recognition and measurement.

Example Balance Sheet (000)

Assets	
Utility Plant	$6,900,000
Less—accumulated depreciation	1,500,000
Total	5,400,000
Less property-related accumulated deferred income taxes	700,000
Total	4,700,000

Current assets:	
Cash	540,000
Accounts receivable (net)	280,000
Materials and supplies	345,000
Total	1,165,000
Total assets	$5,865,000
Capitalization and liabilities	
Capitalization:	
Common stock equity	$1,700,000
Preferred stock	550,000
Long-term debt	2,800,000
Total	5,050,000
Current liabilities:	
Accounts payable	250,000
Customer deposits	30,000
Taxes accrued	40,000
Current deferred income taxes	70,000
Miscellaneous	110,000
Total	500,000
Deferred income taxes	15,000
Accumulated deferred investment tax credits	300,000
Total capitalization and liabilities	$5,865,000

Required

a. Should companies use the same financial reporting methods for their annual report as they use for their federal tax return? Discuss.

b. Explain why there are permanent differences between financial reporting of income and federal tax reporting of income.

c. Explain why a company may be reporting a revenue or expense item in a different period in its financial statements than in its federal tax return.

d. Critically comment on the following: Federal income tax expense should be recognized on the financial statements in the same period that the tax liability is incurred.

e. The Georgia Power position paper states: "Current accounting concepts place much more emphasis on the balance sheet. Concept Statement No. 3 states that deferred taxes, as defined under APB 11, do not meet the definition for proper elements of financial reporting. Deferred taxes must be defined as either liabilities or valuation accounts to be properly recorded in the balance sheet."

    How does the Georgia Power position paper propose to classify deferred taxes on the balance sheet?

f. An important issue to be resolved, if deferred taxes are to be recognized, is the tax rate. How should the tax rate be determined according to the Georgia Power position paper? In your opinion, do you agree with the determination of the tax rate, as proposed by Georgia Power? Comment.

g. Discuss some practical reasons why many firms would prefer that deferred taxes *not* be part of generally accepted accounting principles.

h. Discuss some practical reasons why Georgia Power would prefer that deferred taxes be part of generally accepted accounting principles.

Case 7-2   CONCENTRATION ON OPERATING ASPECTS

The F.W. Woolworth Co., a multinational retailer distributing general merchandise through department stores, had been engaged in an expansion program during the mid-1970s.

During January 1977, the company sold its trade receivables and aggregated approximately $216,100,000, less an initial discount of approximately $2,200,000 to General Electric Credit Corporation (GECC) and the Bank of Montreal (B of M). Most of the accounts were sold with recourse. The company continues to offer credit plans to qualified customers; GECC and B of M have agreed to purchase, without recourse after a transitional period, future trade receivables, as they arise, at discounts ranging from 1.75% to 3% in the United States and 3% to 5% in Canada. In the United States, the company will also pay a fee for each account billed.

The following press release was issued to explain the sale of the accounts receivable to GECC:

From: Ernest C. Downing, Jr.   For Immediate Release
        Carl Byoir & Associates, Inc.
        800 Second Avenue, 986-6100
        New York, New York 10017

For: F.W. Woolworth Co.

WOOLWORTH NEGOTIATING SALE OF
CUSTOMER ACCOUNTS RECEIVABLE

NEW YORK, Sept. 13—F.W. Woolworth Co. has reached a tentative agreement in principle with General Electric Credit Corporation (GECC) whereby GECC would purchase for cash approximately $175 million of customer accounts receivable of the U.S. Woolco and Woolworth operations.

GECC would operate the 1.1 million active account customer credit program under the Woolco and Woolworth names in the approximately 300 stores currently offering credit service.

Lester A. Burcham, chairman of Woolworth, said that the tentative agreement is subject to the formulation of a definitive contract which would then require approval by the boards of directors of both corporations. It is contemplated that the sale would be effective before January 31, 1977.

"Although Woolworth is comfortably strong financially, this action would provide additional financial strength through the improvement of debt ratios and additional latitude for programmed growth," Burcham said, "it also would improve the return on assets employed in the U.S. Woolco and Woolworth operations and in effect take us out of the 'financing business', allowing us to concentrate our corporate management and financial resources in our expanding retail business."

Should the new arrangement go into effect, all present Woolworth and Woolco credit personnel "would be accorded fullest individual consideration for reassignment to other positions within the company, employment by GECC or others," Woolworth pointed out.

The new arrangement would result in no significant changes as far as customers are concerned. The company would still offer the Woolworth and Woolco revolving and time payment credit plans to qualified customers with GECC owning the receivables. Where honored, bank credit cards such as BankAmericard and Master Charge would be continued and their use encouraged.

Woolworth said that estimated overall company costs under the proposed arrangement are not expected to differ materially from levels which would be incurred if the present system were to continue.

A condensed balance sheet of F.W. Woolworth for the fiscal years 1976 and 1975 is presented.

	January 31	
	1976	1975
Assets	(In thousands)	
Current assets:		
Cash	$ 39,100	$ 46,500
Time deposits	10,200	27,700
Trade receivables, less allowance of $4,500 and $10,700	18,200	229,700
Other receivables	74,200	53,500
Merchandise inventories	1,026,300	914,100
Operating supplies and prepaid expenses	21,900	22,600
	1,189,900	1,294,100
Investment in F.W. Woolworth and Co., Limited	180,100	187,400
Properties, net	692,400	661,900
Intangible assets	14,700	14,700
Deferred charges and other assets	15,700	15,000
	$2,092,800	$2,173,100
Liabilities		
Current liabilities:		
Short-term debt		
domestic	—	$ 92,000
foreign	$ 3,900	56,300
Long-term debt payable within one year	17,800	7,000
Accounts payable	262,100	235,200
Accrued compensation and other liabilities	162,700	141,500
Dividends payable	11,100	9,600
Income taxes	45,000	62,000
	502,600	603,600
Long-term debt	428,900	485,800
Other liabilities	24,900	24,100
Deferred income taxes	59,600	54,400
Shareholders' equity	1,076,800	1,005,200
	$2,092,800	$2,173,100

Required   a. Compute the following ratios and comment on your findings for both the year ended January 31, 1976, and the year ended January 31, 1975:
1. working capital
2. current ratio
3. acid test ratio
4. debt to total assets ratio
5. debt to equity ratio

b. Speculate on the major reason for the substantial short-term debt reduction between the two years in relation to the long-term debt reduction during the same period of time.

c. Can the agreement with General Electric Credit Corporation and the Bank of Montreal be expected to influence the operating cycle of F. W. Woolworth Co.? Discuss.

d. The press release states that the receivable action will improve the financial strength of the company. Assume that the financial strength of the company is already comfortably strong. Can you see any possible nonoperating problem with improving an already comfortably strong financial position?

e. Speculate on a possible operating problem related to the agreements with General Electric Credit Corporation and the Bank of Montreal.

f. Speculate on why the allowance for doubtful accounts was $4,500,000 on January 31, 1976 and $10,700,000 on January 31, 1975, although the receivables decreased at a much greater proportion.

g. Would the selling of the receivables represent a contingency under SFAS No. 5, "Accounting for Contingencies"? If it does represent a contingency, how would the contingency be handled in the financial statements?

Case 7-3   OPERATING LEASES DO COUNT

General Host Corporation included the following data in its 1983 annual report.

Consolidated Statement of Income for fiscal year ended December 31, 1983 (Partial)	
Income from continuing operations before income taxes	$31,973,000
Income taxes	14,204,000
Income from continuing operations	$17,769,000
Discontinued operations, after income taxes	180,000
Net income	$17,949,000

Note: The income statement also disclosed interest and debt expense of $19,071,000.

Consolidated Balance Sheet, December 31, 1983 (Partial)	
Liabilities and shareholders' equity	
Total current liabilities	$ 90,672,000
Total long-term debt	202,785,000
Deferred income taxes	14,063,000

Other liabilities and deferred credits	3,053,000
Shareholders' equity	147,014,000
Total liabilities and shareholders' equity	$457,587,000

Note 12: Leases

The Company's capital leases are principally for offices and retail stores, for periods ranging up to 24 years.

At December 31, 1983 future minimum lease obligations under capital leases, included in long-term debt (Note 10), are as follows:

		(in thousands)
Payable in	1984	$ 3,200
	1985	2,968
	1986	2,852
	1987	2,835
	1988	2,768
Payable after 1988		28,781
Total minimum lease obligations		43,404
Executory costs		(576)
Amount representing interest		(22,500)
Present value of net minimum lease obligations		$20,328

Aggregate future minimum rentals to be received under related subleases amount to $555,000.

The Company's operating leases are principally for retail store locations, for periods ranging up to 14 years, and vehicles, for either one or two years. At December 31, 1983 future minimum rental commitments under operating leases with lease terms longer than one year are as follows:

		(in thousands)
Payable in	1984	$12,151
	1985	11,126
	1986	9,956
	1987	8,743
	1988	7,582
Payable after 1988		33,538
Total commitments		83,096
Future sublease rental income		(3,726)
Net commitments		$79,370

Rent expense of continuing operations was $21,672,000 in 1983, $17,168,000 in 1982 and $12,652,000 in 1981. Rent expense includes additional rentals based on retail store sales (in excess of the minimums specified in leases) of $1,961,000 in 1983, $1,424,000 in 1982 and $1,143,000 in 1981, and is reduced by sub-lease rental income of $666,000 in 1983, $246,000 in 1982 and $152,000 in 1981.

Required
a. Compute the following ratios for 1983:
1. times interest earned
2. fixed charge coverage
3. debt ratio
4. debt/equity
b. Compute the debt ratio and the debt/equity ratio considering operating leases.
c. Give your opinion of the significance of considering operating leases in these ratios for General Host Corporation. Give your opinion of the debt position and of the significance of considering operating leases of General Host Corporation.

Case 7-4   CONSIDER THESE CONTINGENCIES

Halliburton Company reported net revenues of $5,522,178,000, $7,257,291,000, and $8,508,133,000 in 1983, 1982, and 1981 respectively. Total assets at the end of 1983 were $5,833,794,000.

Footnote 12 of its 1983 annual report follows:

Note 12: Contingency. In December 1981 Houston Lighting & Power ("HL&P") and all other owners of the South Texas Project, a two-unit nuclear generating power plant, instituted litigation against the Company and Brown & Root, alleging various breaches of, as well as tortious conduct regarding, a 1972 contract between HL&P and Brown & Root under which Brown & Root was, from 1972 to 1981, designing, engineering and constructing the Project. The estimated cost of the Project increased from $1.1 billion in 1973 to $4.4–$4.8 billion in 1981. Completion dates of the two units were estimated in 1973 to be 1980 and 1982 and in 1981 to be 1986 and 1988. Estimates made in 1982, and reaffirmed in 1983, attributed to Bechtel Energy Corp., current engineer and construction manager for the Project, were that the cost of the Project would be $5.5 billion and that the Project would be completed on essentially the same schedule as last estimated above.

The plaintiffs in the litigation, which are, in addition to HL&P, the cities of Austin and San Antonio and Central Power & Light Company, have requested as yet unspecified amounts of damages, including damages resulting from purchases of substitute power. Counsel for the plaintiffs have indicated they may in the future amend their pleadings in the litigation to include claims under the Texas Deceptive Trade Practices Act which, under certain factual circumstances, may increase recoverable damages to three times the amount of actual damages. Such counsel stated in August 1982 that they had not quantified the damages which will be claimed at the time of trial and that no specific amount thereof was being asserted at that time, but, in discussions among counsel for the various parties, counsel to the plaintiffs have characterized such alleged damages as enormous. The trial judge has set a tentative date of trial in March 1985.

Brown & Root believes that the delayed in-service dates and the substantial increases in total costs of the Project are attributable to factors for which it is not responsible. The Company was not a contracting party and expressly denies any responsibility for claims under the contract or otherwise.

Negotiations with the plaintiffs concerning a settlement of the lawsuit have been initiated. In mid-1983 the plaintiffs rejected an offer by the Company to acquire a 75% interest in a lignite power plant under construction in order to sell power to the plaintiffs on favorable terms for a period of ten years. Further settlement discussions are being conducted by the parties on a preliminary and tentative basis. It is anticipated that these will be lengthy and protracted, and, at this time, it is unclear whether they will lead to a final settlement of the lawsuit.

If the litigation is not settled, the Company and Brown & Root will continue to contest the litigation vigorously. If the plaintiffs were to prevail in the litigation with respect to their theories of liability and damages, the Company believes that the losses by its consolidated group would be material to its consolidated financial statements; however, because of the complexity of the factual and legal issues involved in the litigation, the protracted nature of the discovery procedures and the defenses believed to be available, the Company cannot predict the extent of any such losses or the impact thereof on its consolidated financial statements.

Required   Discuss how to incorporate the contingency footnote into an analysis of Halliburton Company.

Case 7-5   EXPENSING INTEREST NOW AND LATER

The 1984 income statement of the Phelps Dodge Corporation is as follows.

PHELPS DODGE CORPORATION
Statement of Consolidated Operations
For Year Ended December 31

(in thousands of dollars)	1984	1983	1982
Sales and other operating revenues	$ 910,067	952,115	923,366
Operating costs and expenses			
Cost of products sold	899,596	880,179	883,420
Depreciation, depletion and amortization	59,836	62,257	53,224
Selling and general administrative expense	35,863	49,823	54,321
Exploration and research expense	14,173	16,438	19,693
	1,009,468	1,008,697	1,010,658
Operating loss from continuing operations	(99,401)	(56,582)	(87,292)
Equity earnings (losses)	4,971	2,803	(9,875)
Losses from continuing operations	(94,430)	(53,779)	(97,167)
Interest expense	(52,405)	(51,914)	(59,627)
Less capitalized interest	6,712	6,179	7,662
Interest and miscellaneous income	23,759	6,692	50,756
Provision for loss on restructure	(110,000)	—	—

Statement of Consolidated Operations   (continued)

(in thousands of dollars)	1984	1983	1982
Loss from continuing operations before			
taxes	(226,364)	(92,822)	(98,376)
Provision for taxes	19,000	38,984	29,197
Loss from continuing operations	(207,364)	(53,838)	(69,179)
Discontinued operations			
Income (loss) from operations of			
energy segment	24,518	(9,659)	(5,117)
Provision for loss on disposition of			
energy segment	(85,000)	—	—
Net loss	$ (267,846)	(63,497)	(74,296)

Required

a. What is the amount of gross interest expense for 1984?
b. What is the net interest expense reported in 1984?
c. What was the amount of interest added to the cost of property, plant, and equipment during 1984?
d. When is capitalized interest recognized as an expense?
e. What was the effect on income of capitalizing interest?

Case 7-6   POSTRETIREMENT BENEFITS REVISITED

Lukens had net sales of $405,297,000, $422,480,000, and $416,384,000 in 1986, 1985, and 1984, respectively. Total assets were $307,304,000 at December 27, 1986. The pension footnote and retiree benefits footnote from the 1986 financial statements follow.

Lukens has several non-contributory defined benefit plans that provide pension and certain survivor benefits for substantially all of our employees. These plans primarily provide benefits based on years of service and employee's compensation near retirement. Plans are funded in accordance with applicable federal law and regulations.

During the first quarter of 1986, Lukens elected to adopt, effective the beginning of 1986, Statement of Financial Accounting Standards No. 87, "Employers' Accounting for Pensions." Pension expense and related disclosures for 1985 and 1984 were not restated.

As a result of adopting the new standard, pension expense in 1986 was reduced approximately $2.9 million compared to pension expense calculated under the previous method. Net earnings were improved by approximately $1.6 million, or $.31 per share. The reduction was primarily attributable to features which resulted in greater recognition of investment gains on plan assets.

The components of 1986 pension expense included:

(dollars in thousands)	
Service cost—benefits earned during the period	$ 3,836
Interest cost on projected benefit obligation	17,637
Actual return on assets	(27,963)
Net amortization and deferral	11,866
Net pension expense	$ 5,376

The following table presents the funded status and amounts recognized in the Consolidated Balance Sheet as of December 27, 1986:

	Pension plans where:	
Dollars in thousands	Assets Exceed Accumulated Benefits	Accumulated Benefits Exceed Assets
Actuarial present value of:		
Vested benefit obligation	$ (8,110)	$ (180,867)
Accumulated benefit obligation	$ (9,130)	$ (192,604)
Projected benefit obligation	$ (9,450)	$ (217,308)
Plan assets at fair value[1]	13,952	177,833
Projected benefit obligation (in excess of) or less than plan assets	4,502	(39,475)
Unrecognized net (gain) loss	(195)	20,035
Unrecognized net (asset) obligation at January 1, 1986	(3,782)	1,199
Net pension asset (liability) recognized in the consolidated balance sheet[2]	$ 525	$ (18,241)

[1]Plan assets primarily consist of listed stocks and bonds, including Lukens' common stock of $8.1 million which was contributed in 1986.

[2]The net pension asset consists of prepaid pension expense of $.7 million included in Other Assets, less accrued pension expenses of $.2 million that is included in Accrued Employment Costs. The net pension liability consists of $8.0 million included in Accrued Employment Costs and $10.2 million included in Other Liabilities.

Assumptions included a 9.5 percent rate of return on plan assets, an 8.1 percent discount rate to measure the projected benefit obligation and a long-term increase in compensation levels of primarily 5 to 6 percent.

Pension expense of $8.5 million in 1985 and $9.0 million in 1984 has not been restated. The actuarial present value of accumulated plan benefits was $201.8 million ($188.9 million vested) as of December 31, 1985, and $187.6 million ($176.4 million vested) as of December 31, 1984. The assumed rate of return used to discount these benefits ranged from 9 to 11.5 percent in 1985 and

10 to 12.1 percent in 1984. The net effect of the changes in assumed rates of future earnings increased the actuarial present value of accumulated plan benefits by approximately $12.9 million in 1985.

Required

a. Determine the total pension cost for 1986, 1985, and 1984. How significant are these costs in relation to net sales?

b. Give a major reason why pension cost declined in 1986 in relation to 1985.

c. The actuarial present value of accumulated plan benefits is influenced by the discount rate used. The discount rate was reduced in 1985 in comparison with 1984. How did this influence the actuarial present value of accumulated benefits? Why?

d. Compare the accumulated benefit obligation with the plan assets at fair value.

e. What proportion of accumulated benefits was vested as of December 27, 1986?

f. What discount rate was used to measure the projected benefit obligation? What was the assumed rate of increase in compensation levels? Do these rates appear to be reasonable?

g. Are there significant unrecognized gains or losses?

h. What is the balance sheet account or accounts recognized at December 27, 1986?

i. Would the balance sheet accounts be significantly influenced if the projected benefit obligation were used in the computation to compute the balance sheet accounts?

j. Give your opinion as to the significance of the pensions to Lukens.

k. Describe postretirement benefits other than pensions. Do these benefits appear to be significant in relation to net sales? Determine the dollar amount of the liability for postretirement benefits other than pensions.

Case 7-7   INSIGHT ON POSTRETIREMENT BENEFITS

Engelhard Corporation had net sales of $2,289,531,000, $2,263,697,000, and $2,510,974,000 in 1986, 1985, and 1984, respectively. Total assets were $1,043,296,000 at December 31, 1986. Footnote 6 from the 1986 annual report follows:

Retirement Plans

The Company and its subsidiaries have pension plans covering substantially all employees. Plans covering most salaried employees provide benefits based on years of service and the employee's final average compensation. Plans covering most hourly employees and union members generally provide benefits of stated amounts for each year of service. The Company generally makes contributions to the plans equal to the amounts accrued for pension expense to the extent such contributions are currently deducted for tax purposes.

Effective April 1, 1986 the Company adopted the provisions of Statement of Financial Accounting Standards No. 87, for all U.S. pension plans. Under the previous standards, 1986 pension expense for these plans would have been $1.5 million. The net pension credit for 1986 for plans covering U.S. employees included the following components:

(in thousands)

Service cost—benefits earned during the period	$ 4,085
Interest cost on projected benefit obligation	9,934
Actual return on assets	(22,282)

Net amortization and deferral	2,567
Net pension credit	$ (5,696)

The following table sets forth the Plan's funded status and amounts recognized in the Company's statement of financial position at December 31, 1986:

(in thousands)

Actuarial present value of benefit obligations	
Vested benefit obligation	$ 91,581
Accumulated benefit obligation	$ 99,450
Projected benefit obligation	$118,797
Plan assets at fair value, primarily listed stocks and U.S. bonds	167,540
Projected benefit obligation less than plan assets	48,743
Unrecognized net loss	71
Unrecognized net assets	(45,104)
Prepaid pension credit recognized on balance sheet	$ 3,710

The weighted-average discount rate and rate of increase in future compensation levels used in determining the actuarial present value of the projected benefit obligation are 8.25 percent and 6.5 percent, respectively. The expected long-term rate of return on assets is 10.5 percent. The weighted-average discount rate above, does not reflect certain plan benefits which were funded with a dedicated bond portfolio. The corresponding dedicated liability is set equal to the market value of assets in the dedicated bond portfolio.

International pension (credit) expense amounted to $(4.6) million in 1986. $2.5 million in 1985 and $2.6 million in 1984. Foreign plans generally are insured or otherwise fully funded.

The Company and its subsidiaries also provide health care and life insurance benefits to retired employees who reach retirement age while employed by the Company. Substantially all salaried employees and certain hourly paid employees under collective bargaining agreements are eligible for these benefits, which are funded through the Company's general health care and life insurance programs. Annual premiums for these programs are charged to income. The approximate amount of such premiums attributable to retirees in 1986, 1985 and 1984 was $2.4 million, $2.1 million and $1.6 million, respectively.

Required

a. Determine the total pension cost (credit) for 1986.

b. Compare the accumulated benefit obligation with the plan assets at fair value at December 31, 1986.

c. Compare the projected benefit obligation with the plan assets at fair value at December 31, 1986.

d. What percentage of accumulated benefit obligation and projected benefit obligation are vested?

e. What interest rate was used to compute the accumulated benefit obligation? Does the rate appear to be reasonable?

f. What was the rate of compensation increase used in computing the projected benefit obligation? Does the rate appear to be reasonable?

g. Are there significant unrecognized gains or losses?

h. Is the unrecognized transition amount an asset or liability? What impact will this have on future pension cost?

i. Note the balance sheet amount that relates to pensions at December 31, 1986.
j. Give your opinion as to the significance of the pensions to Engelhard Corporation.
k. Describe postretirement benefits other than pensions. Do these benefits appear to be significant in relation to net sales? Determine the dollar amount of the liability for postretirement benefits other than pensions.

CHAPTER 8

ANALYSIS OF PROFITABILITY

CHAPTER TOPICS

Profitability Measures
Net Profit Margin
Total Asset Turnover
Return on Assets
DuPont Return on Assets
Operating Income Margin
Operating Asset Turnover
Return on Operating Assets
Sales to Fixed Assets
Return on Investment (ROI)

Return on Total Equity
Return on Common Equity
Gross Profit Margin

Trends in Profitability

Segment Reporting

Gains and Losses That Bypass the Income Statement

Interim Reports

Profitability is the ability of the firm to generate earnings. Analysis of profit is of vital concern to stockholders, since they derive revenue, in the form of dividends, when paid from profit. Further, increased profits can cause a rise in market price, leading to capital gains. Profits are also important to creditors, because profits are one source of funds for debt coverage. Management is vitally interested in profit, too; it is often used as a performance measure.

In analyzing profit, absolute figures are less meaningful than earnings measured in terms relative to a number of bases—the productive assets, the owners' and creditors' capital employed, and the sales from which earnings are the residual.

PROFITABILITY MEASURES

The income statement contains several figures that might be used in analysis. In general, the primary financial analysis of profit ratios should include only income that is expected to occur in subsequent periods. This implies that the following items are excluded:

1. Unusual or infrequent items
2. Discontinued operations
3. Extraordinary items
4. Cumulative effect of change in accounting principle

Trend analysis should generally consider only income that is expected to occur in subsequent periods. An illustration will help justify this reasoning. XYZ Corporation had net income in year one of $100,000 and in year two of $150,000. In year two, however, there was an extraordinary gain of $60,000. In reality, XYZ suffered a drop in profit, as measured in income that is expected to occur in subsequent periods.

Exhibit 3-3 in Chapter 3 illustrates an income statement with nonrecurring items—unusual or infrequent items, discontinued operations, extraordinary item, and cumulative effect of change in accounting principle. These items are normally excluded for the primary analysis of profitability. Review this section on analysis in Chapter 3 before continuing with the discussion of profitability.

The account titles, equity in earnings of nonconsolidated subsidiaries and minority share of earnings, are also important to the analysis of profitability. These titles were discussed in Chapter 3 and should be reviewed; Exhibits 3-5 and 3-9 illustrate these concepts, respectively.

Net Profit Margin

A commonly used profit measure is return on sales, often termed *net profit margin*. If a company reports that it earned 6% last year, this statistic usually means that its profit as a percentage of sales was 6%. Net profit margin is calculated as follows:

$$\text{Net Profit Margin} = \frac{\text{Net Income before Minority Share of Earnings and Nonrecurring Items}}{\text{Net Sales}}$$

This ratio gives a measure of net income dollars generated by each dollar of sales. While it is desirable for this ratio to be high, competitive forces within an industry, economic conditions, use of debt financing, and operating characteristics such as incurring high fixed costs cause the net profit margin to vary between and within industries.

Using the 1989 and 1988 figures for Cooper, the net profit margin is computed in Exhibit 8-1. This analysis shows that the net profit margin improved substantially.

EXHIBIT 8 - 1

COOPER TIRE & RUBBER COMPANY
Net Profit Margin
For the Years Ended December 31, 1989 and 1988

	1989	1988
Net income [A]	$ 58,243,880	$ 41,062,286
Net sales [B]	866,805,462	748,032,206
Net profit margin [A ÷ B]	6.72%	5.49%

Several refinements to the net profit margin ratio can make it more accurate than the ratio computation in this book. Numerator refinements include removal from net income of equity earnings from investments carried on the equity method and "other income" and "other expense" items. These items do not relate to net sales (denominator). Therefore, they can cause a distortion in the net profit margin.

In this book, the net profit margin ratio is not adjusted for these items, because this adjustment often requires an advanced understanding of financial statements that is beyond the level intended here. Also, this chapter covers ratios for operating income margin, operating asset turnover, and return on operating assets. These operating ratios provide a look at the firm on an operating basis.

If you elect to refine a net profit margin computation by removing equity income from net income, then remove equity income using the gross amount, since no tax or an insignificant amount is paid on this income. If "other income" and "other expense" items are removed from net income, do this by removing these items net of the firm's tax rate. Both of these tax-effect suggestions are reasonable approximations of tax effect.

If you do not elect to refine a net profit margin computation by removing equity income, at least observe whether the company has equity income. Equity income distorts the net profit margin on the high side; substantial equity income results in a substantial distortion.

If you do not elect to refine a net profit margin computation for "other income" and "other expense" items, at least observe whether the company has a net "other income" or a net "other expense." A net "other income" distorts the net profit margin on the high side, while a net "other expense" distorts the profit margin on the low side.

The Cooper statement can be used to illustrate the removal of other income. In Exhibit 8-2, the net profit margin is computed with the other income removed for 1989 and 1988. The adjusted computation shows the net profit margin to be 6.52% in 1989 and 5.25% in 1988, compared to the unadjusted net profit margin of 6.72% in 1989 and 5.49% in 1988 (Exhibit 8-1). The adjusted computation results in the 1989 net profit margin being reduced by .20% and the 1988 net profit margin being reduced by .24%. Both of these reductions are substantial enough to observe.

When working the problems in this book, do not remove equity income or "other income" and "other expense" when computing the net profit margin unless the problem asks for this refinement to be made.

Total Asset Turnover

Total asset turnover measures the activity of the assets and the ability of the firm to generate sales through the use of the assets. The formula for total asset turnover is as follows:

$$\text{Total Asset Turnover} = \frac{\text{Net Sales}}{\text{Average Total Assets}}$$

EXHIBIT 8-2

COOPER TIRE & RUBBER COMPANY
Net Profit Margin (Revised Computation)
For the Years Ended December 31, 1989 and 1988

	1989	1988
Net income	$ 58,243,880	$ 41,062,286
Tax rate:		
Provision for income taxes [A]	34,380,000	23,850,000
Income before income taxes [B]	92,623,880	64,912,286
Tax rate [A ÷ B]	37.12%	36.74%
Other income	2,809,069	2,832,616
Other income × (1 − tax rate)	1,766,343	1,791,913
Net income less net of tax on other		
income [C]	56,477,537	39,270,373
Net sales [D]	866,805,462	748,032,206
Adjusted net profit margin [C ÷ D]	6.52%	5.25%

Total asset turnover is computed for Cooper in Exhibit 8-3 for 1989 and 1988. The total asset turnover increased from 1.75 times to 1.80 times.

For the total asset turnover computation, there are refinements that relate to assets (denominator) but that are not related to net sales (numerator). An example would be investments. This refinement is not made in this book, for the same reasons that the net profit margin ratio was not refined further.

If the refinements are not made, observe the investment account and other

EXHIBIT 8-3

COOPER TIRE & RUBBER COMPANY
Total Asset Turnover
For the Years Ended December 31, 1989 and 1988

	1989	1988
Net sales [A]	$866,805,462	$748,032,206
Average total assets [B]	$442,582,462	$413,306,211
	519,892,610	442,582,462
	962,475,072	855,888,673
	÷ 2	÷ 2
	$481,237,536	$427,944,336
Total asset turnover [A ÷ B]	1.80 times	1.75 times

assets that do not relate to net sales. The presence of these accounts distorts the total asset turnover on the low side (actual turnover is better than the computation indicates).

Return on Assets

Return on assets measures the firm's ability to utilize its assets to create profits. This ratio compares profits with the assets that generate the profits. Return on assets is calculated as follows:

$$\text{Return on Assets} = \frac{\text{Net Income before Minority Share of Earnings and Nonrecurring Items}}{\text{Average Total Assets}}$$

The 1989 and 1988 return on assets is computed in Exhibit 8-4 for Cooper. The return on total assets for Cooper increased significantly in 1989.

Theoretically, the best average would be based on month-end figures, which are not available to the outsider user. Computing an average based on beginning and ending figures is at best a rough approximation that does not consider the timing of interim changes in assets; such changes might be related to seasonal factors.

However, even a simple average based on beginning and ending amounts requires two figures; this implies that ratios for two years require three years of balance sheet data. Since an annual report contains only two balance sheets, obtaining the data for averages may be a problem. If so, ending balance sheet figures may be used consistently for ratio analysis. Similar comments could be made about other ratios in this chapter that utilize balance sheet figures.

The net profit margin, the total asset turnover, and return on assets are usually reviewed together, because of the direct influence that the net profit margin and the total asset turnover have on return on assets. These ratios are reviewed together in this text. When these ratios are reviewed together, it is usually called the *DuPont return on assets*, which is reviewed next.

E X H I B I T   8 - 4

COOPER TIRE & RUBBER COMPANY
Return on Assets
For the Years Ended December 31, 1989 and 1988

	1989	1988
Net income [A]	$ 58,243,880	$ 41,062,286
Average total assets [B]	481,237,536	427,944,336
Return on assets [A ÷ B]	12.10%	9.60%

DuPont Return on Assets

The rate of return on assets can be broken down into two component ratios, the net profit margin and total asset turnover. This decomposition of the rate of return ratio allows for improved analysis of changes in the percentage. This method of separating the rate of return ratio into its component parts was developed by E. I. DuPont de Nemours and Company. The DuPont return on assets formula is as follows:

$$\text{Return on Assets} = \text{Net Profit Margin} \times \text{Total Asset Turnover}$$

$$\frac{\substack{\text{Net Income before} \\ \text{Minority Share of} \\ \text{Earnings and} \\ \text{Nonrecurring Items}}}{\text{Average Total Assets}} = \frac{\substack{\text{Net Income before} \\ \text{Minority Share of} \\ \text{Earnings and} \\ \text{Nonrecurring Items}}}{\text{Net Sales}} \times \frac{\text{Net Sales}}{\text{Average Total Assets}}$$

The DuPont return on assets is computed in Exhibit 8-5 for Cooper for 1989 and 1988. Separation of the ratio into the two elements allows for discussion of the causes for the increase in the percentage of return on assets. Exhibit 8-5 indicates that Cooper's return on assets increased mostly because of the substantial increase in net profit margin.

Interpretation through DuPont Analysis

The following examples help to illustrate the use of this analysis.

Example 1

Return on Assets	=	Net Profit Margin	×	Total Asset Turnover
Year one 10%	=	5%	×	2.0
Year two 10%	=	4%	×	2.5

The first example shows how more efficient use of assets can offset rising costs such as labor or materials.

EXHIBIT   8-5

COOPER TIRE & RUBBER COMPANY
DuPont Return on Assets
For the Years Ended December 31, 1989 and 1988

Return on Assets		=	Net Profit Margin	×	Total Asset Turnover
1989	12.10%	=	6.72%	×	1.80 times
1988	9.60%	=	5.49%	×	1.75 times

Example 2

Return on Assets	=	Net Profit Margin	×	Total Asset Turnover
Firm A				
Year one 10%	=	4%	×	2.5
Year two 8%	=	4%	×	2.0
Firm B				
Year one 10%	=	4%	×	2.5
Year two 8%	=	3.2%	×	2.5

Example 2 shows how a trend in return on assets can be better explained through the breakdown into two ratios. The two firms have identical profit trends. Further analysis shows that Firm A is suffering from a slowdown in asset turnover; it is not generating sales for the assets invested. For Firm B, however, the problem is very different. Here expenses are eating up sales revenue, while asset turnover remains constant.

Variation in Computation of DuPont Ratios
Considering Only Operating Accounts

It is often argued that nonoperating assets should not be considered in the return on asset calculation. Similarly, income from operations is the profit generated by manufacturing, retailing, or service functions. Operating income is net sales less cost of sales and operating expenses. It is listed before other income and other expenses. Operating assets exclude investments, intangibles, and the other assets category from total assets.

The operating ratios may give significantly different results from net earnings ratios if a firm has large amounts of nonoperating assets. For example, if a firm has heavy investments in unconsolidated subsidiaries, and if these subsidiaries pay large dividends, then other income may be a large portion of net earnings. The profit picture may not be as good if these earnings from other sources are eliminated by use of the analysis of operating ratios. Since earnings from investments are not derived from the primary business, however, the lower profit figures that represent normal earnings are more meaningful.

The DuPont analysis, considering only operating accounts, requires a computation of operating income and operating assets. The computations of operating income and operating assets for Cooper are shown in Exhibit 8-6. This includes operating income for 1989 and 1988 and operating assets for 1989, 1988, and 1987.

Operating Income Margin

In the formula for operating income margin, only operating income is included in the numerator. The formula is as follows:

$$\text{Operating Income Margin} = \frac{\text{Operating Income}}{\text{Net Sales}}$$

EXHIBIT 8-6

COOPER TIRE & RUBBER COMPANY
Operating Income and Operating Assets
For the Years Ended December 31, 1989 and 1988

	1989	1988
Operating income		
Net sales	$866,805,462	$748,032,206
Less: Cost of products sold	727,323,386	641,613,558
Selling, general, and administrative expenses	45,293,867	39,843,514
Total operating expenses	$772,617,253	$681,457,072
Operating income	$ 94,188,209	$ 66,575,134

	1989	1988	1987
Operating assets			
Total assets	$519,892,610	$442,582,462	$413,306,211
Less: Investments and other assets	(8,232,809)	(432,883)	(340,546)
Operating assets	$511,659,801	$442,149,579	$412,965,665

Exhibit 8-7 indicates the operating income margin for Cooper in 1989 and 1988; it shows a significant increase in the operating income margin percentage.

Operating Asset Turnover

This ratio measures the ability of operating assets to generate sales dollars. The formula is as follows:

$$\text{Operating Asset Turnover} = \frac{\text{Net Sales}}{\text{Average Operating Assets}}$$

Operating asset turnover is computed in Exhibit 8-8 for Cooper in 1989 and 1988; it indicates an increase from 1.75 times to 1.82 times. These figures are similar to those computed for the total asset turnover.

Return on Operating Assets

Adjusting for nonoperating items results in the following formula for return on operating assets:

EXHIBIT 8-7

COOPER TIRE & RUBBER COMPANY
Operating Income Margin
For the Years Ended December 31, 1989 and 1988

	1989	1988
Operating income [A]	$ 94,188,209	$ 66,575,134
Net sales [B]	866,805,462	748,032,206
Operating income margin [A ÷ B]	10.87%	8.90%

EXHIBIT 8-8

COOPER TIRE & RUBBER COMPANY
Operating Asset Turnover
For the Years Ended December 31, 1989 and 1988

	1989	1988
Net sales [A]	$866,805,462	$748,032,206
Average operating assets	$442,149,579	$412,965,665
	511,659,801	442,149,579
	953,809,380	855,115,244
	÷ 2	÷ 2
[B]	$476,904,690	$427,557,622
Operating asset turnover [A ÷ B]	1.82 times	1.75 times

$$\text{Return on Operating Assets} = \frac{\text{Operating Income}}{\text{Average Operating Assets}}$$

The return on operating assets for Cooper is computed in Exhibit 8-9 for 1989 and 1988. This ratio indicates an increase in the return on operating assets from 15.57% in 1988 to 19.75% in 1989.

The return on operating assets can be viewed in terms of the DuPont analysis that follows:

$$\begin{array}{c}\text{DuPont Return} \\ \text{on Operating Assets}\end{array} = \begin{array}{l}\text{Operating Income Margin} \\ \times \ \text{Operating Asset Turnover}\end{array}$$

Exhibit 8-10 indicates the DuPont return on operating assets for Cooper for 1989 and 1988. This figure supports the conclusion that the increase in return on operating assets was mostly caused by an increase in operating income margin.

EXHIBIT 8-9

COOPER TIRE & RUBBER COMPANY
Return on Operating Assets
For the Years Ended December 31, 1989 and 1988

	1989	1988
Operating income [A]	$ 94,188,209	$ 66,575,134
Average operating assets [B]	476,904,690	427,557,622
Return on operating assets [A ÷ B]	19.75%	15.57%

EXHIBIT 8-10

COOPER TIRE & RUBBER COMPANY
DuPont Analysis with Operating Accounts
For the Years Ended December 31, 1989 and 1988

Return on Operating Assets*	=	Operating Income Margin	×	Operating Asset Turnover
1989: 19.75%	=	10.87	×	1.82 times
1988: 15.57%	=	8.90	×	1.75 times

*There are some minor differences due to rounding.

Sales to Fixed Assets

This ratio measures the firm's ability to make productive use of its property, plant, and equipment by generating sales dollars. This ratio may not be meaningful if the fixed assets are old or if the industry is labor-intensive; in these cases, the ratio is substantially higher because of the low fixed asset base. The sales to fixed assets ratio is as follows:

$$\text{Sales to Fixed Assets} = \frac{\text{Net Sales}}{\text{Average Net Fixed Assets}}$$

In Exhibit 8-11, the sales to fixed assets ratio is computed for Cooper for 1989 and 1988; it decreased from 3.99 in 1988 to 3.65 in 1989. Analysts interested in Cooper should monitor this ratio closely in the future. It could be that the substantial increase in net fixed assets has come so rapidly that sales have not been able to keep up at a comparable pace in the short run. This does not automatically indicate a long-term problem.

EXHIBIT 8-11

COOPER TIRE & RUBBER COMPANY
Sales to Fixed Assets
For the Years Ended December 31, 1989 and 1988

	1989	1988
Net sales [A]	$866,805,462	$748,032,206
Net fixed assets:		
Beginning of year	$212,922,909	$162,447,381
End of year	262,444,739	212,922,909
Total	475,367,648	375,370,290
Average [B]	$237,683,824	$187,685,145
Sales to fixed assets [A ÷ B]	3.65 times	3.99 times

Return on Investment (ROI)

Return on investment is a broad term applied to ratios measuring the relationship between the income earned and the capital invested. These types of measures are widely used to evaluate enterprise performance. Since return on investment is return on capital, this ratio measures the ability of the firm to reward those who provide long-term funds and to attract providers of future funds.

$$\text{Return on Investment} = \frac{\substack{\text{Net Income before Minority Share of} \\ \text{Earnings and Nonrecurring Items} + \\ \text{(Interest Expense)} \times (1 - \text{Tax Rate})}}{\text{Average (Long-Term Liabilities + Equity)}}$$

This ratio evaluates the earnings performance of the firm without regard to the way the investment is financed, since the income figure is preinterest. The ratio measures the earnings on investment and indicates how well the firm utilizes its asset base. Return on investment is computed in Exhibit 8-12 for Cooper for 1989 and 1988. From 1988 to 1989, this ratio increased substantially, from 13.04% to 15.69%.

Return on Total Equity

Return on total equity measures the return to both common and preferred shareholders. It is commonly calculated as

$$\text{Return on Total Equity} = \frac{\substack{\text{Net Income before Nonrecurring Items} - \\ \text{Dividends on Redeemable Preferred Stock}}}{\text{Average Total Equity}}$$

EXHIBIT 8-12

COOPER TIRE & RUBBER COMPANY
Return on Investment
For the Years Ended December 31, 1989 and 1988

	1989	1988
Net income	$ 58,243,880	$ 41,062,286
Interest expense	4,373,398	4,495,464
Income before tax	92,623,880	64,912,286
Income tax	34,380,000	23,850,000
$\dfrac{\text{Income Tax}}{\text{Income before Taxes}}$ = Tax Rate	37.12%	36.74%
1 − tax rate	62.88%	63.26%
(Interest expense) (1 − tax rate)	2,749,992	2,843,830
Net income plus (interest expense) (1 − tax rate) [A]	60,993,872	43,906,116
Long-term liabilities and stockholders' equity		
Beginning of year		
Long-term liabilities	98,700,850	95,504,686
Total stockholders' equity	257,756,169	221,566,454
End of year		
Long-term liabilities	110,899,358	98,700,850
Total stockholders' equity	310,063,660	257,756,169
Total	$777,420,037	$673,528,159
Average [B]	$388,710,018	$336,764,079
Return on investment [A ÷ B]	15.69%	13.04%

Preferred stock subject to mandatory redemption is termed *redeemable preferred stock*. The SEC requires that redeemable preferred stock be categorized separately, not combined with other equity securities. This is based on the fact that the shares must be redeemed in a manner similar to the repayment of debt. Most companies do not have redeemable preferred stock. For those firms that do, the redeemable preferred is excluded from total equity and considered part of debt. Similarly, the dividends must be deducted from income. They have not been deducted on the income statement, despite the similarity to debt and interest, because they are still dividends and payable only if declared.

The return on total equity for Cooper is computed in Exhibit 8-13 for 1989 and 1988. It has increased substantially, from 17.13% in 1988 to 20.51% in 1989.

Return on Common Equity

This ratio measures return to the common shareholder, the residual owner. It is calculated as

EXHIBIT 8-13

COOPER TIRE & RUBBER COMPANY
Return on Total Equity
For the Years Ended December 31, 1989 and 1988

	1989	1988
Net income [A]	$ 58,243,880	$ 41,062,286
Total equity		
Beginning of year	257,756,169	221,566,454
End of year	310,063,660	257,756,169
Total	$567,819,829	$479,322,623
Average [B]	$283,909,914	$239,661,311
Return on total equity [A ÷ B]	20.51%	17.13%

$$\text{Return on Common Equity} = \frac{\text{Net Income before Nonrecurring Items} - \text{Preferred Dividends}}{\text{Average Common Equity}}$$

The net income is found on the income statement. The preferred dividends are most commonly available on the statement of retained earnings. Common equity includes common capital stock and retained earnings less common treasury stock. This amount is equal to total equity minus the preferred capital and any minority interest included in the equity section.

The return on common equity is computed in Exhibit 8-14 for Cooper for 1989 and 1988. Cooper's return on common equity is the same as its return on total equity, because it did not have preferred stock.

The Relationship between Profitability Ratios

Technically, a ratio with a profit figure in the numerator and some type of "supplier of funds" figure in the denominator is a type of return on investment. Another frequently used measure is a variation of return on total assets. Its formula is as follows:

$$\text{Return on Total Assets Variation} = \frac{\text{Net Income + Interest Expense}}{\text{Average Total Assets}}$$

This includes return to all suppliers of funds, both long and short term, by both creditors and investors. This ratio differs from the return on assets ratio previously discussed because it includes the interest add-back. This ratio differs from return on investment in that it does not tax-adjust interest, includes short-term funds, and uses average investment. This ratio will not be discussed or utilized

EXHIBIT 8-14

COOPER TIRE & RUBBER COMPANY
Return on Common Equity
For the Years Ended December 31, 1989 and 1988

	1989	1988
Net income	$ 58,243,880	$ 41,062,286
Less preferred dividends	—	—
Adjusted income [A]	$ 58,243,880	$ 41,062,286
Total common equity		
Beginning of year	$257,756,169	$221,566,454
End of year	310,063,660	257,756,169
Total	$567,819,829	$479,322,623
Average common equity [B]	$283,909,914	$239,661,311
Return on common equity [A ÷ B]	20.51%	17.13%

further here, because it does not lend itself to DuPont analysis, as does the return on total assets ratio discussed earlier.

Rates of return have been calculated on a variety of bases. The interrelationship between these ratios is of importance in understanding the return to the suppliers of funds. These ratios of return are displayed in Exhibit 8-15.

Return on assets measures return to all providers of funds, since total assets equal total liabilities and equity. This ratio will usually be the lowest, since it includes all of the assets. Return on investment measures return to only long-term suppliers of funds, and it is usually higher than return on assets, because of the relatively low amount paid for short-term funds. This is especially true of accounts payable, which are not given a return.

EXHIBIT 8-15

COOPER TIRE & RUBBER COMPANY
Comparison of Profitability Measures
For the Years Ended December 31, 1989 and 1988

	1989	1988
Return on assets	12.10%	9.60%
Return on investment	15.69%	13.04%
Return on total equity	20.51%	17.13%
Return on common equity	20.51%	17.13%

The rate of return on equity ratios is usually higher than return on investment, because it measures return only to the shareholders. The return to shareholders is higher than the return on investment if a profitable use has been made of long-term sources of funds from creditors. In other words, more profits have been made on the long-term source of funds from creditors than were paid for these funds.

One might expect common shareholders to absorb the greatest degree of risk and therefore earn the highest return. This is usually true, causing return in common equity to be the highest. For this to be true, however, the return on funds obtained from preferred stockholders must be more than the funds paid to the preferred stockholders. Cooper did not have preferred stock, so return on total equity and return on common equity were the same.

Gross Profit Margin

Gross profit is the difference between net sales revenue and the cost of goods sold. Cost of goods sold is computed as beginning inventory plus purchases minus ending inventory. It represents the cost of the product sold during the period. Since cost of goods sold is such a large expense for merchandising and manufacturing firms, changes in this figure can have a substantial impact on the profit for the period. The best type of analysis is on a vertical common size basis where gross profit is compared to net sales. This ratio is termed *gross profit margin:*

$$\text{Gross Profit Margin} = \frac{\text{Gross Profits}}{\text{Net Sales}}$$

This ratio should then be analyzed by comparison with industry data or by trend analysis over time. Exhibit 8-16 is an example of trend analysis.

In this illustration, gross profit has declined substantially over the three-year period. This could be attributable to a number of factors, such as those listed on the next page.

EXHIBIT 8-16

SIEGRIST ENTERPRISES
Gross Profit Analysis

	1989	1988	1987
Net sales [B]	$5,000,000	$4,500,000	$4,000,000
Cost of goods sold	3,500,000	2,925,000	2,200,000
Gross profit [A]	$1,500,000	$1,575,000	$1,800,000
Gross profit margin [A ÷ B]	30%	35%	45%

1. The cost of buying inventory has increased more rapidly than have selling prices.
2. Selling prices have declined due to competition.
3. The mix of goods has changed to include more products with lower margin.
4. Theft is occurring. If sales are not recorded, the cost of goods sold figure in relation to the sales figure is very high. If inventory is being stolen, the ending inventory will also be low and cost of goods sold will be high.

Gross profit analysis is of value to a number of users. Managers budget gross profit levels into their predictions of profitability. Gross profit margins are also used in cost control. Estimations utilizing gross profit margins can determine inventory levels for interim statements in the merchandising industries. Gross profit is also used to help estimate inventory in insurance losses. In addition, gross profit measures are used by auditors and the Internal Revenue Service to judge the accuracy of accounting systems.

In order to perform gross profit analysis, the income statement must be in multiple-step format. If it is not, the gross profit must be computed. This is the case with Cooper. The gross profit analysis is presented in Exhibit 8-17, which shows that it has increased substantially.

TRENDS IN PROFITABILITY

Exhibit 8-18 shows profitability trends for manufacturing, mining, and trading for the period 1965–1989. Operating profit compared with sales declined substantially over this period. Net income also declined substantially in relation to sales. This decline in profitability is probably due to many factors, including an increase in competition domestically and internationally. The decline in profitability indicates an increase in the risk of doing business.

E X H I B I T   8 - 1 7

COOPER TIRE & RUBBER COMPANY
Gross Profit Analysis
For the Years Ended December 31, 1989 and 1988

	1989	1988
Net sales [B]	$866,805,462	$748,032,206
Less: Cost of goods sold	727,323,386	641,613,558
Gross profit [A]	$139,482,076	$106,418,648
Gross profit margin [A ÷ B]	16.09%	14.23%

EXHIBIT 8 - 1 8

Trends in Profitability
United States Manufacturing, Mining, and Trading
1965–1989

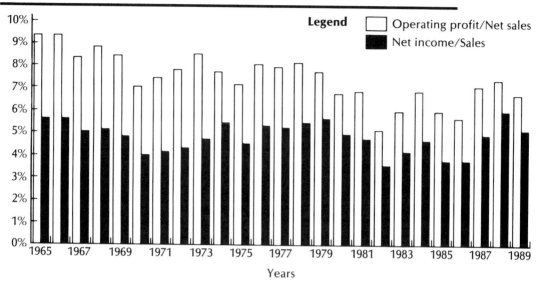

Source: *Quarterly Financial Reports for Manufacturing, Mining, & Trading,* Department of Commerce. Washington, D.C.: Government Printing Office.

SEGMENT REPORTING

Firms frequently operate in more than one line of business. When operations are diversified in this manner, the results of operations of the individual segments may vary. SFAS Statement No. 14, "Financial Reporting for Segments of a Business Enterprise," requires disclosure, on a segmented basis, about such factors as sales, operating income, identifiable assets, aggregate depreciation, depletion and amortization, and capital expenditures. This statement also requires data on foreign operations by geographic area, export sales, and major customers. If a company operates predominantly or exclusively in a single industry, that industry must be identified.

Analysis of segment data can be done both in terms of trends and ratios. Vertical and horizontal common size analyses can be used for trends. Examples of ratios would be relating profits to sales or identifiable assets.

Segment trends are of interest to management and investors. The maximum benefits from this type of analysis come when analyzing a nonintegrated company in terms of product lines, especially where the segments are of relatively similar size.

Cooper does not report segment data. This means that it does not operate in more than one line of business, or that lines of business beyond the major line are immaterial. The 1989 annual report of PepsiCo has been selected to illustrate segment reporting.

Exhibit 8-19 presents the segment reporting for PepsiCo for 1989, 1988, and 1987. Exhibit 8-19 consists of a management discussion of business segments and financial data in terms of industry segments and geographic areas. These data should be reviewed, and consideration should be given to using vertical and horizontal analyses and to computing ratios that appear to be meaningful.

Exhibit 8-20 presents some segment information in vertical common size analysis. In terms of net sales, the growth of PepsiCo has been in soft drinks. The largest decline has been in snack foods. Operating profits were up substantially for soft drinks and down substantially for restaurants. Identifiable assets were up materially for soft drinks and down materially for restaurants. Based on vertical common size analysis, the restaurant segment did well, considering the relative reduction in identifiable assets. The soft drinks segment appears to have done most poorly, considering the substantial increase in identifiable assets, the modest increase in net sales, and the moderate increase in operating profit.

A review of Exhibit 8-21 (segment reporting—ratio analysis) indicates that operating profit to net sales increased moderately for soft drinks, increased substantially for snack foods, and decreased slightly for restaurants. Operating profit to identifiable assets decreased substantially for soft drinks, decreased very materially for snack foods, and increased moderately for restaurants.

E X H I B I T   8 - 1 9

PEPSICO
Industry Segments

Business Segments

This information constitutes a Note to the Consolidated Financial Statements. (Tabular dollars in millions.)

PepsiCo operates on a worldwide basis within three distinct industry segments: soft drinks, snack foods and restaurants. Management's discussion and analysis of PepsiCo's industry segments is presented in the narratives beginning on pages 13, 21 and 29 under the caption "Management's Analysis."

The soft drinks segment primarily manufactures concentrates and markets Pepsi-Cola, Mountain Dew, Slice and their allied brands worldwide and 7UP internationally, and operates soft drink bottling businesses principally in the United States. The soft drinks segment data reflect a number of acquisitions of franchised domestic bottlers, the largest of which were the bottling businesses of General Cinema Corporation and Grand Metropolitan Incorporated acquired in 1989 and 1988, respectively.

The snack foods segment primarily manufactures and markets snack chips. The snack foods segment data reflect the 1989 acquisitions of Smiths Crisps Limited and Walkers Crisps Holdings Limited (Smiths and Walkers), which manufacture and market snack chips in the United Kingdom.

The restaurants segment data include the operations of Pizza Hut, Taco Bell and Kentucky Fried Chicken (KFC) and reflect the acquisitions of several franchised domestic and international restaurant operators, which were not significant in the aggregate. Restaurant net sales include net sales by company-operated restaurants, initial franchise fees, royalty and rental payments from restaurants operated by franchisees, gains on sales of restaurant businesses and net sales to franchisees by PepsiCo's restaurant distribution operation.

All acquisitions were accounted for under the purchase method, and accordingly the results of the acquired businesses are included from their respective dates of acquisition. (See Note to Consolidated Financial Statements on page 43.) The acquisition of Smiths and Walkers had a significant impact on PepsiCo's foreign operations, as reflected in the foreign data presented.

PepsiCo holds a number of equity interests of 50% or less that are reported under the equity method of accounting. Under generally accepted accounting principles, equity in the net income of these joint ventures is excluded from segment operating profits. The equity investments and related equity in net income are not material to the industry segment data. To improve comparability, 1988 and 1987 net sales and operating profits have been restated to report under the equity method of accounting certain previously consolidated KFC foreign joint ventures due to a reduction of PepsiCo's voting interest in early 1989. (See Note to Consolidated Financial Statements on page 43.)

In determining geographic area data, the results of operations of PepsiCo's soft drink concentrate manufacturing facilities in Puerto Rico and Ireland have been allocated based upon actual concentrate sales to the respective geographic areas. Certain centralized foreign administrative expenses in each of the three industry segments have been allocated based upon sales volumes or number of restaurants in the respective geographic areas.

Net corporate expenses primarily consist of interest expense as well as corporate items and interest income that are not allocated to the business segments. Unallocated interest income was $141 million, $100 million and $87 million in 1989, 1988 and 1987, respectively. Net corporate expenses also included equity in net income of joint ventures of $13.4 million, $15.8 million and $19.5 million in 1989, 1988 and 1987, respectively. Because of a 1988 restatement of the 1987 Consolidated Statement of Income, the 1987 equity in net income of joint ventures reflects 100% of the net income of certain previously consolidated domestic soft drink bottling operations contributed to joint ventures in early 1988. The Consolidated Balance Sheet was not restated.

Corporate identifiable assets consist principally of offshore short-term investments and investments in joint ventures. PepsiCo's investments in joint ventures totaled $676 million, $500 million and $178 million at year-end 1989, 1988 and 1987, respectively, and consist principally of foreign businesses operating in all three of PepsiCo's industry segments and a 20% equity interest in a large domestic franchised bottler acquired in 1988.

1989 and 1987 consisted of 52 weeks, while 1988 consisted of 53 weeks.

EXHIBIT 8-19   (continued)

	Net Sales			Operating Profits[a]			Identifiable Assets[b]		
	1989	1988	1987	1989	1988	1987	1989	1988	1987
Industry segments:									
Soft drinks: U.S.	$ 4,623.3	$ 3,667.0	$ 3,112.9	$ 586.9	$ 409.5	$ 363.1			
Foreign	1,153.4	971.2	862.7	103.2	53.4	46.5			
	5,776.7	4,638.2	3,975.6	690.1	462.9	409.6	$ 6,241.9	$ 4,074.4	$2,779.8
Snack foods: U.S.	3,211.3	2,933.3	2,782.8	668.3	587.3	520.0			
Foreign	1,003.7	581.0	419.2	152.6	49.0	27.6			
	4,215.0	3,514.3	3,202.0	820.9	636.3	547.6	3,366.4	1,641.2	1,632.5
Restaurants: U.S.	4,684.8	3,950.3	3,499.5	361.8	307.0	281.6			
Foreign	565.9	430.4	341.0	59.4	44.4	37.8			
	5,250.7	4,380.7	3,840.5	421.2	351.4	319.4	3,095.2	3,105.1	2,782.9
Total: U.S.	12,519.4	10,550.6	9,395.2	1,617.0	1,303.8	1,164.7			
Foreign	2,723.0	1,982.6	1,622.9	315.2	146.8	111.9			
Total	$15,242.4	$12,533.2	$11,018.1	$1,932.2	$1,450.6	$1,276.6	$12,703.5	$ 8,820.7	$7,195.2
Geographic areas:[a],[b],[c]									
United States	$12,519.4	$10,550.6	$ 9,395.2	$1,617.0	$1,303.8	$1,164.7	$ 9,633.2	$ 7,264.6	$5,699.4
Western Europe	739.0	390.8	308.0	55.5	13.0	6.7	1,754.8	187.7	169.1
Canada and Mexico	899.0	726.3	501.5	126.3	55.0	39.9	460.6	348.0	359.8
Other	1,085.0	865.5	813.4	133.4	78.8	65.3	854.9	1,020.4	966.9
							12,703.5	8,820.7	7,195.2
Corporate assets[c]							2,423.2	2,314.6	1,827.5
Total	$15,242.4	$12,533.2	$11,018.1	1,932.2	1,450.6	1,276.6	$15,126.7	$11,135.3	$9,022.7
Interest and other corporate expenses, net				(581.7)	(323.4)	(331.0)			
Income from continuing operations before income taxes				$1,350.5	$1,127.2	$ 945.6			

E X H I B I T   8 - 1 9   (continued)

	Capital Spending			Depreciation and Amortization Expense		
	1989	1988	1987	1989	1988	1987
Soft Drinks	$ 267.8	$ 198.4	$ 202.0	$306.3	$195.7	$166.5
Snack Foods	257.9	172.6	195.6	189.3	156.8	154.1
Restaurants	424.6	344.2	370.8	269.9	271.3	237.1
Corporate	9.2	14.9	6.6	6.5	5.5	5.3
	$ 959.5	$ 730.1	$ 775.0	$772.0	$629.3	$563.0

Supplementary Restaurants Data

	Net Sales			Operating Profits[a]		
	1989	1988	1987	1989	1988	1987
Pizza Hut	$2,453.5	$2,014.2	$1,753.2	$208.6	$153.3	$138.0
Taco Bell	1,465.9	1,157.3	1,004.4	112.6	81.6	91.4
KFC	1,331.3	1,209.2	1,082.9	100.0	116.5	90.0
	$5,250.7	$4,380.7	$3,840.5	$421.2	$351.4	$319.4

(a) Unusual items: Results for the years presented were affected by several unusual credits and charges, the impacts of which were a net credit of $4.4 million ($1.8 after-tax or $0.01 per share) in 1989, a net charge of $23.9 million ($16.3 after-tax or $0.06 per share) in 1988 and a net credit of $19.8 million ($13.7 after-tax or $0.05 per share) in 1987. The unusual items in each industry segment were as follows:

Soft Drinks: 1989 included a $32.5 million credit resulting from a decision to retain a bottling operation in Japan previously held for sale and a $12.3 million reorganization charge to decentralize international operations. 1988 included a $14.5 million reorganization charge to decentralize domestic operations and a $9.4 million loss resulting from the sale of a Spanish winery. 1987 included a $10.3 million gain resulting from the sale of a bottling operation in Puerto Rico.

Snack Foods: 1989 included a $6.6 million reorganization charge to decentralize domestic operations and a $4.3 million credit resulting from a decision to retain a domestic cookie production facility previously held for sale. 1987 included a $10.0 million gain resulting from the sale of another domestic cookie production facility.

Restaurants: 1989 included an $8.0 million reorganization charge to consolidate domestic field operations of KFC and a $5.5 million reorganization charge to consolidate domestic operations of Taco Bell. 1987 included an $8.0 million reorganization charge to consolidate KFC's domestic operations and a $7.5 million gain resulting from the sale of certain Pizza Hut restaurants in Australia.

(b) The identifiable assets were not restated for the previously consolidated KFC foreign joint ventures now reported under the equity method.

(c) At year-end 1989 PepsiCo held an investment of $78 million in a Canadian snack food joint venture and a $122 million investment in the KFC Japan joint venture, which are included in corporate assets.

EXHIBIT 8-20

PEPSICO
Segment Reporting—Common Size Analysis
For the Years 1989, 1988, and 1987

	1989	1988	1987
Industry segments			
Vertical common size analysis			
Net sales			
Soft drinks	37.90	37.01	36.08
Snack foods	27.65	28.04	29.06
Restaurants	34.45	34.95	34.86
Total	100.00%	100.00%	100.00%
Operating profits			
Soft drinks	35.72	31.91	32.08
Snack foods	42.48	43.87	42.90
Restaurants	21.80	24.22	25.02
Total	100.00%	100.00%	100.00%
Identifiable assets			
Soft drinks	49.14	46.19	38.63
Snack foods	26.50	18.61	22.69
Restaurants	24.36	35.20	38.68
	100.00%	100.00%	100.00%

EXHIBIT 8-21

PEPSICO
Segment Reporting—Ratio Analysis
For the Years Ended 1989, 1988, and 1987

	1989	1988	1987
Industry segments			
Operating profit to net sales			
Soft drinks	11.95%	9.98%	10.30%
Snack foods	19.48	18.11	17.10
Restaurants	8.02	8.02	8.32
Operating profit to identifiable assets			
Soft drinks	11.06%	11.36%	14.73%
Snack foods	24.39	38.77	33.54
Restaurants	13.61	11.32	11.48

GAINS AND LOSSES THAT BYPASS THE INCOME STATEMENT

There are a few gains and losses that are not reported on the income statement under current generally accepted accounting principles. These gains and losses result from prior period adjustments, unrealized losses from long-term equity investments (common or preferred stock), and foreign currency translation. The prior period adjustments are charged to retained earnings; the unrealized losses from equity investments are set up in a separate account within stockholders' equity; and the foreign currency translation gain or loss is also set up in a separate account within stockholders' equity. Unrealized gains from equity investments can be used to reduce a previously established unrealized loss account.

These gains and losses that bypass the income statement can potentially be very significant. Therefore, you should review the retained earnings account for prior period adjustments and look for separate accounts within stockholders' equity for unrealized losses from equity investments, as well as foreign currency translation gain or loss. When these items are found, consider them subjectively in your profitability analysis. You may want to change the income figure for the current year and prior years to accommodate these items. This would be done as a supplemental profitability analysis, in addition to your primary analysis.

Prior period adjustments result from certain changes in accounting principles, adjustments that result from the realization of income tax benefits of preacquisition operating loss carryforwards of purchased subsidiaries, a change in accounting entity, and corrections of errors in prior periods.

Exhibit 8-22 includes an example of a prior period adjustment for American Building Maintenance Industries, Inc. The adjustment relates to self-insured insurance claims incurred but not considered, resulting in an understatement of insurance expense and accrued insurance claims. Note that a prior period adjustment will never be recognized on an income statement.

Exhibit 8-23 includes an example of unrealized loss on noncurrent equity investments. This represented a potential loss of $6,941,000 at December 30, 1988 for Kinder Care. A loss could be recognized in a future income statement if the securities are sold or management declares the intent to sell these securities. If management declares the intent to sell the securities, these investments will be classified under current assets in the future.

Exhibit 8-24 includes a shareholders' equity account that has been used for adjustments resulting from *translation* of foreign currency for the financial statements of the Lubrizol Corporation. It indicates a negative balance of $10,076,000 at the end of 1988 and $16,569,000 at the end of 1989. Translation gains and losses are included in this shareholders' equity account; exchange gains and losses resulting from foreign currency *transactions* are included in the statement of income.

EXHIBIT 8-22

AMERICAN BUILDING MAINTENANCE INDUSTRIES, INC.
Prior Period Adjustment
1988 Annual Report

Consolidated Statements of Shareholders' Equity

Years Ended October 31, 1986, 1987 and 1988
(in thousands, except per share amounts)

	Common Stock		Additional Capital	Retained Earnings (Restated) (Note 2)
	Shares	Amount		
Balance October 31, 1985, as previously reported	3,659	$37	$13,670	$50,356
Prior period adjustment (Note 2)				(9,397)
Balance October 31, 1985, as restated	3,659	37	13,670	40,959
Net income as restated				2,763
Dividends ($.88 per common share)				(3,261)
Stock issued under employees' stock purchase plan and for acquisitions	83	—	1,714	
Balance October 31, 1986	3,742	37	15,384	40,461
Net income				4,922
Dividends ($.90 per common share)				(3,424)
Stock issued under employees' stock purchase plan and for acquisitions	99	1	2,055	
Balance October 31, 1987	3,841	38	17,439	41,959
Net income				7,100
Dividends ($.915 per common share)				(3,523)
Stock reacquired	(136)	(1)	(3,362)	
Stock issued under employees' stock purchase plan and for acquisitions	122	1	2,267	
Balance October 31, 1988	3,827	$38	$16,344	$45,536

Notes to Consolidated Financial Statements

2. Adjustment of Prior Years' Financial Statements   The Company is primarily self-insured for property damage and personal liability and workers' compensation coverages, up to certain limits. Based on an analysis of insurance claims, the Company has determined that in certain prior years the effect of claims incurred but not reported was not considered, resulting in an understatement of insurance expense and accrued insurance claims. As a result, the Company has restated net income for 1986 and retained earnings as of October 31, 1985, 1986 and 1987 to provide for increased accrued insurance claims.

The effect of the restatement is to increase the accrued insurance claims liability by $22,506,000, and decrease deferred income taxes by $10,701,000 at October 31, 1987, decrease net income for 1986 by $2,408,000 or $.65 per share, and decrease retained earnings at November 1, 1985 by $9,397,000, and at October 31, 1986 and October 31, 1987 by $11,805,000.

Source: American Institute of Certified Public Accountants, *Accounting Trends and Techniques*, 1989, pp. 331–332.

EXHIBIT 8-23

KINDER CARE LEARNING CENTERS, INC.
Stockholders' Equity—Unrealized Loss
1989 Annual Report

	December 29, 1989	December 30, 1988
Stockholders' equity:		
Common stock, par value $.01; authorized 100,000,000 shares; issued and outstanding 51,740,400 shares at December 29, 1989 and December 30, 1988	517,000	517,000
Additional paid-in capital	$117,769,000	$123,203,000
Unrealized loss on noncurrent marketable equity securities	—	(6,941,000)
Retained earnings (deficit)	(14,490,000)	8,794,000
	$103,796,000	$125,573,000

EXHIBIT 8-24

THE LUBRIZOL CORPORATION
Shareholders' Equity—Accumulated Translation Adjustment
1989 Annual Report

	December 31	
(in thousands of dollars)	1989	1988
Common shares without par value Outstanding 37,008,108 shares in 1989 and 38,009,911 shares in 1988	78,221	77,260
Retained earnings	$601,612	$597,124
Accumulated translation adjustment	(16,569)	(10,076)
Total shareholders' equity	$663,264	$664,308

INTERIM REPORTS

Interim reports are an additional source of information on profitability; these are reports that cover fiscal periods of less than one year. A number of regulations make these interim data available to the investing public. The SEC requires that limited financial data be provided on the form 10-Q. The SEC also requires that companies disclose certain quarterly information in notes to the annual report. The accounting standards that relate to interim reports are APB Opinion No. 28, SFAS No. 3, SFAS No. 16, SFAS No. 69, SFAS Interpretation No. 18, and SFAS Technical Bulletin 79-9.

According to APB Opinion No. 28, the same reporting principles used for annual reports should be employed for interim reports, with the intent that the interim reporting be an integral part of the annual report. APB Opinion No. 28 recognizes that timeliness of data offsets lack of detail, and it requires only minimum data in the interim financial reports. These data include:[1]

1. Income statement amounts:
   a. Sales or gross revenues
   b. Provision for income taxes
   c. Extraordinary items and tax effect
   d. Cumulative effect of an accounting change
   e. Net income
2. Earnings per share—primary and fully diluted
3. Seasonal information
4. Significant changes in income tax provision or estimate
5. Disposal of segments of business and unusual items material to the period
6. Contingent items
7. Changes in accounting principles or estimates
8. Significant changes in financial position

Interim reports contain more estimates in the financial data than annual reports; interim reports are also unaudited. For these reasons, they are less reliable than annual reports.

Income tax expense is an example of a figure that can require considerable judgment and estimation for the interim period. The objective with the interim income tax expense is to use an annual effective tax rate, which may require considerable estimation. Some reasons for this are foreign tax credits and the tax effect of losses in an interim period.

Interim statements must disclose the seasonal nature of the activities of the firm. It is also recommended that firms that are seasonal in nature supplement their interim report by including information for twelve-month periods ended at the interim date for the current and preceding years.

Interim statements can help the analyst determine trends and identify trouble areas before the year-end report is available. The information obtained (such as a lower profit margin) may indicate that trouble is brewing.

---

[1]APB Opinion No. 28, "Interim Financial Reporting" (American Institute of Certified Public Accountants, 1973), par. 30.

SUMMARY

Profitability is the ability of a firm to generate earnings. It is measured relative to a number of bases, such as assets, sales, and investment. The ratios related to profitability covered in this chapter are as follows:

$$\text{Net Profit Margin} = \frac{\text{Net Income before Minority Share of Earnings and Nonrecurring Items}}{\text{Net Sales}}$$

$$\text{Total Asset Turnover} = \frac{\text{Net Sales}}{\text{Average Total Assets}}$$

$$\text{Return on Assets} = \frac{\text{Net Income before Minority Share of Earnings and Nonrecurring Items}}{\text{Average Total Assets}}$$

$$\text{DuPont Return on Assets} = \text{Net Profit Margin} \times \text{Total Asset Turnover}$$

$$\text{Operating Income Margin} = \frac{\text{Operating Items}}{\text{Net Sales}}$$

$$\text{Operating Asset Turnover} = \frac{\text{Net Sales}}{\text{Average Operating Assets}}$$

$$\text{Return on Operating Assets} = \frac{\text{Operating Income}}{\text{Average Operating Assets}}$$

$$\text{DuPont Return on Operating Assets} = \text{Operating Income Margin} \times \text{Operating Asset Turnover}$$

$$\text{Sales to Fixed Assets} = \frac{\text{Net Sales}}{\text{Average Net Fixed Assets}}$$

$$\text{Return on Investment} = \frac{\text{Net Income before Minority Share of Earnings and Nonrecurring Items} + (\text{Interest Expense}) \times (1 - \text{Tax Rate})}{\text{Average (Long-Term Debt + Equity)}}$$

$$\text{Return on Total Equity} = \frac{\text{Net Income before Nonrecurring Items} - \text{Dividends on Redeemable Preferred}}{\text{Average Total Equity}}$$

$$\text{Return on Common Equity} = \frac{\text{Net Income before Nonrecurring Items} - \text{Preferred Dividends}}{\text{Average Common Equity}}$$

$$\text{Gross Profit Margin} = \frac{\text{Gross Profit}}{\text{Net Sales}}$$

QUESTIONS

Q 8-1   Profits might be compared to sales, assets, or owners' equity. Why might all three bases be used? Will trends in these ratios always move in the same direction?

Q 8-2   What is the advantage of segregating extraordinary items in the income statement?

Q 8-3   If profits as a percent of sales decline, what can be said about expenses?

Q 8-4   Would you expect the profit margin of a quality jewelry store to differ from that of a grocery store? Comment.

Q 8-5   The ratio return on assets has net income in the numerator and total assets in the denominator. Explain how each part of the ratio could cause return on assets to fall.

Q 8-6   What is DuPont analysis, and how does it aid in financial statement analysis?

Q 8-7   How does operating income differ from net income? How do operating assets differ from total assets? What is the advantage in removing nonoperating items from the DuPont analysis?

Q 8-8   Why are equity earnings usually greater than cash flow generated from the investment? How can these equity earnings distort profitability analysis?

Q 8-9   Explain how return on assets could decline, given an increase in net profit margin.

Q 8-10   How is return on investment different from return on total equity? How does return on total equity differ from return on common equity?

Q 8-11   What is meant by return on investment? What are some of the types of measures for return on investment? Why is the following ratio preferred? Why is the interest multiplied by $(1 - \text{tax rate})$?

$$\frac{\begin{array}{c}\text{Net Income before Minority Share of}\\\text{Earnings and Nonrecurring items } +\\\text{(Interest Expense)} \times (1 - \text{Tax Rate})\end{array}}{\text{Average (Long-Term Debt } + \text{ Equity)}}$$

Q 8-12   G. Herrich Company and Thomas, Inc., are department stores. For the current year, they reported a net income after tax of $400,000 and $600,000, respectively. Is Thomas, Inc., a more profitable company than G. Herrich Company? Discuss.

Q 8-13   Since interim reports are not audited, they are not meaningful. Comment.

Q 8-14   Speculate on why APB Opinion No. 28 does not mandate full financial statements in interim reports.

Q 8-15   a. Generally accepted accounting principles exclude some gains and losses from the income statement. List three types of gains and losses that are excluded from the income statement.
             b. Discuss the merit of including these items in your profitability analysis.

Q 8-16   The Apple Tree Company disclosed an unrealized loss on noncurrent marketable equity securities in stockholders' equity at December 31, 1990, in the amount of $10,000,000. What is the significance of this disclosure?

Q 8-17   Indicate the difference between the reporting of gains and losses from the translation of foreign currency for the financial statements and the reporting of gains and losses resulting from foreign currency transactions.

PROBLEMS

P 8-1   Ahl Enterprise lists the following data for 1989 and 1988:

	1989	1988
Net income	$ 52,500	$ 40,000
Net sales	1,050,000	1,000,000

	1989	1988
Average total assets	230,000	200,000
Average common equity	170,000	160,000

Required   Calculate the net profit margin, return on assets, total asset turnover, and return on common equity for both years. Comment on the results.

P 8-2   Income statement data for Starr Canning Corporation are as follows:

	1989	1988
Sales	$1,400,000	$1,200,000
Cost of goods sold	850,000	730,000
Selling expense	205,000	240,000
General expense	140,000	100,000
Income tax expense	82,000	50,000

Required   a. Prepare an income statement in comparative form stating each item for both years as a percentage of sales (vertical common size analysis).
b. Comment on the findings in (a).

P 8-3   The balance sheet for the Schultz Bone Company at December 31, 1989, had the following account balances:

Total current liabilities (non-interest-bearing)	$450,000
Bonds payable, 6% (issued in 1972, due in 1998)	750,000
Preferred stock, 5%, $100 par	300,000
Common stock, $10 par	750,000
Premium on common stock	150,000
Retained earnings	600,000

Income before income tax was $200,000, and income taxes were $80,000 for the current year.

Required   Calculate each of the following:

        a. return on assets (using ending assets)
        b. return on total equity (using ending total equity)
        c. return on common equity (using ending common equity)
        d. times interest earned
        e. earnings per share

P 8-4   Revenue and expense data for Vent Molded Plastics, and for the plastics industry as a whole, are as follows:

	Vent Molded Plastics	**Plastics Industry**
Sales	$462,000	100.3%
Sales returns	4,500	.3
Cost of goods sold	330,000	67.1
Selling expenses	43,000	10.1
General expenses	32,000	7.9
Other income	1,800	.4
Other expense	7,000	1.3
Income tax	22,000	5.5

Required   Convert the dollar figures for Vent Molded Plastics into percentages based on net sales. Compare these with the industry average, and comment on your findings.

P 8-5   Day Ko Incorporated presented the following comparative income statements for 1989 and 1988:

	1989	1988
Net sales	$1,589,150	$1,294,966
Other income	22,334	20,822
	1,611,484	1,315,788
Cost and expenses:		
Material and manufacturing costs of products sold	651,390	466,250
Research and development	135,314	113,100
General and selling	526,680	446,110
Interest	18,768	11,522
Other	15,570	7,306
	1,347,722	1,044,288
Earnings before income taxes and minority equity	263,762	271,500
Provision for income taxes	114,502	121,740
Earnings before minority equity	149,260	149,760
Minority equity in earnings	11,056	12,650
Net earnings	$ 138,204	$ 137,110

	For the Years Ended	
	1989	1988
Other relevant financial information:		
Average common shares issued	29,580	29,480
Total long-term debt	$ 209,128	$ 212,702
Total stockholders' equity (all common)	810,292	720,530
Total assets	1,437,636	1,182,110
Operating assets	1,411,686	1,159,666
Dividends per share	1.96	1.86
Stock price (December 31)	53¾	76⅛

Required

a. How did 1989 net sales compare to 1988?
b. How did 1989 net earnings compare to 1988?
c. Calculate the following ratios for 1989 and 1988:

   1. net profit margin
   2. return on assets (using ending assets)
   3. total asset turnover (using ending assets)
   4. DuPont analysis
   5. operating income margin
   6. return on operating assets (use ending assets)
   7. operating asset turnover (use ending assets)
   8. DuPont analysis with operating ratios
   9. return on investment (use ending liabilities and equity)
   10. return on equity (use ending common equity)

d. Based on the above computations, summarize the trend in profitability for this firm.

P 8-6

Dorex, Inc., presented the following comparative income statements for 1989, 1988, and 1987:

	1989	1988	1987
Net sales	$1,600,000	$1,300,000	$1,200,000
Other income	22,100	21,500	21,000
	1,622,100	1,321,500	1,221,000
Costs and expenses:			
Material and manufacturing costs of products sold	740,000	624,000	576,000
Research and development	90,000	78,000	71,400
General and selling	600,000	500,500	465,000
Interest	19,000	18,200	17,040
Other	14,000	13,650	13,200
	1,463,000	1,234,350	1,143,240
Earnings before income taxes and minority equity	159,100	87,150	77,760
Provision for income taxes	62,049	35,731	32,659
Earnings before minority equity	97,051	51,419	45,101
Minority equity in earnings	10,200	8,500	8,100
Net earnings	$ 86,851	$ 42,919	$ 37,601

	For the Years Ended		
	1989	1988	1987
Other relevant financial information:			
Average common shares issued	29,610	29,100	28,800
Average long-term debt	$ 211,100	$ 121,800	$ 214,000
Average stockholders' equity			
(all common)	811,200	790,100	770,000
Average total assets	1,440,600	1,220,000	1,180,000
Average operating assets	1,390,200	1,160,000	1,090,000

Required a. Calculate the following ratios for 1989, 1988, and 1987:

    1. net profit margin   6. return on operating assets
    2. return on assets   7. operating asset turnover
    3. total asset turnover   8. DuPont analysis with operating ratios
    4. DuPont analysis   9. return on investment
    5. operating income margin   10. return on equity

b. Based on the above computations, summarize the trend in profitability for this firm.

P 8-7 Selected financial data for the Squid Company are as follows:

	1989	1988	1987
Summary of operations			
Net sales	$1,002,100	$980,500	$900,000
Cost of products sold	520,500	514,762	477,000
Selling, administrative, and general			
expenses	170,200	167,665	155,700
Nonoperating income	9,192	8,860	6,500
Interest expense	14,620	12,100	11,250
Earnings before income taxes	287,588	277,113	249,550
Provision for income taxes	116,473	113,616	105,560
Net earnings	171,115	163,497	143,990
Financial information			
Working capital	$ 190,400	$189,000	$180,000
Average property, plant, and equipment	302,500	281,000	173,000
Average total assets	839,000	770,000	765,000
Average long-term debt	120,000	112,000	101,000
Average shareholders' equity	406,000	369,500	342,000

Required a. Compute the following ratios for 1989, 1988, and 1987:

    1. net profit margin   5. return on investment
    2. return on assets   6. return on total equity
    3. total asset turnover   7. sales to fixed assets
    4. DuPont analysis

b. Discuss your findings in (a).

P 8-8 The D. H. Muller Company presented the following income statement in its 1989 annual report.

(dollars in thousands except per share amounts)	1989	1988	1987
Net sales	$297,580	$256,360	$242,150
Cost of sales	206,000	176,300	165,970
Gross profit	91,580	80,060	76,180
Selling, administrative, and other expenses	65,200	57,200	56,000
Operating earnings	26,380	22,860	20,180
Interest expense	5,990	5,100	4,000
Other deductions, net	320	1,100	800
Earnings before income taxes, minority interests, and extraordinary items	20,070	16,600	15,380
Income taxes	(8,028)	(6,830)	(6,229)
Net earnings of subsidiaries applicable to minority interests	(700)	(670)	(668)
Earnings before extraordinary items	11,342	9,160	8,483
Gain on sale of investment net of federal and state income taxes of $520		1,050	
Loss due to damages to South American facilities, net of minority interest of $430		(1,600)	
Net earnings	$ 11,342	$ 8,610	$ 8,483

	1989	1988	1987
Earnings per common share			
Earnings before extraordinary items	$2.20	$1.82	$1.65
Extraordinary items	—	—	—
Net earnings	$2.20	$1.76	$1.65

The asset side of the balance sheet is summarized as follows:

(in thousands)	1989	1988	1987
Current assets	$ 89,800	$ 84,500	$ 83,100
Property, plant, and equipment	45,850	40,300	39,800
Other assets (including investments, deposits, deferred charges, and intangibles)	10,110	12,200	13,100
Total assets	$145,760	$137,000	$136,000

Required a. Based on these data, compute the following ratios for 1989, 1988, and 1987. Use ending asset figures in your computations.

1. net profit margin
2. return on assets
3. total asset turnover
4. DuPont analysis
5. operating income margin

6. return on operating assets
7. operating asset turnover
8. DuPont analysis with operating ratios
9. gross profit margin

b. Discuss your findings.

P 8-9   The following financial information is for A. Galler for 1989, 1988, and 1987.

	1989	1988	1987
Income before interest	$4,400,000	$4,000,000	$3,300,000
Interest expense	800,000	600,000	550,000
Income before tax	3,600,000	3,400,000	2,750,000
Tax	1,500,000	1,450,000	1,050,000
Net income	$2,100,000	$1,950,000	$1,700,000

	1989	1988	1987
Current liabilities	2,600,000	2,300,000	2,200,000
Long-term debt	7,000,000	6,200,000	5,800,000
Preferred stock (14%)	100,000	100,000	100,000
Common equity	10,000,000	9,000,000	8,300,000

Required   a. For 1989, 1988, and 1987, determine the following ratios. Use ending balance sheet figures in your computations.
   1. return on assets
   2. return on investment
   3. return on total equity
   4. return on common equity
b. Discuss the trend in these profit figures.
c. Discuss the benefit from the use of long-term debt and preferred stock.

P 8-10   Dexall Company recently had a fire in its store. Management must determine the inventory loss for the insurance company. Since the firm did not have perpetual inventory records, the insurance company has suggested that it might accept an estimate using the gross margin test. The beginning inventory, as determined from the last financial statements, was $10,000. Purchase invoices indicate purchases of $100,000. Credit and cash sales during the period were $120,000. Last year, the gross margin for the firm was 40%, which was also the industry average.

Required   a. Based on these data, estimate the inventory loss.
b. If the industry average gross margin were 50%, why might the insurance company be leery of the estimated loss?

P 8-11   Transactions affect various financial statement accounts.

	Net Profit	Retained Earnings	Total Stockholders' Equity
a. A stock dividend is declared and paid.	_____	_____	_____
b. Merchandise is purchased on credit.	_____	_____	_____
c. Marketable securities are sold above cost.	_____	_____	_____
d. Accounts receivable are collected.	_____	_____	_____
e. A cash dividend is declared and paid.	_____	_____	_____
f. Treasury stock is purchased and recorded at cost.	_____	_____	_____

	Net Profit	Retained Earnings	Total Stockholders' Equity
g. Treasury stock is sold above cost.	_____	_____	_____
h. Common stock is sold.	_____	_____	_____
i. A fixed asset is sold for less than book value.	_____	_____	_____
j. Bonds are converted into common stock.	_____	_____	_____

Required   Indicate the effects of the transactions just listed on each of the following: net profit, retained earnings, and total stockholders' equity. Use + to indicate an increase, − to indicate a decrease, and 0 to indicate no effect.

CASES

Case 8-1   JOHNNY'S SELF-SERVICE STATION

John Dearden and his wife, Patricia, have been taking an annual vacation to Stowe, Vermont, each summer. They like the area very much and would like to retire someday in this vicinity. While in Stowe during the summer, they notice a "for sale" sign in front of a self-service station. John is 55 and is no longer satisfied with commuting to work in New York City. He decides to inquire about the asking price of the station. He is aware that Stowe is considered a good vacation area during the entire year, especially when the ski season is in progress.

On inquiry, John determines that the asking price of the station is $70,000, which includes two pumps, a small building, and ⅛ acre of land.

John asks to see some financial statements and is shown profit and loss statements for 1989 and 1988 that have been prepared for tax purposes by a local accountant. (See page 360.) He is also given an appraiser's report on the property. The land is appraised at $50,000, and the equipment and building are valued at $20,000. The equipment and building are estimated to have a useful life of ten years.

The station has been operated by Jeff Szabo without additional help. He estimates that if help were hired to operate the station, it would cost $10,000 per year. John Dearden anticipates that he will be able to operate the station without additional help. John Dearden intends to incorporate. The anticipated tax rate is 50%.

Required   a. Determine the indicated return on investment if John Dearden purchases the station. Include only financial data that will be recorded on the books. Consider 1989 and 1988 to be representative years for revenue and expenses.
   b. Determine the indicated return on investment if help were hired to operate the station.
   c. Why is there a difference between the rates of return in part (a) and part (b)? Discuss.
   d. Determine the cash flow for 1990 if Mr. Dearden serves as the manager and 1990 turns out to be the same as 1989. Do not include the cost of the hired help. No inventory is on hand at the date of purchase, but an inventory of $10,000 is on hand at the end of the year. There are no receivables or liabilities.
   e. Indicate some other considerations that should be analyzed.
   f. Should John purchase the station?

JOHNNY'S SELF-SERVICE STATION
Statement of Earnings
For the Years Ended December 31, 1989 and 1988

	1989	1988
Revenue	$185,060	$175,180
Expenses:		
Cost of goods sold	160,180	153,280
Depreciation (a)	1,000	1,000
Real estate and property taxes	1,100	1,050
Repairs and maintenance	1,470	1,200
Other expenses	680	725
Total expenses	164,430	157,255
Profit	$ 20,630	$ 17,925
(a) Building and equipment cost	$30,000	
Original estimated life	30 years	
Depreciation per year	$ 1,000	

Case 8-2   **WHAT COST EARNINGS?**

To Our Shareholders

Sales of Chrysler Corporation and consolidated subsidiaries throughout the world in 1970 totaled $7.0 billion, compared with $7.1 billion in 1969. Operations for the year resulted in a net loss of $7.6 million or $0.16 a share, compared with net earnings of $99.0 million or $2.09 a share in 1969.

Net earnings for 1969 are restated to reflect a retroactive change in the company's method of valuing inventories, from a LIFO (last-in, first-out) to a FIFO (first-in, first-out) cost basis, as explained in the notes to financial statements. The LIFO method reduces inventory values and earnings in periods of rising costs. The rate of inflation in costs in 1970 and for the projected short term future is so high that significant understatements of inventory values and earnings result. The use of the LIFO method in 1970 would have reduced inventory amounts at December 31, 1970 by approximately $150 million and did reduce inventory amounts reported at December 31, 1969 by approximately $110 million. Also, the use of the LIFO method in 1970 would have increased the loss for the year by approximately $20.0 million, and its use in 1969 reduced the earnings as reported for that year by $10.2 million. The other three U.S. automobile manufacturers have consistently used the FIFO method. Therefore, the reported loss for 1970 and the restated profit for 1969 are on a comparable basis as to inventory valuation with the other three companies. Prior years' earnings have been restated to make them comparable.

Results of operations for the first three quarters of 1970 were previously reported on the LIFO method of valuing inventories. The restated results, on the FIFO method of valuing inventories, for the four quarters of 1970 are as follows:

	Net Earnings (Loss) (In millions)	Earnings (Loss) (A Share)
1st quarter	$(27.4)	$(0.57)
2nd quarter	10.1	0.21
3rd quarter	2.1	0.05
4th quarter	7.6	0.15
1970	$(7.6)	$(0.16)

CHRYSLER CORPORATION AND CONSOLIDATED SUBSIDIARIES
Consolidated Statement of Net Earnings

	Year Ended December 31	
	1970	1969ᴬ
Net sales	$6,999,675,655	$7,052,184,678
Equity in net earnings (loss) of unconsolidated subsidiaries	(6,210,013)	(6,286,309)
Other income and deductions	(19,962,022)	23,261,424
	6,973,503,620	7,069,159,793
Cost of products sold, other than items below	6,103,250,974	5,966,732,377
Depreciation of plant and equipment	176,758,139	170,305,745
Amortization of special tools	172,568,348	167,194,002
Selling and administrative expenses	386,041,866	431,706,851
Pension and retirement plans	121,406,136	114,577,630
Interest on long-term debt	46,998,713	31,702,530
Taxes on income (credit)	(21,400,000)	91,700,000
	6,985,624,176	6,973,919,135
Net earnings (loss) including minority interest	(12,120,556)	95,240,658
Minority interest in net loss of consolidated subsidiaries	4,517,536	3,730,564
Net earnings (loss)	$ (7,603,020)	$ 98,971,222
Average number of shares of common stock outstanding during the year	48,693,200	47,390,561
Net earnings (loss) a share	$(0.16)	$2.09

ᴬRestated to reflect the change made in 1970 in accounting for inventories and to conform to 1970 classification. The 1969 net earnings and net earnings a share, as previously reported, were $88.8 million and $1.87 respectively. *See* Inventories—Accounting Change note on page [362].

CHRYSLER CORPORATION
Selected Data from Consolidated Balance Sheet

	December 31	
	1970	1969[A]
Assets:		
Current assets:		
Cash	$ 95,807,393	$ 78,768,440
Marketable securities—at cost and accrued interest	60,607,134	230,562,926
Accounts receivable (less allowance for doubtful accounts: 1970—$15,700,000; 1969—$13,400,000)	438,852,496	477,880,423
Refundable United States taxes on income	80,000,000	—
Inventories[B]	1,390,681,228	1,335,198,128
Prepaid insurance, taxes and other expenses	83,299,833	80,087,753
Income taxes allocable to the following year	17,415,554	27,186,281
Total current assets	2,166,663,638	2,229,683,951
Total investments and other assets	767,393,750	680,829,674
Net property, plant and equipment	1,803,223,691	1,753,026,201
Cost of investments in consolidated subsidiaries in excess of equity	78,491,382	78,184,245
Total assets	$4,815,772,461	$4,741,724,071
Liabilities and shareholders' investment:		
Total current liabilities	$1,547,879,351	$1,643,844,815
Total other liabilities	205,977,193	225,873,888
Total long-term debt	791,052,172	586,950,466
International operations reserve	35,500,000	35,500,000
Minority interest in net assets of consolidated subsidiaries	79,742,516	95,149,271
Total shareholders' investment	2,155,621,229	2,154,405,631
Total liabilities and shareholders' investment	$4,815,772,461	$4,741,724,071

[A]Restated to reflect change made in 1970 in accounting for inventories.
[B]*See* Inventories—Accounting Change note on this page.

Selected Notes to Financial Statements

Inventories—Accounting Change   Inventories are stated at the lower of cost or market. For the period January 1, 1957 through December 31, 1969 the last-in, first-out (LIFO) method of inventory valuation had been used for approximately

60% of the consolidated inventory. The cost of the remaining 40% of inventories was determined using the first-in, first-out (FIFO) or average cost methods. Effective January 1, 1970 the FIFO method of inventory valuation has been adopted for inventories previously valued using the LIFO method. This results in a more uniform valuation method throughout the Corporation and its consolidated subsidiaries and makes the financial statements with respect to inventory valuation comparable with those of the other United States automobile manufacturers. As a result of adopting FIFO in 1970, the net loss reported is less than it would have been on a LIFO basis by approximately $20.0 million, or $0.40 a share. Inventory amounts at December 31, 1969 and 1970 are stated higher by approximately $110.0 million and $150.0 million, respectively, than they would have been had the LIFO method been continued.

The Corporation has retroactively adjusted financial statements of prior years for this change. Accordingly, the 1969 financial statements have been restated resulting in an increase in Net Earnings of $10.2 million, and Net Earnings Retained for Use in the Business at December 31, 1969 and 1968 have been increased by $53.5 million and $43.3 million, respectively.

For United States income tax purposes the adjustment to inventory amounts will be taken into taxable income ratably over 20 years commencing January 1, 1971.

Taxes on Income Taxes on income as shown in the consolidated statement of net earnings include the following:

	1970	1969
Currently payable:		
United States taxes (credit)	$(81,800,000)	$50,000,000
Other countries	44,300,000	36,300,000
Deferred taxes	16,100,000	(6,000,000)
As previously reported	—	80,300,000
Adjustment in deferred taxes for change in		
inventory valuation	—	11,400,000
Total taxes on income (credit)	$(21,400,000)	$91,700,000

The change in inventory valuation resulted in a reduction in income taxes allocable to the following year of approximately $56.0 million at December 31, 1969.

Reductions in taxes resulting from the investment credit provisions of the Internal Revenue Code are being taken into income over the estimated lives of the related assets. The amounts of such credits which were reflected in net earnings were $6,300,000 in 1970 and $5,400,000 in 1969.

Note: For computation purposes when working this case, assume a 50% tax rate. All of the information in this case was quoted from the 1970 annual report of the Chrysler Corporation.

Required

   a. What was the amount of taxes that had been deferred because of the use of LIFO as of the beginning of 1970?

   b. Approximate the cost to Chrysler of changing from LIFO to FIFO.

   c. Indicate how the switch to FIFO from LIFO affected the following:

      1. current ratio

      2. debt/equity

      3. cash flow

      4. gross profit

   d. Speculate on reasons why Chrysler made the change from LIFO to FIFO.

Case 8-3   **THE TALE OF THE SEGMENTS***

The segment information from the 1989 annual report of the Procter & Gamble Company is as follows:

8. Segment Information

Sales between geographic areas and those between business segments, included in net sales below, are made at prices approximating market and are eliminated from total net sales. Corporate earnings include interest income and expense, and other general corporate income and expense. Corporate assets include primarily cash and cash equivalents.

Geographic Areas

millions of dollars		United States	International	Corporate	Total
Net sales	1987	$11,805	$5,524	$ (329)	$17,000
	1988	12,423	7,294	(381)	19,336
	1989	13,312	8,529	(443)	21,398
Net earnings	1987*	329	120	(122)	327
	1988	864	305	(149)	1,020
	1989	927	417	(138)	1,206
Assets	1987	8,483	3,849	1,383	13,715
	1988	8,346	4,751	1,723	14,820
	1989	8,669	5,260	2,422	16,351

*Net earnings have been reduced by $357 million in the United States, and $102 million in International by the provision for restructuring.

Business Segments

The Company's operations are characterized by interrelated raw materials and manufacturing facilities and centralized research and administrative staff functions, making any separate profit determination by product group dependent upon necessarily arbitrary assumptions as to allocations of common costs. Different assumptions or physical or organizational arrangements would produce different results.

*Courtesy of the Procter & Gamble Company.

millions of dollars		Laundry and Cleaning	Personal Care	Food and Beverage	Pulp and Chemicals	Corporate	Total
				Product Groups			
Net sales	1987	$5,784	$ 7,512	$2,976	$1,186	$ (458)	$17,000
	1988	6,668	8,676	2,963	1,532	(503)	19,336
	1989	7,138	10,032	3,029	1,778	(579)	21,398
Earnings before income	1987*	510	498	(282)	148	(257)	617
taxes	1988	699	888	32	248	(237)	1,630
	1989	754	1,031	(14)	362	(194)	1,939
Assets	1987	2,690	6,679	1,690	1,273	1,383	13,715
	1988	2,852	7,114	1,721	1,410	1,723	14,820
	1989	2,964	7,511	2,023	1,431	2,422	16,351
Capital expenditures	1987	252	493	148	77	13	983
	1988	285	483	120	117	13	1,018
	1989	273	510	101	138	7	1,029
Depreciation, depletion	1987	120	332	95	77	5	629
and amortization	1988	149	375	88	79	6	697
	1989	151	428	90	90	8	767

*Earnings before income taxes have been reduced by the provision for restructuring, in millions, as follows: Laundry and Cleaning Products—$215; Personal Care Products—$269; Food and Beverage Products—$295; Pulp and Chemicals—$26.

Laundry and Cleaning Products include detergents, hard surface cleaners and fabric conditioners. Personal Care Products include personal cleansing products, deodorants, hair care products, skin care products, oral care products, paper tissue products, disposable diapers, digestive health products, cough and cold remedies and other pharmaceuticals. Sales of disposable diapers represented approximately 17%, 16% and 16% of consolidated sales in 1989, 1988 and 1987 respectively. Food and Beverage Products include shortening and oil, snacks, prepared baking mixes, peanut butter, coffee, soft drinks and citrus products. Products of the Laundry and Cleaning, Personal Care and Food and Beverage segments are distributed primarily through grocery stores and other retail outlets. Pulp and Chemicals are sold direct to customers and through jobbers. Net sales of Pulp and Chemicals include intersegment sales amounting, in millions, to $579 in 1989, $503 in 1988 and $447 in 1987.

Required   a. Perform vertical common size analysis for 1987, 1988, and 1989, using "total" as the base for the following:
  1. Geographic areas
     (a) net sales
     (b) net earnings
     (c) assets
  2. Business segments
     (a) net sales
     (b) earnings before income taxes

           (c) assets

           (d) capital expenditures

           (e) depreciation, depletion, and amortization

    b. Perform horizontal common size analysis, using 1987 as the base, for the following:

        1. Geographic areas

           (a) net sales

           (b) net earnings

           (c) assets

        2. Business segments

           (a) net sales

           (b) earnings before income taxes

           (c) assets

           (d) capital expenditures

           (e) depreciation, depletion, and amortization

    c. Compute the following ratios for 1987, 1988, and 1989:

        1. Geographic areas

           (a) net sales/assets

           (b) net earnings/net sales

           (c) net earnings/assets

        2. Business segments

           (a) net sales/assets

           (b) earnings before income taxes/net sales

           (c) earnings before income taxes/assets

    d. Comment on possible significant insights from the analysis in parts (a), (b), and (c).

Case 8-4   FOLLOW THE SEGMENTS

The segment information from the 1989 annual report of Utilicorp United is as follows:

Note 14: Segment Information

dollars in thousands	Year Ended December 31,				
	1989	1988	1987	1986	1985
Operating revenues:					
Missouri Public Service (electric and gas)	$ 234,139	$ 232,218	$222,869	$222,811	$221,000
Peoples Natural Gas (gas)	312,016	318,143	295,800	356,263	8,681
West Kootenay Power (electric—foreign)	63,093	54,080	16,503	—	—
Michigan Gas Utilities (gas)	52,388	—	—	—	—
Northern Minnesota Utilities (gas)	35,007	33,466	29,768	4,285	—
West Virginia Power (electric)	21,727	21,496	17,007	—	—
Kansas Public Service (gas)	13,563	13,396	12,913	12,446	13,469
Total electric operations	285,862	275,751	227,176	192,575	185,799
Total gas operations	446,071	397,048	367,684	403,230	57,351
Total operating revenues	$ 731,933	$ 672,799	$594,860	$595,805	$243,150

dollars in thousands	Year Ended December 31,				
	1989	1988	1987	1986	1985
Pretax operating income:					
Missouri Public Service (electric and gas)	$ 55,387	$ 53,269	$ 59,172	$ 61,442	$ 62,160
Peoples Natural Gas (gas)*	20,519	18,514	11,958	2,598	(208)
West Kootenay Power (electric—foreign)	19,158	16,299	5,073	—	—
Michigan Gas Utilities (gas)	4,944	—	—	—	—
Northern Minnesota Utilities (gas)	3,979	3,193	2,099	836	—
West Virginia Power (electric)	3,592	3,225	2,722	—	—
Kansas Public Service (gas)	990	1,163	271	1,654	874
Total electric operations	74,514	72,502	67,513	61,534	61,709
Total gas operations	34,055	23,161	13,782	4,996	1,117
Total operating income, before income taxes	108,569	95,663	81,295	66,530	62,826
Less—income taxes	21,680	18,496	19,699	13,817	22,641
Total operating income	$ 86,889	$ 77,167	$ 61,596	$ 52,713	$ 40,185
Investment information:					
Identifiable assets					
Electric operations					
Domestic	$ 515,012	$ 474,726	$449,861	$420,334	$408,822
Foreign	185,561	167,388	144,297	—	—
Total electric operations	700,573	642,114	594,158	420,334	408,822
Gas operations	464,736	283,229	275,221	285,167	297,749
Non-utility operations	267,507	162,379	77,636	37,335	4,455
Total identifiable assets	1,432,816	1,087,722	947,015	742,836	711,026
Corporate assets	34,051	37,224	19,111	22,823	19,740
Total assets	$1,466,867	$1,124,946	$966,126	$765,659	$730,766
Other information:					
Depreciation and amortization					
Electric operations	$ 25,317	$ 23,026	$ 18,478	$ 15,062	$ 14,254
Gas operations	22,754	18,249	21,022	16,111	1,640
Non-utility operations	16,103	4,695	151	36	2
Total depreciation and amortization	$ 64,174	$ 45,970	$ 39,651	$ 31,209	$ 15,896
Capital expenditures					
Electric operations	$ 65,084	$ 55,914	$ 37,921	$ 29,279	$ 28,669
Gas operations	33,230	22,835	18,730	17,704	3,084
Non-utility operations	79,869	74,151	21,470	12,944	—
Total capital expenditures	$ 178,183	$ 152,900	$ 78,121	$ 59,927	$ 31,753

*In 1987, includes pretax effect of change in accounting for unbilled revenues in the amount of $1,475.

Required

a. Perform vertical common size analysis for 1985–1989 for operating revenues. Use total operating revenues as the base.

b. Perform vertical common size analysis for 1985–1989 for pretax operating income. Use total operating income before income taxes as the base.

c. Perform vertical common size analysis for 1985–1989 for total assets. Use total assets as the base.

d. Perform horizontal common size analysis for 1985–1989 for total assets. Use 1985 as the base, except for foreign. For the foreign segment, use 1987 as the base.

e. Perform vertical common size analysis for 1985–1989 for capital expenditures. Use total capital expenditures as the base.

f. Perform horizontal common size analysis for 1985–1989 for capital expenditures. Use 1985 as the base, except for nonutility operations. For nonutility operations, use 1986 as the base.

g. Comment on possible significant insights from the analysis in parts (a)–(e).

CHAPTER 9

ANALYSIS FOR THE INVESTOR

CHAPTER TOPICS

*Leverage and Its Effect
on Earnings*

Definition of Financial Leverage
and Magnification Effects

Computation of the Degree
of Financial Leverage

Summary of Financial Leverage

Earnings Per Common Share

Price/Earnings Ratio

*Percentage of Earnings
Retained*

Dividend Payout

Dividend Yield

Book Value Per Share

Interpretation of Book Value

Stock Options

Stock Appreciation Rights

Certain types of analysis are of particular concern to investors. Although this chapter is not intended as a comprehensive guide to investment analysis, it will introduce certain types of analysis available to the investor. In addition to the analysis covered in this chapter, an investor would also be interested in the liquidity, debt, and profitability ratios covered in prior chapters.

LEVERAGE AND ITS EFFECT ON EARNINGS

Since the common shareholder is the residual owner and is therefore entitled to whatever profits are left, financial and operating decisions affect the level of earnings. For example, the use of debt, called *leverage,* can greatly change the common earnings.

The expense of debt financing is interest, a fixed charge dependent on the amount of financial principal and the rate of interest. Interest must be paid when due; it is a contractual obligation created by the borrowing agreement. In contrast to dividends, the firm must pay the interest regardless of whether it is in a highly profitable period or not. An advantage of interest over dividends is its tax deductibility. Because the interest is subtracted to calculate taxable income, income tax expense is reduced.

Definition of Financial Leverage and Magnification Effects

The use of financing with a fixed charge (such as interest) is termed *financial leverage*. Financial leverage is successful if more can be earned on the borrowed funds than is paid to use the funds. It is not successful if less is earned on the borrowed funds than is paid to use the funds. Using financial leverage results in a fixed financing charge that can materially affect the earnings available to the common shareholders. Exhibit 9-1 illustrates financial leverage and its magnification effect. In this illustration, earnings before interest and tax are $1,000,000. Further, the firm has debt obligations causing interest expense of $200,000 and a tax rate of 40%. The statement illustrates the effect of leverage on the return to the common shareholder. At earnings before interest and tax (EBIT) of $1,000,000, the net income is $480,000. If EBIT increases by 10% to $1,100,000, as in the exhibit, the net income rises by 12.5%. This magnification is caused by the fixed nature of interest expense. While earnings available to pay interest rise, interest remains the same, thus leaving more for the residual owners. Note that since the tax rate remains the same, earnings before tax change at the same rate as earnings after tax on net earnings. Hence, this analysis could be made with either profit figure.

If financial leverage is used, a rise in EBIT will cause an even greater rise in net income. Unfortunately for borrowers, this concept also works in reverse. If

E X H I B I T   9 - 1

DOWELL COMPANY
Financial Leverage
Partial Income Statement to Illustrate Magnification Effects

	Base Year Figures	20% Decrease in Earnings before Interest and Tax	10% Increase in Earnings before Interest and Tax
Earnings before interest and tax	$1,000,000	$800,000	$1,100,000
Interest	200,000	200,000	200,000
Earnings before tax	800,000	600,000	900,000
Income tax (40%)	320,000	240,000	360,000
Net income	$ 480,000	$360,000	$ 540,000
Percentage change in net income (A)		25.0%	12.5%
Percentage change in earnings before interest and tax (B)		20.0%	10.0%
Degree of financial leverage (A ÷ B)		1.25	1.25

financial leverage is utilized, a decrease in EBIT will cause an even greater decrease in net income. Looking again at the statement for Dowell Company, when EBIT declined 20%, net income dropped from $480,000 to $360,000—a decline of $120,000, or 25%, based on the original $480,000. The use of financial leverage, termed *trading on the equity,* is successful only if the rate of earnings on borrowed funds is higher than the fixed charges.

Computation of the Degree of Financial Leverage

The degree of financial leverage is the multiplication factor by which the net income changes as compared to the change in EBIT. One way of computing it is:

$$\frac{\% \text{ Change Net Income}}{\% \text{ Change EBIT}}$$

For Dowell Company,

$$\frac{12.5\%}{10.0\%} = 1.25, \quad \text{or} \quad \frac{25.0\%}{20.0\%} = 1.25$$

The degree of financial leverage is 1.25. From a base EBIT of $1,000,000, any change in EBIT will be accompanied by 1.25 times that change in net income. If net income before interest rises 4%, earnings to the shareholder will rise 5%. If net income before interest falls 8%, earnings to the shareholder will decline 10%. The degree of financial leverage (DFL) can be computed more easily as follows:

$$\text{Degree of Financial Leverage} = \frac{\text{Earnings before Interest and Tax}}{\text{Earnings before Tax}}$$

Again referring to Dowell Company,

$$\frac{\text{Degree of Financial Leverage at Earnings}}{\text{before Interest and Tax on \$1,000,000}} = \frac{\$1,000,000}{\$800,000} = 1.25$$

It must be noted that the degree of financial leverage is for a particular base level of income. The degree of leverage may differ for other levels of income or fixed charges.

The degree of financial leverage formula illustrated as earnings before interest and tax divided by earnings before tax does not work precisely when any of the following items are present in the income statement:

1. Minority share of earnings
2. Equity income
3. Nonrecurring items
   a. Unusual or infrequent item
   b. Discontinued operations
   c. Extraordinary items
   d. Cumulative effect of change in accounting principle

When any of these items are present, they should be eliminated from the numerator and denominator. The all-inclusive formula is as follows:

$$\text{Degree of Financial Leverage} = \frac{\begin{array}{c}\text{Earnings before Interest, Tax,}\\ \text{Minority Share of Earnings,}\\ \text{Equity Income, and Nonrecurring Items}\end{array}}{\begin{array}{c}\text{Earnings before Tax,}\\ \text{Minority Share of Earnings,}\\ \text{Equity Income, and Nonrecurring Items}\end{array}}$$

This formula results in the ratio by which earnings will change before minority share of earnings, equity income, and nonrecurring items in relation to a change in earnings before *interest,* minority share of earnings, equity income, and nonrecurring items. In other words, it results in a leverage factor for recurring earnings excluding minority share of earnings and equity income.

The degree of financial leverage for 1989 and 1988 for Cooper is computed in Exhibit 9-2. The degree of financial leverage is 1.05 for 1989 and 1.07 for 1988. Cooper does not have minority share of earnings, equity income, or nonrecurring items. Therefore, the financial leverage indicates at the end of 1989 that as earnings before interest change, net income will change by 1.05 times that amount. If earnings before interest increase, the financial leverage will be favorable. If earnings before interest decrease, the financial leverage will be unfavorable.

For Cooper, financial leverage is not a major factor, because a leverage of 1.05 is very low. A conservative investor would look favorably on Cooper's low financial leverage.

In periods of relatively low interest rates or declining interest rates, financial leverage is looked on more favorably than in periods of high interest rates or increasing interest rates.

EXHIBIT 9-2

COOPER TIRE & RUBBER COMPANY
Degree of Financial Leverage
Base Years 1989 and 1988

	1989	1988
Income before income taxes [B]	$92,623,880	$64,912,286
Interest and debt expense	4,373,398	4,495,464
Earnings before interest and tax [A]	$96,997,278	$69,407,750
Degree of financial leverage [A ÷ B]	1.05	1.07

Summary of Financial Leverage

Two things are important in looking at financial leverage as part of financial analysis. First, how high is the degree of financial leverage? This is a type of risk (or opportunity) measurement from the viewpoint of the shareholder. The higher the degree of financial leverage, the greater the multiplication factor. Second, in your opinion, is the financial leverage going to work for the owners or against the owners?

EARNINGS PER COMMON SHARE

Earnings per share is the amount of income earned on a share of common stock during an accounting period. It is computed *only* for common stock; moreover, it is a concept that applies only to corporate income statements. Because earnings per share is the financial element of information that receives the greatest attention from the financial community, investors, and potential investors, it will be described in some detail.

Depending on the capital structure of the company, the earnings per share computation can be very simple or very complex. Fortunately, it is not necessary that we compute earnings per share. It must be computed by the company and presented at the bottom of the income statement (per APB Opinion No. 15).

In 1978, the Financial Accounting Standards Board suspended the reporting of earnings per share for "nonpublic enterprises." A nonpublic enterprise was defined as:

> . . . an enterprise other than one (a) whose debt or equity securities trade in a public market on a foreign or domestic stock exchange or in the over-the-counter market (including securities quoted only locally or regionally) or (b) that is required to file financial statements with the Securities and Exchange Commission.[1]

APB Opinion No. 15 distinguishes between two types of corporate capital structures—simple and complex. A simple capital structure consists of common stock, with no material convertible securities, options, warrants, or other rights that upon conversion or exercise could in the aggregate dilute earnings per share.

For a simple capital structure, the earnings per share computation is as follows:

$$\text{Earnings Per Common Share} = \frac{\text{Net Income} - \text{Preferred Dividends}}{\substack{\text{Weighted Average Number of} \\ \text{Common Shares Outstanding}}}$$

---

[1]"Suspension of the Reporting of Earnings per Share and Segment Information by Non-public Enterprise," Statement of Financial Accounting Standards No. 21 (Stamford, Conn.: Financial Accounting Standards Board, 1978), par. 13.

The earnings per common share computation uses only earnings available to common stockholders in the numerator of the computation. To arrive at the income that applies to common stock, preferred dividends are subtracted from net income.

Since earnings pertain to an entire year, they should be related to the common shares outstanding during the year. Thus, the denominator of the equation is the weighted average number of common shares outstanding.

To illustrate, assume that a corporation had 10,000 shares of common stock outstanding at the beginning of the year. On July 1, it issued 2,000 shares, and on October 1, it issued another 3,000 shares. The weighted average number of shares outstanding would be computed as follows:

Months Shares Are Outstanding	Shares Outstanding	×	Fraction of Year Outstanding	=	Weighted Average
January–June	10,000		6/12		5,000
July–September	12,000		3/12		3,000
October–December	15,000		3/12		3,750
Total weighted average common shares					11,750

When the common shares outstanding increase as a result of a stock dividend or stock split, retroactive recognition must be given to these events for all comparative earnings per share presentations. Stock dividends and stock splits do not provide the firm with more funds; they just change the number of outstanding shares. Earnings per share should be related to the outstanding common stock after the stock dividend or stock split. In the weighted average common shares illustration, if it is assumed that a 2-for-1 stock split took place on December 31, the denominator of the earnings per share computation becomes 23,300 (11,750 × 2). The denominator of prior years' earnings per share computations would also be doubled.

If we assume that net income is $100,000 and preferred dividends total $10,000 in the illustration, then the earnings per common share would be $3.83 [($100,000 − $10,000)/23,500].

APB Opinion No. 15 recognizes that a corporation may have a more complex capital structure than the illustration—for example, one that includes financial instruments that may add to the common shares outstanding. Examples would be convertible bonds (bonds that may be converted to common stock by the investor), convertible preferred stock (preferred stock that may be converted to common stock by the investor), stock options (options to buy the common stock at a predetermined price; these are frequently given to employees), and warrants (right to buy the common stock at a predetermined price; warrants are frequently given to buyers of bonds).

Each of the financial instruments that may add to the common shares outstanding is a potential common stock equivalent. APB No. 15 defines a common stock equivalent as a security that, although not in the form of common stock, contains provisions that enable its owner to become a common stockholder.

Financial instruments that may add to the common shares outstanding may reduce (dilute) earnings per share. When the potential dilution is considered to be material, a dual presentation of earnings per share must be presented on the face of the income statement. The dual presentation consists of primary earnings per share and fully diluted earnings per share. Primary earnings per share is a figure that includes most, if not all, of the dilutive financial instruments included under the computation rules prescribed in APB Opinion No. 15. Fully diluted earnings per share includes all dilutive financial instruments included under computation rules that are more conservative than the computation rules for primary earnings per share.

The computation rules for primary and fully diluted earnings per share are complex. For detailed explanations of these rules, refer to any intermediate-level accounting book. The general computation of primary and fully diluted earnings per share is explained and illustrated in this section.

The first step in computing the dual earnings per share (both primary and fully diluted) is to compute the simple earnings per share. Then compute the primary earnings per share.

When computing primary earnings per share, we must test to determine whether simple earnings per share decreases when taking into account the potential additional shares from outstanding options, warrants, convertible preferred stock, and convertible bonds. Dilution is considered only when it decreases earnings per share.

Stock options and warrants are included in the computation under a method referred to as the *treasury stock method*. The steps necessary to implement the treasury stock method for primary earnings per share are summarized as follows:

1. Determine the average market price of common stock during the period.
2. Compute the shares issued per the assumed exercise of all options and warrants.
3. Compute the proceeds received from the assumed exercise. (The investor that owns the options and warrants will need to pay the company a designated amount for each option or warrant exercised.)
4. Compute the assumed shares reacquired by dividing the proceeds by the average market price (step 3 ÷ step 1). (If the assumed shares reacquired are greater than the shares to be issued in step 2, then the options or warrants will not be included this year, for to include a decreased number of shares would increase earnings per share. Earnings per share is never increased by a dilution factor.)
5. Compute the incremental shares (step 2 minus step 4).

To illustrate, assume the same factors that were previously assumed for simple earnings per share:

- 10,000 shares of common stock outstanding at the beginning of the year
- July 1: issued 2,000 shares
- October 1: issued 3,000 shares
- December 31: 2-for-1 stock split
- $10,000 in preferred dividends paid the past year
- $100,000 net income

These factors previously resulted in a numerator of $90,000 and a denominator of 23,500 shares. Now assume that the company has options outstanding to purchase 2,000 shares at $10 each. Also assume an average market price on the stock during the year of $16.

Now test to determine if there will be an increase in the shares outstanding if the options are exercised:

Shares assumed issued per exercise: 2,000
Shares assumed reacquired:

$$\frac{\text{Proceeds}}{\text{Average Market Price}} = \frac{2,000 \times \$10}{\$16} = \frac{\$20,000}{\$16} = \underline{1,250}$$

Assumed increment in common shares for
computing primary earnings per share: $\underline{750}$

This assumed increment in common shares is added to the denominator of the earnings per share computation to get primary earnings per share of $3.71 [$90,000/ (23,500 + 750)].

Now let's assume that our illustration also involves convertible bonds in the amount of $50,000, with an interest rate of 10%. These are bonds in denomination of $1,000 each (50 bonds in total). Assume that the bonds were issued for $50,000 and can be converted to 5,000 shares of common stock. The interest paid on these bonds each year is $5,000 ($50,000 × 10% = $5,000). If the company has a 25% tax rate, this interest will have a net cost to the company of $3,750 [$5,000 × (1 − .25)].

To determine if the potential dilution from the convertible bonds should be included in the primary earnings per share computation, we must perform a test that is called the *effective yield test*. This test is performed only once, when the bonds are originally issued. At that point, it is determined whether these particular convertible bonds will be included in the primary earnings per share computation. Either they will be included each year until conversion of the bonds, or they will never be included until conversion of the bonds. When the bonds are converted, the additional shares issued will always be included in the primary earnings per share computation from that date on.

Convertibles that do not meet the effective yield test will later cause an inconsistency in the primary earnings per share in the year of conversion as against the prior year. The prior year's primary earnings per share computation does not consider the potential shares related to the convertible, but the year of conversion will include the new shares in the primary earnings per share computation.

The effective yield test is formulated as follows:

If: Effective Yield at Issuance $< 66\frac{2}{3}\% \times$ Average AA Corporate Bond
                                                                          Yield at Issuance

then the security is a common stock equivalent.

For the convertible bonds illustration, assume that the average AA corporate bond yield at issuance is 16% and the effective yield is 10%. The cash yield test for these is as follows:

$$10\% < 66\tfrac{2}{3}\% \times 16\%$$
$$10\% < 10.67\%$$

For these convertibles, the effective yield test indicates that the convertibles should be included in the primary earnings per share computation. The opinion is that if the effective yield is less than $66\tfrac{2}{3}\%$ of the average AA corporate bond yield at issuance, then the investor gave up substantial interest income that was available in order to buy the convertible bond. The investor paid a substantial amount for the conversion feature, so these convertibles should be included in primary earnings per share by assuming that the convertible is not outstanding but has been converted and the additional stock issued.

The assumption that the convertible bond has been converted increases the numerator in the primary earnings per share computation by the after-tax interest expense and increases the denominator by the shares assumed to have been issued.

Recall that the primary earnings per share was $3.71 ($90,000/$24,250) before considering the convertible. After considering the convertible, the primary earnings per share becomes $3.21 [($90,000 + $3,750)/(24,250 + 5,000)].

The same effective yield test is made for convertible preferred stocks. However, if the effective yield test results in the convertible stock's being included in the primary earnings per share computation, then the preferred dividend is not subtracted from the numerator of the primary earnings per share computation, and the assumed additional shares are added to the denominator. (The assumption is that the convertible preferred stock has been converted to common stock.)

The rules for computing fully diluted earnings per share are similar to those for primary earnings per share, except for the following:

1. For options and warrants, divide by the ending market price of the common stock, if it is higher than the average market price, when performing the treasury stock method. (This will result in the same dilution as for primary earnings per share, or more dilution if the ending market price is higher than the average market price. It can also result in an inconsistency in the computation of fully diluted earnings per share if year-end market price is used in one year and average market price is used in the other year.)

2. For convertibles, there is no effective yield test. The convertibles are always included in the fully diluted earnings per share computation, except when the inclusion increases earnings per share.

In the illustration, we will assume that the ending market price of the stock is below average for the year. Thus, the same dilution computation would be made as was made for primary earnings per share. The convertible has been included in the primary earnings per share computation, so the same dilution has been included in the primary earnings per share computation for the convertible as will be included for the fully diluted earnings per share computation. Thus, in the illustration, the primary and fully diluted earnings per share is $3.21.

Whether the company will disclose the simple earnings per share at the bottom of the income statement, or the dual presentation of primary earnings per share and fully diluted earnings per share, depends on a test referred to as the *3% test*. If fully diluted earnings per share is 3% or more lower than simple earnings per share, then the dual presentation is made. If fully diluted earnings per share is less than 3% lower than the simple earnings per share, then the simple earnings per share is presented.

In the illustration, the dual presentation would be made, because there is more than a 3% difference between the simple earnings per share ($3.83) and the fully diluted earnings per share ($3.21).

For a firm whose stock is traded publicly, the earnings per share computation is disclosed in the company's 10-K annual report to the SEC, which is available to stockholders.

For a complex capital structure, the earnings per share computation is as follows.

Earnings per common share:

$$\text{Primary and Fully Diluted} = \frac{\text{Net Income} - \text{Preferred Dividends*}}{\substack{\text{Weighted Average Number of} \\ \text{Common Shares Outstanding*}}}$$

*The numerator and denominator are subject to further adjustment based on the rules for computing primary and fully diluted earnings per share.

Reporting standards require that earnings per share be reported for earnings before extraordinary income (loss), disposal of segments, and cumulative effect of a change in accounting principle. Reporting standards also require that earnings per share be reported for net income. Usually, a company elects to report earnings per share for extraordinary items, disposal of segments, and cumulative effect of a change in accounting principle. Therefore, it is usually easy to select the earnings per share for recurring items. Recurring earnings per share is the most significant earnings per share figure for primary analysis.

The one problem in determining the recurring earnings per share occurs when the company has an unusual or infrequent item. The effect of an unusual or infrequent item on earnings per share is not currently reported on the face of the income statement. Some companies disclose such an effect on earnings per share in a footnote that describes the item. In these cases, it is an easy matter to determine earnings per share for recurring items. This book recommends that, for primary financial analysis, the following nonrecurring items should be excluded:

1. Unusual or infrequent items
2. Discontinued operations
3. Extraordinary items
4. Cumulative effect of change in accounting principle

E X H I B I T   9 - 3

COOPER TIRE & RUBBER COMPANY
Earnings Per Share
For the Years Ended December 31, 1989, 1988, and 1987

	1989	1988	1987
Net income per share	$2.84	$2.01	$1.51

For the few companies that report an unusual or infrequent item and do not disclose the effect on earnings per share in a footnote, an estimate of its effect per share will need to be made. For the numerator of the earnings per share computation, remove the item, net of tax. Then divide by the denominator of the earnings per share computation.

For companies that provide the 10-K, this computation is relatively easy; the earnings per share computation is disclosed in the 10-K. Therefore, the denominator of the earnings per share computation will be available. For companies that do not provide the 10-K, it is often difficult or impossible to determine the denominator based on the information disclosed in the annual report. For these companies, use the shares outstanding at the end of the year as your estimated denominator. This is a reasonable estimate of the denominator unless the company has issued substantial additional common shares late in the year and/or has substantial dilution.

Earnings per share for Cooper is presented in Exhibit 9-3. From this simple presentation, we can conclude that there is less than a 3% difference between Cooper's simple earnings per share and its fully diluted earnings per share. Nonrecurring items were not present on Cooper's income statement for either 1989 or 1988.

Earnings per share for Utilicorp United is presented in Exhibit 9-4. The Utilicorp United earnings per share is a complex presentation, and we can conclude that there is more than a 3% difference between the company's simple earnings per share and its fully diluted earnings per share.

PRICE/EARNINGS RATIO

The price/earnings ratio, commonly termed P/E, expresses the relationship between the market price of a share of common stock and that stock's current earnings per share. The formula for the P/E ratio is as follows:

$$\text{Price/Earnings Ratio} = \frac{\text{Market Price Per Share}}{\text{Fully Diluted Earnings Per Share*}}$$

*Simple earnings per share if the company has a simple capital structure.

EXHIBIT 9-4

UTILICORP UNITED
Earnings Per Share
For the Years Ended December 31, 1989, 1988, and 1987

	1989	1988	1987
Primary earnings per common share:			
Earnings before cumulative effect of changes in accounting principles	$2.04	$1.98	$1.80
Cumulative effect of accounting changes	—	—	(.16)
Primary earnings per common share	$2.04	$1.98	$1.64
Fully diluted earnings per common share:			
Earnings before cumulative effect of changes in accounting principles	$1.95	$1.88	$1.70
Cumulative effect of accounting changes	—	—	(.14)
Fully diluted earnings per common share	$1.95	$1.88	$1.56

The text has already discussed the use of fully diluted earnings per share. If used in the P/E ratio, fully diluted earnings per share will give a higher price/earnings ratio. This is a conservative computation of the ratio. It is important to be aware that some financial services use primary earnings per share.

Ideally, the price/earnings ratio should be computed using fully diluted earnings per share after excluding nonrecurring earnings per share. This gives an indication of what is being paid for a dollar of recurring earnings. To adjust the P/E ratio for nonrecurring earnings is usually a simple matter, because the earnings per share for nonrecurring items is customarily presented as part of the earnings per share presentation at the bottom of the income statement (see Exhibit 9-4).

Financial services do not adjust the P/E ratio for nonrecurring items. They use simple earnings per share when the company has a simple capital structure, and they use either primary earnings per share or fully diluted earnings per share when the company has a complex capital structure.

The P/E ratio is computed in Exhibit 9-5 for Cooper for 1989 and 1988. The P/E was 11.40 times at the end of 1989 and 11.94 times at the end of 1988. This indicates that the stock has been selling for about 11 times earnings, which is a moderate multiple. It is important to get a perspective on this ratio by comparing the average P/E for the industry and an average for all of the stocks on the New York Stock Exchange.

The price/earnings ratio is seen by investors as a gauge of the future earning power of the firm. Companies with high growth opportunities generally have high price/earnings ratios; firms with low growth tend to have lower price/earnings ratios. However, investors may be wrong in their estimates of growth potential.

E X H I B I T   9 - 5

COOPER TIRE & RUBBER COMPANY
Price/Earnings Ratio
December 31, 1989 and 1988

	1989	1988
Market price per common share (December 31, close) [A]	32⅜	24
Earnings per share [B]	$2.84	$2.01
Price/earnings ratio [A ÷ B]	11.40	11.94

One fundamental of investing is to be wiser than the market. An example would be buying a stock that has a relatively low P/E ratio, when the prospects for the company are much better than what is reflected in the P/E ratio. This has been the case with Cooper since the early 1980s.

Price/earnings ratios do not have any meaning when a firm has abnormally low profits in relation to the asset base, or when a firm has losses. The P/E ratio in these cases would be abnormally high or negative.

Price/earnings ratios are available from many sources. Two of the sources are *The Wall Street Journal* and *Standard and Poor's Industry Surveys*. When using published price/earnings ratios, remember that they are not usually adjusted for nonrecurring items. Also remember that some sources use primary earnings per share, and some use fully diluted earnings per share. For noncomplex capital structures, simple earnings per share is used.

PERCENTAGE OF EARNINGS RETAINED

This ratio, which measures the proportion of current earnings retained for internal growth, is computed as follows:

$$\text{Percentage of Earnings Retained} = \frac{\text{Net Income} - \text{All Dividends}}{\text{Net Income}}$$

Many firms have a policy on the percentage of earnings that they want retained—for example, between 60% and 75%. In general, new firms, growing firms, and firms perceived as growth firms have a relatively high percentage of earnings retained. This ratio is the same as that called *retained earnings to net income* in the *Almanac of Business and Industrial Financial Ratios*. The phrase *retained earnings* as used in the ratio in the *Almanac* is a misnomer; retained earnings in this ratio does not mean accumulated profits, but rather that portion of income retained in a single year. Hence, these two ratios are computed in the same way, although labeled differently.

Using the 1989 and 1988 figures for Cooper, the percentage of earnings retained is computed in Exhibit 9-6. It appears that Cooper tries to maintain a stable and substantial proportion of its profits for internal use. Cooper would be considered a growing firm. It has been adding substantial production capacity.

DIVIDEND PAYOUT

The dividend payout ratio measures the portion of current earnings per common share that is being paid out in dividends. The formula is as follows:

$$\text{Dividend Payout} = \frac{\text{Dividends Per Common Share}}{\text{Fully Diluted Earnings Per Share}^*}$$

*Simple earnings per share if the company has a simple capital structure.

Earnings per share are fully diluted in the formula, because this is the most conservative viewpoint. Ideally, fully diluted earnings per share is before nonrecurring items, since directors normally look at recurring earnings to develop a stable dividend policy. The fully diluted earnings per share before nonrecurring items may not be readily available. When working problems in this book, use the fully diluted earnings per share.

Most firms have an established dividend policy and hesitate to cause fluctuations in dividends on the downward side, since these types of shifts tend to have adverse effects in the market price. There is no rule of thumb for a correct payout ratio. Some stockholders prefer high dividends; others prefer to have the firm reinvest the earnings in hopes of higher capital gains. In the latter case, the payout ratio would be a relatively smaller percentage.

Exhibit 9-7 computes the dividend payout for 1989 and 1988 for Cooper. The dividend payout ratio decreased from 13.93% in 1988 to 12.32% in 1989. These are very conservative payout ratios. It is often true that if a company is going to

EXHIBIT 9-6

COOPER TIRE & RUBBER COMPANY
Percentage of Earnings Retained
For the Years Ended December 31, 1989 and 1988

	1989	1988
Net income [B]	$58,243,880	$41,062,286
Less: Dividends	7,080,479	5,712,039
Earnings retained [A]	$51,163,401	$35,350,247
Percentage of earnings retained	87.84%	86.09%

EXHIBIT 9-7

COOPER TIRE & RUBBER COMPANY
Dividend Payout
For the Years Ended December 31, 1989 and 1988

	1989	1988
Dividends per share [A]	$ .35	$ .28
Earnings per share [B]	$2.84	$2.01
Dividend payout ratio [A ÷ B]	12.32%	13.93%

attract the type of stockholder who looks favorably on a low dividend payout ratio, it must have a record of earning approximately 15% or better in return on common equity.

Industry averages of dividend payout ratios are available in *Standard and Poor's Industry Surveys*. Although there is no correct payment, even within an industry, the outlook for the industry often makes the bulk of the ratios in a particular industry similar.

The percentage of earnings retained and the dividend payout are usually approximately the reciprocal of each other. An exception to this is when the company has a substantial amount of preferred stock. Preferred dividends are included in the percentage of earnings retained ratio.

In general, new firms, growing firms, and firms perceived as growth firms have a relatively low dividend payout. As previously indicated, Cooper would be considered a growing firm.

DIVIDEND YIELD

The dividend yield indicates the relationship between the dividends per common share and the market price per common share. The formula for dividend yield is as follows:

$$\text{Dividend Yield} = \frac{\text{Dividends Per Common Share}}{\text{Market Price Per Common Share}}$$

The dividend yield for Cooper for 1989 and 1988 is computed in Exhibit 9-8. The dividend yield has been steady and low.

Total earnings from securities include both dividends and price appreciation; again, there is no rule of thumb for dividend yield. It depends on the firm's dividend policy and the market price. If the firm successfully invests the money that is not distributed as dividends, the price should rise. If the dividends are held at low amounts to allow for reinvestment of profits, the dividend yield is likely to be low. Many investors are satisfied with a low dividend yield if the company has a record

EXHIBIT 9-8

COOPER TIRE & RUBBER COMPANY
Dividend Yield
December 31, 1989 and 1988

	1989	1988
Dividends per share [A]	$ .35	$ .28
Market price per share [B]	$32⅜	$24.00
Dividend yield [A ÷ B]	1.08%	1.17%

of above-average return on common equity. Investors who want current income prefer a high dividend yield.

BOOK VALUE PER SHARE

A figure frequently published in annual reports is book value per share, which indicates the amount of stockholders' equity that relates to each share of outstanding common stock. The formula for book value per share is as follows:

$$\text{Book Value Per Share} = \frac{\text{Total Stockholders' Equity} - \text{Preferred Stock Equity}}{\text{Number of Common Shares Outstanding}}$$

Preferred stock equity should be stated at liquidation price if other than book value. This is because the preferred shareholders would be paid this value in the event of liquidation. Liquidation value is sometimes difficult to locate in an annual report; if it cannot be found, the book figure that relates to preferred stock may be used in place of liquidation value. Exhibit 9-9 computes the book value per share for Cooper for 1989 and 1988.

EXHIBIT 9-9

COOPER TIRE & RUBBER COMPANY
Book Value Per Share
December 31, 1989 and 1988

	1989	1988
Stockholders' equity	$310,063,660	$257,756,169
Preferred stock (liquidation value)	—	—
Common equity [A]	$310,063,660	$257,756,169
Shares outstanding [B]	20,564,837	20,455,293
Book value per share [A ÷ B]	$15.08	$12.60

Interpretation of Book Value

The market price of the securities usually does not approximate the book value, since assets are recorded at cost. These historical cost dollars reflect past unrecovered cost of the assets. The market value of the stock, however, reflects the potential of the firm as seen by the investor. For example, land is valued at cost, and this asset value is reflected in the book value. If the asset was purchased several years ago and is now worth substantially more, however, the market value of the stock may recognize this potential.

Book value is of limited use to the investment analyst, since it is based on historical costs. When market value is below book value, investors view the company as lacking potential. A market value above book value indicates that investors view the company as having enough potential to be worth more than the unrecovered cost. It should be noted that Cooper was selling above book value.

When investors are pessimistic about the prospects for stocks, many stocks sell below book value. On the other hand, when investors are optimistic about stock prospects, many stocks sell above book value.

STOCK OPTIONS

Corporations frequently provide stock options for employees and officers of the company, allowing them to purchase stock on favorable terms. The objective of a stock option plan is to provide an incentive for these individuals to be more productive. Whether options actually achieve this objective is debatable. A basic understanding of stock option accounting is needed in order to assess the stock option disclosure of a company. There are two types of stock option plans: noncompensatory and compensatory.

A *noncompensatory plan* attempts to raise capital or encourage widespread ownership of the corporation's stock among officers and employees. This type of plan is available to many employees. A noncompensatory plan does not present major problems in financial statement analysis. Because the employees purchase the stock at only a slight discount from the market price, there is not a substantial dilution of the position of existing stockholders.

A *compensatory plan* is available only to select individuals, such as officers of the company. These plans typically provide the potential for purchasing stock at a bargain rate.

Usually, the company records compensation only to the extent that the option price was below market price on the date of grant of the option. Often the option price is the market price on the date of grant, so no compensation is recorded. Thus, many accountants feel that compensation from stock option plans is understated, because the individual usually purchases stock substantially below market at the date of exercise (the date that the options and cash are exchanged for stock).

Stock options do not require a cash outlay to the company issuing them, but they are a form of potential dilution of the interest of stockholders. Extensive use of stock options would be of concern to existing and potential stockholders. Stock options that are exercised improve the short-run liquidity of the firm and its long-term debt position because of the additional funds. Any improvement is almost always small, however, because of the relatively small amount of funds involved.

The potential dilution of the interest of existing stockholders can be material. In analyzing profitability, the materiality of the number of stock options should be considered in relation to the outstanding shares of common stock. This can be done by relating the number of shares of common stock outstanding. Using this to indicate the materiality of options results in the following formula:

$$\text{Materiality of Options} = \frac{\text{Stock Options Outstanding}}{\text{Number of Shares of Common Stock Outstanding}}$$

Ideally, only compensatory stock options should be included in the formula, since these are the options that have the potential for material dilution of the position of existing stockholders. There may be a problem in identifying noncompensatory and compensatory options based on the footnote disclosure. Seldom are the terms *noncompensatory* and *compensatory* used.

The Cooper footnote indicates that the company's stock option plans provide for granting options to key employees. These can likely be described as compensatory options, so all of them are included in our formula. Cooper had 343,757 options outstanding at December 31, 1989, at a price per share in the range of $9.13–$32.25. The market price of the stock at the close of the year was $32⅜.

The materiality of stock options is computed for Cooper in 1989 and 1988 in Exhibit 9-10. In 1989, the materiality of options came out to be 1.67%, as compared to 2.18% in 1988.

The materiality of options is considered insignificant by many investors if it is below 5%. Because of the cash flow to the company when the options are exercised, a materiality of 5% probably represents only 2% to 3% effective dilution.

Other factors related to stock options should be considered. First, the impact of stock options is already included in earnings per share. As the market price of the common shares increases, however, the diluted impact on earnings per share is greater. Further dilution may also have a future negative impact on market potential.

EXHIBIT   9 - 1 0

COOPER TIRE & RUBBER COMPANY
Materiality of Options
December 31, 1989 and 1988

	1989	1988
Options outstanding at December 31 [A]	343,757	446,051
Number of common shares outstanding at December 31 [B]	20,564,837	20,455,293
Materiality of options [A ÷ B]	1.67%	2.18%

STOCK APPRECIATION RIGHTS

Some firms grant key employees stock appreciation rights instead of stock options or in addition to stock options. With stock appreciation rights, the employee is given the right to receive compensation in cash or stock (or a combination of these) at some future date. This is based on the difference between market price of the stock at the date of exercise and a preestablished price.

The accounting for stock appreciation rights comes under FASB Interpretation No. 28, which directs that the compensation expense recognized each period be based on the difference between the quoted market value at the end of each period and the option price. This compensation expense is then reduced by previously recognized compensation expense on the stock appreciation right. For example, assume that the option price is $10.00 and the market value is $15.00 at the end of the first period of the stock appreciation right. Compensation expense would be recognized at $5.00 ($15.00 − $10.00) per share that is included in the plan. If 100,000 shares are in the plan, the expense to be charged to the income statement would be $500,000 ($5.00 × 100,000 shares). If the market value is $12.00 at the end of the second period of the stock appreciation right, there is a credit to income of $3.00 per share. This is because the total compensation expense for the two years is $2.00 ($12.00 − $10.00). Since $5.00 of expense was recognized in the first year, $3.00 of compensation must be credited in the second year in order to total $2.00 of expense. With 100,000 shares, the credit to income in the second year would be $300,000 ($3.00 × 100,000 shares). Thus, stock appreciation rights can have a material influence on income that is dictated by stock prices.

If a company has outstanding stock appreciation rights, they are described in a footnote to the financial statements. If the number of shares involved is known, a possible future influence on income can be computed based on assumptions made regarding future market prices. For example, if the footnote discloses that the firm has 50,000 shares of stock appreciation rights outstanding, and the stock market price was $10.00 at the end of the year, the analyst can assume a market price at the end of next year and compute the compensation expense for next year. With these facts and an assumed market price of $15.00 at the end of next year, the compensation expense for next year can be computed to be $250,000 [($15.00 − $10.00) × 50,000 shares]. This potential charge to earnings should be considered as the stock is evaluated as a potential investment.

Because stock appreciation rights are tied to the future market price of the stock, they can be practically an unlimited drain on the company. Even a relatively small number of stock appreciation rights outstanding could be considered material. This should be considered by existing and potential stockholders. Some firms have placed limits on the potential appreciation in order to control the cost of appreciation rights.

Cooper has stock options that include stock appreciation rights, but the company has limited its exposure. The Cooper footnote states, "The maximum amount of appreciation on each option share to which the optionee shall be entitled during each year of the option period is limited to 25% of the option exercise price on a cumulative basis." The Cooper footnote is not clear as to the number of appreciation rights outstanding. It does disclose that options granted prior to 1987 include stock appreciation rights.

SUMMARY

This chapter has reviewed certain types of analysis that are of particular concern to investors. The following ratios are particularly relevant to investors:

Degree of Financial Leverage

$$\text{Common Formula} = \frac{\text{Earnings before Interest and Tax}}{\text{Earnings before Tax}}$$

$$\text{All-Inclusive Formula} = \frac{\begin{array}{c}\text{Earnings before Interest, Tax,}\\ \text{Minority Share of Earnings,}\\ \text{Equity Income, and Nonrecurring Items}\end{array}}{\begin{array}{c}\text{Earnings before Tax,}\\ \text{Minority Share of Earnings,}\\ \text{Equity Income, and Nonrecurring Items}\end{array}}$$

Earnings Per Share

$$\text{Simple} = \frac{\text{Net Income} - \text{Preferred Dividends}}{\begin{array}{c}\text{Weighted Average Number of}\\ \text{Common Shares Outstanding}\end{array}}$$

Complex

$$\text{Primary and Fully Diluted} = \frac{\text{Net Income} - \text{Preferred Dividends*}}{\begin{array}{c}\text{Weighted Average Number of}\\ \text{Common Shares Outstanding*}\end{array}}$$

*The numerator and denominator are subject to further adjustment based on the rules for computing primary and fully diluted earnings per share.

$$\text{Price/Earnings Ratio} = \frac{\text{Market Price Per Share}}{\text{Fully Diluted Earnings Per Share*}}$$

*Simple earnings per share if the company has a simple capital structure.

$$\text{Percentage of Earnings Retained} = \frac{\text{Net Income} - \text{All Dividends}}{\text{Net Income}}$$

$$\text{Dividend Payout} = \frac{\text{Dividends Per Common Share}}{\text{Fully Diluted Earnings Per Common Share*}}$$

*Simple earnings per share if the company has a simple capital structure.

$$\text{Dividend Yield} = \frac{\text{Dividends Per Common Share}}{\text{Market Price Per Common Share}}$$

$$\text{Book Value Per Share} = \frac{\text{Total Stockholders' Equity} - \text{Preferred Stock Equity}}{\text{Number of Common Shares Outstanding}}$$

$$\text{Materiality of Options} = \frac{\text{Stock Options Outstanding}}{\text{Number of Shares of Common Stock Outstanding}}$$

QUESTIONS

Q 9-1   Give a simple definition of earnings per share.

Q 9-2   Assume that (a) a corporation does not have debt or equity securities that trade in a public market on a foreign or domestic stock exchange or in the over-the-counter market, and (b) the corporation is not required to file financial statements with the Securities and Exchange Commission. Comment on the requirement for this firm to disclose earnings per share.

Q 9-3   Keller & Fink is a partnership that engages in the wholesale fish market. How would this company disclose earnings per share?

Q 9-4   Dividends on preferred stock total $5,000 for the current year. How would these dividends influence earnings per share?

Q 9-5   The denominator of the earnings per share computation includes the weighted average number of common shares outstanding. Why is the weighted average used instead of the year-end common shares outstanding?

Q 9-6

	Current Year	Prior Year
Primary earnings per share	$1.95	$2.00
Fully diluted earnings per share	$1.93	$1.90

There were no common stock equivalents in either the current year or the prior year, except for convertibles in the prior year.
a. Does it appear that earnings per share improved from the prior year?
b. Explain the inconsistency in the trend of primary earnings per share and fully diluted earnings per share.
c. Should primary earnings per share or fully diluted earnings per share be used in primary financial analysis? Why?

Q 9-7   a. Explain how an increase in the average market price, over the average for the prior year, could have a negative influence on primary earnings per share.
b. Explain how an increase in the year-end market price, over the prior year's year-end market price, could have a negative influence on fully diluted earnings per share.
c. Assume that in the prior year, the year-end market price was very high in relation to the average market price. Assume that in the current year, the year-end market price was very low in relation to the average market price. In both years, there are substantial common stock equivalents that are not the result of convertibles. Explain the inconsistency that

this situation causes in the fully diluted earnings per share but not the primary earnings per share.

Q 9-8   Preferred dividends decreased this year because some preferred stock was retired. How would this influence the earnings per share computation this year?

Q 9-9   Retroactive recognition is given to stock dividends and stock splits on common stock when computing earnings per share. Why?

Q 9-10 Differentiate between a simple capital structure and a complex capital structure in terms of earnings per share.

Q 9-11 How does the 3% test influence whether a firm reports simple earnings per share or makes a dual presentation of primary and fully diluted earnings per share?

Q 9-12 Why do many firms try to maintain a stable percentage of earnings retained ratio?

Q 9-13 Define financial leverage. What is its effect on earnings? When is the use of financial leverage advantageous? When is its use disadvantageous?

Q 9-14 Given a set level of earnings before interest and tax, how will a rise in interest rates affect the degree of financial leverage?

Q 9-15 Why is the price/earnings ratio considered a gauge of future earning power?

Q 9-16 Why does a relatively new firm often have a low dividend payout ratio? Why does a firm with a substantial growth record and/or substantial growth prospects often have a low dividend payout ratio?

Q 9-17 Why would an investor ever buy stock in a firm with a low dividend yield?

Q 9-18 Why is book value often meaningless? What improvements to financial statements would make it more meaningful?

Q 9-19 Why should an investor read the footnote concerning stock options? How might stock options affect profitability?

Q 9-20 Why can a relatively small number of stock appreciation rights prove to be a material drain on future earnings and cash of a company?

Q 9-21 Explain how outstanding stock appreciation rights could increase reported income in a particular year.

PROBLEMS

P 9-1   The McDonald Company shows the following condensed income statement information for the current year:

Revenue from sales	$3,500,000
Cost of products sold	1,700,000
Gross profit	1,800,000

Operating expenses:		
Selling expenses	$425,000	
General expenses	350,000	$ 775,000
Operating income		1,025,000
Other income		20,000
Interest		(70,000)
Operating income before income taxes		975,000
Taxes related to operations		335,000
Income from operations		640,000
Extraordinary loss (less applicable income taxes of $40,000)		80,000
Income before minority interest		560,000
Minority share of earnings		50,000
Net income		$ 510,000

Required   Calculate the degree of financial leverage.

P 9-2   A firm has earnings before interest and tax of $1,000,000, interest of $200,000, and net income of $400,000 in year 1.

Required   a. Calculate the degree of financial leverage in base year 1.
  b. If earnings before interest and tax increase by 10% in year 2, what will be the new level of earnings, assuming the same tax rate as in year 1?
  c. If earnings before interest and tax decrease to $800,000 in year 2, what will be the new level of earnings, assuming the same tax rate as in year 1?

P 9-3   The following information was in the annual report of the Rover Company:

	1990	1989	1988
Earnings per share:			
Primary	$1.20	$1.29	$1.35
Fully diluted	$1.12	$1.20	$1.27
Cash dividends per share (common)	$.90	$.85	$.82
Market price per share	$12.80	$14.00	$16.30
Total common dividends	$21,700,000	$19,500,000	$18,360,000
Shares outstanding end of year	24,280,000	23,100,000	22,500,000
Total assets	$1,280,100,000	$1,267,200,000	$1,260,400,000
Total liabilities	$ 800,400,000	$ 808,500,000	$ 799,200,000
Nonredeemable preferred stock	$ 15,300,000	$ 15,300,000	$ 15,300,000
Preferred dividends	$ 910,000	$ 910,000	$ 910,000
Net income	$ 31,200,000	$ 30,600,000	$ 29,800,000

Required   a. Based on these data, compute the following ratios for 1990, 1989, and 1988:
    1. percentage of earnings retained

2. price/earnings ratio
3. dividend payout
4. dividend yield
5. book value per share
b. Discuss your findings from the viewpoint of a potential investor.

P 9-4   The following data relate to the Edger Company:

	1990	1989	1988
Earnings per share	$ 2.30	$ 3.40	$ 4.54
Dividends per share	$ 1.90	$ 1.90	$ 1.90
Market price end of year	$41.25	$35.00	$29.00
Net income	$9,100,000	$13,300,000	$16,500,000
Total cash dividends	$6,080,000	$ 5,900,000	$ 6,050,000
Order backlog at year end	$5,490,800,000	$4,150,200,000	$3,700,100,000
Net contracts awarded	$2,650,700,000	$1,800,450,000	$3,700,100,000

Note: The stock was selling at 120.5%, 108.0%, and 105.0% of book value in 1990, 1989, and 1988, respectively.

Required   a. Compute the following ratios for 1990, 1989, and 1988:
1. percentage of earnings retained
2. price/earnings ratio
3. dividend payout
4. dividend yield
5. book value per share
b. Comment on your results from (a). Include in your discussion the data on backlog and new contracts awarded.

P 9-5   Dicker Company has the following pattern of financial data for years one and two.

	Years	
	One	Two
Net income	$ 40,000	$ 42,000
Preferred stock (5%)	450,000	550,000
Common shares	38,000	38,500

Required   Calculate simple earnings per share and comment on the trend.

P 9-6   Assume the following facts for the current year:

Common shares outstanding on January 1: 50,000 shares
July 1: 2-for-1 stock split
October 1: a stock issue of 10,000 shares

Required   Compute the denominator of the earnings per share computation for the current year.

P 9-7   The XYZ Corporation reported earnings per share of $2.00 in 1989. In 1990, the XYZ Corporation reported earnings per share of $1.50. Two-for-one stock splits were declared on July 1, 1990, and December 31, 1990.

Required Present the earnings per share for a two-year comparative income statement that includes 1990 and 1989.

P 9-8 The Cook Company shows the following condensed income statement information for the year ended December 31, 1990:

Income before extraordinary gain	$30,000
Plus: Extraordinary gain, net of tax	
expense of $2,000	5,000
Net income	$35,000

The company declared dividends of $3,000 on preferred stock and $5,000 on common stock. At the beginning of 1990, 20,000 shares of common stock were outstanding. On July 1, 1990, the company issued 1,000 additional common shares. The preferred stock is not convertible.

Required a. Compute the earnings per share.
    b. How much of the earnings per share appears to be recurring?

P 9-9 Assume the following facts for the current year:

Net income	$200,000
Common dividends	$ 20,000
Preferred dividends (The preferred stock is	
not convertible.)	$ 10,000
Common shares outstanding on January 1	20,000 shares
Common stock issued on July 1	5,000 shares
Two-for-one stock split on December 31	

Required a. Compute the earnings per share for the current year.
    b. Use the assumptions to compute earnings per share, except that the preferred stock is convertible into 2,000 shares of common stock, prior to the 2-for-1 stock split.
    c. Earnings per share in the prior year was $8.00. Use the earnings per share computed in part (a) and present a two-year earnings per share comparison for the current year and the prior year.

P 9-10 Assume the following facts for the current year:

- 12,000 shares of common stock outstanding at the beginning of the year
- October 1: issued 6,000 shares of common stock
- December 31: 2-for-1 stock split
- $6,000 in preferred dividends paid during the past year
- $80,000 net income
- Options outstanding to purchase 4,000 shares of common stock at $12.00 each
- Average market price on common stock during the past year of $15.00
- Year-end market price on common stock: $18.00

Required a. Compute the earnings per share assuming a simple capital structure.
    b. Compute the earnings per share assuming a complex capital structure.
    c. Which earnings per share should be presented with the income statement? Why?

P 9-11   Smith and Jones, Inc., is primarily engaged in the worldwide production, processing, distribution, and marketing of food products. The following information is extracted from its 1990 annual report.

	1990	1989
Earnings per share		
Primary	$1.12	$1.19
Fully diluted	1.08	1.14
Cash dividends per share (common)	.80	.76
Market price per share	12.94	15.19
Shares outstanding	25,380,000	25,316,000
Total assets	$1,264,086,000	$1,173,924,000
Total liabilities	823,758,000	742,499,000
Nonredeemable preferred stock	16,600,000	16,600,000
Preferred dividends	4,567,000	930,000
Net income	32,094,000	31,049,000

Required   a. Based on these data, compute the following:
    1. percentage of earnings retained   4. dividend yield
    2. price/earnings ratio   5. book value per share
    3. dividend payout
  b. Discuss your findings from the viewpoint of a potential investor.

P 9-12   On December 31, 1990, Farley Camera, Inc., issues 5,000 stock appreciation rights to its president to entitle her to receive cash for the difference between the market price of its stock and a preestablished price of $20.00. The date of exercise is December 31, 1993, and the required service period is the entire three years. The market price fluctuates as follows: 12/31/91—$23.00; 12/31/92—$21.00; 12/31/93—$26.00.

Based on FASB Interpretation No. 28 issued in 1978, Farley Camera accrued the following compensation expense:

1991	$15,000
1992	($10,000)
1993	$25,000

Required   a. What is the executive's main advantage of receiving stock appreciation rights over stock options?
  b. In 1991, a $15,000 expense is recorded. What is the offsetting account?
  c. What is the financial impact on the company of the exercise of the stock appreciation rights in 1993? How does this impact affect financial statement analysis?

P 9-13a   A company has only common stock outstanding.

Required   Answer the following multiple-choice question. Total shareholders' equity divided by the number of shares outstanding represents the
    1. return on equity   3. book value per share
    2. stated value per share   4. price/earnings ratio

P 9-13b   Maple Corporation's stockholders' equity at June 30, 1990, consisted of the following:

Preferred stock, 10%, $50 par value; liquidating value $55 per share; 20,000 shares issued and outstanding	$1,000,000
Common stock, $10 par value; 500,000 shares authorized; 150,000 shares issued and outstanding	1,500,000
Retained earnings	500,000

Required   Answer the following multiple-choice question. The book value per share of common stock is:

1. $10.00   3. $13.33
2. $12.67   4. $17.65

P 9-13c   Selected information for Irvington Company is as follows:

	December 31	
	1990	**1989**
Preferred stock, 8%, par $100, nonconvertible, noncumulative	$125,000	$125,000
Common stock	400,000	300,000
Retained earnings	185,000	75,000
Dividends paid on preferred stock for year ended	10,000	10,000
Net income for year ended	120,000	60,000

Required   Answer the following multiple-choice question. Irvington's return on common stockholders' equity for 1990, rounded to the nearest percentage point, is:

1. 17%   3. 23%
2. 19%   4. 25%

P 9-13d   The following common size income statements are available for Sparky Corporation for the two years ended December 31, 1990 and 1989.

	1990	1989
Sales	100%	100%
Cost of sales	55	70
Gross profit on sales	45	30
Operating expenses (including income tax expense)	20	18
Net income	25%	12%

The trend percentages for sales are as follows:

1990	130%
1989	100%

Required   Answer the following multiple-choice question. What should be the trend percentage for gross profit on sales for 1990?

1. 58.5%   3. 150.0%
2. 130.0%   4. 195.0%

P 9-14

THE WRESTLING FEDERATION OF AMERICA, INC.
Capital Structure and Earnings for the Year 1987

Number of common shares outstanding on December 31, 1987	2,700,000
Number of common shares outstanding during 1987 (weighted average)	2,500,000
Market price per common share on December 31, 1987	$ 25
Weighted average market price per common share during 1987	$ 20
Options outstanding during 1987:	
Number of shares issuable on exercise of options	200,000
Exercise price	$ 15
Convertible bonds outstanding (December 1983 issue):	
Number	10,000
Shares of common issuable on conversion (per bond)	10
Coupon rate	5.0%
Proceeds per bond at issue (= par value)	$ 1,000
Average Aa corporate bond yield at time of issue	8.5%
Net income for 1987	$6,500,000
Tax rate	40.0%

Required   Answer the following questions that relate to earnings per share.

  a. Primary earnings per share for 1987 were:
    1. $2.45
    2. $2.57
    3. $2.62
    4. none of the above
  b. Fully diluted earnings per share for 1987 were:
    1. $2.43
    2. $2.48
    3. $2.54
    4. none of the above

CFA Adapted
June 1988

CASES

Case 9-1   STOCK SPLIT

The May Department Stores Company and subsidiaries reported the following in its 1983 annual report:

	1983	1982	1981
Net earnings	$187,000,000	$141,700,000	$126,200,000
Net earnings per common share	$6.48	$4.87	$4.31
Dividend per common share	$1.95½	$1.79	$1.66

The May Department Stores Company and subsidiaries reported the following in its 1984 annual report:

	1984	1983	1982
Net earnings	$214,100,000	$187,000,000	$141,700,000
Net earnings per common share	$4.96	$4.32	$3.25

Note: There was a 3-for-2 stock split effective October 3, 1984.

The following footnote was in the 1984 annual report:

Common Stock Dividends and Market Prices

During fiscal 1984, the company increased its annual dividend rate twice. Effective with the June 15, 1984, dividend payment, the annual dividend rate was increased 20% to $1.60 per share (40¢ quarterly) from $1.33⅓ per share (33⅓¢ quarterly). Following the September 1984 shareholders meeting, the company raised its annual dividend rate a second time to $1.72 per share (43¢ quarterly), a 7.5% increase from the adjusted pre-split rate and a 29.0% increase from the beginning of the year, effective with the December 15, 1984, dividend payment.

Representing the eleventh dividend increase in ten years, the company has raised its annual dividend rate, effective with the June 15, 1985, payment, to $1.88 per share or 47¢ quarterly, a 9.3% increase and a 17.5% increase from a year ago. The company has paid consecutive quarterly dividends since December 1, 1911.

The quarterly price ranges of the common stock and dividends per share in fiscal 1984 and 1983 were:

	1984 Market Prices		Dividends	1983 Market Prices		Dividends
Quarter	High	Low	Per Share	High	Low	Per Share
First	$34¹/₁₂	$30¹/₁₂	$ .33⅓	$39¼	$29⅔	$ .30⅓
Second	39	32¼	.40	42	35⅙	.33⅓
Third	42½	36¾	.40	40¼	30⅚	.33⅓
Fourth	48⅜	37½	.43	37¹/₁₂	33⁷/₁₂	.33⅓
Year	$48⅜	$30¹/₁₂	$1.56⅓	$42	$29⅔	$1.30⅓

The approximate number of common shareholders as of March 1, 1985, was 36,500.

Required

a. What caused the change in reported earnings per share in 1983 from $6.48 to $4.32?

b. The 1983 annual report reported dividends per common share of $1.95½ for 1983. The 1984 annual report reported dividends per common share of $1.56⅓. Did dividends per common share decrease between 1983 and 1984? Explain.

c. Speculate on reasons for the stock split.

d. How will the book value per share be affected by the stock split?

e. Compute the price/earnings ratio for 1984 and 1983. Use the fourth quarter high in market price.

f. Compute the dividend payout for 1983 and 1984.

g. Compute the dividend yield for 1983 and 1984. Use the fourth quarter high in market price.

Case 9-2   OPTIONS, OPTIONS, OPTIONS

The Hannaford Bros. Co. included the following in its 1986 annual report.

HANNAFORD BROS. CO. AND SUBSIDIARIES
Consolidated Statements of Earnings

	1986	1985	1984
Net sales and other revenues	$898,982,239	$807,018,980	$707,282,486
Expenses:			
Cost of goods sold	669,817,639	610,667,124	539,271,978
Selling, general, and administrative	184,902,165	161,340,672	141,207,454
Interest (note 1G)	5,397,616	6,873,043	4,798,757
	860,117,420	778,880,839	685,278,189
Earnings before income taxes and minority interest	38,864,819	28,138,141	22,004,297
Income taxes (note 9)	19,386,420	12,811,997	9,570,052
Earnings before minority interest	19,478,399	15,326,144	12,434,245
Minority interest	661,495	926,842	1,087,567
Net earnings	$ 18,816,904	$ 14,399,302	$ 11,346,678
Per share of common stock:			
Net earnings	$ 2.05	$ 1.74	$ 1.42
Cash dividends	$ .500	$ .477	$ .389
Weighted average number of common shares outstanding	9,179,143	8,294,541	7,994,376
Shareholders' equity (notes 6 and 8):			
Preferred stock, no par		—	—
Common stock, par value $.75 per share: Issued and outstanding 9,216,603 shares at January 3, 1987 and 9,143,249 shares at December 28, 1985		6,912,452	6,857,437
Additional paid-in capital		43,688,994	42,675,656
Retained earnings		69,199,373	54,975,679
Total shareholders' equity		119,800,819	104,508,772
		$253,592,068	$219,920,564

8. Employee Stock Plans

The 1982 Incentive Stock Option Plan provides that options may be granted with an exercise price not less than 100% of fair market value at the date of grant.

Options for 50% of any grant are exercisable after one year and the remainder after two years. All options expire seven years from the date of grant. All amounts have been adjusted for a three-for-two stock split effected as a 50% stock dividend distributed February 26, 1985 and a three-for-two stock split effected as a 50% stock dividend distributed August 30, 1985. Option activity for the fiscal years ended January 3, 1987 and December 28, 1985 was as follows:

	1986		1985	
	Shares	**Option Price**	**Shares**	**Option Price**
Outstanding at beginning of year	118,715	$5.31–$12.00	187,771	$5.31–$12.00
Granted	none		none	
Exercised	(51,883)	$5.31–$12.00	(59,374)	$5.31–$12.00
Cancelled	(338)		(9,682)	
Outstanding at end of year	66,494	$5.31–$12.00	118,715	$5.31–$12.00
Exercisable at end of year	66,494	$5.31–$12.00	75,787	$5.31–$12.00
Available for future grants	47,147		46,809	

The 1985 Incentive Stock Option Plan provides that options may be granted with an exercise price not less than 100% of fair market value at the date of grant. Options for 50% of any grant are exercisable after one year and the remainder after two years. All options expire seven years from the date of grant. Option activity for the fiscal years ended January 3, 1987 and December 28, 1985 was as follows:

	1986		1985	
	Shares	**Option Price**	**Shares**	**Option Price**
Outstanding at beginning of year	43,801	$23.13–$23.25	none	
Granted	37,475	$36.88	43,801	$23.13–$23.25
Exercised	(2,625)	$23.13–$23.25	none	
Cancelled	(350)	$23.25	none	
Outstanding at end of year	78,301	$23.13–$36.88	43,801	$23.13–$23.25
Exercisable at end of year	19,100	$23.25	none	
Available for future grants	189,074		226,199	

The 1982 Employee Stock Purchase Plan provides for amounts to be withheld from the pay of participating employees. These amounts may be used to purchase shares of Company stock at the option price (90% of the fair market value at the date of grant). Any options not exercised by specified date expire. All amounts have been adjusted for a three-for-two stock split effected as a 50% stock dividend distributed February 26, 1985, and a three-for-two stock split effected as a 50% stock dividend distributed August 30, 1985. Although there are shares available for future grants under this plan, none are contemplated. Option activity for the fiscal years ended January 3, 1987, and December 28, 1985 was as follows:

	1986		1985	
	Shares	**Option Price**	**Shares**	**Option Price**
Outstanding at beginning of year	none		130,510	$11.20
Granted	none		none	
Exercised	none		(64,595)	$11.20
Expired	none		(65,912)	
Outstanding at end of year	none		none	
Exercisable at end of year	none		none	
Available for future grants	65,912		65,912	

Market Price and Dividends

The following table sets forth, for the calendar periods indicated, the high and low sales prices of the common stock on the New York and American Stock Exchange composite tapes, as adjusted to give effect to a three-for-two stock split in the form of a 50% stock dividend distributed on February 26, 1985 and a three-for-two stock split in the form of a 50% stock dividend distributed on August 30, 1985. The common stock was listed on the New York Stock Exchange on July 18, 1986.

	High	**Low**
1985		
January 1–March 31	$18.000	$14.222
April 1–June 30	20.083	17.333
July 1–September 30	27.250	19.750
October 1–December 31	28.125	21.875
1986		
January 1–March 31	$28.875	$24.500
April 1–June 30	37.375	26.250
July 1–September 30	40.500	31.625
October 1–December 31	35.250	32.250

There are approximately 2,925 record holders of the common stock. 1986 was the thirty-eighth consecutive year that dividends were paid on the common stock and the twenty-fourth consecutive year that the aggregate dividend paid per share (after adjusting for stock splits) has increased. Future dividends will depend on the Company's earnings and financial condition.

Required

a. Describe the potential in net earnings that is related to the employee stock plans.

b. Has the potential dilution in net earnings per share of common stock, from outstanding options, been considered for 1986?

c. Is there a potential for employees to receive substantial economic benefits from options they are holding at the end of 1986?

d. Do the number of the options outstanding appear to be material at the end of 1986?

e. In your opinion, would these options outstanding be a major consideration to a potential investor?

Case 9-3   OPTIONS AND APPRECIATION

Trinova included the following note in its 1986 annual report.

7. Capital Stock and Employee Stock Options

The Company has 4,000,000 shares of serial preferred stock authorized for issuance of which 873,208 and 996,558 shares of $4.75 Cumulative Convertible Preferred Stock—Series A were outstanding at December 31, 1986 and 1985, respectively (aggregate liquidation and redemption value at December 31, 1986—$87,320,800). Each share of outstanding preferred stock is entitled to one vote and is convertible into two and one-quarter shares of common stock. On January 22, 1987, the Board of Directors called for redemption on March 2, 1987, all issued and outstanding shares of the Company's $4.75 Cumulative Convertible Preferred Stock for the redemption price of $100 per share plus the 1987 first-quarter dividend. At December 31, 1986, 1,964,718 shares of unissued common stock were reserved for conversion of the preferred stock until expiration of the conversion period on February 25, 1987.

There are 40,000,000 shares of $5 par value common stock authorized for issuance. At December 31, 1986 and 1985, there were 15,118,857 and 20,744,888 shares of common stock outstanding, respectively, and no shares in treasury.

On October 23, 1986, the Board of Directors declared a three-for-two split of the Company's $5 par value common stock in the form of a 50 percent stock dividend, distributed on December 1, 1986 to shareholders of record on November 14, 1986.

On August 26, 1985, the Company sold 3,750,000 shares of $5 par value common stock in a public offering. The net proceeds totaling $115,248,000 were used to reduce outstanding short-term debt. Outstanding short-term debt during 1985 varied from $39,968,000 to amounts in excess of $115,248,000 through August 26, 1985. If the net proceeds had been used to reduce short-term debt outstanding or invested when short-term debt balances were less than $115,248,000 during this period and the 3,750,000 shares had been outstanding at January 1, 1985, pro forma income per share of common stock from continuing operations would have been $2.59 for the year ended December 31, 1985.

The 1982 Stock Option Plan provides for the Board of Directors to grant options, with or without stock appreciation rights, to key employees to purchase up to 750,000 shares of common stock plus any of the shares subject to options outstanding as of January 1, 1982 under the 1975 Plan which were not exercised. Options are granted at prices not less than the fair market value at the date of grant, become exercisable after one year, expire 10 years after date of grant and may be exercised without limitation as to number in any one year. Options are subject to adjustment upon the occurrence of certain events, including stock splits and stock dividends.

Holders of options with stock appreciation rights may, in lieu of exercising stock options, receive payment in an amount not exceeding 100 percent of the difference between the option price and the fair market value of optioned shares. Payment may be in the form of cash and/or common shares, according to the

terms of the right. Stock options surrendered upon the exercise of stock appreciation rights will not be available for the grant of additional options under the 1982
Plan.

At December 31, 1986, options were outstanding with expiration dates ranging to April 27, 1996, to purchase 334,872 shares of common stock at a
weighted-average exercise price of $38.57 per share.

	1986		1985	
	Option Shares	Range of Option Prices	Option Shares	Range of Option Prices
Stock options				
Outstanding at January 1	338,291	$15.58 to $33.92	277,061	$14.75 to $29.92
Granted	240,301	31.92 to 53.17	119,100	29.75 to 33.92
Exercised	(219,203)	15.58 to 33.92	(51,795)	14.75 to 28.33
Expired or cancelled	(24,517)	15.58 to 33.92	(6,075)	15.58 to 33.92
Outstanding at December 31	334,872	15.58 to 53.17	338,291	15.58 to 33.92
Exercisable at December 31	95,996	15.58 to 33.92	221,441	15.58 to 29.92
Available for future grant at December 31	177,150		408,398	
Stock appreciation rights				
Outstanding at January 1	92,682	$15.58 to $33.92	64,512	$14.75 to $29.92
Granted	127,620	31.92 to 53.17	35,520	29.75 to 33.92
Exercised	(15,465)	20.42 to 33.92	—	—
Cancelled	(42,103)	20.42 to 33.92	(7,350)	14.75 to 28.33
Outstanding at December 31	162,734	15.58 to 53.17	92,682	15.58 to 33.92

Quarterly Stock Information

	1986			1985		
Quarter Ended	High	Low	Close	High	Low	Close
Common						
March 31	50.75	31	49.92	33.92	28.42	30.50
June 30	54.17	48	48.67	31.83	28.83	30.50
September 30	50.33	42.33	44.50	33.33	29.83	31.08
December 31	51.17	44.33	47.13	33.42	28.25	32.83
Preferred						
March 31	113	76.50	112	79.50	69	74
June 30	121.50	106	106	75	68.50	72.25

Quarter Ended	1986			1985		
	High	Low	Close	High	Low	Close
September 30	112.50	96	99.50	78.13	72	76.25
December 31	115	101.75	107	80	72	79.25

	1986	1985	1984
Income per share of common stock			
Primary			
Continuing operations	$ 1.87	$ 2.74	$ 3.20
Discontinued operations	5.09	1.07	.68
Primary net income per share	$ 6.96	$ 3.81	$ 3.88
Fully diluted			
Continuing operations	$ 1.90	$ 2.67	$ 3.07
Discontinued operations	4.53	.95	.60
Fully diluted net income per share	$ 6.43	$ 3.62	3.67
Average number of common shares	16,973	18,356	16,969

Required

a. Determine the maximum cash payment related to the outstanding stock appreciation rights at December 31, 1986.

b. Do the number of options outstanding at December 31, 1986, and stock appreciation rights outstanding at December 31, 1986, appear to be material?

c. Has compensation related to option shares and stock appreciation rights been recognized in the 1986 income statement?

d. For the options outstanding, has the potential dilution in earnings per common share been considered?

Case 9-4   THE COMPLEXITIES OF EARNINGS PER SHARE

In its third quarter report to shareholders, Dresser Industries presented the accompanying data related to earnings per share.

Note: This firm's fiscal year ends on October 31. Usage of a year such as 1975 refers to fiscal year ended October 31, 1975. Assume that the conversion occurred in September of 1975 (third quarter of calendar year 1975).

DRESSER INDUSTRIES, INC. AND SUBSIDIARIES
Consolidated Statements of Earnings

In millions except per share data	Three Months Ended July 31,		Nine Months Ended July 31,	
	1976(1)	1975(1)	1976(1)	1975(1)
Net earnings	$ 38.2	$ 30.1	$103.5	$ 80.8
Net earnings available to common shareholders	$ 38.2	$ 28.2	$103.5	$ 73.7

Consolidated Statements of Earnings   (continued)

In millions except per share data	Three Months Ended July 31,		Nine Months Ended July 31,	
	1976(1)	1975(1)	1976(1)	1975(1)
Average common shares outstanding (2) and (3)	38.8	27.5	37.0	26.0
Average fully diluted shares (2), (3) and (4)	38.8	34.8	37.0	34.8
Earnings per share: Primary (2)	$ .98	$ 1.02	$ 2.80	$ 2.84
Fully diluted (2), (3) and (4)	$ .98	$ .86	$ 2.80	$ 2.32

(1) Because the inventory determination under the LIFO method can only be made at the end of each fiscal year based on the inventory levels and costs at that point, interim LIFO determinations must necessarily be based on management's estimates of expected year-end inventory levels and costs. Since future estimates of inventory levels and prices are subject to many forces beyond the control of management, interim financial results are subject to final year-end LIFO inventory amounts.

(2) Earnings per share and share data have been adjusted to reflect the June 1, 1976 two-for-one stock split.

(3) On March 2, 1976, the Company sold 2,000,000 shares of common stock.

(4) Assumes in 1975 that convertible preferred shares were converted and that outstanding options were exercised and the proceeds used to purchase common shares. All preferred shares were converted or redeemed during the third quarter of 1975. Had these conversions and redemptions taken place as of November 1, 1974, the primary earnings per share for 1975 would have been essentially the same as reported fully diluted earnings per share. Thus, this is the only meaningful per share comparison.

These are interim unaudited statements.

Required

a. Footnote (2) indicates that the earnings per share has been adjusted for the stock split. How were the nine months ended July 31, 1975, earnings originally reported?

b. Footnote (3) indicates a stock sale on March 2, 1976. With reference to the three months ended July 31, explain the rise in average shares from 27.5 to 38.8 for primary and from 34.8 to 38.8 for fully diluted.

c. In the periods ending in 1975, the net earnings and net earnings to common shareholders are different. Why? Why is there no difference in the periods ending in 1976?

d. Explain the difference between primary and fully diluted earnings per share in the periods ending in 1975.

e. Why are 1976 primary and fully diluted earnings per share the same? Based on the information given, what must have been true about the stated dividend rate on the preferred in relation to the prime interest rate at the time that it was issued?

f. Why does footnote (4) state that fully diluted earnings per share is the only meaningful comparison?

g. Assuming that only one-half of the convertible preferred shares were converted in 1975, would the company have indicated that fully diluted earnings was the only meaningful comparison?

Case 9-5   WOULD YOU REALIZE THE SIGNIFICANCE?

The following is part of a news release dated April 25, 1979, and issued by Wisconsin Electric Utilities:

From: John Smith, President
The following is being released for publication:

April 25, 1979
Milwaukee—Consolidated net income of Wisconsin Electric Utilities Company increased to $18,049,000 in the first quarter of 1979 compared to $17,697,000 in the same period a year ago, the utility reported today. After preferred stock dividend requirements, earnings available for common stockholders amounted to 81 cents a share compared to 87 cents a share in the same quarter in 1978.

John Smith, Wisconsin Electric Utilities President, said that factors affecting first quarter earnings included greater interest and dividend payments after sales of new bonds and preferred stock last year. In addition, he pointed out that $1,130,000 was written off in the first quarter as part of Wisconsin Electric Utilities' share in the write-off of certain Blackhawk Nuclear Plant project expenditures ordered by the Public Service Commission of Wisconsin.

Smith noted that a 9 percent overall electric rate increase, which took effect on March 15, 1979, had little effect on first quarter earnings.

Required
a. Would the increase in net income or the decrease in earnings per share be considered more significant? Comment.
b. The news release indicates that first quarter earnings were affected by the sale of new bonds. (Assume that the bonds are not convertible bonds.)
   1. Would the sale of the bonds decrease present and/or future net income? Comment.
   2. Would the sale of the bonds decrease earnings per share? Comment.
c. The news release indicates that first quarter earnings were affected by the sale of preferred stock.
   1. Would the sale of preferred stock decrease present and/or future net income? Comment.
   2. Would the sale of preferred stock decrease earnings per share? Comment.
d. The news release indicates that $1,130,000 was written off in the first quarter as part of Wisconsin Electric Utilities' share in the write-off of certain Blackhawk Nuclear Plant project expenditures ordered by the Public Service Commission of Wisconsin. How did this write-off influence net income and earnings per share?

Case 9-6 WILL THE REAL EARNINGS PER SHARE PLEASE STAND UP?

On April 25, 1978, the following article appeared in the *Hartford Courant:*

UTC GOOD NEWS NOT FULLY DILUTED
The big question at United Technologies Corp.'s annual meeting Monday was just how the company fared in the first quarter.

Right at the start, UTC Chairman Harry J. Gray had what sounded like good news: The company's sales were $1.474 billion, up from $1.362 billion in the same period a year before. Net income was $48.3 million, up from $37.2 million in 1977. And, Gray told the group, fully diluted earnings per share were $1.14 per share, up from $1 flat the year before.

It sounded fine. Fully diluted earnings are earnings based on the presumption that all convertible securities of the company have been converted into common stock.

But Donald Ross of Newington left to call his broker during the meeting, and asked him how UTC stock was doing on the market. Poorly, the broker told Ross.

Poorly because the Dow Jones wire had issued a report that the company's earnings were down.

So when Ross returned to the meeting he had a question for Harry Gray: What's going on?

Gray told Ross the company had issued to Dow Jones its press release, and the company can't be responsible for what Dow Jones says.

Ross then had Gray repeat the numbers, and he finally got the catch: What were the primary earnings per share for the quarter? he asked Gray.

Gray reported that primary earnings per share were $1.39 per share. "And would you like them for the year before?" Gray asked.

"Yes, sir."

The 1977 period showed primary earnings per share of $1.41 per share, Gray told him.

"Dow Jones is reporting primary and our stock is going down," Ross told him. "I guess the name of the game is earnings per share primary."

"In the press we reported both of them, primary and fully diluted," Gray said. However, the press release which was issued as Gray's opening talk progressed showed no mention of the unhappy primary earnings per share until the fourth and final page—a statistical chart of the corporation's performance. And the report which UTC issued to two wires disseminating financial news to the press didn't even include the chart, thus making no mention of the primary earnings at all.

A year ago, the text of UTC's first quarter report totally ignored fully diluted 1–1 earnings, supplying only primary earnings per share. However, the reports on subsequent quarters made the distinction and supplied figures for both primary and fully diluted earnings per share.

Gray explained that one reason for the weight now being given to the fully diluted figures is that some 6,876,001 shares were issued during the first quarter as a result of conversion of the company's $8 convertible preferred shares—the stock which the company issued in 1974 when it acquired its Essex Group in a merger. Some 1.1 million shares of the $8 preferred—which can be converted into 4.8 million shares of UTC common stock—are still outstanding.

The effect of the conversions was that the average common shares outstanding in the first quarter of this year was 34.6 million, up from 26.5 million the year before. And even though UTC's net profits advanced by 15.8 percent, when the shares outstanding increase by 30.9 percent, it means lower primary earnings per share.

After Gray explained it all to Ross, the Newington man had one more comment: "The stock is going down; it's very disappointing."

However, the stock showed only a modest loss for the day. It closed at $39.62 per share, down only 25 cents per share from Friday's closing price.

The earnings per share presentation in the first quarter report was:

	Quarter Ended March 31	
	1978	**1977**
Per share of common stock:		
Primary earnings	$1.39*	$1.41*

| | Quarter Ended March 31 | |
	1978	1977
Fully diluted earnings	$1.14	$1.00
Average number of common shares outstanding	34,648,994	26,462,074

*During the three months ended March 31, 1978, 6,876,001 shares of Common Stock were issued upon conversion of 1,547,296 shares of $8.00 Preferred Stock. Had these conversions, as well as conversions of these securities and conversions of 4¼% Convertible Subordinated Debentures which occurred during 1977, taken place on January 1, 1977, primary earnings per share would have been $1.29 and $1.10, respectively, for the quarters ended March 31, 1978 and 1977.

The 1977 discussion of the chairman emphasized the 15% gain in primary earnings per share. The 1978 discussion centered on the 14% gain in fully diluted earnings per share. The reason for the switch in emphasis was the large number of convertible preferred shares that were converted during the first quarter of 1978.

Required

a. Explain why primary earnings per share dropped, while fully diluted earnings per share rose.

b. Refer to the footnote in the earnings per share presentation. Why are the pro forma earnings per share figures lower than those presented in the statements?

c. Speculate on the reasons why the discussion switched from primary to fully diluted. Is the switch in emphasis valid?

d. Does reporting by financial services play a role in this misunderstanding?

e. Do you think that the stock market correctly reacted to the quarterly earnings report issued by United Technologies Corporation?

Case 9-7   HOW ABOUT EARNINGS PER SHARE?*

Financial analysts and investors emphasize a particular type of income figure, earnings per share. Trend analysis of earnings on a per share basis is frequently used measure of performance, which may form a basis for valuation of securities. This extensive utilization requires that the earnings per share data be meaningful and useful.

Objective

The objective of this article is to study the usefulness of earnings per share data. This will be accomplished by reviewing the development of the current earnings per share computations, by examining the reporting of earnings per share data by the financial services, and by a survey of the comprehension of earnings per share by finance oriented users of accounting information.

Development of Earnings Per Share Computations
APB Opinion #9

APB Opinion #9 was issued in 1966. In this Opinion the Board strongly recommended that earnings per share be furnished in conjunction with the statement of income. While

*Note: The authors of the article are Charles H. Gibson and Patricia A. Boyer. Reprinted with permission of *The CPA Journal*, February 1979. Copyright 1979.

some companies complied with this request, others did not. If the computation posed difficulties, as often occurred, the figure could simply be omitted. Further, the Board recommended that two presentations of earnings per share be given:

1. The amount of earnings applicable to each share of common stock or other residual security outstanding; and
2. If potential dilution is material, pro forma computations of earnings per share should be furnished, showing what the earnings would be if the conversions or contingent issuances took place.

Prior to this statement, earnings per share had been computed on the basis of outstanding common stock only, with no consideration for potential dilution and with no concern for common stock equivalents. However, the wording in APB Opinion #9 was vague and caused varying methods of application. "Residual securities" were defined as those deriving a major portion of their value from their conversion rights or common stock characteristics. These "residual securities," as distinguished from "senior securities" such as nonconvertible preferred stock, were to be considered as common stock in the calculation of earnings per share. For example, if a convertible bond selling at $1,000 was convertible into 20 shares of common, selling at $30, then it was considered to be a bond and was classified as a senior security. If the stock price rose to $60, and the bond price to $1,200, then it derived its value from the conversion feature and was to be considered a "residual security." The difficulty is that the classification of convertible securities could change with fluctuations in the stock market, leading to periodic revisions. Further, no designation was specified for stock warrants and options.

While APB Opinion #9 furnished guidelines so that some degree of consistency was obtained and assured that in many cases the data would be subject to examination by auditors, its imprecision posed problems in application. Further, during this period of merger activity a large number of "complex securities" were issued. These were exactly the kind of securities which caused difficulties in the interpretation of Opinion #9, and for these reasons, APB Opinion #15 was developed.

APB Opinion #15, Presentation of Primary and Fully Diluted Earnings

This pronouncement on earnings per share issued in 1969 distinguishes between primary and fully diluted earnings per share. Primary earnings per share is computed by dividing earnings after preferred dividends by the weighted average number of shares of common stock and common stock equivalents outstanding. Stock options and warrants are always treated as common stock equivalents. Convertible debt and convertible preferred stocks are determined to be common stock equivalents if, at time of issue, the cash yield was less than two-thirds of the prime interest rate. This determination is made at time of issue and does not change thereafter. If a security is considered a common stock equivalent, then any effects of dilution related to that security are included in the calculation of primary earnings per share. Fully diluted earnings per share represent the earnings that would occur if all potential dilution occurred; options and warrants are assumed to have been exercised and convertibles exchanged for common stock. A corporation that has potential dilution of less than 3 percent of earnings per common share outstanding is considered to have a simple capital structure. In this case, the dual presentation is ignored and only a single earnings per share computation is presented. This earnings per share concept ignores all dilutive securities.

The Problems of APB Opinion #15

This Opinion took two years to develop and while it apparently solved some of the deficiencies of Opinion #9, it received considerable criticism, including three dissents and five assents with qualifications to the Opinion itself. The advantages and difficulties will be discussed in turn.

First, the Opinion required that earnings per share be shown on the face of the income statement. Next it established a uniform, consistent method of calculating earnings per share, primarily by a strict definition of common stock equivalents. Warrants and options are always considered common stock equivalents. The classification of a security as a common stock equivalent is established at the time of its issue, depending on the cash yield. Primary earnings per share take into account dilution from common stock equivalents.; fully diluted earnings per share represents the results of maximum potential dilution. Uniform computations and reporting on the income statement are achieved.

A *Wall Street Journal* editorial[1] praised the Opinion which tightened the rules on reporting earnings per share. It expressed the opinion that the methods of business acquisitions involving warrants and other complex securities might become less widespread due to this reporting of potential dilution. As termed "funny money," these complex securities would no longer mislead the public.

The theoretical justification of APB Opinion #15 was not universally accepted and questions were raised concerning the ultimate usefulness of the data.

A number of arguments were raised by the Board members, including the following:

1. Common stock equivalents are based on assumptions that may change or may never occur.
2. The cash yield basis for determining equivalency was arbitrary and did not seriously consider the valuation method.
3. Options and warrants may not be exercised and the treasury stock method may be unrealistic.
4. The "if converted" approach to common stock equivalent convertibles is inappropriate in primary earnings per share.
5. Common stock equivalents, such as convertible bonds, should be so classified in the financial statements.

Coupled with these was the argument that the new figures might not be as useful as expected. *Financial Executive* published the results of a questionnaire sent to its members concerning the proposed opinion.[2]

This survey indicated that a large number of respondents, 74 percent, did not agree with the residual security (common stock equivalent) concept. Those who disagreed preferred a single earnings per share presentation based on actual common stock outstanding, supplemented by a pro forma figure based on full potential dilution assuming conversion of all outstanding convertible securities to be presented in a footnote. Second choice was dual presentation, on the face of the statement, of these same two figures.

[1]*Wall Street Journal*, May 19, 1969, p. 22.
[2]*Financial Executive*, March 1969, p. 12.

Financial Services Reporting of Earnings Per Share

The financial services' reporting of earnings per share of Witco Chemical for 1975 was used to determine how the financial services report this information. Witco, a producer of chemical and petroleum products, had the following earnings in 1975: Primary—2.46, Fully Diluted—2.28.

In that year, the difference between primary and fully diluted earnings per share was 7.3 percent, certainly a material amount.

Exhibit 1 summaries the findings of a survey to determine which earnings per share figures were being published by selected financial services.

Most commonly, primary earnings per share was the only number presented. If the fully diluted amount was shown, it was usually in footnote format. This indicates that primary earnings per share figures are the principal subject of financial service reporting.

Empirical Survey of Finance-Oriented Users

A mail survey was made of members of the Eastern Finance Association, whose membership is comprised of academicians and practitioners in finance and closely related fields such as economics and accounting. Its purpose was to determine if a group of professional users would exhibit a clear understanding of the computations and implications contained in Opinion #15. Further, its purpose was to determine whether these users were content with the current dual presentation of data or the format of presentation.

EXHIBIT 1

Summary of Earnings Per Share Presentation by Financial Services

Witco Chemical (1975) Financial Service		Earnings Per Share	
		Primary $2.46	Fully Diluted $2.28*
Barron's		Yes	No
Business Week		Yes	No
Moody's Handbook	Graph	Yes	No
	Statistics	Yes	No
	Interim Earnings	Yes	No
Moody's Industrials		Yes	Yes (footnote)
Standard and Poor's Industry Surveys	Annual	Yes	No
	Interim	Yes	No
Standard and Poor's Stock Reports	Quarterly	Yes	No
	Statistics	Yes	Yes (footnote)
	Text	Yes	Yes
Value Line	Statistics	Yes	No
	Quarterly	Yes	No
Wall Street Journal		Yes	Yes

*Represents a dilution of 7.3 percent from primary earnings.

Nine hundred and ninety-eight (998) questionnaires were mailed. One hundred and fifty-five (155) or 15.5 percent were returned. One hundred and fifty-four or 15.4 percent were usable. Approximately, 80 percent of the respondents were academicians: the remainder were practitioners. These responses were considered sufficient to give meaningful results.

What Are Earnings Per Share?

The computations of earnings per share are sometimes difficult: the underlying theory is complex. Several questions were asked to determine whether these implications were understood by this group of users. Some of the types of questions follow.

Convertibles

Company A issued a material amount of convertible debentures with a stated interest rate of 5 percent at a time when the prime rate was 8 percent. If converted, there will be a dilutive effect on earnings. Which earnings per share figure(s) will reflect this potential dilution? (See Table 1.)

A convertible bond or preferred stock is considered a common stock equivalent if, at the time of issuance, the cash yield is less than two-thirds of the prime interest rate. If a convertible meets this test, then both the primary and fully diluted earnings per share are based on the assumption that conversion had occurred at the beginning of the year or date of issuance, whichever is later.

The correct answer to this question is "both." Only 33.1 percent of the respondents had this correct answer. The largest number of respondents' conclusions was that only the fully diluted figure included the "if converted" assumption. Clearly, there is limited understanding of the common stock equivalency concept of convertibles, which influences primary earnings per share.

Options and Warrants

Company B has outstanding a large number of stock options, which, if exercised, will have a dilutive effect on earnings. Which earnings per share figure(s) will reflect this potential dilution? (See Table 2.)

Options and warrants are regarded as common stock equivalents at all times. Primary and fully diluted earnings per share reflect the dilution that would result from the exercise of these securities and the use of the funds obtained. Therefore, the correct answer is "both." Only 30.5 percent of the respondents indicated the correct answer. Again, the most common

TABLE   1

	Number of Responses	%
Primary	15	9.7
Fully diluted	74	48.1
Both	51	33.1
Neither	9	5.8
No response	5	3.2
	154	100.0

T A B L E   2

	Number of Responses	%
Primary	16	10.4
Fully diluted	69	44.8
Both	47	30.5
Neither	19	12.3
No response	3	1.9
	154	100.0

answer was fully diluted, an indication that the common stock equivalency of options and warrants is not well understood.

Only 24.4 percent of the respondents had the correct response to both of these questions. There were no significant differences between academicians and practitioners as to the percentage responding correctly.

Dilution in Primary Earnings Per Share

Another question was designed to determine the awareness of dilution in primary earnings per share.

Assuming that a firm has securities which offer potential dilution, is any potential dilution ever reflected in primary earnings per share? (See Table 3.)

These percentages indicate that a slight majority of the respondents realize there may be dilution in primary earnings per share. Given the large number of incorrect responses to the two principal types of dilutive securities that were questioned, it is clear that more respondents are aware that a potential dilution can exist in primary earnings per share than those who can correctly identify the proper use of dilutive securities in the computations.

Presentation by Financial Services

The respondents were asked to describe their observation of how the financial services presented earnings per share. Over fifty-one percent (51.3 percent) felt that the figure primary supplemented by the fully diluted would be most common; over twenty-two percent (22.7 percent) felt that both would be presented. About twelve percent (12.3) indicated that primary would be presented alone, which is the most typical case.

T A B L E   3

	Number of Responses	%
Yes	81	52.6
No	69	44.8
No response	4	2.6
	154	100.0

TABLE 4

Methods of Computing Earnings Per Share

Actual earnings per share is computed by dividing the actual earnings applicable to the common shares by the weighted average number of shares outstanding.

Primary earnings per share is computed by dividing the earnings applicable to the common shares by the weighted average number of shares of common stock and common stock equivalents (convertibles meeting a yield test plus warrants and stock options).

Fully diluted earnings per share gives the earnings that would occur if all potential dilution resulted.

Favored Presentation

Three types of earnings per share computations were described for the respondents as shown in Table 4.

For each earnings per share figure, the respondents were asked to indicate whether they felt the presentation of that figure useful, and if so, whether the presentation should be on the face of the statement or in supplementary form.

The results in Exhibit 2 show that the fully diluted information is most strongly favored. However, both actual and primary appear to have strong support with actual having more support than primary. Based on the responses favoring each method, the presentation of actual earnings per share is most favored for the face of statement presentation. However, there is a good majority favoring face of statement presentation for all three figures.

EXHIBIT 2

Type of Earnings Per Share	Should It Be Presented?			Method of Presentation		
Actual	Yes	119	77.3%	Face of statement	103	88.6%
	No	31	20.1%	Supplementary	14	11.8%
	No response	4	2.6%	No response	2	1.7%
		154	100.0%		119	100.0%
Primary	Yes	111	72.1%	Face of statement	83	74.8%
	No	39	25.3%	Supplementary	27	24.3%
	No response	4	2.6%	No response	1	0.9%
		154	100.0%		111	100.0%
Fully diluted	Yes	131	85.1%	Face of statement	85	64.9%
	No	19	12.3%	Supplementary	46	35.1%
	No response	4	2.6%	No response	0	0.0%
		154	100.0%		131	100.0%

Responses concerning these earnings per share figures were then cross tabulated to determine the interrelationships between the responses. The results are shown in Exhibit 3.

There is a distinct preference for having all three earnings per share figures presented. The distant second choice is the combination of actual and fully diluted earnings per share. The requirements of APB Opinion #15 is third, with 15.6 percent of the respondents favoring this presentation. Clearly, a combination including actual earnings per share, eliminating the effects of common stock equivalents, is favored.

Conclusion

Current generally accepted accounting principles require that both primary and fully diluted earnings per share be shown on the face of the Income Statement. Both of these earning per share figures are considered necessary for adequate financial reporting.

The survey of financial services reporting of earnings per share indicates that, most commonly, primary earnings per share was the only number presented. If fully diluted earnings per share was shown, it was usually in footnote format.

This survey of users of earnings per share figures indicates there is considerable misunderstanding of the effects of common stock equivalents in primary earnings per share. Specifically, it is commonly assumed that dilution from convertibles, options and warrants is evident only in fully diluted earnings per share.

Given a choice of earnings per share computations, presentation of actual, primary and fully diluted earnings per share is clearly favored over the primary and fully diluted figures currently required. There is also a preference that earnings per share data be presented on the face of the income statement, which is currently the case.

Since only four respondents indicated that reporting primary earnings only would be most useful, it appears that the financial services could improve their services by reporting both primary and fully diluted earnings per share.

These conclusions indicate that finance oriented users find difficulty in interpreting the current earnings per share figures. Further, financial reporting only increases the magnitude of this problem. The Financial Accounting Standards Board should reevaluate the require-

EXHIBIT 3

Combinations of Earnings Per Share
Data Deemed Useful

	Number of Responses	%
Actual only	3	1.9%
Primary only	4	2.6
Fully diluted only	2	1.3
Actual and primary	11	7.1
Actual and fully diluted	33	21.4
Primary and fully diluted	24	15.6
Actual, primary and fully diluted	72	46.8
None of these	1	.6
No response	4	2.6
	154	100.0%

ments of earnings per share accounting and reporting and the financial services should reevaluate their reporting of this information.

Required a. A corporation that has potential dilution of less than 3% of earnings per common share outstanding is considered to have a simple capital structure. In this case, are dilutive securities considered in the earnings per share presented?

b. The article indicates that the classification of a security as a common stock equivalent is established at the time of its issue, depending on the cash yield. Is this statement still correct?

c. Where does APB Opinion No. 15 require that earnings per share be presented?

d. According to the survey, is there a limited understanding of the common stock equivalency concept of convertibles?

e. Do primary and fully diluted earnings per share reflect dilution that would result from the exercise of outstanding options and warrants?

f. Given a choice, the respondents favored the presentation of what earnings per share numbers?

Case 9-8   SPECIAL ITEMS

The Chevron Corporation presented the following information with its 1989 annual report.

Consolidated Statement of Income

| | Year Ended December 31 | | |
Millions of dollars, except per-share amounts	1989	1988	1987
Revenues			
Sales and other operating revenues*	$31,916	$27,722	$28,106
Equity in net income of affiliated companies	350	422	376
Other income	519	713	638
Total revenues	32,785	28,857	29,120
Costs and other deductions			
Purchased crude oil and products	15,631	12,010	13,627
Operating expenses	6,812	5,220	4,713
Exploration expenses	578	651	466
Selling, general and administrative expenses	1,887	1,758	1,416
Depreciation, depletion and amortization	2,562	2,436	2,514
Taxes other than on income*	3,361	3,255	2,913
Interest and debt expense	648	628	699
Total costs and other deductions	31,479	25,958	26,348
Income before income tax expense	1,306	2,899	2,772
Income tax expense	1,055	1,131	1,522
Net income	$ 251	$ 1,768	$ 1,250
Net income per share of common stock	$.73	$5.17	$3.65
	$2,473	$2,526	$2,091

*Includes consumer excise taxes.

Note 3. Net Income [partial footnote]

Comparability between periods is affected by special items that had a material effect on reported income for 1989, 1988 and 1987. The categories of special items and their net increase (decrease) to net income are as follows:

	Year Ended December 31		
	1989	1988	1987
Asset write-offs and write-downs	$ (631)	$ (8)	$ (97)
Environmental programs	(356)	(145)	—
Prior years' and other tax-related adjustments	(164)	114	126
Asset dispositions	7	173	233
LIFO inventory losses	(3)	(30)	(20)
Other	(63)	(27)	14
Total special items	$(1,210)	$ 77	$256

Asset write-offs and write-downs in 1989 included $445 for the write-down of the company's investment in the Point Arguello Field, located offshore Southern California. (See Note 2 for a discussion of the 1989 change in the accounting policy for determining the impairment of certain oil and gas projects prior to commencement of production.) Write-offs for other oil and gas properties, also mostly offshore Southern California, totaled $153. In addition, the company's $33 investment in the Mount Taylor uranium mine was written off in 1989. Asset write-offs of $97 in 1987 primarily reflected the company's share of certain AMAX Inc. restructuring costs and the company's abandonment of a domestic offshore producing facility.

Charges against earnings of $356 for environmental programs in 1989 were made for expected cleanup costs at certain of the company's U.S. service stations and marketing terminals, refineries and chemical locations. In 1988, environmental charges totaled $145 for certain U.S. refineries and chemical locations, as well as for certain divested operations.

Adjustments relating to prior years' income taxes reduced 1989 earnings by a net $164. Net income for 1988 benefited $114 from income tax and Windfall Profit Tax adjustments, including the enactment of lower statutory rates in Canada and Australia and net favorable adjustments to prior years' taxes. The company's 1987 results included $126 of Windfall Profit Tax refunds and net favorable adjustments to prior years' taxes.

Asset dispositions benefited earnings $7 in 1989. In 1988, net gains of $173 reflected the sales of the company's investment in AMAX and Canada's Irving Oil operations and 20 percent of its interest in the Angolan producing operations. In 1987, dispositions increased net income $233 and included the sales of the company's Denmark producing operations, Puerto Rico refining and marketing operations, and investments in Cetus Corporation, the Harshaw/Filtrol Partnership, and UNC, Inc.

LIFO inventory drawdown losses included the company's share of Caltex LIFO inventory effects, which were immaterial for all three years.

Other special items of $63 in 1989 included charges for various regulatory and other issues and for the company's uranium and geothermal operations. These charges were partially offset by a gain from an insurance recovery. In

1988, provisions of $27 were recorded for streamlining the Port Arthur refinery and reorganizing U.S. exploration and production operations. A $14 benefit was recorded in 1987 from settlement gains related to an early retirement program.

Special items reduced fourth quarter 1989, 1988 and 1987 earnings by $1,206, $266 and $37, respectively. All the 1989 special items were recorded in the fourth quarter except the $7 net gain on asset dispositions, a $20 gain from an insurance settlement and $31 of charges for environmental programs. The largest of the 1988 fourth quarter items was a $155 loss on the sale of the company's Irving Oil investment. The 1987 fourth quarter items included the net effect of the charges for the AMAX restructuring and the offshore producing facility abandonment, partially offset by a favorable tax adjustment.

Other selected data

Preferred stock (authorized 100,000,000 shares, $1.00 par value, none issued).

Common stock (authorized 500,000,000 shares, $3.00 par value, shares issued 356,243,534—1989; 342,109,258—1988).

Treasury stock, at cost (shares 1,219,597—1989; 1,234,728—1988).

Weighted average shares outstanding for the year (in thousands)

1989	341,889
1988	340,849
1987	340,818

Required

a. What are special items?

b. Why are the special items not presented net of tax?

c. What would income tax expense been in 1989, 1988, and 1987 with the special items removed?

d. Comment on the adjusted income before income tax expense in (c) in relation to the trend in net income.

e. Comment on the cash dividends paid per share of common stock as against the net income per share of common stock. Speculate on why these two numbers do not correlate.

f. What are the outstanding shares of common stock at the end of 1989? Why doesn't the weighted average number of shares outstanding for the year agree with the number of outstanding shares? Which share amount is used when computing earnings per share?

CHAPTER **10**

STATEMENT OF CASH FLOWS

CHAPTER TOPICS

WATCH CASH FLOW

Quoth the Banker, "Watch Cash Flow"

Once upon a midnight dreary as I pondered weak and weary
Over many a quaint and curious volume of accounting lore,
Seeking gimmicks (without scruple) to squeeze through some new tax loop-
    hole,
Suddenly I heard a knock upon my door,
  Only this, and nothing more.

Then I felt a queasy tingling and I heard the cash a-jingling
As a fearsome banker entered whom I'd often seen before.
His face was money-green and in his eyes there could be seen
Dollar-signs that seemed to glitter as he reckoned up the score.
  "Cash flow," the banker said, and nothing more.

I had always thought it fine to show a jet black bottom line,
But the banker sounded a resounding, "No,
Your receivables are high, mounting upward toward the sky;
Write-offs loom. What matters is cash flow."
  He repeated, "Watch cash flow."

Then I tried to tell the story of our lovely inventory
Which, though large, is full of most delightful stuff.
But the banker saw its growth, and with a mighty oath
He waved his arms and shouted, "Stop! Enough!
    Pay the interest, and don't give me any guff!"

Next I looked for non-cash items which could add ad infinitum
To replace the ever-outward flow of cash,
But to keep my statement black I'd held depreciation back,
And my banker said that I'd done something rash.
    He quivered, and his teeth began to gnash.

When I asked him for a loan, he responded, with a groan,
That the interest rate would be just prime plus eight,
And to guarantee my purity he'd insist on some security—
All my assets plus the scalp upon my pate.
    Only this, a standard rate.

Though my bottom line is black, I am flat upon my back.
My cash flows out and customers pay slow.
The growth of my receivables is almost unbelievable;
The result is certain—unremitting woe!
And I hear the banker utter an ominous low mutter,
    "Watch cash flow."

—Herbert S. Bailey, Jr.
Reprinted with permission

A REVIEW OF THE FUNDS STATEMENT

The statement of cash flows is a relatively new statement that did not become required until 1988. (Previously, starting in 1971, a similar statement was required: the Statement of Changes in Financial Position.)

A statement that presented a flow of funds existed as early as 1862 in England and 1863 in the United States.[1] This is much later than the first issuance of a balance sheet and income statement. Thus, although the concept of issuing a statement that presented a flow of funds is over 100 years old, it is relatively new when compared with the balance sheet and income statement. This statement is often referred to as the *funds statement*, and this term will be used frequently in this chapter.

A brief historical presentation is included here in order to convey a perspective on the development of the funds statement.

---

[1]L. S. Rosen and Don T. DeCoster, "Funds' Statements: A Historical Perspective," *The Accounting Review* (January 1969), 125.

The original funds statement accounted for the changes in cash in the bank, cash on hand, and stamps. The original statements emphasized the flow of cash, but they had many different formats. The Missouri Pacific Railway Company appears to have been the first organization to highlight changes in all balance sheet accounts, when it presented a funds statement in 1893.[2] At the turn of the century, the United States Steel Corporation presentation began to provide subtotals for current assets and current liabilities, and the presentation reconciled to working capital (current assets less current liabilities).[3] By 1903, there were at least four conceptually different statements that were presented as funds statements. The broad focal points of these statements presented the flow of funds as follows:[4]

1. Cash
2. Current assets
3. Working capital
4. All financial activities in a period

In the period from the 1910s to the late 1920s, an educator named H. A. Finney led a drive to present the funds statement using a format that showed the cause of a change in working capital.[5] Finney was successful, and the working capital approach became the dominant format for presenting the funds statement. Items that increased working capital were regarded as sources of funds, and items that decreased working capital were regarded as users of funds.

The Accounting Principles Board addressed the presentation of the funds statement with the issuance of APB Opinion No. 3 in 1963. In general, this Opinion was vague and left the firm with a great deal of discretion as to the format of the funds statement. It did recommend that firms present a funds statement along with a balance sheet and an income statement. At this time, the funds statement was usually entitled the Statement of Source and Application of Funds.

In 1971, APB Opinion No. 19 was issued. This Opinion made the funds statement a required statement when a firm presented a balance sheet and income statement. Opinion No. 9 concluded that

> When financial statements purporting to present both financial position (balance sheet) and results of operations (statement of income and retained earnings) are issued, a statement summarizing changes in financial position should also be presented as a basic financial statement for each period for which an income statement is presented.[6]

APB Opinion No. 19 gave the funds statement the title of Statement of Changes in Financial Position. The guidelines for the presentation of the funds statement were still fairly flexible. Basically, the funds statement could take whatever form would give the most useful portrayal of the changes in financial position.

[2]Ibid.
[3]Ibid., 126.
[4]Ibid.
[5]Ibid., 130.
[6]"Reporting Changes in Financial Position," APB Opinion No. 19 (New York: AICPA, 1971), par. 7.

At the time of issuance of APB Opinion No. 19, there were two basic presentation formats for the funds statement: the working capital format and the cash and cash equivalents format. In 1971, the working capital format was the dominant approach. During the 1980s, the cash and cash equivalents format became dominant. Because this change in presentation took place without guidance from an official standard, there were many presentation differences, even among firms that used the same basic format.

Some brief comments are in order regarding why the dominant format was switched from the working capital concept to the cash concept. In 1973, the AICPA issued the "Report of the Study Group on the Objectives of Financial Statements." It stated that "an objective of financial statements is to provide information useful to investors and creditors for predicting, comparing, and evaluating potential cash flows to them in terms of amount, timing and related uncertainty."[7]

In 1978, Statement of Financial Accounting Concepts No. 1, "Objectives of Financial Reporting by Business Enterprises," was issued by the FASB. Several of the objectives of financial reporting identified by Concept Statement No. 1 emphasized the importance of cash. For example, paragraph 39 stated that "since an enterprise's ability to generate favorable cash flows affects both its ability to pay dividends and interest and the market prices of its securities, expected cash flows to investors and creditors are related to expected cash flows to the enterprise in which they have invested or to which they have loaned funds."[8]

In December 1980, the FASB issued a Discussion Memorandum entitled "Reporting Funds Flows, Liquidity, and Financial Flexibility." Many of the respondents to the Discussion Memorandum favored the presentation of the funds statement on a cash basis. An important argument in its favor was that cash flows are a major consideration of investors and creditors. When the funds statement is presented on a working capital basis, the cash flow of a company may not be obvious. Thus, the effect on cash flow of large changes in working capital accounts, such as receivables and inventory, may go undetected when the working capital format is used.

In November 1981, the FASB issued an Exposure Draft as a follow-up to the December 1980 Discussion Memorandum. The Exposure Draft proposed focusing the funds statement on cash flow rather than on working capital. An Exposure Draft is typically followed by an FASB Statement, but this did not happen in this case, because of opposition to a required cash format. Time was allowed for discussion and research on the presentation of the funds statement. In 1984, Statements of Financial Accounting Concepts No. 5, "Recognition and Measurement in Financial Statements of Business Enterprises," was issued by the FASB. This Concept Statement also emphasized the importance of cash flow, as did Concept Statement No. 1.

Concept Statement No. 5 recommended that a full set of financial statements

---

[7]"Report of the Study Group on the Objectives of Financial Statements" (New York: American Institute of Certified Public Accountants, 1973), p. 20.
[8]Statement of Financial Accounting Concepts No. 1, "Objectives of Financial Reporting by Business Enterprises" (Norwalk, Conn.: Financial Accounting Standards Board, 1978).

for a period should show cash flows during the period. Paragraph 52 describes the role of information in the statement of cash flows as follows:

> It provides useful information about an entity's activities in generating cash through operations to repay debt, distribute dividends, or reinvest to maintain or expand operating capacity; about its financing activities, both debt and equity; and about its investing or spending of cash. Important uses of information about an entity's current cash receipts and payments include helping to assess factors such as the entity's liquidity, financial flexibility, profitability, and risk.[9]

In 1986, the FASB issued another exposure draft, entitled Proposed Statement of Financial Accounting Standards "Statement of Cash Flows." This Exposure Draft was followed in 1987 by FASB Statement No. 95, "Statement of Cash Flows," which superseded APB Opinion No. 19. Statement No. 95 directed that the cash format be used, changed the title of the statement to the Statement of Cash Flows, and required a fairly specific detailed format. By the time the standard was issued, most firms were using a cash format. Even these firms were affected by the change in the title of the statement and the specific presentation requirements.

FUNDS STATEMENT—WORKING CAPITAL FORMAT

A reasonable understanding of the working capital format is desirable because of its dominance for so many years. Furthermore, such an understanding helps in understanding the cash format.

The basic reason for using the working capital approach is that working capital constantly flows from one current asset or current liability account to another. For example, cash is used to pay accounts payable; these are current obligations from such items as the purchase of inventory. The inventory is sold for cash or accounts receivable, and the receivable is then collected and becomes cash. Working capital, therefore, is thought of as a liquid resource that is available to a firm—current assets less current liabilities.

The working capital funds statement presents the reasons for the change in working capital through analysis of operations and the noncurrent accounts on the balance sheet. Working capital accounts themselves cannot provide an explanation of why working capital changes. For this, one must look to balance sheet accounts other than working capital accounts.

Usually, a major source of funds comes from the operations of the business. Therefore, the statement starts with a reconciliation of net income to funds from operations. Net income does not fairly represent the funds from operations, because items are included in income that do not provide funds, and items are deducted from income that do not use funds.

---

[9]Statement of Financial Accounting Concepts No. 5, "Recognition and Measurement in Financial Statements of Business Enterprises" (Norwalk, Conn.: FASB, 1984), par. 52.

Therefore, the net income figure from the income statement is adjusted for items that affect income but do not provide or use funds. The primary example of such an item is depreciation expense. Depreciation expense reduces operating income but does not require the use of funds. Therefore, depreciation is added back to net income on the funds statement. In this manner, the net income figure is converted to a funds from operations figure for the funds statement. This key figure represents the working capital generated by operations.

Besides working capital from operations, many other items may provide funds for an entity—for example, sales of stock, sales of bonds, and sales of noncurrent assets.

Decreases in funds (net working capital) result from items similar to those that increase funds. For example, there could be a reduction of funds from unprofitable operations, repurchase of the entity's stock, retirement of long-term debt, acquisition of noncurrent assets, and declaration of cash dividends.

In addition to presenting the source and use of working capital, Opinion 19 recommended presenting a schedule that indicates the changes in elements of working capital. This schedule is normally presented at the bottom of the funds statement. The funds statement explains why the working capital changed, and the working capital schedule indicates how each account within working capital changed.

As previously indicated, the working capital approach was dominant in financial reporting for many years. Working capital (current assets less current liabilities) has been in the past, and still is, considered to be one of the prime indicators of liquidity. One of the key ratios that indicates liquidity is the current ratio (current assets ÷ current liabilities). Therefore, it was logical to structure the funds statement around an explanation of the change in working capital. There would be some merit in presenting two funds statements: one focusing on working capital as the pool of funds, and one focusing on cash as the pool of funds. With a working capital focus, working capital accounts are not part of the explanation of the source and application of funds. With a cash focus, working capital accounts are part of the explanation of the source and application of funds—except for the change in cash, because cash is the focal point.

The 1986 Cooper funds statement used working capital as the focal point (see Exhibit 10-1). The Cooper statement closely followed the recommended format described in APB Opinion No. 19, "Reporting Changes in Financial Position."

FUNDS STATEMENT—CASH FORMAT

FASB Statement No. 95, "Statement of Cash Flows," issued in 1987, directs that (1) the statement be prepared on a cash basis; (2) the title be changed to "The Statement of Cash Flows"; and (3) a fairly specific and detailed format be used.

This statement allows the preparer to use a concept of cash that includes not only cash itself but also short-term, highly liquid investments. This is referred to as the "cash and cash equivalent" focus. Cash on hand, cash on deposit, and in-

COOPER TIRE & RUBBER COMPANY
Statement of Changes in Financial Position
Years Ended December 31, 1986, 1985, and 1984

	1986	1985	1984
Sources of working capital:			
Operations:			
Net income	$ 23,017,759	$ 18,470,911	$ 24,578,289
Items not involving working capital in the current period:			
Depreciation and amortization	16,665,785	14,954,645	11,604,615
Deferred federal income taxes	4,126,000	4,200,000	2,100,000
Increase in other long-term liabilities	1,332,000	615,000	692,000
Other	174,126	675,923	164,455
Working capital provided from operations	45,315,670	38,916,479	39,139,359
Increase in long-term debt	50,250,000	11,005,690	8,486,643
Issuance of common stock	568,346	726,677	145,954
	96,134,016	50,648,846	47,771,956
Applications of working capital:			
Additions to property, plant and equipment	26,547,914	23,659,502	57,239,080
Property, plant and equipment of acquired companies	6,607,529	—	—
Reduction in long-term debt	15,365,561	5,596,675	5,399,254
Cash dividends	4,145,914	4,013,095	3,799,298
Additions to investments and other assets	229,375	—	—
	52,896,293	33,269,272	66,437,632
Increase (decrease) in working capital	$ 43,237,723	$ 17,379,574	$(18,665,676)
Changes in components of working capital:			
Increase (decrease) in current assets:			
Cash, including short-term investments	$ 52,382,241	$ 2,349,026	$(15,609,754)
Accounts receivable	15,446,185	(2,601,821)	5,482,209
Inventories	(11,475,651)	7,157,140	591,135
Prepaid expenses	(344,123)	371,020	258,730
	56,008,652	7,275,365	(9,277,680)
Increase (decrease) in current liabilities:			
Accounts payable	6,241,686	(11,322,715)	6,920,813
Federal income taxes	529,259	767,957	1,440,158
Accrued liabilities	5,800,984	178,549	719,025
Current portion of long-term debt	199,000	272,000	308,000
	12,770,929	(10,104,209)	9,387,996
Increase (decrease) in working capital	$ 43,237,723	$ 17,379,574	$(18,665,676)

vestments in short-term, highly liquid investments are all included in the category cash and cash equivalents. The cash flow statement analysis explains the change in these focus accounts by examining all the accounts on the balance sheet other than the focus accounts.

Management may use the statement of cash flows to determine dividend policy, cash generated by operations, and investing and financing policy. Outsiders, such as creditors or investors, may use the statement of cash flows to determine such things as the firm's ability to increase dividends, its ability to pay debt with cash from operations, and the percentage of cash from operations in relation to cash from financing.

The major purpose of the statement of cash flows is to provide the user with information as to why the cash position of the company changed during an accounting period. In addition, the effects of all investing and financing transactions of the period must be disclosed on the cash flow statement or in supporting schedules.

All transactions having cash flow effects must be reported on the statement of cash flows. A company may occasionally have a transaction that involves investing and/or financing activities but has no direct cash flow effect. For example, a company may acquire land in exchange for common stock. This would represent an investing transaction (acquiring the land) and a financing transaction (issuing the common stock). The conversion of long-term bonds into common stock is an example of a transaction involving two financing activities with no cash flow effect. Since one purpose of the statement of cash flows is to show all investing and financing activities, and since transactions such as these will have future effects on cash flows, these transactions are to be disclosed in a separate schedule presented with the statement of cash flows.

The statement of cash flows classifies cash receipts and cash payments by operating, investing, and financing activities.[10] These activities are described as follows:

1. *Operating activities*
   Operating activities include all transactions and other events that are not investing and financing activities. Operating activities include delivering or producing goods for sale and providing services. Cash flows from operating activities are generally the cash effects of transactions and other events that enter into the determination of net income.

2. *Investing activities*
   Investing activities include lending money and collecting on those loans and acquiring and selling investments and productive long-term assets.

3. *Financing activities*
   Financing activities include cash flows relating to liability and owners' equity. In brief, operating activities involve income statement items. Investing activities generally result from changes in long-term asset items; financing activities generally relate to long-term liability and stockholders' equity items.

---

[10]The effect of exchange rate changes on cash is presented separately at the bottom of the statement.

The typical cash flows under operating, investing, and financing activities are as follows:

- *Operating*
  Cash inflows
  - From sale of goods or services
  - From return on loans (interest)
  - From return on equity securities (dividends)
  Cash outflows
  - Payments for acquisitions of inventory
  - Payments to employees
  - Payments to governments (taxes)
  - Payments of interest expense
  - Payments to suppliers for other expenses
- *Investing*
  Cash inflows
  - From receipts from loans collected
  - From sales of debt or equity securities of other corporations
  - From sale of property, plant, and equipment
  Cash outflows
  - Loans to other entities
  - Purchase of debt or equity securities of other entities
  - Purchase of property, plant, and equipment
- *Financing*
  Cash inflows
  - From sale of equity securities
  - From sale of bonds, mortgages, notes, and other short- or long-term borrowings
  Cash outflows
  - Payment of dividends
  - Reacquisition of the firm's capital stock
  - Payment of amounts borrowed

When presenting the statement of cash flows, cash flows from operating activities are presented first, followed by investing activities and then financing activities. The individual inflows and outflows from investing and financing activities are presented separately. The operating activities section can be presented using the *direct method* or the *indirect method*. (The indirect method is sometimes referred to as the *reconciliation method*.) With the direct method, the income statement is essentially presented on a cash receipts and cash payments basis, instead of an accrual basis. With the indirect method, net income is adjusted for items that affected net income but did not affect cash.

SFAS No. 95 encourages enterprises to present cash flows from operating activities using the direct method, but if the direct method is used, the standard requires a reconciliation of net income to cash flow in a separate schedule. Many respondents to the exposure draft claimed that their accounting systems do not presently provide the information necessitated by the direct method (e.g., cash collected from customers). For this reason, SFAS No. 95 permits the use of the indirect method. If a firm uses the indirect method, it must make a separate disclosure of interest paid and income taxes paid during the period.

Skeleton formats of a statement of cash flows using the direct method and indirect method are in Exhibit 10-2.

The 1986 FASB Exposure Draft, "Statement of Cash Flows," indicates that "the principal advantage of the direct method is that it shows the operating cash receipts and payments. Knowledge of where operating cash flows came from and how cash was used in past periods may be useful in estimating future cash flows.

EXHIBIT 10-2

JONES COMPANY
Statement of Cash Flows—Comparison of Presentation of Direct Method and Indirect Method
For the Year Ended December 31, 19XX

Direct Method		
Cash flows from operating activities		
Receipts from customers	$ xxx	
Payments to suppliers	(xxx)	
Income taxes paid	xxx	
Net cash provided by operating activities		$ xxx
Cash flows from investing activities (list of individual inflows and outflows)		xxx
Net cash provided (used) by investing activities		xxx
Cash flows from financing activities (list of individual inflows and outflows)		xxx
Net cash provided (used) by financing activities		xxx
Net increase (decrease) in cash		xxx
Reconciliation of net income to net cash provided by operating activities:		
Net income		xxx
Adjustments to reconcile net income to net cash provided by operating activities		xxx
Net cash provided by operating activities		xxx
Supplemental schedule of noncash investing and financing activities:		
Land acquired by issuing bonds		$ xxx

EXHIBIT 10 - 2   (continued)

Indirect Method

Cash flows from operating activities	
Net income	$ xxx
Adjustments to reconcile net income to net cash provided by operating activities:	xxx
Net cash provided by operating activities	xxx
Cash flows from investing activities (list of individual inflows and outflows)	xxx
Net cash provided (used) by investing activities	xxx
Cash flows from financing activities (list of individual inflows and outflows)	xxx
Net cash provided (used) by financing activities	xxx
Net increase (decrease) in cash	xxx
Supplemental disclosure of cash flow information:	
Cash paid during the year for:	
Interest (net of amount capitalized)	xxx
Income taxes	xxx
Supplemental schedule of noncash investing and financing activities:	
Land acquired by issuing bonds	$ xxx

The indirect method of reporting has the advantage of focusing on the differences between income and cash flow from operating activities."[11]

The 1989 Cooper statement of cash flows is presented in Exhibit 10-3. This statement presents cash from operations using the indirect method. The statement closely follows SFAS No. 95, except that it does not separately disclose interest paid and income taxes paid during the period. Cooper has elected to disclose interest paid and income taxes paid in the footnotes to the financial statements.

In addition to reviewing the flow of funds on an individual year basis, reviewing a flow of funds for a three-year period may be helpful. This can be accomplished by adding a total column to the statement that represents the total of each item for the three-year period. This has been done for Cooper in Exhibit 10-4.

Some observations on the 1989 Cooper statement of cash flows, considering the three-year period ended December 31, 1989, are as follows:

1. Net cash provided by operating activities was the major source of cash each year.

2. Net cash used in investing activities was the major use of cash each year.

3. Financing activities used cash each year.

[11]Financial Accounting Standards Board, Exposure Draft, "Statement of Cash Flows," 1986, p. 21.

E X H I B I T   1 0 - 3

COOPER TIRE & RUBBER COMPANY
Statement of Cash Flows
Years Ended December 31, 1989, 1988, and 1987

	1989	1988	1987
Operating activities:			
Net income	$58,243,880	$41,062,286	$30,679,747
Adjustments to reconcile net income to net cash provided by operating activities:			
Depreciation and amortization	23,393,307	19,872,614	18,436,182
Deferred taxes	2,797,000	1,474,000	2,020,000
Increase in accounts receivable	(6,023,735)	(5,779,124)	(15,607,028)
Decrease (increase) in inventories and prepaid expenses	(3,068,932)	(6,843,493)	962,701
Increase (decrease) in accounts payable and accrued liabilities	13,243,738	(4,106,154)	22,602,888
Increase in other long-term liabilities and other	3,904,508	2,253,798	513,644
Net cash provided by operating activities	92,489,766	47,933,927	59,608,134
Investing activities:			
Additions to property, plant and equipment	(73,181,647)	(70,620,543)	(41,507,210)
Other	58,995	105,792	142,420
Net cash used in investing activities	(73,122,652)	(70,514,751)	(41,364,790)
Financing activities:			
Payments on long-term debt	(2,535,000)	(6,460,836)	(5,720,244)
Issuance of common stock	1,144,090	839,468	409,098
Dividends paid	(7,080,479)	(5,712,039)	(4,673,146)
Net cash used in financing activities	(8,471,389)	(11,333,407)	(9,984,292)
Increase (decrease) in cash and short-term investments	10,895,725	(33,914,231)	8,259,052
Cash and short-term investments at beginning of year	38,690,586	72,604,817	64,345,765
Cash and short-term investments at end of year	$49,586,311	$38,690,586	$72,604,817

4. For the three-year period, net cash provided by operating activities was approximately equal to additions to property, plant, and equipment and dividends paid.

5. For the three-year period, cash dividends were less than 9% of net cash provided by operating activities.

A minority of companies have elected to present cash flow from operations using the direct method. With the direct method, all items presented within cash

EXHIBIT 10-4

COOPER TIRE & RUBBER COMPANY
Statement of Cash Flows, with Three-Year Total
Years Ended December 31, 1989, 1988, and 1987

	Total	1989	1988	1987
Operating activities:				
Net income	$129,985,913	$58,243,880	$41,062,286	$30,679,747
Adjustments to reconcile net income to net cash provided by operating activities:				
Depreciation and amortization	61,702,103	23,393,307	19,872,614	18,436,182
Deferred taxes	6,291,000	2,797,000	1,474,000	2,020,000
Increase in accounts receivable	(27,409,887)	(6,023,735)	(5,779,124)	(15,607,028)
Decrease (increase) in inventories and prepaid expenses	(8,949,724)	(3,068,932)	(6,843,493)	962,701
Increase (decrease) in accounts payable and accrued liabilities	31,740,472	13,243,738	(4,106,154)	22,602,888
Increase in other long-term liabilities and other	6,671,950	3,904,508	2,253,798	513,644
Net cash provided by operating activities	200,031,827	92,489,766	47,933,927	59,608,134
Investing activities:				
Additions to property, plant and equipment	(185,309,400)	(73,181,647)	(70,620,543)	(41,507,210)
Other	307,207	58,995	105,792	142,420
Net cash used in investing activities	(185,002,193)	(73,122,652)	(70,514,751)	(41,364,790)
Financing activities:				
Payments on long-term debt	(14,716,080)	(2,535,000)	(6,460,836)	(5,720,244)
Issuance of common stock	2,392,656	1,144,090	839,468	409,098
Dividends paid	(17,465,664)	(7,080,479)	(5,712,039)	(4,673,146)
Net cash used in financing activities	(29,789,088)	(8,471,389)	(11,333,407)	(9,984,292)
Increase (decrease) in cash and short-term investments	(14,759,454)	10,895,725	(33,914,231)	8,259,052
Cash and short-term investments at beginning of year	64,345,765	38,690,586	72,604,817	64,345,765
Cash and short-term investments at end of year	$ 49,586,311	$49,586,311	$38,690,586	$72,604,817

flow from operations are cash flow items. The 1989 *Accounting Trends and Techniques* reports that of 542 surveyed companies presenting the cash flow statement in 1988, only 16 used the direct method.[12] It is likely that the use of the direct method will increase in the future, as firms adapt their accounting systems to provide the information necessitated by the direct method. As previously indicated, regardless of whether the direct or the indirect method is used, SFAS No. 95 requires that a reconciliation of net income to cash flow from operating activities be presented and that interest and income tax payments be disclosed.

Exhibit 10-5 presents the 1989 cash flow statement of Wausau Paper Mills. This firm presented the cash flows from operating activities using the direct method. The Wausau Paper Mills statement has been restated in Exhibit 10-6, presenting a total column for 1989, 1988, and 1987. Note the following with regard to Exhibit 10-6:

1. Net cash provided by operations represented the major source of cash for each year.
2. Capital expenditures represented the major outflow of cash each year.
3. Capital expenditures were particularly significant in 1989.
4. Borrowings under revolving credit facility were the significant source of financing, and all of it came in 1989.
5. Cash dividends represented less than 11% of cash provided by operations for the three-year period.

For Wausau, the year 1989 has been restated in Exhibit 10-7, viewing inflows and outflows separately. Some observations regarding this exhibit follow:

1. Over 91% of total cash inflow came from operations.
2. Approximately 80% of total cash outflows related to operations.
3. Capital expenditures represented approximately 17% of outflows.
4. Borrowings under revolving credit facility represented approximately 7% of 1989 inflows.
5. Dividends paid represent less than 1% of the outflows.

PROCEDURES FOR DEVELOPMENT
OF THE STATEMENT OF CASH FLOWS

It is useful to consider the accounts that hold the explanations of why cash and cash equivalents changed. The cash inflows and outflows are determined by analyzing all balance sheet accounts other than the cash and cash equivalent accounts. The cash inflows are generated from the accounts listed on page 434.

---

[12]American Institute of Certified Public Accountants, *Accounting Trends and Techniques*, 1989, p. 372. Copyright © 1989, by the American Institute of Certified Public Accountants, Inc. Material is reprinted with permission.

EXHIBIT 10-5

WAUSAU PAPER MILLS COMPANY & SUBSIDIARIES
Consolidated Statement of Cash Flows
Years Ended August 31, 1989, 1988, 1987

(All dollar amounts in thousands)	1989	1988	1987
Increase (decrease) in cash and cash equivalents			
Cash flows from operating activities:			
Cash received from customers	$284,901	$281,366	$248,998
Cash paid to suppliers and employees	(242,868)	(253,088)	(221,367)
Interest received	966	991	647
Interest paid (net of amount capitalized)	(40)	(2,199)	(2,158)
Income taxes paid	(10,226)	(8,688)	(6,713)
Net cash provided by operations	32,733	18,382	19,407
Cash flows from investing activities:			
(Increase) decrease in short-term investments	5,503	(1,693)	(614)
Capital expenditures	(54,540)	(14,900)	(10,550)
Proceeds from property, plant and equipment disposals	47	374	38
Net cash used in investing activities	(48,990)	(16,219)	(11,126)
Cash flows from financing activities:			
Borrowings under revolving credit facility	22,000		
Repayment of long-term debt	(5,781)	(4,511)	(4,425)
Dividends paid	(3,128)	(2,499)	(2,093)
Proceeds from sale of treasury stock	8		18
Net cash provided by (used in) financing activities	13,099	(7,010)	(6,500)
Net increase (decrease) in cash and cash equivalents	(3,158)	(4,847)	1,781
Cash and cash equivalents at beginning of year	5,072	9,919	8,138
Cash and cash equivalents at end of year	$ 1,914	$ 5,072	$ 9,919
Reconciliation of net earnings to net cash provided by operating activities:			
Net earnings	$ 20,912	$ 16,005	$ 12,047
Provision for depreciation, depletion and amortization	7,686	7,274	7,022
Abandonment of fixed assets		1,138	
Increase in receivables	(1,860)	(2,500)	(2,131)
(Increase) decrease in inventories	3,227	(5,018)	1,427
Increase in other assets	(904)	(1,913)	(162)
Increase (decrease) in accounts payable and other liabilities	2,598	3,713	(983)
Increase (decrease) in accrued income taxes	(1,764)	(591)	424
Increase in deferred taxes	2,838	274	1,763
Net cash provided by operations	$ 32,733	$ 18,382	$ 19,407

EXHIBIT 10-6

WAUSAU PAPER MILLS COMPANY & SUBSIDIARIES
Consolidated Statement of Cash Flows, with Three-Year Total
Years Ended August 31, 1989, 1988, 1987

(All dollar amounts in thousands)	Total	1989	1988	1987
Increase (decrease) in cash and cash equivalents				
Cash flows from operating activities:				
Cash received from customers	$815,265	$284,901	$281,366	$248,998
Cash paid to suppliers and employees	(717,323)	(242,868)	(253,088)	(221,367)
Interest received	2,604	966	991	647
Interest paid (net of amount capitalized)	(4,397)	(40)	(2,199)	(2,158)
Income taxes paid	(25,627)	(10,226)	(8,688)	(6,713)
Net cash provided by operations	70,522	32,733	18,382	19,407
Cash flows from investing activities:				
(Increase) decrease in short-term investments	3,196	5,503	(1,693)	(614)
Capital expenditures	(79,990)	(54,540)	(14,900)	(10,550)
Proceeds from property, plant and equipment disposals	454	47	374	38
Net cash used in investing activities	(76,335)	(48,990)	(16,219)	(11,126)
Cash flows from financing activities:				
Borrowings under revolving credit facility	22,000	22,000		
Repayment of long-term debt	(14,717)	(5,781)	(4,511)	(4,425)
Dividends paid	(7,720)	(3,128)	(2,499)	(2,093)
Proceeds from sale of treasury stock	26	8		18
Net cash provided by (used in) financing activities	(411)	13,099	(7,010)	(6,500)
Net increase (decrease) in cash and cash equivalents	(6,224)	(3,158)	(4,847)	1,781
Cash and cash equivalents at beginning of year	23,129	5,072	9,919	8,138
Cash and cash equivalents at end of year	$ 16,905	$ 1,914	$ 5,072	$ 9,919
Reconciliation of net earnings to net cash provided by operating activities:				
Net earnings	48,964	$ 20,912	$ 16,005	$ 12,047
Provision for depreciation, depletion and amortization	22,982	7,686	7,274	7,022
Abandonment of fixed assets	1,138		1,138	
Increase in receivables	(6,491)	(1,860)	(2,500)	(2,131)
(Increase) decrease in inventories	(364)	3,227	(5,018)	1,427
Increase in other assets	(2,979)	(904)	(1,913)	(162)
Increase (decrease) in accounts payable and other liabilities	5,328	2,598	3,713	(983)
Increase (decrease) in accrued income taxes	(1,931)	(1,764)	(591)	424
Increase in deferred taxes	4,875	2,838	274	1,763
Net cash provided by operations	$ 70,522	$ 32,733	$ 18,382	$ 19,407

E X H I B I T   1 0 - 7

WAUSAU PAPER MILLS COMPANY & SUBSIDIARIES
Statement of Cash Flows (Inflows and Outflows by Activity)
For Year Ended August 31, 1989

(All dollar amounts in thousands)	Inflows	Outflows	Inflow Percent	Outflow Percent
Increase (decrease) in cash and cash equivalents				
Cash flows from operating activities:				
Cash received from customers	$284,901		90.3	76.72
Cash paid to suppliers and employees		$242,868		
Interest received	966		.31	
Interest paid (net of amount capitalized)		40		.01
Income taxes paid		10,226		3.23
Cash flow from operating activities	285,867	253,134	91.21	79.96
Cash flows from investing activities:				
(Increase) decrease in short-term investments	5,503		1.76	
Capital expenditures		54,540		17.23
Proceeds from property, plant and equipment				
disposals	47		.01	
Cash flow from investing activities	5,550	54,540	1.77	17.23
Cash flows from financing activities:				
Borrowings under revolving credit facility	22,000		7.02	
Repayment of long-term debt		5,781		1.83
Dividends paid		3,128		.99
Proceeds from sale of treasury stock	8			.003
Cash flow from financing activities	22,008	8,909	7.02	2.81
Total cash provided (used)	$313,425	316,583	100	100
		313,425	—	—
Net decrease in cash		$ 3,158		

1. Decreases in assets (for example, the sale of land for cash)
2. Increases in liabilities (for example, the issuance of long-term bonds)
3. Increases in stockholders' equity (for example, the sale of common stock)

The outflows are generated from the following accounts:

1. Increases in assets (for example, the purchase of a building for cash)
2. Decreases in liabilities (for example, retirement of long-term debt)
3. Decreases in stockholders' equity (for example, the payment of a cash dividend)

Within any individual account, there may be an explanation of both a source and a use of cash. For example, the land account may have increased, but analysis may indicate that there was both an acquisition and a disposal of land.

In order to prepare the statement of cash flows, information from the following is required:

1. The balance sheet for the current period
2. The balance sheet for the prior period
3. Income statement for the current period
4. Supplementary information from the balance sheet accounts, with the exception of the cash equivalent accounts

Steps in developing the statement of cash flows are as follows:

1. Compute the changes in the cash and cash equivalent accounts from the prior period to the end of the current period. This represents the net increase (decrease) in cash to which the statement will balance.
2. Compute the net change in each balance sheet account, except for cash and cash equivalent accounts. The explanation of why the cash and cash equivalent accounts changed is in the balance sheet accounts other than cash and cash equivalent accounts.
3. Determine the cash flows, the noncash investing and financing activities, and the effect of exchange rate changes,[13] using the net change in the balance sheet accounts, the income statement for the current period, and the supplementary information. Segregate the cash flows as cash flows from operating activities, cash flows from investing activities, and cash flows from financing activities.
4. Prepare the statement of cash flows.

Exhibit 10-8 contains the data needed for preparing a statement of cash flows for the ABC Company for the year ended December 31, 1991. These data will be used to illustrate the preparation of the statement of cash flows.

Three techniques may be used to complete the steps in developing the statement of cash flows: (1) the visual method, (2) the T-account method, and (3) the worksheet method. The visual method can be used only when the financial information is not complicated. When the financial information is complicated, either the T-account method or the worksheet method must be used. Only the visual method is illustrated in this book, because the emphasis here is on using financial accounting information, not on the accountant's preparation of financial statements. For an explanation of the T-account method and the worksheet method, consult an intermediate accounting textbook. It is not likely that you will be able to apply either the T-account method or the worksheet method to a complicated situation unless you complete intermediate accounting.

---

[13]Computations for the effect of exchange rate changes are beyond the scope of this book. Therefore, these computations will not be illustrated.

EXHIBIT 10-8

ABC COMPANY
Financial Information for Statement of Cash Flows

	Balance Sheet Information		
	Balances		
Accounts	December 31, 1990	December 31, 1991	Category
Assets			
Cash	$ 2,400	$ 3,000	Cash
Accounts receivable, net	4,000	3,900	Operating
Inventories	5,000	6,000	Operating
Total current assets	11,400	12,900	
Land	10,000	19,500	Investing
Equipment	72,000	73,000	Investing
Accumulated depreciation	(9,500)	(14,000)	Operating
Total assets	$83,900	$91,400	
Liabilities			
Accounts payable	$ 4,000	$ 2,900	Operating
Taxes payable	1,600	2,000	Operating
Total current liabilities	5,600	4,900	
Bonds payable	35,000	40,000	Financing
Stockholders' equity			
Common stock, $10 par	36,000	39,000	Financing
Retained earnings	7,300	7,500	*
Total liabilities and stockholders' equity	$83,900	$91,400	

Income Statement Information For the Year Ended December 31, 1991		Category
Sales	$22,000	Operating
Operating expenses	17,500	Operating
Operating income	4,500	
Gain on sale of land	1,000	Investing
Income before tax expense	5,500	
Tax expense	2,000	Operating
Net income	$ 3,500	

Supplemental Information	Category
(a) Dividends declared and paid are $3,300	Financing
(b) Land was sold for $1,500	Investing
(c) Equipment was purchased for $1,000	Investing
(d) Bonds payable were retired for $5,000	Financing

E X H I B I T   1 0 - 8   (continued)

Supplemental Information	Category
(e) Common stock was sold for $3,000	Financing
(f) Operating expenses includes depreciation expense of $4,500	Operating
(g) The land account and the bond payable account increased by $10,000 because of a noncash exchange.	

*Retained earnings is decreased by cash dividends, $3,300 (financing), and increased by net income, $3,500. Net income can be a combination of operating, investing, and financing activities. In this exhibit all of the net income relates to operating activities except for the gain on sale of land (investing).

Following the steps in developing the statement of cash flows, we first compute the change in cash and cash equivalents. For the ABC Company, this is the increase in the cash account of $600—the net increase in cash.

For the second step, we compute the net change in each balance sheet account other than the cash account. The changes in the balance sheet accounts for the ABC Company are as follows:

Assets

Accounts receivable decrease	$ 100	Operating
Inventories increase	1,000	Operating
Land increase	9,500	Investing
Equipment increase	1,000	Investing
Accumulated depreciation increase (contra-asset—a change would be similar to a change in liabilities)	4,500	Operating

Liabilities

Accounts payable decrease	1,100	Operating
Taxes payable increase	400	Operating
Bonds payable increase	5,000	Financing

Stockholders' equity

Common stock increase	3,000	Financing
Retained earnings increase	200	*

*This is a combination of operating, financing, and investing activities.

For the third step, we consider the changes in the balance sheet accounts along with the income statement for the current period and the supplementary information. The cash flows are segregated as to cash flows from operating activities, cash flows from investing activities, and cash flows from financing activities. Noncash investing and/or financing activities should be shown in a separate schedule with the statement of cash flows.

As previously indicated, cash flows from operating activities are cash flows from operations. Also, there are two methods of presenting cash flow from operating activities: the direct and indirect methods.

To illustrate these two methods, the ABC Company income statement is used, along with the relevant supplemental information and balance sheet accounts. For the direct approach, the revenue and expense accounts on the income statement are presented on a cash basis. For this purpose, the accrual basis income statement is adjusted to a cash basis, as illustrated in Exhibit 10-9.

When the cash provided by operations is presented using the direct approach, the income statement accounts are usually described in terms of receipts or payments. For example, "sales" on the accrual basis income statement is usually described as "receipts from customers" when presented on a cash basis. For the ABC Company, cash provided by operations, using the direct approach, is as follows:

Receipts from customers (from Exhibit 10-9)	$22,100
Payments to suppliers (from Exhibit 10-9)	(15,100)
Income taxes paid (from Exhibit 10-9)	(1,600)
Net cash provided by operating activities	$ 5,400

To compute cash flows from operations using the indirect approach, we start with net income and add back or deduct adjustments necessary to change the income on an accrual basis to income on a cash basis, after eliminating gains or losses that relate to investing or financing activities. On the ABC Company schedule of change from accrual basis to cash basis income statement, notice that the adjustments include non-cash flow items on the income statement, changes in balance sheet accounts related to operations, and gains and losses on the income statement that are related to investing or financing activities.

For the ABC Company, cash provided by operations, using the indirect approach, is as follows (see Exhibit 10-11):

Net income	$3,500
Add (deduct) items not affecting operating cash	
Depreciation expense	4,500
Decrease in accounts receivable	100
Increase in inventories	(1,000)
Decrease in accounts payable	(1,100)
Increase in taxes payable	400
Gain on sale of land	(1,000)
Net cash provided by operating activities	$5,400

E X H I B I T   1 0 - 9

ABC COMPANY
Schedule of Change from Accrual Basis to Cash Basis Income Statement

Accrual Basis		Adjustments*	Add (Subtract)	Cash Basis
Sales	$22,000	Decrease in receivables	100	$22,100
Operating expenses	17,500	Depreciation expense	(4,500)	
		Increase in inventories	1,000	
		Decrease in payables	1,100	15,100
Operating income	4,500			7,000
Gain on sale of land	1,000	This gain is related to		
Income before tax		investing activities	(1,000)	—0—
expense	5,500			7,000
Tax expense	2,000	Increase in taxes payable	(400)	1,600
Net income	$ 3,500			$5,400

*Adjustments are for non-cash flow items in the income statement, changes in balance sheet accounts related to cash flow from operations, and the removal of gains and losses on the income statement that are related to investing or financing activities.

The non-cash flow items in the income statement are removed from the account. For example, depreciation expense may be in cost of goods sold, and this expense would be removed from cost of goods sold.

Change in balance sheet accounts related to cash flow from operations are adjusted to the related income statement account as follows:

Revenue accounts	$XXX
Add decreases in asset accounts and increases in liability accounts	+ XXX
Deduct increases in asset accounts and decreases in liability accounts	− XXX
Cash flow	$XXX
Expense accounts	
Add increases in asset accounts and decreases in liability accounts	+ XXX
Deduct decreases in asset accounts and increases in liability accounts	− XXX
Cash flow	$XXX

Whether an adjustment should be added to or deducted from the net income (or loss) is sometimes confusing, partly because the additions and subtractions do not follow the same rules as were used on the schedule of change from accrual basis to cash basis income statement. For the indirect approach, follow these directions when adjusting the net income (or loss) to net cash flows from operating activities:

Net income (loss)	$ xxx
Non-cash flow items:	
Add expenses	+ xxx
Deduct revenues	− xxx

Changes in balance sheet accounts related to operations:*	
Add decreases in assets and increases in liabilities	+ xxx
Deduct increases in assets and decreases in liabilities	− xxx
Gains and losses on the income statement that are related to investing or financing activities:	
Add losses	+ xxx
Deduct gains	− xxx
Net cash provided by operating activities	$ xxx

*These are usually the current asset and current liability accounts.

The remaining changes in balance sheet accounts (other than those used to compute cash provided by operating activities) and the remaining supplemental information are used to determine the cash flows from investing activities and cash flows from financing activities. These accounts are also used to determine noncash investing and/or financing.

The net cash provided (used) by investing activities and net cash provided (used) by financing activities are computed as follows for the ABC Company:

Cash flow from investing activities:	
Proceeds from sale of land (accounted for by gain on sale of land, $1,000, and decrease in land, $500. The land account increased by $10,000 because of the noncash exchange of land for bonds)	$1,500
Equipment was purchased for (accounted for by increase in equipment account)	(1,000)
Net cash provided by investing activities (see Exhibit 10-10 or Exhibit 10-11)	$ 500
Cash flow from financing activities:	
Dividends declared and paid (dividends declared and paid $3,300 and net income $3,500 account for the increase in retained earnings of $200)	($3,300)
Retirement of bonds payable (the bond payable account decreased $5,000 because of retirement of bonds and increased	(5,000)

EXHIBIT   10-10

Direct Approach for Presenting Cash Flows from Operations
ABC COMPANY
Statement of Cash Flows
For the Year Ended December 31, 1991

Cash flows from operating activities:		
Receipts from customers	$22,100	
Payments to suppliers	(15,100)	
Income taxes paid	(1,600)	
Net cash provided by operating activities		$ 5,400
Cash flows from investing activities:		
Proceeds from sale of land	1,500	
Purchase of equipment	(1,000)	
Net cash provided by investing activities		500
Cash flows from financing activities:		
Dividends declared and paid	($3,300)	
Retirement of bonds payable	(5,000)	
Proceeds from common stock	3,000	
Net cash used for financing activities		(5,300)
Net increase in cash		$ 600
Reconciliation of net income to net cash provided by operating activities:		
Net income		$ 3,500
Adjustments to reconcile net income to net cash provided by operating activities:		
Decrease in accounts receivable		100
Depreciation expense		4,500
Increase in inventories		(1,000)
Decrease in accounts payable		(1,100)
Gain on sale of land		(1,000)
Increase in taxes payable		400
Net cash provided by operating activities		$ 5,400
Supplemental schedule of noncash investing and financing activities:		
Land acquired by issuing bonds		$10,000

$10,000 because of the noncash issuance for land)		
Proceeds from common stock	3,000	
(accounted for by an increase in the common stock account of $3,000)		
Net cash used for financing activities	($5,300)	
(see Exhibit 10-10 or 10-11)		

EXHIBIT 10-11

Indirect Approach for Presenting Cash Flows from Operations
ABC COMPANY
Statement of Cash Flows
For the Year Ended December 31, 1991

Cash flows from operating activities:		
Net income	$ 3,500	
Add (deduct) items not affecting operating activities		
Depreciation expense	4,500	
Decrease in accounts receivable	100	
Increase in inventories	(1,000)	
Decrease in accounts payable	(1,100)	
Increase in taxes payable	400	
Gain on sale of land	(1,000)	
Net cash provided by operating activities		$ 5,400
Cash flows from investing activities:		
Proceeds from sale of land	1,500	
Purchase of equipment	(1,000)	
Net cash provided by investing activities		500
Cash flows from financing activities:		
Dividends declared and paid	($3,300)	
Retirement of bonds payable	(5,000)	
Proceeds from common stock	3,000	
Net cash used for financing activities		(5,300)
Net increase in cash		$ 600
Supplemental disclosure of cash flow information:		
Cash paid during the year for:		
Interest (net of amount capitalized)		0
Income taxes		1,600
Supplemental schedule of noncash investing and financing activities:		
Land acquired by issuing bonds		$10,000

The noncash investing and/or financing activity was the investing activity of acquiring the land ($10,000) and the financing activity of issuing the bonds ($10,000).

Exhibit 10-10 shows the statement of cash flows for the ABC Company using the direct approach for presenting cash flows from operations; Exhibit 10-11 shows the indirect approach.

Some observations on the ABC Company statement of cash flows follow:

1. Net cash provided by operating activities	$5,400
2. Net cash provided by investing activities	$ 500
3. Net cash used for financing activities	$5,300
4. Net increase in cash	$ 600

Additional observations can be determined by preparing the statement of cash flows to present inflows and outflows separately, when the operations section has been presented using the direct method. This has been done in Exhibit 10-12. Some observations from the summary of cash flows in Exhibit 10-12 follow:

Inflows

1. Receipts from customers represent approximately 83% of total cash inflow.
2. Proceeds from common stock sales represent approximately 11% of total cash inflow.
3. Proceeds from sales of land represent approximately 6% of total cash inflow.

EXHIBIT 10-12

ABC COMPANY
Statement of Cash Flows
For the Year Ended December 31, 1991
(Inflows and Outflows, by Activity—Inflows Presented on Direct Basis)

	Inflows	Outflows	Inflow Percent	Outflow Percent
Operating activities:				
Receipts from customers	$22,100		83.1%	
Payments to suppliers		$15,100		58.1%
Income taxes paid		1,600		6.2
Cash flow from operating activities	22,100	16,700	83.1	64.3
Investing activities:				
Proceeds from sale of land	1,500		5.6	
Purchase of equipment		1,000		3.8
Cash flow from investing activities	1,500	1,000	5.6	3.8
Financing activities:				
Dividends declared and paid		3,300		12.7
Retirement of bonds payable		5,000		19.2
Proceeds from common stock	3,000		11.3	
Cash flow from financing activities	3,000	8,300	11.3	31.9
Total cash flows	26,600 26,000	26,000	100.0	100.0
Net increase in cash	$ 600			

Outflows

1. Payment to suppliers represent approximately 58% of total cash outflow.
2. Retirement of bonds payable represent approximately 19% of total cash outflow.
3. Dividends paid represent approximately 13% of total cash outflow.

FINANCIAL RATIOS
AND THE STATEMENT OF CASH FLOWS

Financial ratios that relate to the funds statement were slow in being developed, probably because of several factors. For one thing, most financial ratios relate an income statement item to a balance sheet item. This became the normal way of approaching financial analysis, and the funds statement did not become a required statement until 1971. Thus, it took a while for analysts to become familiar with the statement. Another reason why ratios were slow to develop is that the presentation of the funds statement was very flexible.

Ratios have now been developed that relate to the cash flow statement. Some of the ratios are as follows:

1. Operating cash flow/current maturities of long-term debt and current notes payable
2. Operating cash flow/total debt
3. Operating cash flow per share
4. Operating cash flow/cash dividends

Operating Cash Flow/Current Maturities
of Long-Term Debt and Current Notes Payable

The operating cash flow/current maturities of long-term debt and current notes payable is a ratio that indicates a firm's ability to meet its current maturities of debt. The higher this ratio, the better the firm's ability to meet its current maturities of debt. The higher this ratio, the better the firm's liquidity. This ratio relates to the liquidity ratios discussed in Chapter 6. It is introduced here because it relates to the funds statement.

There is a difference of opinion as to what constitutes cash flow. Some are of the opinion that cash flow from operating activities before nonrecurring items should be used, while others feel that net cash flow from operating activities should be used. The cash flow recommended in this book is cash flow from operating activities before nonrecurring items.[14]

---

[14]Note: Exclude any cash influence from unusual or infrequent items, extraordinary items, discontinued operations, and cumulative effect of accounting change.

The formula for operating cash flow/current maturities of long-term debt and current notes payable is the same as the title of the ratio:

$$\frac{\text{Operating Cash Flow}}{\text{Current Maturities of Long-Term Debt and Current Notes Payable}}$$

The operating cash flow/current maturities of long-term debt and current notes payable is computed for Cooper for 1989 and 1988 in Exhibit 10-13. For Cooper, this ratio is very good, especially in 1989.

Operating Cash Flow/Total Debt

The operating cash flow/total debt ratio indicates a firm's ability to cover total debt with the yearly cash flow. The higher the ratio, the better the firm's ability to carry its total debt. From a debt standpoint, this is considered to be important. It relates to the debt ratios seen in Chapter 7. It is a type of income view of debt, except that operating cash flow is the perspective instead of an income figure. It is introduced here because it relates to the cash flow statement. The operating cash flow amount in this ratio is the same cash flow amount that is computed for the operating cash flow/current maturities of long-term debt and current notes payable. The total debt figure is the same total debt amount that was computed in Chapter 7 for the debt ratio and the debt/equity ratio. For the primary computation of the operating cash flow/total debt ratio, all possible balance sheet debt items are included, as was done for the debt ratio and the debt/equity ratio. This is the more conservative approach to computing the ratio. In practice, many firms are more selective in what is included in debt. Some include only short-term liabilities and long-term items such as bonds payable. The formula for operating cash flow/total debt is as follows:

$$\frac{\text{Operating Cash Flow}}{\text{Total Debt}}$$

EXHIBIT 10-13

COOPER TIRE & RUBBER COMPANY
Operating Cash Flow/Current Maturities of Long-Term Debt and
   Current Notes Payable
For the Years Ended December 31, 1989 and 1988

	1989	1988
Operating cash flow [A]	$92,489,766	$47,933,927
Current maturities of long-term debt and current notes payable [B]	$ 2,060,000	$ 2,532,000
Operating cash flow/current maturities of long-term debt and current notes payable [A ÷ B]	44.90 times	18.93 times

The operating cash flow/total debt ratio is computed in Exhibit 10-14 for Cooper for the years ended December 31, 1989 and 1988. It indicates that the cash flow is significant in relation to total debt.

Operating Cash Flow Per Share

Operating cash flow per share indicates the funds flow per common share outstanding; it is usually substantially higher than earnings per share, because depreciation has not been deducted.

In the short run, operating cash flow per share is a better indication of a firm's ability to make capital expenditure decisions and pay dividends than is earnings per share. This ratio should not be viewed as a substitute for earnings per share in terms of a firm's profitability. For this reason, SFAS No. 95 prohibits firms from reporting cash flow per share on the face of the statement of cash flows. However, it is a complementary ratio that relates to the ratios of relevance to investors (discussed in Chapter 9).

The operating cash flow per share formula is as follows:

$$\frac{\text{Operating Cash Flow} - \text{Preferred Dividends}}{\text{Common Shares Outstanding}}$$

The operating cash flow amount is the same figure that was used in the two previous funds formulas in this chapter. For common shares outstanding, use the shares that were used for the purpose of computing earnings per share assuming full dilution when the firm has a complex capital structure. This figure is available when doing internal analysis; it is also in a firm's 10-K annual report. Some companies disclose the number of shares in the annual report. This share number cannot be computed from information in the annual report, except for very simple situations. To compute the number of shares, it takes an understanding of the rules on how to compute the shares for fully diluted earnings per share. For a firm that has a simple capital structure, use the number of shares used to compute the earnings per share.

EXHIBIT   10-14

COOPER TIRE & RUBBER COMPANY
Operating Cash Flow/Total Debt
For the Years Ended December 31, 1989 and 1988

	1989	1988
Operating cash flow [A]	$ 92,489,766	$ 47,933,927
Total debt [B]	209,828,950	184,826,293
Operating cash flow/total debt [A ÷ B]	44.08%	25.93%

When these share amounts are not available, use the outstanding shares of common stock. This will result in an approximation of the operating cash flow per share. The advantage of using the number of shares used for earnings per share is that this results in an amount that can be compared to earnings per share, and it avoids distortions.

Operating cash flow per share is computed for Cooper for 1989 and 1988 in Exhibit 10-15. Operating cash flow per share was significantly more than earnings per share in both 1989 and 1988. In 1989, there was a very material increase in cash flow per share.

Operating Cash Flow/Cash Dividends

The operating cash flow/cash dividends ratio indicates a firm's ability to cover cash dividends with the yearly operating cash flow. The higher the ratio, the better the firm's ability to cover cash dividends. This ratio relates to the investor ratios discussed in Chapter 9. It is introduced here because it relates to the cash flow statement.

The operating cash flow/cash dividends formula is as follows:

$$\frac{\text{Operating Cash Flow}}{\text{Cash Dividends}}$$

The operating cash flow amount is the same figure that was used in the three previous funds formulas in this chapter. Operating cash flow/cash dividends is computed for Cooper for 1989 and 1988 in Exhibit 10-16. It indicates a very high coverage of cash dividends in both 1989 and 1988. There was a substantial increase in the cash dividends coverage in 1989.

EXHIBIT 10-15

COOPER TIRE & RUBBER COMPANY
Operating Cash Flow Per Share
For the Years Ended December 31, 1989 and 1988

	1989	1988
Operating cash flow	$92,489,766	$47,933,927
Less preferred dividends	—0—	—0—
Operating cash flow after preferred dividends [A]	$92,489,766	$47,933,927
Number of common shares based on the weighted average number of shares outstanding [B]	20,519,236	20,395,635
Operating cash flow per share [A ÷ B]	$4.51	$2.35

EXHIBIT 10-16

COOPER TIRE & RUBBER COMPANY
Operating Cash Flow/Cash Dividends
For the Years Ended December 31, 1989 and 1988

	1989	1988
Operating cash flow [A]	$92,489,766	$47,933,927
Cash dividends [B]	7,080,479	5,712,039
Operating cash flow/cash dividends [A ÷ B]	13.06 times	8.39 times

ALTERNATIVE CASH FLOW

There is no standard definition of cash flow. Often, *cash flow* is used to mean net income plus depreciation expense. This definition of cash flow could be used to compute the cash flow amount for the formulas introduced in this chapter. However, this is a narrow definition of cash flow, and it is considered less useful than the net cash flow from operating activities.

SUMMARY

This chapter has reviewed the development of the funds statement. This statement is now called the *statement of cash flows*. It is a required financial statement, to be included with the balance sheet and income statement. The statement should be reviewed for several time periods in order to determine the major sources of cash and the major uses of cash.

The ratios related to the statement of cash flows are the following:

$$\text{Operating Cash Flow/Current Maturities of Long-Term Debt and Current Notes Payable} = \frac{\text{Operating Cash Flow}}{\text{Current Maturities of Long-Term Debt and Current Notes Payable}}$$

$$\text{Operating Cash Flow/Total Debt} = \frac{\text{Operating Cash Flow}}{\text{Total Debt}}$$

$$\text{Operating Cash Flow Per Share} = \frac{\text{Operating Cash Flow} - \text{Preferred Dividends}}{\text{Common Shares Outstanding}}$$

$$\text{Operating Cash Flow/Cash Dividends} = \frac{\text{Operating Cash Flow}}{\text{Cash Dividends}}$$

QUESTIONS

Q 10-1   If a firm presents an income statement and a balance sheet, why is it necessary that a statement of cash flows also be presented?

Q 10-2   When did the first funds statements appear? Relate the period a funds statement has been presented to the period that a balance sheet and income statement have been presented.

Q 10-3   By 1903, at least four conceptually different statements were presented as the funds statement. List these four statements.

Q 10-4   In what year did the funds statement become required when a balance sheet and income statement are presented? What was the title of that statement? In what year did the cash format become the required format?

Q 10-5   Indicate the basic reason for using the working capital approach to presenting the funds statement.

Q 10-6   Working capital has been considered one of the prime indicators of liquidity. Name the ratio related to working capital that is used as a prime indicator of liquidity.

Q 10-7   When the funds statement is presented on a working capital basis, the cash flow of a company may not be obvious. Explain.

Q 10-8   Indicate how each of the following influenced the selection of the format as the standard for presenting the funds statement.
   a. "Report of the Study Group on the Objectives of Financial Statements" (1973 AICPA).
   b. Statement of Financial Accounting Concepts No. 1, "Objectives of Financial Reporting by Business Enterprises" (1978 FASB Concept Statement)
   c. Statement of Financial Accounting Concepts No. 5, "Recognition and Measurement of Financial Statements of Business Enterprises" (1984 FASB Concept Statement)

Q 10-9   Into what three categories are cash flows segregated on the statement of cash flows?

Q 10-10   Using the descriptions of assets, liabilities, and stockholders' equity, summarize the changes to these accounts for cash inflows and changes to these accounts for cash outflows.

Q 10-11   The land account may be used to explain a use of cash, but not a source of cash. Comment.

Q 10-12   Indicate the three techniques that may be used to complete the steps in developing the statement of cash flows.

Q 10-13   There are two principal methods of presenting cash flow from operating activities: the direct method and the indirect method. Describe these two methods.

Q 10-14   Depreciation expense, amortization of patents, and amortization of bond discount are examples of items that are added to net income when using the indirect method of presenting cash flow from operating activities. Amortization of premium on bonds and a reduction in deferred taxes are examples of items that are deducted from net income when using the indirect method of presenting cash flow from operating activities. Explain why these adjustments to net income are made to compute cash flow from operating activities.

Q 10-15   What is the meaning of the term *cash* in the statement of cash flows?

Q 10-16   What is the purpose of the statement of cash flows?

Q 10-17   Why is it important to disclose certain noncash investing and financing transactions, such as exchanging common stock for land?

Q 10-18   For both the net working capital concept of funds and the cash concept of funds, indicate if the following (1) provide funds, (2) use funds, or (3) do not change funds.

    a. collection of accounts receivable
    b. purchase of land with cash
    c. payment of bonds payable
    d. payment of accounts payable
    e. sale of common stock
    f. purchase of machinery and equipment on account

Q 10-19   Would a write-off of uncollectible accounts against allowance for doubtful accounts be disclosed on a cash flow statement? Explain.

Q 10-20   Fully depreciated equipment costing $60,000 was discarded, with no salvage value. What effect would this have on the statement of cash flows?

Q 10-21   For the current year, a firm reported net income from operations of $20,000 on its income statement and an increase of $30,000 in cash from operations on the statement of cash flows. Explain some likely reasons for the greater increase in cash from operations than net income from operations.

Q 10-22   A firm owed accounts payable of $150,000 at the beginning of the year and $250,000 at the end of the year. What influence does the $100,000 increase have on cash from operations?

Q 10-23   A member of the board of directors is puzzled by the fact that the firm has had a very profitable year but does not have enough cash to pay its bills on time. Explain to the director how a firm can be profitable, yet not have enough cash to pay its bills and dividends.

Q 10-24   Depreciation is often considered a major source of funds. Do you agree? Explain.

Q 10-25   Pickerton started the year with $50,000 in accounts receivable. The firm ended the year with $20,000 in accounts receivable. How did this decrease influence cash from operations?

Q 10-26   Aerco Company acquired equipment in exchange for $50,000 in common stock. Should this transaction be on the statement of cash flows?

Q 10-27   Operating cash flow per share is a better indicator of profitability than is earnings per share. Do you agree? Explain.

Q 10-28   In your primary analysis, you were advised to consider cash provided by operations excluding nonrecurring items. Which nonrecurring items should be excluded?

Q 10-29   The Hornet Company had operating cash flow of $60,000 during a year in which it paid dividends of $11,000. What does this indicate about Hornet's dividend-paying ability?

PROBLEMS

P 10-1   The following material relates to the Darrow Company:

Data	Cash Flows Classification			Effect on Cash		Noncash Transactions
	Operating Activity	Investing Activity	Financing Activity	Increase	Decrease	
a. net loss	_____	_____	_____	_____	_____	_____
b. increase in inventory	_____	_____	_____	_____	_____	_____
c. decrease in receivables	_____	_____	_____	_____	_____	_____
d. increase in prepaid insurance	_____	_____	_____	_____	_____	_____
e. issuance of common stock	_____	_____	_____	_____	_____	_____
f. acquisition of land using notes payable	_____	_____	_____	_____	_____	_____
g. purchase of land using cash	_____	_____	_____	_____	_____	_____
h. payment of cash dividend	_____	_____	_____	_____	_____	_____
i. payment of income taxes	_____	_____	_____	_____	_____	_____
j. retirement of bonds using cash	_____	_____	_____	_____	_____	_____
k. sale of equipment for cash	_____	_____	_____	_____	_____	_____

Required   Place an X in the appropriate columns for each of the situations.

P 10-2

Data	Cash Flows Classification			Effect on Cash		Noncash Transactions
	Operating Activity	Investing Activity	Financing Activity	Increase	Decrease	
a. net income	_____	_____	_____	_____	_____	_____
b. paid cash dividend	_____	_____	_____	_____	_____	_____
c. increase in receivables	_____	_____	_____	_____	_____	_____

	Cash Flows Classification			Effect on Cash		
Data	Operating Activity	Investing Activity	Financing Activity	Increase	Decrease	Noncash Transactions
d. retirement of debt— paying cash	_____	_____	_____	_____	_____	_____
e. purchase of treasury stock	_____	_____	_____	_____	_____	_____
f. purchase of equipment	_____	_____	_____	_____	_____	_____
g. sale of equipment	_____	_____	_____	_____	_____	_____
h. decrease in inventory	_____	_____	_____	_____	_____	_____
i. acquisition of land using common stock	_____	_____	_____	_____	_____	_____
j. retired bonds using common stock	_____	_____	_____	_____	_____	_____
k. decrease in accounts payable	_____	_____	_____	_____	_____	_____

Required   Place an X in the appropriate columns for each of the situations.

P 10-3   The BBB Company balance sheet and income statement follow:

BBB COMPANY
Balance Sheet
December 31, 1991 and 1990

	Balances	
	December 31, 1991	December 31, 1990
Assets		
Cash	$ 4,500	$ 4,000
Marketable securities	2,500	2,000
Accounts receivable	6,800	7,200
Inventories	7,500	8,000
Total current assets	21,300	21,200
Land	11,000	12,000
Equipment	24,000	20,500

	Balances	
	December 31, 1991	December 31, 1990
Accumulated depreciation		
Equipment	(3,800)	(3,000)
Building	70,000	70,000
Accumulated depreciation		
Building	(14,000)	(12,000)
Total assets	108,500	108,700
Liabilities and stockholders' equity		
Accounts payable	7,800	7,000
Wages payable	1,050	1,000
Taxes payable	500	1,500
Total current liabilities	9,350	9,500
Bonds payable	30,000	30,000
Common stock, $10 par	32,000	30,000
Additional paid-in capital	21,000	19,200
Retained earnings	16,150	20,000
	$108,500	$108,700

BBB COMPANY
Income Statement
For the Year Ended December 31, 1991

Sales		$38,000
Operating expenses		
Depreciation expense	$ 2,800	
Other operating expenses	35,000	37,800
Operating income		200
Gain on sale of land		800
Income before tax expense		1,000
Tax expense		500
Net income		$ 500
Supplemental information:		
Dividends declared and paid	$ 4,350	
Land was sold	1,800	
Equipment was purchased	3,500	
Common stock was sold	3,800	

Required   a. Prepare a statement of cash flows for the year ended December 31, 1991. (Present the cash flows from operations using the indirect method.)
              b. Comment on the statement of cash flows.

P 10-4   The income statement and other selected data for the Frish Company are as follows.

FRISH COMPANY
Income Statement
For the Year Ended December 31, 1991

Net sales	$640,000
Expenses	
Cost of goods sold	360,000
Selling and administrative expense	43,000
Other expense	2,000
Total expenses	405,000
Income before income tax	235,000
Income tax	92,000
Net income	$143,000

Other data:
a. Cost of goods sold includes depreciation expense of $15,000
b. Selling and administrative expense includes depreciation expense of $5,000
c. Other expense represents amortization of goodwill, $3,000, and amortization of bond premium $1,000

d. Increase in deferred income taxes (a liability account)	4,000
e. Increase in accounts receivable	27,000
f. Increase in accounts payable	15,000
g. Increase in inventories	35,000
h. Decrease in prepaid expenses	1,000
i. Increase in accrued liabilities	3,000
j. Decrease in income taxes payable	10,000

Required   a. Prepare a schedule of change from accrual basis to cash basis income statement.
              b. Using the schedule of change from accrual basis to cash basis income statement computed in (a), present the cash provided by operations using (1) the direct approach and (2) the indirect approach.

P 10-5   The income statement and other selected data for the Boyer Company are as follows:

BOYER COMPANY
Income Statement
For the Year Ended December 31, 1991

Sales		$19,000
Operating expenses		
Depreciation expense	$ 2,300	
Other operating expenses	12,000	14,300
Operating income		4,700
Loss on sale of land		1,500
Income before tax expense		3,200
Tax expense		1,000
Net income		$ 2,200

Supplemental information:

a. Dividends declared and paid	800
b. Land was purchased for	3,000
c. Land was sold for	500
d. Equipment was purchased for	2,000
e. Bonds payable were retired for	2,000
f. Common stock was sold for	1,400
g. Land was acquired in exchange for common stock	3,000
h. Increase in accounts receivable	400
i. Increase in inventories	800
j. Increase in accounts payable	500
k. Decrease in income taxes payable	400

Required

  a. Prepare a schedule of change from accrual basis to cash basis income statement.
  b. Using the schedule of change from accrual basis to cash basis income statement computed in (a), present the cash provided by operations using (1) the direct approach and (2) the indirect approach.

P 10-6

The Sampson Company's balance sheet for December 31, 1991 and the income statement for the year ended December 31, 1991 follow.

SAMPSON COMPANY
Balance Sheet
December 31, 1991 and 1990

	1991	1990
Assets		
Cash	$ 38,000	$ 60,000
Net receivables	72,000	65,000

	1991	1990
Inventory	98,000	85,000
Plant assets	195,000	180,000
Accumulated depreciation	(45,000)	(35,000)
Total assets	$385,000	$355,000
Liabilities and stockholders' equity		
Accounts payable	85,000	80,000
Accrued liabilities (related to cost of sales)	44,000	61,000
Mortgage payable	11,000	—
Common stock	180,000	174,000
Retained earnings	38,000	40,000
	$358,000	$355,000

SAMPSON COMPANY
Income Statement
For Year Ended December 31, 1991

Net sales	$145,000
Cost of sales	108,000
Gross profit	37,000
Other expenses	6,000
Profit before taxes	31,000
Tax expense	12,000
Net income	$ 19,000

Other data:
1. Dividends paid in cash during 1991 was $21,000.
2. Depreciation is included in cost of sales.
3. The change in the accumulated depreciation account is the depreciation expense for the year.

Required
  a. Prepare the statement of cash flows using the indirect method for net cash flow from operating activities.
  b. Prepare the statement of cash flows using the direct method for net cash flow from operating activities.
  c. Comment on significant items disclosed in the statement of cash flows.

P 10-7   The Arrowbell Company is a growing company. Two years ago, it decided to expand in order to increase its production capacity. The company anticipates that the expansion program can be completed in another two years.

ARROWBELL COMPANY
Sales and Net Income

Year	Sales	Income
1984	$2,568,660	$145,800
1985	2,660,455	101,600
1986	2,550,180	52,650
1987	2,625,280	86,800
1988	3,680,650	151,490

ARROWBELL COMPANY
Balance Sheet

	1991	1990
Assets		
Current assets:		
Cash	$ 250,480	$ 260,155
Accounts receivable (net)	760,950	690,550
Inventories at lower of cost or market	725,318	628,238
Prepaid expenses	18,555	20,250
Total current assets	1,755,303	1,599,193
Plant and equipment:		
Land, buildings, machinery, and equipment	3,150,165	2,646,070
Less: Accumulated depreciation	650,180	525,650
Net plant and equipment	2,499,985	2,120,420
Other assets:		
Cash surrender value of life insurance	20,650	18,180
Other	40,660	38,918
Total other assets	61,310	57,098
Total assets	$4,316,598	$3,776,711
Liabilities and stockholders' equity		
Current liabilities:		
Notes and mortgages payable, current portion	915,180	550,155
Accounts payable and accrued liabilities	1,160,111	851,080
Total current liabilities	$2,075,291	$1,401,235
Long-term notes and mortgages payable, less current portion above	550,000	775,659
Total liabilities	$2,625,291	$2,176,894

	1991	1990
Stockholders' equity:		
Capital stock, par value $1.00, authorized		
(800,000); issued and outstanding 600,000		
(1985 and 1986)	$ 600,000	$ 600,000
Paid in excess of par	890,000	890,000
Retained earnings	201,307	109,817
Total stockholders' equity	1,691,307	1,599,817
Total liabilities and stockholders' equity	$4,316,598	$3,776,711

ARROWBELL COMPANY
Statement of Cash Flows
For the Years Ended December 31, 1991 and 1990

	1991	1990
Cash flows from operating activities:		
Net income	$151,490	$ 86,800
Noncash expenses, revenues, losses, and gains		
included in income:		
Depreciation	134,755	102,180
Increase in accounts receivable	(70,400)	(10,180)
Increase in inventories	(97,080)	(15,349)
Decrease in prepaid expenses in 1991, increase		
in 1990	1,695	(1,058)
Increase in accounts payable and accrued liabilities	309,031	15,265
Net cash provided by operating activities	$429,491	$177,658
Cash flows from investing activities:		
Proceeds from retirement of property, plant, and		
equipment	$ 10,115	$ 3,865
Purchases of property, plant, and equipment	(524,435)	(218,650)
Increase in cash surrender value of life insurance	(2,470)	(1,848)
Other	(1,742)	(1,630)
Net cash used for investing activities	(518,532)	(218,263)
Cash flows from financing activities		
Retirement of long-term debt	(225,659)	(50,000)
Increase in notes and mortgages payable	365,025	159,155
Cash dividends	(60,000)	(60,000)
Net cash provided by financing activities	79,366	49,155
Net increase (decrease) in cash	($ 9,675)	$ 8,550

Required
    a. Comment on the short-term debt position, including computations of current ratio, acid test ratio, cash ratio, and operating cash flow/current maturities of long-term debt and current notes payable.

    b. If you were a supplier to this company, what would you be concerned about?

    c. Comment on the long-term debt position, including computations of the debt ratio, debt/equity, debt to tangible net worth, and operating cash flow/total debt. Review the statement of operating cash flows.

    d. If you were a banker, what would you be concerned about if this company approached you for a long-term loan to continue its expansion program?

    e. What should management consider doing at this point in regard to the company's expansion program?

P 10-8
    The Bernett Company's balance sheet for December 31, 1991, and income statement for the year ended December 31, 1991 follow:

BERNETT COMPANY
Balance Sheet
December 31, 1991 and 1990

	1991	1990
Assets		
Cash	$ 5,000	$ 28,000
Accounts receivable, net	92,000	70,000
Inventory	130,000	85,000
Prepaid expenses	4,000	6,000
Land	30,000	10,000
Building	170,000	30,000
Accumulated depreciation	(20,000)	(10,000)
Total assets	$411,000	$219,000
Liabilities and stockholders' equity		
Accounts payable	$ 49,000	$ 44,000
Income taxes payable	5,000	4,000
Accrued liabilities	6,000	5,000
Bonds payable (current $10,000 at 12/31/91)	175,000	20,000
Common stock	106,000	96,000
Retained earnings	70,000	50,000
Total liabilities and stockholders' equity	$411,000	$219,000

BERNETT COMPANY
Income Statement
For the Year Ended December 31, 1991

Sales	$500,000
Less expenses:	
Cost of goods sold (includes depreciation of $4,000)	310,000
Selling and administrative expenses (includes depreciation of $6,000)	80,000
Interest expense	11,000
Total expenses	401,000
Income before taxes	99,000
Income tax expense	30,000
Net income	$ 69,000

Note: Cash dividends of $49,000 were paid during 1991.

The president of Bernett Company cannot understand why Bernett is having trouble paying current obligations. He notes that business has been very good, as sales have more than doubled, and the company achieved a profit of $69,000 in 1991.

Required

a. Prepare the statement of cash flows for 1991. (Present cash flows from operations using the indirect approach.)
b. Comment on the statement of cash flows.
c. Compute the following liquidity ratios for 1991:
  1. current ratio
  2. acid test ratio
  3. operating cash flow/current maturities of long-term debt and current notes payable
  4. cash ratio
d. Compute the following debt ratios for 1991:
  1. times interest earned
  2. debt ratio
  3. operating cash flow/total debt
e. Compute the following profitability ratios for 1991:
  1. return on assets (use average assets)
  2. return on common equity (use average common equity)
f. Compute the following investor ratio for 1991: operating cash flow/cash dividends.
g. Give your opinion as to the liquidity of Bernett Company.
h. Give your opinion as to the debt position of Bernett Company.
i. Give your opinion as to the profitability of Bernett Company.
j. Give your opinion as to the investor ratio.
k. Give your opinion of the alternatives Bernett Company has in order to ensure that it can pay bills as they come due.

P 10-9   The Zaro Company's balance sheet for December 31, 1991 and income statement for the year ended December 31, 1991 follow:

ZARO COMPANY
Balance Sheet
December 31, 1991 and 1990

	1991	1990
Assets		
Cash	$ 30,000	$ 15,000
Accounts receivable, net	75,000	87,000
Inventory	90,000	105,000
Prepaid expenses	3,000	2,000
Land	25,000	25,000
Building and equipment	122,000	120,000
Accumulated depreciation	(92,000)	(80,000)
Total assets	$253,000	$274,000
Liabilities and stockholders' equity		
Accounts payable	$ 25,500	$ 32,000
Income taxes payable	2,500	3,000
Accrued liabilities	5,000	5,000
Bonds payable (current $20,000 at 12/31/91)	90,000	95,000
Common stock	85,000	85,000
Retained earnings	45,000	54,000
Total liabilities and stockholders' equity	$253,000	$274,000

ZARO COMPANY
Income Statement
For the Year Ended December 31, 1991

Sales	$400,000
Less expenses:	
Cost of goods sold (includes depreciation of $5,000)	280,000
Selling and administrative expenses (includes depreciation expenses of $7,000)	78,000
Interest expense	8,000
Total expenses	366,000
Income before taxes	34,000
Income tax expense	14,000
Net income	$ 20,000

Note: Cash dividends of $29,000 were paid during 1991.

The president of Zaro Company cannot understand how the company was able to pay cash dividends that were greater than net income and at the same time increase the cash balance. He notes that business was down slightly in 1991.

Required

a. Prepare the statement of cash flows for 1991. (Present cash flows from operations using the indirect approach.)
b. Comment on the statement of cash flows.
c. Compute the following liquidity ratios for 1991:
   1. current ratio
   2. acid test ratio
   3. operating cash flow/current maturities of long-term debt and current notes payable
   4. cash ratio
d. Compute the following debt ratios for 1991:
   1. times interest earned
   2. debt ratio
e. Compute the following profitability ratios for 1991:
   1. return on assets (use average assets)
   2. return on common equity (use average common equity)
f. Give your opinion as to the liquidity of Zaro Company.
g. Give your opinion as to the debt position of Zaro Company.
h. Give your opinion as to the profitability of Zaro Company.
i. Explain to the president how Zaro Company was able to pay cash dividends that were greater than net income and at the same time increase the cash balance.

P 10-10

The Ladies Store presented the following statement of cash flows for the year ended December 31, 1991:

LADIES STORE
Statement of Cash Flows
For the Year Ended December 31, 1991

Cash received	
From sales to customers	$150,000
From sales of bonds	100,000
From issuance of notes payable	40,000
From interest on bonds	5,000
Total cash received	$295,000
Cash payments	
For merchandise purchases	$110,000
For purchase of truck	20,000
For purchase of investment	80,000
For purchase of equipment	45,000
For interest	2,000
For income taxes	15,000
Total cash payments	$272,000
Net increase in cash	$ 23,000

Note: Depreciation expense was $15,000.

Required a. Prepare a statement of cash flows in proper form.

b. Comment on the major flows of cash.

P 10-11 Answer the following multiple-choice questions.

a. Which of the following could lead to cash flow problems?
1. tightening of credit by suppliers
2. easing of credit by suppliers
3. reduction of inventory
4. improved quality of accounts receivable
5. selling of bonds

b. Which of the following would not contribute to bankruptcy of a profitable firm?
1. substantial increase in inventory
2. substantial increase in receivables
3. substantial decrease in accounts payable
4. substantial decrease in notes payable
5. substantial decrease in receivables

c. Which of the following current asset or current liability accounts is not included in the computation of cash flows from operating activities?
1. change in accounts receivable
2. change in inventory
3. change in accounts payable
4. change in accrued wages
5. change in notes payable to banks

d. Which of the following items is not included in the adjustment of net income to cash flows from operating activities?
1. increase in deferred taxes
2. amortization of goodwill
3. depreciation expense for the period
4. amortization of premium on bonds payable
5. proceeds from selling land

e. Which of the following represents an internal source of cash?
1. cash inflows from financing activities
2. cash inflows from investing activities
3. cash inflows from selling land
4. cash inflows from operating activities
5. cash inflows from issuing stock

f. How would revenue from services be classified?
1. investing inflow
2. investing outflow
3. operating inflow
4. operating outflow
5. financing outflow

g. What type of account is inventory?
1. investing
2. financing
3. operating
4. noncash
5. sometimes operating and sometimes investing

h. How would short-term investment in marketable securities be classified?
   1. operating activities
   2. financing activities
   3. investing activities
   4. noncash activities
   5. cash and cash equivalents

P 10-12   The Szabo Company presented the following data with the 1991 financial statements.

SZABO COMPANY
Statement of Cash Flows
Years Ended December 31, 1991, 1990, 1989

	1991	1990	1989
Increase (decrease) in cash			
Cash flows from operating activities			
Cash received from customers	$173,233	$176,446	$158,702
Cash paid to supplies and employees	(150,668)	(157,073)	(144,060)
Interest received	132	105	89
Interest paid	(191)	(389)	(777)
Income taxes paid	(6,626)	(4,754)	(845)
Net cash provided by operations	15,880	14,335	13,109
Cash flows from investing activities			
Capital expenditures	(8,988)	(5,387)	(6,781)
Proceeds from property, plant, and equipment disposals	1,215	114	123
Net cash used in investing activities	(7,773)	(5,273)	(6,658)
Cash flows from financing activities			
Net increase (decrease) in short-term debt	—0—	5,100	7,200
Increase in long-term debt	4,100	3,700	5,200
Dividends paid	(6,050)	(8,200)	(8,000)
Purchase of common stock	(8,233)	(3,109)	(70)
Net cash used in financing activities	(10,183)	(2,509)	4,330
Net increase (decrease) in cash and cash equivalents	(2,076)	6,553	10,781
Cash and cash equivalents at beginning of year	24,885	18,332	7,551
Cash and cash equivalents at end of year	$ 22,809	$ 24,885	$ 18,332

SZABO COMPANY
Reconciliation of Net Income to Net Cash Provided by Operating Activities

	1991	1990	1989
Net income	$ 7,610	$ 3,242	$ 506
Provision for depreciation and amortization	12,000	9,700	9,000
Provision for losses on accounts receivable	170	163	140
Gain on property, plant, and equipment disposals	(2,000)	(1,120)	(1,500)
Changes in operating assets and liabilities			
Accounts receivable	(2,000)	(1,750)	(1,600)
Inventories	(3,100)	(2,700)	(2,300)
Other assets	—0—	—0—	(57)
Accounts payable	—0—	5,100	7,200
Accrued income taxes	1,200	—0—	—0—
Deferred income taxes	2,000	1,700	1,720
Net cash provided by operating activities	$15,880	$14,335	$13,109

Required
a. Prepare a statement of cash flows with a three-year total column for 1989–1991.
b. Comment on significant trends you detect in the statement prepared in (a).
c. Prepare a statement of cash flows with inflow/outflow for the year ended December 31, 1991.
d. Comment on significant trends you detect in the statement prepared in (c).

CASES

Case 10-1   HOW GOOD A DETECTIVE ARE YOU? PART I

See the accompanying financial statements for W. T. Grant (pages 466–475).

Required
a. Based on these statements, calculate the following ratios for the years ended January 31, 1971 and 1970.
1. inventory turnover (based on year-end figures)
2. days' sales in receivables
3. current ratio
4. acid test ratio
5. cash ratio
6. debt ratio
7. times interest earned
8. net profit margin
9. total asset turnover (based on year-end figures)
10. return on total assets and DuPont analysis (based on year-end figures)

11. return on common equity

12. dividend payout ratio

b. Prepare a statement of cash flows for the most recent year. For this purpose, use the W. T. Grant statement of source and application of funds. For the working capital accounts, use the W. T. Grant statement of financial position. There is a slight problem with this approach, because the statement of source and application of funds has been rounded to thousands. Add zeros (000s) to the numbers in the statement of source and application of funds. The actual change in working capital was a decrease of $1,211,480. This has been rounded to $1,212,000 in the statement of source and application of funds. The difference of $520 should be presented under cash from operations. Present the increase in sundry accounts, net ($48,000), under investments.

Note: The following numbers should be obtained in the statement of cash flows:

Net decrease in cash flow from operating activities (indirect approach)	($15,319,217)
Net cash outflow from investing activities	($16,625,000)
Net cash inflow from financing activities	32,976,016
Net increase in cash and short-term securities	1,031,799

Prepare the following ratios for 1971 only:

1. cash flow (current) maturities of long-term debt and notes payable
2. cash flow/total debt
3. funds flow per share
4. Comment on the liquidity position of the firm.
5. Comment on the long-term debt position of the firm.
6. Comment on the profitability of the firm.
7. What were the principal sources and uses of cash?
8. Briefly describe the overall financial position of the firm.

W.T. GRANT COMPANY
and Consolidated Subsidiaries
Statement of Financial Position

	January 31	
	1971	**1970***
Assets		
Current assets		
Cash and short term securities	$ 34,008,749	$ 32,976,950
Accounts receivable:		
Customers' installment accounts	433,729,581	381,757,348
Less allowance for doubtful accounts and unearned credit insurance premiums	25,079,275	21,044,723
	408,650,306	360,712,625
Other accounts receivable, claims, etc.	11,080,820	7,554,506
Total accounts receivable, net	419,731,126	368,267,131

Statement of Financial Position   (continued)

	January 31	
	1971	1970*
Merchandise inventories (including merchandise in transit)—at the lower of cost or market determined principally by the retail inventory method	260,492,329	222,127,620
Prepaid taxes, rents, supplies, etc.	5,246,237	5,037,194
Total current assets	719,478,441	628,408,895
Other assets		
Investment in Zeller's Limited, at equity—Note A	21,204,472	17,991,567
Cash surrender value of life insurance	2,732,021	2,702,560
Total other assets	23,936,493	20,694,127
Common stock of W.T. Grant Company 145,400 shares, at cost, held for Deferred Contingent Compensation Plan—Note C	2,381,044	2,381,044
Store properties, fixtures, and improvements—on the basis of cost		
Buildings	545,995	545,995
Furniture & fixtures	96,909,694	89,433,668
Improvements to leased properties	7,748,813	9,433,564
	105,204,502	99,413,227
Less allowance for depreciation and amortization	44,900,240	44,912,336
	60,304,262	54,500,891
Land	1,528,090	809,841
Total store properties, fixtures, and improvements	61,832,352	55,310,732
	$807,628,330	$706,794,798
Liabilities, reserves, and capital		
Current liabilities		
Short-term notes payable	$236,420,216	$180,097,200
Bank loans	10,000,000	2,035,000
Accounts payable	80,681,456	70,853,108
Salaries, wages, and bonuses	15,513,737	15,043,683
Taxes withheld from employees compensation	2,863,885	2,562,850
Taxes other than federal income taxes	5,464,605	6,123,626
Federal income taxes payable	13,566,940	9,559,918
Deferred credits, principally income taxes related to installment sales—Note D	94,488,843	80,443,271
Total current liabilities	458,999,682	366,718,656

*Reclassified to conform with Jan. 31, 1971 presentation.

Statement of Financial Position   (continued)

	January 31	
	1971	**1970***
Long term debt—Note E	$ 32,301,000	$ 35,402,000
Deferred federal income taxes—Note D	8,518,051	8,286,401
Reserves		
For self-insured risks and repainting stores	3,300,000	3,300,000
For deferred contingent compensation	2,473,173	2,399,242
Total reserves	5,773,173	5,699,242
Capital—Notes A and F:		
Capital stock:		
Cumulative preferred—$100 par value:		
Authorized 250,000 shares		
Issued 96,000 and 114,500 shares,		
respectively, of 3¾% series	9,600,000	11,450,000
Common—$1.25 par value:		
Authorized 22,500,000 shares		
Issued 14,544,224 and 14,306,640		
shares, respectively	18,180,280	17,883,300
Paid-in capital	76,637,378	70,224,570
Amounts paid by employees under purchase		
contracts for unissued common stock	1,478,312	1,330,474
Earnings retained for use in the business	230,435,091	211,679,286
	336,331,061	312,567,630
Less 715,119 and 432,764 shares,		
respectively, of treasury common stock,		
at cost	34,294,637	21,879,131
Total capital	302,036,424	290,688,499
Long-term leases and contingent liability—		
Note G		
	$807,628,330	$706,794,798

*Reclassified to conform with Jan. 31, 1971 presentation.
(See notes to financial statements.)

Statement of Operations

	Year ended January 31	
	1971	**1970**
Sales	$1,254,130,857	$1,210,918,068
Income from concessions	4,985,580	3,748,215
	1,259,116,437	1,214,666,283
Cost of merchandise sold, buying and occupancy costs	843,191,987	817,671,347
	415,924,450	396,994,936
Selling, general and administrative expenses	329,767,690	306,628,657
	86,156,760	90,366,279
Add:		
Dividends from Zeller's Limited	1,398,689	1,249,168
Interest earned	780,707	805,734
Other income	695,081	809,063
	2,874,477	2,863,965
	89,031,237	93,230,244
Deduct:		
Interest expense	18,874,134	14,919,228
Other deductions	556,739	585,240
	19,430,873	15,504,468
	69,600,364	77,725,776
Earnings before federal income taxes provision for federal income taxes— Note D:		
Current	21,140,000	24,900,000
Deferred	11,660,000	13,100,000
	32,800,000	38,000,000
Net earnings before Canadian subsidiary	36,800,364	39,725,776
Increase in undistributed equity in Zeller's Ltd.	2,776,723	2,083,524
Net earnings	$ 39,577,087	$ 41,809,300
Earnings per share—Note B	$2.87	$2.99

(See notes to financial statements.)

Statement of Earnings Retained for Use in the Business

	Year ended January 31	
	1971	1970
Balance at the beginning of the year	$211,679,286	$189,606,659
Net earnings for the year	39,577,087	41,809,300
	251,256,373	231,415,959
Deduct:		
Cash dividends:		
3¾% Cumulative Preferred Stock—Four quarterly dividends of 93¾¢ each per share	395,031	456,858
Common Stock—Four quarterly dividends of 37½¢ and 35¢ respectively, each per share	20,426,251	19,279,815
Total cash dividends	20,821,282	19,736,673
Accumulated earnings retained for use in the business at the end of the year	$230,435,091	$211,679,286

Statement of Paid-in Capital

	Year ended January 31	
	1971	1970
Balance at the beginning of the year	$70,224,570	$58,661,960
Excess of proceeds over par value or cost of 199,440 and 232,415 shares respectively, of common stock issued under the employee's stock purchase plan	4,035,962	4,988,060
Excess of the conversion price over par value of 55,789 and 220,005 shares respectively, of common stock issued for 4% convertible debentures	1,474,818	5,811,527
Excess of par value over the cost of 18,500 and 18,000 shares respectively, of 3¾% cumulative preferred stock purchased and cancelled	902,028	763,023
Balance at the end of the year	$76,637,378	$70,224,570

Statement of Source and Application of Funds

	(Years which end January 31 of subsequent years)					
Source of Funds	1970	1969	1968	1967	1966	Five year totals
	(amounts in 000's)					
Net income	$39,577	$41,809	$38,183	$32,993	$31,568	$184,130
Less the increase in equity in Zeller's Limited	2,777	2,083	1,761	1,503	1,073	9,197
	$36,800	$39,726	$36,422	$31,490	$30,495	$174,933
Plus charges to income which involve no cash outlay:						
Depreciation and amortization	9,619	8,972	8,388	8,203	7,524	42,706
Net increase in reserves	74	180	231	130	374	989
Increase in deferred federal income taxes	232	345	390	517	765	2,249
Sale of common stock to employees	5,219	5,278	5,432	4,113	2,695	22,737
Sale of land and buildings	—	—	523	59	30	612
Total funds provided	$51,944	$54,501	$51,386	$44,512	$41,883	$244,226
Application of funds						
Dividends to stockholders	$20,821	$19,737	$17,686	$14,367	$14,091	$ 86,702
Investment in properties, fixtures, and improvements	16,141	14,352	10,626	7,763	15,257	64,139
Purchase of treasury stock	13,224	21,879	3,665	—	—	38,768
Purchase of preferred stock for cancellation	948	1,037	923	155	—	3,063
Retirement of 4¾% sinking fund debentures	1,538	1,687	1,500	1,500	—	6,225
Purchase of common stock for deferred compensation plan	—	223	178	316	441	1,158
Investment in Zeller's Limited	436	—	35	418	269	1,158
Increase in sundry accounts (net)	48	58	458	124	45	732
Working capital increase (decrease)	(1,212)	(4,472)	16,315	19,869	11,780	42,281
Total funds applied	$51,944	$54,501	$51,386	$44,512	$41,883	$244,226

Notes to Financial Statements
January 31, 1971

Note A   The financial statements include the accounts of two wholly owned subsidiaries, W.T. Grant Financial Corporation and Jones & Presnell Studios, Inc.

The Company carries its investment in Zeller's Limited (a 50.5% owned Canadian Subsidiary, cost $8,893,326) at equity and has included in net earnings its share of the increase in the undistributed equity of that company.

Note B   Earnings per share of common stock (equivalent to fully diluted) has been determined based upon the average number of shares outstanding during each year.

Note C   The amount charged to operations for the Deferred Contingent Compensation Plan for the year ended January 31, 1971 was $700,000.

Note D   Gross profits on sales on the installment basis are reflected in the financial statements when the sales are made, whereas, for federal income tax purposes, such gross profits are reported as income as collections are received. The resulting difference between taxes accrued and taxes actually payable is included as "Deferred credits, principally income taxes related to installment sales."

At January 31, 1971, accumulated depreciation of approximately $17,750,000 has been deducted for tax purposes in excess of the deduction (using the straight-line method) in the financial statements. The resulting difference is included in "Deferred Federal Income Taxes."

Investment credit totaling approximately $402,000 has been deducted from the provision for federal income taxes for the year ended January 31, 1971.

Federal income tax returns of the Company have been examined and accepted by the Internal Revenue Service through January 31, 1963.

Note E   Long-term debt:

4¾% Sinking Fund Debentures dated January 1, 1962, and due January 1, 1987 (annual sinking fund payments of $1,500,000)	$28,775,000
4% Convertible Subordinated Debentures dated June 1, 1965 and due June 1, 1990	3,526,000
	$32,301,000

As of January 31, 1971, 125,929 shares of Common Stock of the Company were reserved for conversion of the 4% Convertible Subordinated Debentures at the rate of one share of Common Stock for each $28 principal amount of debentures.

Note F   The 3¾% Cumulative Preferred Stock is redeemable at the Company's option in whole or in part at $100 per share.

At January 31, 1971, 571,450 shares of the Company's unissued Common Stock were reserved under the Employees' Stock Purchase Plans. Contracts for the sales of such shares, on a deferred payment basis, are made at approximate market prices at dates of contracts. Shares are issued after completion of payments. In addition to the shares reserved under these plans, the only other shares of Capital Stock reserved for options, warrants, conversions, and other rights are the 125,929 shares reserved for conversion of debentures and 145,400 shares of issued Common Stock held for the Deferred Contingent Compensation Plan.

During the year, the Company purchased 300,000 shares of its Common Stock and issued 17,645 shares out of Treasury Stock under the 1970 Employees' Stock Purchase Plan. In addition 181,795 shares of unissued common stock were issued under the 1960 Employees' Stock Purchase Plan.

Note G At January 31, 1971, the Company was lessee of real property under 1,089 leases expiring subsequent to January 31, 1974, at aggregate minimum annual rentals of approximately $56,312,000 (exclusive of taxes and other expenses payable under terms of certain of the leases). This amount includes approximately $45,863,000 for minimum annual rentals under 851 leases which were on a percentage of sales basis with specified minimum annual rentals.

Note H The Company has an Employees' Retirement Plan available to all of its employees. The amount charged to operations for the year ended January 31, 1971 for this Plan was $1,217,929. The Company funds pension costs accrued.

Accountant's Report

TO THE BOARD OF DIRECTORS
W.T. GRANT COMPANY
NEW YORK, N.Y.

We have examined the accompanying consolidated financial statements of the W.T. Grant Company and consolidated subsidiaries for the year ended January 31, 1971. Our examination was made in accordance with generally accepted auditing standards, and accordingly included such tests of the accounting records and such other auditing procedures as we considered necessary in the circumstances.

In our opinion the accompanying consolidated statements of financial position, operations, earnings retained for use in the business, paid in capital, and source and application of funds present fairly the consolidated financial position of the W.T. Grant Company and consolidated subsidiaries at January 31, 1971 and the consolidated results of their operations, changes in stockholders' equity and sources and applications of funds for the year then ended, in conformity with generally accepted accounting principles applied on a basis consistent with that of the preceding year.

ERNST & ERNST

March 15, 1971
New York, N.Y.

Comparative Statement of Operations

	(Years ended January 31 of subsequent years)				
	1970	1969	1968	1967	1966
	(amounts in 000's)				
Sales	$1,254,131	$1,210,918	$1,096,152	$979,458	$920,797
Income from concessions	4,985	3,748	2,873	2,786	2,250
Dividends, interest and other income	2,874	2,864	2,528	2,038	1,314
	$1,261,990	$1,217,530	$1,101,553	$984,282	$924,361
Less:					
Cost of merchandise sold, and operating expenses	1,172,960	1,124,300	1,018,548	916,087	860,099
Interest expense and other deductions	19,430	15,504	10,303	9,115	7,935
Earnings before taxes	$ 69,600	$ 77,726	$ 72,702	$ 59,080	$ 56,327
Federal income taxes	32,800	38,000	36,280	27,590	25,832
	$ 36,800	$ 39,726	$ 36,422	$ 31,490	$ 30,495
Equity in Zeller's Ltd.	2,777	2,083	1,761	1,503	1,073
Net earnings	$ 39,577	$ 41,809	$ 38,183	$ 32,993	$ 31,568

Comparative Statement of Financial Position

	(At January 31 of subsequent years)				
	1970	1969	1968	1967	1966
	(amounts in 000's)				
Assets:					
Cash and securities	$ 34,008	$ 32,977	$ 25,639	$ 25,141	$ 39,040
Net accounts receivable	419,731	368,267	312,776	272,450	230,427
Merchandise inventories	260,492	222,128	208,623	183,721	174,631
Prepaid expenses	5,246	5,037	4,402	3,983	4,079
Total current assets	$719,478	$628,409	$551,440	$485,295	$448,177
Investment in Zeller's Ltd.	21,204	17,992	15,908	14,113	12,192
Properties and fixtures	61,832	55,311	49,931	47,578	48,076
Sundry other assets	5,114	5,083	4,830	4,621	4,263
Total assets	$807,628	$706,795	$622,109	$551,607	$512,708
Liabilities:					
Notes payable and bank loans	$246,420	$182,132	$118,125	$ 99,230	$ 97,647
Accounts payable	104,524	94,584	85,099	68,305	61,339
Federal taxes payable	13,567	9,560	16,981	11,368	14,546
Deferred credits (taxes)	94,489	80,443	65,073	56,545	44,667

Comparative Statement of Financial Position   (continued)

	(At January 31 of subsequent years)				
	1970	1969	1968	1967	1966
Total current liabilities	$459,000	$366,719	$285,278	$235,448	$218,199
Long-term debt	32,301	35,402	43,251	62,622	70,005
Deferred federal taxes	8,518	8,287	7,941	7,551	7,034
Reserves	5,773	5,699	5,518	5,288	5,159
Capital:					
Preferred stock	9,600	11,450	13,250	14,750	15,000
Common stock	62,001	67,559	77,264	53,619	43,613
Retained earnings	230,435	211,679	189,607	172,329	153,703
Total liabilities and capital	$807,628	$706,795	$622,109	$551,607	$512,708

Other Items

	1970	1969	1968	1967	1966
Number of stores	1,116	1,095	1,092	1,086	1,104
Pre-tax earnings per sales dollar	5.5¢	6.4¢	6.6¢	6.0¢	6.1¢
Net earnings per share	$2.87	$2.99	$2.71	$2.39	$2.30
Dividends per share	$1.50	$1.40	$1.30	$1.10	$1.10
Working Funds*—in 000's	$354,967	$342,133	$331,235	$306,392	$274,645
Working Funds ratio*	2.0	2.2	2.5	2.7	2.6
Net worth—in 000's	$302,036	$290,688	$280,121	$240,698	$212,316
% earned on net worth	13.1	14.4	13.6	13.7	14.9

*Working Funds consist of current assets less current liabilities, excluding deferred credits for taxes related to install-ment sales. Working Funds Ratio is the ratio between current assets and current liabilities excluding deferred credits.

Case 10-2   HOW GOOD A DETECTIVE ARE YOU? PART II

In the fiscal year 1974, ended January 30, 1975, the W. T. Grant Company suffered a severe turnaround in its profit picture. This decline was evidenced in fiscal 1973, when earnings per share dropped to $.76. As recently as 1969, earnings per share had been $2.99. In fiscal 1974, the loss per share was severe ($12.74). Portions of the fiscal 1974 annual report, including management discussion of the position, are shown on pages 477–486. Use this information for required calculations.

Required   a. Prepare a statement of cash flows for the year ended January 31, 1974. For this purpose, use the statement of changes in financial position provided in the case. The statement of changes in financial position discloses a source of $259 from common stock issued upon conversion of 4% debentures and a use of $262 from conversion of 4% convertible subordinated debentures. These noncash items should balance. In the cash statement, list the $3 difference as a financing activities outflow. (Use the indirect approach.)

b. What provided the most working capital in the year ended January 31, 1974? What was the main use of these funds?

c. Comment on the difference between the working capital provided by operations and the cash provided by operations.

d. In the year ended January 30, 1975, W. T. Grant had a substantial decline in working capital. What were the principal causes of this decline?

e. For the years ended January 30, 1975 (fiscal 1974) and 1974 (fiscal 1973), calculate the following ratios.
   1. inventory turnover (based on year-end inventory)
   2. days' sales receivables
   3. current ratio
   4. acid test ratio
   5. cash ratio
   6. debt ratio
   7. times interest earned
   8. net profit margin on sales
   9. total asset turnover (based on year-end figures)
   10. return on total assets and DuPont analysis (based on year-end figures)
   11. return on equity
   12. dividend payout ratio
       (For 13, 14, and 15, do only for year ended January 31, 1974.)
   13. operating cash flow/current maturities of long-term debt and current notes payable
   14. operating cash flow/total debt
   15. operating cash flow per share

f. Based on the summary of operations, prepare a vertical common size analysis of the income statement for the years ended January 31, 1975 and 1974. Use sales as the base.

g. Quarterly information on dividends and earnings is presented. Discuss this information with respect to dividend payout and dividend policy.

h. Briefly describe the policy adopted by the firm in the last year concerning credit sales.* Speculate as to the reasons for this policy.

i. What action did the company take concerning bad debts? How did this affect the 1975 income?* Were the receivables realistically valued on the January 31, 1974 balance sheet?

j. Comment on the current liquidity position of the firm (January 30, 1975).

k. Considering the current liquidity position, what would be an action suppliers might consider?

l. Comment on the current long-term borrowing position of the firm (January 30, 1975).

m. The going concern principle recommends valuation of assets based on that assumption until such time as there is evidence to the contrary. Does the auditor's opinion give any hint that W. T. Grant Company may not be a going concern?

*52 weeks ended January 30, 1975.

**W.T. GRANT COMPANY
and Consolidated Subsidiaries
Statement of Financial Position**

	January 30, 1975	January 31, 1974*
	($ in thousands)	
Assets		
Current assets		
Cash Notes 4 and 5	$ 79,642	$ 45,951
Customers' installment accounts		
receivable—Notes 1, 3, 4 and 5	518,387	602,305
Less:		
Allowance for doubtful accounts	79,510	16,315
Unearned credit insurance premiums	1,386	4,923
Deferred finance income	37,523	59,748
	399,968	521,319
Merchandise inventories (including		
merchandise in transit)—Notes 4 and 5	407,357	450,637
Other accounts receivable, refundable		
taxes and claims—Note 10	31,223	19,483
Prepaid expenses	6,591	7,299
Total current assets	924,781	1,044,689
Investments in unconsolidated subsidiaries—		
Notes 2, 4, and 5	49,764	44,251
Common stock of W.T. Grant Company		
155,400 shares, at cost, held for Deferred		
Contingent Compensation Plan—Note 8	2,500	2,500
Properties, fixtures, and improvements		
Buildings	2,953	1,475
Furniture and fixtures	142,772	138,827
Improvements to leased properties	13,412	12,620
	159,137	152,922
Less allowance for depreciation and		
amortization	58,108	52,546
	101,029	100,376
Land	903	608
Total properties, fixtures, and		
improvements	101,932	100,984
Unamortized debt expenses and other assets	3,290	2,563
	$1,082,267	$1,194,987

*Restated as described in Note 1.
See notes to financial statements.

Statement of Financial Position   (continued)

	January 30, 1975	January 31, 1974*
	($ in thousands)	
Liabilities and capital		
Current liabilities		
Bank loans—Note 4	$ 600,000	
Short-term commercial notes—Note 4		$ 453,097
Current portion of long-term debt—Note 5	995	
Accounts payable for merchandise	50,067	58,192
Salaries, wages and bonuses	10,808	14,678
Other accrued expenses—Notes 9 and 10	49,095	14,172
Taxes withheld from employees	1,919	4,412
Sales and other taxes	17,322	13,429
Federal income taxes payable—Note 10	17,700	
Deferred income taxes related to		
installment sales—Notes 1 and 10	2,000	103,078
Total current liabilities	749,906	661,058
Other liabilities		
Long-term debt—Note 5	216,341	220,336
Deferred Federal income taxes—Note 10		14,649
Deferred contingent compensation and		
other liabilities	2,183	4,196
Total other liabilities	218,524	239,181
Capital—Notes 1, 4, 5 and 6		
Capital stock		
Cumulative preferred—$100 par value:		
Authorized 250,000 shares		
Issued 74,645 shares of 3¾% series	7,465	7,465
Common—$1.25 par value:		
Authorized 22,500,000 shares		
Issued at 14,879,554 shares	18,599	18,599
Paid-in capital	82,394	84,271
Amounts paid by employees under		
purchase contracts for common stock	1,520	1,638
Earnings retained for use in the business	37,674	219,471
	147,652	331,444
Less 754,824 and 803,054 shares,		
respectively, of treasury common		
stock, at cost	33,815	36,696
Total capital	113,837	294,748
Leases, contingencies and subsequent		
events—Notes 3, 4, 5, 10 and 12		
	$1,082,267	$1,194,987

Statement of Operations

	52 weeks ended January 30, 1975	Year ended January 31, 1974*
	($ in thousands)	
Sales	$1,761,952	$1,849,802
Income from concessions	4,238	3,971
	1,766,190	1,853,773
Cost of merchandise sold, buying and occupancy costs	1,303,267	1,282,945
	462,923	570,828
Selling, general and administrative expenses	540,953	540,230
Store closing expenses—Note 9	24,000	—
Net credit expense—Notes 1 and 3	161,467	5,972
Other interest expense—Note 7	37,771	18,082
	764,191	564,284
	(301,268)	6,544
Other income:		
Interest earned—Note 7	1,390	1,036
Gain on retirement of long-term debt	1,986	1,960
	3,376	2,996
Earnings (loss) before income taxes and equity in net earnings of unconsolidated subsidiaries	(297,892)	9,540
Provision (credit) for Federal, state and local income taxes—Note 10		
Current	(19,439)	(6,021)
Deferred	(98,027)	9,310
	(117,466)	3,289
	(180,426)	6,251
Equity in net earnings of unconsolidated subsidiaries—Note 2	3,086	4,651
Net earnings (loss)	($ 177,340)	$ 10,902
Net earnings (loss) per common share	($12.74)	$ .76

*Restated as described in Note 1.
See notes to financial statements.

Statement of Capital (Partial)
For the Year Ended January 31, 1974
and the 52 Weeks Ended January 30, 1975

	Earnings retained for use in the business
	($ in thousands)
Cash dividends:	
3¾% cumulative preferred stock—Four quarterly dividends of 93¾¢ each per share	(293)
Common stock—Four quarterly dividends of 37½¢ each per share	(20,829)
Cash dividends:	
3¾% cumulative preferred stock—Four quarterly dividends of 93¾¢ each per share	(280)
Common stock—Two quarterly dividends of 15¢ each per share	(4,177)

Statement of Changes in Financial Position

	52 weeks ended January 30, 1975	Year ended January 31, 1974*
	($ in thousands)	
Funds provided by (applied to) operations:		
Net earnings (loss)	($177,340)	$ 10,902
Less undistributed equity in net earnings of unconsolidated subsidiaries	331	3,570
	(177,671)	7,332
Other items not affecting working capital:		
Depreciation and amortization of properties	14,587	13,579
Increase (decrease) in deferred Federal income taxes—non-current	(14,649)	2,723
Decrease in deferred contingent compensation and other liabilities	(2,013)	(498)
Total funds provided by (applied to) operations	(179,746)	23,136
Other sources of funds:		
Notes payable to banks		100,000
Receipts from employees under stock purchase contracts	886	2,584
Common stock issued upon conversion of 4% debentures		259
Total other sources	886	102,843

Statement of Changes in Financial Position   (continued)

	52 weeks ended January 30, 1975	Year ended January 31, 1974*
Other applications of funds:		
Dividends to stockholders	(4,457)	(21,122)
Investment in properties, fixtures and improvements	(15,535)	(23,143)
Decrease in long-term debt	(3,995)	(6,074)
Investment in Granjewel Jewelers & Distributors, Inc:		
Convertible notes	(3,646)	(5,700)
Common stock	(1,536)	
Purchase of cumulative preferred stock, for cancellation		(618)
Purchase of treasury common stock		(133)
Conversion of 4% convertible subordinated debentures		(262)
Increase in other assets—net	(727)	(642)
Total other applications	(29,896)	(57,694)
Working capital increase (decrease)	($208,756)	$ 68,285
Current assets increase (decrease)		
Cash	$ 33,691	$ 15,008
Customers' installment accounts receivable—net	(121,351)	52,737
Merchandise inventories	(43,280)	51,104
Other current assets	11,032	8,935
	(119,908)	127,784
Current liabilities increase (decrease)		
Bank loans	600,000	(10,000)
Short-term commercial notes	(453,097)	73,063
Current portion of long-term debt	995	
Accounts payable for merchandise	(8,125)	(2,781)
Salaries, wages and bonuses	(3,870)	(3,349)
Other accrued expenses	34,923	3,932
Taxes withheld from employees	(2,493)	2,217
Sales and other taxes	3,893	448
Federal income taxes payable	17,700	(8,480)
Deferred income taxes related to installment sales	(101,078)	4,449
	88,848	59,499
Working capital increase (decrease)	($208,756)	$ 68,285

*Restated as described in Note 1.
See notes to financial statements.

Notes to Financial Statements (Partial)

Note 3   Credit Operations

The Company presently has available two types of Company operated credit plans at most locations: a revolving charge account providing for payment in full within 28 days or on terms, based upon balance, ranging up to approximately 24 months, including finance charges which generally do not exceed 1½% per month; and a traditional installment (budget) account, payment terms up to 24 months with finance charges included, ranging up to an annual percentage rate of approximately 19%.

During the 52 weeks ended January 30, 1975, the Company terminated offering its former coupon account plan, payment terms up to 24 months. In December, 1974, the Company reduced from 36 months to 24 months the maximum payment terms on its budget accounts opened after that date, and increased the minimum payment on the majority of its credit accounts to $10 per month.

A summary of the net expense of credit operations is shown below:

	52 weeks ended January 30, 1975	Year ended January 31, 1974
	($ in thousands)	
Finance income (see Note 1)	$ 87,012	$ 86,677
Expenses: Interest expense	48,308	32,965
Provision for doubtful accounts	155,691	21,198
Finance income related to uncollectible accounts	(4,127)	(1,317)
Administration	48,607	39,803
	248,479	92,649
Net credit expense	$161,467	$ 5,972
Credit sales	$402,916	$451,471

Interest expense is allocated to credit operations based on the average borrowing rate of W.T. Grant Financial Corporation applied to average customers' installment accounts receivable, net of allowance for doubtful accounts, unearned credit insurance premiums, deferred finance income and deferred income taxes related to installment sales.

The provision for doubtful accounts consists of net uncollectible accounts written off plus the increase in the allowance for doubtful accounts.

For the 52 weeks ended January 30, 1975 and the year ended January 31, 1974, the Company wrote off accounts receivable based on a nine months recency of payment, or which were otherwise deemed to be uncollectible. Effective January 31, 1975, the Company changed its write-off policy on accounts receivable, to write off accounts which are nine months delinquent based on contractual payment terms. In November 1974, the Company began to provide for an allowance for doubtful accounts on a six month contractual basis and the Company continues to provide for doubtful accounts on such basis. At January 31, 1974, the Company provided for doubtful accounts in accordance with its write-off policy in effect at that time. Modified collection efforts continue subsequent to write-off, and recoveries are applied as a reduction of the provision for doubtful accounts. The Company is also in the process of restructuring its credit and collection procedures. It is not practicable to estimate the effect of such changes in policies and procedures upon the results of operations for the 52 weeks ended January 30, 1975.

Earned credit insurance premiums are reflected as a reduction of administration expenses. During 1974 the Company discontinued the sale of credit insurance.

At January 30, 1975, there were approximately 1.4 million active revolving charge accounts with an average balance of $154 and 1.1 million active budget accounts with an average balance of $268.

Class actions or purported class actions are currently pending in eight states which involve allegations that the finance and related charges under certain of the Company's credit arrangements exceeded the maximum amount permissible under, or otherwise failed to comply with, the laws regulating credit in such states and/or the Federal Truth-in-Lending Act. Some of the actions are directed specifically at the Company's sale of merchandise coupon books. Such sales have been discontinued.

In one action, the Court has handed down an adverse decision which the Company has appealed. In another action, in accordance with an order of the trial court, implementing the opinion of the state supreme court, the Company is presently crediting existing customer receivables, or refunding to customers certain finance charges previously collected under the coupon account plan. The remaining actions are in various stages of pleadings prior to trial.

The ultimate consequences of these actions are not presently determinable. However, based upon present available information, in the opinion of the Company's Management, these actions will not have a material adverse effect on the Company's financial position.

Note 7   Interest

Interest earned for the 52 weeks ended January 30, 1975 and the year ended January 31, 1974 includes $1,261,820 and $777,339, respectively, on investments in debentures of unconsolidated subsidiaries.

For the 52 weeks ended January 30, 1975 and the year ended January 31, 1974, interest expense on long-term debt amounted to $17,527,553 and $11,300,900, respectively.

Other interest expense includes interest not allocated to net credit expense as described in Note 3 to the financial statements, and interest of $4,000,000 accrued to provide for assessments by the Internal Revenue Service as described in Note 10 to the financial statements.

Note 11   Employees' Retirement Plan

The amounts charged to operations for the 52 weeks ended January 30, 1975 and the year ended January 31, 1974 for the Employees' Retirement Plan were $3,648,008 and $1,247,202, respectively.

The Company's policy is to fund pension costs accrued.

The actuarially computed value of vested benefits at June 30, 1974 (the latest valuation date) exceeded the pension fund assets at market value by approximately $13,184,000; however the actuarially computed value of such fund assets exceeded vested benefits by approximately $7,600,000.

In accordance with the provisions of the Employee Retirement Income Security Act of 1974, the Company will make certain amendments to its pension plan, and may make certain changes in the actuarial determination of pension costs required as of January 1, 1976. An estimate of the effect of these changes on future pension costs and unfunded vested benefits will be available upon completion of an actuarial evaluation.

Note 12   Leases and Contingencies

Total rental expenses for all leases amounted to:

	52 weeks ended January 30, 1975	Year ended January 31, 1974
	($ in thousands)	
Financing leases:		
Minimum rentals	$110,025	$101,237
Contingent rentals	1,894	2,300
Other leases:		
Minimum rentals	4,167	3,578
Less: Rentals from subleases	1,966	1,748
	$114,120	$105,367

Contingent rentals are based upon various percentages of sales in excess of specified minimums.

The future minimum rental commitments as of January 30, 1975 for all non-cancellable leases (as defined by ASR No. 147) are as follows, excluding the leases of the 66 stores described in Note 9 to the financial statements:

Years ending last Thursday in January	Financing Leases Real Estate	Equipment	Other Leases Real Estate	Less: Rental from Subleases of Real Estate	Total
	($ in thousands)				
1976	$ 92,292	$9,072	$ 3,095	$1,726	$102,733
1977	89,754	9,072	3,017	1,502	100,341
1978	86,593	9,072	2,985	1,289	97,361
1979	84,245	6,972	2,975	1,157	93,035
1980	82,604	6,972	2,506	967	91,115
1981–1985	364,647	1,859	12,524	3,134	375,896
1986–1990	304,503	1,859	12,522	1,264	317,620
1991–1995	133,017	310	12,522	434	145,415
1996 and subsequent	5,981		5,635	38	11,578

The estimated net present value of the net fixed minimum rental commitments for all non-cancellable financing leases above are summarized below:

	Range of Interest Rates Used	Present Value	
		January 30, 1975	January 31, 1974
		($ in thousands)	
Real estate	2.53% to 11.94%	$386,778	$431,442
Less: Subleases	2.62% to 11.94%	9,355	7,610
Net real estate		377,423	423,832
Equipment	7.36% to 8.04%	28,695	34,465
		$406,118	$458,297

The present values were computed after reducing total rental commitments by estimated amounts, where applicable, of lessors' payments of taxes and insurance.

If all financing leases had been capitalized, it is estimated that the net loss for the 52 weeks ended January 30, 1975 would have been increased by approximately $2,599,000 (no tax effect); and that net earnings for the year ended January 31, 1974 would have been reduced by approximately $1,623,000. This computation assumes that the estimated present values were amortized on a straight-line basis over the terms of the leases and subleases and that interest expense (income) was accrued on the outstanding lease (sublease) obligations at the range of rates shown above. The amounts included in the computation for net amortization of leased and subleased property and net interest expense were approximately $34,602,000 and $34,629,000 in the 52 weeks ended January 30, 1975, and $36,614,000 and $36,038,000 in the year ended January 31, 1974, respectively.

The United States Department of Labor, Office of the Regional Solicitor in Philadelphia, has advised the Company that it intends to file a complaint alleging violations at fourteen of the Company's stores of the provisions of the Fair Labor Standards Act of 1938, as amended, relating to compensation of employees and record-keeping, and seeking back payments for such violations. It is the opinion of management that this litigation may be settled by a consent decree involving self-regulation and periodic reporting, and the payment of a dollar amount which would not have a material adverse effect on the Company's financial position.

Accountant's Report

Board of Directors and Stockholders
W.T. Grant Company
New York, N.Y.

We have examined the consolidated statements of financial position of W.T. Grant Company and consolidated subsidiaries as of January 30, 1975, and January 31, 1974, and the related consolidated statements of operations, capital and changes in financial position for the 52 weeks ended January 30, 1975 and the year ended January 31, 1974. Our examinations were made in accordance with

Accountant's Report   (continued)

generally accepted auditing standards and, accordingly, included such tests of the accounting records and such other auditing procedures as we considered necessary in the circumstances. The financial statements of Zeller's Limited, used as the basis for recording the Company's equity in net earnings of that corporation, were examined by other independent accountants whose reports were furnished to us. Our opinion expressed herein, insofar as it relates to the amounts of net earnings included for Zeller's Limited, is based solely on the reports of the other independent accountants.

As discussed in Note 10 to the financial statements, the Company has protested certain deficiencies in consolidated Federal income taxes proposed by the Internal Revenue Service for the years ended January 31, 1964 through 1971, and is presently in litigation regarding such proposed deficiencies for the years ended January 31, 1964 and 1965. It is not practicable to estimate the additional income taxes and interest payable, if any, at this time. As discussed in Note 2 to financial statements, the continuing value of the Company's total investment in the common stock and convertible notes of Granjewel Jewelers & Distributors, Inc., a 51% owned subsidiary, may be impaired as a result of the potential inability of such subsidiary to continue as a going concern.

In our opinion, based on our examinations and the reports of other independent accountants, subject to the effects, if any, on the financial statements of the ultimate resolution of the matters discussed in the preceding paragraph, the financial statements referred to above present fairly the consolidated financial position of W.T. Grant Company and consolidated subsidiaries at January 30, 1975 and January 31, 1974, and the consolidated results of their operations and the changes in their financial position for the 52 weeks ended January 30, 1975 and the year ended January 31, 1974, in conformity with generally accepted accounting principles applied on a consistent basis after restatement for the change, with which we concur, in the method of accounting for finance income as described in Note 1 to the financial statements.

New York, N.Y.   ERNST & ERNST
April 18, 1975

Case 10-3   READY FOR DEPLOYMENT—DEPLOYMENT

David M. Roderick, Chairman of the Board of United States Steel, stated the following in the "To Our Shareholders" section of the 1980 annual report of United States Steel:

Steel is and has always been U.S. Steel's principal business and it will continue to be as long as it can return a competitive profit. Facility investments in steel operations will be directed toward cost reduction and improvements in productivity, energy efficiency, product quality and customer service, in addition to environmental and other legally mandated expenditures.

Demand for steel is expected to grow at an average of 1½–2 percent per year—less than the rate of growth expected for the economy as a whole. Demand in many of our other businesses is expected to grow at a faster rate than the nation's economy. For U.S. Steel to grow as fast as the economy, a significant portion of facility investments must be directed to those markets having above average growth potential. In addition, a competitive rate of return must be realized wherever an investment is made.

In the "To Our Shareholders" section of the 1981 annual report of United States Steel, David M. Roderick stated the following:

A major action was undertaken in late 1981 to acquire more profitable assets— through a major acquisition which will complement our other businesses. On January 7, 1982, a U.S. Steel subsidiary purchased 30 million shares (approximately 51 percent) of the common shares of Marathon Oil Company. Assuming Marathon shareholder approval of the proposed merger, Marathon will become a wholly-owned subsidiary of U.S. Steel during the first quarter of 1982. In the merger, the remaining Marathon shares (approximately 49 percent) will be converted into the right to receive 12½ percent notes.

This acquisition in no way lessens our dedication to continued modernization and upgrading of existing lines of business where such investment can earn a competitive rate of return. . . .

Longer-term, capital expenditures for the most modern technology for steel production will only be made if the prospect for an attractive return exists. For investors to realize an attractive return, steel prices—and, hence, steel costs— must be competitive.

In the "To Our Shareholders" section of the 1982 annual report of United States Steel, David M. Roderick stated the following:

The year 1982 was one of profound change and challenge for U.S. Steel. The change accompanied our acquisition of Marathon Oil, a merger which altered the structure, product and asset base of the corporation more dramatically than any other event since our founding in 1901.

The statements of changes in financial position for United States Steel for the years ended December 31, 1980, 1981, and 1982 are provided along with the current asset and current liabilities section of the balance sheet for 1982, 1981, and 1980, and partial footnote 18 from the 1982 annual report.

UNITED STATES STEEL
Statement of Changes in Consolidated Financial Position

	1982	1981	1980
	(in millions)		
Additions to working capital			
Net income (loss) (before extraordinary tax credit in 1980)	$ (361)	$1,077	$ 459
Add (deduct): Depreciation, depletion, and amortization	1,031	571	524
Amortization of discounts	41	—	—
Deferred taxes on income	52	517	97

Statement of Changes in Consolidated Financial Position   (continued)

	1982	1981	1980
Unusual items (excludes current portion of $8 in 1982 and $(7) in 1981)	114·	(33)	—
Minority interest—Marathon Oil Company	29	—	—
Gain on disposal of assets	(199)	(753)	(83)
Nontaxable gain on exchange of stock for debt	(87)	—	—
Working capital from operations (excludes extraordinary tax credit in 1980)	620	1,379	997
Increase in long-term debt due after one year	4,211	127	247
Increase in preferred and common stock	668	73	29
Exchange of common stock for long-term debt:			
Common stock issued	89	—	—
Long-term debt retired	(176)	—	—
Nontaxable gain and other items	87	—	—
Disposal of assets	596	863	173
Miscellaneous additions (net)	112	26	49
Total additions	6,207	2,468	1,495
Deductions from working capital			
Acquisition of Marathon Oil Company (net of working capital $882) (Note 23)	5,053	—	—
Expended for property, plant and equipment	1,936	843	742
Dividends paid	188	178	140
Decrease in long-term debt due after one year	729	188	154
Decrease in redeemable preferred stock of consolidated subsidiary	180	—	—
Increase in other long-term receivables and investments	—	—	77
Decrease in estimated long-term shutdown liability	—	—	98
Total deductions	8,086	1,209	1,211
Increase (decrease) in working capital	$(1,879)	$1,259	$ 284

Analysis of increase (decrease) in working capital	1982	1981	1980
Working capital at beginning of year	$2,589	$1,330	$1,046
Cash and marketable securities	(1,827)	1,436	319
Receivables, less allowance for doubtful accounts	(500)	9	243
Inventories	1,119	68	(120)
Other current assets	43	—	—
Notes payable	(224)	(40)	97
Accounts payable	(464)	(24)	(91)

Analysis of increase (decrease) in working capital	1982	1981	1980
Payroll and benefits payable	213	(158)	(115)
Accrued taxes	206	(93)	(65)
Accrued interest	(138)	(1)	1
Long-term debt due within one year	(234)	(11)	12
Current portion of estimated provision for costs attributable to shutdown of facilities	(18)	73	3
Current portion of redeemable preferred stock of consolidated subsidiary	(55)	—	—
Increase (decrease) in working capital	(1,879)	1,259	284
Working capital at end of year	$ 710	$2,589	$1,330

UNITED STATES STEEL
Partial Consolidated Balance Sheet

	December 31		
	1982	1981	1980
	(in millions)		
Current assets:			
Cash	$ 494	$ 880	$ 442
Marketable securities, at cost (approximates market)	42	1,483	485
Receivables, less allowance for doubtful accounts of $48 and $20, and $19	1,351	1,851	1,842
Inventories	2,317	1,198	1,130
Other current assets	43	—	—
Total current assets	4,247	5,412	3,899
Current liabilities			
Notes payable	$ 362	$ 138	$ 98
Accounts payable	1,498	1,034	1,061
Payroll and benefits payable	733	946	788
Accrued taxes	356	562	469
Accrued interest	190	52	—
Long-term debt due within one year	278	44	33
Current portion of estimated provision for costs attributable to shutdown of facilities	65	47	120
Current portion of redeemable preferred stock of consolidated subsidiary	55	—	—
	3,537	2,823	2,569

Partial footnote 18, 1982 annual report:

	1982	1981	1980
Major items included in other income:		(in millions)	
Gain on disposal of assets[a]	$199	$753	$83
Sale of tax benefits[b]	115	—	—

Note (a):

Major 1982 items were: sale of Marathon Oil Company's Canadian Subsidiaries—$89 million gain and sale of Pittsburgh headquarters building for total gain of $164 million, of which $56 million was recognized in 1982. Major items in 1981 include $550 million gain from the sale of certain coal properties to The Standard Oil Company (Ohio), and $85 million gain from the lease assignment and sale of Manor Coal properties. Included in 1980 were $52 million gain from the sale of Universal Atlas Cement and a $23 million gain from the sale of a partnership interest in a New York office building.

Note (b):

In 1982, the Corporation sold tax benefits totaling $115 million. The transactions were structured as leases for tax purposes and did not convey title to property. Accordingly, the Corporation continued to record book depreciation for financial accounting purposes. The Corporation has provided for deferred taxes on the sale of these benefits.

Required   a. Prepare the statement of cash flows for the years ended December 31, 1982, 1981, and 1980. (Use the indirect approach for cash flow from operations.)

b. Comment on the major cash flows for each year.

c. Were there major differences in the change in working capital and the change in cash?

d. Which type of focus do you prefer—working capital focus or cash flow? Why?

Case 10-4   CASH FLOW TAILS

Media General, Inc., included the following financial data in its 1987 annual report.
From the consolidated balance sheets:

Liabilities and Stockholders' Equity
(in thousands, except share amounts)

December 31,	1987	1986
Current liabilities:		
Accounts payable	$ 40,349	$ 42,874
Accrued expenses and other liabilities	52,418	45,973
Taxes on income	4,337	2,290
Current portion of long-term debt and subordinated debentures	363	363
Total current liabilities	97,467	91,500
Long-term debt	236,250	199,000

Liabilities and Stockholders' Equity   (continued)

December 31,	1987	1986
Deferred income taxes	112,763	105,481
Other liabilities and deferred credits	30,448	25,697
Subordinated debentures	3,985	4,348
Contingencies (note 11)		
Stockholders' equity:		
Preferred stock ($5 cumulative convertible), par value $5 per share:		
Authorized 5,000,000 shares; none outstanding		
Common stock, par value $5 per share:		
Class A, authorized 75,000,000 shares; issued 27,674,224 and 13,541,972 shares	138,371	67,710
Class B, authorized 600,000 shares; issued 558,586 and 559,168 shares	2,793	2,796
Additional paid-in capital	13,289	12,919
Retained earnings	193,978	231,034
Total stockholders' equity	348,431	314,459
Total liabilities and stockholders' equity	$829,344	$740,485

See accompanying notes.

From the consolidated statements of income and retained earnings:

Years Ended December 31,	1987	1986	1985
Earnings per common share and equivalent	$1.50	$.60	$1.15
Weighted average common shares and equivalents	28,636,000	28,576,000	28,480,000

Years Ended December 31,	1987	1986	1985
Cash flows from operating activities:			
Net income	$ 42,921	$ 17,107	$ 32,824
Adjustments to reconcile net income to net cash provided by operating activities:			
Special charge	0	30,699	0
Depreciation	41,512	36,504	28,675
Amortization of excess cost of businesses acquired	1,586	1,618	1,579
Provision for discounts and doubtful accounts	13,538	14,559	14,075
Deferred income taxes	8,563	5,852	17,817
Equity in undistributed net income of unconsolidated affiliates	(9,348)	(5,005)	(6,404)

Years Ended December 31,	1987	1986	1985
Change in assets and liabilities net of the effects of the special charge:			
(Increase) in accounts receivable	(22,845)	(18,418)	(25,108)
(Increase) decrease in inventories	2,792	4,993	(5,314)
(Increase) decrease in other current assets	(7,371)	2,318	(7,819)
(Decrease) in accounts payable	(2,525)	(831)	(2,854)
Increase in accrued expenses and other liabilities	6,445	9,017	8,402
Increase in taxes on income	2,047	194	1,141
Other—net	4,321	3,487	(7,532)
Net cash provided by operating activities	81,636	102,094	49,482
Cash flows from investing activities:			
Capital expenditures	(80,593)	(100,314)	(90,621)
Investment in unconsolidated affiliates	(31,110)	(15,000)	(20,152)
Other—net	2,648	1,537	(2,056)
Net cash used in investing activities	(109,055)	(113,777)	(112,829)
Cash flows from financing activities:			
Net increase in long-term debt	37,250	21,000	83,000
Payment of long-term debt and subordinated debentures	(363)	(363)	(12,265)
Cash dividends paid	(9,454)	(8,388)	(8,133)
Other—net	47	91	583
Net cash provided by financing activities	27,480	12,340	63,185
Net increase (decrease) in cash	61	657	(162)
Cash at beginning of year	7,603	6,946	7,108
Cash at end of year	$ 7,664	$ 7,603	$ 6,946
Supplemental disclosures of cash flow information:			
Cash paid during the year for:			
Interest (net of amount capitalized)	$ 16,400	$ 11,984	$ 10,390
Income taxes (net of refunds)	18,099	(3,742)	4,224

See accompanying notes.

Required

a. Compute and comment on the following ratios for 1987 and 1986:
   1. operating cash flow/current maturities of long-term debt and current notes payable
   2. operating cash flow/total debt
   3. operating cash flow per share
b. Comment on the significance of cash dividends paid in relation to net cash provided by operating activities over the three-year period 1987, 1986, and 1985.
c. 1. What was the major source of cash flow over the three-year period?
   2. What was the major source of cash flow in 1985?
   3. What was the major use of cash flow over the three-year period?

d. Why is depreciation added to net income as part of the reconciliation of net income to net cash provided by operating activities?

Case 10-5 WATCH THE CASH

The Mosinee Paper Corporation presented the following statement of cash flows in its 1989 annual report.

	For the Years Ended December 31,		
	1989	1988	1987
(in thousands)			
Increase (decrease) in cash and cash equivalents:			
Cash flows from operating activities:			
Cash received from customers	$230,977	$235,261	$211,602
Cash paid to suppliers and employees	(200,891)	(209,431)	(192,080)
Interest received	176	140	118
Interest paid (net of amount capitalized)	(255)	(519)	(1,036)
Income taxes paid	(8,835)	(6,338)	(1,126)
Net cash provided by operating activities	21,172	19,113	17,478
Cash flows from investing activities:			
Capital expenditures	(11,984)	(7,182)	(9,041)
Proceeds from property, plant and equipment disposals	1,620	152	164
Proceeds from sale of assets of division/subsidiary	—	750	—
Net cash used in investing activities	(10,364)	(6,280)	(8,877)
Cash flows from financing activities:			
Net increase (decrease) in short-term debt	—	(5,100)	5,100
Repayment of long-term debt	(820)	(824)	(11,158)
Proceeds from issuance of company stock	148	—	—
Dividends paid	(1,981)	(2,040)	(2,071)
Purchase of company stock	(8,223)	(3,109)	(70)
Proceeds from notes receivable—sale of stock	—	—	150
Net cash used in financing activities	(10,876)	(11,073)	(8,049)
Net increase (decrease) in cash and cash equivalents	(68)	1,760	552
Cash and cash equivalents at beginning of year	2,671	911	359
Cash and cash equivalents at end of year	$ 2,603	$ 2,671	$ 911
Reconciliation of net income to net cash provided by operating activities:			
Net income	$ 6,651	$ 9,477	$ 5,714
Provision for depreciation, depletion and amortization	9,738	8,991	8,734
Writedown of equipment from restructuring	6,580	—	—
Provision for losses on accounts receivable	112	231	509
Gain on property, plant and equipment disposals	(34)	(388)	(250)

	For the Years Ended December 31,		
	1989	1988	1987
Changes in operating assets and liabilities:			
Accounts receivable	(2,137)	3,314	(4,348)
Inventories	(1,814)	(369)	754
Other assets	(609)	(680)	1,980
Accounts payable and other liabilities	13,993	(1,795)	2,946
Accrued income taxes	(1,132)	1,325	392
Deferred income taxes	(10,176)	(993)	1,047
Net cash provided by operating activities	$ 21,172	$ 19,113	$ 17,478

Required a. Prepare the statement of cash flows, with a total column for the three-year period ended December 31, 1989.

b. Comment on significant cash flow items in the statement prepared in (a).

c. Prepare the statement of cash flows for 1989, with inflows separated from outflows. Present the data in dollars and percentages. Do not include reconciliation of net income to net cash provided by operating activities. (The presentation should be similar to Exhibit 10-7.)

d. Comment on significant cash flow items in the statement prepared in (c).

CHAPTER 11

STATEMENT ANALYSIS: PART II— COOPER TIRE & RUBBER COMPANY

CHAPTER TOPICS

Eleven-Year Summary
Comments Related
   to Eleven-Year Summary

*Management's Discussion
and Analysis*

Five-Year Ratio Comparison
Liquidity
Long-Term Debt-Paying Ability

Profitability
Investor Analysis

*Ratio Comparison
with Industry Averages*
Liquidity
Long-Term Debt-Paying Ability
Profitability
Investor Analysis

Chapter 5 introduced Cooper Tire & Rubber Company and the tire industry. Cooper's 1989 financial statements were used as illustrations of ratios in subsequent chapters. You may want to review the material in Chapter 5 on Cooper and the tire industry before reading this chapter.

Financial statement analysis is an art, not a science. The comments made in this chapter should be regarded as the opinions of the author based on his analysis; some may not agree with these conclusions.

ELEVEN-YEAR SUMMARY

Cooper included an eleven-year summary of operations and financial data with its 1989 annual report. This summary contains a large amount of financial data, including financial ratios. Cooper includes much more extensive data than most companies.

The eleven-year summary is shown in Exhibit 11-1. The data of Exhibit 11-1 has been presented in Exhibit 11-2 and Exhibit 11-3 in horizontal common size analysis. Exhibit 11-2 shows horizontal common size analysis, other than ratios; Exhibit 11-3 shows horizontal common size analysis for ratios.

EXHIBIT 11-1

COOPER TIRE & RUBBER COMPANY
Eleven-Year Summary of Operations and Financial Data
Data Presented by Company in Annual Report
(All Dollar Amounts in Thousands Except Per Share Figures)

	Net Sales	Gross Margin	Operating Margin	Pretax Income	Income Taxes	Net Income	Common Dividends
1989	$866,805	$139,482	$ 94,188	$ 92,624	$34,380	$58,244	$ 7,080
1988	748,032	106,419	66,575	64,912	23,850	41,062	5,712
1987	665,775	93,877	56,031	53,090	22,410	30,680	4,673
1986	577,517	81,515	46,432	43,138	20,120	23,018	4,146
1985	522,639	64,862	34,492	31,151	12,680	18,471	4,013
1984	555,388	73,030	43,447	41,978	17,400	24,578	3,799
1983	457,780	67,666	41,009	39,796	18,390	21,406	3,392
1982	430,354	63,727	38,716	34,898	15,890	19,008	2,521
1981	393,945	56,193	33,828	31,196	13,930	17,266	2,071
1980	323,953	47,714	28,014	24,545	11,720	12,825	1,543
1979	283,236	28,301	11,447	7,812	2,650	5,162	1,493

	Stockholders' Equity	Total Assets	Working Capital	Net Property, Plant & Equipment	Capital Expenditures	Depreciation & Amortization	Long-term Debt
1989	$310,064	$519,893	$150,285	$262,445	$73,182	$23,393	$65,727
1988	257,756	442,582	143,101	212,923	70,621	19,873	67,790
1987	221,566	413,306	154,283	162,447	41,507	18,436	70,059
1986	195,151	367,715	153,538	139,721	26,548	16,666	76,795
1985	175,711	295,161	110,300	123,380	23,660	14,955	41,910
1984	160,526	279,857	92,920	115,329	57,239	11,605	36,501
1983	139,601	243,665	111,586	69,839	18,502	9,527	33,414
1982	121,451	220,901	105,058	60,917	11,978	8,370	38,480
1981	81,806	185,523	71,787	57,475	15,166	7,067	43,461
1980	60,438	181,784	70,638	49,386	7,122	5,870	51,649
1979	48,705	149,855	59,912	48,339	5,183	5,382	51,708

	Return on Beginning Equity	Return on Beginning Assets	Current Ratio	Pretax Margin	Effective Tax Rate	Return on Sales	Long-term Debt to Capitalization
1989	22.6%	13.2%	2.5	10.7%	37.1%	6.7%	17.5%
1988	18.5	9.9	2.7	8.7	36.7	5.5	20.8
1987	15.7	8.3	2.6	8.0	42.2	4.6	24.0
1986	13.1	7.8	3.1	7.5	46.6	4.0	28.2
1985	11.5	6.6	2.8	6.0	40.7	3.5	19.3
1984	17.6	10.1	2.3	7.6	41.4	4.4	18.5
1983	17.6	9.7	2.8	8.7	46.2	4.7	19.3
1982	23.2	10.2	2.9	8.1	45.5	4.4	24.1
1981	28.5	9.5	2.3	7.9	44.7	4.4	34.7
1980	25.8	8.6	2.2	7.6	47.7	4.0	44.1
1979	10.8	3.3	2.6	2.8	33.9	1.8	48.7

E X H I B I T   1 1 - 1   (continued)

	Net Income Per Share*	Equity Per Share*	Assets Per Share*	Dividends Per Share*	Common Shares Average (000)*	Common Shares Year End (000)*	Number of Stockholders
1989	$2.84	$15.08	$25.28	$.35	20,519	20,565	3,871
1988	2.01	12.60	21.64	.28	20,396	20,455	3,627
1987	1.51	10.89	20.31	.23	20,314	20,346	3,516
1986	1.14	9.62	18.12	.21	20.216	20,288	3,138
1985	.92	8.72	14.64	.20	20,064	20,156	3,526
1984	1.23	8.02	13.98	.19	19,995	20,017	3,872
1983	1.07	6.99	12.20	.17	19,952	19,976	4,028
1982	1.10	6.09	11.08	.15	17,212	19,939	3,500
1981	1.03	4.79	10.87	.13	16,697	17,072	3,845
1980	.84	4.01	12.05	.11	14,942	15,081	3,721
1979	.33	3.26	10.04	.10	14,930	14,930	4,478

	Number of Employees	Wages & Benefits	Total Taxes[†]	Research & Development	Stock Price*		Price/ Earnings Average Ratio
					High	Low	
1989	6,041	$233,257	$53,907	$10,300	$39.00	$22.50	10.8
1988	6,031	217,062	41,743	11,200	27.25	14.13	10.3
1987	5,720	189,045	39,056	10,300	19.88	11.13	10.3
1986	5,398	165,458	34,801	8,900	14.38	8.63	10.1
1985	4,876	153,825	26,275	7,300	10.19	7.31	9.5
1984	4,805	148,139	30,845	6,700	9.50	6.31	6.4
1983	4,455	128,844	29,660	6,400	11.38	6.19	8.2
1982	4,169	118,019	25,644	5,900	9.44	3.47	5.9
1981	3,869	103,901	22,802	5,300	5.22	3.06	4.0
1980	3,885	83,030	18,285	3,900	3.47	1.20	2.8
1979	3,687	77,564	8,830	3,100	2.13	1.27	5.2

*Share data reflects stock splits in 1988, 1983 and 1981.
[†]Excluding Federal Excise Taxes.

EXHIBIT 11-2

COOPER TIRE & RUBBER COMPANY
Horizontal Common Size Analysis (Other Than Ratios)
1979–1989 (Data from Exhibit 11-1)

	Base Year 1979	1980	1981	1982	1983	1984	1985	1986	1987	1988	1989
Liquidity:											
Working capital	100.0	117.9	119.8	175.4	186.2	155.1	184.1	256.3	257.5	238.9	250.8
Long-term debt-paying ability:											
Long-term debt	100.0	99.9	84.1	74.4	64.6	70.6	81.1	148.5	135.5	131.1	127.1
Profitability:											
Net sales	100.0	114.4	139.1	151.9	161.6	196.1	184.5	203.9	235.1	264.1	306.0
Gross margin	100.0	168.6	198.6	225.2	239.1	258.0	229.2	288.0	331.7	376.0	492.9
Operating margin	100.0	244.7	295.5	338.2	358.3	379.5	301.3	405.6	489.5	581.6	822.8
Pretax income	100.0	314.2	399.3	446.7	509.4	537.4	398.8	552.2	679.6	830.9	1185.7
Income taxes	100.0	442.3	525.7	599.6	694.0	656.6	478.5	759.2	845.7	900.0	1297.4
Net income	100.0	248.5	334.5	368.2	414.7	476.1	357.8	445.9	594.3	795.5	1128.3
Number of employees	100.0	105.4	104.9	113.1	120.8	130.3	132.2	146.4	155.1	163.6	163.8
Wages and benefits	100.0	107.0	134.0	152.2	166.1	191.0	198.3	213.3	243.7	279.8	300.7
Investor analysis:											
Common dividends	100.0	103.3	138.7	168.9	227.2	254.5	268.8	277.7	313.0	382.6	474.2
Stockholders' equity	100.0	124.1	168.0	249.4	286.6	329.6	360.8	400.7	454.9	529.2	636.6
Total assets	100.0	121.3	123.8	147.4	162.6	186.8	197.0	245.4	275.8	295.3	346.9
Common shares—Average	100.0	100.1	111.8	115.3	133.6	133.9	134.4	135.4	136.1	136.6	137.4
Common shares—Year end	100.0	101.0	114.3	133.5	133.8	134.1	135.0	135.9	136.3	137.0	137.7
Number of stockholders	100.0	83.1	85.9	78.2	90.0	86.5	78.7	70.1	78.5	81.0	86.4
Stock price:											
High	100.0	162.9	245.1	443.2	534.3	446.0	478.4	675.1	933.3	1279.3	1831.0
Low	100.0	94.5	240.9	273.2	487.4	496.9	575.6	679.5	876.4	1112.6	1771.7
Other:											
Net property, plant, and equipment	100.0	102.2	118.9	126.0	144.5	238.6	255.2	289.0	336.1	440.5	542.9
Capital expenditures	100.0	137.4	292.6	231.1	357.0	1104.4	456.5	512.2	800.8	1362.6	1412.0
Depreciation and amortization	100.0	109.1	131.3	155.5	177.0	215.6	277.9	309.7	342.5	369.2	434.7
Total taxes	100.0	207.1	258.2	290.4	335.9	349.3	297.6	394.1	442.3	472.7	610.5
Research and development	100.0	125.8	171.0	190.3	206.5	216.1	235.5	287.1	332.3	361.3	332.3

EXHIBIT 11-3

COOPER TIRE & RUBBER COMPANY
Horizontal Common Size Analysis (Related to Ratios)
1979–1989 (Data from Exhibit 11-1)

	Year										Base Year
	1989	1988	1987	1986	1985	1984	1983	1982	1981	1980	1979
Liquidity:											
Current ratio	96.2	103.8	100.0	119.2	107.7	88.5	107.7	111.5	88.5	84.6	100.0
Long-term debt-paying ability:											
Long-term debt to capitalization	35.9	42.7	49.3	57.9	39.6	38.0	39.6	49.5	71.3	90.6	100.0
Profitability:											
Return on beginning equity	209.3	171.3	145.4	121.3	106.5	163.0	163.0	214.8	263.9	238.9	100.0
Return on beginning assets	400.0	300.0	251.5	236.4	200.0	306.1	293.9	309.1	287.9	260.6	100.0
Pretax margin	382.1	310.7	285.7	267.9	214.3	271.4	310.7	289.3	282.1	271.4	100.0
Effective tax rates	109.4	108.3	124.5	137.5	120.1	122.1	136.3	134.2	131.9	140.7	100.0
Return on sales	372.2	305.6	255.6	222.2	194.4	244.4	261.1	244.4	244.4	222.2	100.0
Investor analysis:											
Net income per share	860.6	609.1	457.6	345.5	278.8	372.7	324.2	333.3	312.1	254.5	100.0
Equity per share	462.6	386.5	334.0	295.1	267.5	246.0	214.4	186.8	146.9	123.0	100.0
Assets per share	251.8	215.5	202.3	180.5	145.8	139.2	121.5	110.4	108.3	120.0	100.0
Dividends per share	350.0	280.0	230.0	210.0	200.0	190.0	170.0	150.0	130.0	110.0	100.0
Price/earnings average ratio	207.7	198.1	198.1	194.2	182.7	123.1	157.7	113.5	76.9	53.8	100.0

Comments Related to Eleven-Year Summary

Comments related to the eleven-year summary have been divided into five categories: liquidity, long-term debt-paying ability, profitability, investor analysis, and other. It should be remembered that the data under any one category is usually interrelated with one or more of the other categories. For example, net sales under profitability would also be of interest to investors.

Liquidity

Working capital and the current ratio have been categorized as liquidity related. Working capital increased approximately 151%, while the current ratio varied from a low of 2.2 to a high of 3.1. At the end of 1989, the current ratio was 2.5. These are indications of a very good liquidity position.

Long-Term Debt-Paying Ability

Long-term debt increased approximately 27% over the eleven-year period (maximum increase was approximately 49% in 1986). This is very low in relation to the increase in some other items, such as total assets and stockholders' equity.

Long-term debt to capitalization[1] decreased to only approximately 36% of the ratio in 1979. This ratio decreased from 48.7% in 1979 to 17.5% in 1989. Thus, long-term debt is very low in relation to capitalization.

Profitability

Items categorized as primarily relating to profitability were as follows: net sales, gross margin, operating margin, pretax income, income taxes, net income, number of employees, wages and benefits, total taxes, return on beginning equity, return on beginning assets, pretax margin, effective tax rates, and return on sales.

Net sales, gross margin, operating margin, and net income increased substantially. Net sales increased from $283,236,000 to $866,805,000, an increase of 206%. Gross margin increased by 393%, from $28,301,000 to $139,482,000. Operating margin increased from $11,447,000 to $94,188,000, an increase of 723%. Net income grew by 1,028%, from $5,162,000 to $58,244,000.

Income taxes increased 1,197%, which was a higher rate than the increase in pretax income (1,086%). Total taxes increased 511%. Thus, tax increases were substantial and greater than the percentage increase in net sales.

The number of employees increased approximately 64%, while wages and benefits went up 201%. These are very favorable numbers when considered in relation to the increase in sales, gross margin, and net income. Thus, absolute numbers related to profitability were very favorable.

Return on sales increased from 1.8% to 6.7%, for an increase of 272%. Return

---

[1]Long-term debt to capitalization is a type of debt ratio. It is not covered in this book. The higher this ratio, the higher the debt in relation to capitalization. Cooper has computed this ratio by relating long-term debt to the total of long-term debt and total stockholders' equity.

on beginning equity increased from 10.8% to 22.6%—an increase of 109%. Return on beginning assets increased from 3.3% to 13.2%, representing an increase of 300%. Pretax margin increased by 282%, from 2.8% to 10.7%. These financial ratios indicate that Cooper is a very profitable company.

Investor Analysis

Items categorized as primarily relating to investor analysis were as follows: common dividends, stockholders' equity, total assets, common shares—average, common shares—year end, number of stockholders, stock price, net income per share, equity per share, assets per share, dividends per share, and price/earnings average ratio.

Common dividends increased from $1,493,000 to $7,080,000, an increase of 374%. This is a substantial increase. However, when considered in relation to net income, it indicates that dividends have been a relatively small percentage of net income. Dividends per share increased from 10¢ to 35¢, an increase of 250%. This increase is impressive, but less than the percentage increase in common dividends. This difference is explained by the increase in the number of shares.

Net income per share increased much more proportionally than dividends per share. Thus, Cooper is reinvesting a high proportion of its earnings.

Stockholders' equity increased from $48,705,000 to $310,064,000, an increase of 537%. This is very favorable in relation to the increase in total assets, which was 247%. Equity per share increased by 363%, from $3.26 to $15.08. The lesser increase in equity per share as compared to stockholders' equity is related to the increase in the number of shares.

Assets per share increased 152%, which is much less than some of the other increases. It is favorable that sales, net income, and other profitability indicators have increased more than assets per share.

Common shares increased approximately 38%, while the number of stockholders decreased by approximately 14%. This indicates an increase in institutional holders and fewer individual stockholders.

The stock price high increased from $2.13 in 1979 to $39.00 in 1989, and the stock price low increased from $1.27 in 1979 to $22.50 in 1989. This represents an increase of 1,731% for the high and 1,672% for the low—very impressive increases. The price/earnings average ratio increased 108%, which is very substantial. The increase in the price/earnings ratio indicates that the stock market now perceives Cooper as having better prospects than in 1979, but not necessarily in relation to other stocks.

Other

Items presented in the eleven-year summary that I have elected to discuss under the category of "other" are net property, plant, and equipment; capital expenditures; depreciation and amortization; and research and development.

Net property, plant, and equipment increased 443%, capital expenditures increased 1,312%, and depreciation and amortization increased 335%. All of these increases are substantial, particularly the increase in capital expenditures. It appears that Cooper is preparing for further increases in sales.

Research and development increased 232%, which is in line with the increase in net sales. Research and development was approximately 1.2% of net sales in 1989. Thus, research and development does not take up a substantial percentage of sales.

MANAGEMENT'S DISCUSSION AND ANALYSIS

The management discussion and analysis included with the annual report is presented in Exhibit 11-4. It was divided into two sections by Cooper: financial conditions and results of operations. Management's discussion and analysis primarily covers 1989 and 1988 and attempts to explain the reasons behind the changes.

E X H I B I T   1 1 - 4

COOPER TIRE & RUBBER COMPANY
Management's Discussion and Analysis
For the Years Ended December 31, 1989 and 1988

Financial Condition

The year-end financial position of the Company reflects continued excellent operating results in 1989. Funds provided by operating activities (net income plus depreciation) were $81.6 million for the year, a $20.7 million increase over the $60.9 million in the prior year. These strong operating flows provided funds for modernization and expansion, and contributed significantly to the strong financial position at December 31, 1989.

Working capital amounted to $150.3 million at year-end 1989 compared to $143.1 million one year earlier. A current ratio of 2.5 and a quick asset ratio (total cash and receivables divided by current liabilities) of 1.8 reflect the excellent financial liquidity position of the Company. These ratios compare favorably to the 2.7 current ratio and 1.8 quick asset ratio in 1988.

Accounts receivable reached $126.4 million, up from $120.4 million at year-end 1988, reflecting higher fourth quarter sales in 1989. Generally, collection experience has been excellent and payment terms are comparable to the prior year. Customer balances are collectible and adequate provisions have been made for possible collection losses.

Total inventories at $70.7 million were up $2.8 million from $67.9 million at year-end 1988. Finished goods inventories were $2.3 million higher than one year ago while work in process inventories were down slightly. Raw material and supplies inventories increased moderately at year-end 1989.

In 1989 additions to property, plant and equipment were a record $73.2 million, a slight increase of $2.6 million from the previous record of $70.6 million in 1988. These expenditures included amounts for expansion and modernization projects begun in 1989 as well as carry over amounts from 1988 projects. Depre-

E X H I B I T 1 1 - 4 (continued)

ciation and amortization was $23.4 million in 1989, an 18 percent increase from $19.9 million in 1988, reflecting the significant capital expenditures in recent years.

Current liabilities of $98.9 million were $12.8 million higher than the $86.1 million at year-end 1988. This increase was primarily due to increases in trade payables and accrued liabilities. Long-term debt decreased $2.1 million from year-end 1988 to $65.7 million reflecting scheduled payments of debt maturities.

Common stockholders' equity increased $52.3 million during the year reaching $310.1 million at year end. Earnings retentions for 1989 (net income less dividends paid) added $51.2 million to common equity while stock issued for the exercise of employee stock options added $1.1 million. Common equity per share was $15.08 at year-end 1989, an increase of 20 percent over $12.60 per share at year-end 1988.

Long-term debt, as a percent of total capitalization, decreased to 17.5 percent at December 31, 1989 from 20.8 percent one year earlier. Total capitalization, comprised of long-term debt and common stockholders' equity, was $375.8 million at year-end 1989. This total compares favorably to $325.5 million at December 31, 1988.

Results of Operations

Sales increased 15.9 percent in 1989 to a record $866.8 million, following an increase of 12.4 percent in 1988, due to escalating customer demand for the Company's tire products.

Sales margins were slightly higher for 1989 as compared to 1988 which was slightly higher than 1987. The effects of changes in product mix, price increases and production efficiencies in 1989 and 1988 exceeded increased raw material costs. In 1987 significant increases in raw material costs were offset by production efficiencies and some modest increases in product prices.

Increases in 1989 and 1988 selling, general and administrative expenses reflected increased sales activity levels, increased advertising and general inflation.

Other income was lower in 1989 compared with 1988, and lower in 1988 than in 1987. These changes reflect differences related to the investments of cash reserves.

Effective income tax rates differed in 1989, 1988 and 1987 due to differences in the statutory Federal tax rates and tax credits. The Financial Accounting Standards Board has issued Statement of Financial Accounting Standards No. 96, "Accounting for Income Taxes," which significantly modifies certain aspects of accounting for income taxes. The Company has not elected to comply with this statement in 1989 and is not required to do so until 1992. It is expected, if financial statements for prior years are not restated, that the cumulative effect of the change in accounting will increase net income.

Increases in net income during 1989 and 1988 resulted from record high sales levels, efficient production schedules and ongoing cost containment programs. Net income during 1988 also benefited from reduced Federal income taxes.

A number of the variables in the eleven-year summary are discussed in management's discussion and analysis. In other cases, further data is introduced. In general, the eleven-year summary included more variables than management's discussion and analysis.

Further liquidity insight is provided in management's discussion and analysis. Funds provided by operating activities is discussed, as are the quick ratio, accounts receivable detail, and inventory detail. In general, management's discussion and analysis gives the impression that Cooper's liquidity position is very good.

Long-term debt disclosure in management's discussion and analysis is similar to the variable disclosed in the eleven-year summary. Long-term debt as a percentage of total capitalization is discussed, as is total capitalization. The general impression is that the company's long-term debt position is very good.

Also reviewed under financial condition are property, plant, and equipment and common stockholders' equity. In general, it is conveyed that the data relating to property, plant, and equipment and common stockholders' equity is favorable.

The section on results of operations primarily discusses profitability data. Some of these data were in the eleven-year summary, and some are new. Explanations are included with the results of operations. For example, the improved sales margin is attributed to changes in product mix, price increases, and production efficiencies.

In general, there are less data in management's discussion and analysis than there are in the eleven-year summary. For much of the data included in management's discussion and analysis, there is an attempt to explain changes.

From management's discussion and analysis, we obtain a favorable impression of liquidity, debt position, and profitability.

FIVE-YEAR RATIO COMPARISON

Exhibit 11-5 is a five-year ratio comparison for Cooper for the years 1985–1989. This is a summary using the ratios presented in this book, computed as explained in previous chapters. The ratios are presented under liquidity, long-term debt-paying ability, profitability, and investor analysis.

Liquidity

The liquidity of receivables improved over the five-year period, with the improvement concentrated in the last three years. The liquidity of inventory also improved over the five-year period. This improvement took place in all five years and was more substantial than the improvement in the liquidity of receivables. Because of the improved liquidity of receivables and inventory, there was a substantial improvement in the operating cycle.

The current ratio, acid test ratio, and cash ratio are all very favorable. In general, there has been a decrease in these ratios (indicating less liquidity), but this must be considered in relation to the apparent improvement in the managing of

E X H I B I T 1 1 - 5

COOPER TIRE & RUBBER COMPANY
Five-Year Comparison for the Years 1985–1989

	Unit	1989	1988	1987	1986	1985
Liquidity:						
Days' sales in receivables	Days	54.12	59.41	63.56	58.93	60.32
Accounts receivable turnover	Times	6.93	6.29	6.17	6.27	6.10
Accounts receivable turnover	Days	52.70	57.99	59.14	58.21	59.83
Days' sales in inventory	Days	35.48	38.63	38.92	46.70	59.74
Merchandise inventory turnover	Times	10.50	9.96	9.20	7.17	6.42
Inventory turnover	Days	34.78	36.66	39.69	50.92	56.89
Operating cycle	Days	87.48	94.65	98.83	109.13	116.72
Working capital	$	150,285,470	143,101,227	154,283,213	153,537,615	110,299,892
Current ratio	Times	2.52	2.66	2.60	3.07	2.80
Acid test	Times	1.78	1.85	1.95	2.22	1.58
Cash ratio	Times	.50	.45	.75	.87	.20
Sales to working capital	Times	5.91	5.03	4.33	4.38	5.14
Cash flow/current maturities of long-term debt and notes payable	Times	44.90	18.93	8.86	9.51	4.29
Long-term debt-paying ability:						
Times interest earned	Times	15.46	10.81	8.56	11.01	8.88
Fixed charge coverage	Times	11.96	8.59	7.02	8.33	6.90
Debt ratio	%	40.36	41.76	46.39	46.93	40.47
Debt equity	%	67.67	71.71	86.54	88.43	67.98
Debt to tangible net worth	%	67.67	71.71	86.54	88.43	67.98
Cash flow/total debt	%	44.08	25.93	31.09	31.44	19.77

EXHIBIT 11-5 (continued)

	Unit	1989	1988	1987	1986	1985
Profitability:						
Net profit margin	%	6.72	5.49	4.61	3.99	3.53
Total asset turnover	Times	1.80	1.75	1.70	1.74	1.82
Return on assets	%	12.10	9.60	7.86	6.94	6.42
Operating income margin	%	10.87	8.90	8.42	8.04	6.60
Operating asset turnover	Times	1.82	1.75	1.71	1.74	1.82
Return on operating assets	%	19.75	15.57	14.36	14.02	12.00
Sales to fixed assets	Times	3.65	3.99	4.41	4.39	4.38
Return on investment	%	15.69	13.04	11.27	9.60	9.41
Return on total equity	%	20.51	17.13	14.72	12.41	10.99
Return on common equity	%	20.51	17.13	14.72	12.41	10.99
Gross profit margin	%	16.09	14.23	14.10	14.18	12.46
Investor analysis:						
Percentage of earnings retained	%	87.84	86.09	84.77	81.99	78.27
Earnings per share	$	2.84	2.01	1.51	1.14	.92
Degree of financial leverage	Times	1.05	1.07	1.12	1.10	1.13
Price/earnings ratio	Times	11.40	11.94	10.10	11.51	10.53
Dividend payout ratio	%	12.32	13.93	15.23	17.98	21.74
Dividend yield	%	1.08	1.17	1.51	1.56	2.06
Book value per share	$	15.08	12.60	10.89	9.62	8.72
Materiality of stock options	%	1.67	2.18	2.64	1.40	1.91
Cash flow per share	$	4.51	2.35	2.93	2.68	1.17
Operating cash flow/cash dividends	Times	13.06	8.39	12.76	13.09	5.88
Year-end market price	$	32.38	24.00	15.25	13.12	9.69

receivables and inventory. It also must be remembered that we want adequate liquidity but not excessive liquidity, which would be negative to profits. It also must be considered that Cooper uses LIFO inventory, which results in a relatively low inventory dollar amount. Thus, the current ratio is better than it appears.

Sales to working capital has improved substantially, as has operating cash flow/ current maturities of long-term debt and notes payable. These ratios were good to start with, and the improvement has been substantial.

Overall, Cooper's liquidity position appears to be impressive. All liquidity indicators reviewed were positive.

Long-Term Debt-Paying Ability

The times interest earned and the fixed charge coverage are very high and have increased in recent years. From an income statement view, the long-term debt-paying ability is excellent.

The debt ratio, debt equity, and debt to tangible net worth indicate relatively low debt in relation to assets and equity. These ratios were approximately the same at the end of 1989 as they were at the end of 1985. These ratios were very good in each year. They did increase substantially in 1986 and then declined over the next three years.

Operating cash flow/total debt was good in 1985 and improved each year to an impressive 44.08% in 1989. Cooper is generating substantial operating cash flow in relation to total debt.

Overall, Cooper's debt position is impressive. All debt indicators reviewed were positive.

Profitability

Net profit margin increased from 3.53% in 1985 to 6.72% in 1989. This represents a substantial increase, and the 1989 net profit margin is very good. Total asset turnover was approximately the same in 1989 as for 1985, after declining in the middle years. Return on assets increased substantially each year, reaching an impressive 12.10% for 1989. Operating income margin also increased substantially each year, and the figure of 10.87% for 1989 is very good. Operating asset turnover was similar to the total asset turnover, having obtained approximately the same turnover in 1989 as for 1985 after declining in the middle years. Considering the substantial increase in total assets and operating assets, the turnover of those assets is very good. Return on operating assets improved each year, reaching an impressive 19.75% for 1989.

Sales to fixed assets declined over the five-year period and was down to 3.65 in 1989. This indicates a less efficient use of fixed assets, but it could be misleading because of the substantial increase in fixed assets in 1989.

Return on investment improved from 9.41% in 1985 to 15.69% in 1989—a very good figure. Return on total equity improved from 10.99% in 1985 to an impressive 20.51% in 1989, as did return on common equity. The gross profit margin improved from 12.46% in 1985 to 16.09% in 1989.

Overall, Cooper's profitability is impressive. The only profitability ratio with a negative trend was sales to fixed assets. As indicated earlier, this may be misleading because of the substantial increase in fixed assets. Total asset turnover and operating asset turnover were neutral, which is very good considering the substantial increase in total assets and operating assets. Other profitability ratios were overwhelmingly positive.

Investor Analysis

Percentage of earnings retained was high in all five years and increased over the five-year period, topping out at 87.84% in 1989. The dividend payout ratio (approximately the reciprocal of the percentage of earnings retained) was low in all five years—down to 12.32% in 1989.

Earnings per share increased impressively from 92¢ in 1985 to $2.84 in 1989. The price/earnings ratio declined slightly in 1989 to 11.40 from 11.94 in 1988. These are slightly better than the price/earnings ratios in the prior years. It is surprising that the price/earnings ratio did not improve substantially, considering the company's impressive liquidity position, favorable debt position, and substantial improvement in profitability. The market price has increased substantially, from $9.69 to $32.38. This increase in market price follows the increase in earnings per share, but the market has not been willing to pay more in relation to earnings in recent years.

The degree of financial leverage was low in all five years, declining to 1.05 in 1989. Thus, there was only a moderate benefit to profitability from using debt. (This also represents minimum risk to profitability from using debt.)

The dividend yield was low in all five years, declining to 1.08% in 1989. Investors who seek current yield would not be interested in Cooper's stock.

Book value per share increased impressively, from $8.72 in 1985 to $15.08 in 1989. Book value is slightly less than half the market price.

The materiality of stock options has been relatively low and declined in 1989. There is some difficulty in interpreting this ratio because of the use of options and stock appreciation rights.

Operating cash flow/cash dividends was high in all five years, and this ratio more than doubled between 1985 and 1989. Operating cash flow per share has been high in relation to earnings per share. This indicates a favorable cash flow from operations in relation to common shares outstanding.

Overall, the investor ratios indicate that the company would normally be classified as a growth company. Earnings per share are increasing substantially, cash flow per share is increasing substantially, operating cash flow/cash dividends is high, percentage of earnings retained is high, dividend payout ratio is low, and dividend yield is low. The fairly stable price earnings/ratio indicates that the market has not labeled the company as a growth company.

The increase in the market price has been impressive and has reasonably correlated with the increase in earnings per share. If Cooper were to be recognized as a growth stock, the market price would be expected to react in a more favorable manner in the future.

RATIO COMPARISON WITH INDUSTRY AVERAGES

In Chapter 4, we discussed a number of reasons why industry comparisons can be difficult. It was noted that caution must be exercised when using industry comparisons. Cooper represents a very difficult situation when it comes to industry comparison. There were approximately 130 tire companies in the United States in 1920. There are now only two publicly held tire companies in the country: Cooper and Goodyear. Cooper and Goodyear are materially different in terms of operations. Cooper is much smaller than Goodyear. Approximately 80% of Cooper's sales are in the tire replacement market, and 20% are in the industrial rubber products market. Goodyear is a much more diversified company, selling a greater variety of automotive products than Cooper and selling tires extensively in the original equipment market. Goodyear is also in chemicals and plastics and has an oil pipeline.

The industry comparison (summarized in Exhibit 11-6) is somewhat limited because of the problems encountered. Instead of comparing only with the tire industry, comparisons were made with the manufacturing industry in general. The index at the bottom of Exhibit 11-6 indicates the source of each comparison.

Liquidity

The industry comparison indicates that Cooper's days' sales in receivables are somewhat higher than the industry's while the company's accounts receivable turnover times is somewhat lower. Accounts receivable turnover days is somewhat higher than for the industry as a whole. A closer examination of these receivable comparisons indicates that Cooper's receivable data are approximately the same as those of the industry. The reason for this conclusion is that the Cooper data were computed using gross receivables, whereas only net receivables figures were available for industry comparison. Furthermore, the Cooper ratios show substantial improvement between 1988 and 1989.

The Cooper days' sales in inventory is substantially better than the industry figure, and the company made a material improvement in its days' sales in inventory during 1989. Much of the more favorable Cooper data can probably be attributed to the fact that Cooper uses LIFO inventory, while the industry used for comparison is a combination of companies using different inventory methods.

Cooper's current ratio, acid test, and cash ratio are substantially better than the

EXHIBIT 11-6

Ratio Comparison with Industry Averages
For the Years Ended December 31, 1989 and 1988

	Unit	Cooper Tire & Rubber		Industry Statistics		Source
		1989	1988	1989	1988	
Liquidity:						
Days' sales in receivables	Days	54.12	59.41	48.53	49.18	DC
Accounts receivable turnover	Times	6.93	6.29	7.66	7.74	DC
Accounts receivable turnover	Days	52.70	57.99	47.65	47.18	DC
Days' sales in inventory	Days	35.48	38.63	86.86	76.45	IN
Merchandise inventory turnover	Times	10.50	9.96	Not available		
Inventory turnover	Days	34.78	36.66	Not available		
Operating cycle	Days	87.48	94.65	Not available		
Current ratio	Times	2.52	2.66	1.96	2.14	IN
Acid test	Times	1.78	1.85	1.09	1.21	IN
Cash ratio	Times	.50	.45	.31	.27	IN
Sales to working capital	Times	5.91	5.03	8.91	8.63	DC
Cash flow/current maturities of long-term debt and notes payable	Times	44.90	18.93	Not available		
Long-term debt-paying ability:						
Times interest earned	Times	15.46	10.81	Not available		
Fixed charge coverage	Times	11.96	8.59	Not available		
Debt ratio	%	40.36	41.76	51.40	50.10	IN
Debt equity	%	67.67	71.71	1.06	1.00	IN
Debt to tangible net worth	%	67.67	71.71	Not available		
Cash flow/total debt	%	44.08	25.93	Not available		

EXHIBIT 11-6 (continued)

	Unit	Cooper Tire & Rubber		Industry Statistics		Source
		1989	1988	1989	1988	
Profitability:						
Net profit margin	%	6.72	5.49	5.20	8.00	IN
Total asset turnover	Times	1.80	1.75	1.49	1.57	IN
Return on assets	%	12.10	9.60	7.77	12.58	IN
Operating income margin	%	10.87	8.90	6.63	7.28	DC
Operating asset turnover	Times	1.82	1.75	1.58	1.57	DC
Return on operating assets	%	19.75	15.57	10.49	11.48	DC
Sales to fixed assets	Times	3.65	3.99	3.40	3.39	DC
Return on investment	%	15.69	13.04	Not available		
Return on total equity	%	20.51	17.13	Not available		
Return on common equity	%	20.51	17.13	Not available		
Gross profit margin	%	16.09	14.23	Not available		
Investor analysis:						
Percentage of earnings retained	%	87.84	86.09	57.44	62.53	IR
Earnings per share	$	2.84	2.01	Not applicable		
Degree of financial leverage	Times	1.05	1.07	Not available		
Price/earnings ratio	Times	11.40	11.94	12.50	11.90	VL
Dividend payout ratio	%	12.32	13.93	42.56	37.47	IR
Dividend yield	%	1.08	1.17	3.01	3.14	IR
Book value per share	$	15.08	12.60	Not applicable		
Materiality of stock options	%	1.67	2.18	Not available		
Cash flow per share	$	4.51	2.35	Not applicable		
Operating cash flow/cash dividend	Times	13.06	8.39	Not applicable		
Year-end market price	$	32.38	24.00	Not applicable		

Index: Industry statistics are directly from or computed from the following sources:
DC U.S. Department of Commerce—Quarterly Financial Report for Manufacturing, Mining, and Trade Corporations.
IN Dun & Bradstreet—Industry Norms & Key Business Ratios—SIC 3052, Rubber & Plastics.
VL Value Line, Inc.—The Value Line Investment Survey.
IR Standard & Poor's, Security Price Index Record, Statistical Service, 1990 Edition (400 Manufacturing Companies).

industry's. Cooper's use of LIFO tends to hold down its current ratio, but the company's current ratio is nevertheless substantially better than the industry comparison.

Cooper's sales to working capital is much lower than that of the industry. This would be expected because of the company's relatively high current ratio.

In summary, Cooper's overall liquidity position appears to be much better than the industry average.

Long-Term Debt-Paying Ability

Cooper's debt ratio and debt equity are substantially better than the industry figures. The company has much less debt in proportion to its total capital structure than the industry average.

Profitability

Cooper's net profit margin, total asset turnover, return on assets, operating income margin, operating asset turnover, and return on operating assets are all substantially better than those of the industry. Furthermore, these ratios for Cooper materially improved during 1989.

Cooper's sales to fixed assets ratio is also better than the industry figure. Cooper's sales to fixed assets declined somewhat in 1989, probably because of the addition of substantial new plant capacity that generated sales for only part of the year.

In summary, a comparison of Cooper's profitability ratios with those of the industry indicates that the company is materially more profitable than the industry.

Investor Analysis

Cooper's percentage of earnings retained is much higher than the industry average. The dividend payout ratio (the approximate reciprocal of the percentage of earnings retained) is much lower than for the industry in general. Retaining a high percentage of earnings is a characteristic of a growth company.

The dividend yield on Cooper stock is much lower than the industry average; this is also characteristic of a growth stock. The price/earnings ratio was less than that of the industry at the end of 1989, and approximately the same at the end of 1988. This indicates that the stock market has not recognized Cooper as a growth company. The fact that Cooper does not have a price/earnings ratio somewhat above the industry average is surprising, considering the company's liquidity position, debt position, and profitability. If investors recognize Cooper as a growth company in the future, this will have a favorable influence on the stock.

SUMMARY

The years 1989 and 1988 were particularly good for Cooper in terms of liquidity, debt position, and profitability. This was especially true of 1989. Cooper appears to be a good company to sell products to on credit (liquidity would be particularly important), lend money to (liquidity and debt position would be particularly important), and invest in (profitability would be particularly important).

CHAPTER 12

ANALYZING THE IMPACT OF INFLATION ON FINANCIAL STATEMENTS

CHAPTER TOPICS

Inflation Accounting Terminology	*Current Cost Accounting*
Constant Dollar (Price-Level) Accounting	*SFAS No. 33, No. 82, and No. 89*

Traditional financial statements are not designed to account for distortions created by inflation. The distortion inflation creates in financial statements has generated years of debate. In the 1970s and 1980s, major attempts were made to solve this problem.

In 1976, the SEC issued Accounting Series Release (ASR) No. 190. This pronouncement required that certain publicly held companies with heavy investment in inventories and gross plant report current replacement cost information on the form 10-K.

In 1979, the Financial Accounting Standards Board issued SFAS No. 33, "Financial Reporting and Changing Prices," which required that certain large publicly held firms present both constant dollar and current cost data. With the full implementation of SFAS No. 33, the SEC dropped ASR No. 190.

In 1984, the Financial Accounting Standards Board amended SFAS No. 33 with SFAS No. 82, "Financial Reporting and Changing Prices: Elimination of Certain Disclosures." The effect of SFAS No. 82 was to reduce the inflation disclosure requirements of SFAS No. 33.

In 1986, the FASB issued SFAS No. 89, which eliminated required inflation disclosure requirements. This SFAS encouraged the disclosure of supplementary information on the effects of changing prices. SFAS No. 89 was effective for financial reports issued after December 2, 1986.

INFLATION ACCOUNTING TERMINOLOGY

Inflation accounting terminology must be understood before attempting to analyze inflation-adjusted statements. The first distinctions that will be made are among current replacement cost, current cost, and constant dollar accounting.

Current replacement cost is the estimated cost of acquiring the best asset available to undertake the function of the asset owned. This may be a different asset.

Current cost is equal to the current replacement cost of the same asset owned, adjusted for the value of any operating advantages or disadvantages of the asset owned. Current cost differs from current replacement cost in that current cost measurement focuses on the cost of the service potential embodied in the actual asset owned by the enterprise, whereas current replacement cost may be a measurement of a different asset, available for use in place of the asset owned. Current cost information attempts to reflect the current value of certain balance sheet items. It measures specific changes in the prices of goods and services.

Constant dollar accounting (formerly termed *price-level accounting*) is a method of reporting financial statement elements in dollars having similar purchasing power. This method simply adjusts historical cost statements for changes in the price level. Constant dollar accounting measures general changes in the prices of goods and services.

Both current cost and constant dollar accounting will be discussed in general terms, followed by specific discussion of the requirements of SFAS No. 33, SFAS No. 82, and SFAS No. 89.

CONSTANT DOLLAR (PRICE-LEVEL) ACCOUNTING

When financial statements are adjusted for inflation, using constant dollar (price-level) accounting, the statements are adjusted to represent the current purchasing power of the historical dollars that are reflected on the traditional statement. The same concepts are used to prepare both types of statements, but historical cost statements are adjusted to reflect changes in the purchasing power of the dollar.

In order to adjust the statements, accounts on the balance sheet are classified as monetary or nonmonetary. *Monetary accounts* are stated in terms of an amount that is fixed or determinable, without reference to future prices of specific goods and services.

Monetary accounts on the balance sheet do not need to be adjusted, because they have fixed dollar balances and therefore are already in terms of current purchasing power. However, a gain or loss in purchasing power does need to be computed for monetary items; there is a loss in purchasing power from holding monetary assets and a gain in purchasing power from holding monetary liabilities during a period of inflation. As an example, if $10,000 in cash is held for a year, during which there is inflation of 5%, the loss in purchasing power is $500. The $10,000 in cash is automatically in terms of the new purchasing power. In other words, the $10,000 cash will now buy fewer goods. If a $10,000 note payable is on the balance sheet for a year when there is 5% inflation, there is a gain of $500 in purchasing power, since the note payable of $10,000 is automatically in terms of the new purchasing power.

Nonmonetary accounts do need to be adjusted in terms of the new purchasing power. On the historical cost statement, they are in terms of the purchasing power of the time when they were acquired. Adjustment of the nonmonetary accounts indirectly affects the income statement, because the income statement reflects figures computed from the adjusted amounts. For example, if the building account has been adjusted upward for inflation, the depreciation expense increases on the income statement. To illustrate, if a building was purchased for $10,000 when the price level was 100, and the level is now 150, then the building would be presented at $150,000 and depreciation based thereon.

The following illustrates some monetary and nonmonetary accounts:

- *Monetary*
  Assets:
     Cash
     Accounts receivable (net of allowance account)
     Notes receivable
     Advances to employees
  Liabilities:
     Accounts payable
     Notes payable
     Accrued expenses payable
     Bonds payable
- *Nonmonetary*
  Assets:
     Inventories
     Property, plant, and equipment
     Patents, trademarks, goodwill
  Liabilities:
     Deferred income (if to furnish goods and services)
  Owners' equity:
     Minority interest
     Preferred stock
     Common stock

Comprehensive constant dollar restatements are computed by applying the following formula to nonmonetary items:

$$\text{Historical Cost} \times \frac{\text{Price Index at Date of Current Balance Sheet}}{\text{Price Index at Time of Original Transaction}} = \text{Adjusted Amount}$$

To determine the purchasing power gain or loss for income statement purposes, a similar computation is applied to monetary accounts.

The Hawkeye Company will be used to illustrate how the traditional financial statements would be adjusted for price-level accounting on a comprehensive basis. The Hawkeye Company statements are initially presented based on current generally accepted accounting principles in Exhibits 12-1 and 12-2. They are then adjusted on a constant dollar basis in Exhibits 12-3, 12-4, and 12-5.

Additional information:

1. The general price index was as follows on the indicated dates:

December 31, 1988	100
December 31, 1989	120
Average index for 1989	110

2. The December 31, 1988 inventory is at an index of 100. The increase in inventory came when the index was 110. LIFO inventory is used.

3. There were no disposals of plant and equipment during 1989. The increase in plant and equipment came on January 1, 1989, when the price index was 100. No depreciation is taken in the year of acquisition. The price index on December 31, 1980, which is when the remainder of the fixed assets were purchased, was 50.

4. The price index was 115 when capital stock of $10,000 was sold in 1989. Prior capital stock of $110,000 was sold when the price index was 50, and the price index was 100 when prior capital stock of $10,000 was sold.

5. Assume an average price index for sales, purchases, and operating expenses. (This does not include depreciation.)

6. Income taxes and interest expenses were paid on December 31, 1989.

EXHIBIT 12-1

THE HAWKEYE COMPANY
Statement of Earnings
For the Year Ended December 31, 1989

Sales		$350,000
Cost of goods sold:		
Inventory, January 1, 1989	$ 30,000	
Net purchases	150,000	
Total inventory available	$180,000	
Less inventory, December 31, 1989	50,000	130,000
Gross profit		220,000
Operating expenses (including depreciation of $10,000)		120,000
Operating profit		100,000
Less interest expense		8,000
Income before income taxes		92,000
Less income taxes		50,000
Net income		$ 42,000

EXHIBIT 12-2

THE HAWKEYE COMPANY
Balance Sheet
December 31, 1988 and 1989

		1988		1989
Assets				
Current assets:				
Cash		$ 45,000		$ 25,000
Accounts receivable (net)		35,000		30,000
Inventory		30,000		50,000
Total current assets		110,000		105,000
Property, plant, and equipment	$140,000		$180,000	
Less: accumulated depreciation	30,000	110,000	40,000	140,000
Total assets		$220,000		$245,000
Liabilities and stockholders' equity				
Current liabilities:				
Accounts payable		$ 40,000		$ 15,000
Accrued payroll		5,000		10,000
Notes payable		40,000		40,000
Total current liabilities		85,000		65,000
Stockholders' equity:				
Capital stock		120,000		130,000
Retained earnings		15,000		50,000
Total stockholders' equity		135,000		180,000
Total liabilities and stockholders' equity		$220,000		$245,000

7. Dividends of $7,000 were paid on December 31, 1989.

8. Assume that the December 31, 1988 retained earnings balance of $15,000 can be converted at December 31, 1989, using the computation $15,000 × 120/100. The first year that a company prepares a constant dollar statement, the opening retained earnings amount is usually forced (not computed directly). The alternative would be to compute retained earnings for each year since the company went into business.

For financial statement analysis, the reader must be aware of the impact that adjusting for constant dollar accounting has on the resulting financial statements. The Hawkeye Company illustration shows how the traditional statements would be adjusted for constant dollar accounting. However, these statements do not represent a general case from which one can draw conclusions that would apply to all

EXHIBIT 12 - 3

THE HAWKEYE COMPANY
Computation of Purchasing Power Gain or Loss
For the Year Ended December 31, 1989

Schedule 1 Monetary Position at the Beginning and End of the Year

	Jan. 1, 1989	Dec. 31, 1989
Monetary assets:		
Cash	$45,000	$25,000
Accounts receivable	35,000	30,000
Total monetary assets	$80,000	$55,000
Monetary liabilities:		
Accounts payable	$40,000	$15,000
Accrued payroll	5,000	10,000
Notes payable	40,000	40,000
Total monetary liabilities	$85,000	$65,000
Net monetary position	($ 5,000)	($10,000)

Schedule 2 Change in Monetary Position and Purchasing Power Gain or Loss
Between January 1, 1989 and December 31, 1989

	Historical Cost	Price Index	Adjusted Basis
Net monetary position, January 1, 1989	($ 5,000)	120/100	($ 6,000)
Add monetary inflows:			
Sales	350,000	120/110	381,818
Sales of stock	10,000	120/115	10,435
Total available	$355,000		$386,253
Less monetary outflows:			
Purchase of inventory	150,000	120/110	163,636
Operating expenses (excluding depreciation)	110,000	120/110	120,000
Interest expense	8,000	120/120	8,000
Income taxes paid	50,000	120/120	50,000
Purchase of fixed assets	40,000	120/100	48,000
Dividends	7,000	120/120	7,000
Total outflows	$365,000		$396,636
Net monetary position, December 31, 1989	($ 10,000)		($ 10,383)
Purchasing power gain			$ 383

EXHIBIT 12-4

THE HAWKEYE COMPANY
Computation of Constant Dollar Adjusted Statement of Earnings
For the Year Ended December 31, 1989

	Historical Cost	Price Index	Adjusted Basis
Sales	$350,000	120/110	$381,818
Cost of goods sold			
Inventory, January 1, 1989	30,000	120/100	36,000
Net purchases	150,000	120/110	163,636
Total inventory available	$180,000		$199,636
Less inventory, December 31,		30,000 ×	
1989	50,000	120/100	36,000
		20,000 ×	
		120/110	21,818
Cost of goods sold	130,000		141,818
Gross profit	220,000		240,000
Operating expenses			
General expenses	110,000	120/110	120,000
Depreciation	10,000	120/50	24,000
Operating profit	100,000		96,000
Less interest expense	8,000	120/120	8,000
Income before income taxes	92,000		88,000
Less income taxes	50,000	120/120	50,000
Earnings before purchasing power gain	42,000		38,000
Purchasing power gain			383
Net earnings	$ 42,000		$ 38,383

companies. The extent of the impact depends on several factors: the amount of inflation that has taken place, the length of time that the monetary assets and liabilities have been held, and the mixture of monetary and nonmonetary accounts found on the statements.

If there were no inflation, there would be no difference between historical cost statements and constant dollar statements. The greater the inflation, the greater the difference between historical cost statements and constant dollar statements. This also applies to the length of time that the nonmonetary assets and liabilities have been held.

Because the effects of general price-level changes can vary greatly from firm to firm, it is difficult to generalize. Some firms may actually have an increase in income; others, a decrease. The following comments briefly describe some of the effects on financial statements.

THE HAWKEYE COMPANY
Computation of Constant Dollar Adjusted Balance Sheet
December 31, 1989

	Historical Cost	Price Index	Adjusted Basis
Assets			
Current assets:			
Cash	$ 25,000		$ 25,000
Accounts receivable (net)	30,000		30,000
Inventory	50,000	30,000 × 120/100	36,000
		20,000 × 120/110	21,818
Total current assets	105,000		112,818
Property, plant, and equipment	180,000	140,000 × 120/50	336,000
		40,000 × 120/100	48,000
Less accumulated depreciation	40,000	40,000 × 120/50	(96,000)
Net property, plant, and equipment	140,000		288,000
Total assets	$245,000		$400,818
Liabilities and stockholders' equity			
Current liabilities:			
Accounts payable	$ 15,000		$ 15,000
Accrued payroll	10,000		10,000
Notes payable	40,000		40,000
Total current liabilities	65,000		65,000
Stockholders' equity:			
Capital stock	130,000	110,000 × 120/50	264,000
		10,000 × 120/100	12,000
		10,000 × 120/115	10,435
Retained earnings	50,000	15,000 × 120/100	18,000
		(42,000 Earnings)	38,383
		(7,000 Dividends)	(7,000)
Total stockholders' equity	180,000		335,818
Total liabilities and stockholders' equity	$245,000		$400,818

From a short-term analysis view, the working capital and the current ratio have increased, principally because of the higher inventory amount in current assets. The acid test ratio would change very little or not at all, because the inventory account is excluded from the computation. Current asset and current liability accounts would essentially be monetary except for inventory, prepaids, and marketable securities. Under these conditions, they would not change. The conclusion can be drawn that the short-term debt-paying ability would show an improvement, based on the constant dollar statement, because of the improved working capital and current ratio. This improvement comes essentially from the increase in inventory. The improvement in the indicated short-term debt-paying ability is particularly significant for a firm that uses LIFO.

A firm that has a large investment in productive fixed assets would find that inflation can have a material influence on the adjusted statement. The fixed assets would increase on the balance sheet, so there would be a larger depreciation expense on the income statement. This would result in decreased earnings and earnings per share. Net income to sales would decrease, as would return on assets and owners' equity. The debt to equity ratio would improve; the adjusted figures would indicate that a smaller proportion of the financing has come from debt than was indicated on the historical statements. The improvement in the debt to equity ratio would be offset by a reduced times interest earned ratio. In summary, the profitability of the firm would decrease, and the long-term debt position would improve, according to the times interest earned, but a smaller proportion of assets would be financed by debt.

A firm that has a large proportion of its financing in debt would find that inflation can also have a material impact on the adjusted statement. This type of firm would have a large monetary gain from holding the monetary liabilities, which would result in an improved profit picture and an improved long-term debt position, in terms of both times interest earned and debt to equity.

Some firms have a mixture of a large investment in productive fixed assets and a large proportion of their financing in debt. Such firms would usually have a net gain from the restatement, because of the large purchasing power gain on monetary liabilities. This would be the case for the typical public utility. This type of firm would show an improved long-term debt position. The times interest earned and the debt ratios would also be improved.

General inflation-adjusted financial statements would result in no change to the statement of cash flows.

CURRENT COST ACCOUNTING

Under current cost accounting, such nonmonetary accounts as inventory and fixed assets are reported on the balance sheet at their current cost. On the income statement, cost of goods sold and depreciation expense are also measured at current cost. The comprehensive current cost approach also recognizes income as the value of nonmonetary assets changes. This change is termed *holding gains* and is unrealized until the asset is sold (as with inventory) or its use recognized (as with fixed assets) and then realized at that point. Unrealized holding gains occur, then, on the unsold portion of inventory and the undepreciated portion of fixed assets.

The Hawkeye Company illustration will now be continued on a current cost basis in Exhibits 12-6, 12-7, and 12-8. Consider the following additional information when referring to Exhibit 12-1 and Exhibit 12-2:

1. Cost of goods sold on a current cost basis at different dates during the year is $150,000. Current cost of the inventory at the end of 1989 is $60,000. Current cost at the beginning of 1989 was $35,000.

2. Current cost of the property, plant, and equipment at the end of 1989, excluding depreciation, is $270,000; the net current cost is $210,000. Current cost of the property, plant, and equipment at the beginning of 1989, excluding depreciation, was $196,000; net current cost is $154,000. Depreciation expense on a current cost basis is $18,000.

3. All other expenses are the same on a historical and a current cost basis.

EXHIBIT 12-6

THE HAWKEYE COMPANY
Summary of Unrealized and Realized Holding Gains
For the Year Ending December 31, 1989

	Historical Cost	Current Cost	Difference
Inventory 1/1/89	$ 30,000	$ 35,000	$ 5,000
Inventory 12/31/89	50,000	60,000	10,000
Cost of goods sold	130,000	150,000	20,000
Property, plant, and equipment (net) 1/1/89	110,000	154,000	44,000
Property, plant, and equipment (net) 12/31/89	140,000	210,000	70,000
Depreciation expense	10,000	18,000	8,000

	Inventory	Property, Plant, and Equipment	Total
Unrealized gains:			
at 12/31/89	$ 10,000	$ 70,000	$80,000
at 1/1/89	5,000	44,000	49,000
Increase in unrealized gains	$ 5,000	$ 26,000	$31,000
Realized gains	20,000	8,000	28,000
Increase in current cost of assets held during the year (total holding gain)	$ 25,000	$ 34,000	$59,000

EXHIBIT 12-7

THE HAWKEYE COMPANY
Current Cost Statement of Earnings and Retained Earnings
For the Year Ended December 31, 1989

Sales	$350,000
Cost of goods sold	150,000
Gross profit	200,000
Operating expenses	110,000
Depreciation	18,000
Operating profit	72,000
Less interest expense	8,000
Income before income taxes	64,000
Less income taxes	50,000
Current cost income before holding gains	14,000
Realized holding gains	28,000
Unrealized holding gains	31,000
Current cost net income	73,000
Retained earnings, January 1, 1989	64,000
	137,000
Cash dividends	7,000
Retained earnings, December 31, 1989	$130,000

As with constant dollar accounting, the increased value of inventory improves the liquidity picture. The profitability situation must be viewed carefully. Higher cost of goods sold and depreciation expense cause current cost income before holding gains to drop, often sharply. However, for some firms (such as high-technology firms), the cost of replacing inventory, plant, and equipment can actually be less than the historical cost. When holding gains are included in profitability analysis, the profit picture may improve substantially, even if the firm is not a high-technology firm. Part of the holding gains, however, is as yet unrealized. The long-term debt-paying ability may look mixed, as debt to equity may increase or decrease but times interest earned decreases, because it is measured before any types of holding gains.

SFAS NO. 33, NO. 82, AND NO. 89

SFAS No. 33, "Financial Reporting and Changing Prices," was an experimental approach to inflation reporting. It applied only to certain large companies—specifically, public enterprises that had either (1) inventories and property, plant, and

EXHIBIT 12 - 8

THE HAWKEYE COMPANY
Current Cost Balance Sheet
December 31, 1988 and 1989

		1988		1989
Assets				
Current assets:				
Cash		$ 45,000		$ 25,000
Accounts receivable (net)		35,000		30,000
Inventory		35,000		60,000
Total current assets		115,000		115,000
Property, plant, and equipment	$196,000		$270,000	
Less: accumulated depreciation	42,000	154,000	60,000	210,000
Total assets		$269,000		$325,000
Liabilities and stockholders' equity				
Current liabilities:				
Accounts payable		$ 40,000		$ 15,000
Accrued payroll		5,000		10,000
Notes payable		40,000		40,000
Total current liabilities		85,000		65,000
Stockholders' equity:				
Capital stock		120,000		130,000
Retained earnings		64,000		130,000
Total stockholders' equity		184,000		260,000
Total liabilities and stockholders' equity		$269,000		$325,000

equipment (before deducting accumulated depreciation) amounting to more than $125 million, or (2) total assets amounting to more than $1 billion (after deducting accumulated depreciation).

The inflation data were presented as supplementary information in published annual reports and were unaudited. The requirements encompassed both a single-year data and a five-year summary.

SFAS No. 33 was first effective for fiscal years ended on or after December 25, 1979. SFAS No. 33 was viewed as a five-year experiment. At the end of five years, the experiment was to be reviewed to determine if it should be modified or deleted. The subsequent review of SFAS No. 33 resulted in an amendment, and SFAS No. 82 was issued. SFAS No. 82 became effective for fiscal years ending on or after December 15, 1984.

There was continued opposition to reporting inflation-adjusted data, after the issuance of SFAS No. 82. Partly because of this opposition, SFAS No. 89 was issued in 1986, eliminating inflation disclosure requirements.

David Masso, an FASB member who dissented from the elimination of inflation disclosure requirements, included the following comments in his dissent:

> The basic proposition underlying Statement 33—that inflation causes historical cost financial statements to show illusory profits and mask erosion of capital—is virtually undisputed. Specific price changes are inextricably linked to general inflation, and the combination of general and specific price changes seriously reduces the relevance, the representational faithfulness, and the comparability of historical cost financial statements.
>
> Although the current inflation rate in the United States is relatively low in the context of recent history, its compound effect through time is still highly significant. High inflation rates prevail in many countries where United States corporations operate. Rates from country to country vary from time to time. Those distortive influences on financial statements will now go unmeasured and undisclosed.
>
> Although Statement 33 had obvious shortcomings, it was a base on which to build. It represented years of due process—research, debate, deliberations, decisions—and application experience. As last amended, it had made significant progress in eliminating alternative concepts and methodologies. Its recision means that much of that due process and application experience will have to be repeated in response to a future inflation crisis. That will entail great cost in terms of time, money, and creative talent and, because due process does not permit quick reaction to crises, it risks loss of credibility for the Board and loss of initiative in private sector standards setting.[1]

Under SFAS No. 89, a firm may voluntarily disclose supplementary information on the effects of changing prices. Both a current-year schedule and a five-year schedule are recommended. The disclosure guidelines for the current-year and the five-year summaries are as follows:

Current-Year Summary

1. Income from continuing operations under the current cost basis, including disclosure of the current cost amounts of cost of goods sold and depreciation, depletion, and amortization expense.

2. Purchasing power gain or loss on net monetary items (excluded from continuing operations).

---

[1]Financial Accounting Standards Board, Statement of Financial Accounting Standards No. 89, "Financial Reporting and Changing Prices," par. 4. This reprint does not include the appendices to SFAS No. 89, "Financial Reporting and Changing Prices." These appendices are an integral part of the document.

3. Current cost (or lower recoverable) amount of inventory and of property, plant, and equipment at the end of the current year.

4. Increase or decrease in the current cost (or lower recoverable) amount of inventory and of property, plant, and equipment, before and after eliminating the effects of inflation (excluded from income from continuing operations).

5. Aggregate foreign currency translation adjustment on a current cost basis, if applicable.[2] [Foreign currency translation is beyond the scope of this book.]

Five-Year Summary

1. Net sales and other operating revenues.

2. Income from continuing operations (and related earnings per share) under the current cost basis.

3. Purchasing power gain or loss on net monetary items.

4. Increase or decrease in the current cost (or lower recoverable) amount of inventory and of property, plant, and equipment, net of inflation.

5. Aggregate foreign currency translation adjustment on a current cost basis, if applicable.

6. Net assets at year-end on a current cost basis.

7. Cash dividends declared per common share.

8. Market price per common share at year-end.[3]

A company may substitute historical cost/constant purchasing power income from continuing operations for income from continuing operations on a current cost basis in the current-year and in the five-year summaries if there is no material difference in these amounts.[4]

In addition, the notes to these disclosures should report (1) the principal types of information used to calculate the current costs and (2) any differences between the depreciation methods, estimates of useful lives, and residual values used for calculations of current cost depreciation and the methods and estimates used in the primary financial statements.

There are additional disclosures for companies that have mineral resource assets. These additional disclosures are beyond the scope of this book.

For the current-year summary, the Statement requires that the constant purchasing power adjustments use the average Consumer Price Index for All Urban Consumers (CPI-U) for the year. For the five-year summary, the information may be presented either in current purchasing power (year end or average for the year) or in the purchasing power of the base period of the Consumer Price Index. (For the CPI-U index, the base period is 1967. 1967 = 100.)

---

[2]"Financial Reporting and Changing Prices," FASB Statement of Financial Accounting Standards No. 89 (Stamford, Conn.: FASB, 1986), par. 11–13.
[3]SFAS No. 89, par. 7 and 8.
[4]SFAS No. 89, par. 20.

A current-year summary and a five-year summary are presented in Exhibits 12-9 and 12-10, respectively.

Cooper did not elect to include inflation data in its 1989 annual report, as was the case with practically all firms. The inflation footnote was never popular with management, and when this footnote was made optional, management elected not to include it. This is unfortunate, in view of the potentially significant information that this footnote can contain.

Some firms elect to include a descriptive inflation footnote in their annual reports. Such a footnote was included in the 1989 annual report of the Brush Wellman Company:

EXHIBIT   12-9

THE INFLATED COMPANY
Disclosure of the Effects of Changing Prices (Current-Year Summary)
For Year Ended December 31, 1989

	As Reported in the Primary Statements	Adjusted for Changes in Specific Prices (Current Cost)
Net sales and other operating revenue	$320,000	$320,000
Cost of goods sold	(120,000)	(142,000)
Depreciation expense	(23,000)	(28,000)
Other operating expenses	(70,000)	(70,000)
Income tax expense	(18,000)	(18,000)
Income from continuing operations	$ 89,000	$ 62,000
Purchasing power gain on net monetary items		$ 3,600

	Inventory	Property, Plant, and Equipment
Current cost: Specific price (current cost) at year end	$120,000	$190,000
Increase (decrease) in current costs: Increase in specific prices	$ 19,000	$ 34,000
Effect of increase in general price level	12,000	21,000
Excess of increase in specific prices over increase in the general price level	$ 7,000	$ 13,000

E X H I B I T   1 2 - 1 0

THE INFLATED COMPANY
Five-Year Summary (Average 1989 Dollars)
For the Five-Year Period Ended December 31, 1989

	1989	1988	1987	1986	1985
Net sales and other operating revenues	$320,000	$315,000	$299,000	$290,000	$270,000
Income from continuing operations:					
Current cost					
Earnings	62,000	63,500	65,000	64,000	63,000
Earnings per share	1.20	1.24	1.27	1.25	1.22
Purchasing power gains on net monetary items	3,600	3,700	4,000	2,000	3,000
Increase (decrease) in the current cost amount of inventory, net of inflation	7,000	4,000	3,500	3,000	2,000
Increase (decrease) in the current cost amount of property, plant, and equipment, net of inflation	13,000	8,000	12,000	16,000	7,000
Net assets at year end, current cost	300,000	270,000	250,000	135,000	120,000
Cash dividends declared per share	.75	.85	1.00	1.15	1.25
Market price of common stock at year end	30.00	29.00	31.00	28.00	27.00

Inflation and Changing Prices

The prices of major raw materials such as copper, steel, nickel and gold purchased by the Company increased during 1989. Such changes in costs are generally reflected in selling price adjustments. The prices of labor and other factors of production have also increased with inflation. Additions to capacity, while more expensive over time, usually result in greater productivity or improved yields. New products, process improvements and product pricing policies have generally enabled the Company to offset the impact of inflation. The Company employs the last-in, first-out (LIFO) inventory valuation method to more closely match current costs with revenues.

SUMMARY

Inflation adjustments, both constant dollar and current cost, can have a major impact on all aspects of a firm's financial position and profitability. Although accounting for inflation is not now required, the reviewer of financial statements should have a reasonable understanding of how inflation can affect the financial statements.

QUESTIONS

Q 12-1   In what way are traditional financial statements not designed to account for inflation?

Q 12-2   Differentiate among replacement cost, constant dollar, and current cost accounting.

Q 12-3   Which inflation adjustments measure specific changes in prices, and which measure general changes in the level of prices? Are these changes necessarily at the same rate?

Q 12-4   What is meant by a monetary account? Give an example of a monetary asset and a monetary liability.

Q 12-5   What is meant by a nonmonetary account? Give an example of a nonmonetary asset and a nonmonetary liability.

Q 12-6   Why is there a loss in purchasing power from holding monetary assets and a gain in purchasing power from holding monetary liabilities during an inflationary period?

Q 12-7   Why do nonmonetary accounts need to be adjusted to state the accounts in terms of their new purchasing power for constant dollar statements?

Q 12-8   When statements are adjusted for general price-level changes, one often finds that the amount of working capital and the current ratio have improved. Often, these results come from the change in inventory. Explain.

Q 12-9   What influence does a large investment in productive fixed assets have on constant dollar statements during a time of inflation?

Q 12-10   What influence does a large proportion of debt have on constant dollar statements during a time of inflation?

Q 12-11   Explain how depreciation expense and cost of goods sold change under current cost accounting.

Q 12-12   What is meant by the term *holding gains?* Differentiate between realized and unrealized holding gains.

Q 12-13   Based on the assumptions that land had been purchased for $20,000 and that the general price level increased by 60% since the acquisition, answer the following questions:
    a. What is the historical cost of the land?
    b. If constant dollar statements are prepared, what figure is used for land?
    c. If current cost statements are prepared, will the figure be higher or lower than the constant dollar figure?

Q 12-14   What is the advantage of adjusting to average for the year in constant dollar statements?

Q 12-15   What is the term used by the FASB for holding gains? Are realized or unrealized gains segregated? Are these gains included as part of income from continuing operations?

Q 12-16   What is the major current asset account affected by inflation accounting? How does inflation affect days' sales in inventory and the current ratio?

Q 12-17   How does inflation affect long-term debt-paying ability, as measured by times interest earned and debt/equity?

Q 12-18   Current cost income is always lower than constant dollar income. Discuss.

Q 12-19 How does inflation affect return on net assets?

Q 12-20 What does an inflation-adjusted price/earnings ratio indicate to the investor?

Q 12-21 Inflation-adjusted dividend payout ratios sometimes exceed 1 to 1. What does this indicate?

Q 12-22 How does inflation affect book value per share? What does this indicate?

Q 12-23 Accountants normally rely on objective data to give them a cost basis for recorded transactions. Are current cost data as objective as traditional historical data? Comment.

Q 12-24 During a period of inflation, which of the following items would result in a purchasing power gain, a purchasing power loss, or neither?
   a. bonds payable
   b. accounts payable
   c. cash
   d. notes receivable
   e. land

Q 12-25 "When prices are going up, they all go up." Comment on this statement and give an example to illustrate your comment.

Q 12-26 During the fiscal year, the Burger Company had a net monetary balance of assets over liabilities; prices rose by 10%. Would this condition give rise to a purchasing power gain or loss? Explain.

Q 12-27 The conventional statements reflect depreciation computed on a historical cost basis. One of the basic assumptions under which financial statements are prepared is the going concern assumption. Comment on how there can be a possible conflict between computing depreciation based on historical cost and the going concern assumption during a long period of inflation.

| PROBLEMS

P 12-1 XYZ, Inc. presented the following simplified balance sheet comparison in 1989:

	December	
	1989	**1988**
Assets		
Cash	$ 60,000	$ 30,000
Receivables	70,000	35,000
Inventory	120,000	90,000
Total current assets	$250,000	$155,000
Plant, property, and equipment, net	150,000	145,000
Total assets	$400,000	$300,000
Liabilities and stockholders' equity		
Current liabilities	$ 90,000	$ 60,000
Long-term debt	100,000	60,000
Stockholders' equity	210,000	180,000
	$400,000	$300,000

The change in monetary accounts came from transactions that occurred evenly throughout the year. The relevant CPI-U indices are the following:

	1989	1988
Year end	250	225
Year average	240	220

Required

a. Separate the accounts into monetary and nonmonetary.
b. Compute the purchasing power gain or loss in year-end 1989 dollars.
c. Compute the purchasing power gain or loss in year-average 1989 dollars.

P 12-2   Integrated Electronics is a retailing operation with leased facilities. The company's maverick accountant elected to experiment with current cost in the first year of business. At the start of the first year, 1989, the company purchased $1,000,000 in inventory and at the end of the year held an inventory of $600,000 on a historical cost basis and $875,000 on a current cost basis. When the inventory was sold, the current cost was $550,000. Sales for the year, incurred evenly, were $800,000. Other expenses including rent were $100,000 on both a current cost and a historical basis. Ignore tax effects.

Required   Prepare a comprehensive current cost income statement.

P 12-3   A series of questions related to inflation accounting follow:
  a. The valuation basis used in conventional financial statements is
     1. market value
     2. original cost
     3. replacement cost
     4. a mixture of costs and market values
     5. none of these
  b. The restatement of historical dollar financial statements to reflect constant dollar changes results in presenting assets at
     1. lower of cost or market values
     2. current appraisal values
     3. costs adjusted for purchasing power changes
     4. current replacement cost
     5. none of the above
  c. During a period of deflation, an entity would have the greatest gain in general purchasing power by holding
     1. cash
     2. plant and equipment
     3. accounts payable
     4. mortgages payable
     5. none of these
  d. In preparing constant dollar financial statements, monetary items consist of
     1. cash items plus all receivables with a fixed maturity date
     2. cash, other assets expected to be converted into cash, and current liabilities
     3. assets and liabilities whose amounts are fixed by contract or otherwise in terms of dollars, regardless of price-level changes
     4. assets and liabilities that are classified as current on the balance sheet

e. If land were purchased at a cost of $20,000 in January 1974, when the general price-level index was 120, and sold in December 1980, when the index was 150, the selling price that would result in no gain or loss would be
   1. $30,000
   2. $24,000
   3. $20,000
   4. $16,000
   5. none of these

f. If the base year is 1967 (when the price index = 100) and land is purchased for $50,000 in 1973 when the general price index is 108.5, the cost of the land restated to 1967 general purchasing power (rounded to the nearest whole dollar) would be
   1. $54,250
   2. $50,000
   3. $46,083
   4. $45,750
   5. none of these

g. Assume the same facts as in item (f). The cost of the land restated to December 31, 1989, general purchasing power when the price index was 119.2 (rounded to the nearest whole dollar) would be
   1. $59,600
   2. $54,931
   3. $46,083
   4. $45,512
   5. none of these

h. In preparing constant dollar financial statements, a nonmonetary item would be
   1. accounts payable in cash
   2. long-term bonds payable
   3. accounts receivable
   4. allowance for uncollectible accounts
   5. none of the above

i. Gains and losses on nonmonetary assets are usually reported in historical dollar financial statements when the items are sold. Gains and losses on the sale of nonmonetary assets should be reported in general price-level financial statements:
   1. in the same period, but the amount will probably differ
   2. in the same period and the same amount
   3. over the life of the nonmonetary asset
   4. partly over the life of the nonmonetary asset and the remainder when the asset is sold
   5. none of the above

                                                                AICPA Adapted

P 12-4   The Arrow Company's primary financial statements report financial information on the basis of prices that were in effect when the transactions occurred (historical costs). Inflation can distort traditional accounting information contained in the statements. The following information has been prepared to portray certain aspects of the economic effects of inflation.

ARROW COMPANY
Disclosure of the Effects of Changing Prices
For the Year Ended December 31, 1989

	As Reported (historical cost)		Adjusted for Changes in Specific Prices (current cost)
Net sales		$380,000	$380,000
Cost of goods sold	$160,000		$180,000
Depreciation	19,000		27,000
Other operating expense	120,000		120,000
Income tax expense	30,000		30,000
Total expenses		329,000	357,000
Income from continuing operations		$ 51,000	$ 23,000
Purchasing power gain on net monetary items			$ 4,500

	Inventory	Property, Plant, and Equipment
Current cost:		
Specific price (current cost) at year end	$105,000	$205,000
Increase (decrease) in current costs:		
Increase in specific prices	$ 23,000	$ 44,000
Effect of increase in general price level	12,400	28,000
Excess of increase in specific prices over increase in the general price level	$ 10,600	$ 16,000

Required

a. The inflation footnote discloses current cost of properties of $205,000 (at December 31, 1989), while the balance sheet discloses plant and properties of $143,000. Indicate the cause of the difference between these two figures.

b. The inflation footnote discloses depreciation as reported (historical cost) at $19,000 and specific prices (current cost) at $27,000 (year ended December 31, 1989). Indicate the cause of the difference between these two figures.

c. In calculating the current cost of properties at December 31, 1989, the company relied on published price indexes, so the current cost relates to assets owned by the company rather than technologically different or superior assets that may be available. Among other important considerations, potential improvements in manufacturing efficiencies and cost savings are not reflected in the adjusted income statement. Does this imply that the income from continuing operations for the year ended December 31, 1989 ($23,000), specific prices, is overstated or understated? Discuss.

d. Is the dollar amount of the inventory reported on the balance sheet more or less than the inventory at current cost amounts at December 31, 1989? Explain.

e. Using current cost, would you expect the working capital and current ratio to be higher than when historical cost is used? Why?

f. The historical cost of products sold was $160,000, and the current cost of products sold was $180,000.

   1. Indicate reasons for the difference.

   2. Speculate on why the historical cost of products sold was similar to the current cost of products sold.

g. For this company, is the effect of general prices on inventories and properties held during the year greater or less than the effect of specific prices of inventories and properties? Discuss.

h. Does it appear that this company holds more monetary liabilities than monetary assets? Explain.

P 12-5   The Gibsonet Company reported the following data in its 1989 annual report:

GIBSONET COMPANY
Five-Year Comparison of Selected Supplementary Financial Data
Adjusted for Effects of Changing Prices
(End-of-Year 1989 Dollars)

	1989	1988	1987	1986	1985
Net sales	$439,000	$405,000	$375,000	$380,000	$380,000
Income from continuing operations:					
Current cost	29,800	35,400	35,400	35,000	31,000
Earnings per share	1.60	1.72	1.75	1.74	1.62
Purchasing power gain on net monetary items	4,400	4,500	6,000	3,800	5,000
Increase in the current cost amount of inventory, net of inflation	8,100	4,200	6,700	6,000	7,000
Increase in the current cost amount of property, plant, and equipment, net of inflation	27,100	13,000	25,000	32,000	10,000
Net assets at year end:					
Current cost	460,000	410,000	351,000	272,000	226,000
Cash dividends declared per share	.95	1.05	1.15	1.25	1.30
Market price of common stock at year end	11.80	11.00	9.80	8.12	5.80

Other data relating to the Gibsonet Company:

   1. The market price of the common stock has increased more than threefold in the five-year period.

2. Gibsonet Company has declared the same cash dividend per share during the 1985–1989 period.
3. Net sales approximately doubled during the 1985–1989 period.
4. Earnings per share increased each year during the period 1985–1989.

Required

a. Comment on the adjusted earnings per share for the period 1985–1989 in comparison with the actual earnings per share.
b. Comment on the adjusted market price of common stock for the period 1985–1989 in comparison with the actual market price.
c. The adjusted data indicate what trend for cash dividends per share?
d. Comment on the effect of changing prices on the sales trend.
e. Does it appear that Gibsonet Company holds more monetary assets or monetary liabilities? Comment.
f. For the Gibsonet Company, was the effect of specific price increases more than the effect of general inflation when considering inventory and property, plant, and equipment? Comment.

P 12-6

Excerpts from the trial balance as of December 31, 1989 include the following accounts:

Inventory, LIFO	$ 60,000
Notes receivable	150,000
Bonds payable	175,000
Depreciation expense—plant and equipment	20,000
Sales	350,000
Land	280,000
Plant and equipment	500,000
Notes payable	80,000

During 1989, the average price index was 130; at December 31, 1989, the price index was 160. The plant and equipment was purchased in 1980, when the index was 110. The LIFO inventory was built up during 1982, when the average index was 114. The land was purchased in 1980, when the index was 109.

Required

a. At what amounts would these accounts be presented in constant dollar financial statements in average-for-the-year dollars?
b. At what amounts would these accounts be presented in constant dollar financial statements in end-of-year dollars?

P 12-7

Presented below are selected price indices:

December 31, 1989	180
Average 1989	175
July 1, 1984	160
January 20, 1980	140
July 20, 1979	138

Selected accounts at December 31, 1989:
  Cash
  Trucks (purchased July 1, 1984)
  Land (purchased January 20, 1980)
  Common stock (issued July 20, 1979)

Depreciation (on trucks purchased July 1, 1984)
Sales
Accounts payable (relate to purchases in 1989)
Purchases
Interest expense (incurred evenly through 1989)

Required   a. Indicate the numerator and the denominator for each account to adjust for constant dollar presentation at December 31, 1989, in end-of-year dollars.
b. Indicate the numerator and the denominator for each account to adjust for constant dollar presentation at December 31, 1989, in average-for-the-year dollars.

P 12-8   Gossett Company showed the following cost of goods sold for 1989:

Inventory, December 31, 1988	$20,000
Purchases	60,000
Cost of goods available for sale	80,000
Less: Inventory, December 31, 1989	12,000
Cost of goods sold	$68,000

The current cost of the inventory was $5.00 at December 31, 1988 and $5.50 at December 31, 1989. The company uses a LIFO cost flow assumption. The December 31, 1988, inventory consisted of 5,000 units purchased on October 1, 1980. The December 31, 1989, inventory consisted of 3,000 units purchased on October 1, 1980. Purchases of 11,430 units were made during 1989.
   The CPI-U index was as follows:

December 31, 1988	160
December 31, 1989	170
Average 1989	165
October 1, 1980	140

Required   a. Current cost of inventory at December 31, 1988.
b. Current cost of inventory at December 31, 1989.
c. Determine the cost of goods sold on a current cost basis.
d. Constant dollar inventory at December 31, 1988, using average 1989 dollars.
e. Constant dollar inventory at December 31, 1989, using average 1989 dollars.
f. Determine the cost of goods sold on a constant dollar basis, using average 1989 dollars.

P 12-9   The Arrow Company is preparing a constant dollar balance sheet for December 31, 1989. The following are selected accounts and their amounts.

Cash	$ 20,000	
Accounts receivable (net)	30,000	(originated when the index was 140)
Inventory	40,000	(originated when the index was 110)
Plant and equipment	100,000	(originated when the index was 100)
Accounts payable	15,000	(originated when the index was 145)
Bonds payable	100,000	(originated when the index was 100)

The average CPI-U for the year was 160, and the end-of-year index was 165.

Required
a. Compute the amounts that would appear in the constant dollar balance sheet at the average CPI-U index.
b. Compute the amounts that would appear in the constant dollar balance sheet at the end-of-year CPI-U index.

P 12-10   The Quickie Rice Company sells Rice-O-Matics, a device that reduces the time required to prepare rice. Inventory at the beginning of the accounting period was one unit at $35. Two more units were purchased during the period, the first at $39 and the second at $43. One unit was sold at $65. Replacement cost at the cost of the accounting period was $46.

Required   The following questions relate to the Quickie Rice Company.
  a. What is the ending inventory under LIFO?
     1. $82
     2. $78
     3. $74
     4. none of the above
  b. What is the gross profit under FIFO?
     1. $30
     2. $26
     3. $22
     4. none of the above
  c. What is the unrealized holding period gain under LIFO?
     1. $10
     2. $12
     3. $18
     4. none of the above
  d. What is the comprehensive income (income including both conventional income and unrealized holding period gains) under FIFO?
     1. $30
     2. $40
     3. $48
     4. none of the above

CFA Adapted
June, 1988

CASES

Case 12-1   INSIGHTS ON INFLATION

Owens-Corning Fiberglas Corporation presented the following data in its 1984 annual report.

Note 19   Financial Reporting and Changing Prices (Unaudited)

The accompanying Statement of Income and the Five Year Comparison of Selected Financial Information have been prepared in accordance with the requirements established in FASB Statement No. 33 as amended. The objective of the information presented is to measure the effects of inflation and changes in specific prices (current costs) on the resources utilized in the Company's operations.

The current cost method of reporting requires restatement of the Company's inventories and plant and equipment in terms of their specific current year cost. The specific current year prices established for the Company's resources are derived by using current cost estimates and by applying appropriate indices to historical costs. Therefore, for current cost purposes the Company's resources and their consumption are measured at current replacement cost rather than at historical cost amounts.

The same accounting principles have been used for both the historical cost financial statements and the current cost financial information, except that the straight-line method of depreciation has been used for developing current cost information. Accordingly, depreciation amounts contained in the historical cost financial statements for cost of sales, depreciation and amortization expense, inventories, plant and equipment, and accumulated depreciation have been restated to straight-line depreciation and then indexed for current cost purposes. The amounts provided for national income taxes in the historical cost financial statements have not been restated in determining net income on the current cost basis.

Consolidated Statement of Net Income Adjusted for Changing Prices for the Year Ended December 31, 1984

	As Reported in Primary Financial Statements	Adjusted for Changes in Specific Prices (Current Cost)
	(In thousands of dollars)	
Net sales and other revenues	$3,050,000	$3,050,000
Cost of sales	2,199,000	2,203,000
Depreciation and amortization expense	118,000	156,000
Operating expenses	427,000	427,000
Cost of borrowed funds	27,000	27,000
Other costs	97,000	97,000
Provision for national income taxes	72,000	72,000
	2,940,000	2,982,000
Income before equity in net income of affiliates	110,000	68,000
Equity in net income of affiliates	4,000	4,000
Net income	$ 114,000	$ 72,000
Gain from decline in purchasing power of net monetary liabilities		$ 6,000

Consolidated Statement of Net Income Adjusted for Changing Prices for the Year Ended December 31, 1984   (continued)

	As Reported in Primary Financial Statements	Adjusted for Changes in Specific Prices (Current Cost)
Increase in value of inventories and net plant and equipment during 1984 for effect of changes in:		
Specific prices (current cost)		$ 130,000
General price level (constant dollar)		71,000
Increase in specific prices over increase in the general price level		$ 59,000
Current cost at December 31, 1984:		
Inventories		$ 327,000
Net plant and equipment		1,601,000

Comparison of Selected Financial Data Adjusted for Changing Prices Based on Consumer Price Index for All Urban Consumers for the Year Ended December 31
(In thousands of dollars, except Consumer Price Index and per share data)

Average consumer price index for all urban consumers:

1984	311.1
1983	298.4
1982	289.3
1981	272.4
1980	246.9

Net sales and other revenues:

1984	$3,050,000
1983	2,908,000
1982	2,585,000
1981	2,745,000
1980	2,915,000

	Total Net Income (Loss)	Net Income (Loss) Per Share	Net Assets at Year End
Current cost information:			
1984	$72,000	$2.45	$1,643,000
1983*	40,000	1.39	1,592,000
1982	(3,000)	(.11)	1,496,000
1981	31,000	1.00	1,690,000
1980	33,000	1.07	1,827,000

*Excludes extraordinary gain of $8,184,000 or $.28 per share.

Increase in specific prices of inventories and net plant and equipment over (under) increase in the general price level:

1984	$59,000
1983	53,000
1982	8,000
1981	(112,000)
1980	(66,000)

Gain from decline in purchasing power of net monetary liabilities:

1984	$6,000
1983	7,000
1982	13,000
1981	23,000
1980	34,000

Other constant dollar information:

	Per Common Share	
	Cash Dividends Paid	Market Price at Year End
1984	$1.30	$31.52
1983	1.25	37.58
1982	1.29	39.68
1981	1.37	24.86
1980	1.51	32.18

Other Data from the 1984 Annual Report

From the Income Statement

Year	Net Sales	Other Revenues
1984	$3,021,183,000	$28,515,000
1983	$2,753,213,000	$35,010,000
1982	$2,373,478,000	$30,808,000

Income before extraordinary item

1984	$113,866,000
1983	79,739,000
1982	29,686,000

Per share income before extraordinary item

1984	$3.87
1983	$2.77
1982	$ .98

Other Data from the 1984 Annual Report   (continued)

From the Balance Sheet	1984	1983
Inventories:		
On first-in, first-out method		
Finished goods	$ 198,931,000	$ 151,934,000
Materials and supplies	127,841,000	112,087,000
Less reserve to reduce inventories to		
last-in first-out methods	(111,227,000)	(99,399,000)
Net inventories	$ 215,545,000	164,622,000
Plant and equipment, at cost:		
Land	$ 33,304,000	$ 31,100,000
Buildings and leasehold improvements	382,576,000	363,261,000
Machinery and equipment	1,262,703,000	1,206,100,000
Mineral properties	132,211,000	131,180,000
Construction in progress	50,312,000	40,423,000
	1,861,106,000	1,772,064,000
Less accumulated depreciation	950,507,000	879,115,000
	$ 910,599,000	$ 892,949,000

Other

Dividends per share (common)		
1984	$1.30	
1983	$1.20	

Required

a. The inflation footnote discloses current cost of net plant and equipment of $1,601,000,000 at December 31, 1984. The balance sheet disclosed net plant and equipment of $910,599,000 at December 31, 1984. Indicate the cause of the difference between the two figures.

b. As reported in the primary financial statements, depreciation and amortization expense totaled $118,000,000. As adjusted for changes in specific prices, depreciation and amortization expense totaled $156,000,000. Indicate the cause of the difference between these two figures.

c. What is the dollar difference between the inventory amount reported on the balance sheet and the current cost amounts for inventories at December 31, 1984?

d. Using current cost, would you expect the working capital and current ratio to be higher than when historical cost is used? Why?

e. The inflation footnote discloses cost of sales, historical cost, of $2,199,000,000 and cost of sales, current cost, of $2,203,000 at December 31, 1984.
   1. Indicate reasons for the difference.
   2. Why is the historical cost of sales similar to the current cost products sold?

f. For 1980–1984, for Owens-Corning Fiberglas Corporation, is the effect of general prices on inventories and properties held during the year greater or less than the effect of specific prices of inventories and properties? Discuss.

g. Why is net sales on the income statement different from the net sales in the inflation footnote?

h. In percentage, using 1982 as the base, has actual net sales increased more than inflation-adjusted net sales? Show your computation.

i. For the years 1980–1984, has Owens-Corning Fiberglas Corporation held more monetary liabilities than monetary assets? Explain.

j. The inflation footnote reports cash dividends per common share of $1.30 in 1984 and $1.25 in 1983. Other data in the annual report disclosed dividends per common share of $1.30 in 1984 and $1.20 in 1983. Why does the inflation footnote report a different dividend trend from the actual dividend trend?

k. Considering inflation, by what percentage has the market price per common share at year end decreased or increased from 1980 to 1984?

Case 12-2   IMPACT OF INFLATION

Eli Lilly Company and its subsidiaries presented the following in its 1984 annual report.

Inflation and Changing Prices

In recent years inflation has affected the company's production costs in varying degrees in the areas of the world in which manufacturing is performed, although the dominant impact has been in the United States, where a majority of production costs are incurred. In most years, the company has been able to compensate for input cost increases by improvement in productivity and by selling-price increases.

The replacement of buildings and equipment will usually require a substantially greater capital investment than was required to purchase the assets that are being replaced. The additional capital investment reflects principally the cumulative impact of inflation on the long-lived nature of these assets.

The schedules on the following page quantify the effects of inflation on the primary historical-dollar financial statements. Dollar amounts of inventories and property and equipment (and related manufacturing costs of products sold and depreciation expense) are restated to amounts that approximate the current cost of items, thereby measuring the impact of inflation in terms of changes in specific prices. The current cost for property and equipment, and the related depreciation expense, is based principally on external price indexes closely related to the items being measured. The current cost of inventories reflects recent purchase and production costs. The current manufacturing costs of products sold reflect current cost at the time the sales were recorded. Adjustments to current cost information, including amounts measured in functional currencies other than the U.S. dollar, to reflect the effects of general inflation, are based on the United States Consumer Price Index for All Urban Consumers published by the Bureau of Labor Statistics.

It is important to recognize the inherent limitations in this information. It reflects only the estimated effect of changing prices (1) on inventories and property and equipment and related manufacturing costs of products sold and depreciation expense and (2) on monetary assets and liabilities. It ignores any technological improvements or efficiencies that would normally be associated with replacement of production capacity.

No adjustments to or allocations of the amounts of income tax expense were made in the computation of the supplemental information shown below. The effective tax rate for 1984 was 36.4 percent on a historical cost basis and 39.2 percent restated for current cost.

The aggregate amount of depreciation and amortization expense for 1984 was $120.7 million on a historical cost basis and $181.7 million restated for current cost.

Income from Continuing Operations Adjusted for Changing Prices
(In average 1984 dollars)

(Dollars in millions) Year Ended December 31, 1984	As Reported in the Primary Statements	Adjusted for Changes in Specific Prices (Current Costs)
Net sales	$3,109.2	$3,109.2
Manufacturing costs	1,128.4	1,151.4
Operating expenses	1,236.5	1,269.3
Operating income	744.3	688.5
Other income (deductions)—net	26.4	26.4
Income before taxes	770.7	714.9
Income taxes	280.5	280.5
Income from continuing operations	$ 490.2	$ 434.4
Loss from decline in purchasing power of net monetary assets		$ (8.8)
Increase in specific prices (current costs) of inventories and property and equipment held during the year*		$ 125.0
Effect of increase in general price level		94.6
Excess of increase in specific prices over increase in general price level		$ 30.4
Translation adjustment for year		$ (113.2)

*At December 31, 1984, current cost of inventory was $709 million and current cost of property and equipment, net of accumulated depreciation, was $1,780 million.

Five-Year Comparison of Selected Supplementary Financial Data Adjusted for Effects of Changing Prices
(In average 1984 dollars)

(Dollars in millions, except per-share data)	1984	1983	1982	1981	1980
Net sales	$3,109.2	$3,163.2	$3,188.5	$3,167.5	$3,225.5
Income from continuing operations	434.4	408.0	376.3	364.4	369.1
Income from continuing operations per common share	$ 5.96	$ 5.46	$ 4.96	$ 4.79	$ 4.88
Excess (deficit) of increase in specific price level over increase in general prices	$ 30.4	$ .6	$ 92.7	$ (123.2)	$ (73.8)
Loss from decline in purchasing power of net monetary assets	(8.8)	(9.0)	(7.4)	(16.5)	(33.3)
Translation adjustment for year	(113.2)	(79.0)	(102.8)	(54.2)	—
Net assets at year-end	2,767.8	2,774.1	2,846.3	2,671.8	2,703.8
Cash dividends declared per common share*	$ 3.05	$ 2.95	$ 2.79	$ 2.79	$ 3.49
Cash dividends paid per common share	2.975	2.87	2.79	2.71	2.77
Market price per common share at year-end	65.08	59.33	61.18	61.18	76.76
Average Consumer Price Index	311.1	298.4	289.1	272.4	246.8

*Includes dividends in the current year, payable in the following year.

Other Data from the 1984 Annual Report

From the Income Statement

Net Sales
1984	$3,109,200,000
1983	$3,033,700,000
1982	$2,962,700,000

From the Balance Sheet

Inventories
1984	$630,200,000
1983	$628,000,000

Other Data from the 1984 Annual Report   (continued)

	1984	1983
Property and Equipment		
Land	$ 35,200,000	$ 32,900,000
Buildings	674,200,000	625,400,000
Equipment	1,294,800,000	1,182,600,000
	2,004,200,000	1,840,900,000
Less allowances for depreciation	723,800,000	628,300,000
	$1,280,400,000	$1,212,600,000

Other

Dividends per share (common)		
1984	$2.975	
1983	2.75	

Required

a. The inflation footnote discloses current cost of property and equipment, net of accumulated depreciation, of $1,780,000,000 at December 31, 1984. The balance sheet disclosed net property and equipment of $1,280,400,000 at December 31, 1984. Indicate the cause of the difference between the two figures.

b. The inflation disclosure indicates that the aggregate amount of depreciation and amortization expense for 1984 was $120,700,000 on a historical cost basis and $181,700,000 restated for current cost. Indicate the cause of the difference between these two figures.

c. Eli Lilly reported income from continuing operations of $434,400,000 adjusted for changes in specific prices. The discussion of inflation and changing prices points out that the current costs have ignored "any technological improvements or efficiencies that would normally be associated with replacement of production capacity." Does the quote imply that income from continuing operations would have been higher than $434,400,000 if technological improvements or efficiencies that would normally be associated with replacement of production capacity had been considered? Discuss.

d. What is the dollar difference between the inventory amount reported on the balance sheet and the current cost amount for inventories at December 31, 1984?

e. Using current cost, would you expect the working capital and current ratio to be higher than when historical cost is used? Why?

f. For Eli Lilly, is the effect of general prices on inventories and property and equipment held during the year greater or less than the effect of specific prices of inventories and property and equipment? Discuss.

g. Why is net sales on the income statement different from the net sales in the inflation disclosure?

h. In percentage, using 1982 as the base, has actual net sales increased more than inflation-adjusted net sales? Show your computation.

i. For the years 1980–1984, has Eli Lilly held more monetary assets than monetary liabilities? Explain.

j. The inflation disclosure reports cash dividends per share of $2.975 in 1984 and $2.87

in 1983. Other data in the annual report disclose dividends per common share of $2.975 in 1984 and $2.75 in 1983. Why do the reported dividends per share amounts vary in 1983?

k. Considering inflation, by what percentage has the market price per common share at year end increased (decreased) from 1980 to 1984?

CHAPTER **13**

EXPANDED UTILITY
OF FINANCIAL RATIOS

CHAPTER TOPICS

Financial Ratios as Perceived by Commercial Loan Departments

Most Significant Ratios and Their Primary Measure

Ratios Appearing Most Frequently in Loan Agreements

Financial Ratios as Perceived by Corporate Controllers

Most Significant Ratios and Their Primary Measure

Key Financial Ratios Included as Corporate Objectives

Financial Ratios as Perceived by Certified Public Accountants

Financial Ratios as Perceived by Chartered Financial Analysts

Financial Ratios Used in Annual Reports

Degree of Conservatism and Quality of Earnings

Inventory
Fixed Assets
Intangible Assets
Pensions
Leases

Forecasting Financial Failure

Univariate Model
Multivariate Model

Analytical Review Procedures

Management Use of Analysis

Use of LIFO Reserves

Graphing Financial Information

This chapter reviews special areas that are related to the usefulness of ratios and financial statement analyses.

FINANCIAL RATIOS AS PERCEIVED
BY COMMERCIAL LOAN DEPARTMENTS

A large number of financial ratios can be used by a commercial loan department to aid the loan officers in deciding whether to grant a commercial loan and in

maintaining control of a loan once it is granted.[1] Knowing how commercial loan departments view specific financial ratios, in general, would be helpful to other commercial loan departments, as well as to borrowing firms when dealing with commercial loan departments. In order to gain insights into how commercial loan departments view financial ratios, a questionnaire was sent to the commercial loan departments of the 100 largest banks in the United States. Usable responses were received from 44% of them.

A list of fifty-nine financial ratios was drawn from financial literature, text-books, and published industry data for this study. The study set as three objectives the determination of (1) the significance of each ratio, in the opinion of commercial loan officers, (2) how frequently each ratio is included in loan agreements, and (3) what a specific financial ratio primarily measures, in the opinion of commercial loan officers. For primary measure, the choices were liquidity, long-term debt-paying ability, profitability, and other. The ratios included in the study are listed in Exhibit 13-1.

Most Significant Ratios and Their Primary Measure

Exhibit 13-2 displays the ten financial ratios that were given the highest significance rating by the commercial loan officers, as well as the primary measure of these ratios. The highest rating is 9, and the lowest rating is 0.

Most of the ratios given a high significance rating were regarded primarily as measures of liquidity or debt. Only two of the top ten ratios measure profitability, while five are debt measures and three are liquidity measures. The two profitability ratios were two different computations of the net profit margin. One of these computations was net profit margin after tax, and the other was net profit margin before tax. The top three ratios rated materially above the others. Two of these were measures of debt, and the other was a measure of liquidity. The debt/equity ratio was given the highest significance rating, with the current ratio second highest. It is reasonable to assume that the financial ratios that were rated most significant by commercial loan officers would have an influence on a loan decision.

Ratios Appearing Most Frequently in Loan Agreements

A commercial bank may elect to include a ratio as part of a loan agreement. This would be a way of using ratios to control an outstanding loan. Exhibit 13-3 contains a list of the ten financial ratios that appear most frequently in loan agreements, along with an indication of what each ratio primarily measures. Two of the ratios

---

[1]C. H. Gibson, "Financial Ratios as Perceived by Commercial Loan Officers," *Akron Business and Economic Review* (Summer 1983), pp. 23–27.

EXHIBIT 13-1

Ratios Rated by Commercial Loan Officers

Ratio	Ratio
Cash ratio	Sales/working capital
Accounts receivable turnover in days	Sales/net worth
Accounts receivable turnover—times	Cash/sales
Days' sales in receivables	Quick assets/sales
Quick ratio	Current assets/sales
Inventory turnover in days	Return on assets:
Inventory turnover—times	before interest and tax
Days' sales in inventory	before tax
Current debt/inventory	after tax
Inventory/current assets	Return on operating assets
Inventory/working capital	Return on total invested capital:
Current ratio	before tax
Net fixed assets/tangible net worth	after tax
Cash/total assets	Return on equity:
Quick assets/total assets	before tax
Current assets/total assets	after tax
Retained earnings/total assets	Net profit margin:
Debt/equity ratio	before tax
Total debt as a % of net working capital	after tax
Total debt/total assets	Retained earnings/net income
Short-term debt as a % of total invested capital	Cash flow/current maturities of long-term debt
Long-term debt as a % of total invested capital	Cash flow/total debt
Funded debt/working capital	Times interest earned
Total equity/total assets	Fixed charge coverage
Fixed assets/equity	Degree of operating leverage
Common equity as a % of total invested capital	Degree of financial leverage
Current debt/net worth	Earnings per share
Net worth at market value/total liabilities	Book value per share
Total asset turnover	Dividend payout ratio
Sales/operating assets	Dividend yield
Sales/fixed assets	Price/earnings ratio
	Stock price as a % of book value

do not have a primary measure indicated, which means that there was no majority opinion as to what the ratio primarily measured. Six of the ratios that appear most frequently in loan agreements were given a primary measure of debt, two were given a primary measure of liquidity, and none was given a primary measure of profitability.

The two top ratios were debt/equity and the current ratio. These are the same

EXHIBIT 13-2

Commercial Loan Departments—Most Significant Ratios and Their Primary Measure

Ratio	Significance Rating	Primary Measure
Debt/equity	8.71	Debt
Current ratio	8.25	Liquidity
Cash flow/current maturities of long-term debt	8.08	Debt
Fixed charge coverage	7.58	Debt
Net profit margin after tax	7.56	Profitability
Times interest earned	7.50	Debt
Net profit margin before tax	7.43	Profitability
Degree of financial leverage	7.33	Debt
Inventory turnover in days	7.25	Liquidity
Accounts receivable turnover in days	7.08	Liquidity

EXHIBIT 13-3

Commercial Loan Departments—Ratios Appearing Most Frequently in Loan Agreements

Ratio	Percentage of Banks Indicating That the Ratio Was Included in 26% or More of Their Loan Agreements	Primary Measure
Debt/equity	92.5	Debt
Current ratio	90.0	Liquidity
Dividend payout ratio	70.0	*
Cash flow/current maturities of long-term debt	60.3	Debt
Fixed charge coverage	55.2	Debt
Times interest earned	52.6	Debt
Degree of financial leverage	44.7	Debt
Equity/assets	41.0	*
Cash flow/total debt	36.1	Debt
Quick ratio	33.3	Liquidity

*No majority primary measure indicated in this survey.

ratios that were given the highest significance rating. The dividend payout ratio was the third most likely to appear in loan agreements, but it was not rated as a highly significant ratio. The logic for this ratio appearing in loan agreements is that it is a means of controlling outflow of cash on dividends.

EXHIBIT 13-4

EXHIBIT 13-4

Corporate Controllers' Most Significant Ratios and Their Primary Measure

Ratio	Significance Rating	Primary Measure
Earnings per share	8.19	Profitability
Return on equity after tax	7.83	Profitability
Net profit margin after tax	7.47	Profitability
Debt/equity ratio	7.46	Debt
Net profit margin before tax	7.41	Profitability
Return on total invested capital after tax	7.20	Profitability
Return on assets after tax	6.97	Profitability
Dividend payout ratio	6.83	Other*
Price/earnings ratio	6.81	Other*
Current ratio	6.71	Liquidity

*Primary measure indicated to be other than liquidity, debt, or profitability. The ratios rated this way tend to be related to stock analysis.

FINANCIAL RATIOS AS PERCEIVED BY CORPORATE CONTROLLERS

In order to get the views of corporate controllers on important issues relating to financial ratios, a questionnaire was sent to the controllers of the companies listed in *Fortune's* 500 largest industrials for 1979.[2] Companies that were 100% owned or controlled by another firm were excluded. The usable response rate was 19.42%. The questionnaire used the same ratios that were used for the commercial loan department survey. Four objectives of this study were the determination of (1) the significance of a specific ratio as perceived by controllers, (2) which financial ratios are included as corporate objectives, (3) the primary measure of each ratio, and (4) what use is being made of inflation accounting data in ratio analysis.

Most Significant Ratios and Their Primary Measure

Exhibit 13-4 displays the ten financial ratios given the highest significance rating by the corporate controllers, along with the primary measure of these ratios. The highest rating is a 9, and the lowest is a 0.

The financial executives gave the profitability ratios the highest significance

[2]The basis of the comments in this section is a study by Dr. Charles Gibson in 1981. The research was done under a grant from the Deloitte Haskins & Sells Foundation.

ratings. The highest-rated debt ratio was debt/equity, and the highest-rated liquidity ratio was the current ratio. In comparing the responses of the commercial loan officers and the controllers, it can be seen that the controllers rate the profitability ratios as having the highest significance, while the commercial loan officers rate the debt and liquidity ratios highest.

Key Financial Ratios Included as Corporate Objectives

Many firms have selected key financial ratios to be included as part of their corporate objectives. The next section of the survey was designed to determine what ratios the firms used in their corporate objectives. Exhibit 13-5 lists the ten ratios that are most likely to be included in corporate objectives according to the controllers. Nine of the ratios included in Exhibit 13-5 are the same ratios as those in Exhibit 13-4. The one ratio that appears in the top ten ratios in relation to corporate objectives that is not in the top ten significant ratios is accounts receivable turnover in days. The one ratio that appears in the top ten ratios in relation to significance that is not in the top ten ratios used for corporate objectives is the price/earnings ratio.

Logically, there would be a high correlation between the ratios that are rated as highly significant and those that are included in corporate objectives. The debt/equity ratio and the current ratio on the objectives list are rated higher on the objectives list than on the significance list. This makes sense, since a firm has to have some balance in its objectives between liquidity, debt, and profitability.

EXHIBIT 13-5

Ratios Appearing in Corporate Objectives and Their Primary Measure

Ratio	Percentage of Firms Indicating That the Ratio Was Included in Corporate Objectives	Primary Measure
Earnings per share	80.6	Profitability
Debt/equity ratio	68.8	Debt
Return on equity after tax	68.5	Profitability
Current ratio	62.0	Liquidity
Net profit margin after tax	60.9	Profitability
Dividend payout ratio	54.3	Other
Return on total invested capital after tax	53.3	Profitability
Net profit margin before tax	52.2	Profitability
Accounts receivable turnover in days	47.3	Liquidity
Return on assets after tax	47.3	Profitability

EXHIBIT 13-6

CPAs' Most Significant Ratios and Their Primary Measure

Ratio	Significance Rating	Primary Measure
Current ratio	7.10	Liquidity
Accounts receivable turnover in days	6.94	Liquidity
After-tax return on equity	6.79	Profitability
Debt/equity ratio	6.78	Debt
Quick ratio (acid test)	6.77	Liquidity
Net profit margin after tax	6.67	Profitability
Net profit margin before tax	6.63	Profitability
Return on assets after tax	6.39	Profitability
Return on total invested capital after tax	6.30	Profitability
Inventory turnover in days	6.09	Liquidity

FINANCIAL RATIOS AS PERCEIVED BY CERTIFIED PUBLIC ACCOUNTANTS

A research study performed in 1984 dealt with financial ratios as perceived by certified public accountants (CPAs).[3] A questionnaire was sent to one-third of the members of The Ohio Society of Certified Public Accountants who were registered as partners in CPA firms. A total of 495 questionnaires were sent, and the usable response rate was 18.8%.

This questionnaire used the same ratios as were used for the commercial loan departments and corporate controllers. The specific objectives of this study were to determine the following from the viewpoint of the CPA:

1. Which financial ratios CPAs view primarily as a measure of liquidity, debt, and profitability
2. The relative importance of the financial ratios viewed as a measure of liquidity, debt, or profitability

Exhibit 13-6 displays the ten financial ratios given the highest significance rating by the CPAs and the primary measure of these ratios. The highest rating is 9, and the lowest is 0.

The CPAs gave the highest significance rating to two liquidity ratios: the current ratio and the accounts receivable turnover in days. The highest-rated profitability ratio was after-tax net profit margin, and the highest rated debt ratio was debt/equity.

[3]C. H. Gibson, "Ohio CPA's Perceptions of Financial Ratios," *The Ohio CPA Journal* (August 1985), pp. 25–30. © 1985. Reprinted with permission of *The Ohio CPA Journal.*

EXHIBIT 13-7

Chartered Financial Analysts—Most Significant Ratios and Their Primary Measure

Ratio	Significance Rating	Primary Measure
Return on equity after tax	8.21	Profitability
Price/earnings ratio	7.65	*
Earnings per share	7.58	Profitability
Net profit margin after tax	7.52	Profitability
Return on equity before tax	7.41	Profitability
Net profit margin before tax	7.32	Profitability
Fixed charge coverage	7.22	Debt
Quick ratio	7.10	Liquidity
Return on assets after tax	7.06	Profitability
Times interest earned	7.06	Debt

*Primary measure indicated to be other than liquidity, debt, or profitability. The ratios rated this way tend to be related to stock analysis.

FINANCIAL RATIOS AS PERCEIVED BY CHARTERED FINANCIAL ANALYSTS[4]

Exhibit 13-7 displays the ten financial ratios that were given the highest significance rating by chartered financial analysts and the primary measure of these ratios. Again, the highest rating is 9, and the lowest is 0.

The surveyed analysts gave the highest significance ratings to profitability ratios. Return on equity after tax was given the highest significance by a wide margin. Four of the next five most significant ratios were also profitability ratios—earnings per share, net profit margin after tax, return on equity before tax and net profit margin before tax.

The price-earnings ratio—categorized by the analysts as an "other" measure—received the second highest significance rating. CFAs apparently view profitability and what is being paid for those profits before turning to liquidity and debt.

The two highest rated debt ratios were fixed charge coverage and times interest earned, rated seventh and ninth, respectively. Both of these ratios indicate a firm's ability to carry debt. The highest rated debt ratio relating to the balance sheet was the debt/equity ratio, rated as the 11th most significant. Surprisingly, more significance was placed on debt ratios relating to the ability to carry debt than on those relating to ability to meet debt obligations.

The highest rated liquidity ratio was the quick ratio, rated eighth. The second highest liquidity ratio was the current ratio, rated 20th.[5]

[4]C. H. Gibson, "How Chartered Financial Analysts View Financial Ratios," *Financial Analysts Journal* (May–June 1987), pp. 74–76.
[5]Ibid., pp. 74, 76.

FINANCIAL RATIOS USED IN ANNUAL REPORTS

Financial ratios are used to interpret and explain financial statements.[6] Used properly, they can be effective tools in evaluating a company's liquidity, debt position, and profitability. Probably no tool is as effective in evaluating where a company has been financially and projecting its financial future as the proper use of financial ratios.

A firm can use its annual report effectively to relate financial data by the use of financial ratios. To determine how effectively firms are using ratios to communicate financial data, the annual reports of one hundred firms identified in the *Fortune* 500 industrial companies in 1979 were reviewed in a research study in 1981. The one hundred firms represented the first twenty of each hundred in the *Fortune* 500 list. The objective of this research project was to determine (1) which financial ratios were frequently reported in annual reports, (2) where the ratios were disclosed in the annual reports, and (3) what computational methodology was used to compute these ratios.

Exhibit 13-8 indicates the ratios disclosed most frequently in the annual reports reviewed and the section of the annual report where the ratios were located. The locations were president's letter, management discussion, management highlights, financial review, and financial summary. In many cases, the same ratio was located in several sections, so the numbers under the sections in Exhibit 13-8 do not add up to the total number of annual reports where the ratio was included.

Exhibit 13-8 indicates that the sections of the annual report where ratios are most frequently located, in order of use, are financial summary, financial highlights, financial review, president's letter, and management discussion. Practically the only ratio disclosed in the management discussion section was dividends per share, and this ratio was only disclosed 10% of the time.

Seven ratios were found more than 50% of the time in one section or another. These ratios and the number of times found were earnings per share (100), dividends per share (98), book value per share (84), working capital (81), return on equity (62), profit margin (58), and effective tax rate (50). The current ratio was found 47 times, and then the next ratio in order of disclosure, which was the debt/capital ratio, fell off to 23 times. From this listing, the reader can conclude that profitability ratios and ratios related to investing were the most popular. Ratios not disclosed at least five times were not listed in Exhibit 13-8.

Logically, profitability ratios and ratios related to investing were the most popular for inclusion in the annual report. A previous study reported in this chapter indicated that profitability ratios were the most popular ratios with management. Including ratios related to investing in the annual report makes sense, because one of the annual report's major objectives is to inform stockholders.

A review of the methodology used indicated that there are wide differences of opinion on how some of the ratios should be computed. This is especially true of

---

[6]C. H. Gibson, "Financial Ratios in Annual Reports," *The CPA Journal* (September 1982), pp. 18–29.

EXHIBIT 13-8

Ratios Disclosed Most Frequently in Annual Reports*

Ratio	Number Included	President's Letter	Management Discussion	Management Highlights	Financial Review	Financial Summary
Earnings per share	100	66	5	98	45	93
Dividends per share	98	53	10	85	49	88
Book value per share	84	10	3	53	18	63
Working capital	81	1	1	50	23	67
Return on equity	62	28	3	21	23	37
Profit margin	58	10	3	21	23	35
Effective tax rate	50	2	1	2	46	6
Current ratio	47	3	1	16	12	34
Debt/capital	23	9	0	4	14	13
Return on capital	21	6	2	8	8	5
Debt/equity	19	5	0	3	8	8
Return on assets	13	4	1	2	5	10
Dividend payout	13	3	0	0	6	6
Gross margin	12	0	1	0	11	3
Pretax margin	10	2	0	3	6	6
Total asset turnover	7	1	0	0	4	4
Price/earnings ratio	7	0	0	0	1	6
Operating margin	7	1	0	2	6	1
Labor per hour	5	0	2	3	2	2

*Numbers represent both absolute numbers and percentages, since a review was made of the financial statements of 100 firms.

the debt ratios. The two debt ratios most frequently disclosed were the debt/capital ratio and the debt/equity ratio. The debt/capital ratio is not covered in this book. It is similar to the debt/equity ratio, except that the denominator includes sources of capital in addition to stockholders' equity.

In the annual reports, the debt/capital ratio was disclosed twenty-three times, and eleven different formulas were used. One firm used average balance sheet amounts between the beginning and the end of the year, while twenty-two firms used ending balance sheet figures. The debt/equity ratio was disclosed nineteen times, and six different formulas were used. All firms used the ending balance sheet accounts to compute the debt/equity ratio.

In general, no major effort is being made to explain financial results by the disclosure of financial ratios in annual reports. Several financial ratios that could be interpreted as important were not disclosed or were disclosed very infrequently. This is particularly important for ratios that cannot be reasonably computed by outsiders because of a lack of data, such as accounts receivable turnover.

At present, no regulatory agency such as the SEC or the FASB accepts responsibility for determining either the content of financial ratios or the format of presentation for annual reports. The exception to this is the ratio earnings per share.

There are many practical and theoretical issues related to the computation of financial ratios. As long as each firm is allowed to exercise its opinion as to the practical and theoretical issues, there will be a great divergence of opinion on how a particular ratio should be computed.

DEGREE OF CONSERVATISM AND QUALITY OF EARNINGS

A review of financial statements, including the footnotes, indicates how conservative the statements are in regard to accounting policies. Accounting policies that result in the slowest reporting of income are the most conservative. When a firm has conservative accounting policies, it is said that its earnings are of high quality. This section reviews a number of areas that often indicate the degree of conservatism of a firm in regard to reporting income.

Inventory

Under inflationary conditions, the matching of current cost against the current revenue results in the lowest income for a period of time. The inventory method that follows this procedure is LIFO. The least conservative method is FIFO, which uses the oldest costs and matches them against revenue. Other inventory methods fall somewhere between the results of LIFO and FIFO.

For a construction firm that has long-term contracts, the two principal accounting methods that relate to inventory are the completed-contract method and the percentage-of-completion method. The completed-contract method recognizes all of the income when the contract is completed, whereas the percentage-of-completion method recognizes income as work progresses on the contract. The completed-contract method is conservative.

Fixed Assets

Two accounting decisions related to fixed assets can have a significant influence on income: the depreciation method and the period of time selected to depreciate an asset.

There are many depreciation methods. The methods that recognize a large amount of depreciation in the early years of the assets are conservative: the accelerated methods of sum of the years' digits and the declining-balance method. The straight-line method recognizes depreciation in equal amounts over each year of the life of the asset. Therefore, the straight-line depreciation method is the least conservative depreciation method.

The shorter the period of time used to depreciate an asset, the sooner the depreciation is taken. There is sometimes a material difference between firms in the lives used for depreciation. Comparing the lives used for depreciation for similar firms can be a clue as to how conservative the firms are in their depreciation. The shorter the period of time used, the lower the income.

Intangible Assets

There are many possible intangible assets, such as goodwill, patents, copyrights, and research and development. The shorter the period of time used to recognize the cost of the intangible asset, the more conservative the accounting.

SFAS No. 2 requires that all firms expense research and development (R&D) costs incurred during each period. Some firms spend very large sums on R&D, and others spend little or nothing on this item. Because of the FASB requirement that R&D costs be expensed in the period incurred, the income of a firm that does considerable research is reduced substantially in the period that the cost is incurred, thus resulting in more conservative earnings.

According to APB No. 17, all intangible assets must be amortized over forty years or less, unless they were acquired prior to 1970. Intangibles that have a legal or economic life that is shorter than forty years should be amortized over the shorter of the legal or the economic life.

An intangible that is frequently material is goodwill. Goodwill results when a firm buys another firm and pays a price that is more than the value of the identifiable assets. Conservative firms expense the goodwill over a relatively short period of time, such as five years. Other firms use the maximum time allowed of forty years.

The amortization of goodwill is not a tax-deductible expense. Therefore, the amortization of goodwill has a dollar-for-dollar effect in reducing financial statement income.

Pensions

Two points relating to pensions should be examined when the firm has a defined benefit plan. One is the assumed discount rate used to compute the actuarial present value of the accumulated benefit obligation and the projected benefit obligation. The higher the interest rate used, the lower the present value of the liability and the lower the immediate pension cost. The other item is the rate of compensation increase used in computing the projected benefit obligations. If the rate is too low, the projected benefit obligation is too low. If the rate is too high, the projected benefit obligation is too high.

Leases

A firm with extensive assets accounted for as operating leases has a permanently more favorable income than a similar firm with capital leases or one that has financed its assets with debt. Examine the footnote that describes the firm's lease obligations. An immaterial amount of operating leases is conservative as to the effect of leases on income.

FORECASTING FINANCIAL FAILURE

There have been many academic studies on the use of financial ratios to forecast financial failure. Basically, these studies try to isolate individual ratios or combinations of ratios that can be considered trends that may forecast failure.

A reliable model that can be used to forecast financial failure can also be used by management to take preventive measures. Such a model can aid investors in selecting and disposing of stocks. Banks can use this model to aid in lending decisions and in monitoring loans. Firms can use the model in making credit decisions and in monitoring accounts receivable. In general, many sources can use such a model to improve the allocation and control of resources. A model that forecasts financial failure can also be valuable to an auditor. Such a model can aid in the determination of audit procedures and in making a decision as to whether the firm will remain as a going concern.

There are many ways of describing financial failure. It can mean liquidation, deferment of payments to short-term creditors, deferment of payments of interest on bonds, deferment of payments of principal on bonds, or the omission of a preferred dividend. One of the problems in examining the literature on forecasting financial failure is that different authors have used different criteria to indicate failure. When reviewing the literature, always determine the criteria used to define financial failure.

In this book, two of the studies that deal with predicting financial failure are reviewed. Based on the number of references to these two studies in the literature, they appear to be particularly significant on the subject of forecasting financial failure.

Univariate Model

William Beaver reported his univariate model in a study published in *The Accounting Review* in October 1968.[7] A univariate model involves the use of a single variable in a prediction model. Such a model would use individual financial ratios to forecast financial failure. For the Beaver study, a firm was classified as a failed firm when any one of the following events occurred in the 1954–1964 period: bankruptcy, bond default, an overdrawn bank account, or nonpayment of a preferred stock dividend.

Beaver paired seventy-nine failed firms with a similar number of successful firms drawn from *Moody's Industrial Manuals*. For each failed firm in the sample, a successful one of similar asset size was selected from the same industry. The Beaver study indicated that the following ratios were the best for forecasting financial failure (in the order of their predictive power):

---

[7]W. H. Beaver, "Alternative Accounting Measures as Predictors of Failure," *The Accounting Review* 43 (January 1968), pp. 113–122.

1. Cash flow/total debt
2. Net income/total assets (return on assets)
3. Total debt/total assets (debt ratio)

Beaver speculated as to the reason for these results: "My interpretation of the finding is that the cash flow, net income, and debt positions cannot be altered and represent permanent aspects of the firm. Because failure is too costly to all involved, the permanent, rather than the short-term, factors largely determine whether or not a firm will declare bankruptcy or default on a bond payment."[8] Assuming that the ratios identified by Beaver are valid in forecasting financial failure, it would be wise to pay particular attention to trends in these ratios when following a firm. Beaver's reasoning for seeing these ratios as valid in forecasting financial failure appears to be very sound.

These three ratios for Cooper for 1989 have been computed in previous chapters. The cash flow/total debt was 47.31%, which appears to be very good. Net income/total assets (return on assets) was 12.10%, which was much better than the industry average. The debt ratio was 40.36%, which is very good. Thus, Cooper appears to have minimal risk of financial failure.

The Beaver study also computed the mean values of thirteen financial statement items for each year before failure. Several important relationships were indicated among the liquid asset items, as follows:[9]

1. Failed firms have less cash but more accounts receivable.
2. When cash and receivables are added together, as they are in quick assets and current assets, the differences between failed and successful firms are obscured, because the cash and receivables differences are working in opposite directions.
3. Failed firms tend to have less inventory.

These results indicate that particular attention should be paid to three current assets when forecasting financial failure: cash, accounts receivable, and inventory. The analyst should be alert for low cash and inventory and high accounts receivable.

Multivariate Model

Edward I. Altman developed a multivariate model to predict bankruptcy.[10] His model uses five financial ratios that are weighted in order to maximize the predictive power of the model. The model produces an overall discriminant score, called a Z value. The Altman model is as follows:

---

[8]Ibid., p. 117.
[9]Ibid., p. 119.
[10]E. I. Altman, "Financial Ratios, Discriminant Analysis and the Prediction of Corporate Bankruptcy," *Journal of Finance* (September 1968), pp. 589–609.

$$Z = .012\,X_1 + .014\,X_2 + .033\,X_3 + .006\,X_4 + .010\,X_5$$

$$Z = \text{Discriminant Score}$$

$$X_1 = \text{Working Capital/Total Assets}$$

This computation is a measure of the net liquid assets of the firm relative to the total capitalization.

$$X_2 = \text{Retained Earnings (balance sheet)/Total Assets}$$

This variable is a measure of cumulative profitability over time.

$$X_3 = \text{Earnings before Interest and Taxes/Total Assets}$$

This variable is a measure of the productivity of the firm's assets, abstracting from any tax or leverage factors.

$$X_4 = \text{Market Value of Equity/Book Value of Total Debt}$$

This variable measures how much the firm's assets can decline in value before the liabilities exceed the assets and the firm becomes insolvent.

Equity is measured by the combined market value of all shares of stock, preferred and common, while debt includes both current and long-term debts.

$$X_5 = \text{Sales/Total Assets}$$

This variable measures the sales-generating ability of the firm's assets.

When computing the Z score, the ratios are expressed in absolute percentage terms. Thus, X_1 (working capital/total assets) of 25% is noted as 25.

The Altman model was developed using manufacturing companies whose asset size was between $1 million and $25 million. The original sample by Altman and the test samples used the period 1946–1965. The model's accuracy in predicting bankruptcies in more recent years (1970–1973) was reported in a 1974 article.[11] Not all of the companies included in the test were manufacturing companies, although the model was initially developed by using only manufacturing companies.

With the Altman model, the lower the Z score, the more likely that the firm will go bankrupt. By computing the Z score for a firm over several years, it can be determined if the firm is moving toward a more likely or less likely position in regard to bankruptcy.

In the more recent study that covered the period 1970–1973, a Z score of 2.675 was established as a practical cutoff point. Firms that scored below 2.675 are assumed to have characteristics similar to those of past failures.[12]

The Altman model is substantially less significant if there is no firm market value for the stock (preferred and common). The reason for this is that variable X_4 in the model requires that the market value of the stock be determined.

The Z score for Cooper at the end of 1989 is computed as follows:

[11]Edward I. Altman and Thomas P. McGough, "Evaluation of a Company as a Going Concern," *The Journal of Accountancy* (December 1974), pp. 50–57.
[12]Ibid., p. 52.

$Z = .012$ (working capital/total assets)
$+ .014$ (retained earnings [balance sheet]/[total assets])
$+ .033$ (earnings before interest and taxes/total assets)
$+ .006$ (market value of equity/book value of total debt)
$+ .10$ (sales/total assets)

$Z = .012$ ([\$249,215,062 − \$98,929,592]/\$519,892,610)
$+ .014$ (\$263,894,759 [balance sheet]/\$519,892,610)
$+ .033$ (\$96,997,278/\$519,892,610)
$+ .006$ ([20,564,837 × \$32.3/8]/[\$98,929,592 + \$65,726,850 + \$16,204,000 + \$28,968,508])
$+ .010$ (\$866,805,462/\$519,892,610)

$Z = .012$ (28.91)
$+ .014$ (50.76)
$+ .033$ (18.66)
$+ .006$ (317.30)
$+ .010$ (166.73)

$Z = .35 + .71 + .62 + 1.90 + 1.67$

$Z = 5.25$

The Z score for Cooper at the end of 1989 came to 5.25. Considering that higher scores are better and that companies with scores below 2.675 are assumed to have characteristics similar to those of past failures, this indicates that Cooper is a very healthy company.

As previously indicated, there are many academic studies on the use of financial ratios to forecast financial failure. These studies help substantiate that firms with weak ratios are more likely to go bankrupt than firms that have strong ratios. No conclusive model has yet been developed to forecast financial failure. The best approach is probably an integrated one, such as the approach suggested in this book. As a supplemental measure, it may also be helpful to compute some of the ratios that appear useful in forecasting financial failure.

ANALYTICAL REVIEW PROCEDURES

Statement of Auditing Standards No. 23, "Analytical Review Procedures," provides guidance for the use of such procedures in audits. The objective of analytical review procedures is to isolate significant fluctuations and unusual items in operating statistics.

Analytical review procedures may be performed at various times during the audit, including the planning stage, during the audit itself, and near the completion of the audit. Some examples of analytical review procedures that may lead to special audit procedures are as follows:

1. Horizontal common size analysis of the income statement may indicate that an item, such as selling expenses, is abnormally high for the period. This could lead to a close examination of the material selling expenses.

2. Vertical common size analysis of the income statement may indicate that cost of goods sold is out of line in relation to sales, in comparison with prior periods.

3. A comparison of accounts receivable turnover with the industry data may indicate that receivables are turning over much more slowly than is typical for the industry. This may indicate that receivables should be analyzed closely.

4. Cash flow in relation to debt may have declined significantly, indicating a materially reduced ability to cover debt from internal cash flow.

5. The acid test ratio may have declined significantly, indicating a materially reduced ability to pay current liabilities with current assets less inventories.

When the auditor spots a significant trend in a statement or ratio, follow-up procedures should be performed to determine why this is happening. Such an investigation can lead to significant findings.

MANAGEMENT USE OF ANALYSIS

There are many ways that management can use financial ratios and common size analysis as aids. Analysis can indicate the relative liquidity, debt, and profitability of a firm. Analysis can also indicate how investors perceive the firm and can help detect emerging problems and strengths in a firm. As indicated previously in this chapter, financial ratios can also be used as part of the firm's corporate objectives. Using financial ratios in conjunction with the budgeting process can be particularly helpful. An objective of the budgeting process is the determination of the firm's game plan. The budget can consist of an overall comprehensive budget and many separate budgets, such as a production budget.

The comprehensive budget relating to financial statements indicates how a firm plans to get from one financial position (balance sheet) to another. The income statement details how the firm changed internally from one balance sheet position to another. The statement of cash flows indicates how the firm's funds changed from one balance sheet to another.

A proposed comprehensive budget should be compared with financial ratios that have been agreed upon as part of the firm's corporate objectives. For example, if corporate objectives include a current ratio of 2:1, a debt equity of 40%, and a return on equity of 15%, then the proposed comprehensive budget should be compared with these corporate objectives before the budget is accepted as the firm's overall game plan. If the proposed comprehensive budget will not result in the firm achieving its objectives, attempts should be made to change the game plan in order to achieve them. If the proposed comprehensive budget cannot be changed satisfactorily to achieve the corporate objectives, this should be known at the time that the comprehensive budget is accepted.

| USE OF LIFO RESERVES

A firm that uses LIFO usually discloses a LIFO reserve account in a footnote or on the face of the balance sheet. If a LIFO reserve account is not disclosed, there is usually some indication of an amount that approximates current cost. In its 1989 annual report, Cooper disclosed in a footnote under the LIFO method, "Inventories have been reduced by approximately $52,204,000 and $49,001,000 at December 31, 1989 and 1988, respectively, from amounts which would have been reported under the first-in, first-out method, which approximates current cost."

This information can be used to improve the analysis of inventory and (in general) the analysis of liquidity, debt, and profitability. Supplemental analysis using this additional inventory information can be particularly significant when there has been substantial inflation.

The disclosure is usually limited as to differences in profit figures when using LIFO or FIFO. A primary reason for this is that the Internal Revenue Service objects to a firm's using LIFO and then disclosing details on what profits would have been based on some other inventory method. When a net income figure is not disclosed, based on inventory at approximate current costs, it can usually be approximated.

For Cooper, an approximation of the increase or decrease in income if inventory were at approximate current costs could be computed by comparing the change in inventory, net of any tax effect. For the year 1989, the approximation of the income if the inventory were at approximate current costs is computed as follows:

1989 net income as reported		$58,243,880
Net increase in inventory reserve		
1989	$52,204,000	
1988	49,001,000	
[a]	$ 3,203,000	
[b] Effective tax rate—federal income taxes (Effective tax rate could be approximated by comparing provision for income taxes to income before income taxes)		

$$\frac{\$34,380,000}{\$92,623,880} = 37.1\%$$

[c] Increase in taxes [a × b] = $1,188,313	
[d] Net increase in income [a − c] $3,203,000 − $1,188,313	2,014,687
Approximate income for 1989 if inventory had been valued at approximate current cost	$60,258,567

This type of computation can be made for each year. The approximate new income figures can then be considered and reviewed over a series of years to obtain an idea of what net income would have been if inventory had been computed using a method that approximated inventory costs closer to current costs than is accomplished with LIFO. Some analysts would consider this adjusted income amount to be more realistic than the unadjusted amount. Others would consider the unadjusted income to be more realistic from an operating basis, because it represents a better matching of current costs against revenue.

Specific liquidity and debt ratios can be recomputed taking into consideration the adjusted inventory figure. To make these computations, add the gross inventory reserve to the inventory disclosed in current assets. The approximate additional taxes are added to the current liabilities.

The additional tax figure is estimated by taking the effective tax rate times the gross LIFO reserve. This tax figure relates to the additional income that would have been reported in the current year, and all prior years, if the higher inventory amounts had been reported. The additional tax amount is a deferred tax amount that is added to current liabilities, to be conservative. The difference between the additional inventory amount and the additional tax amount is added to retained earnings, because it represents the total prior influence on net income. The adjusted figures for Cooper at the end of 1989 are as follows:

Inventory	
As disclosed on the balance sheet	$ 70,690,865
Increase in inventory	52,204,000
	$122,894,865
Deferred current tax liability	
Effective tax rate 37.1% × increase in inventory ($52,204,000)	$ 19,367,684
Retained earnings	
As disclosed on the balance sheet	$263,894,759
Increase in retained earnings ($52,204,000 − $19,367,684)	32,836,316
	$296,731,075

An adjusted cost of goods sold can also be estimated using the change in the inventory reserve. A net increase in inventory reserve would reduce cost of goods sold. A net decrease in inventory reserve would increase cost of goods sold.

Cooper reported cost of goods sold of $727,323,386 and an increase in inventory reserve of $3,203,000 in 1989. This increase in inventory reserve would be deducted from cost of goods sold, resulting in an adjusted cost of goods sold of $724,120,386. The adjusted cost of goods sold could be used when computing several ratios, such as days' sales in inventory. This refinement of cost of goods sold usually has an immaterial influence on the ratios, because the change in inventory reserve is usually immaterial in relation to the cost of goods sold figure. Therefore, this refinement to cost of goods sold is not made for illustrations and problems in this book.

In Exhibit 13-9, selected liquidity, debt, and profitability ratios are displayed for Cooper, comparing the adjusted ratio with the prior computation. The ratios that relate to inventory are not as favorable when the LIFO disclosure is considered as when the LIFO disclosure is not considered. Working capital is more favorable, and the current ratio is slightly more favorable. The acid test and cash ratio are less favorable. The balance sheet-related debt ratios (debt ratio and debt/equity) are slightly less favorable when the LIFO disclosure is considered. The income statement-

EXHIBIT 13-9

COOPER TIRE & RUBBER COMPANY
Selected Liquidity, Debt, and Profitability, Considering LIFO Disclosure
For the Year Ended December 31, 1989

	1989 Considering LIFO Disclosure	1989 Prior Computations
Liquidity ratios		
Days' sales in inventory	61.67	35.48 days
Merchandise inventory turnover	6.07	10.50 times
Inventory turnover in days	60.17	34.78 days
Operating cycle	112.87	87.48 days
Working capital	$183,121,786	$150,285,470
Current ratio	2.55	2.52 times
Acid test	1.49	1.78 times
Cash ratio	.42	.50 times
Debt		
Debt ratio	40.06	40.36%
Debt/equity	66.84	67.67%
Times interest earned	15.97	15.46 times
Profitability		
Net profit margin	7.09	6.72%
Total asset turnover	1.63	1.80 times
Return on assets	10.95	12.10%
Return on total equity	18.44	20.51%

related debt ratio of times interest earned is slightly more favorable. The profitability ratio of net profit margin is more favorable. Total asset turnover, return on assets, and return on total equity are all less favorable.

The adjusted liquidity, debt, and profitability ratios could be considered to be more realistic than the prior computations because of the use of a realistic inventory amount. This is particularly true for the ratios that relate to inventory.

For many of the ratios, we cannot generalize about whether the ratio will improve or decline when the LIFO reserve is used. For example, if the current ratio is above 2.00, then it may not improve when the LIFO reserve is considered, especially if the firm has a high tax rate. When the current ratio is low and/or the tax rate is low, then the current ratio is likely to improve.

GRAPHING FINANCIAL INFORMATION

It has become very popular to use graphs in annual reports to present financial information. This is done to make it easier to grasp key financial information. It is generally agreed that graphs can be a better communicative device than a written report or a tabular presentation, because graphs can communicate by means of pictures and thus create more immediate mental images.

The basic form of a graph is a coordinate surface on which one or more series of figures are placed. The coordinate surface is explained in terms of the x-axis and the y-axis. The x-axis is the horizontal scale, and it is used to represent the independent variable (the numbers go from left to right). The y-axis is the vertical scale, and it is used to represent the dependent variable (the numbers go from bottom to top).

A coordinate surface with the x- and y-axes is illustrated as follows:

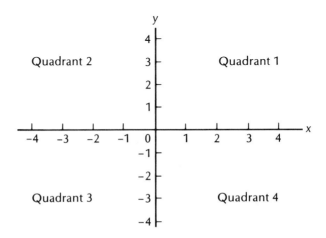

Usually, graphs use only quadrant 1, the one for which both sets of values are positive. Each series of figures is placed at the location of the two related variables (the independent variable and the dependent variable).

There are many forms of graphs. Some popular forms used by accountants are line, column, bar, and pie. These forms will be briefly described here, but a detailed description of these and other forms can be found in reference books and articles.[13]

The line graph uses a set of points connected by a line to show change over time. It is important that the vertical axis be extended to zero and that the vertical axis not be broken. Not extending the vertical axis to zero and/or breaking the

[13]Suggested reference sources:

Anker V. Andersen, "Graphing Financial Information: How Accountants Can Use Graphs to Communicate," National Association of Accountants (1983), p. 50.

Edward Bloches, Robert P. Moffie, and Robert W. Smud, "How Best to Communicate Numerical Data," *The Internal Auditor* (February 1985), pp. 38–42.

Charles H. Gibson and Nicholas Schroeder, "Improving Your Practice—Graphically," *The CPA Journal* (August 1990), pp. 28–37.

Johnny R. Johnson, Richard R. Rice, and Roger A. Roemmich, "Pictures That Lie: The Abuse of Graphs in Annual Reports," *Management Accounting* (October 1980), pp. 50–56.

Calvin F. Schmid and Stanton E. Schmid, *Handbook of Graphic Presentation*, 2nd ed. (New York: Ronald Press, 1979), p. 308.

vertical axis can result in a very misleading presentation. A line graph is illustrated in Exhibit 13-10.

A column graph has columns in vertical form. As in a line graph, it is important that the vertical axis be extended to zero and that the vertical axis not be broken. A column graph is often the best form for presenting accounting data. A column graph is presented in Exhibit 13-11.

A bar graph is similar to a column graph except that the bar is horizontal. A bar graph is illustrated in Exhibit 13-12.

A pie graph is divided into segments. This type of graph makes a comparison of the segments, which must add up to a total or to 100 percent. A pie graph can mislead if it creates an optical illusion. Also, some accounting data do not fit on a pie graph. A pie graph is illustrated in Exhibit 13-13.

SUMMARY

This chapter reviewed special areas related to financial statements. It was noted that commercial loan departments give a high significance rating to selected ratios that primarily measure liquidity or debt. The debt/equity ratio was given the highest

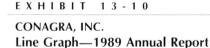

E X H I B I T   1 3 - 1 0

CONAGRA, INC.
Line Graph—1989 Annual Report

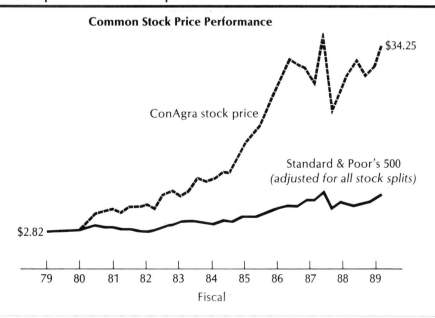

Common Stock Price Performance

EXHIBIT   13-11

THE COCA-COLA COMPANY
Column Graphs—1989 Annual Report

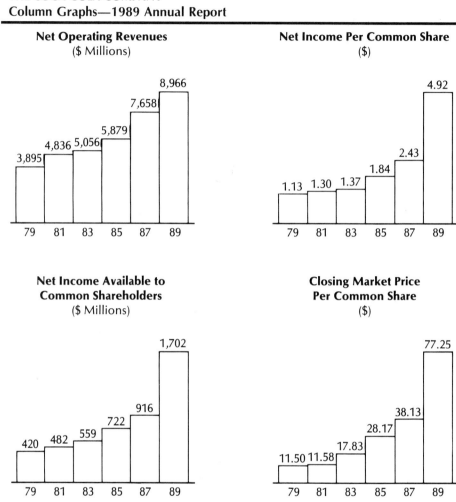

significance rating, and the current ratio was the second-highest rated by the commercial loan officers. A commercial bank may elect to include a ratio as part of a loan agreement. The two ratios that are most likely to be included in a loan agreement are the debt/equity and current ratios.

Financial executives give the profitability ratios the highest significance ratings. Several profitability ratios are rated high by financial executives, with earnings per share and return on investment rated the highest. Many firms have selected key

EXHIBIT 13-12

COLLINS INDUSTRIES, INC.
Bar Graphs—1989 Annual Report

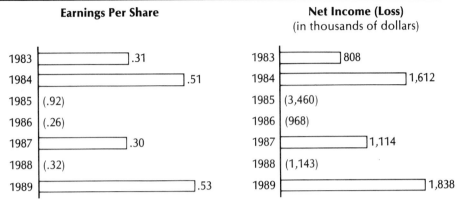

Earnings Per Share

Year	Value
1983	.31
1984	.51
1985	(.92)
1986	(.26)
1987	.30
1988	(.32)
1989	.53

Net Income (Loss)
(in thousands of dollars)

Year	Value
1983	808
1984	1,612
1985	(3,460)
1986	(968)
1987	1,114
1988	(1,143)
1989	1,838

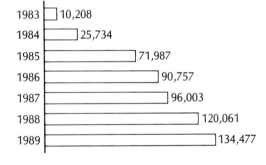

Sales
(in thousands of dollars)

Year	Value
1983	10,208
1984	25,734
1985	71,987
1986	90,757
1987	96,003
1988	120,061
1989	134,477

financial ratios to be included as part of their corporate objectives. Profitability ratios are the most likely to be selected for corporate objectives.

Certified public accountants give the highest significance rating to two liquidity ratios: the current ratio and the accounts receivable turnover in days. The highest-rated profitability ratio was after-tax net profit margin, and the highest-rated debt ratio was debt/equity.

A firm could use its annual report to relate financial data effectively by the use of financial ratios. In general, no major effort is being made to explain financial results by the disclosure of financial ratios in annual reports. A review of the methodology used to compute the ratios disclosed in annual reports indicated that there are wide differences of opinion on how many of the ratios should be computed.

EXHIBIT 13-13

UST
Pie Graph—1989 Annual Report

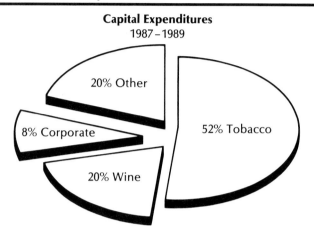

Capital Expenditures
1987–1989

20% Other

8% Corporate

20% Wine

52% Tobacco

A review of the financial statements, including the footnotes, indicates how conservative the statements are in terms of accounting policies. When a firm has conservative accounting policies, it is said that its earnings are of high quality.

There have been many academic studies on the use of financial ratios to forecast financial failure. No conclusive model has yet been developed to forecast financial failure.

Financial analysis can be used by auditors as part of their analytical review procedures. Using financial analysis, significant fluctuations and unusual items in operating statistics can be detected. This can result in a more efficient and effective audit.

Management can use financial analysis in many ways to manage a firm more effectively. A particularly effective use of financial analysis is to integrate ratios that have been accepted as corporate objectives into comprehensive budgeting.

It has become very popular to use graphs in annual reports to present financial information. This is done to make it easier to grasp key financial information. It is generally agreed that graphs can be a better communicative device than a written report or a tabular presentation.

| QUESTIONS

Q 13-1   Profitability financial ratios are regarded as very significant by commercial loan officers. Comment.

Q 13-2   Which two financial ratios are regarded as the most significant by commercial loan officers? Which two ratios appear most frequently in loan agreements?

Q 13-3   The dividend payout ratio was not listed as a highly significant ratio by commercial loan officers, but the officers indicated that the dividend payout ratio was a ratio that appeared frequently in loan agreements. Speculate on the reason for this apparent inconsistency.

Q 13-4   Profitability financial ratios are regarded as very significant by corporate controllers. Comment.

Q 13-5   List the top five financial ratios that are included in corporate objectives according to the study reviewed in this book. Indicate what each of these ratios primarily measures.

Q 13-6   Which two financial ratios are regarded as the most significant by certified public accountants? What is the highest-rated profitability ratio? The highest-rated debt ratio?

Q 13-7   Financial ratios are used extensively in annual reports to interpret and explain financial statements. Comment.

Q 13-8   List the sections of annual reports where ratios are most frequently located, in order of use.

Q 13-9   According to a study of annual reports reviewed in this chapter, what type or types of financial ratios are most likely to be included in annual reports? Speculate on the probable reason for these ratios appearing in annual reports.

Q 13-10   The study of annual reports reviewed in this chapter showed that earnings per share was disclosed in every annual report. Why?

Q 13-11   The study of annual reports reviewed in this chapter indicated that there are wide differences of opinion on how some ratios should be computed. Comment on why this is so.

Q 13-12   What types of accounting policies are described as conservative?

Q 13-13   Indicate which of the following accounting policies are conservative by placing an X under Yes or No. Assume that there are inflationary conditions.

	Conservative	
	Yes	No
a. LIFO inventory	____	____
b. FIFO inventory	____	____
c. completed-contract method	____	____
d. percentage-of-completion method	____	____
e. accelerated depreciation method	____	____
f. straight-line depreciation method	____	____
g. a relatively short estimated life for a fixed asset	____	____
h. short period for expensing intangibles	____	____
i. amortization of goodwill over forty years	____	____
j. high interest rate used to compute the present value of the accumulated benefit obligation	____	____
k. high rate of compensation increase used in computing the projected benefit obligation	____	____
l. extensive assets accounted for as operating leases	____	____

Q 13-14   All firms are required to expense R&D costs incurred each period. Some firms spend very large sums on R&D, while others spend little or nothing on this area. Why is it important to observe whether a firm has substantial or immaterial R&D expenses?

Q 13-15   Indicate some possible uses of a reliable model that can be used to forecast financial failure.

Q 13-16   Describe what is meant by a firm's financial failure.

Q 13-17   According to the Beaver study, which ratios should be watched most closely, in order of their predictive power?

Q 13-18   According to the Beaver study, three current asset accounts should be given particular attention in order to forecast financial failure. List each of these accounts and indicate whether you should look for these accounts to be abnormally high or low.

Q 13-19   What does a Z score below 2.675 indicate, according to the Altman model?

Q 13-20   Indicate a practical problem with computing a Z score for a closely held firm.

Q 13-21   No conclusive model has been developed to forecast financial failure. This indicates that financial ratios are not helpful in forecasting financial failure. Comment.

Q 13-22   You are the auditor of Piedmont Corporation. A review indicates that its receivable turnover has been much slower this period than in prior periods, and that it is also materially lower than the industry average. How might this situation affect your audit plan?

Q 13-23   You are in charge of preparing a comprehensive budget for your firm. Indicate how financial ratios can help determine an acceptable, comprehensive budget.

Q 13-24   Which quadrant, in terms of the x-axis and the y-axis, is usually used for a graph? Why?

Q 13-25   List four popular forms of graphs that are used by accountants.

Q 13-26   List two things that can make a line graph misleading.

Q 13-27   Indicate two possible problems with a pie graph for accounting data.

Q 13-28   The surveyed chartered financial analysts gave the highest significance rating to which type of financial ratio?

Q 13-29   Liquidity ratios are given a high significance rating by chartered financial analysts. Comment.

| *PROBLEMS*

P 13-1

Required   Answer the following multiple-choice questions.
   a. Footnotes to financial statements are beneficial in meeting the disclosure requirements of financial reporting. The footnotes should not be used to
      1. describe significant accounting policies
      2. describe depreciation methods employed by the company
      3. describe principles and methods peculiar to the industry in which the company operates, when these principles and methods are predominantly followed in that industry
      4. disclose the basis of consolidation for consolidated statements
      5. correct an improper presentation in the financial statements
   b. Which one of the following would be a source of funds under a cash concept of funds, but would not be listed as a source under the working capital concept?

1. sale of stock
2. sale of machinery
3. sale of treasury stock
4. collection of accounts receivable
5. proceeds from long-term bank borrowing

c. The concept of conservatism is often considered important in accounting. The application of this concept means that in the event there is some doubt as to how a transaction should be recorded, it should be recorded so as to
   1. understate income and overstate assets
   2. overstate income and overstate assets
   3. understate income and understate assets
   4. overstate income and understate assets
   5. the concept relates to the content of the president's letter that accompanies the statements, not to the statements themselves

d. Early in a period in which sales were increasing at a modest rate, and plant expansion and start-up costs were occurring at a rapid rate, a successful business would likely experience
   1. increased profits and increased financing requirements because of an increasing cash shortage
   2. increased profits and decreased financing requirements because of an increasing cash surplus
   3. increased profits and no change in financing requirements
   4. decreased profits and increased financing requirements because of an increasing cash shortage
   5. decreased profits and decreased financing requirements because of an increasing cash surplus

e. Which of the following ratios would best disclose effective management of working capital by a given firm relative to other firms in the same industry?
   1. a high rate of financial leverage relative to the industry average
   2. a high number of days' sales uncollected relative to the industry average
   3. a high turnover of net working capital relative to the industry average
   4. a high number of days' sales in inventory relative to the industry average
   5. a high proportion of fixed assets relative to the industry average

f. Stock options are frequently provided to officers of companies. Stock options that are exercised would
   1. improve the debt/equity ratio
   2. improve earnings per share
   3. improve the ownership interest of existing stockholders
   4. improve the total asset turnover
   5. improve the net profit margin

g. If a company has a long-term investment in the capital stock of another company, SFAS No. 12, "Accounting for Certain Marketable Securities," requires
   1. that the investment be carried at the lower of cost or market, with any difference between cost and market reported as an unrealized loss on the income statement as an extraordinary item
   2. that the investments be carried at the lower of cost or market, with any difference between cost and market reported as an unrealized loss in the stockholders' equity section of the balance sheet
   3. that the investment be carried at the lower of cost or market, with any difference

between cost and market reported as an unrealized loss on the statement of retained earnings

4. that the investment be carried at cost but the market value be disclosed in a footnote or in parentheses

5. that the investment be carried at the current market value, with any unrealized gain or loss reported on the income statement as an extraordinary item

h. In the preparation of general, price-level adjusted financial statements, monetary items would include all of the following except:

1. accounts receivable
2. accounts payable
3. investments in government bonds
4. bonds payable
5. inventories

CMA Adapted

P 13-2 The following balance sheet, income statement, and related information of the Brief Company pertain to items (a) through (g).

BRIEF COMPANY
Balance Sheet
December 31, 1990

Assets:	
Cash	$ 106,000
Accounts receivable	566,000
Inventories	320,000
Plant and equipment, net of depreciation	740,000
Patents	26,000
Other tangible assets	14,000
	$1,772,000
Equities:	
Accounts payable	$ 170,000
Federal income tax payable	32,000
Miscellaneous accrued payables	38,000
Bonds payable (4%, due 2002)	300,000
Preferred stock ($100 par, 7% cumulative nonparticipating and callable at $110)	200,000
Common stock (no par, 20,000 shares authorized, issued and outstanding)	400,000
Retained earnings	720,000
Treasury stock—800 shares of preferred	(88,000)
	$1,772,000

BRIEF COMPANY
Income Statement
Year Ended December 31, 1990

Net sales	$1,500,000
Cost of goods sold	900,000
Gross margin on sales	600,000
Operating expenses (including bond interest expense)	498,000
Income before federal income taxes	102,000
Income tax expense	37,000
Net income	$ 65,000

Additional information: There are no preferred dividends in arrears; the balance in the accounts receivable and inventory accounts are unchanged from January 1, 1990; and there were no changes in the bonds payable, preferred stock, or common stock accounts during 1990.

Required   Answer the following multiple-choice questions:

a. The current ratio was

1. $\dfrac{922}{170}$ to 1   2. $\dfrac{922}{208}$ to 1   3. $\dfrac{922}{240}$ to 1   4. $\dfrac{672}{208}$ to 1

5. none of the above

b. The number of times bond interest was earned using the theoretically preferable method was

1. $\dfrac{1,500}{12}$ 2. $\dfrac{114}{12}$ 3. $\dfrac{102}{12}$ 4. $\dfrac{650}{120}$

5. none of the above

c. The average number of days' sales in ending inventories was

1. $365\dfrac{(150)}{(32)}$ 2. $365\dfrac{(90)}{(32)}$ 3. $365\dfrac{(1,500)}{(566)}$ 4. $365\dfrac{(32)}{(150)}$

5. none of the above

d. The average number of days in the operating cycle was approximately

1. $365\dfrac{(150}{(32} + \dfrac{1,500)}{566)}$ 2. $365\dfrac{(90}{(32} + \dfrac{1,500)}{566)}$

3. $365\dfrac{(32}{(90} + \dfrac{566)}{1,500)}$ 4. $365\dfrac{(320 + 566)}{1,500}$

5. none of the above

e. The book value per share of common stock was

1. $66   4. $51.60

2. $61.60   5. none of these

3. $56

f. The rate of return based on the year-end common stockholders' equity was:

1. $\dfrac{650}{11,120}$ 2. $\dfrac{566}{10,320}$ 3. $\dfrac{650}{12,320}$ 4. $\dfrac{566}{11,120}$

5. none of the above

g. The debt equity, with debt defined as total liabilities, would be

1. $\dfrac{540}{1,112}$ 2. $\dfrac{540}{1,120}$ 3. $\dfrac{540}{1,232}$ 4. $\dfrac{540}{1,772}$

5. none of the above

AICPA Adapted

P 13-3

Required   Answer the following multiple-choice questions:

a. If business conditions are stable, a decline in the number of days' sales outstanding from one year to the next (based on a company's accounts receivable at year end) might indicate
   1. a stiffening of the company's credit policies
   2. that the second year's sales were made at lower prices than the first year's sales
   3. that a longer discount period and a more distant due date were extended to customers in the second year
   4. a significant decrease in the volume of sales of the second year

b. Trading on the equity (financial leverage) is likely to be a good financial strategy for stockholders of companies having
   1. cyclical high and low amounts of reported earnings
   2. steady amounts of reported earnings
   3. volatile fluctuation in reported earnings over short periods of time
   4. steadily declining amounts of reported earnings

c. The ratio of total cash, trade receivables, and marketable securities to current liabilities is
   1. the acid test ratio
   2. the current ratio
   3. significant if the result is 2 to 1 or below
   4. meaningless

d. The ratio of earnings before interest and taxes to total interest expense is a measure of
   1. liquidity
   2. risk
   3. activity
   4. profitability

e. The calculation of the number of times bond interest is earned involves dividing
   1. net income by annual bond interest expense
   2. net income plus income taxes by annual bond interest expense
   3. net income plus income taxes and bond interest expense by annual bond interest expense
   4. sinking fund earnings by annual bond interest expense

P 13-4   Items (a) through (f) deal with the calculation of ratios and the determination of other factors considered important in analysis of financial statements. Prior to the occurrence of the independent events described, the corporation concerned had current and quick ratios in excess of 1 to 1 and reported a net income (as opposed to a loss) for the period just ended. Income tax effects of the events are to be ignored. The corporation had only one class of shares outstanding.

Required Answer the following multiple-choice questions:
  a. The effect of recording a 100% stock dividend would be to
     1. decrease the current ratio, decrease working capital, and decrease book value per share
     2. leave inventory turnover unaffected, decrease working capital, and decrease book value per share
     3. leave working capital unaffected, decrease earnings per share, and decrease book value per share
     4. leave working capital unaffected, decrease earnings per share, and decrease the debt to equity ratio
  b. Recording the payment (as distinguished from the declaration) of a cash dividend whose declaration was already recorded will
     1. increase the current ratio but have no effect on working capital
     2. decrease both the current ratio and working capital
     3. increase both the current ratio and working capital
     4. have no effect on the current ratio or earnings per share
  c. What would be the effect on book value per share and earnings per share if the corporation purchased its own shares in the open market at a price greater than book value per share?
     1. no effect on book value per share but increase earnings per share
     2. increase both book value per share and earnings per share
     3. decrease book value per share and earnings per share
     4. decrease book value per share and increase earnings per share
  d. If the corporation were to increase the extent to which it successfully "traded on the equity," this fact would likely be manifested in a combination of facts that its
     1. ratio of owners' equity to total assets decreased while its ratio for net income to owners' equity increased
     2. book value and earnings per share increased
     3. working capital decreased while its current ratio increased
     4. asset turnover and return on sales both decreased
  e. The corporation exercises control over an affiliate in which it holds a 40% common stock interest. If its affiliate completed a fiscal year profitably but paid no dividends, how would this affect the investor corporation?
     1. result in an increased current ratio
     2. result in increased earnings per share
     3. increase several turnover ratios
     4. decrease book value per share
  f. What would be the most probable cause of an increase in the rate of inventory turnover while the rate of receivables turnover decreased when compared with the prior period?
     1. sales volume has changed markedly
     2. investment in inventory has decreased while investment in receivables has increased
     3. investment in inventory has increased while investment in receivables has decreased
     4. the corporation has shortened the credit period for customers (tightened credit terms)

AICPA Adapted

P 13-5

Required   Answer the following multiple-choice questions:

   a. Payment of a dividend in stock
      1. increases the current ratio
      2. decreases the amount of working capital
      3. increases total stockholders' equity
      4. decreases book value per share of stock outstanding

   b. Each year, a company has been investing an increasingly greater amount in machinery. Since there are a large number of small items with relatively similar useful lives, the company has been using the straight-line depreciation method at uniform rate to the machinery as a group. The ratio of this group's total accumulated depreciation to the total cost of the machinery has been steadily increasing and now stands at .75 to 1. The most likely explanation of this increasing ratio is that the:
      1. estimated average life of the machinery is greater than the actual average useful life
      2. estimated average life of the machinery is equal to the actual average useful life.
      3. estimated average life of the machinery is less than the actual average useful life.
      4. company has been retiring fully depreciated machinery that should have remained in service.

   c. Companies A and B begin 1990 with identical account balances, and their revenues and expenses for 1990 are identical in amount, except that Company A has a higher ratio of cash to noncash expenses. If the cash balances of both companies increase as a result of operation (no financing or dividends), the ending cash balance of Company A as compared to Company B will be
      1. higher
      2. the same
      3. lower
      4. indeterminate from the information given

   d. Eden Company has outstanding both common stock and nonparticipating, noncumulative preferred stock. The liquidation value of the preferred stock is equal to its par value. The book value per share of the common stock is unaffected by
      1. the declaration of stock dividend on preferred payable in preferred stock when the market price of the preferred is equal to its par value
      2. the declaration of a stock dividend on common payable in common stock when the market price of the common stock is equal to its par value
      3. the payment of a previously declared cash dividend on the common stock
      4. a 2-for-1 split of the common stock

   e. On April 15, 1991, the Rest-More Corporation accepted delivery of merchandise, which it purchased on account. As of April 30, the corporation has not recorded the transaction or included the merchandise in its inventory. The effect of this on its balance sheet for April 30, 1991, would be that
      1. assets and owners' equity were overstated, but liabilities were not affected
      2. owners' equity was the only item affected by the omission
      3. assets and liabilities were understated, but owners' equity was not affected
      4. assets and owners' equity were understated, but liabilities were not affected

   f. Assuming stable business conditions, a decline in the number of days' sales outstanding in a company's accounts receivable at year end from one year to the next might indicate
      1. a stiffening of the company's credit policies
      2. that the second year's sales were made at lower prices than the first year's sales

3. a longer discount period and a more distant due date were extended to customers in the second period.
4. a significant decrease in the volume of sales of the second year.

AICPA Adapted

P 13-6 Items (a), (b), and (c) are based on the following information:

The December 31, 1990, balance sheet of Ratio, Inc., is presented below. These are the *only* accounts in Ratio's balance sheet. Amounts indicated by a question mark (?) can be calculated from the additional information given.

Assets:	
Cash	$ 25,000
Accounts receivable (net)	?
Inventory	?
Property, plant, and equipment	294,000
	$432,000

Liabilities and stockholders' equity:	
Accounts payable (trade)	$?
Income taxes payable (current)	25,000
Long-term debt	?
Common stock	300,000
Retained earnings	?
	$?

Additional information:	
Current ratio (at year end)	1.5 to 1
Total liabilities divided by total stockholders' equity	.8
Inventory turnover based on sales and ending inventory	15 times
Inventory turnover based on cost of goods sold and ending inventory	10.5 times
Gross margin for 1990	$315,000

Required Answer the following multiple-choice questions:

a. What was Ratio's December 31, 1990 balance in the inventory account?
   1. $21,000   2. $30,000   3. $70,000   4. $135,000

b. What was Ratio's December 31, 1990 balance in retained earnings?
   1. $60,000 deficit   3. $132,000 deficit
   2. $60,000   4. $132,000

c. What was Ratio's December 31, 1990 balance in trade accounts payable?
   1. $67,000   2. $30,000   3. $70,000   4. $135,000

d. Trail, Inc. has a current ratio of .65 to 1. A cash dividend declared last month is paid this month. What is the effect of this dividend payment on the current ratio and working capital, respectively?
   1. rise and decline   3. decline and no effect
   2. rise and no effect   4. no effect on either

AICPA Adapted

P 13-7   Thorpe Company is a wholesale distributor of professional equipment and supplies. The company's sales have averaged about $900,000 annually for the three-year period 1988–1990. The firm's total assets at the end of 1990 amounted to $850,000.

The president of Thorpe Company has asked the controller to prepare a report to summarize the financial aspects of the company's operations for the past three years. This report will be presented to the board of directors at its next meeting.

In addition to comparative financial statements, the controller has decided to present a number of relevant financial ratios that can assist in the identification and interpretation of trends. At the request of the controller, the accounting staff has calculated the following ratios for the three-year period 1988–1990.

Ratio	1988	1989	1990
Current ratio	2.00	2.13	2.18
Acid test (quick) ratio	1.20	1.10	0.97
Accounts receivable turnover	9.72	8.57	7.13
Inventory turnover	5.25	4.80	3.80
Percent of total debt to total assets	44	41	38
Percent of long-term debt to total assets	25	22	19
Sales to fixed assets (fixed asset turnover)	1.75	1.88	1.99
Sales as a percentage of 1988 sales	1.00	1.03	1.06
Gross margin percentage	40.0%	33.6%	38.5%
Net income to sales	7.8%	7.8%	8.0%
Return on total assets	8.5%	8.6%	8.7%
Return on stockholders' equity	15.1%	14.6%	14.1%

In preparing his report, the controller has decided first to examine the financial ratios independently of any other data, to determine if the ratios themselves reveal any significant trends over the three-year period.

Required   a. The current ratio is increasing, while the acid test (quick) ratio is decreasing. Using the ratios provided, identify and explain the contributing factor(s) for this apparently divergent trend.

b. In terms of the ratios provided, what conclusion(s) can be drawn regarding the company's use of financial leverage during the 1988–1990 period?

c. Using the ratios provided, what conclusion(s) can be drawn regarding the company's net investment in plant and equipment?

CMA Adapted

P 13-8   The L. Konrath Company is considering extending credit to the D. Hawk Company. It is estimated that sales to the D. Hawk Company would amount to $2,000,000 each year. The L. Konrath Company is a wholesaler that sells throughout the Midwest. The D. Hawk Company is a retail chain operation that has a number of stores in the Midwest. The L. Konrath Company has had a gross margin of approximately 60% in recent years and expects to have a similar gross margin on the D. Hawk Company order. The D. Hawk Company order is approximately 15% of the L. Konrath Company's present sales. Recent statements of the D. Hawk Company are as follows:

	1988	1989	1990
	(in millions)		
Assets			
Current assets:			
Cash	2.6	1.8	1.6
Government securities (cost)	.4	.2	—
Accounts and notes receivable (net)	8.0	8.5	8.5
Inventories	2.8	3.2	2.8
Prepaid assets	.7	.6	.6
Total current assets	14.5	14.3	13.5
Property, plant, and equipment (net)	4.3	5.4	5.9
Total assets	18.8	19.7	19.4
Equities			
Current liabilities:			
Notes payable	3.2	3.7	4.2
Accounts payable	2.8	3.7	4.1
Accrued expenses and taxes	.9	1.1	1.0
Total current liabilities	6.9	8.5	9.3
Long-term debt, 6%	3.0	2.0	1.0
	9.9	10.5	10.3
Shareholders' equity	8.9	9.2	9.1
Total equities	18.8	19.7	19.4

Income Statement

	For the Years Ended December 31		
	1988	1989	1990
	(in millions)		
Net sales	24.2	24.5	24.9
Cost of goods sold	16.9	17.2	18.0
Gross margin	7.3	7.3	6.9
Selling expenses	4.3	4.4	4.6
Administrative expenses	2.3	2.4	2.7
Total expenses	6.6	6.8	7.3
Earning (loss) before taxes	.7	.5	(.4)
Income taxes	.3	.2	(.2)
Net income	.4	.3	(.2)

Required   a. Calculate the following ratios for the year 1990:
     1. rate of return on total assets
     2. acid test ratio
     3. return to sales
     4. current ratio
     5. inventory turnover
  b. As part of the analysis to determine whether or not Konrath should extend credit to Hawk, assume that the ratios below were calculated from D. Hawk Company statements. For each ratio, indicate whether it is a favorable, unfavorable, or neutral statistic in the decision to grant Hawk credit. Briefly explain your choice in each case.

Ratio	1988	1989	1990
Rate of return on total assets	1.96%	1.12%	(.87)%
Return to sales	1.69%	.99%	(.69)%
Acid test ratio	1.73/1	1.36/1	1.19/1
Current ratio	2.39/1	1.92/1	1.67/1
Inventory turnover (times)	4.41	4.32	4.52
Equity relationships			
Current liabilities	36.0%	43.0%	48.0%
Long-term liabilities	16.0	10.5	5.0
Shareholders' equity	48.0	46.5	47.0
	100.0%	100.0%	100.0%
Asset relationships			
Current assets	77.0%	72.5%	69.5%
Property, plant, and			
equipment	23.0%	27.5%	30.5%
	100.0%	100.0%	100.0%

  c. Would you grant credit to D. Hawk Company? Support your answer with facts given in the problem.
  d. What additional information, if any, would you want before making a final decision?

                                                   CMA Adapted

P 13-9   Your company is considering the possible acquisition of Growth Inc. Financial statements of Growth Inc. are as follows:

GROWTH INC.
Statement of Income
Years Ended December 31, 1990, 1989, and 1988

	1990	1989	1988
Revenues	$578,530	$523,249	$556,549
Costs and expenses:			
Cost of products sold	495,651	457,527	482,358
Selling, general and administrative	35,433	30,619	29,582

Statement of Income   (continued)

	1990	1989	1988
Interest and debt expense	4,308	3,951	2,630
	535,392	492,097	514,570
Income before income taxes	43,138	31,152	41,979
Provision for income taxes	20,120	12,680	17,400
Net income	$ 23,018	$ 18,472	$ 24,579
Net income per share	$2.27	$1.85	$2.43

GROWTH INC.
Balance Sheet
December 31, 1990 and 1989

	1990	1989
Assets		
Current assets:		
Cash	$ 64,346	$ 11,964
Accounts receivable, less allowance of $750		
for doubtful accounts	99,021	83,575
Inventories, FIFO	63,414	74,890
Prepaid expenses	834	1,170
Total current assets	227,615	171,599
Investments and other assets	379	175
Property, plant, and equipment:		
Land and land improvements	6,990	6,400
Buildings	63,280	59,259
Machinery and equipment	182,000	156,000
	252,270	221,659
Less accumulated depreciation	113,000	98,000
Total assets	$370,264	$295,433
Liabilities and stockholders' equity		
Current liabilities:		
Accounts payable	$ 32,730	$ 26,850
Federal income taxes	5,300	4,800
Accrued liabilities	30,200	24,500
Current portion of long-term debt	5,500	5,500
Total current liabilities	73,730	61,650
Long-term debt	76,750	41,900

Balance Sheet   (continued)

	1990	1989
Other long-term liabilities	5,700	4,300
Deferred federal income taxes	16,000	12,000
Stockholders' equity		
Capital stock	44,000	43,500
Retained earnings	154,084	132,083
Total stockholders' equity	198,084	175,583
Total liabilities and stockholders' equity	$370,264	$295,433

Partial Footnotes

Under the LIFO method, inventories have been reduced by approximately $35,300 and $41,100 at December 31, 1990 and 1989, respectively, from current cost, which would be reported under the first-in, first-out method.

The effective tax rates were 36.6%, 30.7%, and 31.4%, respectively, for the years ended December 31, 1990, 1989, and 1988.

Required

a. Compute the following ratios for 1990, without considering the LIFO reserve.
   Liquidity ratios:
     1. days' sales in inventory
     2. merchandise inventory turnover
     3. inventory turnover in days
     4. operating cycle
     5. working capital
     6. current ratio
     7. acid test
     8. cash ratio
   Debt ratios:
     1. debt ratio
     2. debt/equity
     3. times interest earned
   Profitability ratios:
     1. net profit margin
     2. total asset turnover
     3. return on assets
     4. return on total equity
b. Compute the ratios in part (a) considering the LIFO reserve.
c. Comment on the apparent liquidity, debt, and profitability, considering both sets of ratios.

P 13-10

Required

For each of the following numbered items, you are to select the lettered item(s) that indicate(s) its effect(s) on the corporation's statements. If more than one effect is applicable to a particular item, be sure to indicate *all* applicable letters. (Assume that the state statutes do not permit declaration of nonliquidating dividends except from earnings.)

	Item		*Effect*

<table>
<tr><td>

1. declaration of a cash dividend due in one month on noncumulative preferred stock
2. declaration and payment of an ordinary stock dividend
3. receipt of a cash dividend, not previously recorded, on stock of another corporation
4. passing of a dividend on cumulative preferred stocks
5. receipt of preferred shares as a dividend on stock held as a temporary investment (this was not a regularly recurring dividend)
6. payment of dividend mentioned in (1)
7. issue of new common shares in a 5-for-1 stock split

</td><td>

a. reduces working capital
b. increases working capital
c. reduces current ratio
d. increases current ratio
e. reduces the dollar amount of total capital stock
f. increases the dollar amount of total capital stock
g. reduces total retained earnings
h. increases total retained earnings
i. reduces equity per share of common stock
j. reduces equity of each common stockholder

</td></tr>
</table>

P 13-11   The following partially condensed financial statements are to be used in computing the items listed on page 589.

X CORPORATION
Statement of Financial Position
December 31, 1990

Cash	$ 63,000
Trade receivables, less estimated uncollectibles of $12,000	238,000
Inventories	170,000
Prepaid expenses	7,000
Property and equipment, cost less $182,000 charged to operations to date	390,000
Other assets	13,000
	$881,000
Accounts and notes payable—trade	$ 98,000
Accrued liabilities	17,000
Estimated federal income tax liability	18,000
First mortgage, 4% bonds, due in 1996	150,000
$7 Preferred stock—no par value (entitled to $110 per share in liquidation); authorized 1,000 shares; in treasury 400 shares; outstanding 600 shares	108,000
Common stock—no par, authorized	100,000
Shares, issued and outstanding	10,000
Shares stated at a normal value of $10 per share	100,000
Excess of amounts paid in for common stock over stated values	242,000
Reserve for plant expansion	50,000
Reserve for cost of treasury stock	47,000

Statement of Financial Position   (continued)

Retained earnings	98,000
Cost of 400 shares of treasury stock	(47,000)
	$881,000

Notes:
(1) Working capital—12/31/89 was $205,000.
(2) Trade receivables—12/31/89 were $220,000 gross, $206,000 net.
(3) Dividends for 1990 have been declared and paid.
(4) There has been no change in amount of bonds outstanding during 1990.

X CORPORATION
Statement of Earnings
Year Ended December 31, 1990

	Cash	Charge	Total
Gross sales	$116,000	$876,000	$992,000
Less: discounts	$ 3,000	$ 12,000	$ 15,000
Returns and allowances	1,000	6,000	7,000
	$ 4,000	$ 18,000	$ 22,000
Net sales	$112,000	$858,000	$970,000
Cost of sales:			
Inventory of finished goods—January 1		$92,000	
Cost of goods manufactured		680,000	
Inventory of finished goods—December 31		(100,000)	672,000
Gross profit on sales			$298,000
Selling expenses		$173,000	
General expenses		70,000	243,000
Net profit on operations			$ 55,000
Other additions and deductions (net)			3,000
Net earnings before federal income tax			$ 58,000
Federal income tax (estimated)			18,000
Net earnings			$ 40,000

Required   From the X Corporation's financial statements, compute the following and choose from the accompanying answers.

	Approximate Answers				
Items to Be Computed	1	2	3	4	5
a. Acid test ratio	3.2:1	2.3:1	2.9:1	2.4:1	3.07:1
b. Average number of days' charge sales uncollected	89	94	35	100	105
c. Average finished goods turnover	7	10.1	10.3	9.7	6.7
d. Number of times bond interest was earned (before taxes)	6⅔	10⅔	7⅔	9⅔	20⅓
e. Earnings per share of common stock	$4.00	$3.30	$3.58	$5.10	$5.38
f. Book value per share of common stock	$33.80	$35.00	$49.80	$48.80	$53.20
g. Current ratio	3.6:1	1.2:7	2.7:1	4.2:1	1.3:6

AICPA Adapted

P 13-12 Ratio analysis is often applied to test the reasonableness of the relationships among current financial data against those of prior financial data. Given prior financial relationships and a few key amounts, a CPA could prepare estimates of current financial data to test the reasonableness of data furnished by the client.

Argo Sales Corporation has in recent prior years maintained the following relationships among the data on its financial statements:

Gross profit rate on net sales	40%
Net profit rate on net sales	10%
Rate of selling expenses to net sales	20%
Accounts receivable turnover	8 per year
Inventory turnover	6 per year
Acid test ratio	2 to 1
Current ratio	3 to 1
Quick-asset composition: 8% cash, 32% marketable securities, 60% accounts receivable	
Asset turnover	2 per year
Ratio of total assets to intangible assets	20 to 1
Ratio of accumulated depreciation to cost of fixed assets	1 to 3
Ratio of accounts receivable to accounts payable	1.5 to 1
Ratio of working capital to stockholders' equity	1 to 1.6
Ratio of total debt to stockholders' equity	1 to 2

The corporation had a net income of $120,000 for 1990, which resulted in earnings of $5.20 per share of common stock. Additional information includes the following:

Capital stock authorized, issued (all in 1970) and outstanding:
   Common, $10 per share par value, issued at 10% premium.

Preferred, 6% nonparticipating, $100 per share par value, issued at a 10% premium.
Market value per share of common at December 31, 1990: $78.
Preferred dividends paid in 1990: $3,000.
Times interest earned in 1990: 33.

The amounts of the following were the same at December 31, 1990, as at January 1, 1990: inventory, accounts receivable, 5% bonds payable—due 1992, and total stockholders' equity.

All purchases and sales were on account.

Required

a. Prepare in good form the condensed balance sheet and income statement for the year ending December 31, 1990, presenting the amounts you would expect to appear on Argo's financial statements (ignoring income taxes). Major captions appearing on Argo's balance sheet are current assets, fixed assets, intangible assets, current liabilities, long-term liabilities, and stockholders' equity. In addition to the accounts divulged in the problem, you should include accounts for prepaid expenses, accrued expenses, and administrative expenses. Supporting computations should be in good form.

b. Compute the following for 1990 (show your computations):
1. rate of return on stockholders' equity
2. price/earnings ratio for common stock
3. dividends paid per share of common stock
4. dividends paid per share of preferred stock
5. yield on common stock

CMA Adapted

P 13-13   Warford Corporation was formed five years ago through a public subscription of common stock. Lucinda Street, who owns 15% of the common stock, was one of the organizers of Warford and is its current president. The company has been successful but currently is experiencing a shortage of funds. On June 10, Street approached the Bell National Bank, asking for a 24-month extension on two $30,000 notes, which are due on June 30, 1989, and September 30, 1989. Another note of $7,000 is due on December 31, 1989, but she expects no difficulty in paying this note on its due date. Street explained that Warford's cash flow problems are due primarily to the company's desire to finance a $300,000 plant expansion over the next two fiscal years through internally generated funds.

The commercial loan officer of Bell National Bank requested financial reports for the last two fiscal years. These reports are as follows:

WARFORD CORPORATION
Statement of Financial Position

	March 31	
	1988	**1989**
Assets:		
Cash	$ 12,500	$ 16,400
Notes receivable	104,000	112,000
Accounts receivable (net)	68,500	81,600
Inventories (at cost)	50,000	80,000

Statement of Financial Position   (continued)

	March 31	
	1988	1989
Plant and equipment (net of depreciation)	646,000	680,000
Total assets	$881,000	$970,000
Liabilities and owners' equity:		
Accounts payable	$ 72,000	$ 69,000
Notes payable	54,500	67,000
Accrued liabilities	6,000	9,000
Common stock (60,000 shares, $10 par)	600,000	600,000
Retained earnings*	148,500	225,000
	$881,000	$970,000

*Cash dividends were paid at the rate of $1.00 per share in fiscal year 1988 and $1.25 per share in fiscal year 1989.

WARFORD CORPORATION
Income Statement
For the Fiscal Years Ended March 31, 1988 and 1989

	1988	1989
Sales	$2,700,000	$3,000,000
Cost of goods sold*	1,720,000	1,902,500
Gross margin	$ 980,000	$1,097,500
Operating expenses	780,000	845,000
Net income before taxes	$ 200,000	$ 252,500
Income taxes (40%)	80,000	101,000
Income after taxes	$ 120,000	$ 151,500

*Depreciation charges on the plant and equipment of $100,000 and $102,500 for fiscal years ended March 31, 1988 and 1989, respectively, are included in cost of goods sold.

Required   a. Calculate the following items for Warford Corporation:
1. current ratio for fiscal years 1988 and 1989
2. acid test (quick) ratio for fiscal years 1988 and 1989
3. inventory turnover for fiscal year 1989
4. return on assets for fiscal years 1988 and 1989
5. percentage change in sales, cost of goods sold, gross margin, and net income after taxes from fiscal year 1988 to 1989

b. Identify and explain what other financial reports and/or financial analyses might be helpful to the commercial loan officer of Bell National Bank in evaluating Street's request for a time extension on Warford's notes.

c. Assume that the percentage changes experienced in fiscal year 1989, as compared with fiscal year 1988, for sales, cost of goods sold, gross margin, and net income after taxes will be repeated in each of the next two years. Is Warford's desire to finance the plant expansion from internally generated funds realistic? Explain.

d. Should Bell National Bank grant the extension on Warford's notes, considering Street's statement about financing the plant expansion through internally generated funds? Explain.

CMA Adapted

P 13-14   The following data apply to items (a) through (g).

JOHANSON COMPANY
Statement of Financial Position
December 31, 1988 and 1989

	1988	1989
	(in thousands)	
Assets		
Current assets:		
Cash and temporary investments	$ 380	$ 400
Accounts receivable (net)	1,500	1,700
Inventories	2,120	2,200
Total current assets	$4,000	$4,300
Long-term assets:		
Land	$ 500	$ 500
Building and equipment (net)	400	4,700
Total long-term assets	$4,500	$5,200
Total assets	$8,500	$9,500
Liabilities and equities		
Current liabilities:		
Accounts payable	$ 700	$1,400
Current portion of long-term debt	500	1,000
Total current liabilities	$1,200	$2,400
Long-term debt	4,000	3,000
Total liabilities	$5,200	$5,400
Stockholders' equity		
Common stock	$3,000	$3,000
Retained earnings	300	1,100
Total stockholders' equity	$3,300	$4,100
Total liabilities and equities	$8,500	$9,500

JOHANSON COMPANY
Statement of Income and Retained Earnings
For the Year Ended December 31, 1989

	(in thousands)	
Net sales		$28,800
Less: Cost of goods sold	$15,120	
Selling expenses	7,180	
Administrative expenses	4,100	
Interest	400	
Income taxes	800	27,600
Net income		$ 1,200
Retained earnings January 1		300
Subtotal		$ 1,500
Cash dividends declared and paid		400
Retained earnings, December 31		$ 1,100

Required   Answer the following multiple-choice questions.

a. The acid test ratio for 1989 for Johanson Company is
   1. 1.1 to 1   4. .2 to 1
   2. .9 to 1   5. .17 to 1
   3. 1.8 to 1

b. The average number of days' sales outstanding in 1989 for Johanson Company is
   1. 18 days   4. 4.4 days
   2. 360 days   5. 80 days
   3. 20 days

c. The times interest earned ratio for 1989 for Johanson Company is
   1. 3.0 times   4. 2.0 times
   2. 1.0 times   5. 6.0 times
   3. 72.0 times

d. The asset turnover in 1989 for Johanson Company is
   1. 3.2 times   4. 1.1 times
   2. 1.7 times   5. .13 times
   3. .4 times

e. The inventory turnover in 1989 for Johanson Company is
   1. 13.6 times   4. 7.0 times
   2. 12.5 times   5. 51.4 times
   3. .9 times

f. The operating income margin in 1989 for Johanson Company is
   1. 2.7%   4. 95.8%
   2. 91.7%   5. 8.3%
   3. 52.5%

g. The dividend payout ratio in 1989 for Johanson Company is

    1. 100%   4. 8.8%

    2. 36%   5. 33.3%

    3. 20%

CMA Adapted

P 13-15   Seaway Food Town, Inc., presented the following consolidated balance sheet for September 27, 1980, September 29, 1979, and September 30, 1978:

	1980	1979	1978
Assets			
Current assets:			
Cash	$ 4,888,465	$ 5,719,264	$ 6,437,834
Marketable securities at cost			
(approximates market)	6,000,000	4,900,000	4,489,625
Notes and accounts receivable, less			
allowance for doubtful accounts			
of $325,000 (1980), $325,000			
(1979), and $300,000 (1978)	4,912,230	4,581,978	4,463,405
Merchandise inventories	24,041,620	22,864,563	18,526,507
Prepaid expenses, including			
deferred income taxes of			
$444,600 (1980), $570,600			
(1979), and $512,600 (1978)	1,320,696	1,272,488	1,180,015
Total current assets	41,163,011	39,338,293	35,097,386
Other assets	2,310,181	2,960,453	1,023,036
Property and equipment, at cost:			
Land	2,663,507	2,260,107	1,613,943
Buildings and improvements	26,300,062	23,891,011	19,648,510
Leasehold improvements	7,162,125	6,351,098	4,901,138
Equipment	31,093,333	25,816,098	21,438,216
	67,219,027	58,318,224	47,601,807
Less accumulated depreciation and			
amortization	24,277,183	20,675,017	17,644,176
Net property and equipment	42,941,844	37,643,207	29,957,631
	$86,415,036	$79,941,953	$66,078,053

	1980	1979	1978
Liabilities and shareholders' equity			
Current liabilities:			
Accounts payable	$20,449,067	$18,522,854	$17,872,527
Income taxes	1,401,578	1,539,437	1,879,543
Accrued liabilities			
Payroll	1,234,580	1,115,312	929,176
Taxes, other than income	1,181,023	988,068	391,195
Other	1,759,767	1,496,854	1,244,878
	4,175,370	3,600,234	2,565,249

	1980	1979	1978
Long-term debt due within one year	690,000	646,000	911,900
Total current liabilities	26,716,015	24,308,525	23,229,219
Deferred income taxes	1,732,020	1,408,020	1,003,020
Shareholders' equity:			
Serial preferred stock without par value; 300,000 shares authorized, none issued	—	—	—
Common stock, without par value (stated value $2 per share): 4,000,000 shares authorized (1980 and 1979), 2,000,000 shares authorized (1978); 1,640,191 shares outstanding (1980), 1,648,363 shares outstanding (1979), and 1,633,919 shares outstanding (1978), after deducting 137,126 shares (1979), and 143,628 (1978)	3,280,382	3,296,726	3,267,838
Capital in excess of stated value	1,522,242	1,500,637	1,472,794
Retained earnings	24,537,613	21,093,178	17,280,417
Total shareholders' equity	29,340,237	25,890,541	22,021,049
	$86,415,036	$79,941,953	$66,078,053
Selected income statement data:			
Net sales	$357,112,740	$325,856,820	$285,214,868
Cost of merchandise sold	290,299,069	264,861,109	233,716,546
Net income	4,587,446	4,756,865	3,325,437
Net income per common share	$2.78	$2.90	$2.05

Partial Footnote 1 (1980 financial statements)

Inventories—Meat and produce inventories are valued at the lower of cost, using the first-in, first-out (FIFO) method, or market. All other merchandise inventories (including store inventories which are determined by the retail inventory method) are valued at the lower of cost, using the last-in, first-out (LIFO) method, or market.

Inventories have been reduced by $10,121,000 and $7,728,000 at September 27, 1980, and September 29, 1979, respectively, from amounts which would have been reported under the FIFO method (which approximates current cost). Had the company valued all of its inventories under the FIFO method, net income would have been approximately $5,800,000 ($3.52 per common share in 1980) and $5,601,000 ($3.41 per common share in 1979), and retained earnings would be increased by approximately $4,968,000 at September 27, 1980, and $3,755,000 at September 29, 1979.

Required   For 1980 compute the following:

a. Percentage increase in net income, over the reported net income, if FIFO had been used.

b. Percentage increase in net income per common share, over the reported net income per common share, if FIFO had been used.

c. For the following ratios compute the ratio from the financial statements (using LIFO), using the inventory data that approximates current cost.

1. days' sales in inventory	4. acid test
2. working capital	5. debt ratio
3. current ratio	6. debt/equity

d. Comment on the difference between the appearance of the firm's profitability, liquidity, and debt position between the LIFO figures and the FIFO figures

e. Comment on the substance between the LIFO and FIFO differences computed in (d).

P 13-16   The statement of financial position for Paragon Corporation at November 30, 1984, the end of its current fiscal year, is presented below. The market price of Paragon Corporation's common stock was $4 per share on November 30, 1984.

Assets
Current assets

Cash			$ 6,000
Accounts receivable		$ 7,000	
Less allowance for doubtful accounts		400	6,600
Merchandise inventory			16,000
Supplies on hand			400
Prepaid expenses			1,000
Total current assets			$30,000
Property, plant, and equipment			
Land			$27,500
Building		$36,000	
Less accumulated depreciation		13,500	22,500
Total property, plant, and equipment			50,000
Total assets			$80,000

Liabilities and stockholders' equity
Current liabilities

Accounts payable	$ 6,400	
Accrued interest payable	800	
Accrued income taxes payable	2,200	
Accrued wages payable	600	
Deposits received from customers	2,000	
Total current liabilities		$12,000
Long-term debt		
Bonds payable—20 year, 8% convertible debentures due December 1, 1989 (Note 1)	$20,000	
Less unamortized discount	200	19,800
Total liabilities		$31,800

Stockholders' equity
   Common stock—authorized 40,000,000
     shares of $1 par value; 20,000,000 shares

issued and outstanding	$20,000	
Paid-in capital in excess of par value	12,200	
Total paid-in capital	$32,200	
Retained earnings	16,000	
Total stockholders' equity		48,200
Total liabilities and stockholders' equity		$80,000

All items are to be considered independent of one another, and any transactions given in the items are to be considered the only transactions to affect Paragon Corporation during the just-completed current or coming fiscal year. Average balance sheet account balances are used in computing ratios involving income statement accounts. Ending balance sheet account balances are used in computing ratios involving only balance sheet items.

Required

a. If Paragon paid back all of the deposits received from customers, its current ratio would be
  1. 2.50 to 1.00   4. 3.00 to 1.00
  2. 2.80 to 1.00   5. 2.29 to 1.00
  3. 2.33 to 1.00

b. If Paragon paid back all of the deposits received from customers, its quick (acid test) ratio would be
  1. 1.06 to 1.00   4. 1.26 to 1.00
  2. 1.00 to 1.00   5. 1.20 to 1.00
  3. 0.88 to 1.00

c. A 2-for-1 common stock split by Paragon would
  1. result in each $1,000 bond being convertible into 600 new shares of Paragon common stock
  2. decrease the retained earnings due to the capitalization of retained earnings
  3. not affect the number of common shares outstanding
  4. increase the total paid-in capital
  5. increase the total stockholders' equity

d. Paragon Corporation's building is being depreciated, using the straight-line method, of $6,000,000. The number of years the building has been depreciated by Paragon as of November 30, 1984, is
  1. 7.5 years   4. 15.0 years
  2. 12.5 years   5. none of these
  3. 9.0 years

e. Paragon's book value per share of common stock as of November 30, 1984, is
  1. $4.00   4. $2.41
  2. $1.61   5. none of these
  3. $1.00

f. If, during the current fiscal year ending November 30, 1984, Paragon had sales of $90,000,000 with a gross margin of 20% and an inventory turnover of five times per year, the merchandise inventory balance on December 1, 1983, was
  1. $14,400,000   4. $20,000,000
  2. $12,800,000   5. $16,000,000
  3. $18,000,000

g. If Paragon has a payout ratio of 80% and declared and paid $4,000,000 of cash dividends during the current fiscal year ended November 30, 1984, the retained earnings balance on December 1, 1983, was

1. $20,000,000
2. $17,000,000
3. $15,000,000
4. $11,000,000
5. none of these

CMA Adapted

P 13-17 Calcor Company has been a wholesale distributor of automobile parts for domestic automakers for 20 years. Calcor has suffered through the recent slump in the domestic auto industry, and its performance has not rebounded to the levels of the industry as a whole.

Calcor's single-step income statement for the year ended November 30, 1984, is as follows:

CALCOR COMPANY
Income Statement
For the Year Ended November 30, 1984 ($000 omitted)

Net sales	$8,400
Expenses	
Cost of goods sold	$6,300
Selling expense	780
Administrative expense	900
Interest expense	140
Total	$8,120
Income before income taxes	$ 280
Income taxes	112
Net income	$ 168

Calcor's return on sales before interest and taxes was 5% in fiscal 1984, compared to the industry average of 9%. Calcor's turnover of average assets of four times and return on average assets before interest and taxes of 20% are both well below the industry average.

Joe Kuhn, president of Calcor, wishes to improve these ratios and raise them nearer to the industry averages. He established the following goals for Calcor Company for fiscal 1985:

Return on sales before interest and taxes	8%
Turnover of average assets	5 times
Return on average assets before interest and taxes	30%

Kuhn and the rest of Calcor's management team are considering the following actions for fiscal 1985, which they expect will improve profitability and result in a 5% increase in unit sales.

Increase selling prices 10%.

Increase advertising by $420,000 and hold all other selling and administrative expenses at fiscal 1984 levels.

Improve customer service by increasing average current assets (inventory and accounts receivable) by a total of $300,000, and hold all other assets at fiscal 1984 levels.

Finance the additional assets at an annual interest rate of 10% and hold all other interest expense at fiscal 1984 levels.

Improve the quality of products carried; this will increase the unit of goods sold by 4%.

Calcor's 1985 effective income tax rate is expected to be 40%—the same as in fiscal 1984.

Required a. Prepare a single-step pro forma income statement for Calcor Company for the year ended November 30, 1985, assuming that Calcor's planned actions would be carried out and that the 5% increase in unit sales would be realized.

b. Calculate the following ratios for Calcor Company for the 1984–1985 fiscal year and state whether Kuhn's goals would be achieved:

   1. return on sales before interest and taxes
   2. turnover of average assets
   3. return on average assets before interest and taxes

c. Would it be possible for Calcor Company to achieve the first two of Kuhn's goals without achieving his third goal of a 30% return on average assets before interest and taxes? Explain your answer.

CMA Adapted

P 13-18   The following data are for the A, B, and C companies.

	Company		
Variable	A	B	C
Working capital	$ 90,000	$120,000	$150,000
Total assets	$300,000	$280,000	$250,000
Retained earnings	$ 80,000	$ 90,000	$ 60,000
Earnings before interest and taxes	$ 70,000	$ 60,000	$ 50,000
Market value of equity	$180,000	$170,000	$150,000
Book value of total debt	$ 30,000	$ 50,000	$ 80,000
Sales	$430,000	$400,000	$200,000

Required a. Compute the Z score for each company.

b. According to the Altman model, which of these firms is most likely to experience financial failure?

P 13-19   At the back of this book is a comprehensive case that includes selected pages of the 1990 annual report of Worthington Industries. *Note:* The market price of the Worthington Industries common stock at May 31, 1990, was $24.25 per share.

Required a. Compute the Z score of Worthington Industries at the end of fiscal 1990.

b. According to the Altman model, does the Z score of Worthington Industries indicate a high probability of financial failure for the company?

P 13-20   The General Company financial statements for 1989 follow:

GENERAL COMPANY
Statement of Income
Years Ended December 31

	1989	1988	1987
Net sales	$860,000	$770,000	$690,000
Cost and expenses:			
Cost of products sold	730,000	630,000	580,000
Selling, general, and administrative expenses	46,000	40,000	38,000
Interest and debt expense	4,000	3,900	6,500
	780,000	673,900	624,500
Income before income taxes	80,000	96,100	65,500
Provision for income taxes	33,000	24,000	21,000
Net income	$ 47,000	$ 72,100	$ 44,500
Net income per share	$2.67	$4.10	$2.54

GENERAL COMPANY
Balance Sheet

	December 31	
	1989	1988
Assets		
Current assets:		
Cash	$ 48,000	$ 39,000
Accounts receivable, less allowance for doubtful accounts of $2,000 in 1989 and $1,400 in 1988	125,000	121,000
Inventories	71,000	68,000
Prepaid expenses	2,500	2,200
Total current assets	246,500	230,200
Property, plant, and equipment		
Land and land improvements	12,000	10,500
Buildings	98,000	89,000
Machinery and equipment	303,000	247,000
	413,000	346,500
Less accumulated depreciation	165,000	144,000
Net property, plant, and equipment	248,000	202,500
Total assets	$494,500	$432,700

Balance Sheet   (continued)

	December 31	
	1989	1988
Liabilities and stockholders' equity		
Current liabilities:		
Accounts payable	$ 56,000	$ 50,000
Income taxes	3,700	3,600
Accrued liabilities	34,000	28,000
Total current liabilities	93,700	81,600
Long-term debt	63,000	64,000
Other long-term liabilities	16,000	6,800
Deferred federal income taxes	27,800	24,000
Stockholders' equity:		
Capital stock	46,000	45,000
Retained earnings	248,000	211,300
Total stockholders' equity	294,000	256,300
Total liabilities and stockholders' equity	$494,500	$432,700

GENERAL COMPANY
Statement of Cash Flows
Years Ended December 31

	1989	1988	1987
Operating activities:			
Net income	$ 47,000	$ 72,100	$ 44,500
Adjustments to reconcile net income to net cash			
provided by operating activities:			
Depreciation and amortization	21,000	20,000	19,000
Deferred taxes	3,800	2,500	2,000
Increase in accounts receivable	(4,000)	(3,000)	(3,000)
Decrease (increase) in inventories	(3,000)	(2,500)	1,000
Decrease (increase) in prepaid expenses	(300)	(200)	100
Increase (decrease) in accounts payable	6,000	5,000	(1,000)
Increase (decrease) in income taxes	100	300	(100)
Increase (decrease) in accrued liabilities	6,000	3,000	(1,000)
Net cash provided by operating activities	76,600	97,200	61,500
Investing activities:			
Additions to property, plant, and equipment	(66,500)	(60,000)	(58,000)

Statement of Cash Flows   (continued)

	1989	1988	1987
Financing activities:			
Payment on long-term debt	(1,000)	(2,000)	(1,500)
Issuance of other long-term liabilities	9,200	1,000	(1,000)
Issuance of capital stock	1,000	—	—
Dividend paid	(10,300)	(9,800)	(9,500)
Net cash used in financing activities	(1,100)	(10,800)	(12,000)
Increase (decrease) in cash	9,000	2,000	(3,000)
Cash at beginning of year	39,000	37,000	40,000
Cash at end of year	$ 48,000	$ 39,000	$ 37,000

Note: The market price of the stock at the end of 1989 was $30.00 per share. Common shares outstanding at December 31, 1989 were 17,603.

Required   a. Compute the Z score of the General Company at the end of 1989.

b. According to the Altman model, does the Z score of the General Company indicate a high probability of financial failure for the company?

P 13-21   Two line graphs are presented with this problem.

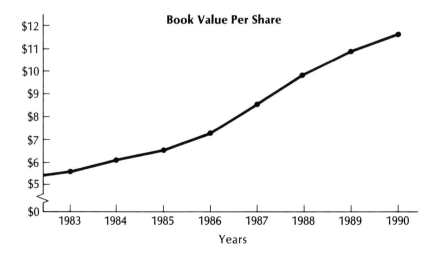

Book Value Per Share

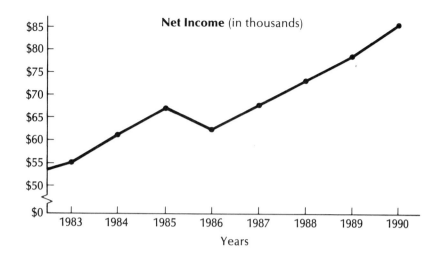

Net Income (in thousands)

Required   Indicate the misleading feature in each graph.

CHAPTER **14**

STATEMENT ANALYSIS FOR SPECIAL INDUSTRIES: BANKS, UTILITIES, OIL AND GAS, TRANSPORTATION, INSURANCE

CHAPTER TOPICS

Banks

Balance Sheet
Income Statement
Ratios for Banks
Earning Assets to Total Assets
Return on Earning Assets
Interest Margin to Average
  Earning Assets
Loan Loss Coverage Ratio
Equity Capital to Total Assets
Deposits Times Capital
Loans to Deposits

Electric Utilities

Ratios for Electric Utilities
Operating Ratio
Funded Debt to Operating
  Property
Percent Earned on Operating
  Property
Operating Revenue
  to Operating Property

Oil and Gas

Successful Efforts versus Full
  Cost
Supplementary Information
  on Oil and Gas Exploration,
  Development, and Production
  Activities
Cash Flow

Transportation

Operating Ratio
Long-Term Debt to Operating
  Property
Operating Revenue
  to Operating Property
Per Mile—Per Person—Per
  Ton—Passenger Load Factor

Insurance

Balance Sheet under GAAP
Income Statement under GAAP
Ratios

All of the preceding chapters have covered material that is most applicable to man-ufacturing, retailing, wholesaling, and service industries. This chapter discusses problems in analyzing five specialized industries: banks, electric utilities, oil and gas, transportation, and insurance. In each case, differences in statements will be noted, and suggested changes or additions to analysis will be presented.

One common characteristic of three of these industries—banks, utilities, and transportation—is that a uniform system of accounts has been established for each, controlled by a federal regulatory agency. The nature of these three industries, however, makes their statements somewhat dissimilar from those of other industries. Insurance companies' statements also differ from those of other industries, and insurance companies must file annual reports with the state insurance departments in accordance with statutory accounting practices. Many of the companies in these industries also file required forms with the Securities and Exchange Commission. The forms filed with the SEC must conform with GAAP.

Oil and gas companies must disclose supplemental resource data. This disclosure, along with the extra importance of cash flow, makes them unique.

BANKS

Banks operate under either a federal or a state charter. National banks are required to submit uniform accounting statements to the comptroller of the currency. State banks are controlled by the state banking departments. In addition, the Federal Deposit Insurance Corporation and the Board of Governors of the Federal Reserve System receive financial and operating statements from all members of the Federal Reserve System. Member banks are required to keep reserves with the Federal Reserve bank of the district. State banking laws also dictate the geographical area within which a bank may function. The range runs from within one county to interstate.

Banking systems usually involve two types of structures—individual banks and bank holding companies. Bank holding companies consist of a parent that owns one or many banks; additionally, the holding company may own bank-related financial services and nonfinancial subsidiaries. In financial statement analysis, the reader must determine what portion of the business is generated by banking services. In order for the specific industry ratios to be meaningful, a large proportion of the services should be bank related.

A substantial part of the 1989 annual report of Huntington Bancshares is presented in Exhibit 14-1. Huntington Bancshares is located in Columbus, Ohio, and has offices in many parts of Ohio, including every major market. It has also purchased several banks in other Midwestern states.

Balance Sheet

The balance sheet of a commercial bank is sometimes termed the *report of condition*. There are two significant differences between the traditional balance sheet and that of a bank. First, the accounts of banks may seem opposite to those of other types of firms. Checking accounts or demand deposits are liabilities to a bank, as it owes the customers money in these cases. Similarly, loans to customers are assets, receivables. Further, the balance sheet accounts do not have to be subdivided into current and noncurrent accounts.

(continues on p. 617)

E X H I B I T   1 4 - 1

HUNTINGTON BANCSHARES INCORPORATED
Selected Data from 1989 Annual Report
Consolidated Statement of Income (in thousands of dollars)

Year Ended December 31,	1989	1988	1987
Interest and fees on loans	$ 785,721	$667,035	$563,969
Investment securities income			
Taxable interest	173,847	115,368	97,271
Tax-exempt interest	29,190	31,166	34,975
Total investment securities income	203,037	146,534	132,246
Trading account interest	850	1,192	1,584
Other interest income	30,528	25,243	36,999
Total Interest Income	1,020,136	840,004	734,798
Interest on deposits			
Domestic	496,481	380,734	328,675
Foreign	3,210	9,460	6,896
Total interest on deposits	499,691	390,194	335,571
Interest on short-term borrowings	117,169	76,719	55,746
Interest on long-term debt	14,305	15,053	15,292
Total Interest Expense	631,165	481,966	406,609
Net Interest Income	388,971	358,038	328,189
Provision for loan and lease losses	39,895	28,471	77,103
Net Credit Income	349,076	329,567	251,086
Non-interest income			
Service charges on deposit accounts	41,146	37,580	35,717
Credit card fees	23,551	20,837	19,217
Trust services	22,870	21,940	20,246
Mortgage banking income	12,764	7,422	6,365
Capital markets income	4,221	4,526	4,566
Investment securities gains	209	565	588
Other	34,759	21,240	27,242
Total Non-Interest Income	139,520	114,110	113,941
Non-interest expense			
Salaries and employee benefits (Note 13)	163,530	148,504	146,501
Equipment expense (Note 7)	25,276	23,352	21,856
Net occupancy expense (Note 7)	23,357	21,105	19,683
Credit card expense	17,240	14,377	12,663
Printing and supplies	11,441	10,449	9,612
Advertising expense	8,096	6,528	6,815
Other	96,064	93,566	86,643
Total Non-Interest Expense	345,004	317,881	303,773
Income Before Income Tax Expense	143,592	125,796	61,254
Less income tax expense (Note 14)	35,614	27,741	3,855
Net Income	$ 107,978	$ 98,055	$ 57,399
Per Common Share (Note 15)[1]			
Net income:			
Primary	$2.11	$1.93	$1.12
Fully diluted	$2.11	$1.91	$1.11
Cash dividends declared	$ .69	$ .61	$ .56
Average common shares outstanding	51,104,228	50,701,325	50,667,119

See notes to consolidated financial statements.

[1]Restated for stock dividend and stock split.

EXHIBIT 14-1 (continued)

Consolidated Balance Sheet

(in thousands of dollars)

December 31,	1989	1988
Assets		
Cash and due from banks (Note 3)	$ 866,444	$ 861,207
Deposits at interest with banks	20,026	135,751
Investment securities — Market value $2,935,935 and $2,077,002, respectively (Note 4)	2,917,512	2,103,786
Trading account assets	992	29,720
Mortgages held for resale	196,789	47,475
Federal funds sold and securities purchased under resale agreements	119,986	304,347
Loans and leases		
Commercial	2,794,861	2,519,407
Foreign	2,468	6,427
Tax-free	123,796	163,518
Real estate — construction	468,734	493,962
Real estate — mortgage	1,048,854	873,540
Consumer (net of $21,142 and $26,648 unearned discount respectively)	2,398,352	2,057,901
Direct lease financing	278,257	254,282
Total loans and leases	7,115,322	6,369,037
Less allowance for loan and lease losses (Note 6)	83,293	73,053
Net loans and leases	7,032,029	6,295,984
Premises and equipment (Note 7)	179,812	172,669
Customers' acceptance liability	57,566	85,758
Accrued income and other assets	288,606	252,704
Total Assets	$11,679,762	$10,289,401
Liabilities and Stockholders' Equity		
Demand deposits:		
Non-interest bearing	$ 1,412,447	$ 1,454,670
Interest bearing	1,818,368	1,960,564
Savings deposits	945,065	979,772
Time CD's $100,000 and over	1,515,397	1,206,359
Other time deposits	2,879,028	2,099,838
Foreign deposits	19,286	68,060
Total deposits	8,589,591	7,769,263
Short-term borrowings (Note 8)	1,949,525	1,479,973
Bank acceptances outstanding	57,566	85,758
Long-term debt (Note 9)	152,625	163,614
Accrued expenses and other liabilities	209,760	150,185
Total liabilities	10,959,067	9,648,793
Commitments and Contingencies (Notes 10 and 11)		
Stockholders' equity		
Preferred stock — authorized 6,617,808 shares		
Common stock — without par value; authorized 100,000,000 shares; issued and outstanding 51,644,162 shares in 1989 and 45,315,517 shares in 1988	494,578	372,601
Less 426,395 treasury shares in 1989 and 188,189 shares in 1988	(8,585)	(3,582)
Surplus	117,249	117,152
Retained earnings	117,453	154,437
Total stockholders' equity	720,695	640,608
Total Liabilities and Stockholders' Equity	$11,679,762	$10,289,401

See notes to consolidated financial statements.

EXHIBIT 14-1 (continued)

Consolidated Statement of Changes in Stockholders' Equity

(in thousands of dollars or shares)

	Preferred Shares	Preferred Stock	Common Shares	Common Stock	Treasury Shares	Treasury Stock	Surplus	Retained Earnings	Total
Balance—January 1, 1987	382	$7,644	34,580	$305,706	—	—	$113,007	$132,589	$558,946
Net income								57,399	57,399
Cash dividends									
Common ($.56 per share)								(23,046)	(23,046)
$2.25 Preferred								(430)	(430)
Stock options exercised			68	744			86	(59)	771
10% stock dividend			2,498	61,699				(61,815)	(116)
Shares issued through									
dividend reinvestment			86	2,088					2,088
Shares issued for PAYSOP			16	414					414
Redemption of $2.25									
preferred stock	(382)	(7,644)						(3,057)	(10,701)
Treasury shares purchased					(114)	$(2,544)		(33)	(2,577)
Change in valuation allowance									
for marketable equity securities ..								(3,832)	(3,832)
Pre-merger transactions of									
pooled banks			116	148			1,153	(4,704)	(3,403)
Balance—December 31, 1987 ..	—	—	37,364	370,799	(114)	(2,544)	114,246	93,012	575,513
Net income								98,055	98,055
Cash dividends ($.61 per share) ...								(26,556)	(26,556)
Stock options exercised			139	1,529	62	1,325	302	(879)	2,277
Five-for-four stock split			7,583		(63)			(120)	(120)
Treasury shares purchased					(587)	(13,354)			(13,354)
Treasury shares sold:									
Stockholder dividend									
reinvestment plan					116	2,534	(30)	(111)	2,393
Employee stock purchase plan ...					398	8,457	133	(228)	8,362
Change in valuation allowance									
for marketable equity securities ..								(1,863)	(1,863)
Pre-merger transactions of									
pooled banks			230	273			2,501	(6,873)	(4,099)
Balance—December 31, 1988 ..	—	—	45,316	372,601	(188)	(3,582)	117,152	154,437	640,608
Net income								107,978	107,978
Cash dividends ($.69 per share) ...								(30,290)	(30,290)
Stock options exercised				(70)	23	451	(65)	(197)	119
15% stock dividend			5,757	115,722	(10)			(115,845)	(123)
Conversion of 5%									
convertible notes			564	6,298					6,298
Treasury shares purchased					(914)	(18,808)			(18,808)
Treasury shares sold:									
Stockholder dividend									
reinvestment plan					158	3,236	(65)	(120)	3,051
Employee stock purchase plan ...					505	10,118	168	(164)	10,122
Change in valuation allowance									
for marketable equity securities ..								5,853	5,853
Pre-merger transactions of									
pooled banks			7	27			59	(4,199)	(4,113)
Balance—December 31, 1989 ..	—	—	51,644	$494,578	(426)	$(8,585)	$117,249	$117,453	$720,695

See notes to consolidated financial statements.

E X H I B I T   1 4 - 1   (continued)

Consolidated Statement of Cash Flows

(in thousands of dollars)

Year Ended December 31,	1989	1988	1987
Operating Activities			
Net income	$ 107,978	$ 98,055	$ 57,399
Adjustments to reconcile net income to net			
cash provided by operating activities:			
Provision for loan and lease losses	39,895	28,471	77,103
Provision for depreciation and amortization	29,708	23,073	26,268
Provision for deferred income taxes	5,483	8,222	(4,524)
Increase in accrued income receivable	(23,648)	(4,982)	(7,227)
Increase/(decrease) in accrued expenses	47,486	40,316	(5,231)
(Increase)/decrease in trading securities and mortgages held for resale	(120,586)	(60,620)	58,044
Gains on sales of securities	(209)	(565)	(588)
Other	(82)	(217)	308
Net Cash Provided by Operating Activities	86,025	131,753	201,552
Investing Activities			
Proceeds from sales and maturities of investment securities	2,968,447	2,842,185	2,333,228
Purchases of investment securities	(3,784,391)	(2,964,629)	(2,627,479)
Net loan originations and repayments	(782,244)	(691,006)	(383,404)
Purchases of premises and equipment	(25,685)	(26,343)	(23,677)
Net decrease in deposits at interest with banks	115,725	154,988	105,159
Net increase in other real estate and other assets	(22,574)	(11,264)	(11,897)
Other	2,459	496	262
Net Cash Used for Investing Activities	(1,528,263)	(695,573)	(607,808)
Financing Activities			
Net increase in total deposits	832,046	546,522	320,989
Net increase in short-term borrowings	469,552	66,442	428,007
Payment of long-term debt	(5,077)	(2,994)	(4,233)
Net increase/(decrease) in other liabilities	6,635	(8,300)	9,626
Dividends on common stock	(27,362)	(24,283)	(21,074)
Dividends on preferred stock	—	—	(430)
Proceeds from exercise of stock options	119	2,277	771
Sales of treasury stock	10,122	8,362	—
Acquisition of treasury stock	(18,808)	(13,354)	(2,577)
Redemption of preferred stock	—	—	(10,701)
Shares issued through PAYSOP	—	—	414
Pre-merger transactions of pooled banks	(4,113)	(4,099)	(3,403)
Net Cash Provided by Financing Activities	1,263,114	570,573	717,389
Change in Cash and Cash Equivalents	(179,124)	6,753	311,133
Cash and Cash Equivalents at Beginning of Year	1,165,554	1,158,801	847,668
Cash and Cash Equivalents at End of Year	$ 986,430	$1,165,554	$1,158,801

See notes to consolidated financial statements.

EXHIBIT 14-1   (continued)

Consolidated Average Balances and Interest Rates (annual data)

Fully Tax Equivalent Basis[1]
(in millions of dollars)

	1989			1988		
	Average Balance	Interest Income/ Expense	Yield/ Rate	Average Balance	Interest Income/ Expense	Yield/ Rate
Assets						
Deposits at interest with banks — foreign	$ 30	$ 3.0	10.09%	$ 78	$ 6.1	7.89%
Deposits at interest with banks — domestic	26	2.5	9.52	44	3.4	7.60
Investment securities						
U.S. Treasury and Federal agencies	1,608	141.7	8.81	1,037	80.1	7.73
States and political subdivisions	422	42.3	10.01	460	45.6	9.91
Other	396	32.7	8.25	423	36.6	8.66
Total investment securities	2,426	216.7	8.93	1,920	162.3	8.45
Trading account	10	1.0	9.66	17	1.3	7.58
Mortgages held for resale	102	10.1	9.87	39	3.9	9.96
Other short-term investments	163	14.9	9.21	146	11.9	8.12
Macro interest rate swaps						
Loans and Leases						
Commercial	2,676	303.1	11.32	2,466	248.1	10.06
Foreign	4	0.4	11.72	49	4.1	8.33
Tax-free	150	17.6	11.76	172	19.8	11.56
Real estate — construction	482	54.6	11.32	459	46.0	10.02
Real estate — mortgage	949	100.8	10.62	712	74.2	10.43
Consumer	2,227	274.6	12.33	2,122	245.3	11.56
Direct lease financing	267	26.7	10.00	227	22.4	9.84
Total loans and leases	6,755	777.8	11.51	6,207	659.9	10.63
Allowance for loan and lease losses/ loan and lease fees	77	15.0		92	14.8	
Net loans and leases	6,678	792.8	11.87	6,115	674.7	11.03
Total earning assets	9,512	$1,041.0	10.94%	8,451	$863.6	10.22%
All other assets	1,133			1,071		
Total Assets	$10,568			$9,430		
Liabilities and Stockholders' Equity						
Demand deposits:						
Non-interest bearing	$ 1,232			$1,203		
Interest bearing	1,749	$ 96.2	5.50%	1,917	$ 99.7	5.20%
Savings deposits	998	50.6	5.07	1,012	51.7	5.10
Time CD's $100,000 and over	1,530	138.7	9.06	1,160	88.0	7.59
Foreign deposits	34	3.2	9.45	127	9.5	7.46
Other time deposits	2,566	211.0	8.22	1,964	141.3	7.20
Total deposits	8,109	499.7	7.27	7,383	390.2	6.31
Short-term borrowings	1,342	117.3	8.73	1,083	76.8	7.09
Long-term debt	158	14.5	9.22	164	15.3	9.34
Interest bearing liabilities	8,377	$ 631.5	7.54%	7,427	$482.3	6.49%
All other liabilities	276			193		
Stockholders' equity	683			607		
Total Liabilities and Stockholders' Equity	$10,568			$9,430		
Net interest rate spread			3.40%			3.73%
Impact of non-interest bearing funds on margin			.90%			.78%
Net Interest Income/Margin		$ 409.5	4.30%		$381.3	4.51%

[1]Fully tax equivalent yields are calculated assuming a 34% tax rate in 1989 and 1988, 40% in 1987, and 46% in years 1984 through 1986.
   Average loan balances include non-accruing loans. Loan income includes cash received on non-accruing loans.

E X H I B I T   1 4 - 1   (continued)

Selected Notes

2. Acquisitions

On December 29, 1989, Huntington acquired First Banc Securities, Inc., a $550 million bank holding company in Morgantown, West Virginia, in exchange for 4,939,413 shares of Huntington's common stock. Also, on December 29, 1989, Huntington acquired First Macomb Bancorp, Inc., a $400 million bank holding company in Mt. Clemens, Michigan, in exchange for 2,498,454 shares of Huntington's common stock.

These acquisitions were accounted for as poolings-of-interests. The 1989 results of operations included $11 million of net income of the acquired banks. All periods presented have been restated to include these companies. The results of operations for Huntington, both pre-acquisition and combined, for 1988 and 1987 follow:

(in thousands of dollars)	Year Ended December 31, 1988		1987	
	Previously Reported	Restated	Previously Reported	Restated
Interest Income	$774,428	$840,004	$676,229	$734,798
Net Interest Income	327,570	358,038	301,324	328,189
Net Income	87,552	98,055	47,827	57,399

On December 28, 1989, The Huntington Mortgage Company purchased the majority of the assets of Farragut Mortgage Company. The assets included servicing rights on $600 million in residential mortgage loans and two residential mortgage origination offices located in Waltham, Massachusetts and Warwick, Rhode Island. This transaction had no significant impact on the consolidated financial statements.

On November 30, 1987, Huntington acquired United Midwest Bancorporation, Ltd., a $400 million bank holding company in Troy, Michigan, in exchange for 2,640,000 shares of Huntington's common stock in a transaction accounted for as a pooling-of-interests.

3. Restrictions on Cash and Due From Banks

The Bank subsidiaries of Huntington are required to maintain reserve balances with the Federal Reserve Bank. During 1989 the average reserve balances of the subsidiaries were $114,997,000.

4. Investment Securities

Investment portfolio—Book and Market Values at December 31, 1989 and 1988 were:

(in thousands of dollars)	1989		1988	
	Book	Market	Book	Market
U.S Treasury and Agencies	$2,344,016	$2,348,584	$1,169,152	$1,142,463
States and Political Subdivisions	406,542	421,693	442,582	447,447
Marketable Equity Securities	7,583	7,897	31,128	31,128
Other	159,371	157,761	460,924	455,964
Total Investment Securities	$2,917,512	$2,935,935	$2,103,786	$2,077,002

Securities pledged to secure public or trust deposits and for other purposes were $838,627,000 and $1,147,135,000 at December 31, 1989 and 1988, respectively.

5. Related Party Loans

The Huntington and its subsidiaries have granted loans to its officers and directors and to their associates. The aggregate dollar amount of these loans was $69,161,000 and $82,908,000 at December 31, 1989 and 1988, respectively. During 1989, $43,078,000 of new loans were made, and repayments totalled $56,825,000. Included in the aggregate amount outstanding at December 31, 1989 were loans to two directors or their related interests which aggregated $24,755,000 and $18,866,000, respectively. Such loans were made in the ordinary course of business at the banking subsidiaries' normal credit terms, including interest rate and collateralization, and do not represent more than normal risk of collection.

6. Allowance for Loan and Lease Losses

A summary of the transactions in the allowance for loan and lease losses for the three years ended December 31 follows:

(in thousands of dollars)	1989	1988	1987
Balance, beginning of year	$73,053	$96,440	$64,161
Allowance of assets acquired (sold)	353	916	(67)
Provision for loan and lease losses	39,895	28,471	77,103
Recoveries credited	9,116	11,907	8,717
Losses charged	(39,124)	(64,681)	(53,474)
Balance, end of year	$83,293	$73,053	$96,440

The provision for loan and lease losses in 1987 included $46,780,000 related to LDC loans.

7. Premises and Equipment

At December 31, 1989 and 1988, premises and equipment were comprised of the following:

(in thousands of dollars)	1989	1988
Land	$ 24,366	$ 24,055
Buildings	124,468	96,205
Leasehold improvements	43,888	50,860
Buildings under capital leases	—	6,657
Furniture and fixtures	154,543	142,022
Total premises and equipment	347,265	319,799
Less accumulated depreciation and amortization*	167,453	147,130
Net premises and equipment	$179,812	$172,669

*Lease amortization is included in depreciation expense.

Depreciation and amortization charged to expense and rentals credited to income were as follows:

(in thousands of dollars)	1989	1988	1987
Occupancy expense	$ 6,692	$ 6,363	$ 6,758
Equipment expense	9,848	8,282	9,393
Depreciation charged	$16,540	$14,645	$16,151
Rental income credited to occupancy expense	$18,107	$22,856	$22,946

EXHIBIT 14-1 (continued)

8. Short-Term Borrowings

At December 31, 1989 and 1988, short-term borrowings were comprised of the following:

(in thousands of dollars)	1989	1988
Federal funds purchased and securities sold under agreements to repurchase	$1,700,854	$1,052,014
Commercial paper*	174,891	155,895
Other	73,780	272,064
Total short-term borrowings	$1,949,525	$1,479,973

*Issued by Huntington Bancshares Financial Corporation, a non-bank subsidiary with principal and interest guaranteed by Huntington Bancshares Incorporated (Parent Company).

During 1989, Huntington increased its ability to borrow under lines of credit from $175,000,000 to $200,000,000 to support commercial paper borrowings or other short-term working capital needs. Under the terms of agreement, a quarterly fee must be paid and there are no compensating balances required. The line is cancellable, by Huntington, upon written notice and terminates September 30, 1992. The amount outstanding at December 31, 1989 was $60,000,000. There were no borrowings under the lines of credit in 1988.

11. Commitments and Contingent Liabilities

In the normal course of business, various commitments and contingent liabilities are outstanding which are not included in the financial statements. Management does not anticipate any material losses as a result of these transactions. A summary of significant commitments and contingent liabilities at December 31 follows:

(in thousands)	1989	1988
Commitments to extend credit	$1,995,128	$2,090,488
Standby letters of credit	308,640	324,872
Commercial letters of credit	146,954	71,375
Commitments to purchase foreign currencies	17,752	36,176

The standby letters of credit primarily support performance bonds and Industrial Revenue Bonds. Maturities of the financial guarantees (standby letters of credit) vary, with approximately three-fourths of the portfolio maturing in less than five years.

In the ordinary course of business, there are various legal proceedings pending against Huntington and its subsidiaries. Management considers that the aggregate liabilities, if any, arising from such actions would not have a material adverse effect on the consolidated financial position of Huntington.

E X H I B I T   1 4 - 1   (continued)

Management's Discussion and Analysis of Financial Condition and Results of Operations
Selected Tables

Table 6

Investment Portfolio	December 31,		
(in thousands of dollars)	1989	1988	1987
U.S. Treasury and Federal agencies	$2,344,016	$1,169,152	$1,184,259
States and political subdivisions	406,542	442,582	498,606
Other	166,954	492,052	301,664
Total	$2,917,512	$2,103,786	$1,984,529

Book and market values by maturity at December 31, 1989			
(in thousands of dollars)	Book	Market	Yield[1]
U.S. Treasury			
Under 1 year	$ 106,015	$ 106,419	8.67%
1-5 years	443,554	446,389	8.39
6-10 years	996	1,011	8.04
Over 10 years	403	302	8.03
Total	550,968	554,121	
Federal agencies			
Mortgage-backed securities			
1-5 years	402,403	403,384	9.38
6-10 years	14,964	14,828	8.90
Over 10 years	781,621	780,526	9.30
Total	1,198,988	1,198,738	
Other agencies			
Under 1 year	96,165	96,403	8.70
1-5 years	487,245	488,724	8.46
6-10 years	357	348	8.24
Over 10 years	10,293	10,250	9.11
Total	594,060	595,725	
Total U.S. Treasury and Federal agencies	2,344,016	2,348,584	
States and political subdivisions			
Under 1 year	41,970	42,172	9.08
1-5 years	231,348	240,088	10.43
6-10 years	123,474	130,046	10.38
Over 10 years	9,750	9,387	8.86
Total	406,542	421,693	
Other			
Under 1 year	12,223	12,200	7.77
1-5 years	111,743	111,195	9.21
6-10 years	12,166	12,014	8.97
Over 10 years	23,239	22,352	4.04
Marketable equity securities	7,583	7,897	14.33
Total	166,954	165,658	
Total Investment Securities	$2,917,512	$2,935,935	

[1]Average yields are calculated via the standard bond formula on a fully tax equivalent basis, assuming a 34% tax rate.

E X H I B I T 1 4 - 1   (continued)

Table 8

Loan and Lease Portfolio Composition	Year Ended December 31,				
(in millions of dollars)	1989	1988	1987	1986	1985
Domestic Loans					
Commercial	$2,795	$2,519	$2,279	$2,271	$1,972
Tax-free	124	164	184	223	202
Real estate — construction	469	494	382	251	249
Real estate — mortgage	1,049	874	648	581	564
Consumer	2,398	2,058	1,945	1,725	1,298
Direct lease financing	278	254	204	197	131
Total domestic loans and leases	7,113	6,363	5,642	5,248	4,416
Foreign Loans, primarily governments and official institutions	2	6	76	101	102
Total loans and leases	$7,115	$6,369	$5,718	$5,349	$4,518

NOTE: There are no loans outstanding which would be considered as a concentration of lending in any particular industry or group of industries.

Table 9

Maturity Schedule of Selected Loans				
(in thousands of dollars)	December 31, 1989			
	Within One Year	After One But Within Five Years	After Five Years	Total
Commercial	$1,767,319	$742,948	$284,594	$2,794,861
Tax-free	34,213	32,969	56,614	123,796
Real estate — construction ...	263,784	204,950	—	468,734
Foreign	—	2,468	—	2,468
Total	$2,065,316	$983,335	$341,208	$3,389,859
Variable interest rates		$750,957	$168,878	
Fixed interest rates		$232,378	$172,330	

E X H I B I T   1 4 - 1   (continued)

Table 10

Summary of Allowance for Loan and Lease Losses and Selected Statistics

(in thousands of dollars)	1989	1988	1987	1986	1985	1984
Balance, beginning of period	$73,053	$96,440	$64,161	$54,758	$45,177	$36,438
Loan and lease losses:						
Commercial	(11,924)	(16,872)	(18,046)	(13,944)	(16,013)	(16,081)
Real estate — construction	(4,077)	(281)	—	(13)	—	(33)
Real estate — mortgage	(657)	(144)	(654)	(2,388)	(448)	(654)
Consumer	(21,418)	(17,246)	(14,616)	(10,783)	(7,522)	(5,752)
Direct lease financing	(1,048)	(703)	(777)	(781)	(1,073)	(981)
LDC	—	(29,435)	(19,381)	(38)	(763)	(490)
Total loan and lease losses	(39,124)	(64,681)	(53,474)	(27,947)	(25,819)	(23,991)
Recoveries:						
Commercial	3,163	3,345	4,848	7,133	5,853	2,420
Real estate — construction	—	—	—	—	—	246
Real estate — mortgage	93	223	67	154	166	13
Consumer	4,897	4,022	3,254	2,829	2,257	2,081
Direct lease financing	214	753	263	173	125	134
LDC	749	3,564	285	95	215	194
Total recoveries	9,116	11,907	8,717	10,384	8,616	5,088
Net loan and lease losses	(30,008)	(52,774)	(44,757)	(17,563)	(17,203)	(18,903)
Provision for loan and lease losses:						
Domestic	39,895	28,471	30,323	25,363	26,316	24,292
LDC	—	—	46,780	(57)	548	3,221
Total provision	39,895	28,471	77,103	25,306	26,864	27,513
Allowance of domestic assets acquired (sold)	353	916	(67)	1,660	(80)	129
Balance, end of period	$83,293	$73,053	$96,440	$64,161	$54,758	$45,177
As a % of average total loans and leases						
Net loan and lease losses[1]	.44%	.85%	.82%	.36%	.40%	.51%
Provision for loan and lease losses	.59%	.46%	1.41%	.51%	.62%	.74%
Allowance for loan and lease losses as a %						
of total loans and leases (end of period)[1]	1.17%	1.15%	1.69%	1.20%	1.21%	1.11%
Net loan and lease loss coverage[2]	6.11x	2.92x	3.09x	6.79x	6.34x	4.95x

[1]Net LDC loan and lease losses as a percentage of average LDC loans were 66.28% and 22.07% in 1988 and 1987, respectively. Excluding LDC, loan and lease losses as a percentage of average loans were .44% and .48% in 1988 and 1987. The LDC allowance as a percentage of total LDC loans was 48.18% in 1987. Excluding LDC, the allowance as a percentage of loans was 1.13%. There were no LDC loans outstanding at December 31, 1988 or 1989.

[2]Income before taxes and the provision for loan and lease losses to net loan and lease losses.

Table 12

Analysis of Non-Interest Income

(in thousands of dollars)	Year Ended December 31,			Percentage Increase (Decrease)	
	1989	1988	1987	1989/88	1988/87
Service charges on deposit accounts	$ 41,146	$ 37,580	$ 35,717	9.5%	5.2%
Credit card fees	23,551	20,837	19,217	13.0	8.4
Trust services	22,870	21,940	20,246	4.2	8.4
Mortgage banking income	12,764	7,422	6,365	72.0	16.6
Capital markets income	4,221	4,526	4,566	(6.7)	(0.9)
Investment securities gains	209	565	588	(63.0)	(3.9)
Other	34,759	21,240	27,242	63.6	(22.0)
Total Non-Interest Income	$139,520	$114,110	$113,941	22.3%	0.1%

Table 13

Analysis of Non-Interest Expense

(in thousands of dollars)	Year Ended December 31,			Percentage Increase (Decrease)	
	1989	1988	1987	1989/88	1988/87
Salaries	$133,501	$121,660	$118,685	9.7%	2.5%
Employee benefits	30,029	26,844	27,816	11.9	(3.5)
Total salaries and employee benefits	163,530	148,504	146,501	10.1	1.4
Equipment expense	25,276	23,352	21,856	8.2	6.8
Net occupancy expense	23,357	21,105	19,683	10.7	7.2
Credit card expense	17,240	14,377	12,663	19.9	13.5
Printing and supplies	11,441	10,449	9,612	9.5	8.7
Advertising expense	8,096	6,528	6,815	24.0	(4.2)
Other	96,064	93,566	86,643	2.7	8.0
Total Non-Interest Expense	$345,004	$317,881	$303,773	8.5%	4.6%

Table 14

Non-Performing Assets and Past Due Loans

(in thousands of dollars)	December 31,					
	1989	1988	1987	1986	1985	1984
Non-accrual loans:						
Domestic	$71,756	$60,914	$40,117	$42,165	$39,855	$48,800
Foreign	—	—	11,425	10,745	11,238	8,720
Total non-accrual loans	71,756	60,914	51,542	52,910	51,093	57,520
Renegotiated loans:						
Domestic	2,370	1,494	814	1,205	9,336	10,077
Foreign	—	—	—	49	539	557
Total renegotiated loans	2,370	1,494	814	1,254	9,875	10,634
Other real estate	11,583	5,428	6,273	6,079	9,068	10,737
Total non-performing assets	$85,709	$67,836	$58,629	$60,243	$70,036	$78,891
Non-performing assets to total loans and leases	1.20%	1.07%	1.03%	1.13%	1.55%	1.94%
Accruing loans past due 90 days or more:						
Domestic	$26,221	$35,114	$29,948	$35,081	$30,634	$28,891
Foreign	—	—	—	—	2,254	450
Total past due loans	$26,221	$35,114	$29,948	$35,081	$32,888	$29,341
Accruing loans past due 90 days or more to total loans and leases	.37%	.55%	.52%	.66%	.73%	.72%

NOTE: For 1989, the amount of interest income which would have been recorded under the original terms for domestic loans classified as non-accrual or renegotiated was $7.5 million. Amounts actually collected and recorded as interest income for these loans totalled $426,000, while amounts collected and recorded as interest income for previously non-accrual foreign loans was $14,000.

Representative assets of a bank may include cash on hand or due from other banks, investment securities, loans, bank premises, and equipment. Closely review the disclosure of assets of a bank. This review may indicate risk or opportunity you were not aware of. For example, a review of the assets may indicate that the bank has a substantial risk if interest rates increase. The general rule is that for 20-year fixed obligations, there is a gain or loss of 8% of principal when interest rates change by 1%. Thus, an investment of $100,000,000 in 20-year bonds would lose approximately $32,000,000 in principal if interest rates increased by 4%. A similar example would be a bank that holds long-term fixed-rate mortgages. The value of these mortgages could decline substantially if interest rates increased. Many bank annual reports do not disclose the amount of fixed-rate mortgages.

Review the disclosure of the market value versus the book value of investments. This review may indicate that investments have a market value substantially above or below the book amount.

Footnote 4 in the Huntington Bancshares annual report discloses investment securities. It indicates that the market value of investment securities was $18,423,000 above book at December 31, 1989. (See Footnote 4, Exhibit 14-1.)

In recent years, Less Developed Country (LDC) loans have become a national issue. In general, LDC loans are perceived as being more risky than domestic loans. On the consolidated balance sheet, Huntington Bancshares discloses foreign loans of $2,468,000 at December 31, 1989. This represented only a small fraction of its loans and leases at December 31, 1989. In the Management's Discussion and Analysis, the following is disclosed: "During 1987 and 1988, Huntington successfully eliminated its LDC credit exposure through an active loan sale program and an aggressive charge-off policy."

As part of the review of assets, review the footnote that describes related party loans. Observe the materiality of related party loans and the trend of these loans. Huntington Bancshares discloses related party loans totaling $69,161,000 at December 31, 1989. This was a significant decrease from the $82,908,000 in related party loans at December 31, 1988.

Review the disclosure of allowance for loan losses. It may indicate a significant change and/or significant losses charged. Huntington Bancshares discloses allowance for loan and lease losses in Footnote 6. There was a significant increase in the allowance for loan and lease losses account at the end of 1989. (See Footnote 6, Exhibit 14-1.)

Review the footnotes for disclosure of nonperforming assets. In general, nonperforming assets are those for which the bank is not receiving income or is receiving reduced income. Examples of nonperforming assets are nonaccrual loans, renegotiated loans, and other real estate. Nonaccrual loans are loans that are significantly behind in payments, so that the bank has stopped accruing interest income on these loans. Renegotiated loans are loans that the bank has renegotiated with a customer because the customer has had trouble meeting the terms of the original loan. For example, a loan in the amount of $10,000,000 at 14% interest may come due. The customer who cannot pay may be allowed to renegotiate the loan with the bank, reducing the principal to $8,000,000 and the interest rate to

10% and gaining a five-year extension. Under current generally accepted accounting principles, no immediate loss will be taken by the bank on the renegotiated loan if the projected cash flow under the renegotiated loan will cover the current book value of the loan. In the example, the projected cash flow comes to $12,000,000 ($8,000,000 in principal and $800,000 in interest for each year for five years). Since this covers the current book figure of $10,000,000, no immediate loss will be recognized. In addition to other factors, banks should consider renegotiated loans when they adjust the loan loss reserve.

Other real estate usually consists of real estate the bank has taken when it foreclosed on a loan. For example, the bank may have made a loan to a company for a hotel and have accepted a mortgage on the hotel as collateral. If the bank must foreclose on the loan, it may take possession of the hotel. The bank would want to sell the hotel, but it may be necessary for the bank to hold and operate the hotel for a relatively long period of time before a buyer can be found.

The amount and trend of nonperforming assets should be observed closely. This can be an early indication of troubles to come. For example, a significant increase in nonperforming assets late in the year may have had an insignificant effect on the past year's profits, but it could indicate a significant negative influence on the future year's profits.

Huntington Bancshares discloses nonperforming assets in its 1989 annual report in Management's Discussion and Analysis. The disclosure indicates that nonperforming assets significantly increased at the end of 1989 in comparison with prior years. The increase in nonperforming assets should be monitored.

Typical liabilities of a bank include savings, time, and demand deposits; loan obligations; and long-term debt. Closely review the disclosure of liabilities for favorable or unfavorable trends. For example, a decreasing amount in savings deposits would indicate that the bank is losing one of its cheapest sources of funds.

As part of the review of liabilities, look for a footnote that describes commitments and contingent liabilities. This footnote may reveal significant additional commitments and contingent liabilities. Footnote 11 of Huntington Bancshares discloses that there were significant commitments to extend credit, standby letters of credit, and commercial letters of credit. It indicates that "management does not anticipate any material losses as a result of these transactions."

Some banks provide a very detailed disclosure of their assets and liabilities. Other banks provide only general disclosure. The quality of review that can be performed can be no better than the disclosure.

The stockholders' equity of a bank is similar to that of other types of firms, except that the total stockholders' equity is usually very low in relation to total assets. A general guide for many years was that a bank should have stockholders' equity of approximately 10% of total assets, but very few banks currently have that much stockholders' equity. In comparison with the industry, stockholders' equity of 6% to 7% would probably be considered favorable. In general, the lower the proportion of stockholders' equity in relation to total assets, the greater the risk of failure. There have been proposals to require banks to increase their stockholders' equity in relation to total assets. This would probably improve the safety of the bank, but the bank would perhaps be less profitable because of the additional capital requirement.

As part of the review of stockholders' equity, review the statement of stockholders' equity and footnotes that relate to stockholders' equity for any significant changes. This is the case with Huntington Bancshares, as significant shares were issued for a stock dividend and for conversion of convertible notes.

The current approach by bank regulators is not only to view the adequacy of stockholders' equity in relation to total assets, but also to view capital in relation to risk-adjusted assets. New guidelines establishing minimum standards for risk-based capital were to be implemented in 1992. Although it is not feasible to calculate risk-based capital ratios from information in the annual report, Huntington does state in Management's Discussion and Analysis that "preliminary estimates show Huntington's current capital position to be well in excess of the adjusted capital requirements."

Income Statement

The principal revenue source is usually interest income from loans, deposits, and investment securities. The principal expense is usually interest expense on deposits and other debt. The difference between interest income and interest expense is termed *net interest income* or *interest margin.*

The interest margin is usually very important to the profitability of the bank. Usually, falling interest rates are positive for a bank's interest margin, because the bank will be able to reduce the interest rate that it is paying for deposits faster than the average rate of return earned on loans and investments. Increasing interest rates are usually negative for a bank's interest margin, because the bank will need to increase the interest rate on deposits, which is usually done at a faster rate than the adjustment of rates on loans and investments.

Bank income statements include a separate section for other income. Typical other income includes trust department fees, service charges on deposit accounts, trading account profits (losses), and securities transactions.

The importance of other income has substantially increased for banks. For example, service charges have increased in importance in recent years, as many banks have turned toward setting service charges at a level to make the service profitable. Some banks have substantial service charge income from providing computer services for other banks and financial institutions.

Noninterest income increased substantially in 1989 for Huntington Bancshares. Two areas with significant increases were service charges on deposit accounts and mortgage banking income.

Expenses other than interest expense include the provision for loan losses, salaries and employer benefits, and occupancy costs. Investors should pay close attention to the provision for loan losses. This expense is usually listed separately from other noninterest expense. An increase in the loan loss provision could be an indication of a problem with asset quality.

Earnings per share must meet the reporting requirements of APB No. 15. For analysis purposes, fully diluted earnings per share would give a conservative and consistent view of earnings per share.

Ratios for Banks

Because of the vastly different accounts and statement formats, few of the traditional ratios are appropriate for banks. Exceptions include return on assets, return on equity, and most of the investment-related ratios. In the following sections are presented ratios that are meaningful in bank analysis, but this is not a comprehensive treatment. The Bank Administration Institute, in its annual *Index of Bank Performance*, includes forty-three ratios and growth statistics. The investment firm of Keefe, Bruyette & Woods, Inc., in its *Bankbook Report on Performance*, lists twenty-one financial ratios. Both are excellent sources of industry averages for banks.

Earning Assets to Total Assets

Earning assets includes loans, leases, investment securities, and money market assets; it excludes cash and nonearning deposits plus fixed assets. This ratio shows how well bank management is putting bank assets to work; high-performance banks have a high ratio. Banks typically present asset data on an average annual basis, but this is not always possible based on the annual report disclosure. Huntington Bancshares provides a schedule of average balances in its annual report. This schedule is used for average balance sheet balances; average earning assets and average total assets are used in computing earning assets to total assets. The ratio of earning assets to total assets is computed for Huntington Bancshares in Exhibit 14-2. Note that this ratio increased slightly between 1988 and 1989.

Return on Earning Assets

Return on earning assets is a profitability measure, to be viewed in conjunction with return on assets and return on equity. It is computed by dividing income before securities transactions by average earning assets. This ratio is computed for

EXHIBIT   1 4 - 2

HUNTINGTON BANCSHARES
Earning Assets to Total Assets
1989 and 1988

	1989	1988
	(in millions of dollars)	
Average earning assets	$9,512	$8,451
Average total assets	$10,568	$9,430
Earning assets to total assets	90.01%	89.62%

EXHIBIT 14-3

HUNTINGTON BANCSHARES
Return on Earning Assets
For the Years Ended December 31, 1989 and 1988

	1989	1988
	(in thousands of dollars)	
Income before securities transactions	$ 107,840	$ 97,682
Average earning assets	$9,512,000	$8,451,000
Return on earning assets	1.13%	1.16%

Huntington Bancshares in Exhibit 14-3; it decreased slightly in 1989 to 1.13%, from 1.16% in 1988.

Interest Margin to Average Earning Assets

This is a key determinant of bank profitability, for it provides an indication of management's ability to control the spread between interest income and interest expense. This ratio is computed for Huntington Bancshares in Exhibit 14-4, indicating a decline in profitability.

Loan Loss Coverage Ratio

The loan loss coverage ratio helps determine the asset quality and level of protection of loans. It is computed by dividing pretax income (before security transactions) plus provision for loan losses by net charge-offs. This ratio is computed for Huntington Bancshares in Exhibit 14-5. Note that this ratio increased substantially in 1989. This was caused by higher earnings for coverage and fewer charge-offs.

EXHIBIT 14-4

HUNTINGTON BANCSHARES
Interest Margin to Average Earning Assets
For the Years Ended December 31, 1989 and 1988

	1989	1988
	(in thousands of dollars)	
Interest margin	$ 409,500	$ 381,300
Average earning assets	$9,512,000	$8,451,000
Interest margin to average earning assets	4.30%	4.51%

E X H I B I T   1 4 - 5

HUNTINGTON BANCSHARES
Loan Loss Coverage Ratio
For the Years Ended December 31, 1989 and 1988

	1989	1988
	(in thousands of dollars)	
Pretax income (before security transactions)	$143,383	$125,231
Provision for loan losses	39,895	28,471
	$183,278	$153,702
Net charge-offs	$ 30,008	$ 52,774
Loan loss coverage ratio	6.11 times	2.91 times

Equity Capital to Total Assets

This ratio is also called *funds to total assets*. It is a measure of the extent of equity ownership in the bank. This ownership provides the cushion against the risk of using debt and leverage. This ratio, computed by using average figures, is presented in Exhibit 14-6 for Huntington Bancshares; it was approximately the same for 1988 and 1989.

Deposits Times Capital

The ratio deposits times capital is of concern to both depositors and stockholders. To some extent, it is a type of debt/equity ratio. More capital implies a greater margin of safety, whereas more deposits gives a prospect of higher return to shareholders, since more money is available for investment purposes. This ratio is also based on average figures; it is computed for Huntington Bancshares in Exhibit 14-7. Deposits to capital decreased slightly in 1989. This ratio shows how high the debt position is for a typical bank.

E X H I B I T   1 4 - 6

HUNTINGTON BANCSHARES
Equity Capital to Total Assets
For the Years Ended December 31, 1989 and 1988

	1989	1988
	(in millions)	
Average equity	$ 683	$ 607
Average total assets	$10,568	$9,430
Equity capital to total assets	6.46%	6.44%

EXHIBIT 14-7

HUNTINGTON BANCSHARES
Deposits Times Capital
For the Years Ended December 31, 1989 and 1988

	1989	1988
	(in millions)	
Total average deposits	$8,109	$7,383
Average stockholders' equity	$ 683	$ 607
Deposits times capital	11.87 times	12.16 times

Loans to Deposits

Loans to total deposits is a type of asset to liability ratio. Loans make up a large portion of the bank's assets, and its principal obligations are the deposits that can be withdrawn on request—within time limitations. This is a type of debt coverage ratio, and it measures the position of the bank with regard to taking risks. This ratio is computed for Huntington Bancshares in Exhibit 14-8 (also based on averages). Loans to deposits decreased slightly in 1989, indicating a slight decrease in risk from a debt standpoint.

ELECTRIC UTILITIES

Electric utilities render a service that is not duplicated and one on which the public depends. Electric utilities are basically monopolies subject to government regulation, including strict rate regulation. In general, the comments in this book that relate to electric utilities also apply to other utilities, such as gas utilities.

Services of electric utilities are consumed in the home or at the business prem-

EXHIBIT 14-8

HUNTINGTON BANCSHARES
Loans to Deposits
For the Years Ended December 31, 1989 and 1988

	1989	1988
	(in millions)	
Average total loans	$6,755	$6,207
Average deposits	$8,109	$7,383
Loans to deposits	83.30%	84.07%

ises. Substitute services are generally not available, and rates are determined primarily by regulatory agencies rather than by competition. Further, service areas are small and localized.

Uniformity of accounting is prescribed by the Federal Energy Regulatory Commission for interstate electric and gas companies and by the Federal Communications Commission for telephone and telegraph companies, as well as by state regulatory agencies. Balance sheet presentation differs mainly in the order in which accounts are presented.

Plant and equipment are the first assets listed, followed by investments and other assets, current assets, and deferred debits. Under liabilities and equity, the first section is capitalization, followed by current liabilities, deferred credits, and other. The capitalization section usually includes all sources of long-term capital, such as common stock, preferred stock, and long-term debt.

The income statement is set up by operating revenues, less operating expenses to arrive at net operating income. Net operating income is adjusted by other income (deductions) to arrive at income before interest charges. Interest charges are then deducted to arrive at net income. Electric utilities deduct on the face of the income statement dividend requirements on preferred and preference stock from net income to arrive at earnings available for common stock.

A substantial part of the 1989 annual report of the Public Service Company of Colorado is presented in Exhibit 14-9. Review this exhibit to become familiar with the form of an electric utility income statement and balance sheet.

Inventories are not a problem for electric utilities. Traditionally, receivables were not a problem, because the services are essential and could be cut off for nonpayment, and because a prepayment is often required of the customer. In recent years, receivables have been a problem for some electric utilities, because some utility commissions have ruled that services could not be cut off during the winter.

A few accounts on the financial statements of an electric utility are particularly important to the understanding of the statements. On the balance sheet, an important account is construction work in progress. Practically all utilities have such an account.

Exhibit 14-9 discloses that Public Service Company of Colorado had construction work in progress of $109,245,000 and $95,685,000 in 1989 and 1988, respectively. Electric utilities that have substantial construction work in progress are usually viewed as being more risky investments than electric utilities that do not. Most utility commissions allow no construction work in progress or only a small amount in the rate base. Therefore, the utility rates essentially do not reflect construction work in progress. It is the utility's intent to have this additional property and plant considered in the rate base when the construction work is completed.

It is possible that the utility commission will not allow all of this property and plant in the rate base. The utility commission may rule that part of the cost was caused by inefficiency and disallow this cost. The commission may also disallow part of the cost on the grounds that the utility used bad judgment and provided for excess capacity. Costs disallowed are in effect charged to the stockholders, as future income will not include a return on disallowed cost. In the long run, everybody

E X H I B I T   1 4 - 9

PUBLIC SERVICE COMPANY OF COLORADO AND SUBSIDIARIES
Electric Utility Company
Selected Financial Statement Data
Consolidated Balance Sheet

December 31, 1989 and 1988 (Thousands of Dollars)

Assets	1989	1988
Property, Plant and Equipment, at cost:		
Electric	**$2,579,761**	$2,497,091
Gas	**717,689**	686,805
Steam and other	**74,403**	69,406
Common to all departments	**262,448**	256,873
Construction in progress	**109,245**	95,658
	3,743,546	3,605,833
Less accumulated provision for depreciation	**1,339,278**	1,258,123
	2,404,268	2,347,710
Fort St. Vrain related property (Note 2)	**81,737**	96,469
Less accumulated provision for depreciation	**17,862**	30,769
	63,875	65,700
Total Property, Plant and Equipment	**2,468,143**	2,413,410
Investments, at cost	**92,841**	101,800
Current Assets:		
Cash	**6,850**	4,819
Temporary cash investments	**46,440**	38,574
Accounts receivable, less provision for uncollectible accounts (1989—$5,235; 1988—$6,360)	**136,223**	146,644
Accrued unbilled revenues (Note 1)	**64,164**	56,442
Recoverable purchased gas and electric energy costs—net (Note 1)	**55,516**	54,286
Fuel inventory, at average cost	**34,368**	27,758
Materials and supplies, at average cost	**76,937**	69,510
Gas in underground storage, at cost (LIFO)	**16,092**	14,681
Prepaid expenses	**6,757**	7,586
Other	**269**	550
Total Current Assets	**443,616**	420,850
Deferred Charges:		
Debt expense (being amortized)	**7,407**	8,087
Recoverable nuclear plant and decommissioning costs (Note 2)	**11,725**	18,425
Other	**21,205**	21,870
	40,337	48,382
Total Assets	**$3,044,937**	$2,984,442

See accompanying notes.

E X H I B I T   1 4 - 9   (continued)

December 31, 1989 and 1988 (Thousands of Dollars)

Capital and Liabilities	1989	1988
Common Equity:		
Common stock (Note 4)	$ 718,296	$ 709,726
Retained earnings	186,284	155,232
	904,580	864,958
Preferred Stock (Note 4):		
Not subject to mandatory redemption	140,008	140,008
Subject to mandatory redemption at par	48,944	51,520
Long-Term Debt (Note 5)	904,129	933,020
	1,997,661	1,989,506
Noncurrent Liabilities:		
Defueling and decommissioning liability (Note 2)	85,100	148,366
Accrued pension liability (Note 9)	—	7,884
	85,100	156,250
Current Liabilities:		
Notes payable and commercial paper (Note 6)	153,208	130,368
Long-term debt due within one year	30,217	29,005
Preferred stock subject to mandatory redemption		
within one year (Note 4)	2,576	2,576
Accounts payable	164,434	142,825
Dividends payable	29,531	29,407
Customers' deposits	14,576	13,612
Accrued taxes	61,462	55,980
Accrued interest	20,185	20,778
Gas refund liability	3,890	10,412
Current portion of defueling and		
decommissioning liability (Note 2)	57,205	13,488
Other	43,043	45,093
Total Current Liabilities	580,327	493,544
Deferred Credits:		
Customers' advances for construction	35,816	32,162
Investment tax credit (being amortized over the productive		
lives of the related property)	144,598	149,865
Accumulated deferred income taxes (Note 10)	191,072	154,052
Other	10,363	9,063
	381,849	345,142
Commitments and Contingencies (Notes 2 and 8)		
Total Capital and Liabilities	$3,044,937	$2,984,442

E X H I B I T   1 4 - 9   (continued)

Consolidated Statement of Income

Years ended December 31, 1989, 1988 and 1987 (Thousands of Dollars Except Per Share Data)

	1989	1988	1987
Operating Revenues:			
Electric	**$1,139,471**	$1,115,964	$1,075,753
Gas	**577,282**	546,342	563,307
Other	**23,913**	22,984	18,375
	1,740,666	1,685,290	1,657,435
Operating Expenses:			
Fuel used in generation	**165,801**	165,709	162,759
Purchased power	**295,025**	255,746	227,702
Gas purchased for resale	**380,078**	356,663	381,586
Other operating expenses	**329,991**	307,149	277,048
Write-down of real estate investments (Note 3)	**—**	—	19,505
Defueling and decommissioning expenses (Note 2)	**—**	63,764	—
Maintenance	**86,755**	94,560	71,859
Depreciation	**102,831**	100,941	104,963
Taxes (other than income taxes) (Note 11)	**67,430**	60,434	58,983
Income taxes (Note 10)	**66,557**	61,045	122,070
	1,494,468	1,466,011	1,426,475
Operating Income	**246,198**	219,279	230,960
Other Income and Deductions:			
Allowance for equity funds used during construction (Note 1)	**1,581**	516	781
Miscellaneous income and deductions—net	**1,485**	5,610	762
	249,264	225,405	232,503
Interest Charges:			
Interest on long-term debt	**77,627**	79,001	73,294
Amortization of debt discount and expense less premium	**1,385**	1,300	1,180
Other interest	**23,456**	20,433	15,598
Allowance for borrowed funds used during construction (Note 1)	**(2,044)**	(348)	(1,248)
	100,424	100,386	88,824
Income Before Cumulative Effect of a Change in Accounting Method	**148,840**	125,019	143,679
Cumulative Effect to January 1, 1987 of Accruing Unbilled Revenues (less applicable income taxes of $22,779) (Note 1)	**—**	—	29,589
Net Income	**148,840**	125,019	173,268
Dividend Requirements on Preferred Stock	**12,645**	12,850	13,165
Earnings Available for Common Stock	**$ 136,195**	$ 112,169	$ 160,103
Shares of Common Stock Outstanding (thousands):			
Year-end	**52,807**	52,458	52,457
Average	**52,559**	52,457	52,414
Earnings Per Average Share of Common Stock Outstanding:			
Before cumulative effect of a change in accounting method	**$2.59**	$2.14	$2.49
Cumulative effect to January 1, 1987 of accruing unbilled revenues	**—**	—	0.56
Total	**$2.59**	$2.14	$3.05
Dividends Per Share of Common Stock:			
Paid	**$2.00**	$2.00	$2.00
Declared	**$2.00**	$2.00	$2.00

See accompanying notes.

EXHIBIT 14-9 (continued)

Consolidated Statement of Cash Flows

Years ended December 31, 1989, 1988 and 1987 (Thousands of Dollars)

	1989	1988	1987
Operating Activities:			
Net income	$ **148,840**	$ 125,019	$ 173,268
Adjustments to reconcile net income to cash flows:			
Write-down of real estate investments	**—**	—	19,505
Defueling and decommissioning expenses	**—**	63,764	—
Depreciation and amortization	**115,763**	115,834	121,790
Investment tax credit-net	**(5,267)**	(6,342)	(4,766)
Deferred income taxes	**37,020**	(8,221)	71,256
Allowance for equity funds used during construction	**(1,581)**	(516)	(781)
Change in accounts receivable	**13,338**	(6,050)	5,923
Change in inventories	**(14,037)**	1,530	13,720
Change in other current assets	**(9,254)**	(3,052)	(83,464)
Change in accounts payable	**21,609**	11,782	(71,252)
Change in other current liabilities	**692**	(11,641)	(93,233)
Change in deferred amounts	**12,319**	15,777	14,354
Change in noncurrent liabilities	**(45,444)**	(1,554)	(1,191)
Other	**15,533**	13,834	929
Net Cash Provided by Operating Activities	**289,531**	310,164	166,058
Investing Activities:			
Construction expenditures	**(174,418)**	(162,806)	(127,610)
Allowance for equity funds used during construction	**1,581**	516	781
Proceeds from disposition of equipment	**2,025**	1,132	4,259
Purchase of other investments	**(129,861)**	(31,974)	(34,848)
Sale of other investments	**137,827**	24,440	29,386
Net Cash Used in Investing Activities	**(162,846)**	(168,692)	(128,032)
Financing Activities:			
Proceeds from sale of common stock	**8,570**	23	1,155
Proceeds from sale of long-term notes and bonds	**19,843**	73,902	94,877
Redemption of long-term notes and bonds	**(47,801)**	(30,171)	(54,788)
Proceeds of short-term borrowings	**222,790**	660,225	865,399
Repayment of short-term borrowings	**(199,950)**	(714,532)	(823,030)
Redemption of preferred stock	**(2,576)**	(2,576)	(17,654)
Dividends on common stock	**(105,002)**	(104,914)	(104,827)
Dividends on preferred stock	**(12,662)**	(12,868)	(13,339)
Net Cash Used in Financing Activities	**(116,788)**	(130,911)	(52,207)
Net Increase (Decrease) in Cash and Temporary Cash Investments	**9,897**	10,561	(14,181)
Cash and Temporary Cash Investments at Beginning of Year	**43,393**	32,832	47,013
Cash and Temporary Cash Investments at End of Year	$ **53,290**	$ 43,393	$ 32,832

See accompanying notes.

EXHIBIT   14-9   (continued)

Selected Footnote

ALLOWANCE FOR FUNDS
USED DURING CONSTRUCTION (AFDC):
AFDC, which does not represent current cash earnings, is defined in the system of accounts prescribed by the FERC and the CPUC as the net cost during the period of construction of borrowed funds used for construction purposes, and a reasonable rate on funds derived from other sources. In accordance with such system of accounts, the Company capitalizes AFDC as a part of the cost of utility plant, with a credit to nonoperating income for the portion of AFDC attributable to equity funds and a reduction of interest charges for the portion of AFDC attributable to borrowed funds. The capitalization of AFDC results in the inclusion of AFDC in rate base and the recovery thereof through future billings to customers. In an order dated November 1977, the CPUC directed that the Company is to capitalize AFDC at its authorized rate of return on rate base, but not to exceed the amount allowed by the formula prescribed by the FERC. The following AFDC rates were used for the years 1989, 1988 and 1987, reflecting either the rates calculated by the FERC formula or the Company's authorized rate of return on rate base:

	1989	1988	1987
First Quarter	9.78%	9.73%	9.49%
Second Quarter	10.21%*	10.07%	8.31%
Third Quarter	10.21%*	10.16%	8.71%
Fourth Quarter	10.21%*	10.21%*	8.68%

* Authorized rate of return on rate base

pays for inefficiency and excess capacity, because disallowed costs are a risk to investors that can drive the stock price down and interest rates up for the utility. This increases the cost of capital for the utility, which in turn may force utility rates up.

For the costs that are allowed, the risk is that the utility commission will not allow a reasonable rate of return. It is important to observe what proportion of total property and plant is represented by construction work in progress. It is also important to be familiar with the political climate of the utility commission that will be ruling on the construction work in progress costs.

The income statement accounts of allowance for equity funds used during construction and allowance for borrowed funds used during construction are accounts that relate to construction work in progress costs on the balance sheet. Both of these accounts are added to construction work in progress costs.

The account allowance for equity funds used during construction represents an assumed rate of return on equity funds used for construction. The account allowance for borrowed funds used during construction represents the cost of borrowed funds that are used for construction. Sometimes these two income statement accounts are referred to as the allowance for funds used during construction.

By increasing the balance sheet account construction work in progress, for an assumed rate of return on equity funds, the utility is building into the cost base an amount for an assumed rate of return on equity funds. As explained previously, this cost base may not be accepted by the utility commission. The costs that have been added into the cost base have also been added to income, through the account allowance for equity funds. Sometimes a significant portion of the utility's net income is represented by the account allowance for equity funds used during construction.

The income statement account allowance for borrowed funds used during construction charges to the balance sheet account construction in progress the interest on borrowed funds used for construction in progress. Thus, this interest is added to the cost base.

Utilities with substantial construction work in progress can have significant cash flow problems. Their reported net income can be substantially higher than the cash flow that is related to the income statement. Sometimes these utilities issue additional bonds and stocks to obtain funds to pay dividends.

Exhibit 14-9 indicates that the Public Service Company of Colorado had a relatively immaterial amount of construction work in progress at the end of 1989. Exhibit 14-9 also shows a relatively immaterial allowance for equity funds used during construction and allowance for borrowed funds used during construction in 1989. This indicates that the company's quality of earnings was relatively good.

Ratios for Electric Utilities

Because of the vastly different accounts and statement formats, few of the traditional ratios are appropriate for electric utilities. Exceptions are return on assets, return on equity, debt/equity, and times interest earned. Investor-related ratios are also of value in analyzing utilities. As previously indicated, cash flow can be a particularly important indicator of the utility's ability to maintain and increase dividends. One such ratio is cash flow per share. Standard & Poor's *Industry Survey* is a good source for composite industry data on utilities.

Operating Ratio

The operating ratio compares operating expenses to operating revenues; it is a measure of efficiency. A profitable utility holds this ratio low. A vertical common size analysis of the income statement will aid in conclusions regarding this ratio. The operating ratio for the Public Service Company of Colorado is computed in Exhibit 14-10. This ratio decreased in 1989, thus improving the overall profitability of Public Service Company of Colorado.

Funded Debt to Operating Property

A key ratio is the comparison of funded debt to net fixed operating property. This ratio is sometimes termed LTD (long-term debt) to net property, because funded debt is long-term debt. Operating property consists of property and plant less the

EXHIBIT 14-10

PUBLIC SERVICE COMPANY OF COLORADO
Operating Ratio
For the Years Ended December 31, 1989 and 1988

	1989	1988
	(in thousands)	
Operating expense	$1,494,468	$1,466,011
Operating revenue	$1,740,666	$1,685,290
Operating ratio	85.86%	86.99%

allowance for depreciation. Construction in progress is included, since it has probably been substantially funded by debt. This ratio is a measure of debt coverage and an indicator of how funds are supplied. It is similar to debt to total assets, with only specialized debt and the specific assets that generate the profits to cover the debt charges. Funded debt to operating property for the Public Service Company of Colorado is computed in Exhibit 14-11. This ratio decreased in 1989, indicating a less risky debt position.

Percent Earned on Operating Property

This ratio is sometimes termed *earnings on net property*. It relates net earnings to the assets primarily intended to generate earnings, net property and plant. For the Public Service Company of Colorado, this ratio is computed in Exhibit 14-12. Note that this ratio increased in 1989, which is a positive sign.

Operating Revenue to Operating Property

This ratio is basically an operating asset turnover ratio. In public utilities, the fixed plant is often much larger than the expected annual revenue, so this ratio will be less than 1. The ratio is computed for the Public Service Company of Colorado in

EXHIBIT 14-11

PUBLIC SERVICE COMPANY OF COLORADO
Funded Debt to Operating Property
For the Years Ended December 31, 1989 and 1988

	1989	1988
	(in thousands)	
Funded debt	$ 904,129	$ 933,020
Operating property	$2,468,143	$2,413,410
Funded debt to operating property	36.63%	38.66%

EXHIBIT 14-12

PUBLIC SERVICE COMPANY OF COLORADO
Percent Earned on Operating Property
For the Years Ended December 31, 1989 and 1988

	1989	1988
	(in thousands)	
Net income	$ 148,840	$ 125,019
Operating property	$2,468,143	$2,413,410
Percent earned on operating property	6.03%	5.18%

Exhibit 14-13, which indicates that there was a increase in the operating revenue to operating property. This represents an favorable trend.

OIL AND GAS

Oil and gas companies' financial statements are affected significantly by the method they choose to account for costs associated with exploration and production. The method chosen is some variation of successful-efforts or full-costing methods, which will be explained along with their effects on the financial statements. Another thing that is particularly important to understand about the financial statements of oil and gas companies is the footnote requirement that relates to supplementary information on oil and gas exploration, development, and production activities. This requirement will be explained in this section.

Cash flow is important to all companies, but particularly to oil and gas companies. Therefore, cash flow must be monitored as part of the analysis of an oil or gas company.

Most of the traditional financial ratios apply to oil and gas companies. This section will not cover special ratios that relate to oil and gas companies.

EXHIBIT 14-13

PUBLIC SERVICE COMPANY OF COLORADO
Operating Revenue to Operating Property
For the Years Ended December 31, 1989 and 1988

	1989	1988
	(in thousands)	
Operating revenue	$1,740,666	$1,685,290
Operating property	$2,468,143	$2,413,410
Operating revenue to operating property	70.53%	69.83%

The 1989 financial statements of the Chevron Corporation will be used to illustrate oil and gas financial statements. Chevron's major business is energy, principally petroleum.

Exhibits 14-14, 14-15, and 14-16 contain data from the 1989 annual report of Chevron, which will be used to illustrate the unique aspects of oil and gas.

EXHIBIT 14-14

CHEVRON CORPORATION
Selected Accounting and Financial Reporting Policies
1989 Annual Report

Oil and gas accounting. The successful efforts method of accounting is used for oil and gas exploration and production activities.

Properties, plant and equipment. All costs for development wells, related plant and equipment (including carbon dioxide and certain other injected materials used in enhanced recovery projects), and mineral interests in oil and gas properties are capitalized. Costs of exploratory wells are capitalized pending determination of whether the wells found proved reserves. Costs of wells that are assigned proved reserves remain capitalized. All other exploratory wells and costs are expensed.

The worldwide portfolio of proved oil and gas properties is regularly assessed for possible impairment. In addition, high-cost, long-lead-time oil and gas projects are individually assessed prior to production start-up.

Depreciation and depletion (including provisions for future abandonment and restoration costs) of all capitalized costs of proved oil and gas producing properties, except mineral interests, are expensed using the unit-of-production method by individual fields as the proved developed reserves are produced. Depletion expenses for capitalized costs of proved mineral interests are determined using the unit-of-production method by individual fields as the related proved reserves are produced. Periodic valuation provisions for impairment of capitalized costs of unproved mineral interests are expensed.

Depreciation and depletion expenses for other mineral assets are determined using the unit-of-production method as the proved reserves are produced. The capitalized costs of all other plant and equipment are depreciated or amortized over estimated useful lives. In general, the declining-balance method is used to depreciate plant and equipment in the United States; the straight-line method is generally used to depreciate non-U.S. plant and equipment and to amortize all capitalized leased assets.

Gains or losses are not recognized for normal retirements of properties, plant and equipment subject to composite group amortization or depreciation. Gains or losses from abnormal retirements or sales are included in income.

Expenditures for maintenance, repairs and minor renewals to maintain facilities in operating condition are expensed. Major replacements and renewals are capitalized.

E X H I B I T   1 4 - 1 5

CHEVRON CORPORATION
Supplemental Information on Oil- and Gas-Producing Activities—Unaudited
1989 Annual Report

In accordance with Statement of Financial Accounting Standards No. 69, "Disclosures about Oil and Gas Producing Activities" (SFAS 69), this section provides supplemental information on oil and gas exploration and producing activities of the company in six separate tables. The first three tables provide historical cost information pertaining to capitalized costs incurred in property acquisitions, exploration and development, and results of operations. Tables IV through VI present information on the company's estimated net proved reserve quantities, standardized measure of estimated discounted future net cash flows related to proved reserves, and estimated changes in discounted future net cash flows.

Table 1—Capitalized Costs Relating to Oil and Gas Producing Activities at December 31

Millions of dollars	United States			Canada			Africa			Other			Total Worldwide		
	1989	1988	1987	1989	1988	1987	1989	1988	1987	1989	1988	1987	1989	1988	1987
Consolidated Companies															
Unproved properties	$ 856	$ 1,071	$ 1,051	$ 372	$ 194	$ 115	$ 16	$ 15	$ 17	$ 42	$ 44	$ 51	$ 1,286	$ 1,324	$ 1,234
Proved properties and															
related producing assets	19,069	20,039	17,545	1,024	924	840	955	926	998	2,488	2,151	2,075	23,536	24,040	21,458
Support equipment	672	729	656	69	66	61	48	46	55	72	62	83	861	903	855
Deferred exploratory wells	64	76	125	69	61	70	40	23	29	68	31	1	241	191	225
Other uncompleted projects	564	547	532	51	51	24	169	85	59	251	475	362	1,035	1,158	977
Gross capitalized costs	21,225	22,462	19,909	1,585	1,296	1,110	1,228	1,095	1,158	2,921	2,763	2,572	26,959	27,616	24,749
Unproved properties valuation	508	521	572	54	55	55	8	6	5	38	41	47	608	623	679
Proved producing properties—															
Depreciation and depletion	9,452	8,888	7,987	528	469	421	469	397	362	1,313	1,185	1,025	11,762	10,939	9,795
Future abandonment															
and restoration	1,071	1,092	1,058	33	31	28	107	90	82	170	160	151	1,381	1,373	1,319
Support equipment depreciation	295	246	207	26	23	20	32	30	29	30	24	33	383	323	289
Accumulated provisions	11,326	10,747	9,824	641	578	524	616	523	478	1,551	1,410	1,256	14,134	13,258	12,082

Net Capitalized Costs

	United States			Canada			Africa			Other			Total Worldwide		
	1989	1988	1987	1989	1988	1987	1989	1988	1987	1989	1988	1987	1989	1988	1987
Consolidated Companies	9,899	11,715	10,085	944	718	586	612	572	680	1,370	1,353	1,316	12,825	14,358	12,667
Equity Share in Affiliate	—	—	—	—	—	—	—	—	—	525	466	441	525	466	441
Total	$ 9,899	$11,715	$10,085	$ 944	$ 718	$ 586	$ 612	$ 572	$ 680	$1,895	$1,819	$1,757	$13,350	$14,824	$13,108

Table II—Costs Incurred in Property Acquisitions, Exploration and Development

Millions of dollars	United States			Canada			Africa			Other			Total Worldwide		
	1989	1988	1987	1989	1988	1987	1989	1988	1987	1989	1988	1987	1989	1988	1987
Consolidated Companies															
Exploration															
Wells	$ 211	$ 190	$ 127	$ 41	$ 33	$ 30	$ 75	$ 64	$ 57	$ 107	$ 79	$ 43	$ 434	$ 366	$ 257
Geological and geophysical	113	136	139	66	68	55	25	19	26	78	67	49	282	290	269
Rentals and other	29	27	28	3	2	6	1	2	7	5	3	11	38	34	52
Total exploration	353	353	294	110	103	91	101	85	90	190	149	103	754	690	578
Property acquisitions[2]															
Proved	5	2,389	4	1	1	1	—	—	—	—	—	18	6	2,390	23
Unproved	20	228	38	197	91	22	4	1	—	1	1	2	222	321	62
Total property acquisitions	25	2,617	42	198	92	23	4	1	—	1	1	20	228	2,711	85
Development	592	560	575	83	101	55	84	57	44	208	212	271	967	930	945
Total Costs Incurred															
Consolidated Companies	970	3,530	911	391	296	169	189	143	134	399	362	394	1,949	4,331	1,608
Equity Share in Affiliate	—	—	—	—	—	—	—	—	—	106	63	55	106	63	55
Total	$ 970	$ 3,530	$ 911	$ 391	$ 296	$ 169	$ 189	$ 143	$ 134	$ 505	$ 425	$ 449	$ 2,055	$ 4,394	$ 1,663

[1] Includes costs incurred whether capitalized or charged to earnings. Excludes support equipment expenditures.

[2] The year 1989 included the purchase of additional interests in Beaufort Sea prospects from Husky Oil. The year 1988 included the acquisition of Tenneco Inc.'s Gulf of Mexico properties and the purchase of the eastern Canadian properties of Columbia Gas Development of Canada Ltd.

EXHIBIT 14-15   (continued)

Table III—Results of Operations for Oil and Gas Producing Activities

The company's results of operations from oil and gas producing activities for the years 1989, 1988 and 1987 are shown below.

Net income from exploration and production activities as reported on Page 36 includes the allocation of corporate overhead and income taxes computed on an effective rate basis. In accordance with SFAS 69, allocated corporate overhead is excluded from the results below, and income taxes are based on statutory tax rates, reflecting allowable deductions and tax credits. Interest expense is excluded from both reported results.

Millions of dollars	United States			Canada			Africa			Other			Total Worldwide		
	1989	1988	1987	1989	1988	1987	1989	1988	1987	1989	1988	1987	1989	1988	1987
Consolidated Companies															
Revenues from net production															
Sales	$1,699	$1,332	$1,743	$ 310	$ 267	$ 244	$ 257	$ 236	$ 330	$ 290	$ 452	$ 500	$2,556	$2,287	$2,817
Transfers	2,444	2,012	2,154	211	184	232	939	721	830	526	304	478	4,120	3,221	3,694
Total	4,143	3,344	3,897	521	451	476	1,196	957	1,160	816	756	978	6,676	5,508	6,511
Production expenses	(2,003)	(1,769)	(1,840)	(148)	(143)	(114)	(95)	(93)	(99)	(211)	(201)	(198)	(2,457)	(2,206)	(2,251)
Proved producing properties depreciation, depletion and abandonment provision	(1,314)	(1,202)	(1,215)	(66)	(55)	(42)	(85)	(90)	(104)	(153)	(175)	(214)	(1,618)	(1,522)	(1,575)
Exploration expenses	(276)	(326)	(221)	(81)	(99)	(71)	(56)	(81)	(65)	(143)	(122)	(91)	(556)	(628)	(448)
Unproved properties valuation	(144)	(147)	(153)	(16)	(12)	(10)	(2)	(2)	(4)	—	(1)	(1)	(162)	(162)	(168)
Other income (expense)[1]	(545)	317	314	16	35	33	15	200	57	(17)	50	85	(531)	602	489
Results before income taxes	(139)	217	782	226	177	272	973	891	945	292	307	559	1,352	1,592	2,558
Income tax expense	42	(88)	(357)	(101)	(77)	(150)	(829)	(499)	(772)	(230)	(238)	(287)	(1,118)	(902)	(1,566)
Results of Producing Operations															
Consolidated Companies	(97)	129	425	125	100	122	144	392	173	62	69	272	234	690	992
Equity Share in Affiliate	—	—	—	—	—	—				146	116	137	146	116	137
Total	$ (97)	$ 129	$ 425	$ 125	$ 100	$ 122	$ 144	$ 392	$ 173	$ 208	$ 185	$ 409	$ 380	$ 806	$1,129

Results Per Unit of Production—
Consolidated Companies

Revenues from net production															
Liquids ($/bbl.)	**$16.13**	$13.06	$15.91	**$16.71**	$13.80	$16.79	**$17.53**	$13.96	$17.08	**$16.21**	$13.33	$16.08	**$16.49**	$13.35	$16.24
Natural Gas ($/MCF)	**1.49**	1.40	1.35	**1.65**	1.46	1.57	**—**	—	—	**2.26**	2.39	2.47	**1.54**	1.45	1.43
Total ($/OEG bbl.)(2)	**12.86**	11.14	12.86	**14.83**	12.54	14.60	**17.53**	13.96	17.08	**15.78**	13.46	15.91	**13.99**	11.95	14.00
Production expenses	**(6.22)**	(5.89)	(6.07)	**(4.21)**	(3.97)	(3.49)	**(1.39)**	(1.36)	(1.46)	**(4.08)**	(3.58)	(3.22)	**(5.15)**	(4.79)	(4.84)
Depreciation, depletion and abandonment provision	**(4.08)**	(4.00)	(4.01)	**(1.88)**	(1.53)	(1.27)	**(1.25)**	(1.31)	(1.54)	**(2.96)**	(3.12)	(3.48)	**(3.39)**	(3.30)	(3.39)
Exploration expenses	**(.86)**	(1.09)	(.73)	**(2.31)**	(2.75)	(2.18)	**(.82)**	(1.18)	(.96)	**(2.77)**	(2.17)	(1.48)	**(1.16)**	(1.36)	(.96)
Unproved properties valuation	**(.45)**	(.49)	(.51)	**(.46)**	(.33)	(.32)	**(.03)**	(.03)	(.05)	**—**	(.02)	(.02)	**(.34)**	(.35)	(.36)
Other income (expense)(1)	**(1.69)**	1.06	1.04	**.46**	.97	1.01	**.22**	2.92	.84	**(.33)**	.89	1.38	**(1.11)**	1.31	1.05
Results before income taxes	**(.44)**	.73	2.58	**6.43**	4.93	8.35	**14.26**	13.00	13.91	**5.64**	5.46	9.09	**2.84**	3.46	5.50
Income tax expense	.13	(.29)	(1.18)	**(2.88)**	(2.14)	(4.61)	**(12.15)**	(7.28)	(11.37)	**(3.37)**	(3.47)	(4.67)	**(2.34)**	(1.96)	(3.37)
Results of Producing Operations	**$ (.31)**	$ .44	$ 1.40	**$ 3.55**	$ 2.79	$ 3.74	**$ 2.11**	$ 5.72	$ 2.54	**$ 2.27**	$ 1.99	$ 4.42	**$ .50**	$ 1.50	$ 2.13

Additional Data for
Consolidated Companies

Average sales price for last month of year:															
Liquids ($/bbl.)	**$17.08**	$12.45	$14.83	**$17.41**	$15.40	$15.91	**$18.43**	$14.44	$16.07	**$16.70**	$12.41	$15.86	**$17.34**	$13.10	$15.35
Natural Gas ($/MCF)	**2.06**	1.58	1.45	**1.72**	1.43	1.35	**—**	—	—	**2.31**	2.32	2.53	**2.06**	1.60	1.51
Investment per barrel of net proved reserves added:															
Additions to capitalized costs	**775**	2,883	823	**105**	90	97	**31**	22	47	**351**	81	115	**1,262**	3,076	1,082
$/OEG bbl. (2)	**3.56**	5.57	4.56	**3.65**	2.49	1.77	**1.37**	.34	.81	**5.31**	1.25	3.86	**3.76**	4.50	3.35

(1) Includes gas processing fees, sulfur revenues, natural gas contract settlements, foreign currency gains and losses, miscellaneous expenses, etc. The United States in 1989 included $889 of before-tax charges related to asset write-offs and write-downs. In 1988, Africa included a before-tax gain of $179 from the sale of 20 percent of the company's interest in the Angolan producing operations, while in 1987, the Other geographic area included a net before-tax gain of $119 from the sales of the Denmark and Ras Al-Khaimah producing operations.

(2) Natural gas converted to Oil Equivalent Gas (OEG) barrels at 6 MCF = 1 OEG barrel.

EXHIBIT 14-15 (continued)

Table IV—Reserve Quantities Information

The company's estimated net proved underground oil and gas reserves and changes thereto for the years 1989, 1988 and 1987 are shown in the following table. These quantities are estimated by the company's reserves engineers and reviewed by the company's Reserves Advisory Committee using reserve definitions prescribed by the Securities and Exchange Commission.

Proved reserves are the estimated quantities that geological and engineering data demonstrate with reasonable certainty to be recoverable in future years from known reservoirs under existing economic and operating conditions. Due to the inherent uncertainties and the limited nature of reservoir data, estimates of underground reserves are subject to change over time as additional information becomes available.

Proved reserves do not include additional quantities recoverable beyond the term of lease or contract, or that may result from extensions of currently proved areas, or from application of secondary or tertiary recovery processes not yet tested and determined to be economic.

Proved developed reserves are the quantities expected to be recovered through existing wells with existing equipment and operating methods.

"Net" reserves exclude royalties and interests owned by others and reflect contractual arrangements and royalty obligations in effect at the time of the estimate.

The company's net proved reserves of carbon dioxide, which are not included in the tables below, were 410 billion cubic feet at December 31, 1989. These reserves are located in the United States.

Chevron owns an equity interest in the Arabian American Oil Company (Aramco) but has no ownership interest in its crude oil reserves. The company provides loaned manpower and technical services to Aramco and continues to have access to Saudi Arabian crude oil; purchases for the years 1989, 1988 and 1987 were 217,000, 271,000 and 284,000 barrels per day, respectively. These amounts are not included in the table below.

Net Proved Reserves of Crude Oil, Condensate and Natural Gas Liquids

Millions of barrels

	United States			Canada			Africa			Other			Total Worldwide		
	1989	1988	1987	1989	1988	1987	1989	1988	1987	1989	1988	1987	1989	1988	1987
Consolidated Companies—At January 1	**1,806**	1,809	1,880	**176**	175	161	**659**	725	737	**295**	301	366	**2,936**	3,010	3,144
Changes attributable to															
Revisions	**50**	79	59	**2**	16	29	**22**	3	56	**55**	41	18	**129**	139	162
Improved recovery	**72**	17	39	**11**	6	4	—	56	—	—	1	—	**83**	80	43
Extensions and discoveries	**26**	19	19	**1**	1	3	**1**	6	—	**2**	1	5	**30**	27	27
Purchases[1]	**1**	72	10	**3**	5	1	—	—	—	—	—	—	**4**	77	11
Sales[2]	**(16)**	(13)	(13)	—	—	—	—	(63)	—	—	—	(35)	**(16)**	(76)	(48)
Production	**(176)**	(177)	(185)	**(25)**	(27)	(23)	**(68)**	(68)	(68)	**(43)**	(49)	(53)	**(312)**	(321)	(329)
Consolidated Companies—December 31	**1,763**	1,806	1,809	**168**	176	175	**614**	659	725	**309**	295	301	**2,854**	2,936	3,010
Equity Share in Affiliate—December 31	—	—	—	—	—	—	—	—	—	**325**	381	338	**325**	381	338
Total Proved Reserves—December 31	**1,763**	1,806	1,809	**168**	176	175	**614**	659	725	**634**	676	639	**3,179**	3,317	3,348
Developed reserves in consolidated companies															
At January 1	**1,635**	1,585	1,646	**164**	167	153	**490**	583	583	**204**	238	283	**2,493**	2,573	2,665
At December 31	**1,565**	1,635	1,585	**159**	164	167	**473**	490	583	**221**	204	238	**2,418**	2,493	2,573

Net Proved Reserves of Natural Gas

Billions of cubic feet

	United States			Canada			Africa			Other			Total Worldwide		
	1989	1988	1987	1989	1988	1987	1989	1988	1987	1989	1988	1987	1989	1988	1987
Consolidated Companies—At January 1	**8,274**	7,078	7,509	**869**	873	825	—	—	—	**1,417**	1,332	1,602	**10,560**	9,283	9,936
Changes attributable to															
Revisions	**201**	475	239	**36**	42	105	—	—	—	**44**	130	50	**281**	647	394
Improved recovery	**4**	1	2	—	1	—	—	—	—	—	—	—	**4**	2	2
Extensions and discoveries	**209**	184	68	**9**	3	—	—	—	—	—	—	—	**218**	187	68
Purchases[1]	**2**	1,324	8	**24**	4	1	—	—	—	—	—	4	**26**	1,328	13
Sales[2]	**(70)**	(48)	(40)	—	—	—	—	—	—	—	—	(274)	**(70)**	(48)	(314)
Production	**(881)**	(740)	(708)	**(58)**	(54)	(58)	—	—	—	**(50)**	(45)	(50)	**(989)**	(839)	(816)
Consolidated Companies—December 31	**7,739**	8,274	7,078	**880**	869	873	—	—	—	**1,411**	1,417	1,332	**10,030**	10,560	9,283
Equity Share in Affiliate—December 31	—	—	—	—	—	—	—	—	—	**160**	150	161	**160**	150	161
Total Proved Reserves—December 31	**7,739**	8,274	7,078	**880**	869	873	—	—	—	**1,571**	1,567	1,493	**10,190**	10,710	9,444
Developed reserves in consolidated companies															
At January 1	**7,617**	6,627	7,085	**854**	858	797	—	—	—	**1,023**	1,051	1,265	**9,494**	8,536	9,147
At December 31	**7,128**	7,617	6,627	**862**	854	858	—	—	—	**1,022**	1,023	1,051	**9,012**	9,494	8,536

[1]Purchases in 1988 included the proved oil and gas reserves attributable to Tenneco Inc.'s Gulf of Mexico properties.

[2]The sales of proved oil and gas reserves in 1988 reflected the sale of 20 percent of Chevron's investment in Angola, while 1987 included the sales of the company's interests in Denmark and Ras Al-Khaimah.

EXHIBIT 14-15   (continued)

Standardized Measure of Future Net Cash Flows Related to Proved Oil and Gas Reserves

The standardized measure of discounted future net cash flows, related to the proved oil and gas reserves disclosed on Page 59, is calculated in accordance with the requirements of SFAS 69. Estimated future cash inflows from production are computed by applying year-end prices for oil and gas to year-end quantities of estimated net proved reserves. Future price changes are limited to those provided by contractual arrangements in existence at the end of each reporting year. Future development and production costs are those estimated future expenditures necessary to develop and produce year-end estimated proved reserves

based on year-end cost indices, assuming continuation of year-end economic conditions. Estimated future income taxes are calculated by applying appropriate year-end statutory tax rates. These rates reflect allowable deductions and tax credits and are applied to estimated future pre-tax net cash flows, less the tax basis of related assets. Discounted future net cash flows are calculated using 10 percent midperiod discount factors. This discounting requires a year-by-year estimate of when the future expenditures will be incurred and when the reserves will be produced.

Table V—Standardized Measure of Discounted Future Net Cash Flows at December 31 of Each Year

Millions of dollars	United States			Canada			Africa			Other			Total Worldwide		
	1989	1988	1987	1989	1988	1987	1989	1988	1987	1989	1988	1987	1989	1988	1987
Consolidated Companies															
Future cash inflows from production	$44,180	$37,830	$37,140	$3,910	$3,500	$3,980	$11,320	$ 9,510	$11,740	$8,360	$6,240	$7,080	$67,770	$57,080	$59,940
Future production and development costs	(22,670)	(19,600)	(19,960)	(1,170)	(1,250)	(1,060)	(1,770)	(1,490)	(1,760)	(3,020)	(2,820)	(2,480)	(28,630)	(25,160)	(25,260)
Future income taxes	(6,370)	(5,690)	(5,260)	(1,210)	(1,130)	(1,460)	(7,180)	(6,250)	(8,470)	(2,480)	(1,460)	(2,550)	(17,240)	(14,530)	(17,740)
Undiscounted future net cash flows	15,140	12,540	11,920	1,530	1,120	1,460	2,370	1,770	1,510	2,860	1,960	2,050	21,900	17,390	16,940
10% midyear annual discount for timing of estimated cash flows	(6,230)	(5,440)	(5,420)	(560)	(370)	(480)	(870)	(730)	(530)	(1,150)	(900)	(790)	(8,810)	(7,440)	(7,220)

Standardized Measure of Discounted Future Net Cash Flows

Consolidated Companies	$ 8,910	$ 7,100	$ 6,500	$ 970	$ 750	$ 980	$ 1,500	$ 1,040	980	$ 1,710	$1,060	$1,260	$13,090	$ 9,950	$ 9,720
Equity Share in Affiliate	—	—	—	—	—	—	—	—	—	770	520	800	770	520	800
Total	$ 8,910	$ 7,100	$ 6,500	$ 970	$ 750	$ 980	$ 1,500	$ 1,040	980	$2,480	$1,580	$2,060	$13,860	$10,470	$10,520

Table VI—Changes in the Standardized Measure of Discounted Future Net Cash Flows from Proved Reserves

Consolidated Companies Millions of dollars	1989	1988	1987
Present value at January 1	$ 9,950	$ 9,720	$ 9,120
Sales and transfers of oil and gas produced, net of production costs	(4,219)	(3,302)	(4,260)
Development costs incurred	967	930	945
Purchases of reserves	18	2,139	20
Sales of reserves	(107)	(523)	(395)
Extensions, discoveries and improved recovery, less related costs	706	193	232
Revisions of previous quantity estimates	2,157	1,981	3,275
Net changes in prices, development and production costs	4,117	(4,807)	780
Accretion of discount	1,691	1,820	1,594
Net change in income tax	(2,190)	1,799	(1,591)
Net change for the year	3,140	230	600
Present value at December 31	$13,090	$ 9,950	$ 9,720

The information provided above does not represent management's estimate of the company's expected future cash flows or value of proved oil and gas reserves. Estimates of proved reserve quantities are imprecise and change over time as new information becomes available. Moreover, probable and possible reserves, which may become proved in the future, are excluded from the above calculations. The arbitrary valuation prescribed under SFAS 69 requires assumptions as to the timing of future production from proved reserves and the timing and amount of future development and production costs. Therefore, the changes in present values between years reflect changes in estimated proved reserve quantities and prices and assumptions used in forecasting production volumes and costs.

Although calculated in accordance with SFAS 69, the company cautions statement users not to place unwarranted reliance on this information. The company believes the information on Page 59 for proved oil and gas reserve quantities — in conjunction with the factual information on capitalized costs, costs incurred, and results of exploration and producing activities provided in Tables I, II and III — is more reliable and meaningful for users of the financial statements.

The price of crude oil has fluctuated significantly over the past several years, with the outlook for crude oil prices remaining uncertain. The company cannot predict if, when or at what level crude oil prices will stabilize, but wishes to re-emphasize that the above calculations are made as of December 31 each year and should not be relied upon as an indication of the company's future cash flows or value of its oil and gas reserves.

EXHIBIT 14-16

CHEVRON CORPORATION
Consolidated Statement of Cash Flows
1989 Annual Report

		Year Ended December 31	
Millions of dollars	**1989**	1988*	1987*
Operating Activities			
Net income	**$ 251**	$1,768	$1,250
Adjustments			
Depreciation, depletion and amortization	**2,562**	2,436	2,514
Dry hole expense related to prior years' expenditures	**52**	106	45
Distributions (less than) greater than equity in affiliates' income	**(183)**	62	(113)
Net before-tax loss (gain) on asset retirements and sales	**772**	(97)	(155)
Net currency translation gain	**(56)**	(92)	(37)
Deferred income tax (credit) provision	**(425)**	(19)	35
Net decrease (increase) in operating working capital	**56**	(1,122)	556
Other	**17**	(49)	(91)
Net cash provided by operating activities	**3,046**	2,993	4,004
Investing Activities			
Capital expenditures	**(3,067)**	(2,459)	(2,116)
Acquisition of Gulf of Mexico properties from Tenneco Inc.	**—**	(2,512)	—
Proceeds from asset sales	**561**	895	767
Net sale of marketable securities	**51**	6	40
Net cash used in investing activities	**(2,455)**	(4,070)	(1,309)
Financing Activities			
Net (payments) borrowings of short-term obligations	**(308)**	883	(24)
Proceeds from issuance of long-term debt	**378**	46	679
Repayment of long-term debt	**(838)**	(808)	(1,935)
Sale of common stock to Employee Stock Ownership Plan	**1,000**	—	—
Cash dividends paid	**(953)**	(869)	(818)
Purchase of treasury shares	**(5)**	(6)	(84)
Net cash used in financing activities	**(726)**	(754)	(2,182)
Effect of Exchange Rate Changes on Cash and Cash Equivalents	**(10)**	4	27
Net Change in Cash and Cash Equivalents	**(145)**	(1,827)	540
Cash and Cash Equivalents at Beginning of Year	**1,297**	3,124	2,584
Cash and Cash Equivalents at Year-End	**$1,152**	$1,297	$3,124

*Certain amounts have been reclassified to conform to the 1989 presentation.
See accompanying notes to consolidated financial statements.

Successful Efforts versus Full Cost

A variation of one of two costing methods is used by an oil or gas company to account for exploration and production costs: the successful-efforts method and the full-costing method.

The successful-efforts method places only exploration and production costs of successful wells on the balance sheet under property, plant, and equipment. Exploration and production costs of unsuccessful (or dry) wells are expensed when it is determined that there is a dry hole. With the full-costing method, exploration and production costs of all the wells (successful and unsuccessful) are placed on the balance sheet under property, plant, and equipment.

Under both methods, exploration and production costs that are placed on the balance sheet are subsequently amortized as expense to the income statement. Amortization costs that relate to natural resources are called *depletion expense.*

The costing method used for exploration and production can have a very significant influence on the balance sheet and the income statement. Under both methods, exploration and production costs are eventually expensed, but there is a significant difference in the timing of the expense.

In theory, the successful-efforts method takes the position that there is a direct relationship between costs incurred and specific reserves discovered. These costs should be placed on the balance sheet. Costs that are associated with unsuccessful efforts are a period expense and should be charged to expense. In theory, the full-costing method takes the position that the drilling of all wells, successful and unsuccessful, is part of the process of finding successful wells. Therefore, all of the cost should be placed on the balance sheet.

In practice, the decision to use the successful-efforts or the full-costing method is probably not significantly influenced by theory, but rather by practicalities. Most relatively small oil and gas companies select a variation of the full-costing method. This results in a much bigger balance sheet and reported profits. It is speculated that the larger balance sheet and the higher reported profits can be used to influence some banks and limited partners, which small oil companies tend to use as sources of funds.

Large oil and gas companies tend to select a variation of the successful-efforts method. This results in a lower balance sheet amount and lower reported income in the short run. The large companies usually depend on bonds and stock as their primary sources of outside capital. Investors in bonds and stock are not likely to be influenced by the larger balance sheet and higher income that results from capitalizing dry wells.

As part of your review of an oil or gas company, note the method it is using to account for exploration and production costs. The method used can have a significant influence on the balance sheet and the income statement. The successful-efforts method is more conservative.

A review of Exhibit 14-14 indicates that Chevron uses the successful-efforts method to account for the cost of oil and gas wells.

Supplementary Information on Oil and Gas Exploration, Development, and Production Activities

Statement of Financial Accounting Standards No. 69 establishes comprehensive disclosures for oil- and gas-producing activities. SFAS No. 69 basically requires three general areas of disclosure. The first one provides historical information about costs and revenues, annual cost incurred, and the results of operations for producing activities. The second contains the company's petroleum engineers' quantity estimates for proved oil and gas reserves and the major factors causing changes in these reserve estimates. The third area indicates a monetary value of proved reserve quantities and changes therein, using a standardized formula.

When reviewing this disclosure, be aware that the second two areas of disclosure are particularly influenced by subjective judgment.

The first area of disclosure reveals capitalized cost, proved properties, and unproved properties. This area also discloses the current year's costs that relate to acquisition of properties, exploration, and development. The major parts of the world where the costs have been incurred are also disclosed. The results of operations for producing activities disclose revenue and costs for producing activities by major parts of the world.

The second area of disclosure reconciles proved developed and underdeveloped reserves from the beginning of the year to the end of the year. Major items on this schedule are typically revisions of previous estimates, improved recovery, discoveries and other additions, and production.

The third area of disclosure contains discounted future net cash flows relating to proved oil and gas reserves. For this disclosure, the company follows guidelines included in SFAS No. 69.

Included in the computation are proved developed and undeveloped reserves, future expected revenues, production and development costs related to future production of proved reserves, income tax, and the future net cash flows discounted at 10%. It should be noted that these data are fairly subjective, but they are the best data available relating to future cash flow from proved oil and gas reserves.

In addition to the three areas of disclosure required by SFAS No. 69, the Securities and Exchange Commission has additional operational and statistical data related to production, drilling, productive wells, and acreage. This disclosure is made by major areas of the world.

This supplementary information on oil and gas exploration, development, and production activities is watched closely by the investment community. It can indicate very significant trends, such as when a company is running out of reserves.

Review Exhibit 14-15 for the supplementary disclosure of Chevron. In Exhibit 14-15, the first three tables provide historical cost information pertaining to capitalized costs; costs incurred in property acquisitions, exploration, and development; and results of operations. Tables IV through VI present information on the company's estimated net proved reserve quantities, a standardized measure of estimated discounted future net cash flows related to proved reserves, and estimated changes in discounted future net cash flows.

Cash Flow

Monitoring cash flow can be particularly important when following an oil or gas company. There is the potential for a significant difference between the reported income and cash flow from operations. One of the reasons is that large sums can be spent for exploration and development, years in advance of revenue from the found reserves. The other reason is that there can be significant differences between when expenses are deducted on the financial statements and when they are deducted on the tax return. Therefore, it is important to observe operating cash flow.

The oil or gas company often discloses cash provided from operations in its annual report, including a five-year or longer period. Cash from operations for a three-year period is disclosed on the statement of cash flows. Exhibit 14-16 includes cash provided by operations for the period 1987–1989. For Chevron, the net cash provided by operating activities was $3,046,000,000 in 1989, while the net income was $251,000,000.

TRANSPORTATION

Three components of the transportation industry will be discussed: air carriers, railroads, and the motor carrier industry. Interstate commercial aviation is regulated by the Civil Aeronautics Board, which requires the use of a uniform system of accounts and reporting. Interstate railroads are regulated by the Interstate Commerce Commission, which also has control over a uniform system of accounts and reporting. Interstate motor carriers whose principal business is transportation services are regulated by the Interstate Commerce Commission; they also have a uniform system of accounts and reports.

The balance sheet format for air carriers, railroads, and motor carriers is similar to that for a manufacturing or retailing firm. As in a heavy manufacturing firm, property and equipment make up a large portion of assets. Also, supplies and parts are the basic inventory items. The income statement format is similar to that of a utility. The system of accounts provides for the grouping of all revenues and expenses in terms of both major natural objectives and functional activities. There is no cost of goods sold calculation; rather, there is operating income, which is revenue (categorized) minus operating expenses. In essence, the statements are a prescribed, categorized form of single-step income statement. They cannot be converted to multiple-step format.

Most of the traditional ratios also apply in the transportation field. Exceptions are inventory turnovers (because there is no cost of goods sold) and gross profit margin. The ratios discussed in the subsections that follow are especially suited to transportation. The traditional sources of industry averages cover transportation.

The federal government accumulates numerous statistics for regulated industries, including transportation. An example is the Interstate Commerce Commission's *Annual Report* on transport statistics in the United States.

For the motor carrier industry, a particularly good source of industry data is the annual publication *Financial Analysis of the Motor Carrier Industry,* published by the American Trucking Association, Inc., 1616 P Street, N.W., Washington, D.C. 20036. This publication includes an economic and industry overview, distribution of revenue by carrier type, and discussion of industry issues. It also includes definitions of terminology that relate to the motor carrier industry.

There are hundreds of motor carrier firms, most of which are relatively small. In the American Trucking Association publication, data are compiled by composite carrier groups. For example, Group A includes composite data for several hundred general freight carriers with annual revenues of less than $5 million. One of the groups includes composite data for the publicly held carriers of general freight.

The composite data in this publication are very extensive. The publication includes industry total dollars for income statement and balance sheet data such as gross revenues. It also includes vertical common size analyses for the income statement and the balance sheet. This publication also includes approximately thirty-six ratios and other analytical data, such as total tons.

The statement of income and balance sheet for Delta Air Lines, Inc. for 1989 are contained in Exhibit 14-17.

Operating Ratio

The operating ratio is computed by comparing operating expenses to operating revenue. It is a measure of cost and should be kept low, but external conditions, such as the level of business activity, may affect this ratio. Operating revenues vary from year to year because of differences in rates, classification of traffic, volume of traffic carried, and distance traffic is transported. Operating expenses change because of variation in the price level, the amount of traffic carried, the type of service performed, and the effectiveness of operating and maintaining the properties. Common size analysis of revenues and expenses is needed to explain changes in the operating ratio. The operating ratio for Delta Air Lines, Inc. is computed in Exhibit 14-18. Notice that the operating ratio declined moderately in 1989. Such a decline in the operating ratio can dramatically affect the profitability of a carrier. In fact, Delta's net income increased from $306,826,000 for 1988 to $460,918,000 in 1989.

Long-Term Debt to Operating Property

Because of the transportation companies' heavy investment in operating assets, such as equipment, the long-term ratios increase in importance. Long-term borrowing capacity is also a key consideration. The ratio of long-term debt to operating property gives a measure of the sources of funds with which property is obtained; it also measures borrowing capacity. Operating property is defined as long-term

DELTA AIR LINES, INC.
1989 Annual Report (Selected Data)

Consolidated Statements of Income For the years ended June 30, 1989, 1988 and 1987

	1989	1988	1987
	(In Thousands, Except Per Share Amounts)		
Operating Revenues:			
Passenger	$7,579,716	$6,443,111	$4,921,852
Cargo	393,662	349,775	280,271
Other, net	116,106	122,491	116,049
Total operating revenues	8,089,484	6,915,377	5,318,172
Operating Expenses:			
Salaries and related costs	3,122,279	2,703,462	2,228,814
Aircraft fuel	988,734	983,590	672,004
Aircraft maintenance materials and repairs	224,500	208,483	127,856
Aircraft rent	329,763	256,656	150,653
Other rent	206,429	178,639	145,473
Landing fees	119,850	109,724	89,519
Passenger service	341,296	290,575	219,834
Passenger commissions	834,407	616,629	432,066
Other cash costs	850,806	716,448	569,453
Depreciation and amortization	393,095	354,087	277,975
Total operating expenses	7,411,159	6,418,293	4,913,647
Operating Income	678,325	497,084	404,525
Other Income (Expense):			
Interest expense	(70,647)	(97,533)	(94,000)
Less: Interest capitalized	31,778	32,329	32,092
	(38,869)	(65,204)	(61,908)
Gain (loss) on disposition of flight equipment	16,562	(1,016)	96,270
Miscellaneous income, net	55,200	24,992	8,312
	32,893	(41,228)	42,674
Income Before Income Taxes	711,218	455,856	447,199
Income Taxes Provided (Note 8)	(279,214)	(180,851)	(219,715)
Amortization of Investment Tax Credits	28,914	31,821	36,245
Net Income	$ 460,918	$ 306,826	$ 263,729
Net Income Per Weighted Average Common Share	$9.37	$6.30	$5.90

EXHIBIT 14-17 (continued)

Consolidated Balance Sheets June 30, 1989 and 1988

ASSETS	1989	1988
	(In Thousands)	
Current Assets:		
Cash and cash equivalents	$ 529,657	$ 822,791
Accounts receivable, net of allowance for uncollectible accounts of $15,878 in 1989 and $13,200 in 1988	752,154	644,527
Maintenance and operating supplies, at average cost	57,024	52,413
Prepaid expenses and other current assets	135,937	131,507
Total current assets	1,474,772	1,651,238
Property and Equipment (Notes 1 and 3):		
Flight equipment owned	5,402,865	4,624,630
Less: Accumulated depreciation	2,298,172	2,125,879
	3,104,693	2,498,751
Flight equipment under capital leases	173,284	221,811
Less: Accumulated amortization	51,014	54,461
	122,270	167,350
Ground property and equipment	1,469,870	1,222,314
Less: Accumulated depreciation	634,783	548,499
	835,087	673,815
Advance payments for new equipment	415,823	226,319
	4,477,873	3,566,235
Other Assets:		
Investments in associated companies (Note 10)	66,651	63,017
Cost in excess of net assets acquired, net of accumulated amortization of $23,401 in 1989 and $14,906 in 1988 (Note 2)	317,853	326,348
Prepaid pension costs (Note 9)	72,247	83,680
Other	74,590	57,837
	531,341	530,882
	$6,483,986	$5,748,355

E X H I B I T   1 4 - 1 7   (continued)

LIABILITIES AND STOCKHOLDERS' EQUITY	1989	1988
	(In Thousands)	
Current Liabilities:		
Current maturities of long-term debt (Note 4)	$ 5,516	$ 5,491
Current obligations under capital leases (Note 5)	11,343	14,793
Short-term notes payable (Note 6)	—	16,163
Accounts payable and miscellaneous accrued liabilities	711,042	503,922
Air traffic liability	746,111	504,083
Accrued vacation pay	132,472	118,344
Transportation tax payable	83,083	67,396
Accrued income taxes	73,242	107,041
Total current liabilities	1,762,809	1,337,233
Noncurrent Liabilities:		
Long-term debt (Note 4)	556,770	563,129
Capital leases (Note 5)	146,244	166,364
Other	160,037	127,634
	863,051	857,127
Deferred Credits:		
Deferred income taxes (Note 8)	519,052	539,908
Unamortized investment tax credits	48,323	79,257
Manufacturers credits	121,921	151,976
Deferred gain on sale and leaseback transactions	545,270	569,279
Other	3,853	4,752
	1,238,419	1,345,172
Commitments and Contingencies (Notes 3, 5 and 12)		
Stockholders' Equity (Note 7):		
Common stock, par value $3.00 per share— Authorized 100,000,000 shares; outstanding 49,265,884 shares at June 30, 1989 and 49,101,271 shares at June 30, 1988	147,798	147,304
Additional paid-in capital	514,079	505,553
Reinvested earnings	1,957,830	1,555,966
	2,619,707	2,208,823
	$6,483,986	$5,748,355

E X H I B I T   1 4 - 1 8

DELTA AIR LINES, INC.
Operating Ratio
For the Years Ended December 31, 1989 and 1988

	1989	1988
	(in thousands)	
Operating expenses	$7,411,159	$6,418,293
Operating revenues	$8,089,484	$6,915,377
Operating ratio	91.61%	92.81%

property and equipment. This ratio is computed for Delta Air Lines in Exhibit 14-19. For Delta, the long-term debt to operating property ratio decreased in 1989 to 15.70% from 20.46%. These are very low and therefore favorable figures.

Operating Revenue to Operating Property

This ratio is a measure of turnover of operating assets. The objective is to generate as many dollars in revenue per dollar of property as possible. This ratio is computed for Delta Air Lines in Exhibit 14-20. The operating revenue to operating property decreased moderately between 1988 and 1989. Part of the reason is that advance payments for new equipment have been included in operating property.

Per Mile—Per Person—Per Ton— Passenger Load Factor

For transportation companies, additional insight can be gained by looking at revenues and expenses on a per unit of usage basis. Examples would be a basis per

E X H I B I T   1 4 - 1 9

DELTA AIR LINES, INC.
Long-Term Debt to Operating Property
For the Years Ended December 31, 1989 and 1988

	1989	1988
	(in thousands)	
Long-term debt	$ 556,770	$ 563,129
Capital leases	146,244	166,364
	$ 703,014	$ 729,493
Operating property	$4,477,873	$3,566,235
Long-term debt to operating property	15.70%	20.46%

EXHIBIT 14-20

DELTA AIR LINES, INC.
Operating Revenue to Operating Property
For the Years Ended December 31, 1989 and 1988

	1989	1988
	(in thousands)	
Operating revenue	$8,089,484	$6,915,377
Operating property	$4,477,873	$3,566,235
Operating revenue to operating property	1.81 times	1.94 times

mile of line or per 10 miles for railroads, or a per passenger mile for air carriers. Although this type of disclosure is not required, it is often presented in highlights.

This type of disclosure is illustrated in Exhibit 14-21, which shows statistics for Delta Air Lines. Statistics in Exhibit 14-21 are available for seat miles, passenger load factor, breakeven load factor, available ton miles, revenue ton miles, passenger revenue per passenger mile, operating expenses per available cost mile, and operating expenses per available ton mile.

INSURANCE

Insurance companies provide two types of services. One is an identified contract service—mortality protection or loss protection. The second is investment management service.

There are basically four types of insurance organizations:

1. *Stock companies.* A stock company is a corporation organized to earn profits for its stockholders. The comments in this insurance section relate specifically to stock companies. Many of the comments are also valid for the other types of insurance organizations.
2. *Mutual companies.* A mutual company is an incorporated entity, without private ownership interest, operating for the benefit of its policyholders and their beneficiaries.
3. *Fraternal benefit societies.* A fraternal benefit society resembles a mutual insurance company in that, although incorporated, it does not have capital stock, and it operates for the benefit of its members and beneficiaries. Policyholders participate in the earnings of the society, and the policies stipulate that the society has the power to assess them in case the legal reserves become impaired.
4. *Assessment companies.* An assessment company is an organized group with similar interests, such as a religious denomination.

Regulation of insurance companies started at the state level. Beginning in 1828, the State of New York required that annual reports be filed with the state control-

EXHIBIT 14-21

DELTA AIR LINES, INC.
Other Financial and Statistical Data
For the Years Ended June 30

(Dollars in thousands, except per share figures)	1989	1988	1987	1986
Total assets	$6,483,986	$5,748,355	$5,342,383	$3,785,462
Long-term debt and capital leases	$ 703,014	$ 729,493	$1,018,417	$ 868,615
Stockholders' equity	$2,619,707	$2,208,823	$1,937,912	$1,301,946
Stockholders' equity per share*	$ 53.17	$ 44.99	$ 39.84	$ 32.45
Shares of common stock outstanding at year end*	49,265,884	49,101,271	48,639,469	40,116,383
Revenue passengers enplaned	64,242,212	58,564,507	48,172,626	39,582,232
Available seat miles (000)	90,741,541	85,833,959	69,013,669	53,336,135
Revenue passenger miles (000)	55,903,857	49,009,094	38,415,117	30,123,387
Passenger load factor	61.61%	57.10%	55.66%	56.48%
Breakeven load factor	56.09%	52.69%	51.09%	56.01%
Available ton miles (000)	11,724,797	11,249,578	8,999,668	6,934,047
Revenue ton miles (000)	6,338,274	5,556,584	4,327,195	3,371,917
Passenger revenue per passenger mile	13.56¢	13.15¢	12.81¢	13.72¢
Operating expenses per available seat mile	8.17¢	7.48¢	7.12¢	8.30¢
Operating expenses per available ton mile	63.21¢	57.05¢	54.60¢	63.82¢

*Adjusted for 2-for-1 stock split distributed December 1, 1981.
The financial and statistical information presented above reflect the Company's acquisition of Western Air Lines, Inc. on December 18, 1986.

ler. Subsequently, other states followed this precedent, and all 50 states now have insurance departments that require annual statements of insurance companies. The reports are filed with the state insurance departments in accordance with statutory accounting practices (SAP). The National Association of Insurance Commissioners (NAIC), a voluntary association, has succeeded in achieving near uniformity among the states, so there are no significant differences in SAP among the states.[1]

Statutory accounting emphasizes the balance sheet. In its concern for protecting the policyholders, it focuses on the financial solvency of the insurance corpo-

[1]Arthur Anderson & Co., *Insurance* (Essex, England: Saffren Press Ltd., 1983), p. 87.

ration. After the annual reports are filed with the individual state insurance departments, a testing process is conducted by the NAIC. This process is based on ratio calculations concerning the financial position of a company. If a company's ratio is outside the prescribed limit, the NAIC brings that to the attention of the state insurance department.

A.M. Best Company publishes *Best's Insurance Reports,* which are issued separately for life-health companies and property-casualty companies. *Best's Insurance Reports* evaluate the financial condition of more than 3,000 insurance companies. The majority of companies are assigned a Best's Rating ranging from A+ (Superior) to C− (Fair). The other companies are classified as "Not Assigned." The "Not Assigned" category has ten classifications to identify why a company has not been given a Best's Rating.

Some of the items included in Best's data include a balance sheet, summary of operations, operating ratios, profitability ratios, leverage ratios, and liquidity ratios. Most of the ratios are industry-specific; it is not practical to describe and explain them in this text. They are described in *Best's Insurance Reports.*

It should be noted that the financial data, including the ratios, are based on the data submitted to the state insurance departments and are thus based on SAP.

Generally accepted accounting principles (GAAP) for insurance companies developed much later than SAP. The annual reports of insurance companies are based on GAAP. GAAP are primarily governed by SFAS No. 60, "Accounting and Reporting by Insurance Enterprises," and SFAS No. 97, "Accounting and Reporting by Insurance Enterprises for Certain Long Duration Contracts and for Realized Gains & Losses from the Sale of Investments."

The 1934 Securities and Exchange Act established national government regulation in addition to the state regulation of insurance companies. Stock insurance companies with assets of $1 million and at least 500 stockholders must register with the SEC and file the required forms, such as the annual form 10-K. Reports filed with the SEC must conform with GAAP.

Exhibit 14-22 contains the income statement, balance sheet, and summary of significant accounting policies from the 1989 annual report of the Aetna Life & Casualty Company. These statements were prepared using GAAP. Review them to observe the unique nature of insurance company financial statements.

Balance Sheet under GAAP

Assets

The balance sheet is not classified by current assets and current liabilities (nonclassified balance sheet). The asset section starts with investments, a classification where most insurance companies maintain the majority of their assets. Many of the investments have a high degree of liquidity, so that prompt payment can be assured in the event of a catastrophic loss. The majority of the investments are typically in bonds, with stock investments often the second-largest investment. Real estate investments are usually present for both property-casualty insurance companies and for life insurance companies. Because liabilities are relatively short term for property-casualty companies, the investment in real estate for these companies is usually immaterial. For life insurance companies, the investment in real estate may be much greater than for property-casualty companies because of the generally longer-term nature and predictability of their liabilities.

Bonds are reported at amortized cost if the company has both the ability and the intent to hold them until maturity. If there is a decline in the market value (other than a temporary decline), the investment is reduced to its net realizable value, and any reduction is reported as a realized loss.

Since temporary decline is a judgment decision, review the disclosure of the market value of bonds. The market value may be significantly below or above the carrying amount, so there may be a potential loss or gain that has not been booked.

E X H I B I T   1 4 - 2 2

AETNA LIFE & CASUALTY COMPANY
Income Statement, Balance Sheet, and Selected Summary
of Significant Accounting Policies
1989 Annual Report

Consolidated Statements of Income

(Millions, except share data)	1989	1988	1987
Revenue:			
Premiums	$13,311.3	$12,038.6	$12,474.9
Net investment income	5,563.8	5,296.7	5,013.8
Other income	550.3	441.4	420.9
Net realized capital gains	246.0	43.5	16.3
Total revenue	19,671.4	17,820.2	17,925.9
Benefits and Expenses:			
Current and future benefits	15,004.4	13,556.7	13,571.0
Amortization of deferred policy acquisition costs	1,343.2	1,415.8	1,311.7
Operating expenses	2,503.8	2,043.7	2,015.3
Total benefits and expenses	18,851.4	17,016.2	16,898.0
Income before income taxes and extraordinary item	820.0	804.0	1,027.9
Federal and foreign income taxes	180.6	104.5	161.1
Income before extraordinary item	639.4	699.5	866.8
Extraordinary item:			
Tax benefit from utilization of loss carryforwards	37.0	13.8	48.5
Net Income	$ 676.4	$ 713.3	$ 915.3
Results Per Common Share:			
Income before extraordinary item	$ 5.69	$ 6.13	$ 7.48
Extraordinary item	.33	.12	.43
Net Income	$ 6.02	$ 6.25	$ 7.91
Weighted average common shares outstanding	111,932,212	112,846,069	113,524,768

See Notes to Financial Statements.

E X H I B I T 1 4 - 2 2 (continued)

Consolidated Balance Sheets

(Millions, except share data)	1989	1988
Assets:		
Investments:		
Fixed maturities, principally at amortized cost		
(market $34,003.3 and $31,117.1)	$33,251.5	$31,924.7
Equity securities, at market (cost $1,160.7 and $1,228.8)	1,348.1	1,228.7
Short-term investments	350.3	357.9
Mortgage loans	23,009.8	21,557.5
Real estate	1,123.6	1,123.5
Policy loans	414.8	418.5
Other	1,693.1	1,816.6
Total investments	61,191.2	58,427.4
Cash and cash equivalents	2,572.4	1,793.6
Accrued investment income	942.4	953.1
Premiums due and other receivables	2,639.7	2,597.4
Deferred policy acquisition costs	1,536.4	1,489.4
Other assets	1,671.3	1,723.1
Separate Accounts assets	16,545.6	14,360.6
Total assets	$87,099.0	$81,344.6
Liabilities:		
Future policy benefits	$13,865.3	$13,170.6
Unpaid claims and claim expenses	14,280.1	13,093.7
Unearned premiums	1,933.4	2,114.4
Policyholders' funds left with the company	29,789.9	28,303.9
Total insurance reserve liabilities	59,868.7	56,682.6
Dividends payable to shareholders	77.5	78.6
Short-term debt	5.7	19.1
Long-term debt	1,037.7	1,096.4
Federal and foreign income taxes:		
Current	80.9	55.3
Deferred	60.2	56.3
Other liabilities	2,311.6	2,279.5
Minority interests and Participating Department	175.0	144.1
Separate Accounts liabilities	16,545.0	14,360.3
Total liabilities	80,162.3	74,772.2
Redeemable Preferred Stock – Class C,		
Less treasury stock	–	118.6
Shareholders' Equity:		
Common stock (No par value; 250,000,000 shares		
authorized; 114,939,275 issued, and		
111,984,979 and 112,231,393 outstanding)	1,421.1	1,421.5
Net unrealized capital gains on investments	142.7	5.3
Retained earnings	5,516.9	5,152.4
Treasury stock, at cost		
(2,954,296 and 2,707,882 shares)	(144.0)	(125.4)
Total shareholders' equity	6,936.7	6,453.8
Total liabilities and shareholders' equity	$87,099.0	$81,344.6
Shareholders' equity per common share	$ 61.94	$ 57.50

See Notes to Financial Statements.

EXHIBIT 14-22 (continued)

Notes to Financial Statements
Note 1   Summary of Significant Accounting Policies (partial)

Investments

Fixed maturity investments include bonds and redeemable preferred stocks and generally are carried at amortized cost. During 1989, the company established certain bond portfolios which are traded to maximize investment returns ("fixed maturity trading securities"). Such fixed maturity trading securities are carried at market value and are included in fixed maturities. Bonds, redeemable preferred stocks and mortgage loans have maturities that generally match the insurance liabilities they support. The distribution of maturities in these fixed investments is monitored, and security purchases and sales are executed with the objective of having adequate funds available at all times to satisfy the company's maturing insurance liabilities. The company also utilizes interest rate and foreign exchange futures, forwards, swaps and options in order to align maturities, interest rates and funds availability with its obligations. Bonds and redeemable preferred stocks are recorded as purchases on the trade date. Mortgage loans are recorded as purchases on the closing date. Redeemable preferred stocks are expected to be retired as a result of regular sinking fund payments by the issuer.

Common stocks and nonredeemable preferred stocks are carried at market value. Purchases are recorded on the trade date. Mortgage loans and policy loans are carried at unpaid principal balances. Real estate investments are generally carried at depreciated cost. The accumulated depreciation for these investments was $71.4 million and $63.4 million at December 31, 1989 and 1988, respectively. Short-term investments, consisting primarily of money market instruments and other debt issues purchased with an original maturity of over ninety days to one year, are stated at amortized cost.

Realized capital gains or losses are the difference between cost and sales proceeds of specific investments sold. Provision for impairments which are other than temporary are included in net realized capital gains. The allowance for potential losses in the value of investments was $306.1 million and $325.9 million at December 31, 1989 and 1988, respectively. Unrealized gains and losses on investments carried at market value, net of related tax, are reflected in shareholders' equity.

Deferred Policy Acquisition Costs

Certain costs of acquiring insurance business have been deferred. These costs, all of which vary with and are primarily related to the production of new business, consist principally of commissions, certain expenses of underwriting and issuing contracts and certain agency expenses. For fixed ordinary life contracts, such costs are amortized over expected premium paying periods. For universal life and certain annuity contracts, such costs are amortized in proportion to estimated gross profits and adjusted to reflect actual gross profits. These costs are amortized over twenty years for annuity and pension contracts, and the contract period for universal life type contracts. For all other lines of business, acquisition costs are amortized over the life of the insurance contract. Deferred policy acquisition costs

EXHIBIT 14-22   (continued)

are written off if it is determined that future policy premiums and investment income or gross profits are not adequate to cover related losses and expenses.

Insurance Reserve Liabilities

Reserves for unpaid claims and claim expenses include provisions for payments to be made on reported losses, losses incurred but not reported and for associated settlement expenses. Estimated amounts of salvage and subrogation, and reinsurance recoverable on unpaid claims are deducted from the liabilities for unpaid claims.

Future policy benefits and policyholders' funds left with the company for universal life and certain fixed annuity contracts are equal to cumulative premiums less charges plus credited interest thereon. Reserves for all other fixed individual and group life, health and annuity contracts are computed on the basis of assumed investment yield, mortality, morbidity and expenses, including a margin for adverse deviation, which generally vary by plan, year of issue and policy duration. Reserve interest rates range from 2.25% to 12.25%. Investment yield is based on company experience. Mortality, morbidity and withdrawal rate assumptions are based on the experience of the company and are periodically reviewed against industry standards and experience. Group life, health and pension insurance reserves on coverages subject to experience rating reflect the rights and expectations of plan participants, group policyholders and the company.

Reinsurance

The company utilizes reinsurance agreements to reduce its exposure to large losses in all aspects of its insurance business. Reinsurance permits recovery of a portion of losses from reinsurers, although it does not discharge the primary liability of the company as direct insurer of the risks reinsured. However, the company treats risks reinsured with other companies as though they are not risks for which it is liable. Deductions from policy and claim reserves for reinsurance ceded were $4.1 billion and $3.8 billion for 1989 and 1988, respectively. Reinsurance premiums ceded were $2.4 billion, $2.5 billion and $2.2 billion for 1989, 1988 and 1987, respectively. Reinsurance premiums assumed were $1.7 billion, $2.0 billion and $1.9 billion for 1989, 1988 and 1987, respectively.

If the insurance company does not intend to hold the bonds until maturity, they are reported at market value. Temporary changes in the market value of these bonds are recognized as unrealized gains or losses, net of applicable income taxes, as a separate component of stockholders' equity.

Redeemable preferred stock is reported in the same manner as bonds.

Common and nonredeemable preferred stocks are reported at market value. Temporary changes to market value are recognized as unrealized gains or losses, net of applicable income taxes, as a separate component of stockholders' equity.

Mortgage loans are reported at par value or at amortized cost if purchased at a discount or premium. This amount is offset for estimated uncollectible amounts. Changes in the estimate for uncollectible amounts are included in realized gains and losses in the income statement. Be aware that the balance in estimated uncollectible amounts is a matter of subjective judgment.

Real estate investments are reported at cost less accumulated depreciation and an allowance for impairment in value. Depreciation is charged to investment income. Changes in the allowance or charges for impairment in value are included in realized gains or losses. Take note if the insurance company under review has substantial investments in real estate. This could represent a risk because of the subjectivity in establishing the allowance for impairment in value.

Loans to life insurance policyholders are carried at the outstanding balance, which includes accumulated interest. These loans may be at a rate of interest below the market rate, which would make their value less than the carrying amount. This is not usually a major problem, because the dollar amount of the loans is usually an immaterial amount of the total under the investment classification. The balance of policy loans should not exceed the cash surrender value or the policy reserve.

Assets Other Than Investments

A number of asset accounts other than investments may be on an insurance company's balance sheet. Some of the typical accounts are described in the paragraphs that follow.

Real estate used in operations is reported at cost less accumulated depreciation. Under SAP, real estate used in operations is expensed.

Deferred policy acquisition costs represent the cost of obtaining policies. Under GAAP, these costs are deferred and charged to expense over the premium-paying period. This is one of the major differences between GAAP reporting and SAP reporting: under SAP reporting, these costs are charged to expense as they are incurred.

Goodwill is an intangible account resulting from acquiring other companies. The same account can be found on the balance sheet of companies other than insurance companies. Under GAAP, the goodwill account is accounted for as an asset and subsequently amortized to expense. Under SAP, neither the goodwill account nor other intangibles are recognized.

Liabilities

Generally, the largest liability is for loss reserves. Reserving for losses involves estimating their ultimate value. The quantification process is subject to a number of estimates, including inflation, interest rates, and judicial interpretations. Mortality estimates are also important for life insurance companies. These reserve accounts should be adequate to pay policy claims under the terms of the insurance policies.

In general, the loss reserves accounts are determined considering the present value of the commitments. There is a great deal of subjectivity involved in setting the reserve amounts. Insurance companies have been accused of underreserving during tough years and overreserving during good years.

Another liability account found on an insurance company's balance sheet is policy and contract claims. This account represents claims that have accrued as of the balance sheet date. These claims are reported net of any portion that can be recovered.

Many other liability accounts are found on an insurance company's balance sheet, such as notes payable and income taxes. These are typically reported in the same manner as other industries report them, except that there is no current liability classification.

Stockholders' Equity

The stockholders' equity section usually resembles the stockholders' equity section of companies in other industries. The account net unrealized gains (losses) on marketable equity securities can be particularly large for insurance companies, because of the expanded use of this account following standards for insurance companies and the material amount of investments that an insurance company may have. Pay close attention to changes in this account, as these unrealized gains or losses have not been recognized on the income statement.

Income Statement under GAAP

The manner of recognizing revenue on insurance contracts is unique for the insurance industry. In general, the duration of the contract governs the revenue recognition.

For contracts of short duration, revenue is ordinarily recognized over the period of the contract in proportion to the amount of insurance protection provided. When the risk differs significantly from the contract period, revenue is recognized over the period of risk in proportion to the amount of insurance protection.[2]

Policies relating to loss protection typically fall under the short-duration contract. An example would be casualty insurance in which the insurance company retains the right to cancel the contract at the end of the policy term.

For long-duration contracts, revenue is recognized when the premium is due from the policyholder. Examples are whole-life contracts and single-premium life contracts.[3] Likewise, acquisition costs are capitalized and expensed in proportion to premium revenue.

However, long-duration contracts that do not subject the insurance enterprise to significant risks arising from policyholder mortality or morbidity are referred to as *investment contracts*. Amounts received on these contracts are not to be reported as revenues but rather as liabilities and accounted for in the same way as interest-

---

[2]Statement of Financial Accounting Standards No. 60, "Accounting and Reporting by Insurance Enterprises" (Stamford, Connecticut: Financial Accounting Standards Board, 1982), par. 13.
[3]Ibid., par. 15.

bearing instruments.[4] These contracts are regarded as investment contracts, since they do not incorporate significant insurance risk. Interestingly, many of the life insurance policies currently being written are of this type.

With the investment contracts, premium payments are credited to the policyholder balance. The insurance company assesses charges against this balance for contract services and credits the balance for income earned. The insurer can adjust the schedule for contract services and the rate at which income is credited.

Investment contracts generally include an assessment against the policyholder on inception of the contract and an assessment when the contract is terminated. The inception fees are booked as recoveries of capitalized acquisition costs, and the termination fees are booked as revenue at the time of termination.

In addition to insurance activities, insurance companies are substantially involved with investments. Realized gains and losses from investments are reported in operations in the period incurred.

Ratios

As previously indicated, many of the ratios relating to insurance companies are industry-specific. An explanation of industry-specific ratios is beyond the scope of this book. The industry-specific ratios are frequently based on SAP financial reporting to the states, rather than the GAAP financial reporting that is used for the annual report and SEC requirements.

Ratios computed from the GAAP-based financial statements are often profitability and investor related. Examples of such ratios are return on common equity, price/earnings ratio, dividend payout, and dividend yield. These ratios are explained in other sections of this book.

Insurance companies tend to have a stock market price at a discount to the average market price (price/earnings ratio). This discount is typically 10% to 20% but at times is as high as 40%. There are many likely reasons for this relatively low market value. Insurance is a highly regulated industry that some perceive as having low growth prospects. It is also an industry with substantial competition. The regulation and the competition put pressure on the premiums that can be charged. The accounting environment also contributes to the relatively low market price for insurance company stocks. The existence of two sets of accounting principles, SAP and GAAP, contributes to the lack of understanding of insurance companies' financial statements. Also, many of the accounting standards are complex and industry-specific.

The nature of the industry leads to standards that allow much subjectivity and possible manipulation of reported profit. For example, insurance companies are perceived to underreserve during tough years and overreserve during good years. Some individuals maintain that insurance companies select which stocks to sell

---

[4]Statement of Financial Accounting Standards No. 97, "Accounting and Reporting by Insurance Enterprises for Certain Long-Duration Contracts and for Realized Gains and Losses from the Sale of Investments" (Stamford, Connecticut: Financial Accounting Standards Board, 1987), par. 15.

based on the potential realized gain or loss or the unrealized gain or loss—selling securities that result in realized gains in down years and selling securities that result in realized losses during good years. (Securities not sold influence unrealized gains and losses that are reported as part of stockholders' equity.)

SUMMARY

Financial statements vary among industries, and they are especially different for banks, utilities, transportation companies, and insurance companies. In each case, the accounting of these firms is subject to a uniform accounting system. Changes in analysis are necessitated by the differences in accounting presentation.

Oil and gas companies' financial statements are affected significantly by the method they choose to account for costs associated with exploration and production. Another important aspect of financial statements of oil and gas companies is the footnote requirement that relates to supplementary information on oil and gas exploration, development, and production activities. Cash flow is also particularly significant to oil and gas companies.

Special industry ratios were reviewed in this chapter. The following ratios are helpful when analyzing a bank:

$$\text{Earning Assets to Total Assets} = \frac{\text{Average Earning Assets}}{\text{Average Total Assets}}$$

$$\text{Return on Earning Assets} = \frac{\text{Income before Securities Transactions}}{\text{Average Earning Assets}}$$

$$\text{Interest Margin to Average Earning Assets} = \frac{\text{Interest Margin}}{\text{Average Earning Assets}}$$

$$\text{Loan Loss Coverage Ratio} = \frac{\text{Pretax Income (before security transactions)} + \text{Provision for Loan Losses}}{\text{Net Charge-Offs}}$$

$$\text{Equity Capital to Total Assets} = \frac{\text{Average Equity}}{\text{Average Total Assets}}$$

$$\text{Deposits Times Capital} = \frac{\text{Average Deposits}}{\text{Average Stockholders' Equity}}$$

The following ratios are helpful in analyzing utility performance:

$$\text{Operating Ratio} = \frac{\text{Operating Expenses}}{\text{Operating Revenues}}$$

$$\text{Funded Debt to Operating Property} = \frac{\text{Funded Debt (long-term)}}{\text{Operating Property}}$$

$$\text{Percent Earned on Operating Property} = \frac{\text{Net Income}}{\text{Operating Property}}$$

$$\text{Operating Revenue to Operating Property} = \frac{\text{Operating Revenue}}{\text{Operating Property}}$$

The ratios that follow are especially suited to transportation. Additional insight can be gained by looking at revenues and expenses on a per unit of usage basis.

$$\text{Operating Ratio} = \frac{\text{Operating Expenses}}{\text{Operating Revenues}}$$

$$\text{Long-Term Debt to Operating Property} = \frac{\text{Long-Term Debt}}{\text{Operating Property}}$$

$$\text{Operating Revenue to Operating Property} = \frac{\text{Operating Revenue}}{\text{Operating Property}}$$

QUESTIONS

Q 14-1 What are the main sources of revenue for banks?

Q 14-2 Why are loans, which are usually accounted for as liabilities, treated as assets for banks?

Q 14-3 Why are savings accounts liabilities for banks?

Q 14-4 Why are banks concerned with their loans/deposits ratios?

Q 14-5 To what agencies and other users of financial statements must banks report?

Q 14-6 Why must the user be cautious in analyzing bank holding companies?

Q 14-7 What is usually the biggest expense item for a bank?

Q 14-8 How does the earnings per share presentation for a bank differ from that of other corporations?

Q 14-9 What does the ratio total deposits times capital measure?

Q 14-10 What ratios are used to indicate profitability for banks?

Q 14-11 Why are banks concerned about the percentage of earning assets to total assets?

Q 14-12 What does the loan loss coverage ratio measure?

Q 14-13 What type of ratio is deposits times capital?

Q 14-14 Give an example of why a review of bank assets may indicate risk or opportunity you were not aware of.

Q 14-15 Why review the disclosure of the market value of investments versus the book amount of investments for banks?

Q 14-16 Why review the disclosure of foreign loans for banks?

Q 14-17   Why review the disclosure of allowance for loan losses for a bank?

Q 14-18   Why review the disclosure of nonperforming assets for banks?

Q 14-19   Why could a review of savings deposit balances be important when reviewing a bank's financial statements?

Q 14-20   Why review the footnote that describes commitments and contingent liabilities for a bank?

Q 14-21   Utilities are very highly leveraged. How is it that they are able to carry such high levels of debt?

Q 14-22   How does demand for utilities differ from demand for other products or services?

Q 14-23   Why are plant and equipment listed first for utilities?

Q 14-24   Are inventory ratios meaningful for utilities? Why?

Q 14-25   What does the funded debt to operating property ratio measure for a utility?

Q 14-26   Is the times interest earned ratio meaningful for utilities? Why, or why not?

Q 14-27   Are current liabilities presented first in utility reporting?

Q 14-28   For a utility, why review the account construction work in progress?

Q 14-29   Describe the income statement accounts allowance for equity funds used during construction and allowance for borrowed funds used during construction.

Q 14-30   Differentiate between successful-efforts and full-cost accounting as applied to the oil and gas industry.

Q 14-31   Some industries described in this chapter are controlled by federal regulatory agencies. How does this affect their accounting systems?

Q 14-32   When reviewing the financial statements of oil and gas companies, why is it important to note the method of costing (expensing) exploration and production costs?

Q 14-33   Oil and gas companies must disclose quantity estimates for proved oil and gas reserves and the major factors causing changes in these resource estimates. Briefly indicate why this disclosure can be significant.

Q 14-34   For oil and gas companies, there is the potential for a significant difference between the reported income and the cash flow from operations. Comment.

Q 14-35   Is it more desirable to have the operating ratios increasing or decreasing for utilities and transportation companies?

Q 14-36   What type of ratio is operating revenue to operating property? Will it exceed 1:1 for a utility?

Q 14-37   What is the most important category of assets for transportation firms?

Q 14-38   Briefly describe the revenue section of the income statement for a transportation firm.

Q 14-39   In a transportation firm, what types of items will change operating revenues? Operating expenses?

Q 14-40   If a transportation firm shows a rise in revenue per passenger mile, what does this rise imply?

Q 14-41   How is the passenger load factor of a bus company related to profitability?

Q 14-42   Explain how the publication *Financial Analysis of the Motor Carrier Industry* could be used to determine what percentage of total revenue a firm has in relation to similar trucking firms.

Q 14-43   Annual reports filed with state insurance departments are in accordance with what accounting standards?

Q 14-44   Annual reports that insurance companies issue to the public are in accordance with what accounting standards?

Q 14-45   Why could an insurance company with substantial investments in real estate represent a risk?

Q 14-46   Describe the difference between GAAP reporting and SAP reporting of deferred policy acquisition costs.

Q 14-47   Briefly describe the difference in accounting for intangibles for an insurance company under GAAP and under SAP.

Q 14-48   Briefly describe the unique aspects of revenue recognition for an insurance company.

Q 14-49   Insurance industry-specific financial ratios are usually prepared from financial statements prepared under what standards?

Q 14-50   Insurance companies tend to have a stock market price at a discount to the average market price (price/earnings ratio). Indicate some perceived reasons for this relatively low price/earnings ratio.

PROBLEMS

P 14-1   The following are statistics from the annual report of the McEttrick National Bank.

	1989	1988
Average loans	$16,000,000	$13,200,000
Average total assets	26,000,000	22,000,000
Average total deposits	24,000,000	20,000,000
Average total capital	1,850,000	1,600,000
Interest expenses	1,615,000	1,512,250
Interest income	1,750,000	1,650,000

Required   a. Calculate the total deposits times capital for each year.
b. Calculate the loans to total deposits for each year.
c. Calculate the capital funds to total assets for each year.
d. Calculate the interest margin to average total assets for each year.
e. Comment on any trends found in the calculations of (a) through (d).

P 14-2   The following are statistics from the annual report of the Dover Bank.

	1989	1988	1987
Average earning assets	$50,000,000	$45,000,000	$43,000,000
Average total assets	58,823,529	54,216,867	52,000,000
Income before securities transactions	530,000	453,000	420,000
Interest margin	2,550,000	2,200,000	2,020,000
Pretax income before securities transactions	562,000	480,500	440,000
Provision for loan losses	190,000	160,000	142,000
Net charge-offs	180,000	162,000	160,000
Average equity	4,117,600	3,524,000	3,120,000
Average net loans	32,500,000	26,000,000	22,500,000
Average deposits	52,500,000	42,500,000	37,857,000

Required   a. Calculate the following ratios for 1989, 1988, and 1987:
   1. earning assets to total assets
   2. return on earning assets
   3. interest margin to average earning assets
   4. loan loss coverage ratio
   5. equity to total assets
   6. deposits times capital
   7. loans to deposits
   b. Comments on trends found in the ratios computed in (a).

P 14-3   Super Power Company reported the following statistics in its statement of income:

	1989	1988
Electric revenues:		
Residential	$11,800,000	$10,000,000
Commercial and industrial	10,430,000	10,000,000
Other	600,000	500,000
	22,830,000	20,500,000
Operating expenses and taxes*	20,340,000	18,125,000
Operating income	2,490,000	2,375,000
Other income	200,000	195,000
Income before interest deductions	2,690,000	2,570,000
Interest deductions	1,200,000	1,000,000
Net income	$ 1,490,000	$ 1,570,000

*Includes taxes of $3,200,000 in 1989 and $3,000,000 in 1988.

Required   a. Calculate the operating ratio and comment on the results.
   b. Calculate the times interest earned and comment on the results.
   c. Perform a vertical common size analysis of revenues, using total revenue as the base, and comment on the relative size of the component parts.

P 14-4   The following statistics relate to the Michgate electric utility.

	1991	1990	1989
	(in thousands, except per share)		
Operating expenses	$ 850,600	$ 820,200	$ 780,000
Operating revenues	1,080,500	1,037,200	974,000
Earnings per share	3.00	2.90	2.60
Cash flow per share	3.40	3.25	2.30
Operating property	3,900,000	3,750,000	3,600,000
Funded debt (long-term)	1,500,000	1,480,000	1,470,000
Net income	280,000	260,000	230,000

Required   a. Calculate the following ratios for 1991, 1990, and 1989.
        1. operating ratio
        2. funded debt to operating property
        3. percent earned on operating property
        4. operating revenue to operating property
      b. Comment on trends found in the ratios computed in (a).
      c. Comment on the trend between earnings per share and cash flow per share.

P 14-5   Local Airways had the following results in the last two years:

	1991	1990
Operating revenues	$ 624,000	$ 618,000
Operating expenses	625,000	617,000
Operating property	365,000	360,000
Long-term debt	280,000	270,000
Estimated passenger miles	7,340,000	7,600,000

Required   Calculate the following ratios for 1991 and 1990.
      a. Calculate the operating ratio and comment on the trend.
      b. Calculate the long-term debt to operating property ratio. What does this tell about debt use?
      c. Calculate the operating revenue to operating property and comment on the trend.
      d. Calculate the revenue per passenger mile. What has caused this trend?

P 14-6   Selected (unaudited) financial data for each quarter within 1980 and 1979 for Alaska Airlines, restated where applicable for the spin-off of Alaska Northwest Properties Inc., are as follows (fiscal year ended December 31):

	1st Quarter		2nd Quarter		3rd Quarter		4th Quarter	
	1980	1979	1980	1979	1980	1979	1980	1979
Airline operating revenues	$21,935	$17,727	$30,986	$26,553	$45,540	$31,159	$32,389	$22,761
Airline operating income	(4,108)	(1,604)	(486)	1,460	7,379	3,797	2,320	(1,374)
Income (loss) before disposed business segment	(2,315)	(1,589)	(921)	797	4,685	2,816	3,679	1,000
Net income (loss)	(2,315)	(1,330)	(921)	895	4,685	2,810	3,679	1,000

Required   a. Discuss the concept of seasonality as related to these data.
              b. Discuss the trend in profits from 1979 to 1980.
              c. Suggest items that would cause operating income before disposed business segment to vary.
              d. Should income before disposed business segment or net income be used in trend analysis? Why?

P 14-7   Chihi Airways had the following results for the last three years:

	1991	1990	1989
		(in thousands)	
Operating expenses	$1,550,000	$1,520,000	$1,480,000
Operating revenues	1,840,000	1,670,400	1,620,700
Long-term debt	910,000	900,500	895,000
Operating property	995,000	990,000	985,000
Passenger load factor	66.5%	59.0%	57.8%

Required   a. Calculate the following ratios for 1991, 1990, and 1989:
                 1. operating ratio
                 2. long-term debt to operating property
                 3. operating revenue to operating property
              b. Comment on trends found in the ratios computed in (a).
              c. Comment on the passenger load factor.

P 14-8   Exhibit 14-17 includes consolidated statements of income for Delta Air Lines, Inc.

Required   a. Prepare a vertical common size analysis of this statement through operating income for 1989, 1988, and 1987. Use total operating revenues as the base.
              b. Comment on trends found in (a).

P 14-9

Required   Answer the following multiple-choice questions related to insurance financial reporting.
              a. Which of the following does not represent a basic type of insurance organization?
                 1. stock companies
                 2. bond companies
                 3. mutual companies
                 4. fraternal benefit societies
                 5. assessment companies
              b. Which of these statements is not correct?
                 1. The balance sheet is a classified balance sheet.
                 2. The asset section starts with investments.
                 3. The majority of the investments are typically in bonds.
                 4. For life insurance companies, the investment on real estate may be much greater than for property-casualty companies.
                 5. Real estate investments are reported at cost less accumulated depreciation and an allowance for impairment in value.
              c. Generally, the largest liability is for loss reserves. The quantification process is subject to a number of estimates. Which of the following would not be one of the estimates?
                 1. investment gains/losses
                 2. inflation rate
                 3. interest rates

    4. judicial interpretations

    5. mortality estimates

  d. The manner of recognizing revenue on insurance contracts is unique for the insurance industry. Which of the following statements is not true?

    1. In general, the duration of the contract governs the revenue recognition.

    2. When the risk differs significantly from the contract period, revenue is recognized over the period of risk in proportion to the amount of insurance protection.

    3. For long-duration contracts, revenue is recognized when the premium is due from policyholders.

    4. Realized gains and losses from investments are reported in operations in the period incurred.

    5. For investment contracts, termination fees are booked as revenue over the period of the contract.

  e. Which of the following statements is not true?

    1. Statutory accounting has emphasized the balance sheet in its concern for protecting the policyholders by focusing on the financial solvency of the insurance corporation.

    2. All 50 states have insurance departments that require annual statements of insurance companies. These annual reports are filed with the state insurance departments in accordance with statutory accounting practices (SAP).

    3. After the annual reports are filed with the individual state insurance departments, a testing process is conducted by the NAIC. If a company's ratio is outside the prescribed limit, the NAIC brings that to the attention of the company.

    4. A. M. Best Company publishes *Best's Insurance Reports,* which are issued separately for life-health companies and property-casualty companies. The financial data, including the ratios, are based on the data submitted to the state insurance departments and are thus based on SAP.

    5. Many stock insurance companies must register with the Securities and Exchange Commission and file the required forms, such as the annual form 10-K. Reports filed with the SEC must conform with GAAP.

| CASES

Case 14-1   ALLOWANCE FOR FUNDS

The following is financial information from the Arizona Public Service Company 1983 annual report:

ARIZONA PUBLIC SERVICE COMPANY
Consolidated Statements of Income
Year Ended December 31

	1983	1982	1981
	(Dollars in Thousands, Except Per Share Amounts)		
Operating revenues:			
Electric	$ 871,875	$ 866,486	730,788
Gas	202,134	197,967	151,366
Total	1,074,009	1,064,453	882,154

Consolidated Statements of Income   (continued)

	1983	1982	1981
Fuel expenses:			
Fuel for electric generation	185,504	177,095	168,227
Purchased power and interchange—net	6,454	27,358	(823)
Purchased gas for resale	141,653	135,715	101,310
Total	333,611	340,168	268,714
Operating revenues less fuel expenses	740,398	724,285	613,440
Other operating expenses:			
Operations excluding fuel expenses	128,412	114,844	105,237
Maintenance	71,431	67,217	71,160
Depreciation and amortization	90,069	85,285	76,178
Income taxes (Note 8)	99,109	89,250	22,381
Other taxes (Note 11)	97,179	97,188	87,566
Total	486,220	453,784	362,522
Operating income	254,198	270,501	250,918
Other income (deductions):			
Allowance for equity funds used during construction	121,832	80,141	57,421
Income taxes (Note 8)	9,288	(2,852)	2,743
Other—net	3,813	6,046	(1,416)
Total	134,933	83,335	58,748
Income before interest deductions	389,131	353,836	309,666
Interest deductions:			
Interest on long-term debt and project financing	176,099	165,931	155,086
Interest on short-term borrowings	11,781	14,917	11,853
Debt discount, premium and expense	2,019	2,265	1,169
Allowance for borrowed funds used during construction—credit	(65,565)	(60,320)	(55,876)
Total	124,334	122,793	112,232
Net income	264,797	231,043	197,434
Preferred stock dividend requirements	43,741	34,816	26,786
Earnings for common stock	$ 221,056	$ 196,227	$ 170,648
Average common shares outstanding	63,865,210	59,549,685	52,289,259
Per share common stock:			
Earnings (based on average shares outstanding)	$3.46	$3.30	$3.26
Dividends declared	$2.56	$2.40	$2.20

See Notes to Consolidatd Financial Statements.

Consolidated Balance Sheet

	December 31	
	1983	1982
Assets	(Thousands of Dollars)	
Utility plant (Notes 4 and 7):		
Plant in service:		
Electric	$2,467,126	$2,402,640
Gas	174,038	151,411
Common, used in all services	90,577	85,131
Total	2,740,741	2,639,182
Construction work in progress	1,986,052	1,539,453
Plant held for future use	34,472	19,831
Total utility plant	4,761,265	4,198,466
Less accumulated depreciation and amortization	727,865	646,517
Utility plant—net	4,033,400	3,551,949
Investments and other assets:		
Investments in and receivables from subsidiaries	44,740	30,269
Time deposits designated for capital expenditures	30,141	49,516
Other investments and notes receivable	5,699	5,750
Total investments and other assets	80,580	85,535
Current assets:		
Cash (Note 6)	11,735	7,930
Temporary cash investments	21,000	—
Special deposits and working funds (Note 6)	3,873	3,877
Accounts receivable:		
Service customers	89,428	80,030
Other	19,686	29,596
Allowance for doubtful accounts	(2,443)	(2,005)
Materials and supplies (at average cost)	41,261	39,937
Fuel (at average cost)	33,264	37,348
Deferred fuel	7,463	8,219
Other	3,691	4,983
Total current assets	228,958	209,915
Deferred debits:		
Unamortized gas exploration cost	14,728	16,497
Unamortized debt issue costs	14,422	11,836
Other	14,224	12,804
Total deferred debits	43,374	41,137
Total	$4,386,312	$3,888,536

Consolidated Balance Sheet   (continued)

	December 31	
	1983	1982
Liabilities		
Capitalization (Notes 2, 3, and 4):		
Common stock	$ 166,777	$ 157,236
Premiums and expenses—net	959,932	883,680
Retained earnings	459,962	401,723
Common stock equity	1,586,671	1,442,639
Nonredeemable preferred stock	218,516	168,561
Redeemable preferred stock	237,400	241,220
Long-term debt less current maturities	1,655,077	1,369,266
Total capitalization	3,697,709	3,221,686
Current liabilities		
Notes payable to banks (Note 6)	86,308	49,516
Commercial paper	—	40,100
Current maturities of long-term debt (Note 4)	115,833	171,153
Accounts payable	91,176	76,604
Accrued taxes	52,369	55,974
Accrued interest	63,112	50,559
Accrued dividends	3,711	3,327
Deferred fuel	14,146	31,785
Other	26,070	21,559
Total current liabilities	452,725	500,577
Deferred credits and other:		
Unamortized credit related to sale of tax benefits (Note 8)	47,020	48,708
Deferred income taxes	73,361	41,585
Deferred investment tax credit	82,118	52,158
Customers' advances for construction	18,039	14,619
Other	15,340	9,203
Total deferred credits and other	235,878	166,273
Commitments and contingencies (Note 10)		
Total	$4,386,312	$3,888,536

See Notes to Consolidated Financial Statements.

Selected Note to Consolidated Financial Statements

Note E

Allowance for funds used during construction—In accordance with the regulatory accounting practice prescribed by the FERC and the ACC, the Company capitalizes an allowance for the cost of funds used to finance its construction program ("AFC"). AFC, which does not represent current cash earnings, is defined as the net cost during the period of construction of borrowed funds used for construction, and a reasonable rate of return on equity funds so used. The calculated amount is capitalized as a part of the cost of utility plant.

AFC has been calculated using composite rates of 13.00%, 13.25%, and 12.25% in 1983, 1982 and 1981 (except for AFC related to project financing which was computed at the actual rate thereon), respectively. In July 1983 the Company began compounding AFC semi-annually and, in October 1983, recording such cost on a "net of tax" basis. AFC ceases to accrue on those portions of construction work in progress allowed in rate base.

Required

a. Describe allowance for funds used during construction.
b. How does capitalizing interest on borrowed funds affect income in the year of capitalization versus not capitalizing this interest? Explain.
c. Would net income tend to be higher than cash flow if there is substantial capitalization of interest on borrowed funds during the current period? Explain.
d. How does capitalizing allowance for equity funds used during construction affect income in the year of capitalization versus not capitalizing these charges?
e. Would net income tend to be higher than cash flow if there is substantial capitalization of allowance for equity funds used during construction for the current year?
f. Describe how a utility that has substantial construction work in progress could have material cash flow problems in relation to the reported income.
g. Compute the following ratios for 1983 and 1982. Comment on each.
   1. operating ratio
   2. funded debt to operating property
   3. percent earned on operating property
   4. operating revenue to operating property
   5. times interest earned
h. Using the balances at December 31, 1983, compute the percentage relationship between construction work in progress and total assets.

Case 14-2   IN PROGRESS

The Toledo Edison Company included the following in its 1983 annual report:

TOLEDO EDISON COMPANY
Selected Income Statement Data
Years Ended December 31

	1983	1982	1981
Allowance for debt funds used during construction	$ 30,443,000	$ 22,505,000	$15,491,000
Allowance for equity funds used during construction	65,385,000	48,706,000	32,498,000
Depreciation and amortization	51,138,000	43,838,000	43,427,000
Net income	128,344,000	105,534,000	83,137,000
Earnings per common share			
Before extraordinary gain	$3.50	$3.18	$2.77
After extraordinary gain	3.50	3.18	3.27
Return on average common equity (before extraordinary gain)	14.5%	13.3%	11.6%

Selected Balance Sheet Data
Years Ended December 31

	1983	1982	1981
Construction work in progress	$1,118,802,000	$ 878,535,000	—
Total assets	$2,401,778,000	$2,124,823,000	—
Other			
Dividends declared per share of common stock	$2.46	$2.38	$2.30
Total dividends declared			
Preferred stock	$ 30,803,000	$ 26,766,000	$24,222,000
Common stock	70,537,000	60,517,000	50,245,000

Required

a. Comment on trends, considering only net income, earnings per common share, return on average common equity, and dividends declared per share of common stock.

b. Comment on trends, considering only allowance for debt funds used during construction, allowance for equity funds used during construction, construction work in progress, and total assets.

c. Comment on cash flow, considering allowance for debt funds used during construction, allowance for equity funds used during construction, and dividends.

Case 14-3   REVIEW THIS UTILITY

The following is financial information from the Central Vermont Public Service Corporation annual report.

Consolidated Statement of Income and Retained Earnings
(dollars in thousands except amounts per share)

			Year Ended December 31			
	1986	1985	1984	1983	1982	1981
Operating revenues	$ 188,081	$ 169,104	$ 155,637	$ 144,009	$ 133,663	$ 117,339
Operating expenses						
Operation						
Purchased power	89,310	82,991	80,121	78,968	64,844	60,237
Production and transmission	13,872	12,131	10,217	8,168	7,795	7,577
Other operation	23,827	19,953	19,691	17,601	16,790	13,672
Maintenance	8,556	8,271	7,868	6,797	6,900	5,863
Depreciation	6,462	5,917	4,916	4,426	4,147	3,805
Other taxes, principally property taxes	6,382	5,804	5,783	5,330	5,085	4,764
Taxes on income (Note 8)	16,607	13,687	10,242	7,618	10,699	7,369
Total operating expenses	165,016	148,754	138,838	128,908	116,260	103,287
Operating income	23,065	20,350	16,799	15,101	17,403	14,052
Other income and deductions						
Equity in earnings of companies not consolidated	4,007	3,446	2,761	2,908	2,541	2,669
Allowance for equity funds during construction	7,504	9,499	8,236	6,608	3,577	2,577
Other income (expenses), net	1,690	(679)	2,574	1,791	(1,478)	1,391
Benefit (provision) for income taxes (Note 8)	(243)	239	(1,154)	(1,083)	705	(799)
Total operating and other income	36,023	32,855	29,216	25,325	22,748	19,890

Interest expense						
Interest on long-term debt	13,963	13,659	11,707	9,890	8,950	7,612
Other interest	612	761	284	931	386	1,441
Allowance for borrowed funds during construction	(4,953)	(5,172)	(4,482)	(3,750)	(2,798)	(3,029)
Net interest expense	9,622	9,248	7,509	7,071	6,538	6,024
Net income	26,401	23,607	21,707	18,254	16,210	13,866
Retained earnings, January 1	60,119	50,601	42,169	35,406	29,149	23,763
	86,520	74,208	63,876	53,660	45,359	37,629
Cash dividends declared						
Preferred stock	2,931	2,024	2,067	2,245	2,403	2,496
Common stock	12,420	12,065	11,208	9,246	7,550	5,984
Total dividends	15,351	14,089	13,275	11,491	9,953	8,480
Retained earnings, December 31	$ 71,169	$ 60,119	$ 50,601	$ 42,169	$ 35,406	$ 29,149
Earnings available for common stock	$ 23,470	$ 21,583	$ 19,640	$ 16,009	$ 13,807	$ 11,370
Average shares of common stock outstanding	6,553,423	6,373,347	6,164,662	5,443,318	4,854,777	4,056,351
Earnings per share of common stock	$3.58	$3.39	$3.19	$2.94	$2.84	$2.80
Dividends per share of common stock	$1.90	$1.90	$1.83	$1.72	$1.62	$1.48

Consolidated Balance Sheet
(dollars in thousands)

	December 31	
	1986	1985
Assets		
Utility plant, at original cost	$273,421	$189,373
Less accumulated depreciation	54,482	50,156
	218,939	139,217
Construction work in progress	6,068	143,986
Nuclear fuel, net	2,632	7,614
Net utility plant	227,639	290,817
Investments in affiliates, at equity (Note 3)	30,546	25,781
Nonutility property, less accumulated depreciation	3,863	4,021
Current assets		
Cash	2,549	1,614
Temporary investments, at cost which approximates market	8,030	2,630
Accounts receivable, less allowance for uncollectible accounts ($553 in 1986 and $598 in 1985)	14,877	13,888
Refundable income taxes	6,575	593
Unbilled revenue	13,352	7,883
Materials and supplies, at average cost	2,758	3,139
Prepayments	1,865	2,227
Other current assets	342	5,650
Total current assets	50,348	37,624
Unrecovered Seabrook investment (Note 2)	70,339	6,396
Other deferred charges	12,505	9,853
	$395,240	$374,492
Capitalization and liabilities		
Capitalization		
Common stock, $6 par value, authorized 14,000,000 shares; outstanding 6,619,730 shares in 1986 and 6,474,069 shares in 1985 (Note 4)	$ 39,718	$ 38,845
Other paid-in capital (Note 4)	42,665	40,227
Retained earnings (Note 4)	71,169	60,119
Total common stock equity	153,552	139,191
Preferred and preference stock (Note 4)	15,146	15,151
Preferred stock with sinking fund requirements (Note 4)	15,200	6,400
Long-term debt (Note 5)	122,270	133,224
	306,168	293,966

Consolidated Balance Sheet   (continued)

	December 31	
	1986	1985
Current liabilities		
Notes payable—banks	—	11,100
Current portion of preferred stock and long-term debt	8,461	3,500
Accounts payable	6,344	6,579
Accounts payable—affiliates	5,136	9,100
Accrued interest	2,259	2,293
Accrued income taxes	1,772	1,220
Other current liabilities	5,363	5,531
Total current liabilities	29,335	39,323
Deferred income taxes (Note 8)	46,628	23,854
Deferred investment tax credits (Note 8)	11,770	16,126
Deferred credits and miscellaneous reserves	1,339	1,223
Commitments and contingencies (Notes 2, 3 and 9)		
	$395,240	$374,492

The accompanying notes are an integral part of these financial statements.

Selected Notes to Consolidated Financial Statements

Note 1   Summary of Significant Accounting Policies

Consolidation: The consolidated financial statements include the accounts of the Company and its wholly owned subsidiaries.

The Company follows the equity method of accounting for its investments in affiliates. See Note 3.

Regulation: The Company is subject to regulation by the Vermont Public Service Board (PSB), the Federal Energy Regulatory Commission (FERC) and, to a lesser extent, the public utilities commissions in other New England states where the Company does business, with respect to rates charged for service, accounting and other matters. The Company's accounting policies generally reflect the rate-making and regulatory policies of these authorities.

Revenues: Estimated unbilled revenues are recorded at the end of accounting periods.

Maintenance: Maintenance and repairs are charged to maintenance expense and include replacements of less than retirement units of property. Replacements of retirement units and betterments are charged to utility plant, and the book cost of units retired plus the cost of removal thereof, less salvage, are charged to accumulated provision for depreciation.

Selected Notes to Consolidated Financial Statements   (continued)

Depreciation: The Company uses the straight-line method of depreciation. Total depreciation expense was between 3.49% and 3.86% of the cost of depreciable utility plant for the years 1981 through 1986.

Income taxes: Deferred income taxes are provided to recognize the income tax effect of reporting certain transactions in different years for income tax and financial reporting purposes in accordance with the rate-making policies of the respective state regulatory authorities. See Note 8. Investment tax credits realized are deferred and amortized to income over the lives of the related properties.

Allowance for funds during construction: Allowance for funds used during construction (AFDC) is the cost, during the period of construction, of debt and equity funds used to finance construction projects. The Company capitalizes AFDC as a part of the cost of major utility plant projects except to the extent that costs applicable to such construction work in progress have been included in rate base in connection with rate-making proceedings. AFDC represents a current non-cash credit to earnings which is expected to be recovered over the life of the property. The AFDC rates used by the Company were 11.89%, 12.05%, 12.22%, 12.76%, 12.80% and 12.74% for the years 1981 through 1986.

Deferred charges: Certain costs are deferred and amortized in accordance with rate-making policies of regulatory authorities. See Note 2. During regular Vermont Yankee refueling shutdowns the increased costs attributable to replacement energy purchased from NEPOOL are deferred and amortized to expense over the estimated period until the next regularly scheduled refueling shutdown. The unamortized deferred replacement energy costs have been included in rate base in recent retail rate cases.

Note 2   Seabrook Project

On November 25, 1986, the Company sold its entire 1.59% ownership share in the Seabrook project for $23,162,000. The Seabrook project is a two-unit nuclear project. As a condition to the sale, the Company continues to have a contingent obligation, if the buyer of the Seabrook project defaults, to pay either (i) certain decommissioning costs with respect to Unit 1 or (ii) certain costs of cancellation with respect to Unit 1 and Unit 2; however, such obligation is limited to $1.3 million under an amendment to the Seabrook Joint Ownership Agreement dealing with the transfer of the Company's ownership interest. Although it is possible that there could be future claims in excess of the $1.3 million due to the Company's participation in the Seabrook project, management believes it is unlikely that any such claims would result in a material loss.

The Seabrook project, which has been under way since 1973, has been subjected to delays. One result of these delays has been the cancellation of Unit 2, with respect to which no construction activities have occurred since September 1983 other than those activities necessary to maintain and protect the assets. The Company had incurred costs of approximately $9,400,000 for Unit 2, approximately 85% of which relates to the Company's retail rate jurisdiction. A PSB rate order dated February 18, 1986 allows recovery of $4,524,000 from retail customers over a four-year period, without a return on the recoverable amount during the recovery period, and requires shareholders to absorb the remainder.

Selected Notes to Consolidated Financial Statements   (continued)

Accordingly, during 1985 the Company charged off $3,000,000 of its investment in Unit 2, which decreased net income by $1,748,000 or 27¢ per common share for 1985. During 1986 an additional $230,000 was written off corresponding to the total PSB retail disallowance. This rate order has been appealed by the Department of Public Service and by the Company to the Vermont Supreme Court. The Company intends to seek recovery of the portion of Unit 2 under FERC jurisdiction which approximates 15% of its investment in the project.

The Company has invested approximately $88,912,000 in Unit 1. Approximately $65,750,000 of the Company's recorded investment was not realized through the sale proceeds and is included in the unrecovered Seabrook investment at December 31, 1986. The Company has requested the PSB for approval to recover its remaining investment in future rates charged to customers. The remaining investment net of deferred taxes is approximately $44,614,000. Management believes that it is probable that the PSB will determine that a portion of the Company's investment was imprudent and will disallow recovery of that portion on that basis. However, management is unable to make a reasonable estimate of the loss that may result from the ultimate rate treatment accorded the Company's investment in Seabrook Unit 1. A PSB decision is expected in May 1987.

In December 1986, the Financial Accounting Standards Board issued a statement entitled "Regulated Enterprises—Accounting for Abandonments and Disallowances of Plant Costs." The new accounting for abandonments under this statement requires loss recognition for discounting, using the Company's incremental borrowing rate, for any recoverable amounts on which the Company is not granted a return. If the new standards were applied in 1986, net income would be approximately $200,000 lower as a result of discounting the PSB rate recovery of Unit 2 over four years. The statement is effective in 1988 and encourages retroactive application to prior financial statements or, alternatively, requires a cumulative adjustment for the accounting change in 1988 financial statements.

Required

a. Compute the following ratios for 1986 and 1985. Comment on each.
   1. operating ratio
   2. funded debt to operating property
   3. percent earned on operating property
   4. operating revenue to operating property
b. In your opinion, how substantial were the following accounts in 1986 and 1985 in relation to net income?
   1. allowance for equity funds during construction
   2. allowance for borrowed funds during construction
c. Comment on the following using the consolidated balance sheet.
   1. construction work in progress
   2. unrecovered Seabrook investment

Case 14-4   LOANS AND PROVISION FOR LOANS

The Sylvania Savings Bank included the following footnote in its 1984 annual report:

Loans

Net loans at December 31, 1984 were $175,617,000, an increase of 23% over $142,264,000 at December 31, 1983. During the year, commercial loans increased by 25%, real estate loans increased by 3%, and consumer loans increased by 74%. Net loans represented 68% of total earning assets at December 31, 1984, compared to 64% at December 31, 1983. The average yield on the loan portfolio for 1984 was 13.2% compared to 12.7% for 1983. Non-earning loans at December 31, 1984 were $2,469,000 as compared to $4,528,000 at December 31, 1983.

During 1984, net loan charge-offs amounted to $1,239,000, compared to $1,414,000 in 1983. To offset these charge-offs, the 1984 provision for possible loan losses was $1,430,000, compared to $1,425,000 in 1983. As a result of these provisions, the Reserve for Possible Loan Losses totaled $1,786,000 at December 31, 1984 and $1,595,000 at December 31, 1983. As a percent of loans less unearned discount, the reserve was 1.01% in 1984 and 1.11% in 1983.

Required   Give your opinion as to significant information in this footnote.

Case 14-5   YOU CAN BANK ON IT

The financial data included in this case are from the 1989 annual report of Mid Am, Inc. and Subsidiaries. These are selected parts of the financial statements.

Consolidated Statement of Condition

	December 31,	
	1989	1988
ASSETS	(Dollars in thousands)	
Cash and due from banks	**$ 37,715**	$ 33,249
Interest-bearing deposits in other banks		2,775
Federal funds sold	**39,930**	11,475
Investment securities (approximate market value of $120,016 and $101,355)	**117,411**	100,578
Mortgage-backed investment securities (approximate market value of $34,091 and $30,001)	**35,042**	31,954
Loans, net of unearned income of $302 and $521	**517,387**	493,530
Allowance for credit losses	**(5,318)**	(4,234)
Net loans	**512,069**	489,296
Bank premises and equipment	**16,755**	15,691
Interest receivable and other assets	**12,124**	12,574
TOTAL ASSETS	**$771,046**	$697,592
LIABILITIES		
Demand deposits (noninterest-bearing)	**$ 85,433**	$ 79,297
Savings deposits	**203,072**	217,300
Other time deposits	**405,309**	323,345
Total deposits	**693,814**	619,942
Federal funds purchased and securities sold under agreements to repurchase	**10,985**	14,209
Capitalized lease obligations and debt	**6,049**	6,332
Interest payable and other liabilities	**8,206**	9,244
	719,054	649,727

SHAREHOLDERS' EQUITY

Common stock - no par value		
Authorized - 10,000,000 shares		
Issued and outstanding at stated value of		
$5 per share - 4,066,617 shares		
and 3,697,806 shares	20,333	18,489
Surplus	23,334	17,341
Retained earnings	8,325	12,035
Commitments and contingencies (Note 11)		
	51,992	47,865
TOTAL LIABILITIES AND SHAREHOLDERS' EQUITY	$771,046	$697,592

Consolidated Statement of Earnings

		Year ended December 31,	
	1989	1988	1987
		(Dollars in thousands)	
Interest income			
Interest and fees on loans	**$60,343**	$50,116	$42,692
Interest on deposits in other banks	**40**	492	488
Interest on federal funds sold	**1,774**	1,014	499
Interest on investments			
Taxable	**9,461**	7,833	9,029
Tax exempt	**2,678**	2,969	3,310
	74,296	62,424	56,018
Interest expense			
Interest on deposits	**40,118**	33,406	30,263
Interest on borrowed funds	**1,786**	1,167	830
	41,904	34,573	31,093
Net interest income	**32,392**	27,851	24,925
Provision for credit losses	**3,677**	3,139	1,502
Net interest income after provision for credit losses	**28,715**	24,712	23,423
Non-interest income			
Trust department	**421**	299	248
Service charges on deposit accounts	**2,663**	2,204	2,015
Net investment securities gains	**173**	254	33
Insurance claim prior to merger			1,034
Other income	**2,297**	2,088	1,741
	5,554	4,845	5,071
Non-interest expense			
Salaries and employee benefits	**11,819**	10,600	9,530
Net occupancy expense	**1,823**	1,737	1,697
Equipment expense	**2,067**	1,871	1,767
Loss from misapplication of funds prior to merger			2,237
Other expenses	**8,544**	7,771	7,199
	24,253	21,979	22,430
Income before income taxes and extraordinary item	**10,016**	7,578	6,064
Applicable income taxes			
Currently payable	**2,833**	1,677	1,625
Deferred	**(761)**	(180)	(431)
Tax effect of loss carryforward	**280**		
	2,352	1,497	1,194
Income before extraordinary item	**7,664**	6,081	4,870

Realization of operating loss carryforward	280		
Net income	$ 7,944	$ 6,081	$ 4,870
Earnings per share before extraordinary item	$ 1.88	$ 1.50	$ 1.20
Earnings per share	$ 1.95	$ 1.50	$ 1.20

Notes to Consolidated Financial Statements

NOTE 1 - ACCOUNTING POLICIES

The accounting and reporting policies followed by Mid Am, Inc. conform to generally accepted accounting principles and to general practices within the banking industry. A summary of the significant accounting policies follows.

Consolidation

The consolidated financial statements of Mid Am, Inc. (the Company) include the accounts of Mid American National Bank and Trust Company (Mid Am Bank), First National Bank Northwest Ohio (First National Bank) and The Farmers Banking Company, N. A. (Farmers Bank). All significant intercompany transactions and accounts have been eliminated in consolidation.

Cash and Due from Banks

The Company is required to maintain average reserve balances with the Federal Reserve Bank. The average reserve balance at December 31, 1989 and 1988 approximated $12,225,000 and $10,338,000, respectively.

Securities

The Company holds its investment and mortgage-backed securities for investment purposes. Such securities are stated at cost, adjusted for amortization of premiums and accretion of discounts computed under the straight-line method, which does not differ materially from the interest method. Such premium amortization and discount accretion are recognized as adjustments to interest income. The Company has the ability and intent to hold such securities to their scheduled maturities. At December 31, 1989 and 1988, neither a disposal, nor conditions that could lead to a decision not to hold such securities to maturity, were reasonably foreseen. The adjusted cost of specific certificates sold is used to compute gains or losses on the sale of investment securities.

Loans

Unearned income on installment loans is recognized using the sum-of-the-months digits method although interest on most installment loans and on all other types of loans is calculated using the simple-interest method on the outstanding principal amounts.

Direct finance leases, which include estimated residual values of leased equipment, are carried net of unearned income. Income from these leases is recognized on a basis which generally produces a level yield on the outstanding balances receivable.

In December 1986, the Financial Accounting Standards Board issued Statement No. 91, "Accounting for Nonrefundable Fees and Costs Associated with Originating or Acquiring Loans and Initial Direct Costs of Leases", which requires that nonrefundable fees and costs associated with lending activities be recognized over the life of the related loan (lease) as an adjustment of yield. In 1988, the Company adopted prospectively the provisions of this Statement. The adoption of this Statement was not material to the consolidated results of operations.

Accrual of interest on loans is discontinued when principal or interest remains due and unpaid for 90 days or more, dependent upon security and collection considerations. Income on such loans is then recognized only to the extent that cash is received and where the future collection of principal is probable. Interest accruals are resumed on such loans only when they are brought fully current with respect to interest and principal and when, in the judgment of management, the loans are estimated to be fully collectible as to both principal and interest. Restructured loans are those loans on which concessions in terms have been granted because of a borrower's financial difficulty. Interest is generally accrued on such loans in accordance with the new terms.

Allowance for Credit Losses

The allowance for credit losses is established through a provision for credit losses charged to expenses. Loans and leases are charged against the allowance for credit losses when management believes that the collectibility of the principal is unlikely. The allowance is an amount that management believes will be adequate to absorb losses inherent in existing loans, leases and commitments to extend credit, based on evaluations of the collectibility and prior loss experience of loans, leases and commitments to extend credit. The evaluations take into consideration such factors as changes in the nature and volume of the portfolio, overall portfolio quality, loan concentrations, specific problem loans, leases and commitments, and current and anticipated economic conditions that may affect the borrowers' ability to pay.

Other Real Estate Owned

Real estate acquired by foreclosure is carried in other assets at the lower of the recorded investment in the property or its fair value. Prior to foreclosure, the value of the underlying loan is written down to the market value of the real estate to be acquired by a charge to the allowance for credit losses, if necessary. Any subsequent write-downs are charged to operating expenses. Carrying costs of such properties, net of related income, and gains and losses on their disposition are charged or credited to operating expenses as incurred.

Bank Premises and Equipment

Bank premises and equipment are stated at cost, less accumulated depreciation which is computed using the straight-line method.

Income Taxes

Provision for income taxes is based on pretax income which differs in some respects from taxable income. When income and expenses are recognized in different periods for financial reporting purposes than for income tax reporting purposes, deferred taxes are provided on such timing differences.

The tax benefit from the utilization of the Farmers Bank operating loss carryforward from 1987 is presented as an extraordinary credit in the consolidated statement of earnings for 1989. No net operating loss carryforwards remain at December 31, 1989.

In December 1987, the Financial Accounting Standards Board issued Statement No. 96, "Accounting for Income Taxes", which requires an asset and liability approach for financial accounting and reporting for income taxes. This Statement is effective for fiscal years beginning after December 15, 1991. The impact that adoption of this Statement is expected to have on the Company's results of operations is not reasonably estimable.

Trust Department

Trust Department income has been recognized on the cash basis (which is not significantly different than the accrual basis) in accordance with general banking practice. Property (other than cash deposits) held by the Company in fiduciary or agency capacities for its customers is not included in the consolidated statement of condition as such items are not assets of the Company.

Earnings per Share

Earnings per share is computed using the weighted average number of shares outstanding during the period, as restated for shares issued in business combinations accounted for as poolings of interests and stock dividends and splits (a 10 percent stock dividend in 1989, a 5 percent stock dividend in 1988 and a two-for-one stock split in 1987), applied to net income. If all stock options outstanding were exercised, there would be no material dilutive effect, and therefore, they have been excluded from the computation. The weighted average number of shares outstanding was 4,066,617 for 1989 and 1988 and 4,065,506 for 1987.

Reclassifications

Certain amounts originally presented in the 1988 and 1987 financial statements have been reclassified to conform with the 1989 presentation. These reclassifications have no effect upon the Company's net income or shareholders' equity accounts.

Statement of Cash Flows

In 1988 the Company adopted prospectively the provisions of Statement No. 95, "Statement of Cash Flows", using the indirect method which requires the reporting of net cash flow from operating activities by adjusting net income to reconcile with cash flow from operating activities, as well as the reporting of net cash flows from investing and financing activities.

NOTE 2 - BANK COMBINATIONS

Effective June 9, 1989, Mid Am, Inc. issued 344,342 shares of common stock in exchange for all of the outstanding stock of FBC Bancshares, Inc. (FBC). FBC was a one-bank holding company which owned all the outstanding common stock of The Farmers Banking Company, N.A. The merger was accounted for as a pooling of interests and accordingly, the consolidated financial statements of the Company for all periods prior to the merger have been restated to include the accounts and results of operations of FBC and subsidiary.

The effect of the restatement is summarized as follows:

	Net Interest Income	Income Before Extraordinary Item	Net Income
	(Dollars in thousands)		
1989			
Mid Am, Inc. prior to merger	$11,697	$2,950	$2,950
Effect of FBC pooling prior to merger	1,664	370	550
Combined subsequent to merger	19,031	4,344	4,444
Combined	$32,392	$7,664	$7,944
1988			
Mid Am, Inc. as previously reported	$24,607	$6,026	$6,026
Effect of FBC pooling	3,244	55	55
Combined	$27,851	$6,081	$6,081
1987			
Mid Am, Inc. as previously reported	$21,911	$5,547	$5,547
Effect of FBC pooling	3,014	(677)	(677)
Combined	$24,925	$4,870	$4,870

Effective March 4, 1988, Mid Am, Inc. issued 870,178 shares of common stock in exchange for all of the outstanding common stock of Tri-State Financial Bancorp, Inc. (Tri-State). Tri-State was a one-bank holding company which owned all the outstanding common stock of First National Bank Northwest Ohio. The terms of such affiliation were set forth in an Agreement and Plan of Reorganization and related Agreement to Merge; pursuant to the terms of such agreements, Tri-State changed its name to Mid Am, Inc. The merger was accounted for as a pooling of interests and accordingly, the consolidated financial statements of the Company for all periods prior to the merger were restated to include the accounts and results of operations of Tri-State and subsidiary. Prior to the date of the merger, the 1988 net interest income and net income of Tri-State and subsidiary amounted to $784,000 and $154,000, respectively. The respective amounts for Mid Am Bank were $2,889,000 and $635,000.

NOTE 3 - INVESTMENT AND MORTGAGE-BACKED SECURITIES

The aggregate carrying value and approximate market value of investment and mortgage-backed securities at December 31 are as follows:

	1989		1988	
	Carrying Value	Approximate Market Value	Carrying Value	Approximate Market Value
	(Dollars in thousands)			
U.S. Treasury Securities	$ 29,828	$ 30,266	$ 33,410	$ 33,294
Securities of other U.S. Government agencies and corporations	50,952	51,569	29,893	29,555
Obligations of states and political subdivisions	33,507	35,080	34,772	36,033
Other securities	3,124	3,101	2,503	2,473
Total	$117,411	$120,016	$100,578	$101,355
Mortgage-backed investment securities	$ 35,042	$ 34,091	$ 31,954	$ 30,001

The carrying value of securities pledged to secure public and trust deposits, securities sold under agreements to repurchase and for other purposes as required by law amounted to $94,348,000 and $79,721,000 at December 31, 1989 and 1988, respectively.

NOTE 4 - LOANS AND ALLOWANCE FOR CREDIT LOSSES

Loans outstanding at December 31 are as follows:

	1989	1988
	(Dollars in thousands)	
Real estate loans		
Construction	$ 9,798	$ 7,563
Mortgage	201,837	210,457
Commercial, financial and		
agricultural loans	207,861	185,900
Installment and credit card loans	83,833	74,090
Industrial development bond loans	10,646	11,613
Lease financing receivables	3,200	3,962
Other loans	514	466
Total	517,689	494,051
Less		
Unearned income	(97)	(293)
Unamortized loan fees	(205)	(228)
Allowance for credit losses	(5,318)	(4,234)
Total net	$512,069	$489,296

In the normal course of business, the Company has made loans to certain directors, executive officers and their associates under terms consistent with the Company's general lending policies. Loans to these individuals amounted to approximately $10,542,000 and $8,884,000 at December 31, 1989 and 1988, respectively. The net increase of $1,658,000 resulted from new loans and advances of $10,691,000 and payments of $9,033,000.

Changes in the allowance for credit losses are as follows:

	1989	1988	1987
	(Dollars in thousands)		
Balance at beginning of year	$ 4,234	$ 3,926	$ 3,318
Additions (reductions)			
Provision for credit losses	3,677	3,139	1,502
Charge-offs	(3,005)	(3,716)	(1,927)
Recoveries on loans charged off	412	885	1,033
Balance at end of year	$ 5,318	$ 4,234	$ 3,926

The allowance for credit losses for federal income tax purposes was $2,085,000 and $2,618,000 at December 31, 1989 and 1988, respectively.

At December 31, 1989 and 1988, the outstanding principal balance of loans placed on non-accrual status amounted to $5,410,000 and $5,483,000, respectively. Loans for which concessions in terms have been granted (restructured loans) are not material.

NOTE 5 - BANK PREMISES AND EQUIPMENT

Bank premises and equipment consist of the following:

	December 31,	
	1989	1988
	(Dollars in thousands)	
Land and land improvements	**$ 2,633**	$ 2,477
Buildings	**16,689**	14,859
Furniture and fixtures	**10,419**	9,430
Leasehold improvements	**246**	162
	29,987	26,928
Less - accumulated depreciation and amortization	**(13,232)**	(11,237)
	$16,755	$15,691

Included in the above are buildings and land and land improvements which secures the capitalized lease and industrial development first mortgage revenue bond obligations with a cost of $7,040,000 less accumulated amortization and depreciation of $1,952,000 and $1,628,000 at December 31, 1989 and 1988, respectively. Mortgage revenue bond obligations totalled $70,000 and $140,000 at December 31, 1989 and 1988, respectively.

Future minimum payments, by year and in the aggregate, under capitalized leases and noncancelable operating leases with remaining terms of one year or more, at December 31, 1989 are as follows:

	Capital Leases	Operating Leases
	(Dollars in thousands)	
1990	$ 572	$ 29
1991	561	29
1992	558	29
1993	545	29
1994	550	29
Thereafter	4,895	113
Total minimum lease payments	7,681	$258
Amounts representing interest	(2,902)	
Present value of minimum lease payments	$4,779	

NOTE 6 - DEPOSITS

Included in other time deposits are certificates of deposit of $100,000 or more totalling $88,148,000 and $57,659,000 at December 31, 1989 and 1988, respectively.

Included in savings deposits are negotiable order of withdrawal (NOW) accounts totalling approximately $66,353,000 and $61,203,000 at December 31, 1989 and 1988, respectively.

The Company paid $41,904,000 and $34,573,000 in interest on deposits and other borrowings in 1989 and 1988, respectively.

NOTE 7 - LONG TERM DEBT

On September 21, 1988, FBC entered into a loan agreement with Merchants National Bank and Trust Company of Indianapolis (Merchants). Upon merger with FBC, the Company assumed the debt. Under the agreement, $1,200,000 was borrowed in a term arrangement with a variable interest rate at Merchant's base rate. Interest payments are due monthly and principal is due in six unequal annual payments beginning on September 30, 1990 as follows: $50,000, $100,000, $150,000, $200,000, $300,000 and $400,000 in 1990 through 1995.

The loan is secured by 100 percent of the issued and outstanding shares of common stock of Farmers Bank. The loan agreement includes various financial covenants, including maintenance of a specified consolidated annual cash flow and maintenance of a specified primary capital level.

As described in Note 1, deferred tax expense results from timing differences in the recognition of revenue and expense for tax and financial reporting purposes. The tax effects of principal timing differences for each of the three years in the period ended December 31, 1989 are presented below:

	1989	1988	1987
		(Dollars in thousands)	
Excess tax depreciation over book	$ 480	$ 515	$ 709
Excess lease financing income over book	(431)	(612)	(534)
Effect of alternative minimum tax		148	(148)
Provision for credit losses for book			
in excess of amount deductible for tax	(654)	(72)	(88)
Other items, net	(156)	(159)	(370)
	$(761)	$(180)	$(431)

The following schedule reconciles the statutory federal income tax rate to the Company's effective tax rate.

	1989	1988	1987
Statutory federal income tax rate	34.0%	34.0%	40.0%
Effect of interest income which			
is not subject to taxation	(12.8)	(18.3)	(29.0)
Nondeductible interest	1.6	2.2	3.3
Net operating losses not recognized			4.7
Other items, net	0.7	1.9	.7
	23.5%	19.8%	19.7%

The Company made income tax payments of $2,220,000 and $1,970,000 during 1989 and 1988, respectively.

NOTE 9 - RETIREMENT PLANS

The Company and its subsidiaries provide retirement benefits for substantially all of its employees under several retirement plans.

The Company has an Employee Stock Ownership and Savings Plan for the benefit of all eligible employees who have completed twelve months of service with the Company and who have not reached the age of sixty-five. The plan provides for annual contributions by the Company based upon income (as defined by the plan) after providing for a specified return on shareholders' equity. The plan was amended effective July 1, 1988 and July 1, 1989 to include eligible employees of First National Bank and Farmers Bank, respectively. The plan was also amended effective July 1, 1989 to include a 401(k) profit-sharing and savings provision. Under this provision, employees may contribute up to eight percent of eligible compensation with a Company match of one-half of such contributions up to a maximum match of three percent. Effective July 1, 1989, the Company implemented an Employee Stock Ownership Pension Plan which provides for an annual contribution by the Company equal to six percent of eligible employees' annual compensation. Expenses relating to these plans amounted to $942,000, $718,000 and $607,000 in 1989, 1988 and 1987, respectively.

Mid Am Bank and Farmers Bank previously maintained defined benefit pension plans. Mid Am Bank terminated its plan effective July 1, 1989 and Farmers Bank terminated its plan effective December 31, 1988. Both plans were substantially funded prior to termination. Plan assets will be (have been) distributed to participants upon Internal Revenue Service approval. Expenses relating to these plans amounted to $63,000, $129,000 and $131,000 in 1989, 1988 and 1987, respectively.

First National Bank had a 401(k) profit sharing and savings plan which required a matching company contribution of a percentage of participants' annual compensation. Effective July 1, 1989, this plan was merged into the Company's Employee Stock Ownership and Savings Plan discussed above.

NOTE 10- STOCK OPTIONS

In October 1986, the Board of Directors of Tri-State adopted an Incentive Stock Option Plan. Options were for ten years becoming exercisable beginning one year from date of grant at 25 percent per year. The Plan allowed for the options and the price per share to be adjusted to reflect future stock dividends and splits. Pursuant to the Agreement and Plan of Reorganization between Tri-State and Mid Am Bank, the terms of the plan were to remain in effect following the effective date of the merger with the options at such date adjusted to reflect the number of shares and exercise price of Mid Am, Inc. No options were exercised during 1989 or 1988. There were options to acquire 33,728 shares outstanding at December 31, 1989 at an option price of $7.91 per share. These options expire in 1996.

NOTE 11 - COMMITMENTS AND CONTINGENCIES

The Company, in the normal course of business, has issued standby letters of credit which are not reflected in the consolidated financial statements. Standby letters of credit, for which the Company is contingently liable, amounted to $14,362,000 and $10,698,000 at December 31, 1989 and 1988, respectively.

There are pending against the Company various lawsuits and claims which arise in the normal course of business. In the opinion of management, any liabilities that may result from such lawsuits and claims will not materially affect the financial position of the Company.

NOTE 12 - LOSS ON LOANS AND INSURANCE CLAIM PRIOR TO MERGER

Prior to the merger between Mid Am, Inc. and FBC, certain loans of FBC's subsidiary, Farmers Bank, were granted by a former loan officer to borrowers who, in 1987, were determined to be fictitious, and certain other loans were granted to borrowers to whom the Board of Directors had directed that no extensions of credit be given. These loans were considered losses, net of existing depository institution bond insurance coverage. A loss of $2,237,000 and income resulting from insurance coverage of $1,034,000 were recorded in 1987. The insurance claim at December 31, 1987 was received in 1988.

NOTE 13 - RELATED PARTY TRANSACTIONS

BancSites, Inc. was incorporated by Mid Am Bank in July 1977. Subsequently, the Bank distributed all of the common stock of BancSites to shareholders of the Bank on a pro-rata basis. Although the Bank does not exercise control of BancSites through an ownership interest, it does significantly influence the operating policies of BancSites through common management. Management believes that all of its transactions with BancSites described below were entered into in the normal course of business and under terms no more favorable then those prevailing in the marketplace.

Included in bank premises and equipment are thirteen branch bank facilities owned by Bancsites and leased to the Bank under long-term lease agreements. Lease payments amounted to $695,000 in 1989, $569,000 in 1988, and $553,000 in 1987. The land on which two of these facilities are built is leased from Bancsites under a long-term lease agreement. Rental payments for the land amounted to $29,000 during 1989, 1988, and 1987. The Bank also leases several parking facilities from Bancsites on a year-by-year basis, rentals for which approximated $31,000 in 1989, $29,000 in 1988, and $28,000 in 1987.

NOTE 14 - RESTRICTIONS ON SUBSIDIARY DIVIDENDS, LOANS OR ADVANCES

Dividends paid by the Company from its assets are mainly provided by dividends from its subsidiaries. However, certain restrictions exist regarding the ability of these banking subsidiaries to transfer funds to the Company in the form of cash dividends, loans or advances. The approval of the Comptroller of the Currency is required to pay dividends in excess of the subsidiaries' earnings retained in the current year plus retained net profits for the preceding two years. As of December 31, 1989, $6,956,000 was available for distribution to the Company as dividends without prior regulatory approval.

Required   a. Compute the following ratios for 1989 and 1988 (use ending balance sheet accounts):
   1. earning assets to total assets
   2. return on earning assets
   3. interest margin to average earning assets
   4. loan loss coverage ratio
   5. equity capital to total assets
   6. deposits times capital
   7. loans to deposits
   b. Comment on the trends indicated by the ratios computed in (a).

Case 14-6   **PROVED RESERVES**

The Standard Oil Company (Indiana) included the information in this problem as part of the supplemental information in its 1983 annual report.

Estimated Proved Reserves

Net proved reserves of crude oil (including condensate), natural gas liquids (NGL), and natural gas at the beginning and end of 1983, 1982, and 1981, with the detail of changes during those years, are presented below. Reported quantities include reserves in which the company holds an economic interest under production-sharing and other types of operating agreements with foreign governments. The estimates were prepared by company engineers and are based on current technology and economic conditions. The company considers such estimates to be reasonable and consistent with current knowledge of the characteristics and extent of proved production. The estimates include only those amounts considered to be proved reserves and do not include additional amounts which may result from extensions of currently proved areas, or amounts which may result from new discoveries in the future, or from application of secondary or tertiary recovery processes not yet determined to be commercial. Proved developed reserves are those reserves which are expected to be recovered through existing wells with existing equipment and operating methods.

	United States			Canada		
	Crude Oil	NGL	Gas	Crude Oil	NGL	Gas
(Crude oil and NGL in millions of barrels)						
(Gas in billions of cubic feet)						
Proved reserves						
December 31, 1980	1,446	217	8,434	188	42	2,106
Revisions of previous estimates	58	47	457	(7)	—	90
Improved recovery applications	15	—	4	—	—	—
Extensions, discoveries, and other additions	44	6	797	3	—	141
Production	(134)	(25)	(835)	(13)	(4)	(93)
December 31, 1981	1,429	245	8,857	171	38	2,244
Revisions of previous estimates	16	12	405	7	1	111
Improved recovery applications	86	—	16	1	—	1
Extensions, discoveries, and other additions	23	—	430	1	1	66
Production	(129)	(22)	(699)	(13)	(4)	(89)
December 31, 1982	1,425	235	9,009	167	36	2,333
Revisions of previous estimates	91	15	687	2	—	1
Improved recovery applications	56	12	23	1	—	1
Extensions, discoveries, and other additions	21	1	360	6	1	20
Sales of reserves in place	(1)	—	(51)	(1)	—	(4)
Production	(127)	(22)	(637)	(13)	(4)	(89)
December 31, 1983	1,465	241	9,391	162	33	2,262
Proved developed reserves						
December 31, 1980	1,415	199	7,762	176	39	1,850
December 31, 1981	1,374	200	7,942	156	35	1,955
December 31, 1982	1,316	205	8,148	150	32	1,972
December 31, 1983	1,361	216	8,788	144	29	1,902

*Includes the reinstatement of approximately 895 billion cubic feet of natural gas in Trinidad which had been eliminated as uneconomic in 1978.

Europe			Other Foreign		Worldwide		
Crude Oil	NGL	Gas	Crude Oil and NGL	Gas	Crude Oil	NGL	Gas
204	22	1,554	530	1,588	2,364	285	13,682
—	—	18	24	779*	75	47	1,344
—	—	—	2	—	17	—	4
—	—	100	126	—	173	6	1,038
(4)	—	(115)	(109)	(92)	(260)	(29)	(1,135)
200	22	1,557	573	2,275	2,369	309	14,933
(14)	—	(1)	29	(73)	38	13	442
—	—	—	16	—	103	—	17
—	—	—	63	161	87	1	657
(4)	—	(104)	(108)	(99)	(253)	(27)	(991)
182	22	1,452	573	2,264	2,344	296	15,058
(1)	—	68	73	(44)	165	15	712
—	—	—	1	—	58	12	24
1	—	16	2	—	30	2	396
—	—	—	—	—	(2)	—	(55)
(9)	—	(110)	(113)	(109)	(261)	(27)	(945)
173	22	1,426	536	2,111	2,334	298	15,190
21	1	1,331	432	747	2,041	242	11,690
18	1	1,211	471	1,177	2,016	239	12,285
29	3	1,137	439	1,087	1,931	243	12,344
59	8	1,273	446	1,279	2,007	256	13,242

Required   a. Prepare a horizontal common size analysis of proved reserves and proved develope[d] reserves. Only use balances at December 31. Use December 31, 1980, as the base.

                    b. Comment on trends indicated by the common size analysis.

PERSONAL FINANCIAL STATEMENTS AND ACCOUNTING FOR GOVERNMENTS AND OTHER NONPROFIT INSTITUTIONS

CHAPTER TOPICS

Personal Financial Statements
Form of the Statements
Illustration of Preparation
  of Statement of Financial
  Condition
Illustration of Preparation
  of Statement of Changes
  in Net Worth

Accounting for Governments and Other Nonprofit Institutions
Accounting for Governments
Nonprofit Institutions Other
  Than Governments
Budgeting by Objectives and/or
  Measures of Productivity

This chapter provides brief coverage of two types of financial reporting that have not been discussed in previous chapters. While previous chapters have covered financial reporting for profit-oriented businesses, this chapter covers accounting and financial reporting for personal financial statements and accounting for governments and other nonprofit institutions. You will find that financial reporting is much different in these areas than it is for businesses.

PERSONAL FINANCIAL STATEMENTS

Personal financial statements are financial statements of individuals, husband and wife, or a larger family group. These statements are prepared for obtaining credit, income tax planning, retirement planning, estate planning, and so on.

Guidelines for the preparation of personal financial statements are covered in Statement of Position 82-1 (SOP 82-1).[1] SOP 82-1 concludes that "the primary

---

[1]Statement of Position 82-1, "Accounting and Financial Reporting for Personal Financial Statements," October 1, 1982, American Institute of Certified Public Accountants.

users of personal financial statements normally consider estimated current value information to be more relevant for their decisions than historical cost information. Lenders require estimated current value information to assess collateral, and most personal loan applications require estimated current value information. Estimated current values are required for estate, gift, and income tax planning, and estimated current value information about assets is often required in federal and state filings of candidates for public office."[2]

SOP 82-1 concludes that personal financial statements should present assets at their estimated current values and liabilities at their estimated current amounts at the date of the financial statements. This is in contrast to commercial financial statements, which predominantly use historical cost information.

SOP 82-1 provides guidelines for determining the estimated current value of an asset and the estimated current amount of a liability. These guidelines are reproduced in Exhibit 15-1.[3]

Form of the Statements

The basic statement prepared for personal financial statements is a *statement of financial condition,* which is similar to a balance sheet.

For the statement of financial condition, assets are presented at estimated current values, and liabilities are stated at estimated current amounts. A tax liability is estimated on the difference between the amounts at which the assets and liabilities are stated and the tax basis of these assets and liabilities. For example, land may have cost $10,000, which would be the tax basis, but have an estimated current value of $25,000. The estimated tax liability on the difference between the $10,000 and the $25,000 would be estimated.

The difference between the total assets and total liabilities is designated *net worth.* Net worth is equivalent to the equity section in a commercial balance sheet.

The statement of financial condition is prepared on the accrual basis. Assets and liabilities are presented in order of liquidity and maturity.

The statement of changes in net worth is optional. It presents the major sources of increases and decreases in net worth. Examples of changes in net worth would be income, increases in the estimated current value of assets, and decreases in estimated income taxes.

The *statement of changes in net worth* is presented in terms of realized increases (decreases) and unrealized increases (decreases). Examples of realized increases (decreases) are salary, dividends, income taxes, and personal expenditures. Examples of unrealized increases (decreases) are increase in value of securities, increase in value of residence, decrease in value of boat, and estimated income taxes on the differences between the estimated current values of assets and the estimated current amounts of liabilities and their tax bases.

(continues on page 698)

[2]Ibid., p. 6.
[3]A good article on this subject is "Personal Financial Statements: Valuation Challenges and Solutions," by Michael D. Kinsman and Bruce Samuelson, *Journal of Accountancy* (September 1987), p. 138.

EXHIBIT 15-1

Guidelines for Determining the Estimated Current Values of Assets and the Estimated Current Amounts of Liabilities

General

12. Personal financial statements should present assets at their estimated current values and liabilities at their estimated current amounts. The estimated current value of an asset in personal financial statements is the amount at which the item could be exchanged between a buyer and seller, each of whom is well informed and willing, and neither of whom is compelled to buy or sell. Costs of disposal, such as commissions, if material, should be considered in determining estimated current values.^ The division recognizes that the estimated current values of some assets may be difficult to determine and the cost of obtaining estimated current values of some assets directly may exceed the benefits of doing so; therefore, the division recommends that judgment be exercised in determining estimated current values.

13. Recent transactions involving similar assets and liabilities in similar circumstances ordinarily provide a satisfactory basis for determining the estimated current value of an asset and the estimated current amount of a liability. If recent sales information is unavailable, other methods that may be used include the capitalization of past or prospective earnings, the use of liquidation values, the adjustment of historical cost based on changes in a specific price index, the use of appraisals, or the use of the discounted amounts of projected cash receipts and payments.

14. In determining the estimated current values of some assets (for example, works of art, jewelry, restricted securities, investments in closely held businesses, and real estate), the person may need to consult a specialist.

15. The methods used to determine the estimated current values of assets and the estimated current amounts of liabilities should be followed consistently from period to period unless the facts and circumstances dictate a change to different methods.

Receivables

16. Personal financial statements should present receivables at the discounted amounts of cash the person estimates will be collected, using appropriate interest rates at the date of the financial statements.

Marketable Securities

17. Marketable securities include both debt and equity securities for which market quotations are available. The estimated current values of such securities are their quoted market prices. The estimated current values of securities traded on securities exchanges are the closing prices of the securities on the date of the financial statements (valuation date) if the securities were traded on that date. If the securities were not traded on that date but published bid and asked prices are available, the estimated current values of the securities should be within the range of those prices.

18. For securities traded in the over-the-counter market, quotations of bid

EXHIBIT 15-1 (continued)

and asked prices are available from several sources, including the financial press, various quotation publications and financial reporting services, and individual broker-dealers. For those securities, the mean of the bid prices, of the bid and asked prices, or of the prices of a representative selection of broker-dealers quoting the securities may be used as the estimated current values.

19. An investor may hold a large block of the equity securities of a company. A large block of stock might not be salable at the price at which a small number of shares were recently sold or quoted. Further, a large minority interest may be difficult to sell despite isolated sales of a small number of shares. However, a controlling interest may be proportionately more valuable than minority interests that were sold. Consideration of those factors may require adjustments to the price at which the security recently sold. Moreover, restrictions on the transfer of a security may also suggest the need to adjust the recent market price in determining the estimated current value.[B]

Options

20. If published prices of options are unavailable, their estimated current values should be determined on the basis of the values of the assets subject to option, considering such factors as the exercise prices and length of the option periods.

Investment in Life Insurance

21. The estimated current value of an investment in life insurance is the cash value of the policy less the amount of any loans against it. The face amount of life insurance the individuals own should be disclosed.

Investments in Closely Held Businesses

22. The division recognizes that the estimated current values of investments in closely held businesses usually are difficult to determine. The problems relate to investments in closely held businesses in any form, including sole proprietorships, general and limited partnerships, and corporations. As previously stated, only the net investment in a business enterprise (not its assets and liabilities) should be presented in the statement of financial condition. The net investment should be presented at its estimated current value at the date of the financial statement. Since there is usually no established ready market for such an investment, judgment should be exercised in determining the estimated current value of the investment.

23. There is no one generally accepted procedure for determining the estimated current value of an investment in a closely held business. Several procedures or combinations of procedures may be used to determine the estimated current value of a closely held business, including a multiple of earnings, liquidation value, reproduction value, appraisals, discounted amounts of projected cash receipts and payments, or adjustments of book value or cost of the person's share of the equity of the business.[c] The owner of an interest in a closely held business may have entered into a buy-sell agreement that specifies the amount (or the basis of determining the amount) to be received in the event of withdrawal, retirement,

or sale. If such an agreement exists, it should be considered, but it does not necessarily determine estimated current value. Whatever procedure is used, the objective should be to approximate the amount at which the investment could be exchanged between a buyer and a seller, each of whom is well informed and willing, and neither of whom is compelled to buy or sell.

Real Estate (Including Leaseholds)

24. Investments in real estate (including leaseholds) should be presented in personal financial statements at their estimated current values. Information that may be used in determining their estimated current values includes—

a. Sales of similar property in similar circumstances.
b. The discounted amounts of projected cash receipts and payments relating to the property or the net realizable value of the property, based on planned courses of action, including leaseholds whose current rental value exceeds the rent in the lease.
c. Appraisals based on estimates of selling prices and selling costs obtained from independent real estate agents or brokers familiar with similar properties in similar locations.
d. Appraisals used to obtain financing.
e. Assessed value for property taxes, including consideration of the basis for such assessments and their relationship to market values in the area.

Intangible Assets

25. Intangible assets should be presented at the discounted amounts of projected cash receipts and payments arising from the planned use or sale of the assets if both the amounts and timing can be reasonably estimated. For example, a record of receipts under a royalty agreement may provide sufficient information to determine its estimated current value. The cost of a purchased intangible should be used if no other information is available.

Future Interests and Similar Assets

26. Nonforfeitable rights to receive future sums that have all the following characteristics should be presented as assets at their discounted amounts:

- The rights are for fixed or determinable amounts.
- The rights are not contingent on the holder's life expectancy or the occurrence of a particular event, such as disability or death.
- The rights do not require future performance of service by the holder.

Nonforfeitable rights that may have those characteristics include—

- Guaranteed minimum portions of pensions.
- Vested interests in pensions or profit sharing plans.
- Deferred compensation contracts.
- Beneficial interests in trusts.
- Remainder interests in property subject to life estates.
- Annuities.
- Fixed amounts of alimony for a definite future period.

Payables and Other Liabilities

27. Personal financial statements should present payables and other liabilities at the discounted amounts of cash to be paid. The discount rate should be the rate implicit in the transaction in which the debt was incurred. If, however, the debtor is able to discharge the debt currently at a lower amount, the debt should be presented at the lower amount.[D]

Noncancellable Commitments

28. Noncancellable commitments to pay future sums that have all the following characteristics should be presented as liabilities at their discounted amounts:

- The commitments are for fixed or determinable amounts.
- The commitments are not contingent on others' life expectancies or the occurrence of a particular event, such as disability or death.
- The commitments do not require future performance of service by others.

Noncancellable commitments that may have those characteristics include fixed amounts of alimony for a definite future period and charitable pledges.

Income Taxes Payable

29. The liability for income taxes payable should include unpaid income taxes for completed tax years and an estimated amount for income taxes accrued for the elapsed portion of the current tax year to the date of the financial statements. That estimate should be based on the relationship of taxable income earned to date to total estimated taxable income for the year, net of taxes withheld or paid with estimated income tax returns.

Estimated Income Taxes on the Differences Between the Estimated Current Values of Assets and the Estimated Current Amounts of Liabilities and Their Tax Bases

30. A provision should be made for estimated income taxes on the differences between the estimated current values of assets and the estimated current amounts of liabilities and their tax bases, including consideration of negative tax bases of tax shelters, if any. The provision should be computed as if the estimated current values of all assets had been realized and the estimated current amounts of all liabilities had been liquidated on the statement date, using applicable income tax laws and regulations, considering recapture provisions and available carryovers. The estimated income taxes should be presented between liabilities and net worth in the statement of financial condition. The methods and assumptions used to compute the estimated income taxes should be fully disclosed. Appendix B to this statement of position illustrates how to compute the provision.

[A]Paragraph 27 defines the estimated current amount of a liability.
[B]For further discussion on valuing marketable securities, see the AICPA Industry Audit Guide, *Audits of Investment Companies* (New York: AICPA, 1973), pp. 15–17.
[C]The book value or cost of a person's share of the equity of a business adjusted for appraisals of specific assets, such as real estate or equipment, is sometimes used as the estimated current value.
[D]For a further discussion of the setting of a discount rate for payables and other liabilities, see APB Opinion 21. *Interest on Receivables and Payables*, paragraph 13.

It may also be desirable to present comparative financial statements. Such a presentation may be more informative than statements of only one period.

The concept of an income statement does not apply to personal financial statements; the statement of changes in net worth replaces the income statement. SOP 82-1 includes guidelines on disclosure (Exhibit 15-1). These guidelines are not intended to be all-inclusive. Examples of disclosure include the methods used in determining current values of major assets, descriptions of intangible assets, and assumptions used to compute the estimated income taxes.

Most individuals do not maintain a complete set of records, so it is necessary to gather the necessary data from various sources. Examples of sources that should be considered are brokers' statements, income tax returns, safe deposit boxes, insurance policies, real estate tax returns, checkbooks, and bank statements.

Suggestions for Reviewing Statement of Financial Condition and Statement of Changes in Net Worth

Statement of Financial Condition

1. Usually, the most important figure is the net worth amount. In effect, this is an indication of the level of wealth.
2. Determine the amount of the assets that you consider to be very liquid (cash, savings accounts, marketable securities, and so on). These assets are readily available.
3. Observe the due period of the liabilities. In general, we would prefer the liabilities to be relatively long term. Long-term liabilities do not represent an immediate pressing problem.
4. When possible, compare specific assets with any related liabilities. This will indicate the net investment in the asset. For example, a residence with a current value of $90,000 and a $40,000 mortgage represents a net investment of $50,000.

Statement of Changes in Net Worth

1. Review realized increases in net worth. Determine the principal sources of realized net worth.
2. Review realized decreases in net worth. Determine the principal items in realized decreases in net worth.
3. Observe whether the net realized amount increased or decreased, and by how much.
4. Review unrealized increases in net worth. Determine the principal sources of unrealized increases in net worth.
5. Review unrealized decreases in net worth. Determine the principal sources of unrealized decreases in net worth.
6. Observe whether the net unrealized amount increased or decreased, and by how much.
7. Observe whether the net change was an increase or decrease, and the amount.
8. Observe the net worth at the end of the year.

Illustration of Preparation of Statement of Financial Condition

For Bill and Mary, assume that the assets and liabilities, the effective income tax rates, and the amount of estimated income taxes are as follows at December 31, 1991:

Account	Tax Bases	Estimated Current Value	Excess of Estimated Current Values over Tax Bases	Effective Income Tax Rates	Amount of Estimated Income Taxes
Cash	$ 8,000	$ 8,000	—	—	—
Savings accounts	20,000	20,000	—	—	—
Marketable securities	50,000	60,000	$10,000	28%	$2,800
Options	—0—	20,000	20,000	28%	5,600
Royalties	—0—	10,000	10,000	28%	2,800
Auto	15,000	10,000	(5,000)	—	—
Boat	12,000	8,000	(4,000)	—	—
Residence	110,000	130,000	20,000	28%	5,600
Furnishings	30,000	25,000	(5,000)	—	—
Mortgage payable	(60,000)	(60,000)	—	—	—
Auto loan	(5,000)	(5,000)	—	—	—
Credit cards	(5,000)	(4,000)	—	—	—
Total estimated income tax					$16,800

BILL AND MARY
Statement of Financial Condition
December 31, 1991

Assets	
Cash	$ 8,000
Savings accounts	20,000
Marketable securities	60,000
Options	20,000
Royalties	10,000
Auto	10,000
Boat	8,000
Residence	130,000
Furnishings	25,000
	$291,000

Statement of Financial Condition   (continued)

Liabilities	
Credit cards	$ 4,000
Auto loan	5,000
Mortgage payable	60,000
Total liabilities	$ 69,000
Estimated income taxes on the difference between the estimated current values of assets and the estimated current amounts of liabilities and their tax bases	$ 16,800
Net worth	205,200
	$291,000

Comments

1. The net worth is $205,200. Many would consider this a relatively high amount.
2. Liquid assets total $88,000 (cash, $8,000; savings accounts, $20,000; and marketable securities, $60,000).
3. Most of the liabilities appear to be long-term (mortgage payable, $60,000).
4. Compare specific assets with related liabilities:

Auto		Residence	
Current value	$10,000	Current value	$130,000
Auto loan	5,000	Mortgage payable	60,000
Net investment	$ 5,000	Net investment	$ 70,000

Illustration of Preparation of Statement of Changes in Net Worth

For Bill and Mary, the changes in net worth for the year ended December 31, 1991 are detailed as follows:

Realized increases in net worth	
Salary	$ 70,000
Dividend income	5,000
Interest income	6,000
Gain on sale of marketable securities	2,000
Realized decreases in net worth	
Income taxes	20,000
Real estate taxes	2,000
Personal expenditures	28,000

Unrealized increases in net worth	
Marketable securities	11,000
Residence	3,000
Unrealized decreases in net worth	
Boat	2,000
Furnishings	4,000
Estimated income taxes on the differences between the estimated current values of assets and current amounts of liabilities and their tax bases	12,000
Net worth at the beginning of year	176,200

BILL AND MARY
Statement of Changes in Net Worth
For the Year Ended December 31, 1991

Realized increases in net worth	
Salary	$ 70,000
Dividend income	5,000
Interest income	6,000
Gain on sale of marketable securities	2,000
	83,000
Realized decreases in net worth	
Income taxes	20,000
Real estate taxes	2,000
Personal expenditures	28,000
	50,000
Net realized increase in net worth	33,000
Unrealized increases in net worth	
Marketable securities	11,000
Residence	3,000
	14,000
Unrealized decreases in net worth	
Boat	2,000
Furnishings	4,000
Estimated income taxes on the differences between the estimated current values of assets and the estimated current amounts of liabilities and their tax bases	12,000
	18,000
Net unrealized decreases in net worth	4,000
Net increase in net worth	29,000
Net worth at the beginning of year	176,200
Net worth at the end of the year	$205,200

Comments

1. Most of the realized increases in net worth came from salary ($70,000).
2. The major decreases in realized net worth were income taxes ($20,000) and personal expenditures ($28,000).
3. Net realized increase in net worth was $33,000.
4. Principal unrealized increase in net worth was in marketable securities ($11,000).
5. Principal unrealized decreases in net worth were the estimated income taxes on the differences between the estimated current value of assets and the estimated current amounts of liabilities and their tax bases ($12,000).
6. Net unrealized decreases in net worth were $4,000.
7. Net increase in net worth was $29,000.
8. Net worth at the end of the year was $205,200.

ACCOUNTING FOR GOVERNMENTS AND OTHER NONPROFIT INSTITUTIONS

A large amount of economic activity in the United States is performed by governments and other nonprofit institutions. Examples of nonprofit institutions are federal, state, and local governments; universities; hospitals; churches; and professional organizations.

The accounting for nonprofit institutions is not uniform from one type of institution to another, and sometimes it is not even uniform among institutions of a particular type. Many organizations provide a source of accounting principles for nonprofit institutions. Examples are the National Council on Governmental Accounting, the American Hospital Association, and the National Association of College and University Business Officers. In 1983, the Governmental Accounting Standards Board was established, to provide more uniformity in reporting standards for nonprofit institutions.

Typically, accounting for nonprofit institutions is very different from accounting for a profit-oriented enterprise. The accounting for a profit-oriented business is centered on the entity concept and the efficiency of the entity. The accounting for a nonprofit institution does not include a single entity concept or efficiency. The accounting for a profit-oriented business has a bottom line—net income. The accounting for a nonprofit institution does not typically have a bottom line.

Accounting for Governments

The accounting terminology utilized by governments is much different from that used by profit-oriented enterprises. Governments use such terms as *appropriations* and *general fund*. Definitions of some of the terms that will be encountered are as follows:

- Appropriations—Provision for necessary resources and the authority for their disbursement
- Debt service—Cash receipts and disbursements related to the payment of interest and principal on long-term debt
- Capital projects—Cash receipts and disbursements related to the acquisition of long-lived assets
- Special assessments—Cash receipts and disbursements related to improvements or services for which special property assessments have been levied
- Enterprises—Operations that are similar to private businesses in which service users are charged fees
- Internal services— Service centers that supply goods or services to other governmental units on a cost reimbursement basis
- General fund—All cash receipts and disbursements not required to be accounted for in another fund
- Proprietary funds—Funds whose intention is to maintain the assets through cost reimbursement by users, or partial cost recovery from users and periodic infusion of additional assets
- Fiduciary funds (nonexpendable funds)—Funds whose principal must remain intact (although typically, revenues earned may be distributed)
- Encumbrances—Future commitments for expenditure

There are thousands of state and local governments in the United States, and they account for a large segment of the gross national product. State and local governments have a major impact on the citizens. No organization has had a clear responsibility for providing accounting principles for state and local governments. The American Institute of Certified Public Accountants, the National Council on Governmental Accounting, and the Municipal Finance Officers Association have provided significant leadership in establishing accounting principles for state and local governments.

During the early 1980s, it was thought that governmental accounting could benefit from the establishment of a board similar to the Financial Accounting Standards Board. A group of government accountants and CPAs organized a committee known as the Governmental Accounting Standards Board Organizing Committee. The committee recommended the establishment of a separate standard-setting body for governmental accounting.

In April 1984, the Financial Accounting Foundation amended its articles of incorporation to accommodate a Governmental Accounting Standards Board. Thus, the Governmental Accounting Standards Board (GASB) became a branch of the Financial Accounting Foundation.

Governmental Accounting Standards Board Statement No. 1, Appendix B, addresses the jurisdictional hierarchy of the GASB and the FASB. Appendix B of Governmental Accounting Standards Board Statement No. 1 establishes the following priorities for governmental units:

a. Pronouncements of the Governmental Accounting Standards Board.

b. Pronouncements of the Financial Accounting Standards Board.

c. Pronouncements of bodies composed of expert accountants that follow a due process procedure, including broad distribution of proposed accounting principles for public comment, for the intended purpose of establishing accounting principles or describing existing practices that are generally accepted.

d. Practices or pronouncements that are widely recognized as being generally accepted because they represent prevalent practice in a particular industry or the knowledgeable application to specific circumstances of pronouncements that are generally accepted.

e. Other accounting literature.[4]

Governmental Accounting Standards Board Statement No. 1 also adopts the National Council on Governmental Accounting pronouncements and the American Institute of Certified Public Accountants audit guide entitled *Audits of State and Local Governmental Units* as the basis for currently existing GAAP for state and local governmental units.

State and local governments serve as stewards of public funds. This stewardship responsibility dominates the accounting for state and local governments.

State and local government accounting revolves around fund accounting. A fund is defined as an "independent fiscal and accounting entity with a self-balancing set of accounts recording cash and/or other resources together with all related liabilities, obligations, reserves, and equities which are segregated for the purpose of carrying on specific activities or attaining certain objectives in accordance with special regulations, restrictions, or limitations."[5]

Government transactions are recorded in one or more funds designed to emphasize control and budgetary limitations. A fund is established for a specific purpose. Examples are highway maintenance, parks, debt repayment, endowment fund, and welfare.

The number of funds that are utilized depends on the responsibilities of the particular state or local government and the grouping of these responsibilities. For example, highway maintenance and bridge maintenance may be grouped together. Each of the funds is in effect a self-balancing fund.

Some governments do their accounting using a method that is close to a cash basis; others use a modified accrual basis; and some use an accrual basis. A single government unit may use more than one basis, depending on the fund. For example, the City of Toledo, Ohio, uses a modified accrual basis for the governmental and expendable trust funds and uses an accrual basis of accounting for the proprietary and nonexpendable trust funds. The trend is away from the cash basis and toward a modified accrual basis. Some states have passed a law requiring governments to use a modified accrual basis.

The manner of handling depreciation can be much different than it is for a

---

[4]Government Accounting Standards Board, Statement No. 1 (July 1984), Appendix B, par. 4.
[5]*Governmental Accounting, Auditing, and Financial Reporting* (Chicago: Municipal Finance Officers Association of the United States and Canada, 1968), p. 6.

commercial business. Review the notes to the financial statements to determine how the state or local government unit is handling depreciation. The City of Toledo, Ohio describes its handling of depreciation in a footnote to its 1989 annual report, as follows: "Depreciation expense relating to Proprietary Fund Fixed assets is charged to operations. Accumulated depreciation on general fixed assets of the City is recorded on a memorandum basis in the General Fixed Assets Account Group."

The 1989 annual report of Lucas County, Ohio, in footnote B, describes the handling of depreciation as follows: "Depreciation is not provided for the General Fixed Assets Account Group. Depreciation for the Proprietary Funds is determined by allocating the cost of fixed assets over the estimated useful lives of the assets on a straight-line basis."

For state and local governments, a detailed plan of operations is prepared for each period. This includes an item-by-item estimate of expenditures. This plan of operation (budget) is approved by the representatives of the citizens (city council, town meeting, and so on). When the representatives of the citizens approve the budget, the individual expenditures become limits. An increase in an approved expenditure will require approval by the same representatives of the citizens. Thus, the representatives of the citizens set up a *legal* control over expenditures. This is much different from the budget for a commercial business, in which the budget is merely a plan of future revenues and expenses.

There is a great variance in quality of disclosure in the financial reporting of state and local governments. Some items that have been particularly poorly reported have been pension liabilities, marketable securities, inventories, fixed assets, and lease obligations.

The Government Finance Officers Association of the United States and Canada presents a Certificate of Achievement for Excellence in Financial Reporting to governmental units and public employee retirement systems whose comprehensive annual financial reports are judged to conform substantially to program standards. These standards are considered to be very rigorous. When analyzing financial statements of a governmental unit, determine whether a Certificate of Achievement for Excellence in Financial Reporting has been received. The municipal bond rating of the governmental unit should also be determined.

Standard & Poor's and Moody's evaluate and grade the quality of a bond relative to the probability of default. It is usual for a governmental unit to have its bonds rated. One rating is assigned to all general obligation bonds (backed by the full faith and credit of the government unit). Bonds that are not backed by the full faith and credit of the government unit are rated individually—for example, industrial revenue bonds. These ratings do not represent the probability of default by the governmental unit.

When reviewing the financial reporting of governmental units, it is helpful to visualize the reporting in a pyramid fashion. The funds are typically grouped into major categories, which are supported by individual funds that serve to account for each of the separate government activities. The pyramid concept of financial reporting for a governmental unit is illustrated in Exhibit 15-2.

The Financial Reporting "Pyramid"

Daniel L. Koulak, "Understanding Your Town's Financial Report," *Management Accounting* (December 1984), p. 54.

Suggestions for Reviewing a Governmental Unit

1. Determine if a Certificate of Achievement has been received.
2. Determine the municipal bond rating of the governmental unit.
3. Review the combined balance sheet.
4. Review the combined statement of revenues, expenditures, and changes in fund balances.
5. Review the disclosure of debt.
6. Review footnotes and other disclosures.
7. In addition to reviewing the absolute numbers, prepare selected common size analyses.

The City of Toledo, Ohio, presents detailed financial statements, and in recent years it has been awarded Certificates of Achievement for Excellence in Financial Reporting. The total financial report consists of more than 100 pages, so it is not feasible to present the entire report here. The parts selected are as follows:

1. Combined Balance Sheet—All Fund Types and Account Groups (Exhibit 15-3).
2. Combined Statement of Revenues, Expenditures and Changes in Fund Balances—All Government Fund Types and Expendable Trust Funds (Exhibit 15-4). (Notice that proceeds from debt are recorded on this statement as revenue. Principal retirement, interest, and fiscal charges are recorded as expenditures.)
3. Partial Footnote 1—Organization and Summary of Significant Accounting Policies (Exhibit 15-5). (Notice that a modified accrual basis of accounting is utilized by the Governmental and Expendable Trust Funds, whereas an accrual basis of accounting is utilized by the Proprietary and Nonexpendable Trust Funds. Agency Fund assets and liabilities are recognized on the modified accrual basis of accounting, since these funds are custodial in nature and do not involve measurement of results of operations.)
4. Income tax revenues (Exhibit 15-6).
5. Ratio of net bonded debt to assessed value and net bonded debt per capita (Exhibit 15-7).

Nonprofit Institutions Other Than Governments

Nonprofit institutions other than governments use forms of financial reporting that vary from the fund type of system to a commercial type of reporting. Often, the system is a hybrid of the fund system and a commercial system.

Exhibit 15-8 shows the 1989 financial statements of the Institute of Internal Auditors. Notice how these financial statements resemble the financial statements of a commercial enterprise. Exhibit 15-9 contains the 1989 financial statements of the National Association of Accountants. Notice how these financial statements follow fund accounting and thus resemble the financial reporting of a governmental institution.

In 1987, the FASB passed SFAS No. 93, "Recognition of Depreciation by Not-for-Profit Organizations." This Standard required all not-for-profit organizations to recognize the cost of using up long-lived tangible assets (depreciation) in general-purpose external financial statements.

An exception provided in SFAS No. 93 to recognizing depreciation expense is for "individual works of art or historical treasures whose economic benefit or service potential is used up so slowly that their estimated useful lives are extraordinarily long."[6]

(continues on page 716)

[6]Financial Accounting Standards Board, Statement of Financial Accounting Standards No. 93, "Recognition of Depreciation by Not-for-Profit Organizations," 1987, par. 6.

EXHIBIT 15-3

CITY OF TOLEDO, OHIO
Combined Balance Sheet—All Fund Types and Account Groups
December 31, 1989 (amounts in thousands)

		GOVERNMENTAL FUND TYPES		
ASSETS AND OTHER DEBITS	GENERAL	SPECIAL REVENUE	DEBT SERVICE	CAPITAL PROJECTS
Equity in pooled cash	$ 3,176	$ 1,932	$ —	$ 21,550
Other cash	19	—	75	—
Investments at cost	125	—	—	—
Funds on deposit — Employees Deferred Compensation Program	—	—	—	—
Receivables (net of allowance for uncollectible accounts):				
Taxes	12,266	—	—	—
Accounts	1,430	923	—	663
Special assessments	—	37,915	6,766	1,337
Notes	—	1,307	—	—
Due from other funds	1,640	—	—	4,516
Due from other governments	—	—	—	—
Prepaid expenditures and expenses	8	458	—	—
Inventory of supplies	1,178	1,526	—	1,221
Restricted assets:				
Equity in pooled cash	—	—	—	—
Investments at cost	—	2,070	43	7,310
Accounts receivable (net of allowance for uncollectible accounts)	—	—	—	—
Due from other funds	—	—	—	—
Due from other governments	—	—	—	—
Property, plant and equipment (net of accumulated depreciation)	—	—	—	—
Deferred debt issuance cost	—	—	—	—
Amount available in Debt Service Funds	—	—	—	—
Amount to be provided for:				
Retirement of general long-term obligations	—	—	—	—
Compensated absences	—	—	—	—
Total assets and other debits	$ 19,842	$ 46,131	$ 6,884	$ 36,597

E X H I B I T   1 5 - 3   (continued)

	PROPRIETARY FUND TYPES		FIDUCIARY FUND TYPES	ACCOUNT GROUPS		
ENTERPRISE	INTERNAL SERVICE	TRUST AND AGENCY	GENERAL FIXED ASSETS	GENERAL LONG-TERM OBLIGATIONS	TOTAL (MEMORANDUM ONLY)
$ 535	$ 7,587	$ 15,648	$ —	$ —	$ 50,428
99	—	26	—	—	219
42,384	—	1,084	—	—	43,593
—	—	16,141	—	—	16,141
—	—	—	—	—	12,266
6,019	—	5	—	—	9,040
—	—	—	—	—	46,018
—	—	1,475	—	—	2,782
—	1,011	—	—	—	7,167
230	—	—	—	—	230
78	—	—	—	—	544
3,155	373	—	—	—	7,453
802	—	—	—	—	802
18,834	—	—	—	—	28,257
1,025	—	—	—	—	1,025
40,102	—	—	—	—	40,102
708	—	—	—	—	708
271,823	16,858	—	81,434	—	370,115
997	—	—	—	—	997
—	—	—	—	4	4
—	—	—	—	123,506	123,506
—	—	—	—	25,719	25,719
$ 386,791	$ 25,829	$ 34,379	$ 81,434	$ 149,229	$ 787,116

E X H I B I T   1 5 - 3   **(continued)**

| | | GOVERNMENTAL FUND TYPES | | |
	GENERAL	SPECIAL REVENUE	DEBT SERVICE	CAPITAL PROJECTS
LIABILITIES				
Accounts payable	$ 1,508	$ 507	$ —	$ 1,389
Escrow	—	140	—	—
Retainages	8	31	—	620
Due to other funds	—	5,129	114	442
Due to other governments	—	11	—	793
Deferred revenue	—	37,915	6,766	6,086
Other current liabilities	3,835	407	—	12
Accrued compensated absences	—	—	—	—
Unfunded Police P.E.R.S. Liability	—	—	—	—
Unfunded Fire P.E.R.S. Liability	—	—	—	—
Payable from restricted assets:				
Accounts payable	—	—	—	—
Escrow	—	—	—	—
Due to other governments	—	—	—	—
Other liabilities	—	—	—	—
Debt:				
Notes payable	—	29,300	—	27,230
General obligation bonds payable	—	—	—	—
Special assessment bonds payable with governmental commitment	—	—	—	—
Revenue bonds payable	—	—	—	—
Capitalized lease obligation	—	—	—	—
Other long-term debt	—	—	—	—
Deferred compensation	—	—	—	—
Total liabilities	5,351	73,440	6,880	36,572
FUND EQUITY AND OTHER CREDITS				
Contributed capital	—	—	—	—
Investment in general fixed assets	—	—	—	—
Retained earnings (deficit):				
Reserved for debt service	—	—	—	—
Reserved for replacement	—	—	—	—
Reserved for improvements	—	—	—	—
Unreserved	—	—	—	—
Fund balances (deficit):				
Reserved for encumbrances	1,449	3,200	—	14,893
Reserved for inventory of supplies	1,178	1,526	—	1,221
Reserved for long-term notes receivable	—	1,307	—	—
Reserved for debt service	—	—	113	—
Reserved for budget stabilization fund	6,445	—	—	—
Unreserved:				
Undesignated	5,419	(33,342)	(109)	(16,089)
Total fund equity (deficit) and other credits	14,491	(27,309)	4	25
Total liabilities, fund equity (deficit) and other credits	$ 19,842	$ 46,131	$ 6,884	$ 36,597

EXHIBIT 15-3 (continued)

	PROPRIETARY FUND TYPES		FIDUCIARY FUND TYPES	ACCOUNT GROUPS		
ENTERPRISE		INTERNAL SERVICE	TRUST AND AGENCY	GENERAL FIXED ASSETS	GENERAL LONG-TERM OBLIGATIONS	TOTAL (MEMORANDUM ONLY)
$ 1,817	$ 740		$ 24	$ —	$ —	$ 5,985
48	—		807	—	—	995
1,258	—		—	—	—	1,917
40,102	1,181		301	—	—	47,269
—	—		5,700	—	—	6,504
—	—		—	—	—	50,767
350	1,134		2,654	—	—	8,392
—	—		4,977	—	25,719	30,696
—	—		—	—	14,574	14,574
—	—		—	—	15,668	15,668
2,859	—		—	—	—	2,859
952	—		—	—	—	952
156	—		—	—	—	156
778	—		—	—	—	778
7,965	—		—	—	205	64,700
8,345	1,120		—	—	52,640	62,105
—	—		—	—	4,046	4,046
55,787	—		—	—	—	55,787
—	—		—	—	29,692	29,692
—	—		—	—	6,685	6,685
—	—		16,141	—	—	16,141
120,417	4,175		30,604	—	149,229	426,668
16,852	42,982		—	—	—	59,834
—	—		—	81,434	—	81,434
6,427	—		—	—	—	6,427
35,009	—		—	—	—	35,009
76,302	—		—	—	—	76,302
131,784	(21,328)		—	—	—	110,456
—	—		—	—	—	19,542
—	—		—	—	—	3,925
—	—		1,475	—	—	2,782
—	—		—	—	—	113
—	—		—	—	—	6,445
—	—		2,300	—	—	(41,821)
266,374	21,654		3,775	81,434	—	360,448
$ 386,791	$ 25,829		$ 34,379	$ 81,434	$ 149,229	$ 787,116

EXHIBIT 15-4

CITY OF TOLEDO
Combined Statement of Revenues, Expenditures, and Changes in Fund Balances
All Governmental Fund Types and Expendable Trust Funds
For the Year Ended December 31, 1989 (amounts in thousands)

| | | GOVERNMENTAL FUND TYPES | | |
	GENERAL	SPECIAL REVENUE	DEBT SERVICE	CAPITAL PROJECTS
Revenues:				
Income taxes	$ 106,702	$ —	$ —	$ —
Property taxes	12,070	—	—	—
Special assessments	—	14,790	960	217
Licenses and permits	2,776	79	—	—
Intergovernmental revenue	14,299	16,320	653	3,837
Charges for services	8,542	925	—	1
Investment earnings	5,418	858	46	457
Fines and forfeitures	3,475	—	—	—
All other revenue	707	54	—	346
Total revenues	153,989	33,026	1,659	4,858
Expenditures:				
Current:				
General government	18,073	256	—	—
Public service	1,902	18,782	—	—
Public safety	85,407	348	—	—
Public utilities	—	2,407	—	—
Community environment	5,206	5,759	—	—
Health	13,299	2,288	—	—
Parks and recreation	5,148	83	—	—
Capital outlay	478	1,511	—	31,075
Debt service:				
Principal retirement	1,090	—	6,482	—
Interest and fiscal charges	2,190	2,456	5,146	1,458
Total expenditures	132,793	33,890	11,628	32,533
Excess (deficiency) of revenues over expenditures	21,196	(864)	(9,969)	(27,675)
Other financing sources (uses):				
Operating transfers in	279	424	9,622	38,374
Operating transfers (out)	(24,161)	(231)	(60)	(24,282)
Bond proceeds	—	—	—	1,395
Other financing sources	18	40	—	69
Total other financing sources (uses)	(23,864)	233	9,562	15,556
Excess (deficiency) of revenues and other financing sources over expenditures and other financing (uses)	(2,668)	(631)	(407)	(12,119)
Fund balances (deficit) at beginning of year	17,680	(26,519)	89	14,009
Residual equity transfers	(591)	—	322	(2,093)
Increase (decrease) in reserve for inventory	70	(159)	—	228
Fund balances (deficit) at end of year	$ 14,491	$ (27,309)	$ 4	$ 25

FIDUCIARY FUND TYPES EXPENDABLE TRUSTS	TOTAL (MEMORANDUM ONLY)
$ —	$ 106,702
1,864	13,934
—	15,967
—	2,855
—	35,109
166	9,634
34	6,813
—	3,475
1,255	2,362
3,319	196,851
2,766	21,095
—	20,684
330	86,085
—	2,407
9	10,974
—	15,587
50	5,281
—	33,064
—	7,572
—	11,250
3,155	213,999
164	(17,148)
157	48,856
(622)	(49,356)
—	1,395
—	127
(465)	1,022
(301)	(16,126)
3,757	9,016
—	(2,362)
—	139
$ 3,456	$ (9,333)

EXHIBIT 15-5

CITY OF TOLEDO, OHIO
Partial Footnote 1—Organization and Summary of Significant Accounting Policies

C. Basis of Accounting

The modified accrual basis of accounting is utilized by the Governmental and Expendable Trust Funds. Under this method of accounting, the City recognizes revenue when it becomes both measurable and available to finance current City operations. Revenues accrued at the end of the year include individual income taxes during the fourth quarter that are received within 60 days after year-end. Property taxes are recognized as revenue in the budget year to which they apply where taxpayer liability has been established and collectibility is assured. Expenditures are recorded when the related fund liability is incurred. Principal and interest on general long-term debt are recorded as fund liabilities when due or when amounts have been accumulated in the debt service fund for payments to be made early in the following year.

The accrual basis of accounting is utilized by the Proprietary and Nonexpendable Trust Funds. Revenues are recognized when earned, and expenses are recognized when incurred. Unbilled Water and Sewer Funds' utility service receivables are recorded at year-end.

Agency Fund assets and liabilities are recognized on the modified accrual basis of accounting since these Funds are custodial in nature and do not involve measurement of results of operations.

EXHIBIT 15-6

CITY OF TOLEDO, OHIO
Income Tax Revenues
Last Ten Years (amounts in thousands)

Fiscal Year	Tax Revenues	Tax Rate
1980	$ 45,822	1½%
1981	46,803	1½%
1982	59,514	1½–2¼%[1]
1983	76,812	2¼%
1984	87,461	2¼%
1985	93,161	2¼%
1986	95,651	2¼%
1987	102,267	2¼%
1988	109,542	2¼%
1989	106,702	2¼%

[1]Tax rate at 1½% from January 1 through June 30, 1982 and at 2¼% from July 1 through December 31, 1982.
Source: City of Toledo, Income Tax Department.

EXHIBIT 15-7

CITY OF TOLEDO, OHIO
Ratio of Net General Bonded Debt
to Assessed Value and Net Bonded Debt Per Capita
Last Ten Years (dollar amounts in thousands, except per capita)

Fiscal Year	Population	Assessed Value	Gross General Bonded Debt	Less Balance in Debt Service Fund
1980	354,635	$2,406,890	$50,120	$ —
1981	354,635	2,431,067	48,391	—
1982	354,635	2,658,209	45,009	882
1983	354,635	2,661,746	54,822	2,349
1984	354,635	2,689,362	50,620	21
1985	354,635	2,763,049	46,510	89
1986	354,635	2,773,893	61,550	31
1987	354,635	2,796,483	66,395	70
1988	354,635	3,091,093	68,820	26
1989	354,635	3,111,062	52,640	113

Fiscal Year	Net General Bonded Debt	Ratio of Net Bonded Debt to Assessed Value	Net Bonded Debt Per Capita
1980	$50,120	2.1%	$141.33
1981	48,391	2.0%	136.45
1982	44,127	1.7%	124.43
1983	52,473	2.0%	147.96
1984	50,599	1.9%	142.68
1985	46,421	1.7%	130.90
1986	61,519	2.2%	173.47
1987	66,325	2.4%	187.02
1988	68,794	2.2%	193.99
1989	52,527	1.7%	148.12

In January 1988, the GASB passed Statement No. 8, "Recognition of Depreciation by Not-for-Profit Organizations, to Certain State and Local Government Entities." This Statement provides that governmental colleges and universities and other governmental entities that use certain specialized industry accounting and reporting principles and practices should not change their accounting and reporting for depreciation of capital assets as a result of SFAS No. 93. Thus, the positions of the FASB and the GASB differed on the issue of recognizing depreciation.

This difference was resolved in late 1989, when the Financial Accounting Foundation's board of trustees altered its position regarding the jurisdictional dispute between the FASB and the GASB. Under the revised position, the GASB retained authority over financial reporting by all governmental entities.

Therefore, some not-for-profit organizations will be recording depreciation, and some will not. Statements of governmentally owned special entities will not be recording depreciation, but other not-for-profit organizations will. Thus, a government-owned hospital will not record depreciation, while a private hospital will do so.

The Institute of Internal Auditors and the National Association of Accountants are not governmentally owned, so they record depreciation. A review of Exhibits 15-8 and 15-9 reveals that both of these not-for-profit organizations do record depreciation expense.

Budgeting by Objectives and/or Measures of Productivity

It was previously mentioned that accounting for nonprofit institutions does not typically include the concept of efficiency. Because of this, there is the tendency to spend all of the funds allocated, for fear that the next year's budget will be reduced if all budgeted funds are not spent.

Some nonprofit institutions have added budgeting by objectives and/or measures of productivity to their financial reporting to incorporate measures of efficiency. The article "Budgeting by Objectives: Charlotte's Experience" reported several objectives that were incorporated in the budget of Charlotte, North Carolina. The budget was guided by four primary objectives: (1) the property tax rate should not increase, (2) continued emphasis should be placed on making the best use of city employees and the present computer capability, (3) any budget increase should be held to a minimum, and (4) a balanced program of services should be presented.[7]

This article also reports measures of productivity that Charlotte has used. These measures of productivity are[8] (1) customers served per $1,000 of sanitation expense, (2) number of tons of refuse per $1,000 expense, and (3) street miles flushed per $1,000 expense.[9]

(continues on page 730)

---

[7]Charles H. Gibson, "Budgeting by Objectives: Charlotte's Experience," *Management Accounting* (January 1978), p. 39.
[8]Ibid., p. 39.
[9]Ibid., p. 48.

EXHIBIT 15-8

THE INSTITUTE OF INTERNAL AUDITORS
Financial Statements
1988–1989 Annual Report

Balance Sheets	ASSETS		
	May 31, 1988	May 31, 1989 (Unaudited)	September 30, 1989
CURRENT ASSETS:			
Cash and temporary cash investments (Note 1)	$ 204,097	$ 444,332	$ 241,369
Accounts receivable	194,574	264,980	330,677
Prepaid expenses and advances	181,495	164,287	196,849
Educational products inventory (Note 1)	126,707	127,804	123,910
	706,873	1,001,403	892,805
INVESTMENTS (Notes 2 and 6)	1,226,557	1,458,000	1,689,200
PROPERTY AND EQUIPMENT (Note 1):			
Land	178,025	178,025	178,025
Buildings and improvements	1,096,790	1,099,165	1,099,151
Furniture and equipment	1,169,280	1,378,704	1,316,214
	2,444,095	2,655,894	2,593,390
Less-accumulated depreciation	(1,390,170)	(1,577,027)	(1,574,569)
	1,053,925	1,078,867	1,018,821
DEFERRED PROJECT COSTS (Note 1)	218,045	107,037	113,374
	$ 3,205,400	$ 3,645,307	$ 3,714,200

LIABILITIES AND FUND BALANCE

	May 31, 1988	May 31, 1989 (Unaudited)	September 30, 1989
CURRENT LIABILITIES:			
Accounts payable and accrued expenses	$ 697,844	$ 604,449	$ 652,529
Deferred revenue (Note 1)	1,231,400	1,263,528	1,491,882
	1,929,244	1,867,977	2,144,411
FUND BALANCE	1,276,156	1,777,330	1,569,789
	$ 3,205,400	$ 3,645,307	$ 3,714,200

E X H I B I T 1 5 - 8   (continued)

Statements of Revenues, Expenses, and Changes in Fund Balance
For the Periods Ended May 31, 1988, and May 31, 1989 (unaudited),
and for the Three Periods Ended September 30, 1989 (four-month period unaudited)

	Twelve Months Ended May 31, 1988	Twelve Months Ended May 31, 1989 (Unaudited)	Four Months Ended September 30, 1989 (Unaudited)	Sixteen Months Ended September 30, 1989	Twelve Months Ended September 30, 1989
REVENUES (Notes 1 and 2):					
Professional Development	$ 3,321,205	$ 4,108,517	$ 1,103,898	$ 5,212,415	$ 3,945,730
Professional Services	1,966,605	2,050,776	692,698	2,743,474	2,059,225
Professional Practices	547,153	768,489	115,234	883,723	756,481
Other Income	173,637	218,004	180,445	398,449	354,786
Total Revenues	6, 008,600	7,145,786	2,092,275	9,238,061	7,116,222
EXPENSES (Note 1):					
Professional Development	2,635,576	3,136,691	1,016,262	4,152,953	3,150,435
Professional Services	1,137,883	1,232,644	391,584	1,624,228	1,205,655
Professional Practices	556,980	682,459	239,901	922,360	719,336
Administrative Services	1,394,812	1,528,487	624,246	2,152,733	1,700,566
Building rental loss, net (Note 3)	28,241	64,331	27,823	92,154	76,453
Total Expenses	5,753,492	6,644,612	2,299,816	8,944,428	6,852,445
EXCESS OF REVENUES OVER EXPENSES	255,108	501,174	(207,541)	293,633	263,777
FUND BALANCE, beginning of period	1,021,048	1,276,156	1,777,330	1,276,156	1,306,012
FUND BALANCE, end of period	$ 1,276,156	$ 1,777,330	$ 1,569,789	$ 1,569,789	$ 1,569,789

E X H I B I T 1 5 - 8 (continued)

Statements of Cash Flows
For the Periods Ended May 31, 1988, and May 31, 1989 (unaudited),
and for the Three Periods Ended September 30, 1989 (four-month period unaudited)

	Twelve Months Ended May 31, 1988	Twelve Months Ended May 31, 1989 (Unaudited)	Four Months Ended September 30, 1989 (Unaudited)	Sixteen Months Ended September 30, 1989	Twelve Months Ended September 30, 1989
CASH FLOWS FROM OPERATING ACTIVITIES:					
Excess of revenues over expenses	$ 255,108	$ 501,174	$ (207,541)	$ 293,633	$ 263,777
Adjustments to reconcile excess of revenues over expenses to net cash provided by operating activities:					
Depreciation	210,057	186,857	61,954	248,811	192,451
Amortization of deferred project costs	99,157	186,700	26,054	212,754	181,922
Change in assets and liabilities:					
(Increase) decrease in accounts receivable	61,135	(70,406)	(65,697)	(136,103)	49,147
(Increase) decrease in prepaid expenses and advances	(18,040)	17,208	(32,562)	(15,354)	40,860
Decrease (increase) in educational products inventory	24,407	(1,097)	3,894	2,797	22,708
Increase in deferred project costs	(102,957)	(75,692)	(32,391)	(108,083)	(99,102)
(Decrease) increase in accounts payable and accrued expenses	72,548	(93,395)	48,080	(45,315)	20,468
Increase (decrease) in deferred revenue	189,172	32,128	228,354	260,482	(27,272)
Net cash provided by operating activities	790,587	683,477	30,145	713,622	644,959
CASH FLOWS FROM INVESTING ACTIVITIES:					
Purchases of investments	(2,098,345)	(1,929,282)	(1,576,665)	(3,505,947)	(3,145,024)
Sales of investments	1,471,788	1,697,839	1,345,465	3,043,304	2,718,824
Purchases of property and equipment, net	(70,848)	(211,799)	(1,908)	(213,707)	(181,423)
Net cash used in investing activities	(697,405)	(443,242)	(233,108)	(676,350)	(607,623)
NET INCREASE (DECREASE) IN CASH AND TEMPORARY CASH INVESTMENTS	93,182	240,235	(202,963)	37,272	37,336
CASH AND TEMPORARY CASH INVESTMENTS, beginning of period	110,915	204,097	444,332	204,097	204,033
CASH AND TEMPORARY CASH INVESTMENTS, end of period	$ 204,097	$ 444,332	$ 241,369	$ 241,369	$ 241,369

EXHIBIT 15-8 **(continued)**

The Institute of
Internal Auditors, Inc.
**Notes to Financial Statements
May 31, 1988, and May 31, 1989
(unaudited), and for the Three
Periods Ended September 30, 1989
(four-month period unaudited)**

1. ORGANIZATION AND SUMMARY OF SIGNIFICANT ACCOUNTING POLICIES:

Organization

The Institute of Internal Auditors, Inc.
(The Institute) is a not-for-profit membership organization exempt from
income tax under Section 501(c)(6) of
the U.S. Internal Revenue Code. The
Institute was formed in 1941 to culti-
vate, promote, and disseminate
knowledge and information concerning internal auditing and related
subjects.

Fiscal Year

The Institute changed its fiscal year
end from May 31 to September 30. This
change was made to better match The
Institute's natural business cycle with
its fiscal year, as well as help facilitate
management's planning and budgeting processes.

The $207,541 loss for the four-month
period ended September 30, 1989, is
consistent with budgeted amounts and
prior experience over several periods.
The relatively high earnings realized
for the period ended May 31, 1989, resulted from unexpected sales of
educational products and attendance
at seminars.

Temporary Cash Investments

Temporary cash investments are
carried at cost which approximates
market.

Educational Products Inventory

Educational products inventory is
carried at the lower of cost (first-in,
first-out basis) or market.

Property and Equipment and Depreciation

Property and equipment is stated at

cost or, if donated, at the approximate
fair market value at the date of donation. Depreciation is computed using
the straight-line method over the
estimated useful lives of the related
assets, which range as follows:

	Years
Buildings and improvements	10-35
Furniture and equipment	3-5

Deferred Project Costs and Amortization

Costs related to seminar and educational product development or revision are deferred until the projects are
completed. Prior to June 1, 1988,
deferred project costs were amortized
straight-line over their estimated
useful lives which ranged from three
to four years. Effective June 1, 1988,
The Institute changed its method of
amortizing deferred educational
product development or revision costs
to more clearly reflect the estimated
lives of current publications and to
better match the higher sales historically experienced in the earlier years.
Such costs are now amortized over
three years, 50 percent the first year
and 25 percent each of the two suc-
ceeding years. This change in estimate
has been accounted for prospectively
and resulted in additional amortization of approximately $80,400 for the
sixteen months ended September 30,
1989.

Basis of Revenue Recognition

The basis of revenue recognition for
each of the revenue-producing functions included in professional development, professional services, and
professional practices is as follows:

Professional Development

Conference and seminar fees are
recognized as income in the period
that the meeting is held. Educational
product sales (publications, video-
tapes, and cassette tapes) are
reflected in income when the related
items are shipped.

Professional Services

Membership dues are recognized as
income monthly during the appli-

E X H I B I T   1 5 - 8   (continued)

cable membership period. Membership application fees (nonrefundable) are recognized as income when received. Subscriptions are reflected in income when the related publications are issued.

Professional Practices
Certification fees are recognized as income in the period that the examination is given. Prior to June 1, 1988, quality assurance review service fees were included in income in the period that the engagement was completed. Effective June 1, 1988, quality assurance review service fees are recognized as income as service is provided, based on percentage of engagement completed. Such change has been adopted in recognition that such service revenues, previously immaterial in their effect, may be material in the future and the new policy more fairly reflects such revenues. The effect of this change on the twelve- and sixteen-month periods ended September 30, 1989, was to increase revenue by approximately $55,000 for each period.

Deferred Revenue
Conference fees, educational product sales, seminar fees, certification fees, membership dues, and subscriptions collected in advance have been included in deferred revenue in the accompanying balance sheets. Such deferred revenue is substantially recognizable within one year.

Revenue and Expense Classifications and Allocations
The Institute has divided its revenue-producing functions into three divisions: professional development, professional services, and professional practices. The expenses directly related to the revenue-producing functions are presented in corresponding classifications, combined with allocations of certain common costs of The Institute such as advertising, in-house printing, and in-house composition services, based on estimated usage. Administrative services include those expenses

related to the President and other administrative departments such as data processing and accounting, as well as certain expenses incurred by The Institute for the benefit of the members and the profession which are not related to specific revenue-producing functions.

2. INVESTMENTS:
In July 1988, The Institute's Board of Directors voted to set aside cash in excess of a certain percentage of the previous year's expenses as a reserve for future needs. At September 30, 1989, investments included $222,200 in money market accounts set aside for this purpose. These funds will be invested mainly in certificates of deposit and may only be used with the approval of The Institute's International Treasurer.

The Institute's investments included $1,467,000 of certificates of deposit at September 30, 1989. These certificates bear interest at rates ranging from 8.75% to 10.8%, with maturities ranging from December 1989 through June 1991. At maturity, management of The Institute intends to reinvest these funds in other long-term investments of a similar nature.

3. BUILDING RENTAL LOSS:
Building rental loss represents rental revenue of $63,114, less related expenses of $155,268 for the sixteen-month period ended September 30, 1989, and rental revenue of $45,300, less related expenses of $121,753 for the twelve-month period ended September 30, 1989. For twelve months ended May 31, 1988, building rental income represented rental revenue of $77,858, less related expenses of $106,099. The rental expenses include utilities, depreciation, maintenance, and similar costs related to those portions of The Institute's buildings which are rented or available for rental to others.

4. PENSION PLAN:
The Institute has a noncontributory, trusteed, defined contribution pension plan which covers substantially all employees. It is The Institute's policy

EXHIBIT 15-8 (continued)

to fund the pension cost accrued, net of any forfeitures available. Costs of the plan totaled approximately $177,500 for the sixteen months ended September 30, 1989, and $138,200 for the twelve months ended same (net of forfeitures of approximately $24,700 during the pension year July 1, 1988, through June 30, 1989) and $160,300 (net of forfeitures of $9,800) for the twelve months ended May 31, 1988.

5. THE INSTITUTE OF INTERNAL AUDITORS RESEARCH FOUNDATION (THE FOUNDATION):

The Foundation is a separate corporation organized for the purpose of promoting research and education in internal auditing. The corporation is managed by a Board of Trustees appointed by its members which consist solely of the Board of Directors of The Institute. The Institute contributes to the Foundation the accounting, managerial, and administrative services necessary for the ordinary operations of the Foundation. Such services have not been reflected separately in the accompanying financial statements as contributions because the amounts are not objectively determinable.

Included in the Accounts Payable are $10,305 and $4,198 at September 30, 1989, and May 31, 1988, respectively, due to the Foundation. These amounts represent various research projects transferred to The Institute for publication and/or distribution. For Projects completed March 1985 through May 1988, a royalty, usually 15 percent of gross sales, is paid to the Foundation. For publication of Foundation Projects completed after May 31, 1988, The Institute remits 66.6 percent of gross sales.

The Foundation's financial position and results of operations have not been included in The Institute's financial statements. Selected financial information of the Foundation as of May 31, 1989, and 1988, and for the years then ended, is as follows:

	May 31,1989	May 31,1988
Total Assets	$429,170	$393,015
Fund balance	$364,368	$363,316
Total revenues	$278,971	$157,282
Excess (deficiency) of revenues over expenses	$ 1,052	$ (5,371)

6. LINE OF CREDIT:

The Institute maintains a $500,000 line-of-credit arrangement with a bank to provide for seasonal working capital requirements. Amounts borrowed on the line bear interest at the prime rate and are secured by long-term investments. No amounts were borrowed on the line during the sixteen months ended September 30, 1989, or the twelve months ended May 31, 1988.

E X H I B I T   1 5 - 9

NATIONAL ASSOCIATION OF ACCOUNTANTS, INC. AND AFFILIATES
1989 Financial Statements

NATIONAL ASSOCIATION OF ACCOUNTANTS, INC. AND AFFILIATES
COMBINED BALANCE SHEET
June 30, 1989 and 1988

(In Thousands)

	NAA, Inc.			1989			1988
	Current Operating Fund	Reserve Fund	Total	ICMA, Inc.	NAAMEF, Inc.	Combined	Combined
ASSETS							
Cash and cash equivalents.............	$ 371	$1,931	$ 2,302	$ –	$ 14	$ 2,316	$ 5,350
Marketable securities at lower of cost or market	–	8,328	8,328	–	–	8,328	5,155
Receivables net of allowance for doubtful accounts ($9 and $5)	730	–	730	5	–	735	685
Plant, property, equipment and software (net)	5,050	–	5,050	109	–	5,159	5,551
Due (to) from funds	4,495	(5,330)	(835)	277	558	–	–
Other assets	212	–	212	–	–	212	210
	10,858	4,929	15,787	391	572	16,750	16,951
LIABILITIES and FUND BALANCE							
Accounts payable and accrued expenses	1,463	–	1,463	137	12	1,612	1,562
Bonds payable	3,705	–	3,705	–	–	3,705	3,770
Deferred revenues							
Membership dues...................	3,516	–	3,516	–	–	3,516	3,613
Research contributions	135	–	135	–	–	135	105
Other...........................	432	–	432	195	–	627	763
Total liabilities	9,251	–	9,251	332	12	9,595	9,813
Fund balance.......................	1,607	4,929	6,536	59	560	7,155	7,138
	$10,858	$4,929	$15,787	$391	$572	$16,750	$16,951

See notes to combined financial statements

EXHIBIT 15-9   (continued)

NATIONAL ASSOCIATION OF ACCOUNTANTS, INC. AND AFFILIATES
COMBINED STATEMENT OF REVENUES AND EXPENSES AND CHANGES IN FUND BALANCES
Years Ended June 30, 1989 and 1988

(In Thousands)

			1989				1988
	NAA, Inc.						
	Current Operating Fund	Reserve Fund	Total	ICMA, Inc.	NAAMEF, Inc.	Combined	Combined*
REVENUES							
Membership dues	$ 6,727	$ –	$ 6,727	$ 297	$ –	$ 7,024	$ 7,114
Professional education program	1,606	–	1,606	–	–	1,606	1,117
Advertising and sales of publications	1,096	–	1,096	34	–	1,130	1,163
Subscriber list rentals	265	–	265	–	–	265	250
Controllers council/business and tax planning board	437	–	437	–	–	437	449
Annual conference	516	–	516	–	–	516	570
ICMA examination fees	–	–	–	755	–	755	710
Research fund contributions applied	–	–	–	–	–	–	10
Academic relations symposia	14	–	14	–	–	14	–
Interest and dividends on investments	476	–	476	–	30	506	314
Gain on security sales	127	164	291	–	18	309	669
Registration fees for membership	–	104	104	85	–	189	163
Treadway commission report sales	22	–	22	–	–	22	–
Other	46	–	46	5	2	53	90
Total revenues	11,332	268	11,600	1,176	50	12,826	12,619
EXPENSES							
Payments to chapters	1,110	–	1,110	–	–	1,110	1,121
Professional education program	1,306	–	1,306	–	–	1,306	872
Technical information and library	176	–	176	–	–	176	148
Technical publications	1,675	–	1,675	–	–	1,675	1,778
Controllers council/business and tax planning board	384	–	384	–	–	384	376
Annual conference	487	–	487	–	–	487	562
ICMA program	–	–	–	1,003	–	1,003	954
Research expenditures	266	–	266	–	–	266	282
Management accounting practices	172	–	172	–	–	172	192
Academic relations	172	–	172	–	–	172	132
Marketing and membership	557	–	557	–	–	557	588
Chapter operations	590	–	590	–	–	590	533
Public relations and promotion	139	–	139	–	–	139	124
Accounting, general office, graphic arts, human resources and food services	1,754	–	1,754	167	–	1,921	1,798
Management information services	500	–	500	–	–	500	559
Occupancy costs	759	–	759	65	–	824	806
Administration	1,007	–	1,007	–	1	1,008	883
Meetings planning	290	–	290	–	–	290	283
International department	56	–	56	–	–	56	84
Long–range strategy/implementation	12	–	12	–	–	12	19
Computer study/development	84	–	84	–	–	84	–
Treadway commission	75	–	75	–	–	75	–
Scholarship awards	–	–	–	–	12	12	9
Total expenses	11,571	–	11,571	1,235	13	12,819	12,103
EXCESS (DEFICIENCY) OF REVENUES OVER EXPENSES	(239)	268	29	(59)	37	7	516
FUND BALANCE, BEGINNING OF YEAR	1,492	4,980	6,472	118	548	7,138	6,602
CAPITAL ADDITIONS							
Building fund contributions	10	–	10	–	–	10	20
TRANSFERS (see notes 2 and 3)							
Reimbursement of funds advanced	(10)	10	–	–	–	–	–
NAA Memorial Education Fund, Inc.	25	–	25	–	(25)	–	–
Reserve Fund	329	(329)	–	–	–	–	–
FUND BALANCE, END OF YEAR	$ 1,607	$4,929	$ 6,536	$ 59	$560	$ 7,155	$ 7,138

*Reclassified to conform to 1989 format

See notes to combined financial statements

EXHIBIT 15-9 (continued)

NATIONAL ASSOCIATION OF ACCOUNTANTS, INC. AND AFFILIATES
COMBINED STATEMENT OF CASH FLOWS
Years Ended June 30, 1989 and 1988
Increase (Decrease) in Cash and Cash Equivalents
(In Thousands)

	1989						1988
	NAA, Inc.						
	Current Operating Fund	Reserve Fund	Total	ICMA, Inc.	NAAMEF, Inc.	Combined	Combined
CASH FLOWS FROM OPERATING ACTIVITIES							
Excess (deficiency) of revenues over expenses	$(239)	$ 268	$ 29	$(59)	$ 37	$ 7	$ 516
Adjustments to reconcile excess (deficiency) of revenues over expenses to net cash							
Depreciation, amortization and valuation allowances..........................	390	–	390	80	–	470	518
(Gain) on sale of securities......................	(127)	(164)	(291)	–	(18)	(309)	(669)
Changes in assets and liabilities							
(Increase) in receivables.........................	(53)	–	(53)	(1)	–	(54)	(199)
Decrease (increase) in due (to) from funds	(87)	140	53	(29)	(24)	–	–
Decrease (increase) in other assets	(4)	–	(4)	2	–	(2)	16
Increase in accounts payable and accrued expenses	37	–	37	9	4	50	145
Increase (decrease) in deferred revenue	(216)	–	(216)	13	–	(203)	49
Net cash provided by (used for) operating activities	(299)	244	(55)	15	(1)	(41)	376
CASH FLOWS FROM INVESTING ACTIVITIES							
Capital expenditures	(59)	–	(59)	(15)	–	(74)	(153)
Purchases of equity investments..................	–	(6,588)	(6,588)	–	–	(6,588)	(3,253)
Proceeds from sales of equity investments	127	3,579	3,706	–	18	3,724	6,526
Reimbursement of funds advanced	(10)	10	–	–	–	–	–
Net cash provided by (used for) investing activities	58	(2,999)	(2,941)	(15)	18	(2,938)	3,120
CASH FLOWS FROM FINANCING ACTIVITIES							
Repayment of current portion of long-term debt	(65)	–	(65)	–	–	(65)	(65)
Building fund contributions	10	–	10	–	–	10	20
Fund transfers	354	(329)	25	–	(25)	–	–
Net cash provided by (used for) financing activities	299	(329)	(30)	–	(25)	(55)	(45)
Net increase (decrease) in cash and cash equivalents.........................	58	(3,084)	(3,026)	–	(8)	(3,034)	3,451
Cash and cash equivalents—							
Beginning of year	313	5,015	5,328	–	22	5,350	1,899
End of year.................................	$ 371	$ 1,931	$ 2,302	$ –	$ 14	$ 2,316	$ 5,350
Supplemental disclosure							
Cash paid for interest	$ 402	–	$ 402	–	–	$ 402	$ 406

See notes to combined financial statements

EXHIBIT 15-9   (continued)

NATIONAL ASSOCIATION OF ACCOUNTANTS, INC. AND AFFILIATES

NOTES TO COMBINED FINANCIAL STATEMENTS
June 30, 1988

Note 1—Summary of significant accounting policies

The combined financial statements include the funds and accounts of the National Association of Accountants, Inc. (NAA, Inc.) and its affiliates, the Institute of Certified Management Accountants, Inc. (ICMA, Inc.) and the National Association of Accountants Memorial Education Fund, Inc. (NAAMEF, Inc.) (see note 3). The combined financial statements do not include the funds and accounts of chapters, regional councils and the Stuart Cameron McLeod Society.

For purposes of the combined statement of cash flows, NAA, Inc. and Affiliates considers cash equivalents to be liquid debt instruments with a maturity of 90 days or less.

Revenue recognition

Membership dues are recorded as revenue during the applicable membership period and no portion of such dues is allocated to subscription revenues in the combined financial statements. Subscription revenue is recorded during the applicable subscription period. Registration and examination fees are recorded as revenue when the related program or examination takes place. Advertising revenues are recorded as revenue when the applicable publications are issued.

Plant, property, equipment and software

Plant, property, equipment and software are recorded at cost. Plant and equipment are depreciated on the straight-line method over their estimated useful lives. Software is amortized on the straight-line method over a period of five years.

Income taxes

NAA, Inc. and NAAMEF, Inc are currently exempt from federal income tax under Internal Revenue Code Section 501(c)(3). ICMA, Inc. is currently exempt from federal income tax under Internal Revenue Code Section 501(c)(6). These organizations are subject to tax on income not related to the exempt purpose of the organization, which is not material.

Note 2—National Association of Accountants, Inc.

Current Operating Fund

The Fund balance as of June 30, 1989 and 1988 consists of the following components:

| | | (In Thousands) | | |
| | | Amount Expended | | |
1989	Authorized	1989	1988	Balance
Computer Study/Development	$ 100	$ 84	$ –	$ 16
Support for the Long-Range Implementation Committee	75	1	–	74
Implementation of the Treadway Commission Report	125	–	–	125
Implementation of a new computer system	400	–	–	400
1988				
Implementation and Development of a Marketing Program	180	180	–	–
Support of NAA's efforts to promote the recommendations of the Treadway Commission	159	53	–	106
Strategic Planning Committee Support for the Long-Range	150	11	18	–*
Totals	$1,189	$329	$18	$ 721

*The unexpended balance of the $150,000 authorized for support of the Long-Range Strategic Planning Committee amounting to $120,622 will remain in the Reserve Fund.

Deferred Research Contributions (Research Fund)

The Research Fund, which is administered by the Committee on Research, was established for the purpose of providing funds for the expansion of the research activities of NAA, Inc. The policy of NAA, Inc. is that funds contributed for research be included in the Current Operating Fund and that expenditures for research will come first from the amount of NAA's annual budget for this purpose. Any excess expenditures will be charged to contributed funds and remaining contributed funds will be deferred and committed to future research expenditures. Funds contributed for research with a specific dedication or restriction to a specific research subject or project will be considered restricted funds and accounted for as such.

The following is a summary of transactions affecting deferred research contributions:

	(In Thousands) June 30	
	1989	1988
Fund balance from operations	$ 122	$ 7
Capital transfers from Reserve Fund (net)	1,485	1,485
Total Fund Balance	$1,607	$1,492

Reserve Fund

The excess funds of NAA, Inc. and NAAMEF, Inc. are commingled, and invested with, those of the Reserve Fund for better management and return on investment (see note 4). Interest, dividends, gains and losses are apportioned to the various funds in proportion to the amounts invested.

In accordance with the bylaws, interest and dividend revenues on Reserve Fund investments are transferred to the Current Operating Fund while gains (losses) on sales of securities remain in the Reserve Fund.

Reserve Fund cash is held by an investment banker and earns interest at a rate which approximates the 30-day dealer commercial paper rate. Cash equivalents consist of short-term master notes of investment bankers.

Expenditures were approved from the Reserve Fund for the purpose of acquiring land and the construction of a building in Bergen County, New Jersey and moving and related costs as required, for which $2,000,000 was transferred to the Operating Fund. The Reserve Fund has been reimbursed to the extent of building fund contributions received aggregating $617,000 of which $10,000 and $20,000 represent 1989 and 1988 contributions, respectively.

The following is a summary of the status of the transfers from the Reserve Fund to the Current Operating Fund authorized by the Board of Directors of NAA, Inc.:

	(In Thousands) June 30	
	1989	1988
Balance, beginning of year	$105	$ 87
Contributions received	21	21
Interest earned	9	7
	135	115
Research Fund contributions applied	—	10
Balance, end of year	$135	$105

Note 3—National Association of Accountants Memorial Education Fund, Inc.

Memorial Education Fund

The Memorial Education Fund was established for the purpose of supporting and furthering the educational goals of NAA, Inc. Contributions for such purposes, and income earned on the Fund's investments, are recorded in the Fund. Earnings on the Fund investments may be expended for research and educational purposes. The Fund is administered by the Board of Trustees of NAAMEF, Inc.

During each year ended June 30, 1989 and 1988, $25,000 was expended for a video education program. At June 30, 1989 and 1988, $59,255 and $68,174, respectively, were available for future expenditures.

Scholarship Fund

The Scholarship Fund was the recipient of a bequest from the late Stuart Cameron McLeod, the first secretary of the National Association of Accountants. The income of the fund is to be used for scholarship programs.

During the years ended June 30, 1989 and 1988, $12,000 and $9,000, respectively, were expended for scholarship awards. At June 30, 1989 and 1988, $88,000 and $64,000, respectively, were available for future awards.

The financial statements of NAAMEF, Inc. include the accounts of the Memorial Education Fund and the Scholarship Fund. As of June 30, 1989 and 1988, the assets and fund balance were as follows:

	(In Thousands) 1989			1988
	Memorial Education Fund	Scholarship Fund	Total	Total
ASSETS				
Cash	$ —	$ 14	$ 14	$ 22
Due from other funds	173	385	558	534
	173	399	572	556
LIABILITIES AND FUND BALANCE				
Liabilities	—	12	12	8
Fund Balance	173	387	560	548
	$173	$399	$572	$556

Interest, dividends and net gains (losses) on sales are apportioned to the respective funds and are reflected in the fund balances at June 30, 1989 and 1988.

EXHIBIT 15-9   (continued)

Note 4—Marketable securities

Following is a summary of marketable securities as of June 30, 1989 and 1988:

	(In Thousands) Reserve Fund June 30	
	1989	1988
Market	$10,786	$ 5,710
Cost	8,328	5,155
Net Unrealized Gain	$ 2,458	$ 555

Included in the net unrealized gain are unrealized losses of $2,497 and $99,202 for 1989 and 1988, respectively.

The amounts shown above as investments of the Reserve Fund include the following amounts invested on behalf of each fund:

(In Thousands)
FUNDS

	NAA,Inc. Current Operating	Reserve	NAAMEF, Inc.	Total
1989				
Market	$ 4,851	$ 5,291	$644	$10,786
Cost	3,746	4,085	497	8,328
Net unrealized gain	$ 1,105	$ 1,206	$147	$ 2,458
1988				
Market	$ 2,518	$ 2,861	$331	$ 5,710
Cost	2,273	2,583	299	5,155
Net unrealized gain	$ 245	$ 278	$ 32	$ 555

Note 5—Plant, property, equipment and software

As of June 30, 1989 and 1988 plant, property, equipment and software consisted of the following:

	(In Thousands)	
	1989	1988
Land	$ 998	$ 998
Building	3,784	3,783
Furniture and equipment	2,986	2,916
Software	684	681
	8,452	8,378
Less accumulated depreciation and amortization	3,293	2,827
	$5,159	$5,551

Property, plant, equipment and software relating to ICMA, Inc. included in the above amounted to:

The funded status of the plans and the unfunded accrued pension cost at June 30, 1989 and 1988 follow:

	(In Thousands) June 30	
	1989	1988
Accumulated benefit obligation including vested benefits of $3,473,876 (1988 – $3,212,704)	$ 3,578	$ 3,306
Plan assets at fair value	4,968	4,498
Projected benefit obligations	(4,091)	(3,797)
Plan assets in excess of projected benefit obligations	877	701
Unrecognized net (gain)	(637)	(416)
Unrecognized prior service costs	81	88
Unrecognized net asset at July 1, 1985 being recognized over 14 years	(535)	(588)
Unfunded accrued pension cost	$ (214)	$ (215)

At June 30, 1989, approximately 71 percent of the plan's assets are invested in an immediate participation guarantee contract plan and 29 percent in a pooled common stock fund, both managed by John Hancock Mutual Life Insurance Company.

Statement of Financial Accounting Standards No. 87 specifies varying dates for the determination of actuarial assumptions. Assumptions made as of the beginning of the fiscal year (July 1, 1988) were used to determine Net Periodic Pension Cost for the year. The calculation of the plan's funded status and amounts recognized in the statement of financial position as of the end of the fiscal year (June 30, 1989) were based upon actuarial assumptions appropriate at that date and are shown below;

	June 30	
	1989	1988
Discount rate	9.00%	9.00%
Expected long-term rate of return on plan assets	9.50%	9.50%
Rates of increase in compensation levels	5.00%	5.00%

As of June 30, 1988 the method of computing the discount rate and the expected rate of return on long-term plan assets was changed from the Pension Benefit Guaranty Corporation rate to the average of the 30-year treasury bond and long-term bond rates to more appropriately reflect the actual experience of the fund. Such change had the effect of decreasing net periodic pension cost for the year ended June 30, 1989 by $124,887 but had no effect on such cost for the prior year.

Under a deferred compensation plan for certain employees, a provision had been accrued annually to provide an amount at age 65 equal to the present value of anticipated payments under the plan. Payments commenced under the plan during the year ended June 30, 1987 and as of June 30, 1989 the balance of the accrual amounted to $43,011.

	(In Thousands) June 30	
	1989	1988
Furniture and equipment	$ 67	$ 52
Software	332	332
	399	384
Less accumulated depreciation and amortization	290	210
	$109	$174

Note 6—Retirement Plans

NAA, Inc. has a noncontributory defined benefit pension plan covering substantially all employees. The plan provides benefits based on the participants' years of service and compensation. NAA, Inc's policy is to record annually amounts intended to provide not only for benefits attributed to service to date but also for those expected to be earned in the future.

Funding of the retirement cost for this plan complies with the minimum funding requirements specified by the Employee Retirement Income Security Act of 1974 (ERISA). No contributions were made or required to be made to the plan for the years ended June 30, 1989 and 1988 as it was subject to the full funding limitation prescribed by ERISA.

Net pension cost (income) for the years ended June 30, 1989 and June 30, 1988 included the following components:

	(In Thousands) June 30	
	1989	1988
Service cost-benefits earned during the period	$154	$175
Interest cost on projected benefit obligations	333	309
Actual return on plan assets	(666)	(18)
Amortization of excess plan net assets:		
Initial transition amount	(53)	(53)
Unrecognized prior service costs	6	6
Amortization of (gain)/loss and deferral of assets (gain)/loss	225	(336)
Net periodic pension cost (income)	$ (1)	$ 83

Note 7—Bonds Payable

A reimbursement agreement dated July 1, 1983 between NAA, Inc. and Manufacturers Hanover Trust Company regarding the issuance of an irrevocable letter of credit by the bank to facilitate the sale of New Jersey Economic Development Authority Bonds contains a provision that NAA, Inc. agrees to pay a fee of 1¼% per annum on the outstanding balance of the letter of credit. At June 30, 1989 the standby Letter of Credit amounted to $3,755,370. The collateral is a first lien on the property and building. For the years ended June 30, 1989 and 1988 the total fees amounted to $51,235 and $51,822, respectively.

The $4,000,000 of Industrial Development Bonds are special obligations of the New Jersey Economic Development Authority guaranteed by NAA, Inc. and require interest payments semiannually on January 1 and July 1 of each year at the rate set forth in the maturity schedule as follows:

MATURITY SCHEDULE
Remaining Serial Bonds

Due July 1	Principal Amount	Interest Rate	Due July 1	Principal Amount	Interest Rate
1989	$70,000	7.50%	1992	$ 90,000	8.25%
1990	80,000	7.75%	1993	100,000	8.50%
1991	80,000	8.00%			

The remaining 9-5/8 percent term bonds totaling $3,285,000 will be retired annually by redemption from July 1, 1994 to July 1, 2008 by lot or other method as determined by the trustee. Interest expense related to the debt amounted to $350,456 and $354,669 for 1989 and 1988, respectively.

Note 8—Commitments

During the year ended June 30, 1989, the Board of Directors of the National Association of Accountants, Inc. authorized the expenditure of $1,399,767, to be expended over the 1989-90 and 1990-91 fiscal years for the acquisition of hardware and software, including implementation costs.

Budgeting by objectives and/or measures of productivity could be added to the financial reporting of any nonprofit institution. The objectives and measures of productivity should be applicable to the particular nonprofit institution.

SUMMARY

This chapter has reviewed financial reporting for personal financial statements and accounting for governments and other nonprofit institutions. The accounting in these areas is quite different from the accounting for profit-oriented businesses.

Guidelines for the preparation of personal financial statements are covered in Statement of Position 82-1. SOP 82-1 concludes that personal financial statements should present assets at their estimated current values and liabilities at their estimated current amounts at the date of the financial statements. This is in contrast to commercial financial statements, which predominantly use historical information.

The accounting for nonprofit institutions is not uniform from one type of institution to another, and sometimes it is not even uniform among institutions of a particular type. State and local governments' accounting revolves around fund accounting. Nonprofit institutions other than governments use forms of financial reporting that vary from the fund type of system to a commercial type of reporting. Often, the system is a hybrid of the fund system and a commercial system.

QUESTIONS

Q 15-1   May personal financial statements be prepared only for an individual? Comment.

Q 15-2   What is the basic personal financial statement?

Q 15-3   Is a statement of changes in net worth required when presenting personal financial statements?

Q 15-4   Are comparative financial statements required when presenting personal financial statements?

Q 15-5   Should assets and liabilities be presented on the basis of historical cost or estimated current value when presenting the statement of financial position?

Q 15-6   What is the equity section called in the statement of financial condition?

Q 15-7   What statement should be prepared when an explanation of changes in net worth is desired?

Q 15-8   Is the presentation of a personal income statement appropriate?

Q 15-9   Generally accepted accounting principles as they apply to personal financial statements use the cash basis. Comment.

Q 15-10   Is the concept of working capital used with personal financial statements? Comment.

Q 15-11   List some sources of information that may be available when preparing personal financial statements.

Q 15-12   Give examples of disclosure in footnotes with personal financial statements.

Q 15-13   If quoted market prices are not available, a personal financial statement cannot be prepared. Comment.

Q 15-14   List some objectives that could be incorporated into the financial reporting of a professional accounting organization.

Q 15-15   Do all nonprofit institutions use fund accounting? Comment.

Q 15-16   Fortunately, the accounting for nonprofit institutions is uniform within a particular type of institution. Comment.

Q 15-17   The accounting for a nonprofit institution is centered on the entity concept and the efficiency of the entity. Comment.

Q 15-18   Define the following types of funds.
1. general fund
2. proprietary fund
3. fiduciary fund

Q 15-19   How many funds will be used by a state or local government?

Q 15-20   The budget for a state or local government is not as binding as the budget for a commercial business. Comment.

Q 15-21   Which organization provides a service whereby it issues a certificate of conformance to governmental units having financial reports that meet its standards?

Q 15-22   The rating on an industrial revenue bond is representative of the probability of default of bonds issued with the full faith and credit of a governmental unit. Comment.

Q 15-23   The accounting for nonprofit institutions does not typically include the concept of efficiency. Indicate how the concept of efficiency can be incorporated in the financial reporting of a nonprofit institution.

Q 15-24   Could a profit-oriented enterprise use fund accounting practices? Comment.

| *PROBLEMS*

P 15-1   For each of these situations, indicate the amount to be placed on a statement of financial condition at December 31, 1991.
a. Bill and Pat Konner purchased their home at 2829 Willow Road in Stow, Ohio, in August 1980, for $80,000. The unpaid mortgage is $20,000. Several improvements were added to the home immediately after purchase, for a total of $10,000. Real estate prices in Stow increased 40% since the time of purchase.

From the facts given, determine the estimated current value of the home.
b. Joe Best drives a Toyota for which he paid $10,000 when it was new. Joe believes

that since he maintains the car in good condition, he could sell it for $12,000. The average selling price for this model of Toyota is $9,000.

From the facts given, determine the estimated current value of Joe's car.

c. Sue Bell is 40 years old and has an IRA with a balance of $20,000. The IRS penalty for early withdrawal is 10%. The marginal tax rate of Sue Bell is 30% (tax on gross amount).

What is the estimated current value of the IRA and the estimated income taxes on the difference between the estimated current values of assets and the estimated current amounts of liabilities and their tax bases?

d. Bill Kell guaranteed a loan of $8,000 for his girlfriend to buy a car. Bill's girlfriend is behind in payments on the car.

What liability should be shown on Bill Kell's statement of financial condition?

e. Dick Better bought a home in 1976 for $70,000. Currently, the mortgage on the home is $45,000. Because of the current high interest rates, the bank has offered to retire the mortgage for $40,000.

What is the estimated current value of this liability?

P 15-2 For each of these situations, indicate the amount to be placed on a statement of financial condition at December 31, 1991.

a. Raj Reel owns the following securities:
1,000 shares of Ree's
2,000 shares of Bell's

Ree's is traded on the New York Stock Exchange. The prices from the most recent trade day were as follows:

Open	19
High	20½
Low	19
Close	20

Bell's is a local company whose stock is sold by brokers on a workout basis (the broker tries to find a buyer). The most recent selling price was $8.

What is the estimated current value of these securities? (Assume that the commission on Ree's would be $148 and the commission on Bell's would be $170.)

b. Charlie has a certificate of deposit with a $10,000 balance. Accrued interest is $500. The penalty for early withdrawal would be $300.

What is the estimated current value of the certificate of deposit?

c. Jones has an option to buy 500 shares of ABC Construction at a price of $20 per share. The option expires in one year. ABC Construction shares are now selling for $25.

What is the estimated current value of these options?

d. Carl Jones has a whole-life insurance policy with face amount of $100,000, cash value of $50,000, and a loan of $20,000 outstanding against the policy. Susan Jones is the beneficiary.

What is the estimated current value of the insurance policy?

e. Larry Solomon paid $60,000 for a home ten years ago. The unpaid mortgage on the home is $30,000.

Larry estimates the current value of the home to be $90,000. This estimate is partially based on the selling price of homes recently sold in the neighborhood. Larry's home is assessed for tax purposes at $50,000. Assessments in the area average one-half of market value. The house has not been inspected for assessment during the past two years. Larry would sell through a broker, who would charge 5% of the selling price. What is the estimated current value of the home?

P 15-3 For Bob and Carl, the assets and liabilities and the effective income tax rates are as follows at December 31, 1991:

Accounts	Tax Bases	Estimated Current Value	Excess of Estimated Current Values over Tax Bases	Effective Income Tax Rates	Amount of Estimated Income Taxes
Cash	$ 20,000	$ 20,000	—	—	_____
Marketable securities	45,000	50,000	5,000	28%	_____
Life insurance	50,000	50,000	—	—	_____
Residence	100,000	125,000	25,000	28%	_____
Furnishings	40,000	25,000	(15,000)	—	_____
Jewelry	20,000	20,000	—	—	_____
Autos	20,000	12,000	(8,000)	—	_____
Mortgage payable	(90,000)	(90,000)	—	—	_____
Note payable	(30,000)	(30,000)	—	—	_____
Credit cards	(10,000)	(10,000)	—	—	_____

Required
a. Compute the estimated tax liability on the differences between the estimated current value of the assets and liabilities and their tax bases.
b. Present a statement of financial condition for Bob and Carl at December 31, 1991.
c. Comment on the statement of financial condition.

P 15-4 For Mary Lou and Ernie, the assets and liabilities and the effective income tax rates are as follows at December 31, 1991:

Accounts	Tax Bases	Estimated Current Value	Excess of Estimated Current Values over Tax Bases	Effective Income Tax Rates	Amount of Estimated Income Taxes
Cash	$ 20,000	$ 20,000	—	—	_____
Marketable securities	80,000	100,000	20,000	28%	_____
Options	—0—	30,000	30,000	28%	_____
Residence	100,000	150,000	50,000	28%	_____
Royalties	—0—	20,000	20,000	28%	_____
Furnishings	40,000	20,000	(20,000)	—	_____
Auto	20,000	15,000	(5,000)	—	_____
Mortgage	(70,000)	(70,000)	—	—	_____
Auto loan	(10,000)	(10,000)	—	—	_____

Required
a. Compute the estimated tax liability on the differences between the estimated current value of the assets and liabilities and their tax bases.

b. Present a statement of financial condition for Mary Lou and Ernie at December 31, 1991.

c. Comment on the statement of financial condition.

P 15-5   For Bob and Sue, the changes in net worth for the year ended December 31, 1991, are detailed as follows:

Realized increases in net worth	
Salary	$ 60,000
Dividend income	2,500
Interest income	2,000
Gain on sale of marketable securities	500
Realized decreases in net worth	
Income taxes	20,000
Interest expense	6,000
Personal expenditures	29,000
Unrealized increases in net worth	
Stock options	3,000
Land	7,000
Residence	5,000
Unrealized decreases in net worth	
Boat	3,000
Jewelry	1,000
Furnishings	4,000
Estimated income taxes on the differences between the estimated current values of assets and the estimated current amounts of liabilities and their tax bases	15,000
Net worth at the beginning of year	150,000

Required   a. Prepare a statement of changes in net worth for the year ended December 31, 1991.

b. Comment on the statement of changes in net worth.

P 15-6   For Jim and Carl, the changes in net worth for the year ended December 31, 1991 are detailed as follows:

Realized increases in net worth	
Salary	$ 50,000
Interest income	6,000
Realized decreases in net worth	
Income taxes	15,000
Interest expense	3,000
Personal property tax	1,000
Real estate taxes	1,500
Personal expenditures	25,000
Unrealized increases in net worth	
Marketable securities	2,000
Land	5,000
Residence	3,000
Stock options	4,000

Unrealized decrease in net worth	
Furnishings	3,000
Estimated income taxes on the	
differences between the estimated	
current values of assets and the	
estimated current amounts of	
liabilities and their tax bases	12,000
Net worth at the beginning of year	130,000

Required
a. Prepare a statement of changes in net worth for the year ended December 31, 1991.
b. Comment on the statement of changes in net worth.

P 15-7
Use Exhibit 15-4, City of Toledo Combined Statement of Revenues, Expenditures, and Changes in Fund Balances.

Required
a. Prepare a vertical common size statement for Exhibit 15-4 using total revenues and expenditures. Use the total memorandum column as the base. Relate the amount in each fund to the total column. For example, property taxes in the general fund ($12,070) would be compared with the total column ($13,934).
b. Comment on significant items in the vertical common size analysis.
c. Are any of the revenue items in Exhibit 15-4 inappropriate for a profit enterprise? Identify the items.
d. Are any of the expense items in Exhibit 15-4 inappropriate for a profit enterprise? Identify the items.

P 15-8
Use Exhibit 15-4, City of Toledo Combined Statement of Revenues, Expenditures and Changes in Fund Balances.

Required
a. Prepare a vertical common size analysis of total revenues and expenditures for 1989. Use total revenues as the base. (Use only the total memorandum column.)
b. Comment on significant items in the vertical common size analysis in (a).
c. Prepare a vertical common size analysis of revenues and expenditures for the general fund. Use total revenues as the base.
d. Comment on significant items in the vertical common size analysis in (c).

P 15-9
Use Exhibit 15-6, City of Toledo Income Tax Revenues.

Required
a. Prepare a horizontal common size analysis of taxes collected. Use 1980 as the base.
b. Comment on significant trends indicated in the horizontal common size analysis prepared for (a).

P 15-10
Use Exhibit 15-7, City of Toledo Ratio of Net General Bonded Debt to Assessed Value and Net Bonded Debt Per Capita.

Required
a. How much has assessed value increased from 1980 to 1989?
b. How much has net general bonded debt increased from 1980 to 1989?
c. Give your opinion of the significance of the change in debt between 1980 and 1989.

P 15-11
Use Exhibit 15-8, the Institute of Internal Auditors financial statements.

Required   a. Compute the working capital for May 31, 1988 and September 30, 1989.

b. Compute the current ratio for May 31, 1988 and September 30, 1989.

c. What was the major reason for the change in working capital and the change in the current ratio between 1988 and 1989?

d. Prepare a horizontal common size analysis for revenue and expenses. Use 1988 as the base. (Compare the twelve months ended May 31, 1988 with the twelve months ended May 31, 1989.)

e. Prepare a vertical common size analysis for revenue and expenses for 1988 and 1989. Use total revenues as the base. (Use the twelve months ended May 31, 1988 and the twelve months ended May 31, 1989.)

f. Comment on significant items in the horizontal and vertical common size analyses in (d) and (e).

g. Comment on any separate corporation that is related to the Institute of Internal Auditors, Inc. (Review the footnotes.)

P 15-12   Use Exhibit 15-9, National Association of Accountants financial statements.

Required   a. How much was the combined change in fund balance between 1988 and 1989?

b. Prepare a horizontal common size analysis for total revenue and expenses for 1988 and 1989. (Use 1988 as the base.)

c. Prepare a vertical common size analysis for the combined revenues and expenses for 1988 and 1989. (Use total revenues as the base.)

d. Comment on significant items in the horizontal and vertical common size analyses.

| CASES

Case 15-1   GOVERNOR LUCAS—THIS IS YOUR COUNTY

The 1989 Lucas County, Ohio financial report contains 164 pages, of which this case includes selected parts (pages 738–746). The Lucas County financial report has consistently received the Certificate of Achievement for Excellence in Financial Reporting.

Required   a. Prepare a vertical common size analysis of the combined balance sheet. Use the total column as the base.

b. 1. Which fund has the most total assets?

   2. What is the total for cash and cash equivalents?

   3. What is the total accrued wages and benefits?

c. Notes to the financial statements

   1. How much interest was capitalized in 1989?

   2. Where were the proprietary fund types?

   3. What was the basis of accounting for Governmental and Fiduciary Funds?

   4. Briefly describe the accounting for employee health care benefits.

d. Table 3

   1. Total nominal expenditures—prepare a horizontal common size analysis. Use 1980 as the base.

   2. Total real expenditures—prepare a horizontal common size analysis. Use 1980 as the base.

     3. Compare the trend in (2) with the trend in (1).
     4. Total real expenditures for 1989 are stated in terms of what year? Show the computation of the 1989 total real expenditures ($100,524,000).

  e. Table 4
     1. Using horizontal common size analysis, determine the tax revenue by source that increased the most between 1980 and 1989.
     2. Convert Table 4 to a vertical common size analysis. Use total revenue as the base.
     3. Comment on major trends found in (2).

LUCAS COUNTY, OHIO
COMBINED BALANCE SHEET
ALL FUND TYPES AND ACCOUNT GROUPS
DECEMBER 31, 1989
(AMOUNTS IN 000's)

	GOVERNMENTAL FUND TYPES			
	General Fund	Special Revenue	Debt Service	Capital Projects
Assets and other debits:				
Pooled cash and cash equivalents...............	$ 2,085	$ 27,826	$ 548	$ 5,639
Segregated cash accounts...........................	-	-	-	-
Receivables (net of allowances for uncollectables)				
Taxes (Note J)......................................	737	3,266	-	165
Accounts	291	131	-	-
Special assessments	27	-	10,870	-
Accrued interest...................................	119	-	-	-
Interfund loan (Note D)	91	-	-	-
Due from other funds (Note D)	18	110	-	-
Due from other governments.......................	842	179	-	-
Prepayments	3	10	-	-
Inventory: materials and supplies................	-	62	-	-
Property, plant and equipment (Note E)-				
Land	-	-	-	-
Land improvements....................................	-	-	-	-
Buildings, structures and improvements..	-	-	-	-
Furniture, fixtures and equipment.............	-	-	-	-
Less: accumulated depreciation..............	-	-	-	-
Construction-in-progress (Note E)	-	-	-	-
Amount available in debt service fund	-	-	-	-
Amount to be provided for retirement of general long-term obligations	-	-	-	-
Total assets and other debits	$ 4,213	$ 31,584	$ 11,418	$ 5,804

Proprietary Fund Types		Fiduciary Fund Types	Account Groups		1989 Totals (Memorandum Only)	1988 Totals (Memorandum Only)
Enterprise	Internal Service	Trust and Agency	General Fixed Assets	General Long Term Obligations		
$ 2,262	$ 4,814	$ 13,355	$ -	$ -	$ 56,529	$ 56,108
-	-	12,516	-	-	12,516	10,425
-	-	-	-	-	4,168	4,045
1,734	38	-	-	-	2,194	2,733
-	-	-	-	-	10,897	9,552
-	-	-	-	-	119	58
-	-	-	-	-	91	17
-	49	-	-	-	177	839
-	644	-	-	-	1,665	1,276
-	-	-	-	-	13	46
11	50	-	-	-	123	205
393	89	-	11,531	-	12,013	12,042
53,085	-	-	-	-	53,085	50,477
4,784	30	-	69,600	-	74,414	71,067
11,991	1,115	-	15,049	-	28,155	26,988
(27,033)	(466)	-	-	-	(27,499)	(25,498)
-	-	-	14,160	-	14,160	9,104
-	-	-	-	559	559	603
-	-	-	-	62,535	62,535	62,690
$ 47,227	$ 6,363	$ 25,871	$ 110,340	$ 63,094	$ 305,914	$ 292,777

LUCAS COUNTY, OHIO
COMBINED BALANCE SHEET
ALL FUND TYPES AND ACCOUNT GROUPS -(continued)
DECEMBER 31, 1989
(Amounts in 000's)

	GOVERNMENTAL FUND TYPES			
	General Fund	Special Revenue	Debt Service	Capital Projects
Liabilities:				
Accounts payable..	$ 346	$ 2,845	$ -	$ 31
Contracts payable..	348	1,058	-	364
Accrued wages and benefits	2,068	3,272	-	-
Due to other funds (Note D)	40	136	-	-
Interfund loan payable	-	43	-	-
Due to other governments...........................	361	151	-	-
Due to pooled cash and cash equivalents...	-	-	-	-
Deferred revenue (Note J)	559	2,402	10,751	121
Matured bonds payable	-	-	91	-
Matured interest payable	-	-	17	-
Accrued interest payable	-	-	-	228
Unapportioned monies	-	-	-	-
Deposits held due to others.........................	-	-	-	-
Payroll withholdings.....................................	-	-	-	-
Deferred compensation payable-employees	-	-	-	-
Legal settlement payable (Note Q)..............	-	-	-	-
Notes payable (Note F).................................	-	-	-	11,610
Bonds payable (Note G)	-	-	-	-
OWDA loans payable (Note G).....................	-	-	-	-
Obligations under capital leases (Note G)	-	-	-	-
Other long-term obligations (Note G)	-	-	-	-
Total liabilities	3,722	9,907	10,859	12,354
Fund equity and other credits:				
Contributed capital.......................................	-	-	-	-
Investments in general fixed assets..............	-	-	-	-
Retained earnings: unreserved.....................	-	-	-	-
Fund balances (deficit)				
Reserved-				
Reserved for encumbrances...................	807	3,792	3	2,164
Reserved for inventory............................	-	62	-	-
Reserved for prepayments......................	3	10	-	-
Unreserved-				
Designated for uninsured contingencies.....................................	-	-	-	-
Designated for charity	-	71	-	-
Undesignated...	(319)	17,742	556	(8,714)
Total fund equity and other credits......	491	21,677	559	(6,550)
Total liabilities and fund equity	$ 4,213	$ 31,584	$ 11,418	$ 5,804

PROPRIETARY FUND TYPES		FIDUCIARY FUND TYPES	ACCOUNT GROUPS		1989 Totals (Memorandum Only)	1988 Totals (Memorandum Only)
Enterprise	Internal Service	Trust and Agency	General Fixed Assets	General Long-Term Obligations		
$ 89	$ 948	$ -	$ -	$ -	$ 4,259	$ 4,508
181	12	-	-	-	1,963	2,484
346	41	-	-	6,847	12,574	11,461
-	1	-	-	-	177	839
-	48	-	-	-	91	17
43	-	-	-	-	555	357
-	-	-	-	-	-	2,362
-	-	-	-	-	13,833	12,763
-	-	-	-	-	91	140
17	-	-	-	-	34	24
337	20	-	-	-	585	473
-	-	10,544	-	-	10,544	11,463
-	-	3,878	-	-	3,878	3,649
-	-	545	-	-	545	608
-	-	8,654	-	-	8,654	6,794
-	-	-	-	-	-	347
-	1,030	-	-	-	12,640	6,430
1,850	-	-	-	32,354	34,204	34,118
9,833	-	-	-	2,852	12,685	13,095
-	-	-	-	21,041	21,041	21,710
3	7	-	-	-	10	58
12,699	2,107	23,621	-	63,094	138,363	133,700
28,746	-	-	-	-	28,746	27,082
-	-	-	110,340	-	110,340	101,097
5,782	4,256	-	-	-	10,038	9,304
-	-	-	-	-	6,766	6,021
-	-	-	-	-	62	126
-	-	-	-	-	13	46
-	-	563	-	-	563	1,534
-	-	71	-	-	71	73
-	-	1.687	-	-	10.952	13.794
34.528	4.256	2.250	110.340	-	167.551	159.077
$ 47.227	$ 6.363	$ 25.871	$ 110.340	$ 63.094	$ 305.914	$ 292.777

LUCAS COUNTY, OHIO
NOTES TO THE FINANCIAL STATEMENTS
DECEMBER 31, 1989

Note A - *Description of Lucas County and Basis of Presentation*

The County: Lucas County is a political subdivision of the State of Ohio. The County was formed by an act of the Ohio General Assembly in 1835. The three member **Board of County Commissioners** is the legislative and executive body of the County. The **County Auditor** is the chief fiscal officer. In addition, there are seven other elected administrative officials, each of whom is independent as set forth in Ohio law. These officials are: **Clerk of Courts, Coroner, Engineer, Prosecutor, Recorder, Sheriff,** and **Treasurer**. There are also **eight Common Pleas Court Judges, two Domestic Relations Court Judges, one Juvenile Court Judge, one Probate Court Judge** and **four Court of Appeals Judges** elected on a county-wide basis to oversee the County's justice system.

The County's combined financial statements include accounts of all County operations. The County's major operations include human and social services, certain health care and community assistance services, civil and criminal justice systems, road and bridge maintenance and general administrative services. In addition, a water supply and sanitary sewer system is operated by the County.

The County's combined financial statements include all government departments, agencies, institutions, commissions, public authorities and other governmental organizations over which the County exercises significant oversight responsibility or management control. Oversight responsibility is determined upon the basis of the County's participation with each entity in the following areas: financial interdependence, selection of governing authority, designation of management, ability to significantly influence operations and accountability for fiscal matters.

Boards and organizations for which the Lucas County Board of Commissioners exercise significant fiscal responsibility but do not exercise management control are included in the accompanying financial statement as follows:

- Board of Community Mental Health-provides mental health services and programs.
- Board of Children Services-provides child care programs and other related services.
- Board of Mental Retardation-provides care and services to the mentally retarded.
- Emergency Medical Service-provides emergency medical care to citizens of, and visitors to, Lucas County.

The following were excluded from the Lucas County reporting entity. Although the following entities meet the scope of public service criterion (GASB codification 2100.112) the degree of oversight by the County is so remote that to include these entities in the County financial statements would be misleading. The

governing authorities of these excluded entities are selected independently of Lucas County officials. Each individual governing authority: designates its own management; has total control over operations; is solely responsible for reviewing, approving and revising its budget; has the ability to issue and is responsible for its own debt; function as fiscal managers by controlling the collection and disbursement of funds and holding the title to assets; and has the ability to generate their own revenue through public tax levys or charges:

- Metropolitan Park District, Lucas County Board of Health, Lucas County Soil and Water Conservation District - Based on the structure of Ohio Counties, the County Auditor and County Treasurer serve respectively as the fiscal officers and custodian of funds for certain non-County entities. In the case of these districts and boards, the county serves as fiscal agent, but does not exercise primary oversight responsibility.

- Toledo - Lucas County Port Authority, Lucas County Recreation Inc., Lucas County Improvement Corporation, Toledo Zoological Society, Toledo Area Sanitary District, Lucas County Board of Education, Toledo - Lucas County Convention and Visitors Bureau.. The County serves no fiscal or custorial function for these entities.

Basis of Presentation: The accounts of the County are organized on the basis of funds or account groups, each of which is considered a separate accounting entity. The operations of each fund are accounted for with a set of self-balancing accounts that comprise its assets, liabilities, fund equity, revenues, expenditures/expenses and statement of cash flows as appropriate. The various funds are summarized by type in the general purpose financial statements.

Amounts in the "1989 Totals (Memorandum Only)" and "1988 Totals (Memorandum Only)" columns of the financial statements represent a summation of the combined financial statement line items of the fund types and account groups. These amounts are presented for analytical purposes only.The summation includes fund types and account groups that use different basis of accounting, both restricted and unrestricted amounts, and the caption "amount to be provided", which is not an asset in the usual sense. Interfund transactions have not been eliminated. Consequently, amounts shown in the "1989 Totals (Memorandum Only)" and "1988 Totals (Memorandum Only)" columns are not comparable to a consolidation and do not represent the total resources/revenues or expenditures/expenses of the County.

The County uses the following fund types and account groups:

Governmental Fund Types:

- General Fund: This fund accounts for the general operating revenues and expenditures of the County not recorded elsewhere. The primary revenue sources are sales and use taxes, property taxes, state and local government fund receipts, investment earnings and charges for service.

LUCAS COUNTY, OHIO
NOTES TO THE FINANCIAL STATEMENTS-(continued)
DECEMBER 31, 1989

Note A - *Description of Lucas County and Basis of Presentation-(continued)*

- Special Revenue Funds: These funds are used to account for specific governmental revenues (other than major capital projects) requiring separate accounting because of legal or regulatory provisions or administrative action. These funds include: Public Assistance, the Board of Mental Retardation and the Motor Vehicle and Gas Tax funds, which are major funds of the County.

- Debt Service Fund: The Debt Service fund is used to account for revenues received and used to pay principal and interest on debt reported in the County's general long-term obligations account group.

- Capital Projects Funds: These funds are used to account for the acquisition or construction of capital assets. Revenues and financing sources are derived from the issuance of debt or receipts from the General Fund and Special Revenue funds.

Proprietary Fund Types:

- Enterprise Funds: These funds are used to account for operations that provide services which are financed primarily by user charges, or activities where periodic measurement of income is appropriate for capital maintenance, public policy, management control or other purposes.

- Internal Service Funds: These funds are used to account for the goods or services provided by certain County departments to other County funds, departments and other governmental units, on a cost reimbursement basis.

Fiduciary Fund Types:

- Trust and Agency Funds: These funds are used to account for and maintain assets held by the County in a trustee capacity or as an agent for individuals, private organizations, other governmental units and other funds. These assets include: property and other taxes, as well as other intergovernmental resources which have been collected and which will be distributed to other taxing districts located in Lucas County.

Account Groups:

- General Fixed Assets Account Group: This account group is used to present the general fixed assets of the County utilized in its general operations, exclusive of those used in Enterprise and Internal Service funds. General fixed assets of Lucas County include land, buildings, structures and improvements, furniture, fixtures and equipment, capital leases and construction in progress.

- General Long-Term Obligations Account Group: This account group is used to account for all long-term obligations of the County.

Note B - *Summary of Significant Accounting Policies*

The accompanying financial statements of the County are prepared in conformity with generally accepted accounting principles *(GAAP)* for local government units as prescribed in statements and interpretations issued by the *GASB* and other recognized authoritative sources.

Measurement Focus: Governmental and Expendable Trust Funds are accounted for on a spending, or "financial flow," measurement focus. Governmental and Expendable Trust Fund operating statements represent increases and decreases in net current as-

sets. Their reported fund balance is considered a measure of available spendable resources.

Proprietary Fund Types are accounted for on a cost of services, or "capital maintenance," measurement focus. Proprietary Fund Type income statements represent increases and decreases in net total assets.

Basis of Accounting: All financial transactions for Governmental and Fiduciary Funds are reported on the modified accrual basis of accounting. Under this accounting method, revenues are recognized when measurable and available to finance County operations. Revenues accrued at the end of the year consist of: reimbursements from other governments for grant expenditures, amounts receivable from charges for services, licenses and permits, fines, special assessments, and property taxes. Governmental Fund expenditures are accrued when the related fund liability is incurred, except interest on long-term debt, which is recorded when due. Proprietary Fund financial transactions are recorded on the accrual basis of accounting; revenues are recognized when earned and measurable; expenses are recognized as incurred.

Budgetary Accounting and Control: Under Ohio law, the Board of County Commissioners must adopt an appropriations budget by January 1st of a given year, or adopt a temporary appropriation measure with final passage of a permanent budget by April 1st, for all funds except Fiduciary Fund Types. Budgets are legally required for each organizational unit by object (personal services, materials and supplies, charges for services, and capital outlays and equipment).

Each County department prepares a budget which is approved by the Board of County Commissioners. Modifications to the original budget within expenditure objects can be made by the budget manager in the Auditor's Office. The County maintains budgetary control within an organizational unit and fund by not permitting expenditures and encumbrances to exceed appropriations at the object level (the legal level of control). Unencumbered and unexpended appropriations lapse at year-end. Encumbered and unpaid appropriations (reserved for encumbrances) are carried forward to the next year as authority for expenditures.

The County's budgetary process accounts for certain transactions on a basis other than GAAP. The major difference between the budget basis and the GAAP basis are:

(1) Revenues are recorded when received in cash (budget) as opposed to when susceptible to accrual (GAAP).

(2) Expenditures are recorded when encumbered, or paid in cash (budget), as opposed to when susceptible to accrual (GAAP).

LUCAS COUNTY, OHIO
NOTES TO THE FINANCIAL STATEMENTS-(continued)
DECEMBER 31, 1989

Note B - *Summary of Significant Accounting Policies-(continued)*

The actual results of operations, compared to the final appropriation, which include amendments to the original appropriation, for each fund type by expenditure function and revenue source are presented in the *Combined Statement of Revenues, Expenditures and Changes in Fund Balances-Budget and Actual (non-GAAP Budgetary Basis)- All Governmental Fund Types*. The reserve for encumbrances is carried forward as part of the budgetary authority for the next year and is included in the revised budget amounts shown in the budget to actual comparisons.

Cash Equivalents: The county considers cash equivalents as short-term, highly liquid deposits and investments that are either readily convertible to known amounts of cash or so near their maturity date that they present insignificant risk of changes in value because of changes in interest rates. County investments with an original maturity of three months or less are included in this category.

Inventory of Supplies: Inventory is valued at cost using the first-infirst-out method. Inventory is recorded as an expenditure/expense when consumed.

Fixed Assets and Depreciation: All fixed assets which are acquired or constructed for general governmental purposes are reported as expenditures in the fund that finances the asset acquisition and are capitalized in the General Fixed Assets Account Group, if they meet the County's capitalization criteria. Real property (except for infrastructure assets) is recorded at estimated historical cost based on an appraisal performed in 1984, or at cost. Donated and contributed fixed assets are recorded at their fair market value on the date donated to the County. Infrastructure assets (public domain general fixed assets such as roads, bridges, streets, sidewalks, curbs and gutters, drainage systems, lighting systems and the like) are not included in the financial statements as general fixed assets of the County. However, water supply and sanitary sewer lines are capitalized in the Water Supply and Sanitary Engineer funds, respectively, of the Enterprise funds. These assets are classified as land improvements when the Sanitary Engineer has accepted them.

Depreciation is not provided for the General Fixed Assets Account Group. Depreciation for the Proprietary Funds is determined by allocating the cost of fixed assets over the estimated useful lives of the assets on a straight-line basis. A full year of depreciation expense is taken in the year of acquisition, and none in the year of disposal.

The estimated useful lives are as follows:

- Furniture, fixtures and equipment- 5 to 20 years
- Buildings, structures, improvements- 20 to 40 years
- Land improvements (water and sewer lines)- 40 years

Capitalization of Interest: The County's policy is to capitalize interest on Governmental and Proprietary fund construction projects until substantial completion of the project. Capitalized interest on Proprietary fund construction is amortized on a straight-line basis over the estimated useful life of the asset. For 1989, interest capitalized for Governmental fund and Proprietary fund construction was $237 thousand.

Contributed Capital: Contributed capital represents resources from other governments, funds, special assessments, developers, and grants provided to Proprietary funds, and are not subject to repayment. These assets are recorded at cost on the date the asset is purchased. Depreciation on those assets acquired by the capital grants externally restricted for capital acquisitions is expensed, and closed to the contributed capital fund equity account.

Grants and Other Intergovernmental Revenues: Local Government fund revenues are recorded as receivables and revenue when measurable and available. Assistance awards made on the basis of entitlement are recorded as intergovernmental receivables and revenues when entitlement occurs. Federal and State reimbursement type grants for the acquisition or construction of fixed assets in Proprietary funds are recorded as receivables and contributed capital when the related expenses are incurred. All other Federal and State reimbursement type grants are recorded as receivables and revenues when the related expenditures/expenses are incurred.

Interfund Transactions: During the normal course of operations, the County has numerous transactions between funds. These transactions include charges for services provided by an Internal Service fund to other funds and operating transfers. Operating transfers represent transfers of resources from a fund receiving revenue to a fund through which those resources will be expended and are recorded as other financing sources (uses) in Governmental Fund Types and as operating transfers in Proprietary funds.

The Internal Service funds record charges for services to all County funds, departments and other governmental units as operating revenue. Both Governmental and Proprietary funds record these payments to the Internal Service funds as operating expenditures/expenses.

Compensated Absences: The County records accumulated unpaid vacation and overtime pay, and vested sick time benefits as accrued wages and

LUCAS COUNTY, OHIO
NOTES TO THE FINANCIAL STATEMENTS-(continued)
DECEMBER 31, 1989

Note B - *Summary of Significant Accounting Policies-(continued)*

benefits payable when earned by employees. For Governmental Fund Types the portion of the liability which is not currently due and payable is recorded in the General Long-Term Obligations Account Group (GLTOAG).

Ohio law requires that vacation time not be accumulated for more than three years. Normally, all vacation time is to be taken in the year available unless administrative written approval for carry over is obtained. Employees with a minimum of one year of service become vested in accumulated unpaid vacation time. Unused vacation is payable upon termination of employment. Unused sick time may be accumulated until retirement. Employees with a minimum of ten years of service are paid one third of accumulated sick time upon retirement. In general, employees are eligible to be paid for unused compensation time upon termination of employment. All sick, vacation and compensation payments are made at employees current wage rate.

Self-Funded Insurance: The County is self-funded for employee health care benefits. The program is administered by Blue Cross, which provides claims review and processing services. Each County fund is charged for its proportionate share in accounts payable of covered employees. The County records a liability for incurred but unreported claims at year end based upon an actuarial estimate by Blue Cross.

Encumbrances: Encumbrance accounting is utilized by County funds in the normal course of operations for purchase orders and contract related expenditures. An encumbrance is a reserve on the available spending authority due to a commitment for a future expenditure and does not represent a liability. Encumbrances outstanding at year end appear as a reserve to the fund balance on a GAAP basis and as the equivalent of expenditures on a non-GAAP budgetary basis in order to demonstrate legal compliance. This encumbrance authority is carried forward to the next fiscal year and is reported in the "**Revised Budget**" amount for budgetary comparisons. If the actual expenditures are less than the amount encumbered, the excess-reserve is closed to the unreserved fund balance.

Fund Balance Reservations and Designations: The County reserves portions of fund balances which are legally segregated for specific future uses or which do not represent available, spendable resources and therefore are not appropriable for expenditures. Designations of fund balances are amounts that have been designated by management for a specific future use, which are not legally segregated. Undesignated fund balances are not reserved nor designated and are appropriable in future periods.

Note C - *Pooled Cash and Cash Equivalents, Segregated Cash, Investments and Deposits*

Pooled Cash and Cash Equivalents: Cash resources of a majority of individual funds are combined to form a pool of cash and investments which is managed by the County Treasurer. All investments are recorded at cost which approximates market value. Interest earned on investments is accrued as earned and distributed to the General and Metroparks funds utilizing a formula based on the average month end balance of cash and cash equivalents of all funds.

Certain monies for the Water Supply System, and Trust and Agency funds are invested by the Treasurer in individual segregated bank accounts for those funds. Monies of all other funds of the County are held or invested in a group of bank accounts and investments. Collectively, these bank accounts and investments represent the pooled cash and cash equivalents account.

Legal Provisions: The County Treasurer is permitted by Ohio law to deposit or invest County monies provided that they mature or are redeemable within two years from date of purchase. The Treasurer is permitted to invest or deposit in the following classification of obligations:

1) Obligations of, or backed by the faith of, the United States Government

2) Obligations issued by any Federal agency

3) Deposits in institutions eligible under Ohio law. All deposits are collateralized with eligible securities, as described by state statutes, which are pledged to a collateral pool for each individual financial institution, in amounts equal to at least 110 % of the carrying value of all public deposits held by each institution.

4) Obligations of the State

5) Repurchase agreements with institutions eligible under Ohio law not to exceed 30 days, where the institution agrees unconditionally to repurchase any of the securities listed in (1) or (2).

The Governmental Accounting Standard Board (GASB Statement 3) has established credit risk categories for deposits and investments.

- Category 1- Investments that are insured or registered, or securities held by the County or its agent in the County's name.

  Deposits that are insured or collateralized with securities held by the County or its agent in the County's name.

TABLE 3
LUCAS COUNTY, OHIO
GENERAL GOVERNMENTAL EXPENDITURES AND REVENUES
ADJUSTED FOR INFLATION[1]
LAST TEN FISCAL YEARS
(Amounts in 000's)

Fiscal[2] Year	Total Nominal Expenditures	Total Nominal Revenues	Average[3] CPI-U	Total Real Expenditures	Total Real Revenues	Fiscal[2] Year
1980	$ 83,029	$ 71,873	246.8	$ 61,061	$ 52,856	1980
1981	98,420	76,116	272.4	65,577	50,716	1981
1982	116,881	96,900	289.1	73,379	60,835	1982
1983	127,715	119,253	298.1	77,760	72,608	1983
1984	135,918	134,438	315.5	78,191	77,339	1984
1985	142,806	138,016	322.2	80,445	77,746	1985
1986	158,787	152,876	328.4	87,757	84,491	1986
1987	167,470	169,090	340.4	89,294	90,158	1987
1988	187,964	185,417	361.5	94,371	93,093	1988
1989	205,313	201,671	370.7	100,524	98,741	1989

[1] Between 1980 and 1989 real expenditures increased by 64.63% or $39.4 million, while real revenues increased by 86.81% or $45.9 million over the same period.

[2] Fiscal year 1984 was the first year on a modified accrual accounting system conforming to Generally Accepted Accounting Principles (GAAP).

[3] Average Consumer Price Index for all Urban Consumers. 1977 is the base year when the Average CPI-U was 181.5.

Source: Lucas County Auditor

TABLE 4
LUCAS COUNTY, OHIO
TAX REVENUES BY SOURCE
LAST TEN FISCAL YEARS
(Amounts in 000's)

Fiscal[1] Year	General Property Tax	Tangible[2] Personal Tax	Property Transfer Tax	County[3] Sales Tax	Total	Fiscal[1] Year
1980	$ 14,374	$ 5,552	$ 376	$ 9,035	$ 29,337	1980
1981	14,802	5,530	336	10,275	30,943	1981
1982	19,933	7,235	284	12,664	40,116	1982
1983	20,554	7,345	465	20,467	48,831	1983
1984	21,299	7,400	527	24,117	53,343	1984
1985	21,696	7,776	651	25,761	55,884	1985
1986	26,022	9,059	771	28,431	64,283	1986
1987	35,025	10,399	755	31,229	77,408	1987
1988	36,763	10,300	773	34,662	82,498	1988
1989	41,227	10,549	734	35,351	87,861	1989

[1] Fiscal year 1984 was the first year on a modified accrual accounting system conforming to Generally Accepted Accounting Principles (GAAP).

[2] Tangible Personal Tax includes: personal property tax, mobile home tax and grain tax.

[3] Includes county sales tax and hotel lodging tax.

Source: Lucas County Auditor

COMPREHENSIVE CASE— WORTHINGTON INDUSTRIES

Worthington Industries began in 1955, when John H. McConnell started a steel brokerage business in his basement. The company began as a processor of flat rolled steel. In the early years, the company only "slit" or changed the width of steel. Today, at eleven plants in eight states, Worthington performs a wide variety of processes. Portions of its 1990 annual report follow.

Consolidated Statement of Earnings
Worthington Industries, Inc. and Subsidiaries

In thousands, except per share	Year Ended May 31	1990	1989	1988
Net sales and revenues		**$915,913**	$939,247	$841,405
Cost of goods sold		**768,961**	783,474	702,816
	Gross Margin	**146,952**	155,773	138,589
Selling, general and administrative expense		**55,093**	51,294	47,948
Interest expense		**4,245**	4,404	3,888
	Earnings From Continuing Operations Before Income Taxes	**87,614**	100,075	86,753
Income taxes		**32,417**	37,083	33,255
	Earnings From Continuing Operations	**55,197**	62,992	53,498
Discontinued operation, earnings (loss), net of taxes:				
From operations		**(1,272)**	1,184	2,617
On disposal		**(750)**	—	—
	Earnings (Loss) From Discontinued Operation	**(2,022)**	1,184	2,617
	Net Earnings	**$ 53,175**	$ 64,176	$ 56,115
	Average Common Shares Outstanding	**40,045**	40,608	40,977
Earnings (loss) per share:				
Continuing operations		**$1.38**	$1.55	$1.31
Discontinued operation		**(.05)**	.03	.06
	Net Earnings	**$1.33**	$1.58	$1.37

Consolidated Statement of Shareholders' Equity
Worthington Industries, Inc. and Subsidiaries

Dollars in thousands, except per share	Common Shares	Additional Paid-in Capital	Retained Earnings
Balance at June 1, 1987	$414	$63,205	$197,307
Net earnings			56,115
Cash dividends declared ($.41 per share)			(16,756)
Sale of 79,675 shares under stock option plan	1	703	
Sale of 39,620 shares under dividend reinvestment plan		783	
Purchase and retirement of 923,000 common shares	(9)	(1,417)	(14,147)
Balance at May 31, 1988	406	63,274	222,519
Net earnings			64,176
Cash dividends declared ($.46 per share)			(18,621)
Sale of 42,300 shares under stock option plan		470	
Sale of 41,124 shares under dividend reinvestment plan		889	
Purchase and retirement of 595,100 common shares	(5)	(944)	(11,713)
Balance at May 31, 1989	401	63,689	256,361
Net earnings			53,175
Cash dividends declared ($.57 per share)			(22,856)
Sale of 52,765 shares under stock option plan	1	592	
Sale of 44,740 shares under dividend reinvestment plan		1,003	
Purchase and retirement of 377,477 common shares	(4)	(597)	(7,329)
Balance at May 31, 1990	**$398**	**$64,687**	**$279,351**

See notes to consolidated financial statements.

Consolidated Balance Sheet
Worthington Industries, Inc. and Subsidiaries

Dollars in thousands	May 31	1990	1989
ASSETS			
Current Assets			
Cash and cash equivalents		$ 47,943	$ 40,766
Short-term investments		2,075	2,327
Accounts receivable, less allowances of			
$1,227 and $1,585 at May 31, 1990 and 1989		129,339	135,091
Inventories			
Raw materials		66,105	77,530
Work in process and finished products		54,171	65,247
		120,276	142,777
Prepaid expenses and other current assets		13,310	11,989
	Total Current Assets	312,943	332,950
Other Assets		11,926	14,415
Property, Plant and Equipment			
Land		8,579	8,353
Buildings		71,137	66,661
Machinery and equipment		248,679	248,490
Construction in progress		37,310	20,552
		365,705	344,056
Less accumulated depreciation		129,958	133,634
		235,747	210,422
		$560,616	$557,787
LIABILITIES AND SHAREHOLDERS' EQUITY			
Current Liabilities			
Accounts payable		$ 71,982	$ 76,557
Accrued compensation, contributions to			
employee benefit plans and related taxes		28,086	30,824
Other accrued items		18,966	26,202
Income taxes		9,980	12,008
Current maturities of long-term debt		4,239	4,120
	Total Current Liabilities	133,253	149,711
Accrued Pension Cost		1,672	1,681
Long-Term Debt		42,468	46,868
Deferred Income Taxes		38,787	39,076
Contingent Liabilities — Note H			
Shareholders' Equity			
Preferred shares, $1.00 par value, authorized —			
1,000,000 shares, issued and outstanding — none			
Common shares, $.01 par value, authorized —			
100,000,000 shares, issued and outstanding —			
1990 — 39,845,515 shares; 1989 — 40,125,487 shares		398	401
Additional paid-in capital		64,687	63,689
Retained earnings		279,351	256,361
		344,436	320,451
		$560,616	$557,787

See notes to consolidated financial statements.

Consolidated Statement of Cash Flows
Worthington Industries, Inc. and Subsidiaries

In thousands Year Ended May 31	1990	1989	1988
OPERATING ACTIVITIES			
Earnings from continuing operations	**$55,197**	$62,992	$53,498
Adjustments to reconcile earnings from continuing			
operations to net cash provided by operating activities:			
Depreciation	**20,790**	18,769	17,088
Provision for deferred income taxes	**391**	340	(1,176)
Changes in assets and liabilities:			
Decrease (increase) in short-term investments	**252**	4,275	(1,778)
Decrease (increase) in accounts receivable	**(4,656)**	(11,303)	(11,521)
Decrease (increase) in inventories	**7,932**	(2,111)	(40,203)
Decrease (increase) in other current assets	**(563)**	(3,588)	5,499
Decrease (increase) in other assets	**2,359**	(173)	(1,853)
Increase (decrease) in accounts payable			
and accrued expenses	**(11,905)**	16,260	27,707
Increase (decrease) in accrued pension cost	**(9)**	(201)	(385)
Increase (decrease) in long-term deferred			
income taxes	**(90)**	(146)	(13)
Net Cash Provided By Operating Activities	**69,698**	85,114	46,863
INVESTING ACTIVITIES			
Investment in property, plant and equipment, net	**(54,558)**	(43,564)	(29,133)
Cash provided (used) by discontinued operation	**25,435**	4,268	(3,302)
Net Cash Used By Investing Activities	**(29,123)**	(39,296)	(32,435)
FINANCING ACTIVITIES			
Proceeds from long-term borrowings	**5,000**	4,300	4,000
Principal payments on long-term debt	**(9,208)**	(5,582)	(7,058)
Proceeds from issuance of common shares	**1,596**	1,359	1,487
Repurchase of common shares	**(7,930)**	(12,662)	(15,573)
Dividends paid	**(22,856)**	(18,621)	(16,756)
Net Cash Used By Financing Activities	**(33,398)**	(31,206)	(33,900)
Increase (decrease) in cash and cash equivalents	**7,177**	14,612	(19,472)
Cash and cash equivalents at beginning of year	**40,766**	26,154	45,626
Cash and Cash Equivalents at End of Year	**$47,943**	$40,766	$26,154

See notes to consolidated financial statements.

Industry Segment Data

Worthington Industries, Inc. and Subsidiaries

In thousands Year Ended May 31	1990	1989	1988	1987	1986
Net Sales and Revenues					
Processed steel products	**$652,479**	$658,575	$622,406	$540,547	$500,215
Custom products	**165,351**	182,085	155,113	143,989	142,530
Cast products	**98,083**	98,587	63,886	81,634	61,241
	$915,913	$939,247	$841,405	$766,170	$703,986
Earnings From Continuing Operations					
Before Income Taxes					
Processed steel products	**$ 73,946**	$ 77,806	$ 77,760	$ 65,474	$ 66,771
Custom products	**7,838**	15,889	12,276	14,295	15,368
Cast products	**10,075**	10,784	605	2,498	2,225
Interest expense	**(4,245)**	(4,404)	(3,888)	(4,064)	(4,488)
	$ 87,614	$100,075	$ 86,753	$ 78,203	$ 79,876
Identifiable Assets					
Processed steel products	**$334,927**	$318,357	$293,800	$245,702	$238,518
Custom products	**91,121**	78,386	66,764	53,220	52,037
Cast products	**59,560**	56,370	44,875	47,386	61,724
Corporate	**75,008**	65,587	59,804	73,736	46,783
Continuing Operations	**560,616**	518,700	465,243	420,044	399,062
Discontinued Operation	**—**	39,087	41,387	35,169	36,655
	$560,616	$557,787	$506,630	$455,213	$435,717
Depreciation Expense					
Processed steel products	**$ 10,983**	$ 9,965	$ 8,533	$ 7,072	$ 6,647
Custom products	**4,246**	3,667	3,545	3,081	2,692
Cast products	**5,561**	5,137	5,010	5,518	5,184
	$ 20,790	$ 18,769	$ 17,088	$ 15,671	$ 14,523
Capital Expenditures					
Processed steel products	**$ 33,561**	$ 21,147	$ 18,743	$ 10,076	$ 18,592
Custom products	**12,653**	11,299	5,752	5,639	4,172
Cast products	**8,344**	11,118	4,638	3,177	7,263
	$ 54,558	$ 43,564	$ 29,133	$ 18,892	$ 30,027

( ) Indicates deduction

Corporate expenses have been allocated on a consistent basis among industry segments over the five-year period. "Capital expenditures" are net of normal disposals and exclude amounts in connection with acquisitions and divestitures.

See notes to consolidated financial statements.

Notes To Consolidated Financial Statements
Worthington Industries, Inc. and Subsidiaries

NOTE A — Summary of Significant Accounting Policies
Consolidation: The consolidated financial statements include the accounts of Worthington Industries, Inc. and Subsidiaries (the Company). Significant intercompany accounts and transactions are eliminated.

Cash and Cash Equivalents: For purposes of the consolidated statement of cash flows, the Company considers all highly liquid investments purchased with a maturity of three months or less to be cash equivalents.

Short-Term Investments: Short-term investments consist principally of stocks and bonds carried at the lower of cost or market. Cost was $2,193,000 at May 31, 1990, and $2,413,000 at May 31, 1989.

Inventories: Inventories are valued at the lower of cost or market. Cost is determined using the specific identification method for steel processing and the first-in, first-out method for all other businesses.

Property and Depreciation: Property, plant and equipment are carried at cost and depreciated on the straight-line method over the estimated useful lives of the assets. Accelerated depreciation methods are used for income tax purposes.

Capitalized Interest: Interest is capitalized in connection with construction of qualified assets. In 1990, interest totaling $445,000 was capitalized under this policy. No interest was capitalized during 1989 or 1988.

Income Taxes: Income taxes are based on amounts included in the consolidated statement of earnings. Deferred taxes are provided for those items reported in different periods for income tax and financial statement purposes. On December 30, 1987, the Financial Accounting Standards Board issued Statement No. 96, "Accounting for Income Taxes," which must be adopted no later than fiscal 1993. The Company has not completed the complex analyses required to determine the impact of the Statement; however, adoption is not expected to have an adverse impact on the Company's financial position.

NOTE B — Discontinued Operation
On January 16, 1990, the Company sold all of the capital stock of U-Brand Corporation, a manufacturer and distributor of pipe fittings, to the Mueller Brass Company. Net proceeds from the sale totaled approximately $24 million in cash. U-Brand's operating results, and a $750,000 capital loss(no tax benefit) on the sale of the business, are presented under the caption "Discontinued Operation." All prior period results are restated to reflect the sale.

Net sales and operating results of the discontinued operation, for the current year through the date of disposal and for the years ended May 31, 1989 and 1988, are summarized below. Earnings before taxes for these periods include interest expense of $260,000, $349,000 and $361,000, respectively. Interest expense was allocated to U-Brand based on net assets employed in the business.

In thousands	1990	1989	1988
Net sales and revenues	$36,477	$66,831	$62,827
Earnings (loss) before income taxes	(2,015)	1,792	3,755
Income taxes (benefit)	(743)	608	1,138
Net earnings (loss)	$ (1,272)	$ 1,184	$ 2,617

NOTE C — Preferred Shares
The Board of Directors is empowered to determine the issue prices, dividend rates, amounts payable upon liquidation, voting rights and other terms of the preferred shares.

NOTE D — Long-Term Debt
Long-term debt is summarized as follows:

In thousands May 31	1990	1989
Industrial development revenue bonds and notes	$25,207	$28,465
Note payable to bank — unsecured	7,000	7,000
9.25% unsecured promissory notes, due in graduated installments through 1999	14,500	15,000
All other debt		523
	46,707	50,988
Less current maturities	4,239	4,120
	$42,468	$46,868

The industrial development revenue bonds and notes (IRBs) represent loans to purchase or obligations to lease facilities and equipment costing $49,326,000. The leases are accounted for as lease purchases with ownership passing to the Company at the expiration dates for nominal amounts. The bonds and notes mature serially through 2001 and may be retired in whole or in part at any time. Approximately $6,270,000 of the IRBs have fixed interest rates of 5.5% to 8.0%. The remaining $18,937,000 carry variable interest rates based upon a percentage of the prime rate. At May 31, 1990, these interest rates ranged from 6.5% to 8.3%.

The note payable to bank is due September 1991. At May 31, 1990, the interest rate was 8.94%, based on the thirty-day London Interbank Offered Rate plus a fixed percent.

Various debt agreements place restrictions on financial conditions and require maintenance of certain ratios. The most significant of these restrictions limits cash dividends and certain other payments to $3,000,000 plus 75% of net earnings, as defined, subsequent to May 31, 1976. Retained earnings of $190,778,000 were unrestricted at May 31, 1990.

Principal payments on all long-term debt, including lease purchase obligations, in the next five fiscal years are as follows: 1991 — $4,239,000; 1992 — $11,710,000; 1993 — $3,811,000; 1994 — $3,400,000; 1995 — $3,640,000; and thereafter — $19,907,000.

During the year ended May 31, 1988, the Company obtained IRB financing of $4,000,000 for expansion of its steel processing facility in Jackson, Michigan. A portion of the proceeds are invested until needed to pay construction costs and are included in other assets on the balance sheet. These funds totaled $938,000 and $889,000 at May 31, 1990 and 1989, respectively.

The Company is guarantor on bank loans for two separate joint ventures. The guarantees totaled $20,400,000 at May 31, 1990.

The Company has established lines of credit permitting short-term, unsecured borrowings totaling $40,000,000, at rates below the prime rate. These lines of credit were unused at May 31, 1990, and do not require compensating balances.

Notes To Consolidated Financial Statements
Worthington Industries, Inc. and Subsidiaries

NOTE E – Income Taxes
Income taxes for the years ended May 31, 1990, 1989 and 1988 were as follows:

In thousands	1990	1989	1988
Current: Federal	**$28,189**	$32,811	$30,202
State and local	**3,837**	3,932	4,229
Deferred: Federal	**496**	20	(657)
State	**(105)**	320	(519)
	$32,417	$37,083	$33,255

The components of deferred income tax expense resulted from the use of the following:

In thousands	1990	1989	1988
Accelerated depreciation	**$ 1,815**	$ 1,754	$ 1,634
Other items	**(1,424)**	(1,414)	(2,810)
	$ 391	$ 340	$ (1,176)

The federal statutory rate was 34% in 1990 and 1989, and 35% in 1988. The effective income tax rate was 3% higher for these years, due to state and local income taxes, net of federal tax benefit.

NOTE F – Employee Benefit Plans
Nonunion employees of the Company participate in a current cash profit sharing plan and a deferred profit sharing plan. Contributions to and costs of these plans are determined as a percentage of the Company's operating income.

Certain operations have non-contributory defined benefit pension plans covering a majority of their employees qualified by age and service. Company contributions to these plans comply with the minimum funding requirements of ERISA.

In fiscal 1988, the Company adopted Financial Accounting Standards Board Statement No. 87, "Employers' Accounting for Pensions," for all defined benefit plans. The effect was to reduce 1988 pension expense by approximately $560,000. As allowed by this statement, the Company deferred, until fiscal 1990, the recognition of the unfunded liability of these plans. The implementation of this provision had no impact on net earnings or cash flow and its effect is shown below under the caption, "Adjustment to recognize minimum liability."

A summary of the components of net periodic pension cost for the defined benefit plans in 1990, 1989 and 1988, and the contributions charged to pension expense for the defined contribution plans follows:

In thousands	1990	1989	1988
Defined benefit plans:			
Service cost (benefits earned during the period)	**$1,053**	$ 997	$ 677
Interest cost on projected benefit obligation	**2,316**	2,219	1,892
Actual return on plan assets	**(3,123)**	(3,027)	(573)
Net amortization and deferral	**323**	488	(2,069)
Net pension cost of defined benefit plans	**569**	677	(73)
Defined contribution plans	**2,591**	2,914	2,708
Total pension expense	**$3,160**	$3,591	$2,635

Pension expense was calculated assuming a weighted average discount rate and an expected long-term rate of return on plan assets of 8%. Plan assets consist principally of listed equity securities and fixed income instruments. The following table sets forth the funded status and amounts recognized in the Company's consolidated balance sheet for defined benefit pension plans at May 31, 1990 and 1989:

In thousands	Plans Whose Assets Exceed Accumulated Benefits		Plans Whose Accumulated Benefits Exceed Assets	
	1990	1989	1990	1989
Actuarial present value of benefit obligations:				
Vested	**$26,974**	$25,186	**$4,500**	$4,800
Accumulated	**$27,078**	$25,264	**$4,619**	$5,101
Projected benefit obligation	**$27,078**	$25,264	**$4,748**	$5,101
Plan assets at fair value	**29,010**	25,974	**4,178**	4,430
Projected benefit obligation less than (in excess of) plan assets	**$ 1,932**	$ 710	**$ (570)**	$ (671)
Comprised of:				
Accrued pension cost	**$(1,231)**	$(1,480)	**$ (441)**	$ (323)
Prepaid pension cost	**120**			71
Unrecognized:				
net gain (loss)	**1,450**	368	**47**	(358)
prior service cost	**(2,804)**	(3,011)	**(357)**	(281)
Unrecorded net asset at transition, net of amortization	**4,397**	4,833	**27**	220
Adjustment to recognize minimum liability			**154**	
	$ 1,932	$ 710	**$ (570)**	$ (671)

NOTE G – Stock Options
The Company reserved 1,800,000 common shares for issuance under the Amended 1980 Stock Option Plan for certain salaried employees. The plan, which allowed for the issuance of an equal number of incentive and non-qualified options, expired during fiscal 1990. Options outstanding are exercisable at the rate of 20% a year beginning one year from date of grant and generally expire ten years thereafter. Common shares under option:

	Price Range Per Share	Number of Options	
		1990	1989
Exercised	$7.92-$18.38	**52,765**	42,300
At May 31,			
Outstanding	$5.90-$21.38	**1,530,841**	914,306
Exercisable		**645,861**	619,206
Available for grants		**0**	667,077

The options outstanding at May 31, 1990, were held by 228 persons, had an average exercise price of $16.15 per share and had expiration dates ranging from January 1993 to February 2000.

Report of Independent Auditors

NOTE H — Contingent Liabilities

The Company is a defendant in certain legal actions. In the opinion of management, the outcome of these actions, which is not clearly determinable at the present time, would not significantly affect the Company's consolidated financial position.

NOTE I — Industry Segment Data

Industry segment descriptions under the "Business Segments" section and segment data on page 16 of the annual report are an integral part of these financial statements.

Sales for processed steel products and custom products include $107,147,000 in 1990, $113,011,000 in 1989 and $102,760,000 in 1988 to a major manufacturer purchasing through decentralized divisions and subsidiaries in different geographical areas.

NOTE J — Related Party Transactions

During 1990, the Company purchased $78 million of raw materials and services, at prevailing market prices, from affiliated companies and other related parties. Accounts payable at May 31, 1990 included $13.6 million due to this group.

NOTE K — Quarterly Results of Operations (Unaudited)

Financial results previously reported for the first and second quarters of 1990 and each of the four quarters of 1989 are restated to reflect the sale of U-Brand Corporation, as more fully described in Note B. Net sales and revenues and gross margin reflect only the Company's continuing operations. Net earnings and net earnings per share, for the periods noted above, were not affected by the restatement.

The following is a summary of the unaudited quarterly results of operations for the years ended May 31, 1990 and 1989.

In thousands, except per share	Three Months Ended			
	Aug.	Nov.	Feb.	May
1990				
Net sales and revenues	**$212,989**	**$223,851**	**$221,996**	**$257,077**
Gross margin	**32,209**	**33,182**	**35,017**	**46,544**
Earnings (loss) from:				
Continuing operations	**11,500**	**11,970**	**12,663**	**19,064**
Discontinued operation	**(365)**	**31**	**(1,688)**	—
Net earnings	**11,135**	**12,001**	**10,975**	**19,064**
Earnings (loss) per share:				
Continuing operations	**.29**	**.30**	**.31**	**.48**
Discontinued operation	**(.01)**	**.00**	**(.04)**	—
Net earnings	**$.28**	**$.30**	**$.27**	**$.48**
1989				
Net sales and revenues	$209,241	$227,275	$237,267	$265,464
Gross margin	32,820	35,732	40,479	46,742
Earnings (loss) from:				
Continuing operations	12,557	14,226	16,378	19,831
Discontinued operation	304	402	(509)	987
Net earnings	12,861	14,628	15,869	20,818
Earnings (loss) per share:				
Continuing operations	.31	.35	.40	.49
Discontinued operation	.01	.01	(.01)	.02
Net earnings	$.32	$.36	$.39	$.51

Shareholders and Board of Directors
Worthington Industries, Inc.

We have audited the accompanying consolidated balance sheet of Worthington Industries, Inc. and Subsidiaries as of May 31, 1990 and 1989, and the related consolidated statements of earnings, shareholders' equity and cash flows for each of the three years in the period ended May 31, 1990. These financial statements are the responsibility of the Company's management. Our responsibility is to express an opinion on these financial statements based on our audits.

We conducted our audits in accordance with generally accepted auditing standards. Those standards require that we plan and perform the audit to obtain reasonable assurance about whether the financial statements are free of material misstatement. An audit includes examining, on a test basis, evidence supporting the amounts and disclosures in the financial statements. An audit also includes assessing the accounting principles used and significant estimates made by management, as well as evaluating the overall financial statement presentation. We believe that our audits provide a reasonable basis for our opinion.

In our opinion, the financial statements referred to above present fairly, in all material respects, the consolidated financial position of Worthington Industries, Inc. and Subsidiaries at May 31, 1990 and 1989, and the consolidated results of their operations and their cash flows for each of the three years in the period ended May 31, 1990, in conformity with generally accepted accounting principles.

Ernst + Young

Columbus, Ohio
June 14, 1990

Part I   *Directions for two-year analyses (1990 and 1989).* Alternative directions for five-year analysis follow these directions.

Required   a. Prepare the following ratio analyses for Worthington Industries for 1990 and 1989. Comment on each ratio and make general comments about liquidity, long-term debt-paying ability, profitability, and investor analysis.

Liquidity
  1. days' sales in receivables
  2. accounts receivable turnover (gross receivables, 1988—$125,302,000)
  3. accounts receivable turnover in days
  4. days' sales in inventory
  5. merchandise inventory turnover (1988 inventory—$143,554,000)
  6. inventory turnover in days
  7. operating cycle
  8. working capital
  9. current ratio
 10. acid test
 11. cash ratio
 12. operating cash flow/current maturities of long-term debt and current notes payable

Long-Term Debt-Paying Ability
 13. times interest earned
 14. debt ratio
 15. debt/equity ratio
 16. debt to tangible net worth
 17. operating cash flow/total debt

Profitability
 18. net profit margin
 19. total asset turnover (total assets 1988—$506,630,000)
 20. return on assets
 21. operating income margin
 22. operating asset turnover (total operating assets 1988—$506,630,000)
 23. return on operating assets
 24. sales to fixed assets (fixed assets 1988—$176,610,000)
 25. return on investment (1988 long-term debt + equity $334,607,000)
 26. return on total equity (1988 total equity $286,199,000)
 27. gross profit margin

Investor Analysis
 28. percentage of earnings retained
 29. earnings per common share
 30. degree of financial leverage
 31. price/earnings ratio (market price 1990, $24¼; 1989, $21⅜.
 32. dividend payout
 33. dividend yield
 34. book value per share

     b. Prepare a vertical common size analysis of the statement of income for 1990, 1989, and 1988. Use net sales and revenues as the base, and stop with earnings from continuing operations. Comment on the findings. (Round to one decimal place.)

c. Prepare a horizontal common size analysis for the statement of income for 1988–1990. Use 1988 as the base year and exclude discontinued operations. Comment on the findings. (Round to one decimal place.)

d. Prepare a vertical common size analysis of the balance sheet for 1990 and 1989. Use total assets as the base. Comment on the findings. (Round to one decimal place.)

e. Prepare a horizontal common size analysis of the balance sheet for 1990 and 1989. Use 1989 as the base year. Comment on the findings. (Round to one decimal place.)

f. Industry segment data
   1. Using common size, compare net sales and revenues in 1990 with 1986 (exclude intersegment sales). Comment on your findings. (Round to one decimal place.)
   2. Using common size, compare earnings from continuing operations before income taxes in 1990 with 1986 (exclude corporate interest expense). Comment on your findings. (Round to one decimal place.)
   3. Using common size, compare capital expenditures with identifiable assets in 1989 and 1990 for processed steel products, custom products, and cast products. Comment on the findings. (Round to one decimal place.)

Advanced Topics

a. Review the accounting policies of Worthington Industries, Inc. Would you describe its policies as conservative or liberal (conservative in terms of the lowest possible income and liberal in terms of the highest possible income)?

b. 1. Explain why deferred taxes decreased in 1990.
   2. How firm a liability is deferred income taxes?

c. Earnings per share
   1. The earnings per share presentation indicates what type of capital structure?
   2. Does the Worthington Industries earnings per share consider dilution?
   3. Does Worthington Industries have any potential dilution to earnings per share?

d. How material is pension expense in relation to net sales and revenues?

e. Give your opinion of the materiality of outstanding options at the end of 1990 and 1989.

f. Explain capitalized interest. How significant was capitalized interest during 1990, 1989, and 1988?

g. The company is guarantor on bank loans for two separate joint ventures. The guarantees totaled $20,400,000 at May 31, 1990. How do accountants describe this guarantee of debt?

h. The company is the defendant in certain legal actions. How is this potential liability accounted for?

i. For fiscal 1990, the market price of the common stock ranged from $20.25 to $25.50. The par value of the common stock was $.01. Why the significant difference between the market value and the par value?

j. Comment on apparent seasonal influences to net sales and revenues and net earnings.

Part II   *Alternative directions for five-year analysis.* Note: Part II requires the use of the computer assist package. The package includes an input screen that enables users to perform a five-year analysis.

Required   a. Prepare the following ratio analyses for Worthington Industries for 1990, 1989, 1988, 1987, and 1986. Make general comments about liquidity, long-term debt-paying ability, profitability, and investor analysis. Use the end-of-year numbers for balance sheet data when computing the financial ratios. This will enable you to do a five-year analysis with five years of balance sheet data.

Liquidity
1. days' sales in receivables
2. accounts receivable turnover
3. accounts receivable turnover in days
4. days' sales in inventory
5. merchandise inventory turnover
6. inventory turnover in days
7. operating cycle
8. working capital
9. current ratio
10. acid test
11. cash ratio
12. sales to working capital
13. operating cash flow/current maturities of long-term debt and current notes payable

Long-Term Debt-Paying Ability
1. times interest earned
2. fixed charge coverage
3. debt ratio
4. debt/equity
5. debt to tangible net worth
6. operating cash flow/total debt

Profitability
1. net profit margin
2. total asset turnover
3. return on assets
4. operating income margin
5. operating asset turnover
6. return on operating assets
7. sales to fixed assets
8. return on investment
9. return on total equity
10. return on common equity
11. gross profit margin

Investor Analysis
1. degree of financial leverage
2. earnings per common share
3. price/earnings ratio
4. percentage of earnings retained
5. dividend payout
6. dividend yield
7. book value per share
8. materiality of options
9. operating cash flow per share
10. operating cash flow/cash dividends

b. Prepare a vertical common size analysis of the statement of income for 1990, 1989, 1988,

1987, and 1986. Use net sales and revenues as the base, and stop with earnings from continuing operations. Comment on the findings.

c. Prepare a horizontal common size analysis for the statement of income for 1986–1990. Use 1986 as the base year, and exclude discontinued operations. Comment on the findings.

d. Prepare a vertical common size analysis of the balance sheet for 1990, 1989, 1988, 1987, and 1986. Use total assets as the base. Comment on the findings.

e. Prepare a horizontal common size analysis of the balance sheet for 1990, 1989, 1988, 1987, and 1986. Use 1986 as the base year. Comment on the findings.

Advanced Topics

Answer the advanced topics questions that are included with Part I.

GLOSSARY

Most of the terms in this glossary are explained in the text. Also, some terms that are not explained in the text are included here because they are frequently found in annual reports.

Accelerated depreciation: Any depreciation method in which the charges in earlier periods are greater than those in later periods.

Accounts receivable: Monies due on accounts from customers arising from sales or services rendered.

Accrual basis: The accrual basis of accounting dictates that revenue is recognized when it is realized (realization concept) and expenses are recognized when incurred (matching concept).

Accrued expenses: Expenses that have been incurred but are not recognized in the accounts.

Accrued revenues: Revenues for which the service has been performed or the goods have been delivered, but the revenues have not been recorded.

Accumulated depreciation: Depreciation is the process of allocating the cost of buildings and machinery over the periods of benefits. The depreciation expense taken each period is accumulated in the account accumulated depreciation.

Administrative expense: Expense resulting from the general administration of the company's operation.

Adverse opinion: An audit opinion issued whenever financial statements contain departures from GAAP that are too material to warrant only a qualification. This opinion states that the financial statements do not present fairly the financial position, results of operations, or cash flows of the entity in conformity with GAAP.

Allowance for uncollectible accounts: A contra accounts receivable account showing the estimated total of the as yet unidentified accounts receivable that will not be collected.

Amortization: The periodic allocation of the cost of an intangible asset over its useful life.

Annual report: A report containing financial statements and other important information, which is prepared by the management of a corporation once a year.

Appropriated retained earnings: A restriction of retained earnings that indicates that a portion of a company's assets are to be used for purposes other than paying dividends.

Assets: Assets are probable future economic benefits obtained or controlled by a particular entity as a result of past transactions or events.

Audit report (Accountant's report): The mechanism for communicating the results of an audit.

Auditor: A person who conducts an audit.

Authorized stock: The maximum number of shares a corporation may issue without changing its charter with the state.

Average cost method (inventory): Averaging methods lump the costs of inventory to determine a midpoint.

Balance sheet: Financial statement showing the financial position of an accounting entity as of a particular date. The balance sheet consists of assets, which are the resources of the firm; liabilities, which are the debts of the firm; and stockholders' equity, which is the owners' interest in the firm.

Balance sheet (account form): A form in which the total of the assets appears as an amount equal to the total of the liabilities and owners' equity. The assets are usually set on one side, with the liabilities and owners' equity on the other.

Balance sheet (Classified balance sheet): A form in which the assets and liabilities are segregated into current and noncurrent.

Balance sheet (financial position form): A form in which current liabilities are deducted from current assets to show working capital. The remaining assets are added and the remaining liabilities deducted to derive the residual stockholders' equity.

Balance sheet (unclassified): A form in which the assets and liabilities are not segregated into current and noncurrent.

Bond: A security, usually long-term, representing money borrowed by a corporation.

Bonds payable: A debt security, normally issued with $1,000 par and requiring semiannual interest payments based on the coupon rate.

Bond sinking fund: A fund established by the segregation of assets over the life of the bond issue to satisfy investors that money will be available to pay the bondholders at maturity.

Bonds (serial): An issue of bonds which matures in periodical installments.

Buildings: Structures are valued at cost plus the cost of permanent improvements. Buildings are depreciated over their estimated useful life.

Business entity: The separate entity viewpoint is that the business (or entity) for which the financial statements are prepared is separate and distinct from the owners of the entity.

Callable bonds: Bonds that a corporation has the option of buying back and retiring at a given price before maturity.

Callable preferred stock: Preferred stock that may be redeemed and retired by the corporation at its option.

Capital: Owners' equity in an unincorporated firm.

Capital lease: Long-term lease in which the risk of ownership lies with the lessee and whose terms resemble a purchase or sale; recorded by entering on the books an asset and a corresponding liability at the present value of the lease payments.

Cash: Cash, the most liquid of the assets, includes negotiable checks and unrestricted balances in checking accounts, as well as any cash on hand.

Common size analysis (horizontal): Common size analysis involves expressing comparisons in percentages. In horizontal analysis, a dollar figure for an account is expressed in terms of that same account figure for a selected base year.

Common size analysis (vertical): Common size analysis involves expressing comparisons in percentages. In vertical analysis, a figure from the year's statement is compared with a base selected from the same statement.

Common stock: The stock representing the most basic rights to ownership of a corporation.

Conservatism: The concept of conservatism directs that the measurement with the least favorable effect on net income and financial position in the current period be selected.

Conservative analysis: A relatively strict interpretation of the value of assets and what constitutes debt.

Consistency: The consistency concept requires the entity to give the same treatment to comparable transactions from period to period. When a change in accounting methods is made, the justification for the change must be disclosed, along with an explanation of the effect on the statements, such as the effect on income.

Consolidated financial statements: When one corporation holds substantial voting rights in an-

other corporation, the corporation that owns the stock is described as the *parent corporation* and the corporation that is invested in is described as the *subsidiary*. When a parent corporation has control of voting rights, the financial statements of the parent and the subsidiary are combined into consolidated financial statements.

Constant dollar accounting (Price-level accounting): The method of reporting financial statement elements in dollars having similar purchasing power. Constant dollar accounting measures general changes in the prices of goods and services.

Contingent liabilities: Liabilities that may result in payment but are dependent, for now, on a particular occurrence such as settlement of litigation or a ruling of tax court.

Contra account: An account used to offset a primary account in order to show a net position or valuation—e.g., accounts receivable (primary account) less allowance for doubtful accounts (contra account).

Convertible bonds: Bonds that may be exchanged for other securities of the corporation, usually common stock.

Convertible preferred stock: Preferred stock that can be converted into common stock.

Copyright: An exclusive right granted by the federal government to the possessor to publish and sell literary, musical, and other artistic materials.

Corporation: A body of persons granted a charter legally recognizing it as a separate entity having its own rights, privileges, and liabilities distinct from those of its members.

Cost of goods manufactured: The total cost of goods completed in the manufacturing process during an accounting period.

Cost of goods sold (Cost of sales): Includes the cost of goods that were sold during an accounting period.

Cost principle: The accounting principle that holds that historical cost is the appropriate basis of initial accounting recognition of all acquisitions, liabilities, and owners' equity.

Cumulative effect of change in accounting principle: The effect that a new accounting principle would have had on net income of prior periods if it had been used instead of the old principle.

Cumulative preferred stock: Preferred stock on which unpaid dividends accumulate over time and must be satisfied in any given year before a dividend may be paid to common stockholders.

Current assets: Assets (1) in the form of cash, (2) that will normally be realized in cash, or (3) that conserve the use of cash during the operating cycle of a firm or for one year, whichever is longer.

Current cost: The current replacement cost of the same asset owned, adjusted for the value of any operating advantages or disadvantages of the asset owned.

Current liabilities: Current liabilities are obligations whose liquidation is reasonably expected to require the use of existing current assets or the creation of other current liabilities within a year or an operating cycle, whichever is longer.

Current replacement cost: The estimated cost of acquiring the best asset available to undertake the function of the asset owned.

Debenture bonds: Bonds issued on the general credit of a company.

Declining-balance depreciation: The declining-balance method applies double the straight-line depreciation rate times the declining book value (cost minus accumulated depreciation) to achieve a declining depreciation charge over the estimated life of the asset.

Deferral: The postponement of the recognition of an expense already paid or of a revenue already received.

Deferred charge: A long-term expense prepayment. (This account is amortized to expense.)

Deferred taxes: Any case in which revenue or expense is recognized in a different time period for the tax return than for the financial statements will create a deferred tax situation. Deferred taxes is a balance sheet account that could be classified as an asset or a liability, depending on the nature of the timing differences.

Depletion: Recognition of the wearing away or using up of a natural resource.

Depreciation expense: Depreciation is the process of allocating the cost of buildings and machinery over the periods of benefit.

Disclaimer of opinion: Inability to render an audit opinion because of lack of sufficient evidence or lack of independence.

Discontinued operations: The income statement items that relate to a discontinued operation.

Dividends (cash): Dividends return profits (cash) to the owners of a corporation.

Dividends (cumulative): Dividends, at a fixed annual rate, on preferred stock. If not paid in one year, they are carried forward as an additional priority of preferred shareholders in future income distributions.

Dividends in arrears: The accumulated unpaid dividends on cumulative preferred stock from prior years.

Dividend payout: A current liability on the balance sheet, resulting from the declaration by the board of directors of a dividend to be paid.

Dividends (stock): A firm issues a percentage of outstanding stock as new shares to existing shareholders.

Earnings per share: Net income (after preferred dividends) per share of common stock.

Equity: Synonymous with shareholders' equity.

Equity in earnings of unconsolidated subsidiaries: When a firm has investments in stocks, the equity method of accounting is utilized and the investment is not consolidated, then the investor reports equity earnings. Equity earnings are the proportionate share of the earnings of the investee.

Estimated liability: A definite obligation of the entity, the exact amount of which cannot be determined until a later date.

Expenses: Outflows or other using up of assets or incurrences of liabilities (or a combination of both) during a period from delivery or producing goods, rendering services, or carrying or other activities that constitute an entity's ongoing major or central operations.

Extraordinary items: Material events and transactions distinguished by their unusual nature and by the infrequency of their occurrence.

Financial Accounting Standards Board (FASB): A body that has responsibility for developing and issuing rules on accounting practice.

Financial leverage: The amount of debt financing in relation to equity financing.

Financial statements: Generally considered to be the balance sheet, the income statement, and the statement of cash flows.

Finished goods: Manufacturer's inventory ready for sale.

First-in, first-out (FIFO) (inventory): The flow pattern assumed here is that the first unit purchased is the first sold—first-in, first-out.

Fiscal year: Any twelve-month accounting period used by an economic entity. (It does not necessarily correspond to the calendar year.)

Footnotes: Used for presenting additional information on items included in the financial statements and for presenting additional relevant information.

Form 10-K: A Securities and Exchange Commission form required to be filed within ninety days of a company's fiscal year end. It is like an annual report, but with more detail.

Form 10-Q: A Securities and Exchange Commission form required to be filed within 45 days of the end of a company's first, second, and third fiscal year quarters. It contains interim information on a company's operations and financial position.

Franchise: A contractual privilege granted by one person to another permitting the sale of a product, use of a trade name or provision of a service within a specified territory and/or in a specified manner.

Full-cost accounting: The method of accounting whereby all costs of exploring for and developing oil and gas reserves within a defined area are capitalized, subject only to the limitation that costs attributable to developed reserves should not exceed their estimated present value.

Full disclosure: The accounting reports must disclose all facts that may influence the judgment of an informed reader.

Fully diluted earnings per share: Net income applicable to common stock divided by the sum of the weighted-average common stock and common stock equivalents. (The rules are more conservative than for primary earnings per share.)

Fund accounting: Accounting procedures in which a self-balancing group of accounts is provided for each accounting entity established by legal, contractual, or voluntary action.

Generally accepted accounting principles (GAAP): Accounting principles that have substantial authoritative support.

Generally accepted auditing standards: Auditing standards that have been established in a particular jurisdiction by formal recognition by a standard-setting body or by authoritative support.

Going concern or continuity: The assumption that the entity that is being accounted for will remain in business for an indefinite period of time.

Goodwill: Arises from the acquisition of a business for a sum greater than the physical asset value, usually because the business has unusual earning power.

Governmental funds: General, special revenue, project, debt service, and special assessment funds; each is designed for a specific purpose and is used by a state or local government to account for its normal operations.

Human resource accounting: Attempts to account for the services of employees.

Income statement: A summary of revenues and expenses and gains and losses, ending with net income for a particular period of time.

Income taxes: Federal, state, and local income taxes, based on reported accounting profit. Income tax expense includes both tax paid and tax deferred.

Industry practices: Some industry practices lead to accounting reports that do not conform to the general theory that underlies accounting.

Intangibles: Nonphysical assets, such as legal rights. Intangibles are recorded at historical cost, which is then reduced by systematic amortization.

Interim reports: Financial reports that cover fiscal periods of less than one year.

Inventories: The balance of goods on hand.

Investments: Usually stocks and bonds of other companies held for the purpose of maintaining a business relationship or exercising control. To be classified as long term, it must be the intent of management to hold these assets for a long time. Long-term investments are differentiated from marketable securities, where the intent is to hold the assets for short-term profits and to achieve liquidity.

Issued stock: The shares of stock sold or otherwise transferred to stockholders.

Joint ventures: An association of two or more businesses established for a special purpose. Some joint ventures are in the form of partnerships and unincorporated joint ventures; others are in the form of corporations that are jointly owned by two or more other firms.

Land: Land is shown at acquisition cost and is not depreciated. However, lands containing resources that will be used up, such as mineral deposits and timberlands, are subject to depletion.

Land improvements: Expenditures incurred in the process of putting land into a usable condition—e.g., clearing, grading, paving, etc.

Last-in, first-out (LIFO) (inventory): Last-in, first-out assumes that those units purchased last are sold first.

Lease: An agreement conveying the right to use property, plant, or equipment (land and/or depreciable assets), usually for a stated period of time. A lease involves a lessee and a lessor.

Leasehold: A payment made to secure the right to a lease.

Lease improvement: An improvement to leased property that becomes the property of the lessor at the end of the lease.

Lessee: The party to a lease who acquires the right to use the property, plant, and equipment.

Lessor: The party to a lease giving up the right to use the property, plant, and equipment.

Liabilities: Probable future sacrifices of economic benefits arising from present obligations of a particular entity to transfer assets or provide services to other entities in the future, as a result of past transactions or events.

LIFO liquidation: The reduction of inventory levels below previous levels. This has the effect of increasing income by the amount by which current prices exceed the historical cost of the inventory under LIFO.

Liquidating dividend: A dividend that exceeds retained earnings.

Long-term liabilities: Liabilities due in a period exceeding one year or one operating cycle, whichever is longer.

Lower of cost or market (LCM) rule (inventory): An inventory pricing method under which the inventory is priced at an amount below cost if the replacement (market) value is less than cost.

Machinery: Equipment is listed at historical cost, including delivery and installation, plus any material improvements that extend its life or increase the quantity or quality of service. Machinery is also depreciated over its estimated useful life.

Marketable securities: Ownership and debt instruments of the government and other companies that can be readily converted into cash.

Market value (stock): The price investors are willing to pay for a share of stock.

Matching: The matching concept addresses when to recognize the costs that are associated with the revenue. The basic intent is to determine the revenue and then match the appropriate cost against this revenue.

Materiality: It is essential that material items be properly handled on the financial statements. Immaterial items are not subject to the concepts and principles that bind the accountant and may be handled in the most economical and expedient manner possible. The accountant is faced with a judgment situation when determining materiality.

Minority interest (balance sheet account): Reflects the ownership of minority shareholders in the equity of consolidated subsidiaries that are less than wholly owned.

Minority share of earnings: The portion of income that belongs to the minority owners of a firm that is consolidated.

Monetary assets: Cash and other assets that represent the right to receive a specific amount of cash.

Monetary liabilities: Accounts payable and other liabilities that represent the obligation to pay a specific amount of cash.

Monetary unit: Money is the unit used for the purpose of measuring financial transactions.

Mortgage payable: A type of liability secured by real property.

Multiple-step income statement: Form of the income statement that arrives at net income in steps.

Natural business year: A twelve-month period ending on a date that is especially appropriate for the year end of the business because it coincides with the end of an operating cycle.

Neutrality: A qualitative characteristic of accounting information that involves the faithful reporting of business activity without bias to one view or another.

Noncurrent or long-term assets: Assets that do not qualify as current assets. In general, they take longer than a year to be converted to cash or to conserve cash in the long run.

Notes payable: Payables in the form of a written promissory note.

Off-balance-sheet financing: Refers to a company taking advantage of debt-like resources without these obligations appearing as debt on the face of the balance sheet.

Operating cycle: The time between the acquisition of inventory and the realization of cash from selling the inventory.

Operating expenses: Consist of two types: selling and administrative. Selling expenses result from the company's efforts to create sales. Administrative expenses relate to the general administration of the company's operations.

Operating lease: Periodic payment for the right to use an asset, recorded in a manner similar to the way in which rent expense payments are recorded.

Organizational costs: The legal costs incurred when a business is organized. These costs are carried as an asset and are usually written off over a period of five years or longer.

Other income and expenses: These categories are nonoperating in nature; they are secondary activities of the firm not directly related to the operations.

Parent company: A company that owns a controlling interest in another company.

Par value: An amount set by the board and approved by the state. (The par value does not relate to the market value.)

Patent: Exclusive legal rights granted to an inventor for a period of seventeen years.

Payables: Short-term obligations created by the acquisition of goods and services, such as for materials or goods bought for use or resale, wages payable, taxes payable, and the like.

Pension fund: A fund, established through contributions from an employer and sometimes from employees, that pays pension benefits to employees after retirement.

Periodic inventory method: A method of accounting for inventory under which the inventory is determined periodically.

Perpetual inventory method: A method of accounting for inventory under which the sales and purchases of individual items of inventory are recorded continuously.

Personal financial statements: Financial statements of individuals, husband and wife, or a larger family group.

Predictive value: A qualitative characteristic of accounting information based on its relevance and usefulness to a decision maker in forecasting a future event or condition.

Preferred stock: Stock that has some preference over common stock.

Prepaid: An expenditure made in advance of the use of the service or goods.

Present value consideration: The characteristic that money received or paid out in the future is not worth as much as money available today is referred to as the *time value* of money or the *present value*. Accountants consider the time value of money when preparing the financial statements for such areas as long-term leases, pensions, and other long-term situations in which the future payments or receipts are not indicative of the present value of the asset or the obligation.

Primary earnings per share: Net income applicable to common stock divided by the sum of the weighted-average common stock and common stock equivalents. (The rules are less conservative than for fully diluted earnings per share.)

Property, plant, and equipment: Tangible assets of a long-term nature, used in the continuing operation of the business.

Proxy statement: Information provided in a formal written form to shareholders prior to a company's regular annual meeting.

Qualified opinion: An audit opinion rendered under circumstances of one or more material scope restrictions or departures from GAAP.

Qualitative characteristics: Standards for judging the information accountants provide to decision makers; the primary criteria are relevance and reliability.

Ratio analysis: A means of stating a meaningful relationship between components of financial statements.

Raw materials: Goods purchased for direct use in manufacturing a product, which become part of the product.

Realization: The realization principle is that revenue should be recognized when (1) the earning process is virtually complete and (2) the exchange value can be objectively determined.

Redeemable preferred stock: Preferred stock subject to mandatory redemption requirements or having a redemption feature that is outside the control of the issuer.

Relevance: Qualitative characteristic requiring that accounting information bear directly on the economic decision for which it is to be used; one of the primary qualitative characteristics of accounting information.

Reliability: Qualitative characteristic requiring that accounting information be faithful to the original data and that it be neutral and verifiable; one of the primary qualitative characteristics of accounting information.

Representational faithfulness: The agreement of information with what it is supposed to represent.

Residual value (Salvage value): The estimated net scrap or trade-in value of a tangible asset at the estimated date of disposal.

Retained earnings: The undistributed earnings of a corporation—in general, the net income for all past periods minus the dividends that have been declared.

Sale and leaseback: The sale of an asset, with the purchaser concurrently leasing the asset to the seller.

Sales or revenues: Revenue on goods or services sold to a customer; may also include lease revenue or royalties, depending on the product

of the business. Revenues included here are for the principal products of the firm.

Securities and Exchange Commission (SEC): An agency of the federal government that has the legal power to set and enforce accounting practices.

Selling expenses: Result from the company's efforts to create sales.

Serial bonds: A bond issue with several different maturity dates.

Sinking fund: An accumulation of cash or securities in a special fund dedicated to pay, or redeem, an issue of bonds or preferred stock.

Single-step income statement: Form of the income statement that arrives at net income in a single step.

Social accounting: Attempts to account for the benefits to the social environment within which the firm operates.

Specific identification (inventory): The items in inventory are identified as coming from specific purchases.

Stated value: A value assigned by the board of directors to no-par stock.

Statement of cash flows: Provides information as to why the cash position of the company changed during an accounting period. The statement gives detailed information on cash flows resulting from operating, investing, and financing activities.

Statement of retained earnings: Summarizes the changes to retained earnings for a period of time.

Stock appreciation rights: Give the holder the right to receive compensation at some future date, based on the market price of the stock at the date of exercise over a preestablished price.

Stock certificate: A document issued to a stockholder in a corporation, indicating the number of shares of stock owned by the stockholder.

Stock options: Allow the holder to purchase stock on favorable terms.

Stock split: Increase in the number of shares of a class of capital stock, with no change in the total dollar amount of the class, but with a converse reduction in the par or stated value of the shares.

Straight-line depreciation: Depreciation is recognized in equal amounts over the estimated life of the asset.

Subordinated debt: Some form of long-term debt that is "junior," or in a secondary position, vis-a-vis the claim on a company's assets for the payment of its other debt obligations.

Subsequent events: Events that occur after the balance sheet date but before the statements are issued.

Subsidiary: A company whose stock is more than 50% owned by another company.

Successful-efforts accounting: The method of accounting whereby only the costs that result in the discovery of oil and gas reserves are capitalized.

Sum-of-the-years'-digits depreciation: For this method, a fraction is taken each year times the cost less salvage value. The numerator of the fraction changes each year, and it is the remaining number of years of life. The denominator of the fraction remains constant, and it is the sum of the digits representing the years of life.

Summary annual report: A simplified annual report. Under this approach, the full data required by the SEC is supplied in the proxy statement and the form 10-K.

Supplies: Items used indirectly in the production of goods or services.

Tangible assets: The physical facilities used in the operation of the business.

Term bonds: Bonds for which the entire issue matures at the same time.

Timeliness: The qualitative characteristic of accounting information that reaches the user in time to help in making a decision.

Time period: The assumption is made that the entity can be accounted for reasonably accurately for a particular period of time. In other words, the decision is made to accept some inaccuracy

because of incomplete information about the future, in exchange for more timely reporting.

Trademarks: Distinctive names or symbols. Rights are granted to the holder for twenty-eight years, with option for renewal.

Transaction approach: The accountant records only events that affect the financial position of the entity and at the same time can be reasonably determined in monetary terms.

Translation gains and losses: Gains and losses that are due to fluctuations in exchange rates.

Treasury stock: Capital stock of a company, either common or preferred, that has been issued and reacquired by the issuing company but has not been reissued or retired. It reduces stockholders' equity.

Unconsolidated subsidiaries: Subsidiaries that have not been consolidated.

Unearned income: A company's liability either current or long-term, for income received prior to the delivery of goods or the rendering of services (also described as deferred income).

Unit-of-production depreciation: Relates depreciation to the output capacity of the asset, estimated for the life of the asset.

Unqualified opinion: An audit opinion not qualified for any material scope restrictions or departures from GAAP.

Unrealized decline in market value of noncurrent equity investments: A stockholders' equity account that results from adjusting long-term equity securities to the lower of cost or market value.

Unusual or infrequent item: Certain income statement items that are unusual or occur infrequently, but not both.

Verifiability: The qualitative characteristic of accounting information that it can be confirmed or duplicated by independent parties using the same measurement technique.

Vesting: The accrual to an employee of pension rights, arising from employer contributions, which are not contingent upon the employee's continuing service with the employer.

Warranty obligations: Estimated obligations arising out of product warranties.

Working capital: The excess of current assets over current liabilities.

Work in process: Goods started but not ready for sale.

Zero coupon bond: A bond that does not pay periodic interest but is a promise to pay a fixed amount at the maturity date.

BIBLIOGRAPHY

1. Fundamental Concepts and Introduction to Financial Statements

Beaver, W.H. "What Should Be the FASB's Objectives?" *Journal of Accountancy* (August 1973), 49–56.

Beaver, W.H. *Financial Reporting: An Accounting Revolution*. Englewood Cliffs, N.J.: Prentice-Hall, 1981.

Benston, G.J. "An Analysis of the Role of Accounting Standards for Enhancing Corporate Governance and Social Responsibility," *Journal of Accounting and Public Policy* (Fall 1982), 5–17.

Beresford, D.R. "A Practitioner's View of the FASB Conceptual Framework," *Ohio CPA Journal* (Spring 1981), 65–67.

Beresford, D. R. "The Balancing Act in Setting Accounting Standards," *Accounting Horizons* (March 1988), 1–7.

Bierman, Harold. "Extending the Usefulness of Accrual Accounting," *Accounting Horizons* (September 1988), 10–14.

Bishop, Ashton, and Rasoul H. Tondkar. "Development of a Professional Code of Ethics," *Journal of Accountancy* (May 1987), 97–100.

Bruns, William J., and Kenneth A. Merchant. "The Dangerous Morality of Managing Earnings," *Management Accounting* (August 1990), 22–25.

Chatov, R. "Should the Public Sector Take Over the Function of Determining Generally Accepted Accounting Principles?" *The Accounting Journal* (Spring 1977), 117–123.

Christenson, Charles. "The Methodology of Positive Accounting," *The Accounting Review* (January 1983), 1–22.

Cooper, K., and G.D. Keim. "The Economic Rationale for the Nature and Extent of Corporate Financial Disclosure Regulation: A Critical Assessment," *Journal of Accounting and Public Policy* (Fall 1983).

Cullather, James. "Accounting: Kin to the Humanities," *The Accounting Review* (October 1959), 525–527.

Dawson, J.P., P.M. Neupert, and C.P. Stickney. "Restating Financial Statements for Alternative GAAPs: Is It Worth the Effort?" *Financial Analysts Journal* (November–December 1980), 38–46.

Dhaliwal, D.S. "Some Economic Determinants of Management Lobbying for Alternative Methods of Accounting: Evidence from the Accounting for Interest Costs Issue," *Journal of Business Finance and Accounting* (Summer 1982), 255–265.

Foster, G. "Accounting Policy Decisions and Capital Market Research," *Journal of Accounting and Economics* (March 1980), 29–62.

Foster, G. "Externalities and Financial Reporting," *The Journal of Finance* (May 1980), 521–533.

Gerboth, Dale L. "The Conceptual Framework: Not Definitions, But Professional Values," *Accounting Horizons* (September 1987), 1–8.

Govindarajan, V. "Objectives of Financial Reporting by Business Enterprises: Some Evidence of User Preference," *Journal of Accounting, Auditing and Finance* (Summer 1979), 339–343.

Halder, W.W., and K.H. Eudy. "A Framework for Building an Accounting Constitution," *Journal of Accounting, Auditing and Finance* (Winter 1982), 110–125.

Horngren, C.T. "Accounting Principles: Private or Public Sector?" *The Journal of Accountancy* (May 1972), 37–41.

Horngren, C.T. "The Marketing of Accounting Standards," *The Journal of Accountancy* (October 1973), 61–69.

Ijiri, Yuji, and Robert Jaedicke. "Reliability and Objectivity of Accounting Methods," *The Accounting Review* (July 1966), 474–483.

Koeppen, David R. "Using the FASB's Conceptual Framework: Fitting the Pieces Together," *Accounting Horizons* (June 1988), 18–26.

Lee, Charles, and Dale Morse. "Summary Annual Reports," *Accounting Horizons* (March 1990), 39–50.

Lowe, Herman J. "Ethics in Our 100-Year History," *Journal of Accountancy* (May 1987), 78–87.

May, Robert, and Gary Sundem. "Research for Accounting Policy: An Overview," *The Accounting Review* (October 1976), 747–763.

Morris, R.D. "Corporate Disclosure in a Substantially Unregulated Environment," *Abacus* (June 1984), 52–86.

Nair, R.D., and Larry E. Rittenberg. "Summary Annual Reports: Background and Implications for Financial Reporting and Auditing," *Accounting Horizons* (March 1990), 25–38.

Rimerman, Thomas W. "The Changing Significance of Financial Statements," *Journal of Accountancy* (April 1990), 79–83.

Schreuder, H. "Employees and the Corporate Social Report: The Dutch Case," *Accounting Review* (April 1981), 294–307.

Stamp, Edward. "Why Can Accounting Not Become a Science Like Physics?" *Abacus* (Spring 1981), 13–27.

Sterling, Robert R. "Toward a Science of Accounting," *Financial Analysts Journal* (September–October 1975), 28–36.

Szepan, S.B. "Corporate Social Responsibility—An Update," *Journal of Accountancy* (July 1980), 77–81.

Watts, Ross L. "Corporate Financial Statements, a Product of the Market and Political Processes," *Australian Journal of Management* (April 1977), 33–75.

Watts, Ross L., and Jerald L. Zimmerman. "Towards a Positive Theory of the Determination of Accounting Standards," *The Accounting Review* (January 1978), 112–134.

Wyatt, Arthur. "Accounting Standards: Conceptual or Political?" *Accounting Horizons* (September 1990), 83–88.

2. *Balance Sheet*

Burton, J.C. "Emerging Trends in Financial Reporting," *Journal of Accountancy* (July 1981), 54–66.

Flamholtz, Eric G., D. Gerald Searfoss, and Russell Coff. "Developing Human Resource Accounting As a Human Resource Decision Support System," *Accounting Horizons* (September 1988), 1–9.

Lebar, M.A. "A General Semantics Analysis of Selected Sections of the 10-K, the Annual Report to Shareholders and the Financial Press Release," *Accounting Review* (January 1982), 176–184.

Moonitz, Maurice. "The Changing Concept of Liabilities," *Journal of Accountancy* (May 1960), 41–46.

Romans, D.B. "Drafting a Meaningful Annual Report," *Financial Executive* (June 1979), 26–30.

Stanga, K.G. "Disclosure in Published Annual Reports," *Financial Management* (Winter 1976), 42–52.

Urbancie, F.R. "Reporting Preferred Stock: Debt or Equity?" *Mergers and Acquisitions* (Spring 1980), 15–20.

Walker, E.W., and J.W. Petty, III. "Financial Differences between Large and Small Firms," *Financial Management* (Winter 1978), 61–68.

Walker, Robert G. "Asset Classification and Asset Valuation," *Accounting and Business Research* (Autumn 1974), 286–296.

3. Income Statement and Statement of Retained Earnings

Asquith, Paul, Paul Healy, and Krishna Palepu. "Earnings and Stock Splits," *The Accounting Review* (July 1989), 387–403.

Bremser, W.G. "The Earnings Characteristics of Firms Reporting Discretionary Accounting Changes," *The Accounting Review* (July 1975), 563–573.

Eiseman, P.C., and E.A. Moses. "Stock Dividends: Management's View," *Financial Analysts Journal* (July–August 1978), 77–80.

Horngren, Charles J. "How Should We Interpret the Realization Concept?" *The Accounting Review* (April 1965), 323–333.

Horwitz, B., and R. Kolodny. "Segment Reporting: Hindsight after Ten Years," *Journal of Accounting, Auditing and Finance* (Fall 1980), 20–35.

Lilien, Steven, Martin Mellman, and Victor Pastena. "Accounting Changes: Successful Versus Unsuccessful Firms," *The Accounting Review* (October 1988), 642–656.

May, Gordon S., and Douglas K. Schneider. "Reporting Accounting Changes: Are Stricter Guidelines Needed?" *Accounting Horizons* (September 1988), 68–74.

Mobley, Jybit C. "The Concept of Realization: A Useful Device," *The Accounting Review* (April 1966), 292–296.

Myers, John H. "The Critical Event and Recognition of Net Profit," *The Accounting Review* (October 1959), 528–532.

Neuhausen, B.S. "Consolidation and the Equity Method—Time for an Overhaul," *Journal of Accountancy* (February 1982), 54–66.

Schwartz, K.B. "Accounting Changes by Corporations Facing Possible Insolvency," *Journal of Accounting, Auditing and Finance* (Fall 1982), 32–43.

Smisewska, M.E., and R.L. Hagerman. "An Income Strategy Approach to the Positive Theory of Accounting Standard Setting/Choice," *Journal of Accounting and Economics* (August 1981), 129–149.

Story, Reed K. "Revenue Realization, Going Concern and Measurement of Income," *The Accounting Review* (April 1959), 232–238.

4. Basics of Analysis

Chang, L.S., K.S. Most, and C.W. Brain. "The Utility of Annual Reports: An International Study," *Journal of International Business Studies* (Spring/Summer 1983), 63–84.

Gibson, C.H., and P.A. Boyer. "An Inventory of Industry Average Financial Ratios," *Journal of Commercial Bank Lending* (August 1979), 59–64.

Gibson, C.H., and P.A. Boyer. "Need for Disclosure of Uniform Financial Ratios," *Journal of Accountancy* (May 1980), 78.

Wittington, G. "Some Basic Properties of Accounting Ratios," *Journal of Business Finance and Accounting* (Summer 1980), 219–232.

6. Liquidity of Short-Term Assets and the Related Short-Term Debt-Paying Ability

Backer, M., and M.L. Gosman. "The Use of Financial Ratios in Credit Downgrade Decisions," *Financial Management* (Spring 1980), 53–56.

Bonsack, R.A. "Inventory Ratios—Reader Beware," *Management Controls* (May–June 1977), 24–29.

Campbell, W.A. "Liquidity—Some New Findings," *Cost and Management* (July–August 1979), 48–52.

Fadel, H., and J.M. Parkinson. "Liquidity Evaluation by Means of Ratio Analysis," *Accounting and Business Research* (England) (Spring 1978), 101–107.

Granof, M.H., and D.G. Short. "Why Do Companies Reject LIFO?" *Journal of Accounting, Auditing and Finance* (Summer 1984), 323–333.

Halloran, J.A., and H.P. Lanser. "The Credit Policy Decision in an Inflationary Environment," *Financial Management* (Winter 1981), 31–38.

Heath, L.C. "Is Working Capital Really Working?" *Journal of Accountancy* (August 1980), 55–62.

Johnson, J.M., et al. "Problems in Corporate Liquidity," *Financial Executive* (March 1980), 44–53.

Morse, D. "LIFO . . . FIFO?" *Financial Executive* (February 1980), 14–17.

Peles, Y.C., and M.L. Schneller. "Liquidity Ratios and Industry Averages—New Evidence," *Abacus* (June 1979), 13–22.

Scherr, F.C. "Ratio Analysis for Credit Decisions on Marginal Accounts: A Statistical Approach," *Akron Business and Economic Review* (Fall 1980), 12–16.

7. Long-Term Debt-Paying Ability

Backer, M., and M.L. Gosman. "The Predictive Value of Financial Reporting in Bank Term Loan Decisions," *Journal of Commercial Bank Lending* (March 1979), 53–67.

Burianek, F.G. "Using Financial Ratios to Analyze Pension Liabilities," *Financial Executive* (January 1981), 29–36.

Cason, R., and E. Williams. "Earnings to Fixed Charges Ratio—Useful?" *CPA Journal* (January 1977), 74–76.

Deakin, Edward B. "Accounting for Contingencies: The Pennzoil-Texaco Case," *Accounting Horizons* (March 1989), 21–28.

Dieter, R., and A.R. Wyatt. "Get It Off the Balance Sheet," *Financial Executive* (January 1980), 42–48.

Dietrich, J., and R.S. Kaplan. "Empirical Analysis of the Commercial Loan Classification Decision," *Accounting Review* (January 1982), 18–38.

Findlay, M.C., III, and E.F. Williams. "Toward More Adequate Debt Service Coverage Ratios," *Financial Analysts Journal* (November–December 1975), 58–61.

Gibson, C.H., and P.A. Boyer. "The Effects of 'Accounting for Leases' on Financial Statements of Lessees," *Michigan CPA* (November–December 1978), 7–14.

Heian, James B., and James B. Thies. "Consolidation of Finance Subsidiaries: $230 Billion in Off-Balance-Sheet Financing Comes Home to Roost," *Accounting Horizons* (March 1989), 1–9.

Hulslander, R.E. "Better Debt Coverage Ratio," *Journal of Commercial Bank Lending* (August 1979), 54–58.

Ingberman, M., J. Ronen, and George H. Sorter. "How Lease Capitalization Under FASB Statement No. 13 Will Affect Financial Ratios,"

Financial Analysts Journal (January–February 1979), 28–31.

Lasman, D.A., and R.L. Weil. Adjusting the Debt-Equity Ratio," *Financial Analysts Journal* (September–October 1978), 49–58.

Regan, P.J. "Credit Ratings and Pension Costs," *Financial Analysts Journal* (March–April 1979), 6–7.

Strait, C.M. "Measuring Debt-Service Capacity: A Medium-Sized Bank's Approach," *Journal of Commercial Bank Lending* (April 1978), 58–63.

Strait, C.M., and J.J. Zautra. "Debt-Service Capacity Revisited," *Journal of Commercial Bank Lending* (September 1980), 26–36.

Wyman, H.E. "Stabilized Debt Coverage Ratios," *Accounting Review* (April 1977), 503–507.

8. *Analysis of Profitability*

Barton, M.F., Jr., W.B. Carper, and T.S. O'Connor. "Chartered Financial Analysts Speak Out on the Need and Information Content of Interim Financial Reports," *Ohio CPA* (Winter 1979), 28–32.

Cheney, R.E. "How Dependable Is the Bottom Line?" *Financial Executive* (January 1971), 10–15.

Gibson, C.H., and P.A. Boyer. "How about Earnings per Share?" *CPA Journal* (February 1979), 36–41.

Salamon, G.L., and D.S. Dhaliwal. "Company Size and Financial Disclosure Requirements with Evidence from the Segmental Reporting Issue," *Journal of Business Finance and Accounting* (Winter 1980), 555–568.

Smith, J.L. "Improving Reported Earnings," *Management Accounting* (September 1981), 49–52.

Worthy, F.S. "Manipulating Profits: How It's Done," *Fortune* (June 15, 1984), 50–54.

9. *Analysis for the Investor*

Arnold, J., and P. Maizer. "A Survey of the Methods Used by UK Investment Analysts to Appraise Investments in Ordinary Shares," *Accounting and Business Research* (Summer 1984), 195–207.

Baker, H.K., and J.A. Haslem. "Information Needs of Individual Investors," *Journal of Accountancy* (November 1973), 64–69.

Basu, S. "Information Content of Price-Earnings Ratios," *Financial Management* (Summer 1975), 53–64.

Beaver, W., and D. Morse. "What Determines Price-Earnings Ratios?" *Financial Analysts Journal* (July–August 1978), 65–76.

Bentley, T.J. "Return on Capital Employed (ROCE)," *Management Accounting* (England) (March 1977), 123.

Bowen, R.M., L.A. Daley, and C.C. Huber. "Evidence on the Existence and Determinants of Inter-Industry Differences in Leverage," *Financial Management* (Winter 1982), 10–20.

Chambers, A.E., and S.H. Penman. "Timeliness of Reporting and the Stock Price Reaction to Earnings Announcements," *Journal of Accounting Research* (Spring 1984), 21–47.

Clemente, Holly A. "What Wall Street Sees When It Looks at Your P/E Ratio," *Financial Executive* (May/June 1990), 40–44.

Coggin, T.D., and J.E. Hunter. "Analysts' EPS Forecasts Nearer Actual Than Statistical Models," *The Journal of Business Forecasting* (Winter 1982–1983), 20–23.

Coughlan, John W. "Anomalies in Calculating Earnings Per Share," *Accounting Horizons* (December 1988), 80–88.

Kross, W., and D.A. Schroder. "An Empirical Investigation of the Effect of Quarterly Earnings Announcement Timing on Stock Returns," *Jour-*

nal of Accounting Research (Spring 1984), 153–176.

Leftwich, R. "Market Failure Fallacies and Accounting Information," *Journal of Accounting and Economics* (December 1980), 193–211.

Livingston, D.T., and J.B. Henry. "Effect of Employee Stock Ownership Plans on Corporate Profits," *Journal of Risk and Insurance* (September 1980), 491–505.

O'Connor, M.C. "On the Usefulness of Financial Ratios to Investors in Common Stock," *Accounting Review* (April 1973), 339–352.

Pares, A. "Return on Equity Decomposition (ROED) and Its Importance to Financial Statement Analysis," *Journal of Business Finance and Accounting* (Autumn 1980), 365–375.

Soter, D.S. "The Dividend Controversy—What It Means for Corporate Policy," *Financial Executive* (May 1979), 38–43.

Welsch, J.A., and J.F. White. "Return on Investment or Liquidity? A Manager's Dilemma," *Journal of Small Business Management* (April 1978), 14–21.

10. *Statement of Cash Flows*

Casey, C.J., and N.J. Bartczak. "Cash Flow—It's Not the Bottom Line," *Harvard Business Review* (July–August 1984), 61–66.

Fahnestock, R.T., and R.F. Briner. "How to Use the Cash-basis Funds Statement as an Analytical Tool," *Practical Accountant* (March 1981), 37–41.

Heath, Lloyd, C. "Financial Reporting and the Evaluation of Solvency," *Accounting Research Monograph* No. 3 (1978), AICPA.

Langay, J.A., III, and C.P. Stickney. "Cash Flows, Ratio Analysis and the W.T. Grant Company Bankruptcy," *Financial Analysts Journal* (July–August 1980), 51–54.

Lee, T.A. "A Case for Cash Flow Reporting," *Journal of Business Finance and Accounting* (Summer 1972), 27–36.

Kronquist, Stacey L., and Nancy Newman-Limata. "Reporting Corporate Cash Flows," *Management Accounting* (July 1990), 31–36.

Mason, Perry. "Cash Flow Analysis and the Funds Statement," *Accounting Research Study* No. 2 (1961), AICPA.

Moonitz, Maurice. "Reporting on the Flow of Funds," *The Accounting Review* (July 1956), 378–385.

Rosen, L.S., and Don T. DeCoster. "Funds' Statement: A Historical Perspective," *The Accounting Review* (January 1969), 124–136.

Sorter, George H. "An Events Approach to Basic Accounting Theory," *The Accounting Review* (January 1969), 12–19.

Spiller, Earl A., and Robert L. Virgil. "Effectiveness of APB Opinion No. 19 in Improving Funds Reporting," *Journal of Accounting Research* (Spring 1974), 112–133.

Strischek, D. "Analyzing the Quantity and Quality of Cash Flow for Long-Term Borrowing," *Journal of Commercial Lending* (May 1980), 30–44.

Thomas, Barbara S. "Deregulation and Cash Flow Reporting: One Viewpoint," *Financial Executive* (January 1983), 20–24.

Yu, S.C. "A Flow of Resources Statement of Business Enterprises," *The Accounting Review* (July 1969), 571–582.

12. *Analyzing the Impact of Inflation on Financial Statements*

Bates, H.L., and M.J. Reckens. "Does Replacement Cost Data Make a Difference?" *Journal of Accountancy* (June 1979), 42.

Boatsman, James, and Elba Baskin. "Asset Valuation with Incomplete Markets," *The Accounting Review* (January 1981), 38–53.

Connor, J.E. "Inflation Accounting: An Attestor's View," *Journal of Accountancy* (July 1980), 76–77.

Davidson, S., and R.W. Weil. "Inflation Accounting: What Will General Price Level Adjusted Income Statements Show?" *Financial Analysts Journal* (January–February 1975), 27–31, 70–84.

Heylton, D.P. "Should We Dismantle the Balance Sheet?" *Financial Executive* (August 1977), 16–19.

Kaplan, Robert. "Purchasing Power Gains on Debt: The Effect of Expected and Unexpected Inflation," *The Accounting Review* (April 1977), 369–378.

Ketz, J.E. "Effect of General Price-Level Adjustments on the Predictive Ability of Financial Ratios," *Journal of Accounting Research* (1978), 273–300.

Nichols, Donald. "Operating Income and Distributable Income under Replacement Cost Accounting: The Long-Life Asset Replacement Problem," *Financial Analysts Journal* (January–February 1982), 68–73.

Randall, M.R. "Inflation, Taxes, and Financial

Reports," *Akron Business and Economic Review* (Winter 1981), 7–11.

Rappaport, A. "Inflation Accounting and Corporate Dividends," *Financial Executive* (February 1981), 20–22.

Reusine, Lawrence. "Inflation Accounting for Debt," *Financial Analysts Journal* (May–June 1981), 20–29.

Rosenfeld, P. "A History of Inflation Accounting," *Journal of Accountancy* (September 1981), 95–126.

Seed, A.H. "Measuring Financial Performance in an Inflationary Environment," *Financial Executive* (January 1982), 40–50.

Short, D.G. "Impact of Price-Level Adjustments on the Meaning of Accounting Ratios," *Journal of Business Finance and Accounting* (Autumn 1980), 377–391.

Sterling, Robert. "Relevant Financial Reporting in an Age of Price Changes," *Journal of Accountancy* (February 1975), 42–51.

Vancil, Richard. "Inflation Accounting—The Great Controversy," *Harvard Business Review* (March–April 1976), 58–67.

13. *Expanded Utility of Financial Ratios*

Altman, E. "Financial Ratios, Discriminant Analysis and the Prediction of Corporate Bankruptcy," *Journal of Finance* (September 1968), 589–609.

Altman, E.I., and M. Brenner. "Information Effects and Stock Market Response to Signs of Firm Deterioration," *Journal of Financial and Quantitative Analysis* (March 1981), 35–51.

Altman, E.I., R.G. Haldeman, and P. Narayanan. "Zeta Analysis: A New Model to Identify Bankruptcy Risk of Corporations," *Journal of Banking and Finance* (June 1977), 29–54.

Beaver, W.H. "Financial Ratios as Predictors of Failure," *Journal of Accounting Research* (1967), 71–111.

Beaver, W.H. "Alternative Accounting Measures as Predictors of Failure," *Accounting Review* (January 1968), 113–122.

Beaver, W.H. "Market Prices, Financial Ratios, and the Prediction of Failure," *Journal of Accounting Research* (Autumn 1968), 179–192.

Belkaoui, A. "Financial Ratios as Predictors of Canadian Takeover," *Journal of Business Finance and Accounting* (Spring 1978), 93–107.

Belkaoui, A., K. Alfred, and J. Josette. "Information Needs of Financial Analysts: An International Comparison," *International Journal of Accounting: Education and Research* (Fall 1977), 19–27.

Benjamin, J.J., and K.G. Stanga. "Differences in Disclosure Needs of Major Users of Financial Statements," *Accounting and Business Research* (Summer 1977), 187–192.

Bird, R.G., and A.J. McHugh. "Financial Ratios—An Empirical Study," *Journal of Business Finance and Accounting* (Spring 1977), 29–45.

Blum, M. "Failing Company Discriminant Analysis," *Journal of Accounting Research* (Spring 1974), 1–25.

Bonocure, J.J. "A New Era of Financial Reporting," *Financial Executive* (December 1981), 30–34.

Buzby, S. "Selected Items of Information and Their Disclosures in Annual Reports," *Accounting Review* (July 1974), 432–435.

Casey, C.J., Jr. "Variation in Accounting Information Load: The Effect on Loan Officers' Prediction of Bankruptcy," *Accounting Review* (January 1980), 36–49.

Chandra, G. "A Study of the Consensus on Disclosures among Public Accountants and Security Analysts," *Accounting Review* (October 1974), 733–742.

Chandra, G. "Information Needs of Security Analysts," *Journal of Accountancy* (December 1975), 65–70.

Chen, K.H., and T.F. Shimerda. "An Empirical Analysis of Useful Financial Ratios," *Financial Management* (Spring 1981), 51–60.

Dambolena, I.G., and S. J. Khorvry. "Ratio Stability and Corporate Failure," *Journal of Finance* (September 1980), 1017–1026.

Dawson, J.P., P.M. Neupert, and C.P. Stickney. "Restating Financial Statements for Alternative GAAPs: Is It Worth the Effort?" *Financial Analysis Journal* (November–December 1980), 38–46.

Deakin, E.B. "A Discriminant Analysis of Predictors of Business Failure," *Journal of Accounting Research* (Spring 1972), 167–179.

Deakin, E.B. "Distributions of Financial Accounting Ratios: Some Empirical Evidence," *Accounting Review* (January 1976), 90–96.

Edminster, R.O. "An Empirical Test of Financial Ratio Analysis for Small Business Failure Prediction," *Journal of Financial and Quantitative Analysis* (March 1972), 1477–1493.

Edmunds, S.W. "Performance Measures for Small Businesses," *Harvard Business Review* (January–February 1979), 172–176.

Elliott, T.L. "Analytic Approaches and Financial Ratios for Review Engagements," *Georgia Journal of Accounting* (Spring 1980), 132–140.

Firth, M. "A Study of the Consensus of the Perceived Importance of Disclosure of Individual Items in Corporate Annual Reports," *International Journal of Accounting: Education and Research* (Fall 1978), 57–70.

Frishkoff, P. *Reporting of Summary Indicators: An Investigation of Research and Practice.* Stamford, Conn.: Financial Accounting Standards Board, 1981.

Gibson, C.H. "How Industry Perceives Financial Ratios," *Management Accounting* (April 1982), 13–19.

Gibson, C.H. "Financial Ratios in Annual Reports," *The CPA Journal* (September 1982), 18–29.

Gibson, C.H. "Financial Ratios as Perceived by Commercial Loan Officers," *Akron Business and Economic Review* (Summer 1983), 23–27.

Gibson, C.H. "Ohio CPAs' Perceptions of Financial Ratios," *The Ohio CPA Journal* (Autumn 1985), 25–30.

Gibson, C.H. "How Chartered Financial Analysts View Financial Ratios," *Financial Analysts Journal* (May–June 1987), 74–76.

Gibson, C.H., and P.A. Boyer. "The Need for Disclosure of Uniform Financial Ratios," *The Journal of Accountancy* (May 1980), 78–86.

Gombola, M.J., and J.E. Ketz. "Financial Ratio Patterns in Retail and Manufacturing Organizations," *Financial Management* (Summer 1983), 45–56.

Grant, E.B. "The Financial Executive's Role in External Reporting," *Financial Executive* (February 1981), 24–27.

Hoeven, J.A. "Predicting Default of Small Business Loans," *Journal of Commercial Bank Lending* (April 1979), 47–59.

Imhoff, E.A., Jr. "Analytical Review of Income Elements," *Journal of Accounting, Auditing and Finance* (Summer 1981), 333–351.

Jaggi, B. "Which Is Better, D & B or Zeta, in Forecasting Credit Risk?" *Journal of Business Forecasting* (Summer 1984), 13–16, 22.

Kennedy, H.A. "Behavioral Study of the Usefulness of Four Financial Ratios," *Journal of Accounting Research* (Spring 1975), 97–116.

Laurent, C.R. "Improving the Efficiency and Effectiveness of Financial Ratio Analysis," *Journal of Business Finance and Accounting* (Autumn 1979), 401–413.

Lev, B., and S. Sunder. "Methodological Issues in the Use of Financial Ratios," *Journal of Accounting and Economics* (December 1979), 187–210.

Libby, R. "Accounting Ratios and the Prediction of Failure: Some Behavioral Evidence," *Journal of Accounting Research* (Spring 1975), 150–161.

Lincoln, M. "An Empirical Study of the Usefulness of Accounting Ratios to Describe Levels of Insolvency Risk," *Journal of Banking and Finance* (June 1984), 321–340.

McDonald, B., and M.H. Morris. "The Statistical Validity of the Ratio Method in Financial Analysis: An Empirical Examination," *Journal of Business Finance and Accounting* (Spring 1984), 89–97.

Makeever, D.A. "Predicting Business Failures," *The Journal of Commercial Bank Lending* (January 1984), 14–18.

Ohlson, J.A. "Financial Ratios and the Probabilistic Prediction of Bankruptcy," *Journal of Accounting Research* (Spring 1980), 109–131.

Patrone, F.L., and D. duBois. "Financial Ratio Analysis in the Small Business," *Journal of Small Business Management* (January 1981), 35–40.

Reckers, P.M.R., and A.J. Stagliano. "How Good Are Investor's Data Sources?" *Financial Executive* (April 1980), 26–32.

Rege, V.P. "Accounting Ratios to Locate Take-Over Targets," *Journal of Business Finance and Accounting* (Autumn 1984), 301–311.

Reynolds, P.D. "Comparisons, Differences and Ratios for Management Information," *Accountant's Magazine* (January 1980), 15–16.

Schiedler, P. "Using Accounting Information to Assess Risk," *Management Accounting* (June 1981), 38–40.

Steinbart, Paul John. "The Auditor's Responsibility for the Accuracy of Graphs in Annual Reports: Some Evidence of the Need for Additional Guidance," *Accounting Horizons* (September 1989), 60–70.

Wetzell, R.F. "Statement of Ratio Analysis," *Michigan CPA* (May–June 1976), 8–9.

14. *Statement Analysis for Special Industries: Banks, Utilities, Oil and Gas, Transportation, Insurance*

Agnich, J.F. "How Utilities Account to the Regulators," *Management Accounting* (February 1981), 17–22.

Backer, M., and M.L. Gosman. "The Predictive Value of Financial Ratios in Bank Term Loan Decisions," *The Journal of Commercial Bank Lending* (March 1979), 53–67.

Barefeld, R.M., and E.E. Comiskey. "The Accuracy of Bank Earnings Forecasts," *Business Economics* (May 1976), 59–63.

Barniv, Ran. "Accounting Procedures, Market Data, Cash-Flow Figures, and Insolvency Classification: The Case of the Insurance Industry," *The Accounting Review* (July 1990), 578–604.

Black, T.G. "Constant Dollar Accounting—Its Usefulness to Utility Investors," *Public Utilities* (May 1980), 29–31.

Boyer, P.A., and M.E. Phillips. *Inflation Reporting by the Banking Industry.* Park Ridge, Ill.: Bank Administration Institute, 1980.

Cates, D.C. "Are Summary Ratios Workable in Bank Analysis?" *Bankers Magazine* (Winter 1976), 113–116.

Ho, T., and A. Saunders. "A Catastrophe Model of Bank Failure," *The Journal of Finance* (December 1980), 1189–1207.

Lilien, S., and V. Pastena. "Intramethod Comparability: The Case of the Oil and Gas Industry," *Accounting Review* (July 1981), 690–703.

Ricketts, D., and R. Stover. "Examination of Commercial Bank Financial Ratios," *Journal of Bank Research* (Summer 1978), 121–124.

Rose, P.L., and W.L. Scott. "Return-on-Equity Analysis of Eleven Largest U.S. Bank Failures," *Review of Business and Economic Research* (Winter 1980–1981), 1–11.

Shick, R.A., and L.F. Sherman. "Bank Stock Prices as an Early Warning System for Changes in Condition," *Journal of Bank Research* (Autumn 1980), 136–146.

Stanga, K.G., and J.J. Benjamin. "Information Needs of Bankers," *Management Accounting* (June 1978), 17–21.

15. *Personal Financial Statements and Accounting for Governments and Other Nonprofit Institutions*

American Institute of Certified Public Accountants Statement of Position 82-1, "Accounting and Financial Reporting for Personal Financial Statements." New York: AICPA, 1982.

Caldwell, K. "Efficiency and Effectiveness Measurement in State and Local Government," *Government Finance* (November 1973), 19–21.

Charnes, A., and W. Cooper. "Auditing and Accounting for Program Efficiency and Management Effectiveness in Not-for-Profit Entities," *Accounting Organizations and Society*, 5 (1980), 87–108.

Copeland, R., and R. Ingram. "Municipal Financial Reporting Deficiencies, Causes and Solutions," *Government Finance* (November 1979), 21–24.

Downs, G.W., and D.M. Rocke. "Municipal Budget Forecasting with Multivariate ARMA Models," *Journal of Forecasting* (October–December 1983), 377–387.

Field, H. "Traits in Performance Ratings—Their Importance in Public Employment," *Public Personnel Management* (September–October 1975), 327–330.

Groves, S., M. Godsey, and M. Shulman. "Financial Indicators for Local Government," *Public Budgeting and Finance* (Summer 1981), 5–19.

Hay, E., and James F. Antonio. "What Users Want in Government Financial Reports," *Journal of Accountancy* (August 1990), 91–98.

Henke, E. "Performance Evaluation for Not-for-Profit Organizations," *Journal of Accountancy* (June 1973), 51–55.

Horton, R. "Productivity and Productivity Bargaining in Government: A Critical Analysis," *Public Administration Review* (July–August 1976), 407–414.

Ives, Martin. "Accountability and Governmental Financial Reporting," *Journal of Accountancy* (October 1987), 130–134.

Kinsman, Michael D., and Bruce Samuelson. "Personal Financial Statements: Valuation Challenges and Solutions," *Journal of Accountancy* (September 1987), 138–148.

INDEX